WORKING IN AMERICA

Continuity, Conflict, and Change

For 2/5 = 2, 17, 36, 40
2/6   16, 20, 22, 32

For 2/19 = 8, 25, 27, 28
2/20   21, 24, 33, 43

245-6520

WORKING IN AMERICA
Continuity, Conflict, and Change
Third Edition

Amy S. Wharton

Washington State University

Boston   Burr Ridge, IL   Dubuque, IA   Madison, WI   New York
San Francisco   St. Louis   Bangkok   Bogotá   Caracas   Kuala Lumpur
Lisbon   London   Madrid   Mexico City   Milan   Montreal   New Delhi
Santiago   Seoul   Singapore   Sydney   Taipei   Toronto

To my father, William Wharton, and the
memory of my mother, Marilyn Wharton (1921–1964)

Higher Education

WORKING IN AMERICA: CONTINUITY, CONFLICT, AND CHANGE
Published by McGraw-Hill, a business unit of The McGraw-Hill Companies, Inc., 1221 Avenue of
the Americas, New York, NY, 10020. Copyright © 2006, 2002, 1998 by The McGraw-Hill Companies,
Inc. All rights reserved. No part of this publication may be reproduced or distributed in any form
or by any means, or stored in a database or retrieval system, without the prior written consent of
The McGraw-Hill Companies, Inc., including, but not limited to, in any network or other electronic
storage or transmission, or broadcast for distance learning. Some ancillaries, including electronic
and print components, may not be available to customers outside the United States.

This book is printed on acid-free paper.

1 2 3 4 5 6 7 8 9 0 DOC/DOC 0 9 8 7 6 5

ISBN   0-07-352801-3

Editor in Chief: *Emily Barrosse*
Publisher: *Phillip A. Butcher*
Sponsoring Editor: *Sherith H. Pankratz*
Development Editor: *Larry Goldberg*
Permissions Coordinator: *Sheri Gilbert*
Senior Marketing Manager: *Daniel M. Loch*
Managing Editor: *Jean Dal Porto*
Senior Project Manager: *Diane M. Folliard*
Production Service: *Marilyn Rothenberger*
Design Manager: *Laurie J. Entringer*
Text Designer: *Cher Marie Ruden*
Cover Designer: *Leslie Nayman*
Cover Credit: *Digital Design*
Production Supervisor: *Jason I. Huls*
Composition: *10/12 Book Antiqua by GTS-India*
Printing: *PMS Black, 45 # New Era Matte, R.R. Donnelley, Crawfordsville, Indiana*

Library of Congress Cataloging-in-Publication Data

Wharton, Amy S.
      Working in America: continuity, conflict, and change / Amy S. Wharton.—3rd ed.
         p. cm.
      ISBN 0-07-352801-3 (alk. paper)
         1.   Work—Sociological aspects. 2.   Work—Social aspects—United States. I. Title.
      HD4904 .W485 2006
      306.3'6—dc22

The Internet addresses listed in the text were accurate at the time of publication. The inclusion of a
Web site does not indicate an endorsement by the authors of McGraw-Hill, and McGraw-Hill does
not guarantee the accuracy of the information presented at these sites.

www.mhhe.com

Preface

College students today are more anxious about their futures than in the past, particularly with respect to their places in the world of work. The social contract that promised steadily increasing wages and secure employment has unraveled, leaving many uncertain about their lives and livelihoods. In these times, a sociological perspective on work is more important than ever. Analysis and understanding of the societal conditions that shape people's work lives may be the best tools for conquering their anxiety and uncertainty. To prepare for and reshape the future demands knowledge of the social forces that influenced the past and help structure the present.

The study of work is central to the discipline of sociology. From the industrial revolution to the service economy, sociologists have contributed much to our understanding of the forces shaping workers' lives and the workplace. This anthology contains a sampling of some of the best that sociologists of work have to offer. Through a variety of methods and approaches, the readings address several pertinent questions about the American work-

place: What have been the most important changes in workers' lives and work organization during the twentieth century? What factors shape employment today? What does the 21st century hold for work and workers? By examining how sociologists have pursued answers to these questions, I hope students will acquire tools to address their own concerns and come away better equipped to make sense of their past, present, and future work experiences.

Selecting the readings for this anthology was both a challenge and a pleasure. It was challenging because my colleagues have produced such a tremendous amount of valuable research on the workplace that I could have filled several volumes easily; deciding what to exclude was a difficult task. At the same time, compiling these readings provided me an opportunity to explore and appreciate sociologists' contributions to our knowledge about workers and work. This process reaffirmed my belief that a sociological perspective remains the best vantage point from which to understand the social world.

In the end, the readings that appear here were selected with several considerations in mind. First, I aimed for a degree of comprehensiveness in the coverage of topics. While no anthology can address everything, anthologies remain one the best vehicles for presenting information to students on a range of topics. Second, I wanted to present the key pieces of research in a particular area. I include some classics, but primarily use examples of contemporary research that have made an impact. Third, attending to gender, racial, and ethnic differentiation in the workplace was important to me. Hence, these issues are addressed throughout the anthology. Finally, I selected readings with a student audience in mind. When all is said and done, this anthology is for them.

Acknowledgements

Intellectual work is, at its best, a collective enterprise. In editing this anthology, I benefited from the valuable comments and suggestions of many colleagues around the country. Some of them have been involved with this project from the beginning, and I am especially grateful for their help. The reviewers for the second and third editions include: Robert Althauser, Indiana University; Spencer Blakeslee, Framingham State College; William T. Clute, University of Nebraska, Omaha; Linda Geller-Schwartz, Florida Atlantic University; Richard H. Hall, University at Albany; Kevin D. Henson, Loyola University, Chicago; Linda Markowitz, Southern Illinois University, Edwardsville; Peter F. Meiksins, Cleveland State University; Nancy Plankey-Videla, Texas A&M University; Carol Ray, San Jose State University; Raymond Russell, University of California, Riverside; and Denise Scott, University of New York, Geneseo.

I would also like to thank Sherith Pankratz and her staff at McGraw-Hill for their cooperation and enthusiasm for this project. Special thanks to my friend and former editor, Serina Beauparlant. Finally, I am especially grateful to all of the book's contributors, whose research and writing on workers and the workplace have made this anthology possible.

Amy S. Wharton

Changes to the Third Edition

The American workplace is constantly changing, and the selections in this third edition aim to capture some of these developments, while preserving the book's original intent:

- The changing workplace and its implications for workers are addressed explicitly in the new selections by Powell and Smith in Readings 9 and 10.
- Most of the readings in the Work and Inequality section are new as well; this section devotes more attention than previous editions to issues of globalization, immigration, and unionization.
- Welfare reform has swelled the ranks of the working poor, and the 24/7 economy has created challenges for many families. Both issues are addressed in the last section of Part III.

- Issues of work and family are of special interest to me and this edition contains an expanded discussion of care work as a global issue affecting families, children, and workers.
- The General Introduction remains, and Discussion Questions—new to this edition— appear at the end of each part.

As with previous editions, the amount of cutting-edge sociological research on the workplace far exceeds what I have been able to include here. Nevertheless, I hope that the selections I have included will inform and inspire readers to think more critically about the contemporary workplace and the global society in which we live.

About the Editor

Amy S. Wharton is professor of sociology at Washington State University in Vancouver. She has been teaching courses on work and workers for twenty years. She is especially interested in gender inequality in the workplace and has published her research on this topic in journals such as the *American Sociological Review, Social Forces,* and *Work and Occupations.* She is the author of *The Sociology of Gender: An Introduction to Theory and Research* (Blackwell, 2005). She lives in Portland, Oregon, with her partner and daughter.

Contents

General Introduction

The beginning of a new century offers an opportune time to assess the past, reflect on the present, and imagine the future. As the millennium begins, a course in the sociology of work can provide a conceptual and theoretical platform from which to explore a variety of enduring sociological issues. Though this anthology focuses mainly on the contemporary workplace, it also looks at workplaces of the past and the future through a critical, sociological lens. Work is among the most important social institutions; indeed, in the late 19th and early 20th centuries, sociologists Karl Marx, Max Weber, and Emile Durkheim placed work at the center of their analyses. Contemplating the development of capitalism in the West and the burgeoning industrial revolution, these "founding fathers of sociology" understood that the organization of work helps to determine the fates of individuals as well as their societies.

Three major themes guided the selection of readings for this anthology—the first reflects a methodological concern, the second stems from an empirical observation, and the third emphasizes conceptual and theoretical issues. Each theme has continuity with past efforts to understand the American workplace, yet each also directs attention to important questions about the present and future.

The first theme is that workers' lives are shaped not only by daily life on the job but also by larger trends that are transforming work in the country and across the globe. This theme has methodological implications because it suggests that any study of work must concern itself not only with workers' experiences but also with the larger historical, economic, and social contexts within which these experiences occur. Multiple levels of analysis are thus necessary to address the important questions in the sociology of work.

The second major theme is that workers are demographically more diverse than ever, and this changing demography plays an important role in the organization and experience of work. This theme is drawn from an empirical observation: The American workplace—like the larger society—has always been composed of workers from diverse racial and ethnic backgrounds, genders, ages, religions, and sexual orientations—to name but a few characteristics. As American society moves into the 21st century, this demographic diversity is increasing: Most new entrants to the labor force are expected to be nonwhites, females, or immigrants (Johnston and Packer 1987). Sociologists have come to believe that we cannot fully understand work without considering the characteristics of the people who perform it.

The third theme of this book is perhaps the most significant to sociologists: Work is not strictly an instrumental activity, nor can it be understood only in economic terms. Instead, as Friedland and Robertson (1990, p. 25) explain, "Work provides identities as much as it provides bread for the table; participation in commodity and labor markets is as much an expression of who you are as what you want." Moreover, from this perspective work is not an isolated institution, closed off from the rest of society but is profoundly interconnected with the larger social world. Not only are its boundaries permeable, making the workplace subject to influences from other institutions, but the influence of work on other aspects of society is also great. Indeed, work shapes every aspect of life—from people's conceptions of self to the degree of inequality in a society. Through the years sociologists studying work have disagreed as to which effects of work they consider most important, but there has been no dispute with the basic premise that the study of work is a vehicle for examining some of the most fundamental aspects of social life.

Linking the Micro and the Macro in Sociological Studies of Work

Like the field of sociology as a whole, teaching and scholarship in the sociology of work reflect a range of approaches, which typically have been characterized as either *micro* or *macro*. Micro-level approaches tend to focus on individuals or small groups in a particular workplace and examine processes or outcomes that operate at these levels of analysis. Though by no means is all micro-level research ethnographic, many researchers prefer qualitative methodologies that allow for close, in-depth scrutiny of particular social phenomena. Indeed, there is a long and rich tradition of micro-level ethnographic research in the sociology of work. This research has provided useful accounts of many jobs, offering the student a way to experience life vicariously as a machine shop worker, a medical student, a flight attendant, or a McDonald's employee (Roy 1959; Becker, Geer, Hughes, and Strauss 1961; Hochschild 1983; Leidner 1993).

In contrast, macro-level studies in the sociology of work tend to be less concerned with "flesh-and-blood workers" and more attentive to larger processes, trends, and outcomes (Simpson 1989, p. 565). Studies of this type typically analyze data collected from representative samples of people, jobs, or workplaces and seek to identify patterns and relationships between key variables. Macro-level research thus is often quantitative, driven by the desire to test hypotheses or produce generalizable results. The popularity of macro-level research has grown in recent years, as sociologists have borrowed concepts and theories from economists. Sociological studies of wage determination, for example, attempt to explain what factors determine the "worth" of jobs and cause some jobs to command higher wages than others (Tomaskovic-Devey 1993).

Micro and macro research traditions are often perceived as distinct, and sometimes even conflicting, approaches. Courses in the sociology of work have thus traditionally emphasized one approach, but not both. Ideally, however, micro and macro studies should inform one another, as no single approach can address everything. Moreover, in my view, important sociological questions cannot be answered by only one type of study or approach but require a "division of labor" among researchers. For example, to understand the role of race in the workplace we need both fine-grained, ethnographic studies *and* more large-scale, quantitative analyses. The former can help us understand such issues as workers' experiences of discrimination and the meaning of race to employers (Kirschenman and Neckerman 1991), and the latter may address such issues as the racial gap in earnings or the consequences of corporate restructuring for the employment chances of African Americans (Wilson 1996). This view is reflected in the selection of readings for this anthology, which incorporates studies employing diverse methodologies and approaches. By studying both the micro and the macro dimensions of work, we can begin to see how work is shaped by its social context and, conversely, how workplace dynamics may shape the larger society.

The Changing Demographics of the Workplace

Anyone who takes even a cursory look around any place of work in industrialized countries can see that workers doing the same or similar jobs tend to be of the same gender and racial and ethnic group. In a workplace in New York City—for instance, a handbag factory—a walk through the various departments might reveal that the owners and managers are white men; their secretaries and bookkeepers are white and Asian women; the order takers and data processors are African-American women; the factory hands are Hispanic men cutting pieces and Hispanic women sewing them together; African-American men

are packing and loading the finished product; and non-English-speaking Eastern European women are cleaning up after everyone. (Lorber 1994, p. 194)

Although the labor force is becoming increasingly diverse, jobs and workplaces continue to be highly segregated along gender, racial, and ethnic lines. The continuing association between jobs and workers of a particular gender, race, or ethnic background suggests that these social categories are as powerful in shaping life inside the workplace as they have been shown to be in shaping life in other societal institutions.

Gender, race, and ethnicity in the workplace are often studied by focusing on discrimination and inequality, and these remain important topics. Despite widespread social changes, as well as the passage of legislation and social policies designed to prevent discrimination and reduce inequality, the costs and rewards of work remain unevenly distributed across social categories. The desire to understand the sources of these work-related inequalities, the forces that perpetuate them, and the consequences of these inequalities for workers and their families has generated a tremendous amount of research in recent years. We thus know a great deal about some aspects of gender, racial, and ethnic inequality in the workplace. Changes in the organization of work brought on by a global economy and the changing demographics of workers raise new questions for analysis, however. How will these changes affect the costs and rewards of work? More important, how will the relative situations of different groups of workers be affected by the changing workplace? Will economic inequality increase or diminish in the 21st century? Questions such as these are important topics for research and debate.

The impacts of gender, race, and ethnicity on the workplace are not confined to their roles in producing inequality and discrimination, nor do these factors affect only the personal consequences of work. Rather, sociologists argue that, at a more fundamental level, the structure and organization of work also reflect the influences of gender, race, and ethnicity. From this perspective, gender, race, and ethnicity are not just characteristics of workers but may also be considered characteristics of work roles and jobs or seen as embedded in work arrangements and technologies (Acker 1991). Understanding how the workplace is gendered and learning how it is imbued with racial symbolism have become important concerns in recent years. Addressing these issues requires us to examine how work structures and practices that may appear "neutral" in design or application may nevertheless contribute to the construction and maintenance of gender and racial distinctions in the workplace. Including issues pertaining to gender, race, and ethnicity throughout this anthology, instead of confining them to a section on discrimination, allows the reader to see the many ways in which these social categories shape work experience and organization.

Work and Society

Viewing work through a sociological lens enables us to consider the varied ways in which work and society are interrelated. For example, at the individual level, work shapes identity, values, and beliefs, as well as a host of other outcomes ranging from mental and physical health to political attitudes (see, e.g., Brint 1985; Karasek and Theorell 1990; and Kohn and Schooler 1983). Thus, while sociologists tend to view families as the primary agents of socialization in American society, it is also important to recognize the ways in which people are socialized by their jobs and work experiences. Indeed, some argue that work is an increasingly

"greedy" institution, capable of "outcompeting" other institutions for people's time, emotional energies, and commitments.

One often overlooked feature of work is that it typically brings people into contact with others—co-workers, subordinates, supervisors, and, increasingly for many, the public. Hence, social interaction and group dynamics are just as important in the workplace as they are in other social arenas. An early, influential sociological study first called attention to the ways that the social relations of work shaped workers' reactions to their jobs (Mayo 1933). For contemporary researchers, this insight is reflected in the claim that workers are not "atomized optimizers," unaffected by their interactions with other workplace members (Baron and Pfeffer 1994). Instead, both the content and quality of these relations are seen as important for understanding the consequences and significance of work. Along these lines, some suggest that it is not so much workers' own characteristics that shape their views and behavior but, rather, the relation between their characteristics and the characteristics of those with whom they interact. From this perspective, workplaces are settings in which both expressive and instrumental ties between people are important—not only for understanding workers' responses to their jobs but also for understanding the broader ways in which work shapes meanings and life experience. As Marks (1994, p. 855) explains, "With the help of co-workers, ethnic statuses may get reaffirmed and enlivened, and age and gender identities may be consolidated, celebrated, reorganized, and even transformed. The same is true, of course, of worker identities."

Though the workplace has never been truly separate from other societal institutions and trends, its interdependence with the larger environment has perhaps never been greater. This point can best be illustrated by considering the relations between work and another important social institution: family life. Societal changes, such as women's rising participation in the labor force, declining birth rates, and changing gender roles, have transformed relations between families and work. In the process, new conceptual approaches have emerged, and there has been a change in the way social institutions, including work, are understood. In particular, there has been a move away from rigid dichotomies, such as public and private or impersonal and personal, that compartmentalized work and family life, toward more complex portrayals of these social institutions and those who negotiate the work-family boundary (Marks 1994). Work, family, and the relations between them are not static but, rather, reflect and respond to developments in the wider society.

People's lives in advanced, capitalist societies are largely dependent on forces emanating from the workplace. The organization and availability of work determine—to a great extent—the social and economic well-being of individuals, neighborhoods, cities, and societies. Work is thus among the most important social institutions, with influential consequences for just about all arenas of social life.

REFERENCES

Acker, Joan. 1991. "Hierarchies, Jobs, Bodies: A Theory of Gendered Organizations." Pp. 162–179 in *The Social Construction of Gender*, edited by Judith Lorber and Susan A. Farrell. Newbury Park, CA: Sages.

Baron, James N., and Jeffrey Pfeffer. 1994. "The Social Psychology of Organizations and Inequality." *Social Psychology Quarterly* 57: 190–209.

Becker, Howard S., Blanche Geer, Everett C. Hughes, and Anselm L. Strauss. 1961. *Boys in White: Student Culture in Medical School.* Chicago: University of Chicago Press.

Brint, Steven G. 1985. "The Political Attitudes of Professionals." *Annual Review of Sociology* 11: 389–414.

Friedland, Roger, and A. F. Robertson. 1990. "Beyond the Marketplace." Pp. 3–49 in *Beyond the Marketplace*, edited by Roger Friedland and A. F. Robertson. New York: Aldine de Gruyter.

Hochschild, Arlie Russell. 1983. *The Managed Heart.* Berkeley: University of California Press.

Johnston, William B., and Arnold E. Packer. 1987. *Workforce 2000: Work and Workers for the 21st Century.* Indianapolis, IN: Hudson Institute.

Karasek, Robert, and Tores Theorell. 1990. *Healthy Work: Stress, Productivity, and the Reconstruction of Working Life.* New York: Basic Books.

Kirschenman, Joleen, and Kathryn M. Neckerman. 1991. "We'd Love to Hire Them, but . . . : The Meaning of Race for Employers." Pp. 203–232 in *The Urban Underclass*, edited by C. Jencks and P. E. Peterson. Washington, DC: The Brookings Institution.

Kohn, Melvin L., and Carmi Schooler. 1983. *Work and Personality: An Inquiry into the Impact of Social Stratification.* Norwood, NJ: Ablex.

Leidner, Robin. 1993. *Fast Food, Fast Talk: Service Work and the Routinization of Everyday Life.* Berkeley: University of California Press.

Lorber, Judith. 1994. *Paradoxes of Gender.* New Haven, CT: Yale University Press.

Marks, Stephen R. 1994. "Intimacy in the Public Realm: The Case of Co-Workers." *Social Forces* 72: 843–858.

Mayo, Elton. 1933. *The Human Problems of an Industrial Civilization.* New York: Macmillan.

Roy, Donald. 1959. " 'Banana Time': Job Satisfaction and Informal Interaction." *Human Organization* 18: 158–168.

Simpson, Ida Harper. 1989. "The Sociology of Work: Where Have the Workers Gone?" *Social Forces* 67: 563–581.

Tomaskovic-Devey, Donald. 1993. *Gender and Racial Inequality at Work.* Ithaca, NY: ILR Press.

Wilson, William Julius. 1996. *When Work Disappears: The World of the New Urban Poor.* New York: Knopf.

PART I

Historical and Conceptual Foundations

▓▓▓ HISTORICAL FOUNDATIONS ▓▓▓

∽ READING 1 ∽

The Way It Was

Factory Labor Before 1915

Sanford M. Jacoby

At the beginning of the nineteenth century, most commodities in the United States were produced either in the workshops of artisans or at home. Skilled tradesmen—carpenters, cobblers, potters—crafted their wares in small shops, owned by merchants or master craftsmen, that had not yet been significantly affected by machine methods. Goods made at home were usually consumed there, although in urban areas the putting-out system was common: Merchants distributed raw materials and tools to household workers, who then wove the cloth or made the shoes and returned the finished product to the merchants for distribution and sale. By the end of the century, however, everything had changed: Most commodities were now manufactured in factories, which were enormous agglomerations of machinery and men.

America's first factories were New England's textile mills, which supplanted home methods of production between 1790 and 1840. These early mills shared a number of features that distinguished the factory system from other modes of production: a reliance on power-driven machinery; the integration of different production processes at a single site; an elaborate division of labor; and finally, new methods of administration based on the overseer or foreman.

The overseer was the key figure in the early New England mills. Large mills employed a number of them, each in charge of a room full of machinery and workers. Although there was an agent who dealt with the mill's owners, the overseer did most of the work of maintaining mechanical and human order. In addition to tending machines, he selected the workers, assigned them to their tasks, and made sure that they labored diligently. Indeed, one advantage of the textile factories was that they permitted more effective labor supervision than was previously possible. Under the putting-out system, merchants could manipulate only the piece prices they paid; effort was controlled by the worker, who could take anywhere from two days to two weeks to turn in his goods. But in the factory, workers had less discretion over their work pace and methods. As one Rhode Island merchant wrote in 1809, "We have several hundred pieces now out weaving, but a hundred looms in families will not weave so much cloth as ten at least constantly employed under the immediate inspection of a workman."[1]

Until the 1840s, the factory system was limited chiefly to the textile industry. By 1880, it had become the dominant production mode

"The Way It Was: Factory Labor Before 1915" from *Employing Bureaucracy: Managers, Unions, and the Transformation of Work in American Industry, 1900–1945* by Sanford M. Jacoby, New York: Columbia University Press, 1985. Reprinted with permission of the author.

in most manufacturing industries. As Carroll D. Wright observed in his introduction to the census of manufactures for 1880:

> Of the nearly three millions of people employed in mechanical industries of this country at least four-fifths are working under the factory system. Some of the other [than textiles] remarkable instances of the application of this system are to be found in the manufacture of boots and shoes, of watches, musical instruments, clothing, agricultural implements, metallic goods generally, firearms, carriages and wagons, wooden goods, rubber goods, and even the slaughtering of hogs. Most of these industries have been brought under the factory system during the past thirty years.

Despite this dramatic growth, the factory did not immediately displace older organizational forms. In the iron and steel industry, rural forges and small foundries coexisted during the 1860s and 1870s with giant rail mills employing more than a thousand workers. Similarly, although steam-powered machinery provided the impetus to establish shoe factories in the 1850s, certain types of women's shoes and slippers were manufactured on a putting-out basis until the end of the century.[2]

Older methods persisted in yet another way. Many of the industries that shifted to the factory system after 1850 continued to depend on techniques from the earlier period. In these industries, the factory was often no more than a congeries of artisanal workshops which had been mechanized and enlarged. A steady infusion of craft skills was still required, particularly when the factory turned out small batches of an unstandardized product. As a result, proprietors in these industries were content to let their foremen and skilled workers make most of the decisions about the timing and manner of production.[3]

At one extreme, this practice took the form of internal contracting, which was less a system of production management than a ceding of managerial control to the contractor. The contractor, who was a highly skilled foreman, arranged with the proprietor to deliver the product within a specified time at a specified cost. The proprietor provided the contractor with tools, materials, and money, and then left him in charge of production. The contractor hired and supervised a group of skilled workers, who in turn might employ their own unskilled helpers. This system was most common in metalworking industries—sewing machinery, locomotives, guns—where a high degree of skill was needed to process component parts to exacting tolerances.[4]

At the other extreme were industries that left production decisions entirely to the skilled workers, with no foreman or contractor involved. For instance, at the Columbus Iron Works during the early 1870s, workers negotiated with the firm's owners on a tonnage rate for each rolling job undertaken by the firm. The gang members decided collectively how to pay themselves, how to allocate assignments, whom to hire, and how to train helpers. Unlike internal contracting, this was a highly egalitarian method for production management; no one interposed between the skilled workers and the owners.[5]

Neither the syndicalism of the rolling mill workers nor internal contracting was, however, very common. Rather, in most nineteenth-century factories, salaried foremen and skilled workers shared responsibility for administering production. Although the salaried foreman occupied a position inferior to the internal contractor's, he nevertheless had authority to make most of the decisions about how a production task was to be accomplished, including work methods, technical processes, and work organization.

The foreman exercised his authority within limits set by the skilled workers, who guarded their autonomy in production through a multitude of working rules that governed methods of shop organization and through what one historian has called the craftsman's "moral code." The code included output quotas set by the workers to protect themselves from overexertion, as well as an ethos of manly defiance to any foreman who tried to subvert traditional shop rules.[6]

Foremen had their own moral code, one which owed a great deal to the skilled worker's shop culture. They were arrogant, proud, conservative men, mindful of the position to which their skill and knowledge had elevated them. Often they wore white shirts to work and seated themselves at raised desks in the middle of the shop floor. But despite their former status as skilled workers, most foremen were strenuously antiunion. They were well aware that their authority depended on severing ties to their pasts. As one observer noted, "They spurn the rungs by which they did ascend."[7]

By the 1880s, winds of change were beginning to erode the power of foremen and skilled workers over production management. The new industries, such as electrical machinery and chemicals, were based on a technology that had little continuity with artisanal techniques. The older industries, like iron and steel, had mechanized to the point where craft skills were no longer essential to production. After the introduction of continuous flow methods in steel manufacturing, the foreman was left with little authority. Most production decisions were now made by engineers and metallurgists. Among skilled steelworkers, who had once been "strong, even arrogant in their indispensability," the "strong sense of independence disappeared." In machine-paced industries like textiles, the overseer was forced to share authority with an increasing number of specialists equal or superior in rank: the chief

engineer, the chief electrician, and the supervisors of piping and the waste house. Other than making occasional repairs or inspecting goods to insure their quality, the overseer had fewer and fewer responsibilities in production. In textiles, as in steel and other industries, most of the foreman's tasks were related to employing and supervising labor. Here, however, the methods of the 1850s persisted, with little modification.[8]

I. Foremen in Control, 1880–1915

Whereas the foreman's degree of control over production varied by industry, his authority in employment matters was uniform across industries. Whether in a machine shop or on the assembly line, the foreman was given free rein in hiring, paying, and supervising workers. To the worker, the foreman was a despot—rarely benevolent—who made and interpreted employment policy as he saw fit. Any checks on the foreman's power emanated from the workers he supervised, not from the proprietor.

Recruiting and Hiring

The foreman's control over employment began literally at the factory gates. On mornings when the firm was hiring—a fact advertised by signs hung outside the plant, by newspaper ads, or by word of mouth—a crowd gathered in front of the factory, and the foreman picked out those workers who appeared suitable or had managed to get near the front. At one Philadelphia factory, the foreman tossed apples into the throng; if a man caught an apple, he got the job. Foremen could be less arbitrary. For instance, they frequently hired their friends, the relatives of those already employed, and even their own relatives: "Oftentimes he [the foreman] is connected by blood ties with those who come under his control and he will inevitably be swayed by considerations of previous friendship no matter how hard he may strive not to be." New foremen might dismiss current employees to make room for their friends and relatives, as occurred in a Lawrence textile mill during the 1880s. The overseers "made changes very freely in the departments committed to them, and the result was that for several months a feeling of great insecurity prevailed among the hands."[9]

In addition to blood ties, foremen relied on ethnic stereotypes to determine who would get a job and which job they would get. The Irish and Germans were considered good skilled workers, while Poles and "Hunkies" were thought to be suited for heavy labor. Jews were said to be dexterous, Rumanians dishonest, Slovaks stupid, and Italians "so susceptible to the opposite sex that they could not be satisfactorily employed." When an investigator in the steel mills asked for a job on a blast furnace, he was told "only Hunkies work on those jobs, they're too damn dirty and too damn hot for a white man."[10]

To get a job, workers often resorted to bribing the foreman with whiskey, cigars, or cash, a practice that one study found to be "exceedingly common" in Ohio's factories. The study included an affidavit from an immigrant worker who, to get a factory job, had paid the foreman a five-dollar bribe. Several days later the foreman told the man that he would be fired unless he paid another five dollars right away, because someone else had just paid ten dollars for a similar job.[11]

Assignment to a job was determined in large part by favoritism or ethnic prejudice. The foreman had little interest in or knowledge of an employee's previous work experience. If a newly hired employee proved unsatisfactory, he was easily replaced by someone else. Although intradepartmental promotions occurred, transfers and promo-

tions between departments were rare, as were definite lines of promotion (except on skilled work). The foreman had a parochial view of the factory and was reluctant to give up his best workers to another foreman.

Few companies kept detailed employment records before 1900. Only the foreman knew with any accuracy how many workers were employed in his shop and how much they were paid. In a large firm, a worker could quit his job in the morning and get taken on by the foreman of another department in the afternoon. In 1915, the top managers of a large hosiery factory reported that they had little idea of how many people their firm hired and dismissed each week.[12]

The one exception to this lack of information was the bureau that specialized in screening skilled labor for open-shop employers. Henry Leland, founder of the Cadillac Motor Company, started the Employers' Association of Detroit in 1897 to ensure that Detroit remained an open-shop city. The organization kept records on every individual who had worked for a member firm and blacklisted those who were "agitators" and union supporters. To get a job at a member firm, a worker had to apply through the Employers' Association. By 1911, the association's employment bureau had in its files names of more than 160,000 workers, a figure equalling nearly 90 percent of the Detroit labor force. Other employer organizations (including the National Metal Trades Association and the National Founders Association) set up similar local agencies to blacklist radicals and trade unionists and to supply member firms with the names of "good men" who needed work.[13]

Although direct recruitment was common during the nineteenth century, it was not usually done by the foreman. Instead, employers either sent their own special recruiters to the New York docks to secure immigrant workers or else relied on private agencies like the American Emigrant

Company, which kept scouts in several foreign ports to recruit emigrating workers. After the 1890s, however, immigration flows had become large enough and cyclically sensitive enough to meet industrial demand. Consequently, direct recruitment was rare, except in sectors like construction and the railroads, where work was seasonal and labor requirements for certain projects could run into the thousands.[14]

During the heyday of mass immigration, employers recruited through the immigrants' own informal network: Newcomers to America headed for areas where their countrymen, often men from the same European villages, had found jobs. As more men of a given nationality arrived, benefit societies were organized, priests appeared, and wives and children were sent for. Gradually a new ethnic community developed in the area. The news that a company was seeking help was transmitted to friends and relatives in the old country; sometimes, tickets were purchased for them. Letters might also warn of a shortage of jobs.[15]

Wages and Effort

The foreman also had considerable power in determining the wages of the workers he hired, whether for piecework or daywork. As a result, different individuals doing the same job were often paid very different rates. Because top management monitored labor costs but not the wage determination process, the foreman had an incentive to hire individuals at the lowest rate possible. It was common practice for a foreman "to beat the applicant down from the wage he states he wishes to the lowest which the interviewer believes he can be induced to accept." Moreover, by being secretive about wage rates and production records, foremen could play favorites, varying the day rate or assigning workers to jobs where piece rates were loose. Since each foreman ran his shop

autonomously, rate variations across departments were also common. In their report on the stove industry, Frey and Commons found that "molding [piece] prices were far from equal on similar work in the same shop or district."[16]

Despite—or perhaps because of—the latitude they gave him in determining rates, the firm's owners expected the foreman to hold down labor costs. This meant paying a wage no greater than the "going rate" for a particular job. But it also meant keeping effort levels up in order to reduce unit costs. When the going rate rose, effort became the key variable to be manipulated by the foreman.

The methods used by foremen to maintain or increase effort levels were known collectively as the "drive system": close supervision, abuse, profanity, and threats. Informal rules regulating such work behavior as rest periods were arbitrarily and harshly enforced. Workers were constantly urged to move faster and work harder. Sumner Slichter defined the drive system as "the policy of obtaining efficiency not by rewarding merit, not by seeking to interest men in their work . . . but by putting pressure on them to turn out a large output. The dominating note of the drive policy is to inspire the worker with awe and fear of the management, and having developed fear among them, to take advantage of it."[17]

Driving was more prevalent with daywork, where the effort wage was indeterminate. But it occurred with straight piecework too, when foremen sought to prevent workers from restricting output. An official of the machinists complained that "in many cases the rapidity with which the workingmen have been driven under the piecework and similar systems have been the means of driving the mechanics to the insane asylum." Under the bonus wage systems that began to appear after 1890, wages did not rise in proportion to output. Thus, unit labor costs fell with additional production, creating an incentive for the foreman to drive his men even harder and arousing the unions' anger over these new "scientific" payment plans.[18]

The drive system depended, ultimately, on fear of unemployment to ensure obedience to the foreman. Workers were more submissive when jobs were scarce, as was often the case before World War I. A discharge was usually devastating, since few workers had savings to cushion the hardships of unemployment and only meager relief was available. On the other hand, a tight labor market tended to undermine the foreman's authority, forcing him to rely more heavily on discharges to maintain discipline. Data from a metalworking plant illustrate this point. In 1914, a depressed year, the plant had 225 dismissals, many of them for "unadaptability" or "slow work"; this suggests that workers who could not keep up to standard were fired during hard times. By 1916, when the economy had improved and workers could afford to be feisty, the number of dismissals rose to 467, and a relatively large number of workers were fired for "insubordination," "troublemaking," and "positive misconduct." But whether times were tough or easy, the foreman was free to fire anyone as he saw fit, and discharges were meted out liberally. One critic of this system told the story of an assistant superintendent making his rounds through the shop: "Bill," he said to the foreman, "has anyone been fired from this shop today?" "No," the foreman meekly replied. "Well, then, fire a couple of 'em!" barked the assistant superintendent, in a voice that carried. "It'll put the fear of God in their hearts."[19]

Employment Security

Employment instability involved more than high dismissal rates. In its cyclical and seasonal forms, unemployment regularly touched a large portion of the working class. Between 1854 and 1914, recessions or depressions occurred every three or four years, with about twenty-five of these sixty years spent in contraction. In Massachusetts, unemployment was high even during relatively prosperous periods such as 1900–1906, when about one in every five of the state's manufacturing workers was unemployed for at least part of each year. Even Massachusetts' trade union members, a relatively skilled group, were not immune to job loss. An average of 29 percent of these workers had a spell of joblessness each year between 1890 and 1916. The amount of time spent in unemployment was considerable: In 1890 and again in 1900, over 40 percent of the nation's unemployed were jobless for more than four months.[20]

Because of dismissals and seasonal instability, unemployment was widespread throughout the labor force even during good years. Paul H. Douglas, the noted labor economist, estimated that approximately two-thirds of the unemployment that occurred in the three decades after 1896 was due to seasonal and chronic, as opposed to cyclical, causes. During the 1900s, workers in highly seasonal industries—men's clothing, glass containers, textiles—were on average employed only about three-fourths of a full working year. Employment tended to be more stable in consumer goods industries which produced items unaffected by style changes. But in 1909 even the most stable industry—bread and bakery goods—had monthly employment levels that varied 7 percent from peak to trough. That same year, the industrial average fluctuated 14 percent over the year, rising to 45 percent in the automobile industry. The seasonal instability of employment perpetuated the drive system. Activity became frenzied during the busy season as firms rushed to fill orders. Capacity utilization rates and employment levels rose by magnitudes rarely encountered today. A Fall River textile worker said that during the industry's busy season, "The Board of Trade drives the agent, the agent drives the superintendent, he drives the overseer, and the overseer drives the operative. They drive us, and we drive each other."[21]

However, the existence of widespread unemployment is not by itself an indication of the impermanence of the employment relationship. Had there been some understanding that laid-off workers would be recalled when needed, periodic unemployment need not have severed the relationship. But few firms made systematic attempts to rehire their workers after layoffs. For example, statistics from a large Chicago metalworking plant, whose records distinguished between new hires and rehires, reveal that only 8 percent of all new hires during the 1908–1910 period were rehires of workers who had been laid off during the depression that began late in 1907. Average industrial rehire rates were probably much lower. Of course, rehiring was more common in seasonal industries, since layoffs and their durations were more predictable. Even here, however, reemployment was by no means guaranteed. A government study of seven dressmaking establishments found that from 32 percent to 75 percent of those employed during the spring busy season were rehired after the summer lull.[22]

In addition to rehiring, mechanisms to maintain the employment relationship during downturns included guaranteed employment plans and work-sharing arrangements. By 1920, only 15 companies had employment guarantee plans. Work-sharing plans, though more prevalent, were usually initiated by trade unions in cooperation with unionized employers. Employers in nonunion firms maintained that work-sharing was cumbersome and inefficient.[23]

Few workers had anything resembling equity in their jobs. When layoffs came, it was the rare employer who ordered his foremen to reduce the work force systematically. Employment security was determined by the same arbitrary criteria as hiring. Bribes were a common means of ensuring job security. Shortly after the turn of the century, a group of Lithuanian workers in a rubber factory were forced to hand over a regular portion of their wages to the foreman as a sort of unemployment insurance. In other shops, according to an article in *Engineering Magazine*, everyone had to "pay some sort of tribute to his foreman. The tribute is usually in the form of money or service, but there are cases where the tribute is of a nature which cannot be mentioned in an open paper."[24]

In short, prior to World War I employment for most manufacturing workers was unstable, unpredictable, and frequently unjust. The worker's economic success and job satisfaction depended on a highly personal relationship with his foreman, with management and "the company" playing only a minor role. A foreman interviewed in 1920 noted that "before the war, most workmen worked where they did not so much because of the company they worked for but because of the foreman. To them the foreman represented the company, and workers in the barroom and other hangouts didn't talk so much about this company or that company as they did about this foreman or that foreman they had worked for." There *was* an implicit system of employment here, but it was not bureaucratic. Foremen had many favors to offer those whom they had befriended or those who had bought their friendship. Personal ties and loyalty counted for much, although later reformers were horrified by the particularism and brutality that infused the drive system. Those changes that made employment practices more rational, stable, and equitable were not a managerial innovation; rather, they were imposed from below.[25]

II. The Union Response

Trade unionism helped to curb the foreman's arbitrary exercise of power and gave the skilled worker some control over the terms of his employment. The trade union ensured that strict rules and equitable procedures would govern allocative decisions. While only a minority of all workers belonged to unions, those unions were a persistent reminder that the employer's authority, and that of his agents, could be circumscribed through collective action.[26]

Prior to the 1880s, local trade unions unilaterally adopted working rules or "legislation" that governed wages and working conditions for union members. Enforcement depended upon members' refusing—under threat of punishment by the union—to obey any order that contravened the union's rules. But after 1880, as the unions and their national organizations grew more powerful, the status of these rules changed from unilateral group codes to contractual and bargained restrictions on the employer and his foremen. These contracts were extensive documents that strictly regulated work methods and effort norms as well as such issues as apprenticeship standards and wage scales. An 1889 Memorandum of Agreement for members of the Amalgamated Association of Iron, Steel and Tin Workers at the Homestead Works contained fifty-eight pages of "footnotes" defining work rules for union members.[27]

Hiring

Controlling access to a trade was a fundamental element of the unions' power, and regulating apprenticeship standards was an important method for effecting this control. By limiting the number of apprentices or by lengthening the time required to become a journeyman, the union ensured that there would not be an oversupply of men in the trade and thus that the living standards to which union members were accustomed would not deteriorate. Moreover, by overseeing the training process, the union made certain that persons entering the trade were exposed to the virtues of unionism and had absorbed its moral code.

By the turn of the century, however, the apprenticeship system was fading out in many occupations where an ever finer division of labor reduced the demand for versatile craftsmen who knew all the "secrets" of a trade. The ratio of apprentices to the total number employed in manufacturing steadily declined, from 1:33 in 1860 to 1:88 in 1900. In testimony to Congress in 1901, Samuel Gompers noted that "the apprenticeship system is not so generally in vogue now as formerly. The introduction of new machinery . . . and the division and subdivision of labor have rendered a high class of skill, in which workmen have whole work, scarcely necessary (except the demand for the highest skill in a particular branch)."[28]

Nevertheless, the unions had other ways to bolster their control. One important mechanism was the closed or preferential shop, which restricted the foreman's discretion to hire whomever he chose and enhanced the demand for union labor. This protected union members against discrimination in hiring and guaranteed that vacancies would be filled by them. In some trades, the closed shop led to more restrictive union admissions policies so that a fixed number of potential vacancies could be divided among a smaller body of members. Some unions required that the foreman apply to a union hiring hall when in need of labor; this practice allowed the union to dispense jobs to the workers of its choice. Such arrangements also allowed unions to provide employment for older members and to prohibit the use of tests and other screening devices deemed objectionable. But basically they were a powerful demonstration to the worker that his well-being was best served by allegiance to the union rather than to his foreman.[29]

Wages and Effort

In their approach to wage determination, trade unions sought to protect not only absolute wage levels but also relative and effort wages. The central feature of this approach was the so-called standard rate, which all union members were supposed to receive. Reflecting the principle of equal pay for equal work, the standard rate ruled out all incentive wage systems under which earnings did not rise in proportion to output and effort, as well as all payment systems which "graded" workers: that is, classified them by some criterion such as merit or competence or sometimes even seniority. (One union said that seniority allowed the employer to get "first class service from a man getting less than a first class wage.") The unions' strong emphasis on the standard rate was based on the premise that foremen would always prefer to deal with individuals and that grading was the surest way to divide and conquer.

The unions were opposed to grading on other grounds as well. First, they argued that grading was unnecessary since apprenticeship standards insured that all journeymen were equally competent. Second, they feared that grouping workers by competence would undercut the standard rate and lead inevitably to the substitution of relatively cheap labor for higher priced men. Third, they believed that grading encouraged specialization within the trade, thereby lessening the demand for all-around craftsmen and eroding wage levels. Finally, they viewed grading and other meritocratic wage determination methods as an affront to their egalitarianism and their insistence on occupational autonomy. When the United Typothetae, an employers' association, proposed a graded wage

system in 1887, the Typographical Union replied that "it would be impossible to satisfactorily grade all workmen except by an elaborate system of examination which would be appalling to undertake."[30]

In practice, however, the unions permitted the payment of different rates for the various steps within a trade and for especially skilled or dangerous work. Among machinists and molders, for example, journeymen who had recently advanced from apprenticeship could be paid wages below the standard rate. Other unions allowed grading by skill, but only if the different grades were nonsubstitutable. The photo-engravers permitted half-tone etchers to be paid more than line-etchers, but the latter—however capable—were never permitted to do half-tone work.[31]

The standard rate represented a level of well-being for which union members had fought and to which they felt entitled. Consequently, organized workers viewed wage cuts as a threat to their living standards and stood ready to strike in defense of the standard rate. As early as 1870, textile manufacturers in Fall River, and then coal operators in Ohio's Hocking Valley, deliberately provoked strikes by cutting the wages of their unionized workers, hoping to break the unions in the ensuing disputes.[32]

Unions were equally concerned about how hard members had to work to receive their pay. To check the foreman's driving and to protect the effort wage, skilled workers made effective use of "the stint," the deliberate restriction of output. In many instances, the union specified output limits in the trade agreement and imposed fines on pieceworkers whose earnings were excessive. Typically, however, union members policed themselves. Skilled workers who restricted their output did not think of themselves as Luddites but instead as "sober and trustworthy masters of the trade" whose stinting demonstrated "unselfish brotherhood."[33]

While the stint was also used to deter foremen from playing favorites in assigning piecework jobs, the unions had other ways to limit favoritism. For example, in 1896 the molders demanded that piece rates be listed in a price-book, so as to prevent foremen from paying different rates for similar work. In one stovemaking shop, both the foreman and a union representative were given keys to the locker in which the price-book was kept. In the Chicago meatpacking industry, the cattle butchers devised a detailed system of promotion lines governed by seniority that was intended to curtail favoritism in job allocation and to create a sense of equity among the union's members. Foremen and other managers were strongly opposed to the practice. As John R. Commons observed, "These rules of promotion do not find favor with the superintendents, who contend that forced promotion takes a man away from work he does well."[34]

Elsewhere, promotion lines were devised primarily to enhance the prospects of a shop's incumbent workers. During the 1870s, unskilled helpers in the steel industry demanded that they be given preference over outsiders whenever a skilled position became vacant. By the late 1880s, the steelworkers' union had adopted rules calling for promotion lines governed by seniority. "We endeavor," said the union, "to prevent men from learning the skilled positions before they have served in the minor ones. If they are permitted to learn the skilled jobs, it would necessarily mean that those holding the minor positions would have no opportunity for improvement."[35] . . .

III. The Less Skilled

The unskilled worker dissatisfied with his job had few options. He could complain to higher officials, but they invariably supported the foreman in any dispute. Daniel McCallum, president of the Erie Railroad, justified this practice by asserting that "obedience cannot be enforced where the foreman is interfered with by a superior officer giving orders directly to his subordinates." More was involved here than the application of a military model to industry. As one economist perceptively observed, managers feared that any show of liberality would "give the workmen exaggerated notions of their rights and management desires to keep the workers' minds off their rights." In the early 1900s a group of nineteen unskilled rubber workers presented their employer with signed affidavits that described how they had been forced to bribe a foreman to retain their jobs. All nineteen were fired within two weeks.[36]

Occasionally the unskilled were able to establish their own workplace organizations, which regulated employment in much the same way as the craft unions did. During the 1880s, the Knights of Labor included local assemblies made up of less skilled workers who banded together to press for higher wages and to protect themselves from arbitrary foremen. Some of the locals even achieved the closed shop and a seniority-based layoff system. But unskilled workers had relatively little bargaining power and were rarely able to sustain sizable, stable organizations.

The absence of organization did not, however, deter them from engaging in militant activity. In steel, for instance, pitched battles were fought at Cleveland (1899), East Chicago (1905), McKees Rocks (1909), and Bethlehem (1910), with the unskilled, immigrant work force on one side and the militia and police on the other. The particularly violent strike at McKees Rocks was touched off when the company fired a group of workers who had protested pay practices and fee-charging by the company's foremen. But these strikes, while spectacular, were sporadic and seldom successful.[37]

Limitation of output was a somewhat more effective means of checking the foreman. The Commissioner of Labor's 1904 report on *Regulation and Restriction of Output* found that stints and slowdowns were "enforced in nonunion establishments" and were widely accepted "among all wage earners." But lacking the discipline provided by a union, and sundered by ethnic conflicts and language barriers that stymied cooperation, unskilled workers—even those belonging to assemblies of the Knights of Labor—had less success with this method than did their skilled counterparts.[38]

Because his actions were so ineffectual, the unskilled worker seeking higher wages or better working conditions usually had no alternative but to quit. Data from the 1900s and 1910s show labor turnover levels that were extraordinarily high by modern standards, especially among less skilled workers. Many companies experienced monthly separation rates in excess of 10 percent. In one Milwaukee engine factory, whose experience was typical of other factories, the separation rates for unskilled and semiskilled workers in 1912 were three times as high as the rates for skilled workers in the tool and pattern department. A government official termed labor turnover "the individualistic strike": Just as the number of strikes by skilled trade unionists tended to increase during a recovery period, so did the number of quits by the less skilled.[39]

High turnover rates also reflected the immigrant backgrounds of the unskilled. Almost two-thirds of the immigrants arriving in the United States between 1870 and 1910 were unskilled, and they became the backbone of the manufacturing labor force. Around the turn of the century, when the foreign-born constituted nearly one-quarter of the labor force, they represented about half of all unskilled laborers in manufacturing. Foreign-born workers accounted for 58 percent of all workers in iron and steel

manufacturing, 61 percent in meatpacking, 62 percent in bituminous coal mining, and 69 percent in the cotton mills.[40]

While it is well known that immigration flows were large and cyclically sensitive, it is less well known that emigration flows followed the same pattern. Between 1870 and 1914, one person left the United States for every three that arrived. While emigration decreased and immigration increased during good years, the annual proportion of emigrants to immigrants never fell below 20 percent. Emigration rose during depressed years, as recent immigrants—the first to lose their jobs—decided to return home. Ninety percent of the Bulgarians who made up most of the unskilled labor force in an Illinois steel mill had left town by the end of the 1908 depression. That year, immigration fell, and the national proportion of emigrants to immigrants rose to 75 percent. Although more immigrants stayed than left, the large backflow contributed to the instability of the unskilled labor force and to high rates of turnover.[41]

Immigrants often came to the United States with no intention of permanently settling here. Many were single men or married men with families back home. This was true of about half of the unskilled Italian laborers living in Buffalo in 1905, and of four in five of the nation's immigrant steelworkers. These men came to make their "stake," planning to return to Europe to buy land, open shops, or pay off debts. The transience of the immigrant labor force was part of an older European pattern of peasant mobility. In Italy, landless day laborers roamed from place to place looking for work, often spending weeks or months away from home. Slovaks worked seasonally on their plots and then supplemented their incomes as roving peddlers; Polish peasants went to Germany. The fact that many immigrant workers viewed their stay in the United States as temporary made it difficult to organize them into unions. A strike just lengthened the time a man was away from home and family, while the prospect of returning home made one's privations more bearable.[42]

Finally, quitting was a form of resistance to the rigors of factory life. Here there was a continuity of experience among the early New England textile workers, their French-Canadian and Irish replacements, and the southeastern Europeans who filled the factories after 1880. Each group brought to the factories a preindustrial work ethic that was attuned to the seasons, migratory, and uncomfortable with industrial discipline. Ellen Collins quit the mill at Lowell in the 1840s complaining about her "obedience to the ding-dong of the bell—just as though we were so many living machines." During the 1870s, managers of New England textile mills complained that absenteeism and quits made it difficult to run their machines on the hottest summer days. One manufacturer said in 1878 that "our mill operatives are much like other people and take their frequent holidays for pleasure and visiting." Forty years later, the quit rate at a Connecticut silk mill quadrupled during the hot summer months of 1915. Thus, each group successively went through the process of internalizing factory discipline; this was one of the props to high turnover before 1920.[43]

Although they were relatively less mobile, skilled workers also had a tradition of itinerancy that formed at the intersection of artisanal work habits and the requisites of learning a trade. It was supported by craft institutions, especially the trade union, and by repeated waves of immigrant artisans carrying similar traditions to the United States.

A familiar figure in industrializing societies, the footloose craftsman moved from shop to shop, acquiring the secrets of his trade. Employers often approved of this type of mobility. The labor supervisor at National Cash Register wrote in 1907 that

for a skilled worker, "it is of value, not a detriment, if he has had several employers—he is learning the trade." Reinforcing this mobility was a work ethic that emphasized manliness and independence. Acceptance of demeaning working conditions, or even long tenure, would compromise that ethic. One trade union representative noted that, for many skilled workers, "a job may be satisfactory in every respect, quite as good as they are likely to find anywhere, yet they will leave because they do not want to remain in one shop too long. . . . It rests upon a fear of losing their independence, of getting into a frame of mind wherein they will come to attach disproportionate importance to the retention of a certain job."[44]

The craft union facilitated the skilled worker's propensity to move. The constitutions of the early national unions required local secretaries to furnish reports on the conditions of the trade in their area and to help traveling members find jobs. Some unions loaned their members money to finance a search for work if none was to be found near home. But this loan system was on the decline by the beginning of this century, partly "because, as in the case of the iron molders, it was made use of to secure a free holiday."[45]

IV. A Market of Movement

Because the employment relationship was one of weak attachment on both sides, the industrial labor market prior to 1915 was a market of movement, characterized by high rates of mobility. Indeed, the few available company records indicate a pattern of continuously high turnover rates before World War I. The earliest turnover data come from the New England textile industry of the 1830s and 1840s, and they show that the young Yankee women who worked in the mills were an unstable labor force. Most were unmarried and could return to their parents' farms if they were dissatisfied or if work was scarce. But the immigrants who began to replace native workers in the 1850s had high turnover rates too. A study of 151 Scottish weavers recruited by Lyman Mills in 1853 found that nearly 80 percent of the women had left the firm within three years.[46]

A similar picture emerges in other companies, especially those employing relatively more men. A Massachusetts firm that manufactured textile machinery recruited large numbers of French-Canadians between 1860 and 1890. But "so rapid was the turnover" that, of every three workers hired, only one stayed with the firm. Rates of persistence were also very low at the Boston Manufacturing Company. For quinquennial periods between 1850 and 1865, only 10–12 percent of the male workers employed at the beginning of a period were still working for the firm five years later.[47]

Nineteenth-century employers sometimes complained about what one of them called "the nomadic system of employing men." Employers often responded to high quit rates by withholding the wages of those who left without prior notice, a practice that also deterred strikes. When a Massachusetts mill owner was asked in the 1870s to explain these wage forfeitures, he replied, "If a mill did not keep back workers' wages, it would simply awake to find all its hands gone by the morning."[48]

The better records available for the first two decades of the twentieth century show continuing high levels of turnover throughout the manufacturing sector. But because the overall data are so fragmentary, especially for the nineteenth century, some other source of information is needed to gauge labor turnover levels. . . .

. . . There is no doubt that employment under the drive system was a tenuous relationship. Both parties in the relationship took full advantage of their legal rights, acquired early in the nineteenth century, to quit or to dismiss at will. In fact, this was the only worker right consistently recognized by the courts of the day, and most managers did little to discourage its exercise. During the McKees Rocks dispute of 1909, the president of the struck company was succinct in his opinion of the strikers: "If a man is dissatisfied, it is his privilege to quit."[49]

NOTES

1. Samual Batchelder, *Introduction and Early Progress of the Cotton Manufacture in the United States* (Boston, 1863), passim; Stephen Marglin, "What Do Bosses Do? The Origins and Functions of Hierarchy in Capitalist Production," *Review of Radical Political Economics* (Summer 1974), 6:33–60; Caroline F. Ware, *The Early New England Cotton Manufacture* (Boston, 1931), pp. 23, 50–51, 263–266; Howard M. Gitelman, "The Waltham System and the Coming of the Irish," *Labor History* (Fall 1967), 8:227–253; Hannah Josephson, *The Golden Threads: New England's Mill Girls* (New York, 1949), pp. 220–221; Thomas Dublin, *Women at Work: The Transformation of Work and Community in Lowell, Massachusetts, 1826–1860* (New York, 1979).

2. Carroll D. Wright, "The Factory System of the United States," U.S. Bureau of the Census, *Report of the United States at the Tenth Census* (Washington, D.C., 1883), p. 548; Victor S. Clark, *History of Manufacturers in the United States* (Washington, D.C., 1929), 3:15–16, 76–80, 473; Daniel Nelson, *Managers and Workers: Origins of the New Factory System in the United States, 1880–1920* (Madison, Wis., 1975), p. 4.

3. The authority of the foreman and the skilled worker, said Frederick W. Taylor, come from "knowledge handed down to them by word of mouth. . . . This mass of rule-of-thumb or traditional knowledge may be said to be the principal asset or possession of every tradesman." *The Principles of Scientific Management* (New York, 1912), pp. 31–32.

4. Dan Clawson, *Bureaucracy and the Labor Process: The Transformation of U.S. Industry, 1860–1920* (New York, 1980), pp. 75–83, 115; John Buttrick, "The Inside Contract System,"

Journal of Economic History (September 1952), 12:205–221; Nelson, *Managers and Workers,* pp. 31, 38.

5. David Montgomery, "Workers' Control of Machine Production in the Nineteenth Century," *Labor History* (Fall 1976), 17:488–489; Clawson, *Bureaucracy,* pp. 130–166.

6. George S. Gibb, *The Whitesmiths of Taunton: A History of Reed and Barton, 1824–1843* (Cambridge, Mass., 1943), pp. 282–286; Clawson, *Bureaucracy,* pp. 126–130; Nelson, *Managers and Workers,* p. 40; Montgomery, "Workers' Control," p. 491.

7. Alexander Hamilton Church, "The Twelve Principles of Efficiency: The Eleventh Principle—Written Standard Practice Instructions," *The Engineering Magazine* (June 1911), 41:445; Gibb, *Whitesmiths,* p. 184; Ordway Tead, "The Importance of Being a Foreman," *Industrial Management* (June 1917), 53:353.

8. David Brody, *Steelworkers in America: The Nonunion Era* (New York, 1969), p. 85; "The Characteristics of a Foreman," *The Engineering Magazine* (February 1909), 36:847; Evelyn H. Knowlton, *Pepperell's Progress: History of a Cotton Textile Company, 1844–1945* (Cambridge, Mass., 1948), pp. 159–161.

9. Joseph H. Willits, "Steadying Employment," *The Annals* (May 1916), vol. 65, suppl., p. 72; H. Keith Trask, "The Problem of the Minor Executive," *The Engineering Magazine* (January 1910), 38:501; "Fall River, Lowell, and Lawrence," Massachusetts Bureau of the Statistics of Labor, *Thirteenth Annual Report* (Boston, 1882), p. 381.

10. Brody, *Steelworkers,* p. 120; Virginia Yans-McLaughlin, *Family and Community: Italian Immigrants in Buffalo, 1880–1930* (1977; reprint, Urbana, Ill., 1982), p. 43; Arthur Hanko, "Reducing Foreign Labor Turnover," *Industrial Management* (May 1921), 61:351.

11. Fred H. Rindge, Jr., "From Boss to Foreman," *Industrial Management* (July 1917), 53:508–509; C. J. Morrison, "Short-Sighted Methods in Dealing with Labor," *The Engineering Magazine* (January 1914), 46:568.

12. Charles E. Fouhy, "Relations Between the Employment Manager and the Foreman," *Industrial Management* (October 1919), 58:336; Henry Eilbirt, "The Development of Personnel Management in the United States," *Business History Review* (Autumn 1959), 33:346; Willits, "Steadying," p. 72.

13. "Detroit's Great Growth Due to Its Open Shop Policy," *Iron Trade Review* (July 15, 1915), 57:143–145; Clarence E. Bonnett, *Employer's Associations in the United States* (New York, 1922), p. 80; Edwin E. Witte, *The Government in Labor Disputes* (New York, 1932), pp. 211–218.

14. Charlotte Erickson, *American Industry and the European Immigrant, 1860–1885* (Cambridge, Mass., 1957), pp. 17–28, 67–87; Brody, *Steelworkers,* p. 109; Don D. Lescohier, "Working Conditions," in J. R. Commons et al., *History of Labor in the United States* (New York, 1935), 3:188; Isaac A. Hourwich, *Immigration and Labor* (New York, 1912), pp. 93–101; Harry Jerome, *Migration and Business Cycles* (New York, 1926).

15. Yans-McLaughlin, *Italian Immigrants,* pp. 59–64, 72–73; William I. Thomas and Florian Znaniecki, *The Polish Peasant in Europe and America,* abridged by Eli Zaretsky (1918; reprint, Urbana, Ill., 1984), pp. 139–255.

16. Sumner H. Slichter, *The Turnover of Factory Labor* (1919; reprint, New York, 1921), p. 319; Dwight T. Farnham, "Adjusting the Employment Department to the Rest of the Plant," *Industrial Management* (September 1919), 58:202; Commission of Inquiry, Interchurch World Movement, *Report on the Steel Strike of 1919* (New York, 1920), p. 139; Nelson, *Managers and Workers,* pp. 44–45; John P. Frey and John R. Commons, "Conciliation in the Stove Industry," U.S. Bureau of Labor Statistics (BLS) Bulletin No. 62 (Washington, D.C., 1906), p. 128.

17. John R. Commons, "Labor Conditions in Meat Packing and the Recent Strike," *Quarterly Journal of Economics* (November 1904), 19:8; Nelson, *Managers and Workers,* p. 43; Slichter, *Turnover,* p. 202.

18. Lloyd Ulman, *The Rise of the National Trade Union* (Cambridge, Mass., 1955), p. 549.

19. Philip Klein, *The Burden of Unemployment* (New York, 1923), pp. 13–37; Paul F. Brissenden and Emil Frankel, *Labor Turnover in Industry: A Statistical Analysis* (New York, 1922), pp. 80–81; Slichter, *Turnover,* p. 184; *Industrial Relations* (also known as *Bloomfield's Labor Digest*) (May 12, 1923), 15:1530.

20. Alexander Keyssar, "Men Out of Work: A Social History of Unemployment in Massachusetts, 1870–1916" (Ph.D. dissertation, Harvard University, 1977), pp. 43, 72, 76–77, 79,

107; Robert A. Gordon, *Business Fluctuations* (New York, 1961), p. 251.

21. Paul H. Douglas, "Can Management Prevent Unemployment?" *American Labor Legislation Review* (September 1930), 20:273; Mary Van Kleeck, "The Effect of Unemployment on the Wage Scale," *The Annals* (September 1915), 61:97–98; Irene O. Andrews, "The Relation of Irregular Employment to the Living Wage for Women," *American Labor Legislation Review* (June 1915), 5:319–374; Massachusetts Commission on Minimum Wage Boards, *Report* (Boston, 1912), passim; U.S. Bureau of the Census, *Census of Manufacturers: 1909* (Washington, D.C., 1912), pt. 1, pp. 37–54; "Fall River," p. 306.

22. Slichter, *Turnover*, pp. 126–127, 129.

23. Keyssar, "Out of Work," p. 129; "How to Meet Hard Times: A Program for the Prevention and Relief of Abnormal Unemployment," Mayor's Committee on Unemployment, City of New York (New York, 1917), p. 24; "Guaranteed Wages: Report to the President by the Advisory Board," Office of War Mobilization and Reconversion and Office of Temporary Controls (Washington, D.C., 1947), app. C, pp. 290, 293.

24. Keyssar, "Out of Work," p. 153; Morrison, "Short-Sighted," p. 568.

25. *Industrial Relations* (December 11, 1920), 5:484.

26. At its pre-Wagner Act peak in 1920, the proportion of nonagricultural employees who belonged to unions was 18.5 percent. Leo Wolman, *Ebb and Flow in Trade Unions* (New York, 1936), pp. 172–193.

27. F. W. Hilbert, "Trade-Union Agreements in the Iron Molders' Union," in Jacob H. Hollander and George E. Barnett, *Studies in American Trade Unionism* (London, 1906), pp. 221–260; Bruno Ramirez, *When Workers Fight: The Politics of Industrial Relations in the Progressive Era, 1898–1916* (Westport, Conn., 1978), pp. 17–48; Brody, *Steelworkers*, p. 52.

28. James M. Motley, *Apprenticeship in American Trade Unions* (Baltimore, 1907); Paul H. Douglas, *American Apprenticeship and Industrial Education* (New York, 1921), p. 74; "Testimony of Samuel Gompers," in U.S. Industrial Commission, *Report on the Relations and Conditions of Capital and Labor* (Washington, D.C., 1901), 7:620.

29. Sumner H. Slichter, *Union Policies and Industrial Management* (Washington, D.C., 1941), p. 63;

"Gompers," p. 603; Sanford M. Jacoby and Daniel J. B. Mitchell, "Development of Contractual Features of the Union-Management Relationship," *Labor Law Journal* (August 1982), 33:515; Howard T. Lewis, "The Economic Basis of the Fight for the Closed Shop," *Journal of Political Economy* (November 1912), 20:928–952; D. P. Smelser, *Unemployment and American Trade Unions* (Baltimore, 1919), pp. 57–74.

30. Sidney and Beatrice Webb, *Industrial Democracy* (1897; reprint, London, 1920), pp. 279–323; David A. McCabe, *The Standard Rate in American Trade Unions* (Baltimore, 1912), pp. 101–111; William H. Buckler, "The Minimum Wage in the Machinists' Union," in Hollander and Barnett, *Studies*, pp. 111–151.

31. Ulman, *National Trade Union*, pp. 483–484.

32. Montgomery, "Workers' Control," p. 496.

33. "Regulation and Restriction of Output," Eleventh Special Report of the U.S. Commissioner of Labor (Washington, D.C., 1904); Slichter, *Union Policies*, pp. 166–167; Montgomery, "Workers' Control," p. 491; G. G. Groat, *An Introduction to the Study of Organized Labor in America* (1916; reprint, New York, 1926), pp. 358–365. Unions also practiced output limitation as a way to stave off unemployment. Smelser, *Unemployment*, pp. 46–50.

34. Ulman, *National Trade Union*, pp. 542–543; Frey and Commons, "Stove Industry," pp. 128, 157; Commons, "Meat Packing," p. 17.

35. Quoted in Bernard L. Elbaum, "Industrial Relations and Uneven Development: Wage Structure and Industrial Organization in the British and U.S. Iron and Steel Industries, 1870–1970" (Ph.D. dissertation, Harvard University, 1982), p. 171.

36. McCallum quoted in Richard Edwards, *Contested Terrain: The Transformation of the Workplace in the Twentieth Century* (New York, 1979), p. 31; Slichter, *Turnover*, p. 387; Keyssar, "Out of Work," p. 153.

37. Montgomery, "Workers' Control," p. 489; Perlman, *History*, pp. 98–99, 116; Brody, *Steelworkers*, pp. 138–139.

38. "Restriction of Output," pp. 22, 29; Montgomery, "Workers' Control," p. 499. Also see Stanley B. Mathewson, *Restriction of Output Among Unorganized Workers* (New York, 1931).

39. Brissenden and Frankel, *Labor Turnover*, pp. 41, 48; Slichter, *Turnover*, pp. 57–69; William B.

Wilson, "Labor Program of the Department of Labor," BLS Bulletin No. 247 (1918), p. 166. At a large metalworking plant, the number of quits rose from 581 in 1914, a depressed year, to 3,035 in 1916. The plant's proportion of quits due to "dissatisfaction" rose from 27 percent in 1914 to 34 percent in 1915, the beginning of the recovery; by 1916, these accounted for 64 percent of all quits. Slichter, *Turnover*, p. 180.

40. Stanley Lebergott, *Manpower in Economic Growth: The American Record Since 1800* (New York, 1964), p. 28; Hourwich, *Immigration*, p. 503; Walter Fogel, "Immigrants and the Labor Market: Historical Perspectives and Current Issues," in D. G. Papademetriou and M. J. Miller, eds., *The Unavoidable Issue: U.S. Immigration Policy in the 1980s* (Philadelphia, 1983), p. 73.

41. Ulman, *National Trade Union*, p. 9; Jerome, *Migration*, p. 106; Federated American Engineering Societies, *Waste in Industry* (New York, 1921), p. 300; Brody, *Steelworkers*, pp. 105–106.

42. Yans-McLaughlin, *Italian Immigrants*, pp. 26–30, 49, 78; Brody, *Steelworkers*, pp. 97–98; Stephen Hickey, "The Shaping of the German Labor Movement: Miners in the Ruhr," in Richard J. Evans, ed., *Society and Politics in Wilhelmine Germany* (New York, 1978), pp. 215–240.

43. Herbert Gutman, *Work, Culture and Society in Industrializing America* (New York, 1976), p. 28; Massachusetts Bureau of Statistics of Labor, *Tenth Annual Report* (Boston, 1978), cited in Daniel T. Rodgers, *The Work Ethic in Industrializing America, 1850–1920* (Chicago, 1978), p. 162; Slichter, *Turnover*, p. 184.

44. Gutman, *Work, Culture and Society*, pp. 38–40; H. A. Worman, "How to Secure Factory Workers," in Clarence M. Wooley et al., *Employer and Employee* (New York, 1907), p. 57; A. J. Portenar, "Centralized Labor Responsibility from a Labor Union Standpoint," *The Annals* (May 1917), 71:193.

45. Ulman, *National Trade Union*, pp. 57–59; E. J. Hobsbawm, "The Tramping Artisan," in his *Labouring Men: Studies in the History of Labour* (London, 1964), p. 34; John Davidson, *The Bargain Theory of Wages* (New York, 1898), p. 178; Smelser, *Unemployment*, pp. 75–108.

46. Ware, *Cotton Manufacture*, pp. 224–226; Norman Ware, *The Industrial Worker, 1840–1860* (Boston, 1924), p. 149; Ray Ginger, "Labor in a Massachusetts Cotton Mill: 1853–1860," *Business History Review* (March 1954), 28:84, 87.

47 Thomas R. Navin, *The Whitin Machine Works Since 1831: A Textile Machinery Company in an Industrial Village* (Cambridge, Mass., 1950), pp. 160–161; Howard M. Gitelman, *Workingmen of Waltham: Mobility in American Urban Industrial Development, 1850–1890* (Baltimore, 1974), p. 71.

48. Rodgers, *Work Ethic*, p. 164. In an 1853 case involving a weaver who quit without giving prior notice, a Maine court said that, "The only valuable protection which the manufacturer can provide against such liability to loss and against what are in these days denominated 'strikes,' is to make an agreement with his laborers that if they willfully leave their machines and his employment without notice, all or a certain amount of wages that may be due to them shall be forfeited." *Harmon v. Salmon Falls Mfg. Co.*, 35 Me. 450 (1853).

49. Sanford M. Jacoby, "The Duration of Indefinite Employment Contracts in the United States and England: An Historical Analysis," *Comparative Labor Law* (Winter 1982), 5:85–128; Brody, *Steelworkers*, p. 78.

[handwritten note at top: Upshot: W/ the advent of the $ economy (in W.) in the 19th century, ♀'s place in the home became devalued as econ. changed & HHs/ indiv. were defined differently of — ♀ moved from being part of a "productive HH" to "dependents" - Did not chna until 1970s → then in US & not v. thoroug]

READING 2

How Mothers' Work Was "Disappeared"

The Invention of the Unproductive Housewife

Ann Crittenden

> I go to professional gatherings as my husband's wife and when I say I'm at home with two children, people never talk to me about anything serious. . . . They say, "Oh, it's so important what you're doing." I have actually said in reply, "You don't really believe that. Everything in this culture tells me that what I was doing before was more important. The rest of it is vacuous, empty words."
>
> —A Former Vice President of a Washington-Based Trade Association

Any woman who has devoted herself to raising children has experienced the hollow praise that only thinly conceals smug dismissal. In a culture that measures worth and achievement almost solely in terms of money, the intensive work of rearing responsible adults counts for little. One of the most intriguing questions in economic history is how this came to be; how mothers came to be excluded from the ranks of productive citizens. How did the demanding job of rearing a modern child come to be trivialized as baby-sitting? When did caring for children become a "labor of love," smothered under a blanket of sentimentality that hides its economic importance?

In recent years a new generation of female scholars—historians, law professors, economists, and sociologists—have begun to piece this story together. Their research, to put it bluntly, explains how mothers were robbed; how the hardest-working people on earth came to be defined as "dependents" who "don't work" and who have to be "supported" by a spouse who is officially the only "working" member of the household.

The early feminists, most of whom were wives and mothers, did not accept the denial of a mother's worth without a fight. Before the Civil War, feminists claimed that a married woman's unpaid labors entitled her to nothing less than an equal share of family wealth and income. But this demand proved far too radical, and the women's movement increasingly concentrated on the more attainable goal of female suffrage. Not until the 1970s were the assets accumulated in a marriage deemed to belong to both spouses. And as for so-called "family" income, to this day it remains the exclusive property of the spouse who earns it.

In the precapitalist era a "good wife" was considered a major *economic* asset. "Four things necessary in a house are a chimney, a cat, a hen, and a good wife," declared John Florio in the early seventeenth century, equating a spouse with other useful animals and appliances. A wife's skills at "housewifery" were considered as important to a family's standard of living as a husband's skills of yeomanry. The sturdy "good wife"—that bustling candle maker, pie baker, and chicken plucker now celebrated in reconstructed colonial villages all over New England—supported her husband with her labor, and no man of substance could be without one.

Yet the fruits of female labor legally belonged to men. Until the middle of the nineteenth century, married women had no right to property of their own. The common law gave a woman's husband an absolute right to her "services," including any outside income she might earn. Unless her family was wealthy enough to provide property for her in trust, a woman entered marriage as a dependent, and a dependent she remained. Wives had no legal say in family financial decisions, and widows were treated as an "encumbrance" on a man's estate, which was passed on to his heirs. As the first feminists often pointed out, it was hard to distinguish this servile state from that of a slave.

When most families lived at a bare subsistence level, these glaring inequities were somewhat irrelevant. Husband and wife shared bed and board with no great economic disparities between the two. But in the nineteenth century, as the cash economy spread, men gradually began to work for wages or were able to accumulate money through commercial transactions, while women for the most part remained in the barter economy of the family. "Work" or "labor" became synonymous with cash income and with "men's" work. The stage was set for the assumption—still with us—that men "supported" their wives at home, as if unpaid work were not productive and not part of the "real" economy.[1]

One of the first appearances of the monetary definition of "productive" is in Alexander Hamilton's 1791 *Report on Manufactures,* an argument for national investment in manufacturing industries. Only goods that could be sold to create revenue were included in Hamilton's definition of "the total produce" of society. He attributed a "superiority of . . .

productiveness" to labor whose product was geared for exchange outside the household. Thus he argued that women and children "are rendered more useful" by going to work in manufacturing establishments and earning cash than by remaining at home.[2] In *A Vindication of the Rights of Woman,* written at about the same time, Mary Wollstonecraft pointed out that under the new political and economic system that was emerging, "Either women can become [like] men, and so full citizens; or they continue at women's work, which is of no value for citizenship."[3]

As women's family labor lost status as "work," it was increasingly sentimentalized as a "labor of love." Feminist economist Nancy Folbre put it neatly: "The moral elevation of the home was accompanied by the economic devaluation of the work performed there."[4] In the late eighteenth and early nineteenth centuries the frugal, hardworking colonial wife was slowly replaced in popular mythology by the "angel of the hearth," a moral exemplar who tended to the spiritual, emotional, and physical needs of her brood, leaving the material aspects of life to her husband.

For men was reserved the world of money, commerce, and industry. For middle- and upper-middle-class white women, the ideal was to become the embodiment "of pure disinterested love, such as is seldom found in the busy walks of a selfish and calculating world," as one New Hampshire gentleman wrote in 1827.[5] Under this doctrine of "separate spheres," the "true woman" was the upholder of private morality and the caring sentiments. She would never stoop to ask for any monetary compensation for her labors. She was put on a high pedestal but asked to carry a very heavy load.*

---

*This ideology is still alive and well in the twenty-first century. Mothers at home are "the moral backbone of the country," wrote social conservative David Gelernter in a 1998 fund-raising letter for the Family Research Council, a lobbying group for the traditional father-headed family.

It has been suggested that this ideology served to keep educated, relatively privileged women from taking the republican ideals of liberty and equality to heart. After the French and the American Revolutions, many educated women had presumed to dream that they too might be liberated from arbitrary authority. Wollstonecraft's *A Vindication of the Rights of Woman* expressed these hopes in impassioned polemic, devoured by female readers on both sides of the Atlantic. Wollstonecraft posed the perfectly logical question: How could societies founded on the principles of universal human rights deny those rights to women?

The ingenuous solution to this challenge to patriarchal dominance was to cede to women the exalted task of nurturing the new free men. Rather than seeking their own personal gratification, women were urged to find fulfillment in the all-important task of creating the citizens of the new republic.

The emerging ideology of "separate spheres" thus served a dual purpose: it discouraged women from demanding greater participation in public and economic life, and it gave mothers license—and the moral authority—to rear their children as they saw fit. It ratified the withdrawal of fathers from the home and the expansion of mothers' responsibilities within it. Women's new assignment brought with it a significant strengthening of their domestic position. Prior to this time, the family had been a "patriarchal sovereignty," in the words of one satisfied early-eighteenth-century paterfamilias. Fathers had sole legal custody and could apprentice or marry off their children without a mother's consent. A woman's duty to her offspring took a distant second to her obligations to her husband, the rooster who ruled in every roost. All of this gradually changed, until by the mid–nineteenth century American women in many states had won the right to share joint custody of their children. Writer Lydia Sigourney could assure her female readers that their dominion over their young ones, which had hitherto known "bounds and obstructions," was now "entire and perfect."[6]

On the other hand, the new emphasis on conscientious motherhood did succeed in keeping American women out of the mainstream, as numerous foreign travelers observed. A visitor to the United States during the 1830s, Francis Grund, attributed the general ill health of married women "to the great assiduity with which American ladies discharge their duties as mothers. No sooner are they married than they begin to lead a life of comparative seclusion; and once mothers, they are actually buried to the world."[7]

Alexis de Tocqueville was also struck by the "extreme dependence" of American women and the degree to which they were "confined within the narrow circle of domestic life." "American women never manage the outward concerns of the family or conduct a business or take a part in political life. . . . Nor have the Americans ever supposed that one consequence of democratic principles is the subversion of marital power," he wrote. "They hold . . . that the natural head of the conjugal association is man." American women, he concluded, paid for their lofty moral and intellectual stature with "social inferiority" and arduous toil.[8]

But the increasing weight given to the job of caring for children was far more than just a strategy to distract women from participating in public life. It was also necessary to the development of a vibrant capitalist economy. By the late eighteenth century in France, England, and the United States, the countries with the most dynamic economies of the day, the rising bourgeoisie understood that their children would have to become educated, motivated little achievers if they were going to improve or even maintain their station in life.[9]

This required a new approach to childrearing. In a static, agrarian economy people cannot, and need not, make huge investments of time or emotion in their children. Early in life, with little or no schooling, children are able to become valuable economic assets, who work in the fields and the kitchen, tend the babies, care for the animals, and help in the family enterprise. An Indian baby in Guatemala can be safely tucked in a hammock all day with no harm done to his future as a subsistence farmer. A peasant child in Europe could be harshly treated and kept in line with no risk to his future as an underling. Even an aristocratic child could be treated with indifference and still safely count on inheriting his class privileges.

But these practices provide poor preparation for success in a fluid and meritocratic society. It takes years of hard, patient work to mold infants into individuals who have the imagination to find a place for themselves in a competitive, mobile world, the self-confidence to strive, and the self-discipline to plan for an uncertain future. "Breaking the will" or even benign neglect are not the best ways to ensure that a child will have what it takes to be a real go-getter.[10]

Upper- and middle-class fathers, increasingly drawn away from the home by commerce and industry, were not in a position to undertake this new parental challenge. Thus mothers were exhorted to step into the father's traditional place as the family's principal teacher, disciplinarian, and moral arbiter. As Benjamin Rush of Philadelphia, one of the signers of the Declaration of Independence, put it: since men would not have the time to govern their offspring as they had in the past, mothers would have to assume the task. If they were to meet the challenge, Rush predicted, they would need education and training, because raising children was becoming an increasingly complex job.

The mounting demands of child-rearing thus provided the rationale for the education of women. The education of girls for the crucial assignment of producing workers with "a capitalistic spirit" as well as "Christian virtue" became a distinctive feature of early-nineteenth-century America. Numerous special schools for girls were established, with the express purpose of preparing women for enlightened motherhood. Between 1790 and 1850, female literacy in the United States rose at an unprecedented rate, unmatched anywhere in the world. By the middle of the nineteenth century, the literacy rate for white American women was roughly equal to that for white men. By 1860, only 5 percent of white women in New England and 20 percent of white women in the South could not read.[11]

Literate mothers devoured magazines offering "how-to" advice on child health and discipline and reminding them that they were shaping "the character of the whole of society." Again and again, the message of the educational reformers of the Enlightenment was repeated: Successful child-rearing requires a kinder, gentler, more patient hand, and an enormous amount of care and vigilance. Cold, rigid authoritarianism could not do the job of instilling in children the desirable qualities of self-reliance, honesty, industry, and thrift.[12] Thus women were recruited to the crucial task of producing the kind of human capital that the modern industrial economy needed.[13]

This story has been left out of economic history. As the story of the family is conventionally told, virtually all serious economic activity had left the household by the mid–nineteenth century, as manufacturing migrated from farms into factories. The household evolved from a workplace, where most necessities were produced, into a place of leisure, consumption, and emotional replenishment; a "haven in a heartless world." Ostensibly, industrialization put families, and the women in them, "out of business."

In fact, the family remained an intrinsic part of the economy. There was simply a

"A free ride on wives' unpaid labor"

transformation of the type of goods and services produced in the home. The new domestic product was the intensively raised child. According to anthropologist Wanda Minge-Klevana: "During the transition from preindustrial society to industrial society, the family underwent a qualitative change as a labor unit—from one that produced food to one whose primary function was to socialize and educate laborers for an industrial labor market."[14] By producing new worker-citizens, families became, in the words of Shirley Burggraf, "the primary engine of economic growth."[15]

Child-rearing, of course, was still only a small part of the work of the nineteenth-century household. As the economy became more commercial, women by default had to perform what had been men's and even children's domestic work—for children too were leaving the home, to go to school.* The family's unpaid labor force was shrinking down to the adult women, who had to handle chores with animals, gardens, and repairs on top of the traditional work of cooking, cleaning, and child care.[16] The angel of the hearth was increasingly on her own, up to her elbows in coal dust and soapsuds.

Commentaries of the period refer to wives' overwork and lack of leisure in language reminiscent of contemporary complaints about the "second shift." In a letter to the editor of a New England newspaper in 1846, "Cleo Dora" suggested that husbands needed to be reminded of the meaning of the word "helpmeet." It meant to *help*, she wrote, not to perform *all* of the family labor, and certainly not to be kept hard at work long after her husband had come home to relax. "I pray you . . . now and then exhort husbands to do their parts," she concluded.[17] The sheer demands of everyday household management are reflected in the advice manuals for middle-class women of the antebellum period. In her enormously popular 1841 *Treatise on Domestic Economy,* for example, Catherine Beecher argued that the economy of housework required the "wisdom, firmness, tact, discrimination, prudence, and versatility" of a politician and the "system and order" of a business. In Beecher's opinion, domestic accounting procedures actually surpassed the often "desultory" practices of business.[18]

Jeanne Boydston, the leading historian of the nineteenth-century domestic economy, argues that both husbands and employers enjoyed a free ride on wives' unpaid labor. Boydston has calculated that the cash value of the work done by working-class and middle-class wives was far greater than the cost of their maintenance. Their activities enabled employers to pay extremely low wages, a factor that "was critical to the development of industrialization in the antebellum Northeast." Wives were a bargain, which explains why young men, if they wanted to get ahead, were advised to marry.[19]

Thus, behind the myth of the "true woman," whose calling was emotional and moral, lurked the reality of the overworked mother, whose output was economically productive. And behind the myth of the male breadwinner and the self-made man lurked the free labor provided by a wife.[20]

For decades neither sex challenged the gendered split between "work" and "home." Women imagined that their moral and domestic authority compensated for their lack of economic and political power. And men imagined women as givers of love and arbiters of virtue too pure for the marketplace—conveniently overlooking the

---

*Nineteenth-century governments as well as families contributed to the production of human capital by banning child labor and establishing public primary schools that all children were required to attend. But the principal producers of and "investors" in the new worker-citizens were their own families.

fact that as long as women had no right to property or access to cash income, their domestic "gifts" were given in return for food, shelter, and protection.[21]

The reigning family myth—that men "supported" women as well as children—prevented the great majority of women from seeing themselves as valuable economic players and equal marriage partners. They couldn't feel cheated of the fruits of their labor if they didn't believe that what they were doing *was* labor. Even as accomplished and astute a woman as Harriet Beecher Stowe couldn't see through the ideological veil. In 1850 she wrote to her sister-in-law, relating her recent activities: the household had moved to Maine the spring before; she had made two sofas, a chair, diverse bedspreads, pillowcases, pillows, bolsters, and mattresses; painted rooms; revarnished furniture; given birth to her eighth child; run a huge household; and somehow also managed to make her way through the novels of Sir Walter Scott—all within a year.

"And yet," she confided, "I am constantly pursued and haunted by the idea that I don't do anything."[22]

The Joint Property Claim

These were the circumstances in which the early women's rights movement emerged in the eastern United States in the 1840s. And not surprisingly, most of its leaders were educated middle-class married mothers who had begun to question the idea that their work was "unproductive" and hence unworthy of material recognition.

Elizabeth Cady Stanton, the best-known advocate of women's rights in the nineteenth century, had seven children. Her feminism developed in her early thirties, after she moved with her husband and several young children to a new town, Seneca Falls, New York, where she knew no one. Her husband traveled most of the time, leaving her feeling isolated and overworked.[23]

Although Stanton had household help, as her prominence grew she was continually struggling to find time for her lectures and political activities. In a note to Susan B. Anthony in 1853, she asks her friend to find a lawyer who can look up some points of law for her. "You see," she explains, "while I am about the house, surrounded by my children, washing dishes, baking, sewing, etc., I can think up many points, but I cannot search books. . . . I seldom have one hour undisturbed in which to sit down and write. Men who can, when they wish to write a document, shut themselves up for days with their thoughts and their books, know little of what difficulties a woman must surmount to get off a tolerable production."[24]

In 1857, while Stanton was nursing her sixth child, the unmarried Anthony complained that "those of you who have talent to do honor to poor—oh! how poor—womanhood have all given yourselves over to baby-making; and left poor brainless me to do battle alone."[25]

But Susan B. Anthony was the exception. Most early feminists did it all.

Antoinette Brown Blackwell, the first female minister in the United States, had seven children, as did Martha Coffin Wright, an adviser to Anthony and Stanton who later became an officer of the National Woman Suffrage Association. Lucy Stone, a teacher who kept her own name after marrying Antoinette Blackwell's brother-in-law, raised one child, made her own yeast, bread, and soap, cured meat, kept chickens and cows, and grew vegetables. Lydia Maria Child supported herself and her husband by writing, and noted in her diary that in one year she prepared 722 meals and made thirty-six pieces of clothing and seventeen items of household furnishing. Ida B. Wells, who as a courageous young journalist documented southern lynchings, later raised six children while organizing African-American women in Chicago to demand the vote.

These feminist foremothers knew first-hand about a wife's contributions to the household economy. They could speak from experience to women like the anonymous author of "The Revolt of Mother," a short story based on the writer's memories of farm life in pre–Civil War Massachusetts. The storyteller described a farm wife, Mrs. Penn, who toiled for years in silent resignation—raising the children, preparing the food, washing and ironing the clothes, cleaning the house—while all of the family's earnings were poured into the husband's farm business. When Mr. Penn decided yet again to make a big expenditure on what interested *him* (a new barn) instead of what *she* wanted (a spruced-up house), an avalanche of accumulated anger and resentment came pouring down on him: "You see this room, here, father, you look at it well. You see there ain't no carpet on the floor an' you see the paper is all dirty, an' droppin' off the walls. . . . You see this room, father, it's all the one I've had to work in an' eat in and sit in since we was married."

This fictitious wife found a solution: she moved the family into the new barn.[26]

The early leadership of the woman's rights movement had close ties to the antislavery movement and saw obvious parallels between the institution of slavery and the institution of marriage. But rather than attack marriage itself, as some nineteenth-century utopian socialists and communitarians had done, the antebellum feminists came up with a strategy that took the doctrine of separate spheres literally. If women's work in the home is so exalted, they asked, why isn't it valued equally with men's work? By virtue of their labor, they argued, wives earned joint rights to all the property accumulated during a marriage.

This joint property claim was on the agenda of the First National Woman's Rights Convention, held in 1850 at Worcester, Massa-

chusetts. The convention's resolutions opened with a demand for women's suffrage and closed with a vow to remember the million and a half women trapped in slavery in the South. In between, the delegates resolved to revise the marital property laws "so that all rights may be equal between (married parties);—that the wife may have, during life, an equal control over the property gained by their mutual toil and sacrifices, be heir to her husband precisely to the extent that he is heir to her, and entitled, at her death, to dispose by will of the same share of the joint property as he is."[27]

In the following year's convention at Worcester, the joint property claim was spelled out in greater detail. It was resolved: "That since the economy of the household is generally as much the source of family wealth as the labor and enterprise of man, therefore the wife should, during life, have the same control over the joint earnings as her husband."[28]

In 1854, Stanton, then age thirty-eight, gave her first major public address, before the New York state senate. In a black silk dress with a white lace collar secured with a diamond pin, she made a bold bid for full legal citizenship for women, and for female equality in marriage. She demanded for married women the right to earn money and inherit property, a share of marital property, shared custody of children, and the right to divorce.

This was an uncompromisingly radical agenda. The attempt to win legal and economic equality for women *in the family* was far more sweeping than the demand for the vote, and far more threatening to men's economic dominance. Indeed, more than a century later, the vote has long been won, but mothers are still waiting for full economic equality in the family.

Stanton's demands, and subsequent campaigning, did achieve results. The New York state legislature had in 1848 passed the Married Women's Property Act, allowing married women to hold property in their own

[Handwritten at top: Acts passed for property rights but mean little for ♀ w/ no wages earned (ie most white women)]

names, and insulating their separate estates from a husband's debts. In 1857 and again in 1860, the act was amended to give married women, for the first time, the right to collect their own earnings, to share joint custody of their children, and to inherit equally with their children when widowed. This was the most liberal marital property reform that had ever been adopted in the United States.

[Handwritten left margin: ❀ T rights added to act in NY]

In the 1860s and 1870s, similar laws were enacted in other states, granting wives rights to the land and property they brought into a marriage and the right to their own earnings. But these Married Women's Property Acts, or "earnings statutes," passed by all-male legislatures, did not affect the economic status of the great majority of women, who had little if any property or outside earnings of their own.

[Handwritten left margin: But didn't have much meaning]

In 1860, when New York state finally granted a wife the right to her own earnings, only 15 percent of all free women in the United States had any earnings from paid labor, and most of these women were single or widowed. As late as 1890, the national census counted only 3.3 percent of all white married women as working for wages (compared with roughly 40 percent of all African-American women).[29]

Many feminists immediately recognized that the 1860 New York statute would still leave husbands in full control of all property created during a marriage. It was a help to poor women who had to work for a living, one feminist wrote. "But what shall the great mass of women, the wives of the middling classes . . . do? What right have they in the property obtained after marriage?" The answer was poignantly conveyed in this 1876 letter from an anonymous farm woman to the editor of a suffrage magazine:

> Married in pioneer times a poor man, and by our joint efforts have made us a home worth several thousand dollars; have borne nine children, and took the whole care of them. Five are men grown, four of them voters. The first twenty years I did all my house-work, sewing, washing and mending, except a few weeks at the advent of the babies. For the last sixteen years have had help part of the time; but have had from two to four grandchildren to care for the last three years, one of them a baby. And now I want to go to the Centennial and cannot command a sixpence for all my labor. Husband owns and controls everything and says we have nothing to spend for such foolishness. Have no more power than a child. Now if my labor has been of any value in dollars and cents I want those dollars and cents to do as I please with. I feel like advising every woman not to do another day's labor unless she can be the owner of the value of it.
>
> All the property that I possess in my own right is this pen and holder; a present from my brother in California.
> PEN HOLDER

The nation's courts were deaf to such cries. Wives' labor within the home was presumed to be rendered *voluntarily* on behalf of the family, and not in expectation of financial reward. The Iowa Supreme Court, for example, found that the state's earnings statute, passed in 1873, "did not intend . . . to release and discharge the wife from her common law and scriptural obligation and duty to be a 'help-meet' to her husband. If such a construction were to be placed upon the statute, then the wife would have a right of action against the husband for any domestic service. . . . For her assistance in the care, nurture, and training of his children, she could bring an action for compensation. She would be under no obligation to superintend or look after any of the affairs of the household unless her husband paid her wages for so doing. Certainly, such consequences were not intended by the legislature."[30]

[Handwritten right margin: why HH econ. = was so scary]

Handwritten margin notes:

- Transition from old HH to indiv. as econ. unit
- Bc of 'threat', own focused on ♀'s on legal (not econ.) equality
- Prop. rights dropped
- Began challenging trad. div. of labor instead
- Chng in census
- 1870s Homemakers no longer "productive employees"

26   *Ann Crittenden*

Certainly not!

———

After the Civil War, in the face of this kind of unyielding opposition, the women's rights movement in the United States gradually turned away from the issue of economic equality between husbands and wives. The leadership increasingly focused on legal equality, including the right to hold office, to be tried by peers, to equal treatment under the criminal code, and, most notably, the right to vote. By the 1880s the claim that wives had a right to joint marital property had been dropped from the suffragists' legislative agenda.

Instead of demanding that equal *value* be placed on women's work of child care and homemaking, many women's rights advocates began to challenge the traditional gender division of labor itself. American feminists began to describe work within the family as labor that women had to *escape*, if they were ever to achieve equality and freedom. They began to imagine two-career marriages and schemes for cooperative housekeeping that would free women to earn an income and relieve them from the drudgery of housework. In other words, they began to sound like contemporary feminists in their assumption that women could only avoid subservience and economic dependency by becoming wage earners.

This shift reflected the dramatic changes in the U.S. economy taking place after the Civil War. By 1870, for the first time in American history, more men were employed, earning wages, than were producing their own livelihood themselves. In the new money economy, wives increasingly depended on their husbands for income to run the household. The principal economic unit was no longer considered the household, but the individual, whose wages were legally his alone.

Fifty years earlier, when the federal census first began to measure economic activity it had tallied the number of families, not individuals, engaged in agriculture, commerce, and manufacturing. It was assumed that all members of a household contributed to the family enterprise, whether it was a farm, a handicraft, or a business. As working for wages became more common, however, the federal census began to inquire into the occupations of *individuals*. The 1850 census wanted to know the "profession, occupation, or trade" of each male person over fifteen years of age. In 1860 this question was extended to women, the great majority of whom described their occupation as "housekeeper."[31]

In 1870 Francis Walker, a prestigious economist who later served as president of the Massachusetts Institute of Technology, took command of the U.S. census. A Civil War veteran who liked to be addressed as "General," Walker did not believe that women's household work was of particular economic value. "We may assume that speaking broadly, [a wife] does not produce as much as she consumes," he confidently wrote.[32] Under Walker's aegis, the census explicitly stipulated that those who described themselves as "housekeepers" had to be people receiving wages for the service. "Women keeping house for their own families, or for themselves, without any other gainful employment, will be entered as 'keeping house,'" he decreed. Thus the work of family maintenance—all of the gardening and canning and cooking and cleaning, the animal raising, the sewing and mending, the care of the sick and the elderly—not to mention the task of rearing the next generation of productive workers, was stricken from the list of productive employments.

Precise on this point, Walker was surprisingly cavalier about the systemic undercounting of the cash earnings that women did have. His census takers, by his own admission, overlooked most women's income, earned by taking in boarders and lodgers, for example, or contracting industrial piecework from manufacturing firms. As a result, virtually all of women's toil from dawn to dusk was dismissed as irrelevant to the real productive activity of the bustling, growing nation.

This massive slight did not go unnoticed. Speaking at a woman's congress in 1874, Mary Livermore argued that "women had a monetary value as wives and mothers, and they ought to insist upon a recognition of that value. Eight millions of American women were wives and housekeepers, but according to the census they were 'doing nothing.'" In 1878 a protest was issued by the Association for the Advancement of Women, a group of the most highly educated women of the time, including Maria Mitchell, a Harvard astronomer, Julia Ward Howe, a prominent feminist activist, and Melusina Fay Pierce, an advocate for the collectivization of housework.

In a letter to Congress these notables complained that "more than twelve millions of American women [were] overlooked as laborers or producers or left out . . . and not even incidentally named as in any wise affecting the causes of increase or decrease of population or wealth." They suggested that a more accurate accounting could be obtained if the Census Bureau employed "intelligent women to collect vital statistics concerning women and children."[33]

The suggestion was ignored. By 1900, wives and daughters without paying jobs were officially classified as "dependents." As the new century began, the married woman had become "just a housewife." In 1900, in an essay published in *Cosmopolitan* magazine, one Flora Thompson penned these words: "Women have forced economic recognition of their labor in men's spheres, but especial woman's work remains the economic cipher. Domestic labor is accorded no rational recognition in the mind of political economy or in the heart of labor reform."[34]

One hundred years later, this is still true.

Interestingly, the state of Massachusetts, the home of so many educated and distin-guished women, held out against the trend longer than most. In the Massachusetts census of 1875, unpaid housewives were included in an occupational category along with housekeepers, servants, nurses, and washerwomen. Married women were not automatically assumed to be either productive or unproductive. Some were described as "having nothing to do but superintend the households," and others, in the census's own words, were "simply ornamental." (By some unknown method of accounting, these were estimated to be fewer than 2 percent of all wives.) Gradually, however, the Massachusetts census bowed to the inevitable. By 1905, housework was listed in the "not gainful" class, along with students, retirees, those unemployed for twelve months, and dependents.[35]

The British census evolved in a similar fashion. Before 1851, British census takers, like those in the United States, had inquired after the occupations of families rather than individuals. When individual occupations were first listed, "wives, mothers and mistresses" were placed in a category by themselves, distinct from the class of "dependents," which included children, the sick and infirm, gypsies and vagrants, and certain "ladies and gentlemen of independent means."[36]

The censuses of Britain and of England and Wales from 1851 to 1871 were under the direction of the renowned medical statistician William Farr, who viewed a nation's population as its "living capital." In one section of his 1851 report, Farr defined the head of the family as "the husband-and-wife." Farr also had a strong appreciation of the value of the work of child-rearing. "The most important production of a country is its population," he wrote in 1851. In 1861 he elaborated: "These women [wives and widows] are sometimes returned as of no occupation. But the occupation of wife and mother and housewife is the most important in the country, as will be immediately apparent if it be assumed for a moment to be suppressed."[37]

By 1871, however, the head of household had been redefined as "the householder, master, husband, or father." In 1881, all women engaged in unpaid domestic duties were explicitly placed in the "Unoccupied Class." In 1891, a year in which as many women were engaged as wives and mothers as men were engaged in all the other occupations, the British census dropped the category of wives and mothers altogether. The bureaucrats apparently felt a little guilty about erasing mothers from the rolls of the fruitful: "The most important, however, of all female occupations . . . is altogether omitted from the reckoning, namely the rearing of children and the management of domestic life."

The great English neoclassical economist Alfred Marshall had no qualms about this bold stroke. Testifying before a parliamentary committee in 1898, Marshall held up a recent German census as an example of superior methodology. It described married women as "dependents."

In Australia as well the work of women was "disappeared." By 1890 the population had been divided into two categories: breadwinners and dependents. Women doing domestic work were "dependents," along with children and "all persons depending upon private charity, or whose support is a burthen on the public revenue."[38]

Thus all over the Anglo-Saxon world by the beginning of the twentieth century, the notion that women at home were "dependents" had acquired the status of a scientific fact. The idea that money income was the only measure of human productivity had triumphed. With official blessing, husbands could consider wives not as economic assets but as liabilities.

The theft was breathtaking.

So complete was this victory that it was accepted by some of the most prominent turn-of-the-century feminists. In 1909 two women's organizations sponsored a debate between Charlotte Perkins Gilman, the celebrated author, and Anna Howard Shaw, the president of the National American Woman Suffrage Association. The topic was the economic value of a wife's household labor.

Gilman took the position that the vast majority of American women, the "immense middle class," were unproductive parasites. Even though a wife might work ten to fourteen hours a day for the family, raising the children, maintaining the home, and extending the purchasing power of her husband's wages by her thrift, Gilman maintained that "her labor is not productive industry." An "unpaid wife," Gilman declared, was "a domestic servant in the extremely wasteful and expensive class of one servant to one man."

Gilman's position was elaborated in her widely acclaimed book, *Women and Economics* (which was said to be "the Bible of the student body at Vassar"). In it she ridiculed the notion that "the wife [is] an equal factor with the husband in producing wealth" and insisted that women are supported by their husbands. She repudiated the struggles of earlier feminists by denying that work for the family could have any claim to equal status or reward. "There is no equality in class between those who do their share in the world's work in the largest, newest, highest ways and those who do theirs in the smallest, oldest, lowest ways," she wrote of the traditional division of labor in marriage. For Gilman, only the collectivization of domestic labor and the "break up [of] that relic of the patriarchal age—the family as an economic unit" could emancipate women. She wanted to abolish the private home and have people live in apartment houses, with professionally staffed facilities for meals, cleaning, laundry, and child care.

It is not hard to detect in this program a profound distaste for family life. For Charlotte Gilman, maternity had none of the solace that might have mitigated its oppressions. She lumped the care of children with all of the other menial labor women were assigned, as if child care were equivalent to dishwashing, and as if women could flee their children as easily as they could run away from dirty laundry. She literally threw the baby out with the bathwater.

Gilman's thinking was strangely congruent with that of male-dominated legislatures and courts, which also denigrated the economic importance of women's "labor of love." She was in effect abandoning a position—that wives had an equal right to marital property—that had threatened the very foundations of male economic power.

In the historic 1909 debate, Anna Shaw challenged Gilman's assumption that mothers were analogous to servants. She made a fundamental distinction between the work of a mother and that of a domestic servant. The former, she explained, creates a *home* for her children; the other merely maintains it. Shaw claimed that wives "put something economically valuable into [the husband's income] which has increased, if not its incoming power, at least its outgoing power." For that, she concluded, wives and mothers should be compensated with earnings proportionate to the position that their family held in society.[39]

A reporter covering the debate for the *New York Evening Call* reported that the female audience had no problem deciding which side of the argument they were on. At the close of the debate, when the audience was asked whether a wife was supported by her husband, " [a] few scattered ayes were heard, but when the judge asked for the 'noes' the answers were so vigorous and numerous that it was easily apparent that the vast majority of the audience had no doubts."

Shaw won the debate but lost the battle.

As that evening in New York illustrated, at the turn of the twentieth century, the women's movement contained two contradictory strands: one that denigrated women's role within the family, and one that demanded recognition and remuneration for it. The first argued that only one road could lead to female emancipation, and it pointed straight out of the house toward the world of paid work. The second sought equality for women within the family as well and challenged the idea that a wife and mother was inevitably an economic "dependent" of her husband.

For the rest of the twentieth century, the women's movement followed the first path, and it led to innumerable great victories. But in choosing that path, many women's advocates accepted the continued devaluation of motherhood, thereby guaranteeing that feminism would not resonate with millions of wives and mothers.

Married women in the United States were to remain legally and economically subservient to their husbands for several more generations. Until 1970, husbands still had sole power to manage all property acquired during the marriage. A wife had no clear legal remedies to prevent her husband's mismanagement of marital property, and no clear right even to know the extent or location of the communal assets. A married woman with no separate property of her own could not even obtain credit without her husband's consent.

In the 1970s, the joint property claim finally became the law of the land. Assets accumulated during a marriage, except for those that are inherited, are deemed to belong to both spouses. But to this day, in only three states—California, Louisiana, and New Mexico—are wives unequivocally entitled to half of marital assets. (In six other states there is a judicial presumption that marital assets are owned fifty-fifty.)[40] Moreover, in many courts of law it is still considered *unnatural* for a wife and mother to claim a material reward for her labors on behalf of the family. If a wife is promised benefit from her husband in exchange for the performance of household labor, and he reneges on his part of the bargain, no court will assist her in enforcing the agreement. The courts have declared that her labor was "presumed gratuitous" or "rendered freely," with no expectation of any quid pro quo.

As recently as 1993, for example, a California court refused to enforce an agreement made between a married couple after the husband suffered a stroke. Although he had been advised by his doctors to enter a nursing home, his wife had consented to nurse him at home in return for inheriting certain properties. She provided the care, but he died without keeping his promise. The judge declared that he would abide by "the long-standing rule that a spouse is not entitled to compensation for support." "Even if few things are left that cannot command a price, marital support remains one of them," this judge opined, in a ruling that brought the full weight of history down on the hoodwinked wife.[41]

Free riding in the family endures.

NOTES

1. A detailed history of women's unpaid domestic labor, and how it came to be redefined as industrialism spread, is described in Jeanne Boydston, *Home and Work: Housework, Wages, and the Ideology of Labor in the Early Republic* (New York: Oxford University Press, 1990).

2. Boydston, *op. cit.,* pp. 46–47.

3. Mary Wollstonecraft, *A Vindication of the Rights of Women* (Mineola, N.Y.: Dover Publications, 1996).

4. Nancy Folbre, "The Unproductive Housewife," *Signs: Journal of Women in Culture and Society* 16, no. 31 (1991): 465.

5. Charles Burroughs, *An Address on Female Education, Delivered in Portsmouth, N.H.,* October 29, 1827.

6. Ann Douglas, *The Feminization of American Culture* (New York: Alfred A. Knopf, 1977), pp. 74–75. The quote is from Lydia Sigourney's *Letters to Mothers,* written in 1838.

7. Quoted in Boydston, *op. cit.,* pp. 81–82.

8. Alexis de Tocqueville, *Democracy in America, Volume II* (New York: Vintage Books, 1945), pp. 223–25.

9. As Olivier Bernier wrote in *Pleasure and Privilege* (Garden City, N.Y.: Doubleday, 1981), a history of late-eighteenth-century Europe and America, "Middle class children would one day be expected to earn money and further the family fortunes; they had to be educated accordingly."

10. Mary P. Ryan, *The Empire of the Mother* (New York: Harrington Park Press, 1985), pp. 48–49.

11. Jane Rendell, *The Origins of Modern Feminism: Women in Britain, France, and the United States, 1780–1860* (New York: Macmillan, 1985), pp. 145–46.

12. *Ibid.,* pp. 209–10.

13. In the 1970s some feminist scholars viewed the cultural shift toward more intensive childrearing as a step backward for women. Writing at a time when women were just emerging from "the feminine mystique," they concluded that the weighty importance suddenly attached to mothering sounded ominously familiar and repressive. The nineteenth-century "cult of motherhood" was characterized as the "bonds of womanhood," an enormous scam to keep women busy in the home while men monopolized the marketplace, the money, and the public power.

   But even if the glorification of the role of the mother did play a part in channeling educated women away from public life, as it clearly did, that does not alter the fact that the feminization of child-rearing practices had profound economic consequences.

14. Wanda Minge-Klevana, "Does Labor Time Decrease with Industrialization? A Survey of Time-Allocation Studies," *Current Anthropology* 21, no. 3 (June 1980): 279.

15. Shirley Burggraf, *op. cit.*

16. Boydston, *op. cit.,* p. 102.

17. *Ibid.,* p. 104.

18. *Ibid.,* p. 114.

19. *Ibid.,* pp. 132–37.

20. Elizabeth Fox-Genovese, *op. cit.,* p. 57; Stephanie Coontz, *The Way We Never Were* (New York: Basic Books, 1992), pp. 52–53; and Robert Bellah, *Habits of the Heart: Individualism and Commitment in American Life* (New York: Harper & Row, 1986), p. 40.

21. Coontz, *op. cit.,* p. 55.

22. Boydston, *op. cit.,* pp. 162–63.

23. Elizabeth Griffith, *In Her Own Right: The Life of Elizabeth Cady Stanton* (New York: Oxford University Press, 1984), p. iii.

24. Theodore Stanton and Harriet S. Blatch, eds., *Elizabeth Cady Stanton as Revealed in Her Letters, Diary, and Reminiscences,* 1922, pp. 54–55, quoted in Reva Siegel, "Home as Work: the First Woman's Rights Claims Concerning

Wives' Household Labor, 1850–1880," *Yale Law Journal* 103, no. 5 (March 1994): 1090–91.

25. Griffith, *op. cit.*, p. 91.

26. Boydston, *op. cit.*, p. 97.

27. Reva B. Siegel, *op. cit.*, p. 1113.

28. *Ibid.*, p. 1115.

29. Alice Kessler Harris, *Out to Work: A History of Wage-Earning Women in the United States* (New York, Oxford University Press, 1982), pp. 46–48.

30. Siegel, *op. cit.*, pp. 1083, 1183–85.

31. Folbre, "The Unproductive Housewife," pp. 474–75.

32. Siegel, *op. cit.*, p. 1092.

33. Folbre, *op. cit.*, pp. 483–84.

34. Cited in Barnet Wagman and Nancy Folbre, "Household Services and Economic Growth in the United States, 1870–1930," *Feminist Economics* 2, no. 1 (spring 1996): 43.

35. Folbre, "The Unproductive Housewife," pp. 478–79.

36. *Census of Great Britain, 1851*, quoted in Folbre, *ibid.*, p. 471.

37. *Census of England and Wales, 1961 and 1871*, quoted in Folbre, *ibid.*, p. 471.

38. Desley Deacon, "Political Arithmetic: The Nineteenth-Century Australian Census and the Construction of the Dependent Woman," *Signs* 2, no. 11 (autumn 1985): 34–35.

39. Siegel, *op. cit.*, pp. 1203–9.

40. The six states in which there is a legal presumption that marital property should be divided fifty-fifty are Idaho, Nevada, Arkansas, West Virginia, North Carolina, and New Hampshire. In these states a judge has to have a good reason for deviating from the principle of an equal division of property.

41. Reva B. Siegel, "The Modernization of Marital Status Law: Adjudicating Wives' Rights to Earnings, 1860–1930," *Georgetown Law Journal* 82, no. 7 (September 1994): 2197–99. Also see an analysis of this case by Joan Williams, *Unbending Gender*, pp. 18, 119–21.

⊂∞ READING 3 ∞⊃

The Evolution of the New Industrial Technology

Stephen Meyer III

I have heard it said, in fact I believe that it's quite a current thought, that we have taken skill out of work. We have not. We have put a higher skill into planning, management, and tool building, and the results of that skill are enjoyed by the man who is not skilled.[1]

—Henry Ford, 1922

. . . The experience of the Ford Motor Company represents an important case study for the integration of the history of technology and social history. For the early twentieth century, it provides an example for the detailed examination of the interrelationship

Reprinted by permission from *The Five Dollar Day: Labor Management and Social Control in the Ford Motor Company, 1908–1921* by Stephen Meyer III, the State University of New York Press © 1981, State University of New York. All rights reserved.

between industrial technology and work. Undoubtedly, automotive production technology established the pattern for technical change in the modern mass production industries through the twentieth century. In the matter of a few years, a single industrial establishment demonstrated the transition from traditional craft forms of work to modern industrial ones. Additionally, in the popular mind, Henry Ford and the Ford Motor Company gave the world mass production with its modern dilemma of work and its discontents. While this popular view was only a partial truth, technical and organizational innovation in the Highland Park factory did represent, as Alfred Chandler noted, "the culmination of earlier developments in the metal working industries." Here, "the new technology was most fully applied" and "brought an enormously swift expansion in the output and productivity of a single factory." If the concept of mass production did not exactly originate in the Ford factory, Ford innovations nevertheless allowed the nearly universal extension of the American system of production and the general adoption of its principles. Through the 1920s, Fordization and Fordism characterized by true standardization and interchangeability of parts, work rationalization, and line production methods, became the label for modern industrial techniques in Detroit, the United States, and the entire world in industry after industry.[2]

Generally, American advances in industrial technology have been attributed to a shortage of skilled labor. Most certainly, such was the case for the Ford factory. Technical change was the result of a phenomenal growth in the volume of Model T production and the concommitant expansion of Ford labor force. In 1908, the Ford Motor Company employed an estimated 450 persons. By 1913, it grew to more than 14,000 workers. This growth created a monumental labor problem—a severe shortage of skilled

mechanics who could machine and assemble parts for the popular Model T Ford. Consequently, the company hired large numbers of less-skilled and non-skilled American and immigrant workers. Prior to the rapid expansion in the workforce, Ford production workers were predominantly skilled American and German craftsmen. By 1914, threequarters of the workforce was foreign-born and slightly more than half of the workforce came from southern and eastern Europe. Indeed, the workforce lacked traditional industrial skills. So, in the design of machines, the rationalization of work tasks and routines, and the rearrangement and integration of work processes, Ford managers and engineers found their technical solution to a social and economic problem. With advanced machine-tool technology, the division and subdivision of labor, and the novel techniques of line production and assembly, they relied on the traditional American solution to labor shortages. Technical and organizational innovation displaced skill. It permitted unskilled labor to perform work of high quality and in large quantities.[3]

Specifically, Ford managers and engineers redesigned what they labelled the "mechanical element" of production. The "human element" had to conform to its new work tasks and routines. The result was the destruction of traditional patterns of work and discipline and the overall deterioration of conditions of work in the newly mechanized factory. In order to produce their incredibly popular automobile and to overcome their shortage of skilled labor, Ford managers and engineers brought together and implemented a number of interconnected technical and managerial innovations. In the end, they revolutionized automobile production and factory production in the modern world.

The specific components for the new Ford industrial system were not entirely new. Yet, taken together and systematically applied, they completely transformed factory production. First, Ford managers and engineers standardized the design of their product. This enabled them to specialize and routinize machine and work processes throughout the Ford plant. Second, they used the most recent advances in machine-tool technology. The new machines "transferred" skill into the design of sophisticated and complicated machines. Third, they analyzed, rationalized, and reorganized work tasks and routines. In effect, they "Taylorized" work processes and eliminated wasteful moments and motions in the performance of work. In other words, they followed the proposals of Frederick W. Taylor, the originator of scientific management. Finally, they developed and extended the unique concepts of progressive production and progressive assembly. And, ultimately, they created an integrated industrial system. The result was a complete change in tasks and routines, a new occupational structure, and new forms of control in the various shops and departments of the Ford factory.

Founded in 1903, the Ford Motor Company followed the pattern of development of other early automobile manufacturers. Generally, the evolution of Ford manufacturing processes mirrored the pattern of growth for the industry. Automobile manufacture was a complicated process—first, the foundry production of castings and their machine production into individual parts; second, the assembly of these individual parts into components, such as a magneto or an engine; and, finally, the assembly of thousands of parts and components into the motor vehicle. The manufacture of parts and components often involved a substantial capital expenditure. At the same time, the infant automobile industry suffered from a volatile and fluctuating demand for its luxury product. Consequently, the Ford enterprise, like other early automobile manufacturers, reduced its financial risk through its concentration on the final assembly of automobiles.

The company subcontracted the manufacture of various parts and components to outside machine shops and foundries. Gradually, as the company grew, it began to produce more and more of its own parts and components, such as engines, axles, transmissions, chassis, bodies, and so forth. By the 1920s, most automobile manufacturers produced all of their major parts and components and left the minor small ones to outside shops and factories. In the Ford Motor Company, the subsumption of part and component manufacture began in 1906 and rapidly accelerated with the manufacture of the popular Model T in 1908 and with the construction of the Highland Park plant in 1910.[4]

Against this background, from the early years until the arrival of assembly lines in 1914, the Ford shops relied on customary craft methods for the organization of production. To be sure, a long tradition of innovation and change existed in American workshops and factories. But, at the same time, a strong craft tradition delineated the boundaries for change in machines, work routines, and shop organization.

As David Montgomery and Daniel Nelson have noted, the late nineteenth- and early twentieth-century shop regimen relied on the work patterns of the "autonomous craftsman" and on the social relations of the "inside contract" and "helper" systems. "The functional autonomy of the craftsman," Montgomery wrote, "rested on both their superior knowledge, which made them self-directing at their tasks, and the supervision which they gave to one or more helpers." Many skilled workers, and sometimes even machine tenders and operators and journeymen machinists and fitters, "exercised broad discretion in the direction of their own work and that of their helpers. They often hired and fired their own helpers and paid the latter some fixed proportion of their earnings." Accordingly, Montgomery noted that custom and tradition ruled the shop in the form of output quotas and a "manly" bearing toward the boss and among fellow workers. Moreover, union work rules and the workers' ethic of mutual support were social and cultural manifestations of shop customs and traditions. As Nelson noted, the inside contract and helper systems centered around the contractor or skilled craftsman who directed small and relatively autonomous work groups. These skilled workers controlled their colleagues and assigned work tasks within their particular craft.[5]

For the craftsman, the skilled worker, or the contractor, their skill and knowledge translated into power. Craft skills and knowledge meant status, authority, and control over the performance of tasks within work groups. Indeed, from the 1890s to the 1920s, the development of systematic and scientific forms of management and control represented an effort to break the hold of the autonomous craftsman on the work force and on work procedures.

These customs and traditions formed the backdrop for the work patterns in the early automobile shops and factories. And, most certainly, they contained and restrained technical innovation in the Ford shops. For example, as late as 1912, Ford assembly procedures seemed rather routine. A photograph of the Ford engine assembly room showed a large room with row upon row of assembly benches. At the center of each bench was an engine block, on the side a vise, and behind the block bins of parts. H. L. Arnold, an industrial journalist, described traditional assembly operations in the Ford plant:

> Ordinary shop practice stations the principal component in a convenient place on the shop floor . . . and proceeds with the assembly by bringing other components to the principal component and applying or fixing them to the principal component which remains in place until the assembly is completed.

Even in June 1913, Fred H. Colvin, another industrial journalist, described traditional assembly procedures for the engine:

> Here motors in all stages of completion, the one in front simply having its valves in position, while the one behind it having its crankshaft put in place. The convenient arrangement of the assembling benches will be noted, the bins containing the parts to bring in the center of the benches so as to be easily reached by the assemblers on either side of the benches.

These three fragments of evidence suggested the customary Ford assembly procedures, work routines, and relationships among workers.[6]

At the assembly bench, the skilled worker occupied a central place. He began with a bare motor block, utilized a wide range of mental and manual skills, and attached part after part. Not only did he assemble parts, but he also "fitted" them. If two parts did not go together, he placed them in his vise and filed them to fit. The work routines contained variations in tasks and required considerable amounts of skill and judgment. Additionally, unskilled truckers served the skilled assemblers. When an assembler completed his engine, a trucker carried it away and provided a new motor block. The laborer also kept the assembler supplied with an adequate number of parts and components. Here, the division of labor was relatively primitive—essentially, the skilled and the unskilled. Under normal conditions, a Ford motor assembler needed almost a full day of work to complete a single engine.[7]

The Ford foundry also relied on traditional shop practices. In this period, the foundry relied on the skill and knowledge of the molder. Usually, the molder prepared a sand mold which accepted the molten metal and which hardened to form a rough casting. The coremaker, another highly skilled worker, prepared the core for the hollow part of the casting. Generally, the molder prepared the mold and poured the molten metal from his ladle, but sometimes he had the aid of helpers. Flaskers made the container to hold the mold, rammers forced the sand around the pattern for the mold, pourers poured the molten metal, skimmers removed impurities from the metal, and shakers shook the sand from the casting. Henry Ford described his early foundry:

> Our foundry used to be like other foundries. When we cast our first 'Model T' cylinders in 1910, everything in the place was done by hand; shovels and wheelbarrows abounded. The work was skilled or unskilled; we had moulders and we had laborers.

In this instance, the term molder referred to one of the many skilled specialties within the craft. Nonetheless, skilled molders surely exercised supervisory authority over their less-skilled helpers and laborers.[8]

In the Ford machine shops, the social relationships were much more dynamic and much less certain. From the 1880s on, factory managers and engineers devoted considerable attention to the productive efficiency of the machine shop. Yet, despite the efforts of Taylor and other systematic and scientific managers, craft customs and traditions, technological limitations, and market considerations hindered the efforts to manage and control independent machinists. For in spite of an increasing division of labor and an increasing technical sophistication, machinists still retained sufficient skill and knowledge to maintain some degree of functional autonomy.

By the turn of the century, technical and organizational innovation narrowed the range of the traditional machinist's skill. Both work tasks and basic machine tools became more specialized. But, the machinist still needed practical knowledge and manual ability. By this time, the division of labor

progressed along the line of specialized work within the craft or the operation of specialized machine tools. For example, general workman, vise hand, die sinker, and tool maker represented specialities of the trade, lathe, planer, and milling machine operator represented specialized machine occupations. Nevertheless, even the specialized machinist exercised considerable intellectual and manual skills within a narrower range.

In 1900, while attempting to categorize the impact of machine-tool technology on work, United States Census officials first formulated the idea of three grades of factory workers on the basis of "experience" and "judgment." This was a forerunner to the contemporary classification of skilled, semiskilled, and unskilled workers. In addition to foremen and "all-around" workmen, the "first class of skill" also included the "specialist, who, though he operates one kind of high grade machine, does important work with this to a high degree of perfection." In its definition of a competent workman, an International Association of Machinists' contract noted that the worker "shall be able to take any piece of work, pertaining to his class, with drawings and blue prints, and prosecute the work to completion within a reasonable time." The worker also had either to serve an apprenticeship or to work at the trade for four years. To be sure, machine hands and tenders operated some highly specialized and partially automatic machines. The trade was in a considerable state of flux. But, machinists who first entered the Ford shops in the early 1900s possessed the sophisticated intellectual and manual skills which translated blue prints into first-rate pieces of work.[9]

Until the full mechanization of the Ford factory, which began around 1910, assemblers, molders, machinists, and many other production workers were skilled craftsmen. Additionally, large numbers of less-skilled and unskilled workers—helpers, assistants, laborers, truckers, and so forth—complemented and assisted this highly skilled workforce. Indeed, until its technological and organizational transformation, the early Ford factory was "a congeries of craftsmen's shops rather than an integrated plant."[10]

The popular and practical design of the Model T Ford facilitated the technological and administrative transformation of the Ford factory. Gradually, as Model T sales increased and as production schedules stabilized, Ford and his engineers and managers began to realize the profound impact of product design on their factory operations. The standard design of the Model T influenced machine selection, work and task organization, and the integration of the entire plant. It facilitated the division of labor through the simplification of work routines. This, in turn, meant that some operations could be designed into machines. Finally, the systematic analysis of work and machines logically resulted in an equally systematic examination of the interconnected operations of the entire plant. To this end, the standard design proved a catalyst for innovation and for the integration of the entire Ford industrial system.

Henry Ford's personal contribution to this process was his dogged determination to realize his imaginative concept for the Model T Ford. "I will build," he proclaimed:

> a motor car for the great multitude. It will be large enough for the family, but small enough for the individual to care for. It will be constructed of the best materials, by the best men to be hired, after the simplest designs that modern engineering can devise.

In another instance, he suggested a relationship between design and production methods:

> The way to make automobiles is to make one automobile just like another automobile, to make them all alike, to make them come through the factory alike—just like one pin is like another pin when it comes from the pin factory, or one match is like another match when it comes from the match factory.

Indeed, Ford had a deceptively simple idea—"a motor car for the great multitude," a complicated product for a mass market, with "the simplest designs." He wanted to produce a standardized automobile that could be manufactured like a pin or a match.[11]

A stream of industrial journalists, engineers and others who visited the Ford plant testified to the advantage of standard design as the foundation of the remarkable technical and commercial success of the Ford enterprise. In 1914, H. L. Arnold noted the technological merits of a single and standard product: "The Ford car holds so closely to one unchanged model that it becomes commercially possible to equip the shops with every special tool, great or small, simple or complex, cheap or costly, which can be made to reduce production-labor costs." H. F. Porter elaborated on the varied economic and engineering benefits of Model T design. With the production of a single model, he noted that managers and engineers devoted their complete attention to the handling of men, machines, materials, and work routines. The Model T's "unlimited run" resulted in "a free hand in the selecting and developing machinery, special tools, dies, and men." Engineers and tool makers directed "their attention to changes in equipment and methods that will effect further cost reductions or increase the output per unit of floor space." Furthermore, supervisors and inspectors became more specialized and experienced in their work. Hence, the quality of the work improved and the amount of waste declined. Additionally, workers became more specialized and experienced in their repeated tasks and routines. Machine operators, he observed, "engaged regularly in repetitive work become highly proficient. The entire organization, in fact, becomes a body of specialized experts."[12]

Finally, Porter described how product design influenced work patterns and integrated industrial processes. "Nothing," he wrote:

is quite so demoralizing to the smooth commercial operation of a factory as incessant changes in design. Even small changes at the beginning of the season occasion much confusion for weeks or months; meanwhile, production is curtailed and costs go skyward.

The problem involved the interaction of workers and machines. Both needed adjustments to the new conditions of changed product design. Workers had to change their tasks and routines. Machines required redesign.[13]

Porter cited an instance where "minor changes" in the design of the Model T sharply reduced worker productivity. Ford engineers changed the metallic composition of some parts and the appearance of the hood and fenders. "The first month," Porter noted, "saw production curtailed by fifty per cent; and it was nearly three months before the entire organization could be geared up for the stipulated work." A changed product meant alterations in machines and work tasks. Managers and workers had to rediscover the most efficient way to produce or assemble the different part of component.[14]

Once initiated, the process of standardization had its own inexorable inner logic. It influenced each routine and operation throughout the entire plant. In 1916, John R. Lee, a Ford factory manager described this process:

For the past eight years, the plan of the company has been steadfastly toward standardization. A single model chassis

with a very limited number of bodies have been built in large quantities with the exercise of exacting thought and care in the development of mechanism and material which are especially adapted to the product.

Consequently, the factory became an integrated industrial system. As Porter observed, the flow of materials to and through the plant had to be balanced perfectly. "Lapses," he related:

. . . would, if given any leeway here, cause untold havoc. Thorough standardization in one department, therefore, entails equally thorough standardization in all other interdependent departments.

As in the eighteenth century textile mills, innovation in one area of production necessitated innovation in others. Technical advance in one shop created bottlenecks in other shops. And, these bottlenecks spurred innovation in technologically backward departments.[15]

For Porter, the standardized product was "Ford's great lesson for other manufacturers." He continued:

let standardization begin with the design of the product itself. Ford believes in spending plenty of time to perfect the model in the first place. Thereafter, he tolerates no changes that are not justified fully by economic considerations.

Within this context, Ford had a sound economic logic in his oft-repeated statement that the customer could choose any color so long as it was black. Another color meant a deviation from a standard design and from standardized production procedures.[16]

In the development of their novel methods and techniques of production, Ford managers and engineers worked within a rapidly evolving tradition of American technological innovation. In 1912, a special subcommittee of the American Society of Mechanical Engineers (ASME) detailed this tradition in its survey of "the present state of the art of industrial management." In this study, American mechanical engineers attempted to synthesize the new industrial ideas and practices which bore the general label, "scientific management." The subcommittee wanted to amalgamate the ideas of Taylor and his followers and successors. In the process, it developed the notion of "labor-saving management." And, it concluded that the new art of management emphasized two older principles, the division of labor and the transference of skill, and a more recent one, the new "mental attitude" on the part of industrial engineers and managers.[17]

Indeed, the elements of this technical and managerial tradition provided the basis for innovation and change in the Ford factory. First, the ASME subcommittee cited the classical political economists, Adam Smith and Charles Babbage, for their definition of the division of labor. Smith and Babbage also provided examples on how the division and subdivision of work tasks and routines resulted in higher productivity. Second, the subcommittee pointed to Henry Maudsley's eighteenth-century invention of the lathe slide rest as an early and important illustration of the transference of skill from worker to machine. In its design, the survey noted, this mechanical device "substituted for the skillful control of hand tools." Finally, the ASME subcommittee noted a new attitude on the part of engineers:

> an attitude of questioning, of research, of careful investigation of everything affecting the problems in hand, of seeking for exact knowledge and then shaping action on the discovered facts.

This new mental attitude brought the method of science to industry. The result was "to extend the principle of the transference of skill to production, so that it completely embraces every activity in manufacture." Ultimately, each principle related to the skill of workers: the division of labor simplified skills, the transfer of skill shifted it to the machine, and the new mental attitude uncovered its fundamental elements, and relocated skills in the design of work tasks and routines, of machines, and of the entire integrated industrial system.[18]

The new "scientific" division of labor was an important element in the evolution of mass production in the Ford factory. While Ford denied that "scientific management" or "Taylorism" formed the basis of his new industrial methods, most surely some elements of the new managerial tradition influenced the reorganization of work tasks and routines in the Highland Park plant. In 1912, the ASME also issued a report on "modern shop practice." It noted:

> One of the noteworthy improvements in modern shop practice is the application of the principles of scientific management. . . . Undoubtedly the fundamental principles are coming to be more thoroughly understood and are being quite generally applied.

Ford managers and engineers may not have followed a specific program, but they surely followed general principles. The new ideas on industrial management readily diffused through the community of factory owners, managers, engineers, superintendents, and foremen in the nation's more modern factories and particularly in Detroit's automobile plants.[19]

In fact, Taylor himself visited Detroit several times. In 1914, he addressed an assemblage of Detroit factory managers, superintendents, and foremen. Here, he commented favorably on the application and, in some instances, the autonomous development of his principles in the automobile industry. This industry, he said, was "the first instance in which a group of manufacturers had undertaken to install the principles of scientific management without the aid of experts." In Detroit, the practical men in automobile shops and factories independently developed and expanded on Taylor's general principles. And, Ford and his managers and skilled workers were at the forefront of technical innovation and change.[20] . . .

Henry Ford detailed how the division of labor through time study changed the assembly procedures for pistons and rods. The "old plan" of assembly, he related, was:

> . . . a very simple operation. The workman pushed the pin out of the piston, oiled the pin, slipped the rod in place, put the pin through the rod and piston, tightened on screw, and opened another screw. That was the whole operation. The foreman, examining the operation, could not discover why it should take as much as three minutes. He analyzed the motions with a stopwatch. He found that four hours of a nine-hour day were spent walking. The assembler did not go off anywhere, but he did shift his feet to gather in his materials and to push away his finished piece. In the whole task, each man performed six operations. The foreman devised a new plan; he split the operation into three divisions, put a slide on the bench and three men on each side of it, and an inspector at the end. Instead of one man performing the whole operation, one man then performed only one-third of the operation—he performed only as much as he could do without shifting his feet.

The reorganization of work resulted in a phenomenal increase in worker productivity. Under the old method, twenty-eight men assembled 175 pistons and rods in a nine-hour day; under the new one, seven men assembled 2,600 in an eight-hour day.[21]

Arnold reported on the division of labor for hand and automatic machine work throughout the entire Ford plant. Managers and engineers possessed "actual stop-watch time" for thousands of operations. "Minute division of labor," he concluded:

> is effective in labor-cost reducing in two ways: first by making the workman extremely skilled, so that he does his part with no needless motions, and secondly by training him to perform his operation with the least expenditure of will-power, and hence with the least brain fatigue.

In this instance, Arnold revealed an important aspect of the managerial attitude about technical and organizational achievements. Needless to say, his concept of skill differed considerably from that of the craftsman. Moreover, his ideal worker was the mindless automaton who applied himself constantly and consistently with little thought.[22]

In other instances, Ford managers and engineers established specific tasks and standards for machine and assembly operations. As early as 1908, William A. Klann, a machinist who became general foreman of motor assembly, related: "I was setting work standards. They didn't call it the Time Study Department then. It was work standards." In 1912, O. J. Abell, the Midwestern correspondent for *Iron Age*, noted that machine ratings for individual machines determined the work standards for Ford workers. The engineers determined the most efficient "possible rate of production and then made an allowance of perhaps 10 per cent for time when the operator was not at the machine. . ." In other words, each machine operation had a predetermined output which the worker had to meet. The same was true for assembly operations. Surely, Taylor's "task idea" prevailed in the Ford shops. In both cases, the specific task determined the amount of a worker's effort.[23]

Next, improvements in machine-tool technology constituted a powerful force for the transformation of work routines and factory procedures. In fact, Ford industrial expansion occurred at the same time that machine tools underwent notable improvements in their design and construction. Until the early twentieth century, the general-purpose machine tool, which relied on the varied and complex skills of the machinist, prevailed in American workshops and factories. To be sure, some nineteenth-century industries developed their specialized machines for the volume production of nearly identical parts. Indeed, the automatic screw machine was a classic nineteenth-century example of the automatic and special-purpose machine. Additionally, the small arms, sewing machine, agricultural implement, and bicycle industries all made important contributions in the design of specialized machines for the manufacture of nearly identical parts. Nonetheless, due to technical limitations of the machines, these parts were not truly interchangeable, because they often required skilled mechanics to file and to "fit" the parts together. Undoubtedly, the new automobile industry sparked a most intense phase in the design and specialization of machine tools in the first decades of the twentieth century. As the new machine-tool technology acquired technical sophistication, the volume production of duplicate parts required little, if any skill. Furthermore, assembly operations no longer needed skilled machinists. And, Ford engineers and tool makers were in the forefront of technical innovation in machine shop practices.[24]

In the short period from 1905 to 1912, the American Society of Mechanical Engineers reported on the significant advances in the design of industrial machinery. The basic principle was the transfer of skill from the worker to the machine. The special committee on machine shop practice reported:

. . . "The transference of skill" by the machine designer from the operators to the machines has embodied in the latter much of the accumulated experience of many mechanics working on simpler and more primitive tools; . . . much of the improvement in machine shop practice has appeared in the improvement of machine tools themselves in one way or another.

In the same year, the report on the art of industrial management also noted the significance of the transfer of skill. The committee reported:

After the traditional skill of a trade, or the peculiar skill of a designer or inventor, has been transferred to a machine, an operator with little or no previously acquired skill can learn to handle it and turn off the product.

The transfer of skill involved an accumulation of small innovations and changes in the design and construction of machine tools.[25] . . .

From 1913 to 1914, Ford managers and engineers further refined their notion of progressive or continuous production with the creation of moving lines for the assembly of parts into automobile components and for the final assembly of parts and components into the Model T Ford. As late as 1913, Colvin described rather traditional methods and techniques for the assembly of engines, axles, and the final product. To be sure, some experimentation was under way. For automobile assembly, the work-process was divided and subdivided and workers performed specialized operations. At first, teams of workmen moved from car to car and attached their part or component. However, materials did not move in the same manner as in the machine shops. Two examples illustrated the evolution and the advantages of the Ford assembly lines. One was the magneto assembly line, the first to develop; and the other was the chassis assembly line, the most difficult to implement,

Assembly line emerge

into which all other parts and components flowed.[26]

The flywheel magneto provided the electrical charge to ignite the fuel of the Ford automobile. It was the first component to be assembled on a moving assembly line. Prior to May 1913, one Ford worker put together approximately 35 to 40 magnetos in a nine-hour day. A skilled assembler constructed the entire component. "The work was done by experienced men," H. L. Arnold noted, "but was not so uniformly satisfactory as was desired, and was costly . . . as all one-man assembly must of necessity be forever." In May 1913, Ford managers and engineers analyzed the work and subdivided it into twenty-nine separate operations. As in existing progressive machining operations, the assemblers passed the component from worker to worker by hand. The managers and engineers continued to redesign and to restructure the work and the assembly processes. They added a chain-driven conveyor to move the component from one worker to another. And, after March 1914, productivity dramatically increased—fourteen workers assembled 1,335 magnetos in an eight-hour day. Even though the working day was reduced by one hour, the assemblers more than doubled their average productivity and produced an average of 95 magnetos per person each day.[27]

Ford engineers duplicated this procedure with varying degrees of difficulty in other assembly departments throughout the Highland Park factory from the late summer of 1913 through 1914. They created a coordinated and synchronized industrial system as a result of their efforts to provide for the progressive machine production of parts and the progressive assembly of these parts into components and finally the Model T Ford. As Sorensen recalled:

> What was worked at Ford was the practice of moving work from one quarter to

another until it became a complete unit, then arranging the flow of these units at the right time and the right place to a moving assembly line from which came a finished product.

According to Sorensen, Clarence Avery tackled the problem of the coordination and synchronization of the newly mechanized plant. Trained over a period of eight months in each department, Avery:

> worked out the timing schedules necessary before the installation of conveyor assembly systems to motors, fenders, magnetos, and transmissions. One by one those operations were revamped and continuously moving conveyors delivered assembled parts to the final assembly floor. Savings in labor time were enormous; some parts were put together six times as fast.

Hands, rollways, gravity slides, chain and belt conveyors, and overhead cranes moved materials from location to location. Men, machines and materials became an intricately interconnected mechanical organism.[28]

Eventually, everything flowed to the chassis assembly line, where "from 1,000 to 4,000 separate pieces of each chassis component" streamed "daily, infallibly, and constantly." Begun in the late summer of 1913 and completed in the late spring of 1914, chassis assembly lines presented the greatest difficulty to Ford engineers. Until August 1913, Ford workers assembled the Model T chassis as a single location. H. L. Arnold described the early method for chassis assembly:

> First, the front and rear axles were laid on the floor, then the chassis frame with springs in place was assembled with the axles, next the wheels were placed on the axles, and the remaining components were successively added to complete the chassis. All the components needed to make the chassis had to be

brought by hand to each chassis assembly location.

At the time, 250 skilled assemblers with the assistance of 80 "component carriers" assembled 6,182 chassis in the course of one month. Colvin reported that the assemblers moved from chassis to chassis to attach their pieces or component. It required an average of 12½ hours of one workman's time to put together a single chassis.[29]

In August 1913, Ford managers and engineers began to analyze, experiment with, and systematize their procedures for chassis assembly. In September 1913, they connected the Model T chassis to a "rope and windlass" device and pulled it along a row of parts and components. Six assemblers and their helpers walked along with the chassis and attached the necessary parts and components as they went down the line. This resulted in a dramatic reduction of the assembly time for each chassis. It fell to an average of five hours and fifty minutes of a workman's time—a reduction of 50 percent. Next, in October, the mechanical device pulled the chassis along a line of 140 stationary assemblers. They stood at stations near supplies of parts and components and attached them as the chassis passed. The assembly time now averaged slightly less than three hours per worker. Additional changes in the length of the line and the number of stations further reduced the chassis assembly time. In January 1914, the engineers developed an "endless chain-driven" conveyor to pull the chassis along the line. In April 1914, they created a "man high" line to eliminate unnecessary and unproductive movements on the part of the workers. In the end, these experiments reduced chassis assembly time from 12½ hours to one hour and thirty-three minutes.[30]

By June 1914, Ford managers and engineers perfected the new chassis assembly line to their satisfaction and introduced it as a part of the normal industrial operations of the new mechanized Highland Park plant. Eighteen workmen performed the first two operations which set the chassis frames on two assembly lines. On these lines, unskilled assemblers performed the remaining forty-three operations to put together the Model T chassis. Mechanical conveyors delivered the parts and components to their stations. One hundred and forty-two workers assembled an average of 600 chassis in an eight-hour day. The average assembly time for each chassis under normal, as opposed to experimental, conditions was slightly under two hours of a worker's time. This was approximately one-sixth of the time that traditional methods and techniques of assembly required.[31]

The chassis assembly line capped the Ford system of mass production. A commonplace fact of our industrial world, Ford industrial processes fascinated and overwhelmed contemporary observers in 1914. They even impressed H. L. Arnold, a man thoroughly familiar with the very latest and most advanced industrial systems of this time. The Ford assembly lines, he said, afforded "a highly impressive spectacle." He described:

> Long lines of slowly moving assemblies in progress, busy troups of successive operators, the rapid growth of the chassis as component after component is added from overhead sources of supply, and, finally the instant start into self-moving power.

The main assembly line, he continued, excited "the liveliest interest and imagination" as "the varied elements" came together and formed "the new and seemingly vivified creation."[32]

In a few brief years, modern mass production became a reality in the Ford Highland factory. Within an extremely short period of time, Ford engineers and skilled workers transformed traditional industrial process and broke ground for modern forms of integrated and synchronized production. Although difficult, the technical and organizational problems were not insurmountable. Nevertheless, the new industrial technology was a mixed social blessing, perhaps even a curse. It promised a material cornucopia for all. Yet, at the same time, it contained incredible social costs. The world of work would never be the same again. The new industrial technology made the worker's daily routine more monotonous and more repetitive. It dramatically altered the social structure of the shop, the factory, and, in fact, modern industrial society. And, it possessed or required new patterns of authority and control over the workforce. Indeed, the new industrial technology had a profound impact on modern social existence.

NOTES

1. Henry Ford, *My Life and Work* (Garden City, N.Y., 1922), p. 78.

2. Alfred D. Chandler, *The Visible Hand: The Managerial Revolution in American Business* (Cambridge, Mass., 1977), p. 280. On the development of mass production, see John B. Rae, "Rationalization of Production" in Kranzberg and Pursell, *Technology,* vol. 2, pp. 37–52 and Siegfried Giedion, *Mechanization Takes Command* (New York, 1955), pp. 14–127.

3. On the expansion of the Ford workforce, see Allan Nevins, *Ford: The Times, the Man, the Company* (New York, 1954), p. 648. On the number of immigrant workers, see "Automobile Trade Notes," *New York Times,* November 15, 1914, sec. 7, p. 6.

4. John B. Rae, *The American Automobile: A Brief History* (Chicago, 1965), pp. 17–68 Ralph C. Epstein, *The Automobile Industry: Its Economic and Commercial Development* (Chicago, 1928), pp. 23–101; and Nevins, *Ford,* pp. 220–386.

5. Montgomery, *Workers' Control,* pp. 11 and 12–27 and Nelson, *Managers and Workers,* pp. 17–54. See also, John Buttrick, "The Inside Contract System," *Journal of Economic History,* 12 (Summer 1952), pp. 205–21; Benson Soffer, "A Theory of Trade Union Development: The Role of the 'Autonomous' Workman," *Labor History,* 1 (Spring 1960), pp. 141–63; Katherine Stone, "The Origins of Job Structures in the Steel Industry," *Review of Radical Political Economics,* 6 (Summer, 1974), pp. 113–73; R. R. Lutz, *The Metal Trades* (Philadelphia, 1916); and George E. Barnett, *Chapters on Machinery and Labor* (Cambridge, Mass., 1926).

6. O. J. Abell, "Making the Ford Motor Car," *Iron Age,* 89 (June 6, 1912), p. 1391; H. L. Arnold, "Ford Methods and the Ford Shops: Inspection and Assembling Methods and Practices," *Engineering Magazine,* 47 (July 1914), p. 510; and Fred H. Colvin, "Machining Ford Cylinders—II," *American Machinist,* 38 (June 12, 1913), p. 975.

7. H. L. Arnold and Fay L. Faurote, *Ford Methods and the Ford Shops* (New York, 1916), pp. 115–16.

8. "Glossary" in United States, Bureau of the Census, *Special Reports: Employees and Wages* (Washington, 1903), pp. 1182–3 and Ford, *Life and Work,* p. 87.

9. "Glossary," p. 1168 and "International Association of Machinists Agreement," Folder 3, Box 45, File A, Series 11, American Federation of Labor Papers, Wisconsin State Historical Society, Madison, Wisconsin.

10. Nelson, *Managers and Workers,* p. 41.

11. Ford, *Life and Work,* p. 77; Ford quoted in Alfred D. Chandler, *Giant Enterprise: Ford, General Motors, and the Automobile Industry* (New York, 1964), p. 28.

12. H. L. Arnold, "Ford Methods and the Ford Shops: The Stock System and Employment Methods," *Engineering Magazine,* 47 (May 1914), p. 179 and H. F. Porter, "Four Big Lessons from Ford's Factory," *System,* 31 (June 1917), pp. 640–1.

13. Porter, "Four Big Lessons," p. 640.

14. Porter, "Four Big Lessons," p. 640.

15. John R. Lee, "The So-called Profit Sharing System at the Ford Plant," *Annals AAPSS,* 65 (May 1916), p. 298 and Porter, "Four Big Lessons," p. 642.

16. Porter, "Four Big Lessons," p. 640.

17. American Society of Mechanical Engineers (Hereafter ASME), "The Present State of the Art of Industrial Management," *Transactions ASME,* 34 (1912), pp. 1133–9.

18. ASME, "Industrial Management," pp. 1133 and 1137.

19. ASME, "Developments in Machine Shop Practice in the Last Decade," *Transactions ASME,* 34 (1912), p. 851.

20. Taylor quoted in Nevins, *Ford,* p. 469.

21. Ford, *Life and Work,* p. 88.

22. Arnold and Faurote, *Ford Methods,* p. 245.

23. Ford Motor Company Archives, *The Reminiscences of Mr. William C. Klann* (September 1955), p. 7; O. J. Abell, "Making the Ford Motor Car," *Iron Age,* 89 (June 13, 1912), p. 1457; and Frederick Winslow Taylor, *The Principles of Scientific Management* (New York, 1967), pp. 120–2.

24. Robert S. Woodbury, *Studies in the History of Machine Tools* (Cambridge, Mass., 1972); Nathan Rosenberg, "Technological Change in the Machine Tool Industry, 1840–1910" in *Perspectives on Technology* (New York, 1976), pp. 9–31; Chandler, *The Visible Hand,* pp. 240–83; and David Allen Hounshell, "From the American System to Mass Production: The Development of Manufacturing Technology in the United States, 1850–1920." Ph.D. dissertation, University of Delaware, 1978.

25. ASME, "Machine Shop Practice," p. 847 and ASME, "Industrial Management," pp. 1133–4.

26. Colvin, "Cylinders—II," p. 975; Fred H. Colvin, "Special Machines for Small Auto Parts," *American Machinist,* 39 (September 11, 1913), p. 442; and Colvin, "Building an Automobile," pp. 761–2.

27. Arnold, "Inspection and Assembling," pp. 522–3.

28. Sorensen, *Ford,* pp. 116 and 130.

29. H. L. Arnold, "Ford Methods and the Ford Shops: How the Work in the Ford Factory Is Actually Done," *Engineering Magazine,* 47 (June 1914), pp. 331–2; H. L. Arnold, "Ford Methods and the Ford Shops: Ford Motor-Test Blocks and Chassis Assembling Lines," *Engineering Magazine,* 47 (August 1914), pp. 672–3 and 677; and Colvin, "Building an Automobile," pp. 657–62.

30. Arnold, "Chassis Assembling Lines," pp. 677–80.

31. Arnold, "Chassis Assembling Lines," p. 680.

32. Arnold, "Chassis Assembling Lines," p. 672.

CONCEPTUAL FOUNDATIONS

∞ **READING 4** ∞

Alienated Labour

Karl Marx

We started from the presuppositions of political economy. We accepted its vocabulary and its laws. We presupposed private property, the separation of labour, capital, and land, and likewise of wages, profit, and ground rent; also division of labour; competition; the concept of exchange value, etc. Using the very words of political economy we have demonstrated that the worker is degraded to the most miserable sort of commodity; that the misery of the worker is in inverse proportion to the power and size of his production; that the necessary result of competition is the accumulation of capital in a few hands, and thus a more terrible restoration of monopoly; and that finally the distinction between capitalist and landlord, and that between peasant and industrial worker disappears and the whole of society must fall apart into the two classes of the property owners and the propertyless workers.

Political economy starts with the fact of private property; it does not explain it to us. It conceives of the material process that private property goes through in reality in general abstract formulas which then have for it a value of laws. It does not understand these laws, i.e. it does not demonstrate how they arise from the nature of private property. Political economy does not afford us any explanation of the reason for the separation of labour and capital, of capital and land. When, for example, political economy defines the relationship of wages to profit from capital, the interest of the capitalist is the ultimate court of appeal, that is, it presupposes what should be its result. In the same way competition enters the argument everywhere. It is explained by exterior circumstances. But political economy tells us nothing about how far these exterior, apparently fortuitous circumstances are merely the expression of a necessary development. We have seen how it regards exchange itself as something fortuitous. The only wheels that political economy sets in motion are greed and war among the greedy, competition.

It is just because political economy has not grasped the connections in the movement that new contradictions have arisen in its doctrines, for example, between that of monopoly and that of competition, freedom of craft and corporations, division of landed property and large estates. For competition, free trade, and the division of landed property were only seen as fortuitous circumstances created by will and force, not developed and comprehended as necessary, inevitable, and natural results of monopoly, corporations, and feudal property.

So what we have to understand now is the essential connection of private property,

selfishness, the separation of labour, capital, and landed property, of exchange and competition, of the value and degradation of man, of monopoly and competition, etc.—the connection of all this alienation with the money system.

Let us not be like the political economist who, when he wishes to explain something, puts himself in an imaginary original state of affairs. Such an original state of affairs explains nothing. He simply pushes the question back into a grey and nebulous distance. He presupposes as a fact and an event what he ought to be deducing, namely the necessary connection between the two things, for example, between the division of labour and exchange. Similarly, the theologian explains the origin of evil through the fall, i.e. he presupposes as an historical fact what he should be explaining.

We start with a contemporary fact of political economy:

The worker becomes poorer the richer is his production, the more it increases in power and scope. The worker becomes a commodity that is all the cheaper the more commodities he creates. The depreciation of the human world progresses in direct proportion to the increase in value of the world of things. Labour does not only produce commodities; it produces itself and the labourer as a commodity and that to the extent to which it produces commodities in general.

What this fact expresses is merely this: the object that labour produces, its product, confronts it as an alien being, as a power independent of the producer. The product of labour is labour that has solidified itself into an object, made itself into a thing, the objectification of labour. The realization of labour is its objectification. In political economy this realization of labour appears as a loss of reality for the worker, objectification as a loss of the object of slavery to it, and appropriation as alienation, as externalization.

The realization of labour appears as a loss of reality to an extent that the worker loses his reality by dying of starvation. Objectification appears as a loss of the object to such an extent that the worker is robbed not only of the objects necessary for his life but also of the objects of his work. Indeed, labour itself becomes an object he can only have in his power with the greatest of efforts and at irregular intervals. The appropriation of the object appears as alienation to such an extent that the more objects the worker produces, the less he can possess and the more he falls under the domination of his product, capital.

All these consequences follow from the fact that the worker relates to the product of his labour as to an alien object. For it is evident from this presupposition that the more the worker externalizes himself in his work, the more powerful becomes the alien, objective world that he creates opposite himself, the poorer he becomes himself in his inner life and the less he can call his own. It is just the same in religion. The more man puts into God, the less he retains in himself. The worker puts his life into the object and this means that it no longer belongs to him but to the object. So the greater this activity, the more the worker is without an object. What the product of his labour is, that he is not. So the greater this product the less he is himself. The externalization of the worker in his product implies not only that his labour becomes an object, an exterior existence but also that it exists outside him, independent and alien, and becomes a self-sufficient power opposite him, that the life that he has lent to the object affronts him, hostile and alien.

Let us now deal in more detail with objectification, the production of the worker, and the alienation, the loss of the object, his product, which is involved in it.

The worker can create nothing without nature, the sensuous exterior world. It is the matter in which his labour realizes itself, in which it is active, out of which and through which it produces.

But as nature affords the means of life for labour in the sense that labour cannot live without objects on which it exercises itself, so it affords a means of life in the narrower sense, namely the means for the physical subsistence of the worker himself.

Thus the more the worker appropriates the exterior world of sensuous nature by his labour, the more he doubly deprives himself of the means of subsistence, firstly since the exterior sensuous world increasingly ceases to be an object belonging to his work, a means of subsistence for his labour; secondly, since it increasingly ceases to be a means of subsistence in the direct sense, a means for the physical subsistence of the worker.

Thus in these two ways the worker becomes a slave to his object: firstly he receives an object of labour, that is he receives labour, and secondly, he receives the means of subsistence. Thus it is his object that permits him to exist first as a worker and secondly as a physical subject. The climax of this slavery is that only as a worker can he maintain himself as a physical subject and it is only as a physical subject that he is a worker.

(According to the laws of political economy the alienation of the worker in his object is expressed as follows: the more the worker produces the less he has to consume, the more values he creates the more valueless and worthless he becomes, the more formed the product the more deformed the worker, the more civilized the product, the more barbaric the worker, the more powerful the work the more powerless becomes the worker, the more cultured the work the more philistine the worker becomes and more of a slave to nature.)

Political economy hides the alienation in the essence of labour by not considering the immediate relationship between the worker (labour) and production. Labour produces works of wonder for the rich, but nakedness for the worker. It produces palaces, but only hovels for the worker; it produces beauty, but cripples the worker; it replaces labour by machines but throws a part of the workers back to a barbaric labour and turns the other part into machines. It produces culture, but also imbecility and cretinism for the worker.

The immediate relationship of labour to its products is the relationship of the worker to the objects of his production. The relationship of the man of means to the objects of production and to production itself is only a consequence of this first relationship. And it confirms it. We shall examine this other aspect later.

So when we ask the question: what relationship is essential to labour, we are asking about the relationship of the worker to production.

Up to now we have considered only one aspect of the alienation or externalization of the worker, his relationship to the products of his labour. But alienation shows itself not only in the result, but also in the act of production, inside productive activity itself. How would the worker be able to affront the product of his work as an alien being if he did not alienate himself in the act of production itself? For the product is merely the summary of the activity of production. So if the product of labour is externalization, production itself must be active externalization, the externalization of activity, the activity of externalization. The alienation of the object of labour is only the résumé of the alienation, the externalization in the activity of labour itself.

What does the externalization of labour consist of then?

Firstly, that labour is exterior to the worker, that is, it does not belong to his essence. Therefore he does not confirm himself in his work, he denies himself, feels miserable instead of happy, deploys no free physical and intellectual energy, but mortifies

his body and ruins his mind. Thus the worker only feels a stranger. He is at home when he is not working and when he works he is not at home. His labour is therefore not voluntary but compulsory, forced labour. It is therefore not the satisfaction of a need but only a means to satisfy needs outside itself. How alien it really is is very evident from the fact that when there is no physical or other compulsion, labour is avoided like the plague. External labour, labour in which man externalizes himself, is a labour of self-sacrifice and mortification. Finally, the external character of labour for the worker shows itself in the fact that it is not his own but someone else's, that it does not belong to him, that he does not belong to himself in his labour but to someone else. As in religion the human imagination's own activity, the activity of man's head and his heart, reacts independently on the individual as an alien activity of gods or devils, so the activity of the worker is not his own spontaneous activity. It belongs to another and is the loss of himself.

The result we arrive at then is that man (the worker) only feels himself freely active in his animal functions of eating, drinking, and procreating, at most also in his dwelling and dress, and feels himself an animal in his human functions.

Eating, drinking, procreating, etc. are indeed truly human functions. But in the abstraction that separates them from the other round of human activity and makes them into final and exclusive ends they become animal.

We have treated the act of alienation of practical human activity, labour, from two aspects. (1) The relationship of the worker to the product of his labour as an alien object that has power over him. This relationship is at the same time the relationship to the sensuous exterior world and to natural objects as to an alien and hostile world opposed to him. (2) The relationship of labour to the act of production inside labour. This relationship is the relationship of the worker to his own activity as something that is alien and does not belong to him; it is activity that is passivity, power that is weakness, procreation that is castration, the worker's own physical and intellectual energy, his personal life (for what is life except activity?) as an activity directed against himself, independent of him and not belonging to him. It is self-alienation, as above it was the alienation of the object.

We now have to draw a third characteristic of alienated labour from the two previous ones.

Man is a species-being not only in that practically and theoretically he makes both his own and other species into his objects, but also, and this is only another way of putting the same thing, he relates to himself as to the present, living species, in that he relates to himself as to a universal and therefore free being.

Both with man and with animals the species-life consists physically in the fact that man (like animals) lives from inorganic nature, and the more universal man is than animals the more universal is the area of inorganic nature from which he lives. From the theoretical point of view, plants, animals, stones, air, light, etc. form part of human consciousness, partly as objects of natural science, partly as objects of art; they are his intellectual inorganic nature, his intellectual means of subsistence, which he must first prepare before he can enjoy and assimilate them. From the practical point of view, too, they form a part of human life and activity. Physically man lives solely from these products of nature, whether they appear as food, heating, clothing, habitation, etc. The universality of man appears in practice precisely in the universality that makes the whole of nature into his inorganic body in that it is both (i) his immediate means of subsistence and also (ii) the material object

and tool of his vital activity. Nature is the inorganic body of a man, that is, in so far as it is not itself a human body. That man lives from nature means that nature is his body with which he must maintain a constant interchange so as not to die. That man's physical and intellectual life depends on nature merely means that nature depends on itself, for man is part of nature.

While alienated labour alienates (1) nature from man, and (2) man from himself, his own active function, his vital activity, it also alienates the species from man; it turns his species-life into a means towards his individual life. Firstly it alienates species-life and individual life, and secondly in its abstraction it makes the latter into the aim of the former which is also conceived of in its abstract and alien form. For firstly, work, vital activity, and productive life itself appear to man only as a means to the satisfaction of a need, the need to preserve his physical existence. But productive life is species-life. It is life producing life. The whole character of a species, its generic character, is contained in its manner of vital activity, and free conscious activity is the species-characteristic of man. Life itself appears merely as a means to life.

The animal is immediately one with its vital activity. It is not distinct from it. They are identical. Man makes his vital activity itself into an object of his will and consciousness. He has a conscious vital activity. He is not immediately identical to any of his characterizations. Conscious vital activity differentiates man immediately from animal vital activity. It is this and this alone that makes man a species-being. He is only a conscious being, that is, his own life is an object to him, precisely because he is a species-being. This is the only reason for his activity being free activity. Alienated labour reverses the relationship so that, just because he is a conscious being, man makes his vital activity and essence a mere means to his existence.

Handwritten margin notes:

man works for something other than himself

human relationship w/ nature world

Humans depend on nature for subsistence & nothing more

(?—maybe) It takes our natural exch. w/ the earth for subsistence & makes us run thru an intermediary for which we must labor

species being

Species-being: Cognizance of oneself/one's ego & intentions

(Doesn't this sum the main themes in all lit.?)

The practical creation of an objective world, the working-over of inorganic nature, is the confirmation of man as a conscious species-being, that is, as a being that relates to the species as to himself and to himself as to the species. It is true that the animal, too, produces. It builds itself a nest, a dwelling, like the bee, the beaver, the ant, etc. But it only produces what it needs immediately for itself or its offspring; it produces one-sidedly whereas man produces universally; it produces only under the pressure of immediate physical need, whereas man produces freely from physical need and only truly produces when he is thus free; it produces only itself whereas man reproduces the whole of nature. Its product belongs immediately to its physical body whereas man can freely separate himself from his product. The animal only fashions things according to the standards and needs of the species it belongs to, whereas man knows how to produce according to the measure of every species and knows everywhere how to apply its inherent standard to the object; thus man also fashions things according to the laws of beauty.

How humans' species-being differentiated us from other animals

Thus it is in the working over of the objective world that man first really affirms himself as a species-being. This production is his active species-life. Through it nature appears as his work and his reality. The object of work is therefore the objectification of the species-life of man; for he duplicates himself not only intellectually, in his mind, but also actively in reality and thus can look at his image in a world he has created. Therefore when alienated labour tears from man the object of his production, it also tears from him his species-life, the real objectivity of his species and turns the advantage he has over animals into a disadvantage in that his inorganic body, nature, is torn from him.

1st step in affirmation of species being

Upshot

Similarly, in that alienated labour degrades man's own free activity to a means, it turns the species-life of man into a means for his physical existence.

More conseq. of alienated labor

Thus consciousness, which man derives from his species, changes itself through alienation so that species-life becomes a means for him.

Therefore alienated labor:

(3) makes the species-being of man, both nature and the intellectual faculties of his species, into a being that is alien to him, into a means for his individual existence. It alienates from man his own body, nature exterior to him, and his intellectual being, his human essence.

Alienates humanity from nature

(4) An immediate consequence of man's alienation from the product of his work, his vital activity and his species-being, is the alienation of man from man. When man is opposed to himself, it is another man that is opposed to him. What is valid for the relationship of a man to his work, of the product of his work and himself, is also valid for the relationship of man to other men and of their labour and the objects of their labour.

Man alienated from man

In general, the statement that man is alienated from his species-being, means that one man is alienated from another as each of them is alienated from the human essence.

Summ.

The alienation of man and in general of every relationship in which man stands to himself is first realized and expressed in the relationship with which man stands to other men.

Thus in the situation of alienated labour each man measures his relationship to other men by the relationship in which he finds himself placed as a worker.

Back to worker

We began with a fact of political economy, the alienation of the worker and his production. We have expressed this fact in conceptual terms: alienated, externalized labour. We have analysed this concept and thus analysed a purely economic fact.

Let us now see further how the concept of alienated, externalized labour must express and represent itself in reality.

→ *How tearing away of species-being leads to alienation*

If the product of work is alien to me, opposes me as an alien power, whom does it belong to then?

If my own activity does not belong to me and is an alien, forced activity to whom does it belong then?

To another being than myself.

Who is this being?

The gods? Of course in the beginning of history the chief production, as for example, the building of temples etc. in Egypt, India, and Mexico was both in the service of the gods and also belonged to them. But the gods alone were never the masters of the work. And nature just as little. And what a paradox it would be if, the more man mastered nature through his work and the more the miracles of the gods were rendered superfluous by the miracles of industry, the more man had to give up his pleasure in producing and the enjoyment in his product for the sake of these powers.

The alien being to whom the labour and the product of the labour belongs, whom the labour serves and who enjoys its product, can only be man himself. If the product of labour does not belong to the worker but stands over against him as an alien power, this is only possible in that it belongs to another man apart from the worker.

If his activity torments him it must be a joy and a pleasure to someone else. This alien power above man can be neither the gods nor nature, only man himself.

Consider further the above sentence that the relationship of man to himself first becomes objective and real to him through his relationship to other men. So if he relates to the product of his labour, his objectified labour, as to an object that is alien, hostile, powerful, and independent of him, this relationship implies that another man is the alien, hostile, powerful, and independent master of this object. If he relates to his own activity as to something unfree, it is a relationship to an activity that is

under the domination, oppression, and yoke of another man.

Every self-alienation of man from himself and nature appears in the relationship in which he places himself and nature to other men distinct from himself. Therefore religious self-alienation necessarily appears in the relationship of layman to priest, or, because here we are dealing with a spiritual world, to a mediator, etc. In the practical, real world, the self-alienation can only appear through the practical, real relationship to other men. The means through which alienation makes progress are themselves practical. Through alienated labour, then, man creates not only his relationship to the object and act of production as to alien and hostile men; he creates too the relationship in which other men stand to his production and his product and the relationship in which he stands to these other men. Just as he turns his production into his own loss of reality and punishment and his own product into a loss, a product that does not belong to him, so he creates the domination of the man who does not produce over the production and the product. As he alienates his activity from himself, so he hands over to an alien person an activity that does not belong to him.

Up till now we have considered the relationship only from the side of the worker and we will later consider it from the side of the non-worker.

Thus through alienated, externalized labour the worker creates the relationship to this labour of a man who is alien to it and remains exterior to it. The relationship of the worker to his labour creates the relationship to it of the capitalist, or whatever else one wishes to call the master of the labour. Private property is thus the product, result, and necessary consequence of externalized labour, of the exterior relationship of the worker to nature and to himself.

Thus private property is the result of the analysis of the concept of externalized labour, i.e. externalized man, alienated work, alienated life, alienated man.

We have, of course, obtained the concept of externalized labour (externalized life) from political economy as the result of the movement of private property. But it is evident from the analysis of this concept that, although private property appears to be the ground and reason for externalized labour, it is rather a consequence of it, just as the gods are originally not the cause but the effect of the aberration of the human mind, although later this relationship reverses itself.

It is only in the final culmination of the development of private property that these hidden characteristics come once more to the fore, in that firstly it is the product of externalized labour and secondly it is the means through which labour externalizes itself, the realization of this externalization.

[handwritten annotation:] Upshot: ① B/c humanity works not for itself, its own subsistence, its own creative freedom, humanity is alienated from the objects it produces, its own labor, from nature, & from other people. ② Industrial work is unnatural; antithetical to "man's species-being"

∞ READING 5 ∞

Bureaucracy

Max Weber

I: Characteristics of Bureaucracy

Modern officialdom functions in the following specific manner:

I. There is the principle of fixed and official jurisdictional areas, which are generally ordered by rules, that is, by laws or administrative regulations.

1. The regular activities required for the purposes of the bureaucratically governed structure are distributed in a fixed way as official duties.

2. The authority to give the commands required for the discharge of these duties is distributed in a stable way and is strictly delimited by rules concerning the coercive means, physical, sacerdotal, or otherwise, which may be placed at the disposal of officials.

3. Methodical provision is made for the regular and continuous fulfillment of these duties and for the execution of the corresponding rights; only persons who have the generally regulated qualifications to serve are employed.

In public and lawful government these three elements constitute "bureaucratic authority." In private economic domination, they constitute bureaucratic "management." Bureaucracy, thus understood, is fully developed in political and ecclesiastical communities only in the modern state, and, in the private economy, only in the most advanced institutions of capitalism. Permanent and public office authority, with fixed jurisdiction, is not the historical rule but rather the exception. This is so even in large political structures such as those of the ancient Orient, the Germanic and Mongolian empires of conquest, or of many feudal structures of state. In all these cases, the ruler executes the most important measures through personal trustees, table-companions, or court-servants. Their commissions and authority are not precisely delimited and are temporarily called into being for each case.

II. The principles of office hierarchy and of levels of graded authority mean a firmly ordered system of super- and subordination in which there is a supervision of the lower offices by the higher ones. Such a system offers the governed the possibility of appealing the decision of a lower office to its higher authority, in a definitely regulated manner. With the full development of the bureaucratic type, the office hierarchy is monocratically organized. The principle of hierarchical office authority is found in all bureaucratic structures: in state and ecclesiastical structures as well as in large party organizations and private enterprises. It does not matter for the character of bureaucracy whether its authority is called "private" or "public."

When the principle of jurisdictional "competency" is fully carried through, hierarchical subordination—at least in public office—does not mean that the "higher" authority is simply authorized to take over the business of the "lower." Indeed, the opposite is the rule. Once established and having fulfilled its task, an office tends to continue in existence and be held by another incumbent.

III. The management of the modern office is based upon written documents ("the files"), which are preserved in their original or draught form. There is, therefore, a staff of subaltern officials and scribes of all sorts. The body of officials actively engaged in a "public" office, along with the respective apparatus of material implements and the files, make up a "bureau." In private enterprise, "the bureau" is often called "the office."

In principle, the modern organization of the civil service separates the bureau from the private domicile of the official, and, in general, bureaucracy segregates official activity as something distinct from the sphere of private life. Public monies and equipment are divorced from the private property of the official. This condition is everywhere the product of a long development. Nowadays, it is found in public as well as in private enterprises; in the latter, the principle extends even to the leading entrepreneur. In principle, the executive office is separated from the household, business from private correspondence, and business assets from private fortune. The more consistently the modern type of business management had been carried through the more are these separations the case. The beginnings of this process are to be found as early as the Middle Ages.

It is the peculiarity of the modern entrepreneur that he conducts himself as the "first official" of his enterprise, in the very same way in which the ruler of a specifically modern bureaucratic state spoke of himself as "the first servant" of the state. The idea that the bureau activities of the state are intrinsically different in character from the management of private economic offices is a continental European notion and, by way of contrast, is totally foreign to the American way.

IV. Office management, at least all specialized office management—and such management is distinctly modern—usually presupposes thorough and expert training. This increasingly holds for the modern executive and employee of private enterprises, in the same manner as it holds for the state official.

V. When the office is fully developed, official activity demands the full working capacity of the official, irrespective of the fact that his obligatory time in the bureau may be firmly delimited. In the normal case, this is only the product of a long development, in the public as well as in the private office. Formerly, in all cases, the normal state of affairs was reversed: official business was discharged as a secondary activity.

VI. The management of the office follows general rules, which are more or less stable, more or less exhaustive, and which can be learned. Knowledge of these rules represents a special technical learning which the officials possess. It involves jurisprudence, or administrative or business management.

The reduction of modern office management to rules is deeply embedded in its very nature. The theory of modern public administration, for instance, assumes that the authority to order certain matters by decree—which has been legally granted to public authorities—does not entitle the bureau to regulate the matter by commands given for each case, but only to regulate the matter abstractly. This stands in extreme contrast to the regulation of all relationships through individual privileges and bestowals of favor, which is absolutely dominant in patrimonialism, at least in so far as such relationships are not fixed by sacred tradition.

2: The Position of the Official

All this results in the following for the internal and external position of the official:

I. Office holding is a "vocation." This is shown, first, in the requirement of a firmly prescribed course of training, which demands the entire capacity for work for a long period of time, and in the generally prescribed and special examinations which are prerequisites of employment. Furthermore, the position of the official is in the nature of a duty. This determines the internal structure of his relations, in the following manner: Legally and actually, office holding is not considered a source to be exploited for rents or emoluments, as was normally the case during the Middle Ages and frequently up to the threshold of recent times. Nor is office holding considered a usual exchange of services for equivalents, as is the case with free labor contracts. Entrance into an office, including one in the private economy, is considered an acceptance of a specific obligation of faithful management in return for a secure existence. It is decisive for the specific nature of modern loyalty to an office that, in the pure type, it does not establish a relationship to a *person*, like the vassal's or disciple's faith in feudal or in patrimonial relations of authority. Modern loyalty is devoted to impersonal and functional purposes. Behind the functional purposes, of course, "ideas of culture-values" usually stand. These are *ersatz* for the earthly or supramundane personal master: ideas such as "state," "church," "community," "party," or "enterprise" are thought of as being realized in a community; they provide an ideological halo for the master.

The political official—at least in the fully developed modern state—is not considered the personal servant of a ruler. Today, the bishop, the priest, and the preacher are in fact no longer, as in early Christian times, holders of purely personal charisma. The supra-mundane and sacred values which they offer are given to everybody who seems to be worthy of them and who asks for them. In former times, such leaders acted upon the personal command of their master; in principle, they were responsible only to him. Nowadays, in spite of the partial survival of the old theory, such religious leaders are officials in the service of a functional purpose, which in the present-day "church" has become routinized and, in turn, ideologically hallowed.

II. The personal position of the official is patterned in the following way:

1. Whether he is in a private office or a public bureau, the modern official always strives and usually enjoys a distinct *social esteem* as compared with the governed. His social position is guaranteed by the prescriptive rules of rank order and, for the political

official, by special definitions of the criminal code against "insults of officials" and "contempt" of state and church authorities.

The actual social position of the official is normally highest where, as in old civilized countries, the following conditions prevail: a strong demand for administration by trained experts; a strong and stable social differentiation, where the official predominantly derives from socially and economically privileged strata because of the social distribution of power; or where the costliness of the required training and status conventions are binding upon him. The possession of educational certificates—to be discussed elsewhere—are usually linked with qualification for office. Naturally, such certificates or patents enhance the "status element" in the social position of the official. For the rest this status factor in individual cases is explicitly and impassively acknowledged; for example, in the prescription that the acceptance or rejection of an aspirant to an official career depends upon the consent ("election") of the members of the official body. This is the case in the German army with the officer corps. Similar phenomena, which promote this guild-like closure of officialdom, are typically found in patrimonial and, particularly, in prebendal officialdoms of the past. The desire to resurrect such phenomena in changed forms is by no means infrequent among modern bureaucrats. For instance, they have played a role among the demands of the quite proletarian and expert officials (the *tretyj* element) during the Russian revolution.

Usually the social esteem of the officials as such is especially low where the demand for expert administration and the dominance of status conventions are weak. This is especially the case in the United States; it is often the case in new settlements by virtue of their wide fields for profit-making and the great instability of their social stratification.

2. The pure type of bureaucratic official is *appointed* by a superior authority. An official elected by the governed is not a purely bureaucratic figure. Of course, the formal existence of an election does not by itself mean that no appointment hides behind the election—in the state, especially, appointment by party chiefs. Whether or not this is the case does not depend upon legal statutes but upon the way in which the party mechanism functions. Once firmly organized, the parties can turn a formally free election into the mere acclamation of a candidate designated by the party chief. As a rule, however, a formally free election is turned into a fight, conducted according to definite rules, for votes in favor of one of two designed candidates.

In all circumstances, the designation of officials by means of an election among the governed modifies the strictness of hierarchical subordination. In principle, an official who is so elected has an autonomous position opposite the superordinate official. The elected official does not derive his position "from above" but "from below," or at least not from a superior authority of the official hierarchy but from powerful party men ("bosses"), who also determine his further career. The career of the elected official is not, or at least not primarily, dependent upon his chief in the administration. The official who is not elected but appointed by a chief normally functions more exactly, from a technical point of view, because, all other circumstances being equal, it is more likely that purely functional points of consideration and qualities will determine his selection and career. As laymen, the governed can become acquainted with the extent to which a candidate is expertly qualified for office only in terms of experience, and hence only after his service. Moreover, in every sort of selection of officials by election, parties quite naturally give decisive weight not to expert considerations but to the services a follower renders to the party boss. This holds for all kinds of procurement of officials by elections, for the designation of formally free, elected officials by party bosses when they determine the slate of candidates, or the free appointment by a chief who has himself been elected. The contrast, however, is relative: substantially similar conditions hold where legitimate monarchs and their subordinates appoint officials, except that the influence of the followings are then less controllable.

Where the demand for administration by trained experts is considerable, and the party followings have to recognize an intellectually developed, educated, and freely moving "public opinion," the use of unqualified officials falls back upon the party in power at the next election. Naturally, this is more likely to happen when the officials are appointed by the chief. The demand for a trained administration now exists in the United States, but in the large cities, where immigrant votes are "corralled," there is, of course, no educated public opinion. Therefore, popular elections of the administrative chief and also of his subordinate officials usually endanger the expert qualification of the official as well as the precise functioning of the bureaucratic mechanism. It also weakens the dependence of the officials upon the hierarchy. This holds at least for the large administrative bodies that are difficult to supervise. The superior qualification and integrity of federal judges, appointed by the President, as over against elected judges in the United States is well known, although both types of officials have been selected primarily in terms of party considerations. The great changes in American metropolitan administrations demanded by reformers have proceeded essentially from elected mayors working with an apparatus of officials who were appointed by them. These reforms have thus come about in a "Caesarist" fashion. Viewed technically, as an organized form of authority, the efficiency of "Caesarism," which often grows out of democracy, rests in general upon the position of the "Caesar" as a free trustee of the masses (of the army or of the citizenry), who is unfettered by tradition. The "Caesar" is thus the unrestrained master of a body of highly qualified military officers and officials whom he selects freely and personally without regard to tradition or to any other considerations. This "rule of the personal genius," however, stands in contradiction to the formally "democratic" principle of a universally elected officialdom.

3. Normally, the position of the official is held for life, at least in public bureaucracies; and this is increasingly the case for all similar structures. As a factual rule, *tenure for life* is presupposed, even where the giving of notice or periodic reappointment occurs. In contrast to the worker in a private enterprise, the official normally holds tenure. Legal or actual life-tenure, however, is not recognized as the official's right to the possession of office, as was the case with many structures of authority in the past. Where legal guarantees against arbitrary dismissal or transfer are developed, they merely serve to guarantee a strictly objective discharge of specific office duties free from all personal considerations. In Germany, this is the case for all juridical and, increasingly, for all administrative officials.

Within the bureaucracy, therefore, the measure of "independence," legally guaranteed by tenure is not always a source of increased status for the official whose position is thus secured. Indeed, often the reverse holds, especially in old cultures and communities that are highly differentiated. In such communities, the stricter the subordination under the arbitrary rule of the master, the more it guarantees the maintenance of the conventional seigneurial style of living for the official. Because of the very absence of these legal guarantees of tenure, the conventional esteem for the official may rise in the same way as, during the Middle Ages, the esteem of the nobility of office rose at the expense of esteem for the freemen, and as the king's judge surpassed that of the people's judge. In Germany, the military officer or the administrative official can be removed from office at any time, or at least far more readily than the "independent judge," who never pays with loss of his office for even the grossest offense against the "code of honor" or against social conventions of the salon. For this very reason, if other things are equal, in the eyes of the master stratum the judge is considered less qualified for the social intercourse than are officers and administrative officials, whose greater dependence on the master is a greater guarantee of their conformity with status conventions. Of course, the average official strives for a civil-service law, which would materially secure his old age and provide increased guarantees against his arbitrary removal from office. This striving, however, has its limits. A very strong development of the "right to the office" naturally makes it more difficult to staff them with regard to technical efficiency, for such a development decreases the career-opportunities of ambitious candidates for office. This makes for the fact that officials, on the whole, do not feel their dependency upon those at the top. This lack of a feeling of dependency, however, rests primarily upon the inclination to depend upon one's equals rather than upon the socially inferior and governed strata. The present conservative movement among the Badenia clergy, occasioned by the anxiety of a presumably threatening separation of church and state, has been expressly determined by the desire not to be turned "from a master into a servant of the parish."

4. The official receives the regular *pecuniary* compensation of a normally fixed *salary* and the old age security provided by a pension. The salary is not measured like a wage in terms of work done, but according to "status," that is, according to the kind of function (the "rank") and, in addition, possibly, according to the length of service. The relatively great security of the official's income, as well as the rewards of social esteem, make the office a sought-after position, especially in countries which no longer provide opportunities for colonial profits. In such countries, this situation permits relatively low salaries for officials.

5. The official is set for a *"career"* within the hierarchical order of the public service. He moves from the lower, less important, and lower paid to the higher positions. The average official naturally desires a mechanical fixing of the conditions of promotion: if not the offices, at least of the salary levels. He wants these conditions fixed in terms of "seniority," or possibly according to grades achieved in a developed system of expert examinations. Here and there, such examinations actually form a character *indelebilis* of the official and have lifelong effects on his career. To this is joined the desire to qualify the right to office and the increasing tendency toward status group closure and economic security. All of this makes for a tendency to consider the offices as "prebends" of those who are qualified by educational certificates. The necessity of taking general personal and intellectual qualifications into consideration, irrespective of the often subaltern character of the educational certificate, has led to a condition in which the highest political offices, especially the positions of "ministers," are principally filled without reference to such certificates.

In relation to Marx's comments: Does Taylor really think workers get much out of being efficient (even in making "lots" of $)?

∞ READING 6 ∞

Fundamentals of Scientific Management

Frederick Winslow Taylor

main goal of mgmt

Essentially giving exact opposite of Marx's argument

Not all ALL a Marxist: workers & mgmt should get along!

desc

The principal object of management should be to secure the maximum prosperity for the employer, coupled with the maximum prosperity for each employé.

The words "maximum prosperity" are used, in their broad sense, to mean not only large dividends for the company or owner, but the development of every branch of the business to its highest state of excellence, so that the prosperity may be permanent.

In the same way maximum prosperity for each employé means not only higher wages than are usually received by men of his class, but, of more importance still, it also means the development of each man to his state of maximum efficiency, so that he may be able to do, generally speaking, the highest grade of work for which his natural abilities fit him, and it further means giving him, when possible, this class of work to do.

It would seem to be so self-evident that maximum prosperity for the employer, coupled with maximum prosperity for the employé, ought to be the two leading objects of management, that even to state this fact should be unnecessary. And yet there is no question that, throughout the industrial world, a large part of the organization of employers, as well as employés, is for war rather than for peace, and that perhaps the majority on either side do not believe that it *(mm)*

is possible so to arrange their mutual relations that their interests become identical.

The majority of these men believe that the fundamental interests of employés and employers are necessarily antagonistic. Scientific management, on the contrary, has for its very foundation the firm conviction that the true interests of the two are one and the same; that prosperity for the employer cannot exist through a long term of years unless it is accompanied by prosperity for the employé, and *vice versa*; and that it is possible to give the workman what he most wants—high wages—and the employer what he wants—a low labor cost—for his manufactures.

Sci. mgmt: workers & managers can align interests *?!*

It is hoped that some at least of those who do not sympathize with each of these objects may be led to modify their views; that some employers, whose attitude toward their workmen has been that of trying to get the largest amount of work out of them for the smallest possible wages, may be led to see that a more liberal policy toward their men will pay them better; and that some of those workmen who begrudge a fair and even a large profit to their employers, and who feel that all of the fruits of their labor should belong to them, and that those for whom they work and the capital invested in the business are entitled to little or nothing, may be led to modify these views.

Efforts @ compromise! (v. pro-business tho)

No one can be found who will deny that in the case of any single individual the greatest prosperity can exist only when that individual has reached his highest state of efficiency; that is, when he is turning out his largest daily output.

Humanity's ultimate satisfaction: Marx = creativity & freedom. Taylor = efficiency/max. prosperity

The truth of this fact is also perfectly clear in the case of two men working together. To illustrate: if you and your workman have become so skilful that you and he together are making two pairs of shoes in a day, while your competitor and his workman are making only one pair, it is clear that after selling your two pairs of shoes you can pay your workman much higher wages than your competitor who produces only one pair of shoes is able to pay his man, and that there will still be enough money left over for you to have a larger profit than your competitor.

In the case of a more complicated manufacturing establishment, it should also be perfectly clear that the greatest permanent prosperity for the workman, coupled with the greatest prosperity for the employer, can be brought about only when the work of the establishment is done with the smallest combined expenditure of human effort, plus nature's resources, plus the cost for the use of capital in the shape of machines, buildings, etc. Or, to state the same thing in a different way: that the greatest prosperity can exist only as the result of the greatest possible productivity of the men and machines of the establishment—that is, when each man and each machine are turning out the largest possible output; because unless your men and your machines are daily turning out more work than others around you, it is clear that competition will prevent your paying higher wages to your workmen than are paid to those of your competitor. And what is true as to the possibility of paying high wages in the case of two companies competing close beside one another is also true as to whole districts of the country and even as to nations which are in competition. In a word, that maximum prosperity can exist only as the result of maximum productivity. Later in this paper illustrations will be given of several companies which are earning large dividends and at the same time paying from 30 per cent. to 100 per cent.

higher wages to their men than are paid to similar men immediately around them, and with whose employers they are in competition. These illustrations will cover different types of work, from the most elementary to the most complicated.

If the above reasoning is correct, it follows that the most important object of both the workmen and the management should be the training and development of each individual in the establishment, so that he can do (at his fastest pace and with the maximum of efficiency) the highest class of work for which his natural abilities fit him.

These principles appear to be so self-evident that many men may think it almost childish to state them. Let us, however, turn to the facts, as they actually exist in this country and in England. The English and American peoples are the greatest sportsmen in the world. Whenever an American workman plays baseball, or an English workman plays cricket, it is safe to say that he strains every nerve to secure victory for his side. He does his very best to make the largest possible number of runs. The universal sentiment is so strong that any man who fails to give out all there is in him in sport is branded as a "quitter," and treated with contempt by those who are around him.

When the same workman returns to work on the following day, instead of using every effort to turn out the largest possible amount of work, in a majority of the cases this man deliberately plans to do as little as he safely can—to turn out far less work than he is well able to do—in many instances to do not more than one-third to one-half of a proper day's work. And in fact if he were to do his best to turn out his largest possible day's work, he would be abused by his fellow-workers for so doing, even more than if he had proved himself a "quitter" in sport. Underworking, that is, deliberately working slowly so as to avoid doing a full day's work, "soldiering," as it is called in this country, "hanging it out," as it is called in England, "ca canae," as it is called in Scotland, is almost universal in industrial establishments, and prevails also to a large extent in the building trades; and the writer asserts without fear of contradiction that this constitutes the greatest evil with which the working-people of both England and America are now afflicted.

It will be shown later in this paper that doing away with slow working and "soldiering" in all its forms and so arranging the relations between employer and employé that each workman will work to his very best advantage and at his best speed, accompanied by the intimate cooperation with the management and the help (which the workman should receive) from the management, would result on the average in nearly doubling the output of each man and each machine. What other reforms, among those which are being discussed by these two nations, could do as much toward promoting prosperity, toward the diminution of poverty, and the alleviation of suffering? America and England have been recently agitated over such subjects as the tariff, the control of the large corporations on the one hand, and of hereditary power on the other hand, and over various more or less socialistic proposals for taxation, etc. On these subjects both peoples have been profoundly stirred, and yet hardly a voice has been raised to call attention to this vastly greater and more important subject of "soldiering," which directly and powerfully affects the wages, the prosperity, and the life of almost every working-man, and also quite as much the prosperity of every industrial establishment in the nation.

The elimination of "soldiering" and of the several causes of slow working would so lower the cost of production that both our home and foreign markets would be greatly enlarged, and we could compete on more than even terms with our rivals. It would remove one of the fundamental causes for dull times, for lack of employment, and for poverty, and therefore would have a more permanent and far-reaching effect upon these misfortunes than any of the curative remedies that are now being used to soften their consequences. It would insure higher wages and make shorter working hours and better working and home conditions possible.

Why is it, then, in the face of the self-evident fact that maximum prosperity can exist only as the result of the determined effort of each workman to turn out each day his largest possible day's work, that the great majority of our men are deliberately doing just the opposite, and that even when the men have the best of intentions their work is in most cases far from efficient?

There are three causes for this condition, which may be briefly summarized as:

First. The fallacy, which has from time immemorial been almost universal among workmen, that a material increase in the output of each man or each machine in the trade would result in the end in throwing a large number of men out of work.

Second. The defective systems of management which are in common use, and which make it necessary for each workman to soldier, or work slowly, in order that he may protect his own best interests.

Third. The inefficient rule-of-thumb methods, which are still almost universal in all trades, and in practising which our workmen waste a large part of their effort.

This paper will attempt to show the enormous gains which would result from the substitution by our workmen of scientific for rule-of-thumb methods.

To explain a little more fully these three causes:

First. The great majority of workmen still believe that if they were to work at their best speed they would be doing a great injustice to the whole trade by throwing a lot of men out of work, and yet the history of the development of each trade shows that each improvement, whether it be the invention of a new machine or the introduction of a better method, which results in increasing the productive capacity of the men in the trade and cheapening the costs, instead of throwing men out of work makes in the end work for more men.

The cheapening of any article in common use almost immediately results in a largely increased demand for that article. Take the case of shoes, for instance. The introduction of machinery for doing every element of the work which was formerly done by hand has resulted in making shoes at a fraction of their former labor cost, and in selling them so cheap that now almost every man, woman, and child in the working-classes buys one or two pairs of shoes per year, and wears shoes all the time, whereas formerly each workman bought perhaps one pair of shoes every five years, and went barefoot most of the time, wearing shoes only as a luxury or as a matter of the sternest necessity. In spite of the enormously increased output of shoes per workman, which has come with shoe machinery, the demand for shoes has so increased that there are relatively more men working in the shoe industry now than ever before.

The workmen in almost every trade have before them an object lesson of this kind, and yet, because they are ignorant of the history of their own trade even, they still firmly believe, as their fathers did before them, that it is against their best interests for each man to turn out each day as much work as possible. Under this fallacious idea a large proportion of the workmen of both countries each day deliberately work slowly so as to curtail the output. Almost every labor union has made, or is contemplating making, rules which have for their object curtailing the output of their members, and those men who have the greatest influence with the working-people, the labor leaders as well as many people with philanthropic feelings who are helping them, are daily spreading this fallacy and at the same time telling them that they are overworked.

A great deal has been and is being constantly said about "sweat-shop" work and conditions. The writer has great sympathy with those who are overworked, but on the whole a greater sympathy for those who are *under paid*. For every individual, however, who is overworked, there are a hundred who intentionally underwork—greatly underwork—every day of their lives, and who for this reason deliberately aid in establishing those conditions which in the end inevitably result in low wages. And yet hardly a single voice is being raised in an endeavor to correct this evil.

As engineers and managers, we are more intimately acquainted with these facts than any other class in the community, and are therefore best fitted to lead in a movement to combat this fallacious idea by educating not only the workmen but the whole of the country as to the true facts. And yet we are practically doing nothing in this direction, and are leaving this field entirely in the hands of the labor agitators (many of whom are misinformed and misguided), and of sentimentalists who are ignorant as to actual working conditions.

Second. As to the second cause for soldiering—the relations which exist between employers and employés under almost all of the systems of management which are in common use—it is impossible in a few words to make it clear to one not familiar with this problem why it is that the *ignorance of employers* as to the proper time in which work of various kinds should be done makes it for the interest of the workman to "soldier."

The writer therefore quotes herewith from a paper read before The American Society of Mechanical Engineers, in June, 1903, entitled "Shop Management," which it is hoped will explain fully this cause for soldiering:

"This loafing or soldiering proceeds from two causes. First, from the natural instinct and tendency of men to take it easy, which may be called natural soldiering. Second, from more intricate second thought and reasoning caused by their relations with other men, which may be called systematic soldiering.

"There is no question that the tendency of the average man (in all walks of life) is toward working at a slow, easy gait, and that it is only after a good deal of thought and observation on his part or as a result of example, conscience, or external pressure that he takes a more rapid pace.

"There are, of course, men of unusual energy, vitality, and ambition who naturally choose the fastest gait, who set up their own standards, and who work hard, even though it may be against their best interests. But these few uncommon men only serve by forming a contrast to emphasize the tendency of the average.

"This common tendency to 'take it easy' is greatly increased by bringing a number of men together on similar work and at a uniform standard rate of pay by the day.

"Under this plan the better men gradually but surely slow down their gait to that of the poorest and least efficient. When a naturally energetic man works for a few days beside a lazy one, the logic of the situation is unanswerable. 'Why should I work hard when that lazy fellow gets the same pay that I do and does only half as much work?'

"A careful time study of men working under these conditions will disclose facts which are ludicrous as well as pitiable.

"To illustrate: The writer has timed a naturally energetic workman who, while going and coming from work, would walk at a speed of from three to four miles per hour, and not infrequently trot home after a day's work. On arriving at his work he would immediately slow down to a speed of about one mile an hour. When, for example, wheeling a loaded wheelbarrow, he would go at a good fast pace even up hill in order to be as short a time as possible under load, and immediately on the return walk slow down to a mile an hour, improving every opportunity for delay short of actually sitting down. In order to be sure not to do more than his lazy neighbor, he would actually tire himself in his effort to go slow.

"These men were working under a foreman of good reputation and highly thought of by his employer, who, when his attention was called to this state of things, answered: 'Well, I can keep them from sitting down, but the devil can't make them get a move on while they are at work.'

"The natural laziness of men is serious, but by far the greatest evil from which both workmen and employers are suffering is the systematic soldiering which is almost universal under all of the ordinary schemes of management and which results from a careful study on the part of the workmen of what will promote their best interests.

"The writer was much interested recently in hearing one small but experienced golf caddy boy of twelve explaining to a green caddy, who had shown special energy and interest, the necessity of going slow and lagging behind his man when he came up to the ball, showing him that since they were paid by the hour, the faster they went the less money they got, and finally telling him that if he went too fast the other boys would give him a licking.

"This represents a type of *systematic soldiering* which is not, however, very serious, since it is done with the knowledge of the employer, who can quite easily break it up if he wishes.

"The greater part of the *systematic soldiering,* however, is done by the men with the deliberate object of keeping their employers ignorant of how fast work can be done.

"So universal is soldiering for this purpose that hardly a competent workman can be found in a large establishment, whether he works by the day or on piece work, contract work, or under any of the ordinary systems, who does not devote a considerable part of his time to studying just how slow he can work and still convince his employer that he is going at a good pace.

"The causes for this are, briefly, that practically all employers determine upon a maximum sum which they feel it is right for each of their classes of employees to earn per day, whether their men work by the day or piece.

"Each workman soon finds out about what this figure is for his particular case, and he also realizes that when his employer is convinced that a man is capable of doing more work than he has done, he will find sooner or later some way of compelling him to do it with little or no increase of pay.

"Employers derive their knowledge of how much of a given class of work can be done in a day from either their own experience, which has frequently grown hazy with age, from casual and unsystematic observation of their men, or at best from records which are kept, showing the quickest time in which each job has been done. In many cases the employer will feel almost certain that a given job can be done faster than it has been, but he rarely cares to take the drastic measures necessary to force men to do it in the quickest time, unless he has an actual record proving conclusively how fast the work can be done.

"It evidently becomes for each man's interest, then, to see that no job is done faster than it has been in the past. The younger and less experienced men are taught this by their elders, and all possible persuasion and social pressure is brought to bear upon the greedy and selfish men to keep them from making new records which result in temporarily increasing their wages, while all those who come after them are made to work harder for the same old pay.

"Under the best day work of the ordinary type, when accurate records are kept of the amount of work done by each man and of his efficiency, and when each man's wages are raised as he improves, and those who fail to rise to a certain standard are discharged and a fresh supply of carefully selected men are given work in their places, both the natural loafing and systematic soldiering can be largely broken up. This can only be done, however, when the men are thoroughly convinced that there is no intention of establishing piece work even in the remote future, and it is next to impossible to make men believe this when the work is of such a nature that they believe piece work to be practicable. In most cases their fear of making a record which will be used as a basis for piece work will cause them to soldier as much as they dare.

"It is, however, under piece work that the art of systematic soldiering is thoroughly developed; after a workman has had the price per piece of the work he is doing lowered two or three times as a result of his having worked harder and increased his output, he is likely entirely to lose sight of his employer's side of the case and become imbued with a grim determination to have no more cuts if soldiering can prevent it. Unfortunately for the character of the workman, soldiering involves a deliberate attempt to mislead and deceive his employer, and thus upright and straightforward workmen are compelled to become more or less hypocritical. The employer is soon looked upon as an antagonist, if not an enemy, and the mutual confidence which should exist between a leader and his men, the enthusiasm, the feeling that they are all working for the same end and will share in the results is entirely lacking.

"The feeling of antagonism under the ordinary piece-work system becomes in many cases so marked on the part of the men that any proposition made by their employers, however reasonable, is looked upon with suspicion, and soldiering becomes such a fixed habit that men will frequently take pains to restrict the product of machines which they are running when even a large increase in output would involve no more work on their part."

Third. As to the third cause for slow work, considerable space will later in this paper be devoted to illustrating the great gain, both to employers and employés, which results from the substitution of scientific for rule-of-thumb methods in even the smallest details of the work of every trade. The enormous saving of time and therefore increase in the output which it is possible to effect through eliminating unnecessary motions and substituting fast for slow and inefficient motions for the men working in any of our trades can be fully realized only after one has personally seen the improvement which results from a thorough motion and time study, made by a competent man.

To explain briefly: owing to the fact that the workmen in all of our trades have been taught the details of their work by observation of those immediately around them, there are many different ways in common use for doing the same thing, perhaps forty, fifty, or a hundred ways of doing each act in each trade, and for the same reason there is a great variety in the implements used for each class of work. Now, among the various methods and implements used in each element of each trade there is always one method and one implement which is quicker and better than any of the rest. And this one best method and best implement can only be discovered or developed through a scientific study and analysis of all of the methods and implements in use, together with accurate, minute, motion and time study. This involves the gradual substitution of science for rule of thumb throughout the mechanic arts.

This paper will show that the underlying philosophy of all of the old systems of management in common use makes it imperative that each workman shall be left with the final responsibility for doing his job practically as he thinks best, with comparatively little help and advice from the management. And it will also show that because of this isolation of workmen, it is in most cases impossible for the men working under these systems to do their work in accordance with the rules and laws of a science or art, even where one exists.

The writer asserts as a general principle (and he proposes to give illustrations tending to prove the fact later in this paper) that in almost all of the mechanic arts the science which underlies each act of each workman is so great and amounts to so much that the workman who is best suited to actually doing the work is incapable of fully understanding this science, without the guidance and help of those who are working with him or over him, either through lack of education or through insufficient mental capacity. In order that the work may be done in accordance with scientific laws, it is necessary that there shall be a far more equal division of the responsibility between the management and the workmen than exists under any of the ordinary types of management. Those in the management whose duty it is to develop this science should also guide and help the workman in working under it, and should assume a much larger share of the responsibility for results than under usual conditions is assumed by the management.

The body of this paper will make it clear that, to work according to scientific laws, the management must take over and perform much of the work which is now left to the men; almost every act of the workman should be preceded by one or more preparatory acts of the management which enable him to do his work better and quicker than he otherwise could. And each man should daily be taught by and receive the most friendly help from those who are over him, instead of being, at the one extreme, driven or coerced by his bosses, and at the other left to his own unaided devices.

This close, intimate, personal cooperation between the management and the men is of the essence of modern scientific or task management.

It will be shown by a series of practical illustrations that, through this friendly cooperation, namely, through sharing equally in every day's burden, all of the great obstacles (above described) to obtaining the maximum output for each man and each machine in the establishment are swept away. The 30 per cent. to 100 per cent. increase in wages which the workmen are able to earn beyond what they receive under the old type of management, coupled with the daily intimate shoulder to shoulder contact with the management, entirely removes all cause for soldiering. And in a few years, under this system, the workmen have before them the object lesson of seeing that a great increase in the output per man results in giving employment to more men, instead of throwing men out of work, thus completely eradicating the fallacy that a larger output for each man will throw other men out of work.

It is the writer's judgment, then, that while much can be done and should be done by writing and talking toward educating not only workmen, but all classes in the community, as to the importance of obtaining the maximum output of each man and each machine, it is only through the adoption of modern scientific management that this great problem can be finally solved. Probably most of the readers of this paper will say that all of this is mere theory. On the contrary, the theory, or philosophy, of scientific management is just beginning to be understood, whereas the management itself has been a gradual evolution, extending over a period of nearly thirty years. And during

this time the employés of one company after another, including a large range and diversity of industries, have gradually changed from the ordinary to the scientific type of management. At least 50,000 workmen in the United States are now employed under this system; and they are receiving from 30 per cent. to 100 per cent. higher wages daily than are paid to men of similar caliber with whom they are surrounded, while the companies employing them are more prosperous than ever before. In these companies the output, per man and per machine, has on an average been doubled. During all these years there has never been a single strike among the men working under this system. In place of the suspicious watchfulness and the more or less open warfare which characterizes the ordinary types of management, there is universally friendly cooperation between the management and the men.

Several papers have been written, describing the expedients which have been adopted and the details which have been developed under scientific management and the steps to be taken in changing from the ordinary to the scientific type. But unfortunately most of the readers of these papers have mistaken the mechanism for the true essence. Scientific management fundamentally consists of certain broad general principles, a certain philosophy, which can be applied in many ways, and a description of what any one man or men may believe to be the best mechanism for applying these general principles should in no way be confused with the principles themselves.

It is not here claimed that any single panacea exists for all of the troubles of the working-people or of employers. As long as some people are born lazy or inefficient, and others are born greedy and brutal, as long as vice and crime are with us, just so long will a certain amount of poverty, misery, and unhappiness be with us also. No system of management, no single expedient within the

[handwritten: Taylorism did have a profound intl. impact]

control of any man or any set of men can insure continuous prosperity to either workmen or employers. Prosperity depends upon so many factors entirely beyond the control of any one set of men, any state, or even any one country, that certain periods will inevitably come when both sides must suffer, more or less. It is claimed, however, that under scientific management the intermediate periods will be far more prosperous, far happier, and more free from discord and dissen-

sion. And also, that the periods will be fewer, shorter and the suffering less. And this will be particularly true in any one town, any one section of the country, or any one state which first substitutes the principles of scientific management for the rule of thumb.

That these principles are certain to come into general use practically throughout the civilized world, sooner or later, the writer is profoundly convinced, and the sooner they come the better for all the people.

[handwritten: Upshot: - Industrial work should be done as efficiently, uniformly, & scientifically as possible. - Sci. mgmt will ↑ wages, create "intimacy" b/w mgmt & worker, & (most imp) ↑ production. - This will reduce "soldiering," or the inclination of workers to underwork for 3 main reasons.]

READING 7

The Division of Labor

Harry Braverman

[handwritten: Cap's 1st innovation: The manuf. division of labor]

The earliest innovative principle of the capitalist mode of production was the manufacturing division of labor, and in one form or another the division of labor has remained the fundamental principle of industrial organization. The division of labor in capitalist industry is not at all identical with the phenomenon of the distribution of tasks, crafts, or specialties of production throughout society, for while all known societies have divided their work into productive specialties, no society before capitalism systematically subdivided the work of each productive specialty into limited operations. This form of the division of labor becomes generalized only with capitalism. . . .

Our concern at this point, therefore, is not with the division of labor in society at large,

but within the enterprise; not with the distribution of labor among various industries and occupations, but with the breakdown of occupations and industrial processes; not with the division of labor in "production in general," but within the capitalist mode of production in particular. It is not "pure technique" that concerns us, but rather the marriage of technique with the special needs of capital.

The division of labor in production begins with the *analysis of the labor process*—that is to say, the separation of the work of production into its constituent elements. But this, in itself, is not what brings into being the detail worker. Such an analysis or separation, in fact, is characteristic in every labor process organized by workers to suit their own needs. *[handwritten: Internalized Sci. mgmt @ work]*

For example, a tinsmith makes a funnel: he draws the elevation view on sheetmetal, and from this develops the outline of an unrolled funnel and its bottom spout. He then cuts out each piece with snips and shears,

"The Division of Labor" From of *Labor and Monopoly Capital* by Harry Braverman. Copyright © 1974 by Harry Braverman. Reprinted by permission of Monthly Review Foundation.

rolls it to its proper shape, and crimps or rivets the seams. He then rolls the top edge, solders the seams, solders on a hanging ring, washes away the acid used in soldering, and rounds the funnel to its final shape. But when he applies the same process to a quantity of identical funnels, his mode of operation changes. Instead of laying out the work directly on the material, he makes a pattern and uses it to mark off the total quantity of funnels needed; then he cuts them all out, one after the other, rolls them, etc. In this case, instead of making a single funnel in the course of an hour or two, he spends hours or even days on each step of the process, creating in each case fixtures, clamps, devices, etc. which would not be worth making for a single funnel but which, where a sufficiently large quantity of funnels is to be made, speed each step sufficiently so that the saving justifies the extra outlay of time. Quantities, he has discovered, will be produced with less trouble and greater economy of time in this way than by finishing each funnel individually before starting the next.

In the same way a bookkeeper whose job it is to make out bills and maintain office records against their future collection will, if he or she works for a lawyer who has only a few clients at a time, prepare a bill and post it at once to the proper accounts and the customer statement. But if there are hundreds of bills each month, the bookkeeper will accumulate them and spend a full day or two, from time to time, posting them to the proper accounts. Some of these postings will now be made by daily, weekly, or monthly totals instead of bill by bill, a practice which saves a great deal of labor when large quantities are involved; at the same time, the bookkeeper will now make use of other shortcuts or aids, which become practicable when operations are analyzed or broken up in this way, such as specially prepared ledger cards, or carbon forms which combine into a single operation the posting to the customer's account and the preparation of a monthly statement.

Such methods of analysis of the labor process and its division into constituent elements have always been and are to this day common in all trades and crafts, and represent the first form of the subdivision of labor in detail. It is clear that they satisfy, essentially if not fully, the three advantages of the division of labor given by Adam Smith in his famous discussion in the first chapter of *The Wealth of Nations*:

> This great increase in the quantity of work, which, in consequence of the division of labour, the same number of people are capable of performing, is owing to three different circumstances; first, to the increase of dexterity in every particular workman; secondly, to the saving of the time which is commonly lost in passing from one species of work to another; and lastly, to the invention of a great number of machines which facilitate and abridge labour, and enable one man to do the work of many.

The example which Smith gives is the making of pins, and his description is as follows:

> One man draws out the wire, another straightens it, a third cuts it, a fourth points it, a fifth grinds it at the top for receiving the head; to make the head requires two or three distinct operations; to put it on, is a peculiar business, to whiten the pins is another; it is even a trade by itself to put them into the paper; and the important business of making a pin is, in this manner, divided into about eighteen distinct operations, which, in some manufactories, are all performed by distinct hands, though in others the same man will sometimes perform two or three of them.

In this example, the division of labor is carried one step further than in the examples of the tinsmith and the bookkeeper. Not only are the operations separated from each other, but *they are assigned to different workers.* Here we have not just the analysis of the labor process but the creation of the detail worker. Both steps depend upon the scale of production: without sufficient quantities they are impracticable. Each step represents a saving in labor time. The greatest saving is embodied in the analysis of the process, and a further saving, the extent varying with the nature of the process, is to be found in the separation of operations among different workers.

The worker may break the process down, but he never voluntarily converts himself into a lifelong detail worker. This is the contribution of the capitalist, who sees no reason why, if so much is to be gained from the first step—analysis—and something more gained from the second—breakdown among workers—he should not take the second step as well as the first. That the first step breaks up only the process, while the second dismembers the worker as well, means nothing to the capitalist, and all the less since, in destroying the craft as a process under the control of the worker, he reconstitutes it as a process under his own control. He can now count his gains in a double sense, not only in productivity but in management control, since that which mortally injures the worker is in this case advantageous to him.

The effect of these advantages is heightened by still another which, while it is given surprisingly little mention in economic literature, is certainly the most compelling reason of all for the immense popularity of the division of tasks among workers in the capitalist mode of production, and for its rapid spread. It was not formulated clearly nor emphasized strongly until a half-century after Smith, by Charles Babbage.

In "On the Division of Labour," Chapter XIX of his *On the Economy of Machinery and Manufactures,* the first edition of which was published in 1832, Babbage noted that "the most important and influential cause [of savings from the division of labor] has been altogether unnoticed." He recapitulates the classic arguments of William Petty, Adam Smith, and the other political economists, quotes from Smith the passage reproduced above about the "three different circumstances" of the division of labor which add to the productivity of labor, and continues:

> Now, although all these are important causes, and each has its influence on the result; yet it appears to me, that any explanation of the cheapness of manufactured articles, as consequent upon the division of labour, would be incomplete if the following principle were omitted to be stated.
>
> *That the master manufacturer, by dividing the work to be executed into different processes, each requiring different degrees of skill or of force, can purchase exactly that precise quantity of both which is necessary for each process; whereas, if the whole work were executed by one workman, that person must possess sufficient skill to perform the most difficult, and sufficient strength to execute the most laborious, of the operations into which the art is divided.*

To put this all-important principle another way, in a society based upon the purchase and sale of labor power, dividing the craft cheapens its individual parts. To clarify this point, Babbage gives us an example drawn, like Smith's, from pin manufacture. He presents a table for the labor employed, by type (that is, by age and sex) and by pay, in the English manufacture of those pins known in his day as "Elevens."

Drawing wire	Man	3s. 3d. per day
Straightening wire	Woman	1s. 0d.
	Girl	0s. 6d.
Pointing	Man	5s. 3d.
Twisting and	Boy	0s. 4½ d.
cutting heads	Man	5s. 4½ d.
Heading	Woman	1s. 3d.
Tinning or	Man	6s. 0d.
whitening	Woman	3s. 0d.
Papering	Woman	1s. 6d.

It is clear from this tabulation, as Babbage points out, that if the minimum pay for a craftsman capable of performing all operations is no more than the highest pay in the above listing, and if such craftsmen are employed exclusively, then the labor costs of manufacture would be more than doubled, *even if the very same division of labor were employed and even if the craftsmen produced pins at the very same speed as the detail workers.*

Let us add another and later example, taken from the first assembly line in American industry, the meatpacking conveyor (actually a *disassembly* line). J. R. Commons has realistically included in this description, along with the usual details, the rates of pay of the workers:

It would be difficult to find another industry where division of labor has been so ingeniously and microscopically worked out. The animal has been surveyed and laid off like a map; and the men have been classified in over thirty specialties and twenty rates of pay, from 16 cents to 50 cents an hour. The 50-cent man is restricted to using the knife on the most delicate parts of the hide (floorman) or to using the ax in splitting the backbone (splitter); and wherever a less-skilled man can be slipped in at 18 cents, 18½ cents, 20 cents, 21 cents, 22½ cents, 24 cents, 25 cents, and so on, a place is made for him, and an occupation mapped out. In working on the hide

alone there are nine positions, at eight different rates of pay. A 20-cent man pulls off the tail, a 22½-cent man pounds off another part where good leather is not found, and the knife of the 40-cent man cuts a different texture and has a different "feel" from that of the 50-cent man.

Babbage's principle is fundamental to the evolution of the division of labor in capitalist society. It gives expression not to a technical aspect of the division of labor, but to its social aspect. Insofar as the labor process may be dissociated, it may be separated into elements some of which are simpler than others and each of which is simpler than the whole. Translated into market terms, this means that the labor power capable of performing the process may be purchased more cheaply as dissociated elements than as a capacity integrated in a single worker. Applied first to the handicrafts and then to the mechanical crafts, Babbage's principle eventually becomes the underlying force governing all forms of work in capitalist society, no matter in what setting or at what hierarchical level.

In the mythology of capitalism, the Babbage principle is presented as an effort to "preserve scarce skills" by putting qualified workers to tasks which "only they can perform," and not wasting "social resources." It is presented as a response to "shortages" of skilled workers or technically trained people, whose time is best used "efficiently" for the advantage of "society." But however much this principle may manifest itself at times in the form of a response to the scarcity of skilled labor—for example, during wars or other periods of rapid expansion of production—this apology is on the whole false. The capitalist mode of production systematically destroys all-around skills where they exist, and brings into being skills and occupations that correspond to its needs. Technical capacities are henceforth distributed on a strict "need to know" basis. The generalized distribution of knowledge of the productive process among all its participants becomes, from this point on, not merely "unnecessary," but a positive barrier to the functioning of the capitalist mode of production.

Labor power has become a commodity. Its uses are no longer organized according to the needs and desires of those who sell it, but rather according to the needs of its purchasers, who are, primarily, employers seeking to expand the value of their capital. And it is the special and permanent interest of these purchasers to cheapen this commodity. The most common mode of cheapening labor power is exemplified by the Babbage principle: break it up into its simplest elements. And, as the capitalist mode of production creates a working population suitable to its needs, the Babbage principle is, by the very shape of this "labor market," enforced upon the capitalists themselves.

Every step in the labor process is divorced, so far as possible, from special knowledge and training and reduced to simple labor. Meanwhile, the relatively few persons for whom special knowledge and training are reserved are freed so far as possible from the obligations of simple labor. In this way, a structure is given to all labor processes that at its extremes polarizes those whose time is infinitely valuable and those whose time is worth almost nothing. This might even be called the general law of the capitalist division of labor. It is not the sole force acting upon the organization of work, but it is certainly the most powerful and general. Its results, more or less advanced in every industry and occupation, give massive testimony to its validity. It shapes not only work, but populations as well, because over the long run it creates that mass of simple labor which is the primary feature of populations in developed capitalist countries.

READING 8

The Managed Heart

Arlie Russell Hochschild

The one area of her occupational life in which she might be "free to act," the area of her own personality, must now also be managed, must become the alert yet obsequious instrument by which goods are distributed.

—C. WRIGHT MILLS

In a section in *Das Kapital* entitled "The Working Day," Karl Marx examines depositions submitted in 1863 to the Children's Employment Commission in England. One deposition was given by the mother of a child laborer in a wallpaper factory: "When he was seven years old I used to carry him [to work] on my back to and fro through the snow, and he used to work 16 hours a day. . . . I have often knelt down to feed him, as he stood by the machine, for he could not leave it or stop." Fed meals as he worked, as a steam engine is fed coal and water, this child was "an instrument of labor."[1] Marx questioned how many hours a day it was fair to use a human being as an instrument, and how much pay for being an instrument was fair, considering the profits that factory owners made. But he was also concerned with something he thought more fundamental: the human cost of becoming an "instrument of labor" at all.

On another continent 117 years later, a twenty-year-old flight attendant trainee sat with 122 others listening to a pilot speak in the auditorium of the Delta Airlines Stewardess Training Center. Even by modern American standards, and certainly by standards for women's work, she had landed an excellent job. The 1980 pay scale began at $850 a month for the first six months and would increase within seven years to about $20,000 a year. Health and accident insurance is provided, and the hours are good.*

The young trainee sitting next to me wrote on her notepad, "Important to smile. Don't forget smile." The admonition came from the speaker in the front of the room, a crewcut pilot in his early fifties, speaking in a Southern drawl: "Now girls, I want you to go out there and really *smile*. Your smile is your biggest *asset*. I want you to go out there and use it. Smile. *Really* smile. Really *lay it on*."

---

*For stylistic convenience, I shall use the pronoun "she" when referring to a flight attendant, except when a specific male flight attendant is being discussed. Otherwise I shall try to avoid verbally excluding either gender.

The pilot spoke of the smile as the *flight attendant's* asset. But as novices like the one next to me move through training, the value of a personal smile is groomed to reflect the company's disposition—its confidence that its planes will not crash, its reassurance that departures and arrivals will be on time, its welcome and its invitation to return. Trainers take it as their job to attach to the trainee's smile an attitude, a viewpoint, a rhythm of feeling that is, as they often say, "professional." This deeper extension of the professional smile is not always easy to retract at the end of the workday, as one worker in her first year at World Airways noted: "Sometimes I come off a long trip in a state of utter exhaustion, but I find I can't relax. I giggle a lot, I chatter, I call friends. It's as if I can't release myself from an artificially created elation that kept me 'up' on the trip. I hope to be able to come down from it better as I get better at the job."

As the PSA jingle says, "Our smiles are not just painted on." Our flight attendants' smiles, the company emphasizes, will be more human than the phony smiles you're resigned to seeing on people who are paid to smile. There is a smile-like strip of paint on the nose of each PSA plane. Indeed, the plane and the flight attendant advertise each other. The radio advertisement goes on to promise not just smiles and service but a travel experience of real happiness and calm. Seen in one way, this is no more than delivering a service. Seen in another, it estranges workers from their own smiles and convinces customers that on-the-job behavior is calculated. Now that advertisements, training, notions of professionalism, and dollar bills have intervened between the smiler and the smiled upon, it takes an extra effort to imagine that spontaneous warmth can exist in uniform—because companies now advertise spontaneous warmth, too.

At first glance, it might seem that the circumstances of the nineteenth-century factory child and the twentieth-century flight attendant could not be more different. To the boy's mother, to Marx, to the members of the Children's Employment Commission, perhaps to the manager of the wallpaper factory, and almost certainly to the contemporary reader, the boy was a victim, even a symbol, of the brutalizing conditions of his time. We might imagine that he had an emotional half-life, conscious of little more than fatigue, hunger, and boredom. On the other hand, the flight attendant enjoys the upper-class freedom to travel, and she participates in the glamour she creates for others. She is the envy of clerks in duller, less well-paid jobs.

But a close examination of the differences between the two can lead us to some unexpected common ground. On the surface there is a difference in how we know what labor actually produces. How could the worker in the wallpaper factory tell when his job was done? Count the rolls of wallpaper; a good has been produced. How can the flight attendant tell when her job is done? A service has been produced; the customer seems content. In the case of the flight attendant, the *emotional style of offering the service is part of the service itself,* in a way that loving or hating wallpaper is not a part of producing wallpaper. Seeming to "love the job" becomes part of the job; and actually trying to love it, and to enjoy the customers, helps the worker in this effort.

In processing people, the product is a state of mind. Like firms in other industries, airline companies are ranked according to the quality of service their personnel offer. Egon Ronay's yearly *Lucas Guide* offers such a ranking; besides being sold in airports and drugstores and reported in newspapers, it is cited in management memoranda and passed down to those who train and supervise flight attendants. Because it influences consumers, airline companies use it in setting their criteria for successful job performance by a flight attendant. In 1980 the *Lucas Guide* ranked Delta Airlines first in service out of fourteen airlines that fly regularly between the United States and both Canada and the British Isles. Its report on Delta included passages like this:

[Drinks were served] not only with a smile but with concerned enquiry such as, "Anything else I can get you, madam?" The atmosphere was that of a civilized party—with the passengers, in response, behaving like civilized guests. . . . Once or twice our inspectors tested stewardesses by being deliberately exacting, but they were never roused, and at the end of the flight they lined up to say farewell with undiminished brightness. . . .

[Passengers are] quick to detect strained or forced smiles, and they come aboard wanting to *enjoy* the flight. One of us looked forward to his next trip on Delta "because it's fun." Surely that is how passengers ought to feel."[2]

The work done by the boy in the wallpaper factory called for a coordination of mind and arm, mind and finger, and mind and shoulder. We refer to it simply as physical labor. The flight attendant does physical labor when she pushes heavy meal carts through the aisles, and she does mental work when she prepares for and actually organizes emergency landings and evacuations. But in the course of doing this physical and mental labor, she is also doing something more, something I define as *emotional labor.**

———

*I use the term *emotional labor* to mean the management of feeling to create a publicly observable facial and bodily display; emotional labor is sold for a wage and therefore has *exchange value.* I use the synonymous terms *emotion work* or *emotion management* to refer to these same acts done in a private context where they have *use value.*

This labor requires one to induce or suppress feeling in order to sustain the outward countenance that produces the proper state of mind in others—in this case, the sense of being cared for in a convivial and safe place. This kind of labor calls for a coordination of mind and feeling, and it sometimes draws on a source of self that we honor as deep and integral to our individuality.

Beneath the difference between physical and emotional labor there lies a similarity in the possible cost of doing the work: the worker can become estranged or alienated from an aspect of self—either the body or the margins of the soul—that is *used* to do the work. The factory boy's arm functioned like a piece of machinery used to produce wallpaper. His employer, regarding that arm as an instrument, claimed control over its speed and motions. In this situation, what was the relation between the boy's arm and his mind? Was his arm in any meaningful sense his *own?*

This is an old issue, but as the comparison with airline attendants suggests, it is still very much alive. If we can become alienated from goods in a goods-producing society, we can become alienated from service in a service-producing society. This is what C. Wright Mills, one of our keenest social observers, meant when he wrote in 1956, "We need to characterize American society of the mid-twentieth century in more psychological terms, for now the problems that concern us most border on the psychiatric."[3]

When she came off the job, what relation had the flight attendant to the "artificial elation" she had induced on the job? In what sense was it her *own* elation on the job? The company lays claim not simply to her physical motions—how she handles food trays—but to her emotional actions and the way they show in the ease of a smile. The workers I talked to often spoke of their smiles as being *on* them but not *of* them. They were seen as an extension of the make-up, the uniform, the recorded music, the soothing pastel colors of the airplane decor, and the daytime drinks, which taken together orchestrate the mood of the passengers. The final commodity is not a certain number of smiles to be counted like rolls of wallpaper. For the flight attendant, the smiles are a *part of her work,* a part that requires her to coordinate self and feeling so that the work seems to be effortless. To show that the enjoyment takes effort is to do the job poorly. Similarly, part of the job is to disguise fatigue and irritation, for otherwise the labor would show in an unseemly way, and the product—passenger contentment—would be damaged.* Because it is easier to disguise fatigue and irritation if they can be banished altogether, at least for brief periods, this feat calls for emotional labor.

The reason for comparing these dissimilar jobs is that the modern assembly-line worker has for some time been an outmoded symbol of modern industrial labor; fewer than 6 percent of workers now work on assembly lines. Another kind of labor has now come into symbolic prominence—the voice-to-voice or face-to-face delivery of service—and the flight attendant is an appropriate model for it. There have always been public-service jobs, of course; what is new is that they are now socially engineered and thoroughly organized from the top.

---

*Like a commodity, service that calls for emotional labor is subject to the laws of supply and demand. Recently the demand for this labor has increased and the supply of it drastically decreased. The airline industry speed-up since the 1970s has been followed by a worker slowdown. The slowdown reveals how much emotional labor the job required all along. It suggests what costs even happy workers under normal conditions pay for this labor without a name. The speed-up has sharpened the ambivalence many workers feel about how much of oneself to give over to the role and how much of oneself to protect from it.

Though the flight attendant's job is no worse and in many ways better than other service jobs, it makes the worker more vulnerable to the social engineering of her emotional labor and reduces her control over that labor. Her problems, therefore, may be a sign of what is to come in other such jobs.

Emotional labor is potentially good. No customer wants to deal with a surly waitress, a crabby bank clerk, or a flight attendant who avoids eye contact in order to avoid getting a request. Lapses in courtesy by those paid to be courteous are very real and fairly common. What they show us is how fragile public civility really is. We are brought back to the question of what the social carpet actually consists of and what it requires of those who are supposed to keep it beautiful. The laggards and sluff-offs of emotional labor return us to the basic questions. What is emotional labor? What do we do when we manage emotion? What, in fact, is emotion? What are the costs and benefits of managing emotion, in private life and at work?

The Private and Public Faces of an Emotional System

Our search for answers to these questions leads to three separate but equally relevant discourses: one concerning labor, one concerning display, and one concerning emotion.

Those who discuss labor often comment that nowadays most jobs call for a capacity to deal with people rather than with things, for more interpersonal skills and fewer mechanical skills. In *The Coming of Post-Industrial Society* (1973), Daniel Bell argues that the growth of the service sector means that "communication" and "encounter"— "the response of ego to alter and back"—is the central work relationship today.* As he puts it, "The fact that individuals now talk to other individuals, rather than interact with a machine, is the fundamental fact about work

in the post-industrial society." Critics of labor studies, such as Harry Braverman in *Labor and Monopoly Capital* (1974), point out a continual subdivision of work in many branches of the economy. Complex tasks in which a craftsman used to take pride are divided into simpler, more repetitive segments, each more boring and less well paid than the original job. Work is deskilled and the worker belittled. But celebrants and critics alike have not inspected at close hand or with a social-psychological eye what it is that "people jobs" *actually require* of workers. They have not inquired into the actual nature of this labor. Some do not know exactly what, in the case of emotional labor, becomes deskilled.

A second discourse, closer to the person and more remote from the overall organization of work, concerns the display of feeling. The works of Erving Goffman introduce us to the many minor traffic rules of face-to-face interaction, as they emerge at a card game, in an elevator, on the street, or at the dining table of an insane asylum. He prevents us from dismissing the small as trivial by showing how small rules, transgressions, and punishments add up to form the longer strips of experience we call "work." At the same time, it is hard to use Goffman's focus to explain why companies train flight attendants in smiling, or how emotional tone is supervised, or what profit is ultimately tied to emotional labor. It is hard, in other words, to draw on this discourse alone and see how "display work" fits into the larger scheme of things.

---

*Jobs that Bell includes in the service sector are those in transportation and utilities, distribution and trade, finance and insurance, professional and business services, jobs deriving from demands for leisure activities (recreation and travel), and jobs that deal with communal services (health, education, and government). Only some of these service-sector jobs call for much emotion management.

The third discourse takes place in a quiet side street of American social science; it deals with the timeless issues of what an emotion is and how we can manage it. . . .

To uncover the heart of emotional labor, to understand what it takes to do it and what it does to people, I have drawn on elements from all three discourses. Certain events in economic history cannot be fully understood unless we pay attention to the filigreed patterns of feeling and their management because the details of these patterns are an important part of what many men and women do for a living.

Because such different traditions are joined here, my inquiry will have a different relevance for different readers. Perhaps it will be most relevant for those who do the work it describes—the flight attendants. But most of us have jobs that require some handling of other people's feelings and our own, and in this sense we are all partly flight attendants. The secretary who creates a cheerful office that announces her company as "friendly and dependable" and her boss as "up-and-coming," the waitress or waiter who creates an "atmosphere of pleasant dining," the tour guide or hotel receptionist who makes us feel welcome, the social worker whose look of solicitous concern makes the client feel cared for, the salesman who creates the sense of a "hot commodity," the bill collector who inspires fear, the funeral parlor director who makes the bereaved feel understood, the minister who creates a sense of protective outreach but even-handed warmth—all of them must confront in some way or another the requirements of *emotional labor.*

Emotional labor does not observe conventional distinctions between types of jobs. By my estimate, roughly one-third of American workers today have jobs that subject them to substantial demands for emotional labor. Moreover, of all *women* working, roughly one-half have jobs that call for emotional labor. . . . Thus this inquiry has special relevance for women, and it probably also describes more of their experience. As traditionally more accomplished managers of feeling in private life, women more than men have put emotional labor on the market, and they know more about its personal costs.

This inquiry might at first seem relevant only to workers living under capitalism, but the engineering of a managed heart is not unknown to socialism; the enthusiastic "hero of labor" bears the emotional standard for the socialist state as much as the Flight Attendant of the Year does for the capitalist airline industry. Any functioning society makes effective use of its members' emotional labor. We do not think twice about the use of feeling in the theater, or in psychotherapy, or in forms of group life that we admire. It is when we come to speak of the *exploitation* of the bottom by the top in any society that we become morally concerned. In any system, exploitation depends on the actual distribution of many kinds of profits—money, authority, status, honor, well-being. It is not emotional labor itself, therefore, but the underlying system of recompense that raises the question of what the cost of it is. . . .

Private and Commercial Uses of Feeling

A nineteenth-century child working in a brutalizing English wallpaper factory and a well-paid twentieth-century American flight attendant have something in common: in order to survive in their jobs, they must mentally detach themselves—the factory worker from his own body and physical labor, and the flight attendant from her own feelings and emotional labor. Marx and many others have told us the factory worker's story. I am interested in telling the flight attendant's story in order to promote a fuller appreciation of the costs of what she does. And I want to base this appreciation on a prior demonstration of what can happen to any of us when we become estranged from our feelings and the management of them.

We feel. But what is a feeling? I would define feeling, like emotion, as a sense, like the sense of hearing or sight. In a general way, we experience it when bodily sensations are joined with what we see or imagine. Like the sense of hearing, emotion communicates information. It has, as Freud said of anxiety, a "signal function." From feeling we discover our own viewpoint on the world.

We often say that we *try* to feel. But how can we do this? Feelings, I suggest, are not stored "inside" us, and they are not independent of acts of management. Both the act of "getting in touch with" feeling and the act of "trying to" feel may become part of the process that makes the thing we get in touch with, or the thing we manage, *into* a feeling or emotion. In managing feeling, we contribute to the creation of it.

If this is so, what we think of as intrinsic to feeling or emotion may have always been shaped to social form and put to civic use. Consider what happens when young men roused to anger go willingly to war, or when followers rally enthusiastically around their king, or mullah, or football team. Private social life may always have called for the management of feeling. The party guest summons up a gaiety owed to the host, the mourner summons up a proper sadness for a funeral. Each offers up feeling as a momentary contribution to the collective good. In the absence of an English-language name for feelings-as-contribution-to-the-group (which the more group-centered Hopi culture called *arofa*), I shall offer the concept of a gift exchange.[4] Muted anger, conjured gratitude, and suppressed envy are offerings back and forth from parent to child, wife to husband, friend to friend, and lover to lover. . . .

What gives social pattern to our acts of emotion management? I believe that when we try to feel, we apply latent feeling rules. . . . We say, "I shouldn't feel so angry at what she did," or "given our agreement, I have no right to feel jealous." Acts of emotion management are not simply private acts; they are used in exchanges under the guidance of feeling rules. Feeling rules are standards used in emotional conversation to determine what is rightly owed and owing in the currency of feeling. Through them, we tell what is "due" in each relation, each role. We pay tribute to each other in the currency of the managing act. In interaction we pay, overpay, underpay, play with paying, acknowledge our dues, pretend to pay, or acknowledge what is emotionally due another person. In these ways, . . . we make our try at sincere civility.

Because the distribution of power and authority is unequal in some of the relations of private life, the managing acts can also be unequal. The myriad momentary acts of management compose part of what we summarize in the terms *relation* and *role*. Like the tiny dots of a Seurat painting, the microacts of emotion management compose, through repetition and change over time, a movement of form. Some forms express inequality, others equality.

Now what happens when the managing of emotion comes to be sold as labor? What happens when feeling rules, like rules of behavioral display, are established not through private negotiation but by company manuals? What happens when social exchanges are not, as they are in private life, subject to change or termination but ritually sealed and almost inescapable?

What happens when the emotional display that one person owes another reflects a certain inherent inequality? The airline passenger may choose not to smile, but the flight attendant is obliged not only to smile but to try to work up some warmth behind it. What happens, in other words, when there is a *transmutation* of the private ways we use feeling?

One sometimes needs a grand word to point out a coherent pattern between occurrences that would otherwise seem totally unconnected. My word is "transmutation." When I speak of the transmutation of an emotional system, I mean to point out a link between a private act, such as attempting to enjoy a party, and a public act, such as summoning up good feeling for a customer. I mean to expose the relation between the private act of trying to dampen liking for a person—which overcommitted lovers sometimes attempt—and the public act of a bill collector who suppresses empathy for a debtor. By the grand phrase "transmutation of an emotional system" I mean to convey what it is that we do privately, often unconsciously, to feelings that nowadays often fall under the sway of large organizations, social engineering, and the profit motive.

Trying to feel what one wants, expects, or thinks one ought to feel is probably no newer than emotion itself. Conforming to or deviating from feeling rules is also hardly new. In organized society, rules have probably never been applied only to observable behavior. "Crimes of the heart" have long been recognized because proscriptions have long guarded the "preactions" of the heart; the Bible says not to covet your neighbor's wife, not simply to avoid acting on that feeling. What is new in our time is an increasingly prevalent *instrumental stance* toward our native capacity to play, wittingly and actively, upon a range of feelings for a private purpose and the way in which that stance is engineered and administered by large organizations.

This transmutation of the private use of feeling affects the two sexes and the various social classes in distinctly different ways. . . . As a matter of tradition, emotion management has been better understood and more often used by women as one of the offerings they trade for economic support. Especially among dependent women of the middle and upper classes, women have the job (or think they ought to) of creating the emotional tone of social encounters: expressing joy at the Christmas presents others open, creating the sense of surprise at birthdays, or displaying alarm at the mouse in the kitchen. Gender is not the only determinant of skill in such managed expression and in the emotion work needed to do it well. But men who do this work well have slightly less in common with other men than women who do it well have with other women. When the "womanly" art of living up to *private* emotional conventions goes public, it attaches itself to a different profit-and-loss statement.

Similarly, emotional labor affects the various social classes differently. If it is women, members of the less advantaged gender, who specialize in emotional labor, it is the middle and upper reaches of the class system that seem to call most for it. And parents who do emotional labor on the job will convey the importance of emotion management to their children and will prepare them to learn the skills they will probably need for the jobs they will probably get.

In general, lower-class and working-class people tend to work more with things, and middle-class and upper-class people tend to work more with people. More working women than men deal with people as a job. Thus, there are both gender patterns and class patterns to the civic and commercial use of human feeling. That is the social point.

But there is a personal point, too. There is a cost to emotion work: it affects the degree to which we listen to feeling and sometimes our very capacity to feel. Managing feeling is an art fundamental to civilized living, and I assume that in broad terms the cost is usually worth the fundamental benefit. Freud, in *Civilization and Its Discontents*, argued analogously about the sexual instinct: enjoyable as that instinct is, we are wise in the long run to give up some gratification of it. But when the transmutation of the private use of feeling is successfully accomplished—when we succeed in lending our feelings to the organizational engineers of worker-customer relations—we may pay a cost in how we hear our feelings and a cost in what, for better or worse, they tell us about ourselves. When a speed-up of the human assembly line makes "genuine" personal service harder to deliver, the worker may withdraw emotional labor and offer instead a thin crust of display. Then the cost shifts: the penalty becomes a sense of being phony or insincere. In short, when the transmutation works, the worker risks losing the signal function of feeling. When it does not work, the risk is losing the signal function of display.

Certain social conditions have increased the cost of feeling management. One is an overall unpredictability about our social world. Ordinary people nowadays move through many social worlds and get the gist of dozens of social roles. Compare this with the life of the fourteenth-century baker's apprentice described in Peter Laslett's *The World We Have Lost* (1968): it is a life that begins and ends in one locale, in one occupation, in one household, within one world view, and according to one set of rules.[5] It has become much less common that given circumstances seem to dictate the proper interpretation of them or that they indicate in a plainly visible way what feeling is owed to whom, and when, and how. As a result, we moderns spend more mental time on the question "What, in this situation, should I be feeling?" Oddly enough, a second condition more appropriate to Laslett's baker's apprentice has survived into more modern and fluid times. We still, it seems, ask of ourselves, "Who am I?" as if the question permitted a single neat answer. We still search for a solid, predictable core of self even though the conditions for the existence of such a self have long since vanished.

In the face of these two conditions, people turn to feelings in order to locate themselves or at least to see what their own reactions are to a given event. That is, in the absence of unquestioned external guidelines, the signal function of emotion becomes more important, and the commercial distortion of the managed heart becomes all the more important as a human cost.

We may well be seeing a response to all this in the rising approval of the unmanaged heart, the greater virtue now attached to what is "natural" or spontaneous. Ironically, the person like Rousseau's Noble Savage, who only smiles "naturally," without ulterior purpose, is a poor prospect for the job of waiter, hotel manager, or flight attendant. The high regard for "natural feeling," then, may coincide with the culturally imposed need to develop the precise opposite—an instrumental stance toward feeling. We treat spontaneous feeling, for this reason, as if it were scarce and precious; we raise it up as a virtue. It may not be too much to suggest that we are witnessing a call for the conservation of "inner resources," a call to save another wilderness from corporate use and keep it "forever wild."

With the growing celebration of spontaneity have come the robot jokes. Robot humor plays with the tension between being human—that is to say, having feeling—and being a cog in a socioeconomic machine. The charm of the little robot R2-D2, in the film *Star Wars*, is that he seems so human. Films like this bring us the familiar in reverse: every day, outside the movie house, we see human beings whose show of feeling has a robot quality. The ambiguities are funny now.

Both the growing celebration of spontaneity and the jokes we tell about being robots suggest that in the realm of feeling,

Orwell's 1984 came in disguise several years ago, leaving behind a laugh and perhaps the idea of a private way out.

NOTES

Epigraph: C. Wright Mills, *White Collar*, p. 184.
1. Marx, *Capital* (1977), pp. 356–357, 358.
2. *Lucas Guide 1980*, pp. 66, 76. (Fourteen aspects of air travel at the stages of departure, arrival, and the flight itself are ranked. Each aspect is given one of sixteen differently weighted marks. For example, "The friendliness or efficiency of the staff is more important than the quality of the pilot's flight announcement or the selection of newspapers and magazines offered.")
3. Mills (1956), p. xx.
4. Lee (1959) discusses the concept of *arofa*.
5. Laslett (1968); Stone (1965); Swidler (1979).

REFERENCES

Laslett, Peter. 1968. *The World We Have Lost*. London: Methuen.
Lee, Dorothy. 1959. *Freedom and Culture*. New York: Prentice-Hall.
Marx, Karl. 1977. *Capital*, Vol. 1. Intro. by Ernest Mandel. Tr. Ben Fowkes. New York: Vintage.
Mills, C. Wright. 1956. *White Collar*. New York: Oxford University Press.
Stone, Lawrence, ed. 1965. *Social Change and the Revolution in England, 1540–1640*. London: Longmans.
Swidler, Ann. 1979. *Organization Without Authority*. Cambridge, MA, and London: Harvard University Press.

Discussion Questions for Part I

1. Discuss the "drive system" as a technique for supervising and controlling early factory workers. Is a "carrot" or a "stick" a better method of control and motivation?
2. Compare the conditions under which mothers' work was "disappeared" in the 19th century with today. Has this work gained greater recognition?
3. Compare the description of Ford Motor Company with the early factories described in Reading 1. How did Ford transform the organization of work? How did these changes alter the social relations of the workplace?
4. Have any of the elements of alienation as described by Marx been reduced in the modern workplace? Increased?
5. Compare Weber's description of bureaucracy with bureaucracies that you have experienced. In what ways is Weber's characterization accurate? In what ways is it inaccurate?
6. What management problems did Taylor's system of scientific management attempt to solve? How did Ford apply Taylor's system?
7. As Braverman (Reading 7) notes, "dividing the craft cheapens its individual parts." How did Ford and Taylor apply this principle?"
8. How does emotional labor differ from mental or manual labor?
9. Marx's discussion of alienation focuses on manual labor—that is, the labor involved in the production of commodities. Can the performance of emotional labor also produce feelings of alienation?

PART II

The Social Organization of Work

████ **THE NEW WORKPLACE** ████

⌕ READING 9 ⌕

The Capitalist Firm in the Twenty-First Century

Emerging Patterns in Western Enterprise

Walter W. Powell

The past decade was a confusing period for citizens, policymakers, and pundits alike. The pace of economic and technological change appears relentless, but the direction is unfamiliar. Joseph Schumpeter (1934) was one of the first analysts to observe that innovation brings with it the winds of creative destruction, but few were prepared for the gales of the 1990s. Consider just a few of the discordant trends in the U.S. and global economy.

Alongside the tremendous upsurge of startup companies, created in the United States and aboard as well, we see the creation of global giants in a number of key industries. The startups are regaled for their swiftness, their impressive array of new products and services, and their new business practices. But in banking, oil, autos, and telecommunications, we see the making of global corporate behemoths, the product of mergers such as Exxon and Mobil, Travelers Group and Citibank, Vodaphone Group and Air Touch, and Daimler Benz, Chrysler, and Mitsubishi, which are among the largest deals in history. And corporations continue to acquire and grow even as evidence accumulates

that the hoped-for synergies and integration are seldom achieved. Moreover, many of the startups continue the founding and acquisition cycle. In the e-commerce field, the dream of many founders has been to grow large enough to be noticed and bought up. Of course, some startups eventually grow large, and companies like America Online, Microsoft, or Cisco Systems have acquired hundreds of other firms along the way.

But which companies represent the old economy and which ones the new? Cisco Systems had only 250 or so employees back in 1989, but by January 2000 it had more than 26,000 and a market capitalization in excess of $320 billion, one of the largest of any company in the world. Cisco is a designer and maker of computer networking equipment, much of which it sells to traditional companies that are developing Internet services. In so doing, Cisco makes the lines between the new and old economy much blurrier. And the growing reshaping of corporate purchasing through business-to-business e-commerce renders the distinction between the old and the new economy even less meaningful.

Are the new-economy companies in computers, wireless communications, electronic commerce, the life sciences, and genomics creating a new industrial transformation or just a phenomenal amount of speculative excess? *Red Herring* magazine and its Web site, one of many new business publications that has grown fatter and fatter with dot-com ads, routinely warns that Internet company valuations are completely unrealistic even as it touts a new company or the latest technological application. Thus the speculative frenzy increases, and even though caution is warranted, people everywhere are afraid of being left out of the game, falling behind as others make their fortunes, and getting stuck in the "old world" as the "new world" companies ascend. People know that most of the new ventures are unrealistic, but the problem is they do not know which ones are and which ones are not.

Wages and employment offer another puzzle. Unemployment is presently at a thirty-year low, but job security appears tenuous to many employees. Despite impressive performance, many U.S. companies continue to revamp jobs and organizational structures as if the economy were in a tailspin. More jobs were lost to downsizing in 1999 than in any previous year during the 1990s.[1] On the upside, nearly twenty-two million new jobs were created in the United States in the 1990s.[2] Some organizations now complain about the lack of corporate loyalty as employers have become buyers in a seller's market, forgetting that it was their practices of downsizing and contracting out that eroded worker loyalty. Consequently, both voluntary and involuntary departures from jobs have increased (Bernhardt et al. 1998; Capelli et al. 1997; Farber 1996; Osterman 1999, ch. 2).

Despite economic growth, productivity gains, and tight labor markets, there is widening income disparity as growth in the incomes of the winners far outpaces the modest wage gains of others. Moreover, the success of the winners is more and more tied to the fluctuations of the stock market. Industry sources estimate that 48 percent of the U.S. population now has money invested in stocks or stock funds, and roughly ten million workers hold equity in their own companies.[3] But for those whose jobs do not offer such opportunities, the gap grows wider. Silicon Valley is the epitome of these contradictions. In Palo Alto, the local mantra in 1999 was that sixty-four millionaires were created daily, and this success drove the cost of housing to stratospheric levels, making it harder and harder for policemen, school teachers, fire fighters, and assistant professors, not to mention administrative or service workers, to be able to afford to live in the valley.

Finally, consider the emerging political resistance that has coalesced against the specter of globalization and international economic integration. The amalgam of left and right that has brought together environmentalists and dockworkers, French farmers and American steelworkers, has highlighted a backlash against economic change. Anxiety and uncertainty are growing at the same time that more newcomers, from Ireland to Finland to Israel to Bangalore to Taiwan, prosper from the internationalization of production. In sum, economic change has been so rapid and so profound that few seem to understand its dynamics and shape, and much traditional social science is hard pressed to measure its scope and consequence.

The core claim of this chapter is that, behind the confusion and divergent trends of recent years, we can discern the outlines of a fundamental change in the way work is organized, structured, and governed. This transformation, I suggest, is sufficiently far-reaching that looking back from the twenty-first century to the end of the twentieth, many will view the struggles of the 1990s as a disruptive and costly period of adjustment to a new logic of organizing. Just as the shift to the era of the assembly line, vertical integration, and mass production brought with it

[1]Reported in "Career Evolution," *The Economist* (29 January 2000): 89–92.
[2]Reported in "The Great American Jobs Machine," *The Economist* (15 January 2000): 25.

[3]Reported in Carolyn Lochhead, "Old World Discovers New Economy's Money," *San Francisco Chronicle*, 12 December 1999, sec. A1, p. 23.

a great transformation, so will the change to what today we inarticulately term the "new economy" or decentralized capitalism. . . .

Causes and Consequences of the Reshaping of Work and Organization . . .

Downsizing and Restructuring

Unquestionably, one of the most dramatic changes of the past fifteen years has been the willingness of large corporations to downsize, shedding themselves of thousands of formerly "safe" white-collar employees. Although downsizing was first regarded as a response to the economic downturn of the late 1980s, it continued throughout the 1990s even as the economy surged. And companies that had long histories of employment security joined the trend. For example, back in January of 1996, on the first business day of the new year, AT&T—a highly profitable company that was known for its job security—announced it would lay off forty thousand employees. The Vice President for Human Resources at AT&T, James Meadows, subsequently opined to the *New York Times* (13 February 1996) that

> People need to look at themselves as self-employed, as vendors who come to this company to sell their skills. In AT&T, we have to promote the concept of the whole work force being contingent [i.e., on short-term contract, no promises], though most of our contingent workers are inside our walls. Jobs are being replaced by projects and fields of work, giving rise to a society that is increasingly "jobless but not workless."

In tandem with the downsizing wave has been a rapid increase in various forms of contingent employment. Benner (1996) dubs temporary employees the shock absorbers of the flexible economy. Various forms of

contingent employment have grown rapidly (Barker and Christensen 1998; Carnoy, Castells, and Benner 1997). The idea that workers should be employed only when there is immediate need for their services is hardly new, but clearly the use of this practice grew considerably over the 1990s. Just how rapidly is hotly contested and very much contingent on how one defines the employment practice. Does the term include part-time work, self-employment, contract work, home-based work, temporary-help service employment, or a job without long-term security? Regardless of definition, the expansion of such temporary employment firms as Manpower Incorporated is ample proof to many observers that employees are increasingly regarded as another factor in the process of just-in-time production.

There is little doubt that downsizing has exerted a considerable toll on employees and communities. But just how potent a force is it and is the quest for labor-force flexibility the driving force behind organizational change? Despite the headlines, David Gordon (1996, ch. 2) marshals data suggesting that the proportion of managers and supervisors in private non-farm employment has not shrunk. Moreover, throughout the 1980s, he tells us, the proportion of managerial and administrative employment was more than three times as high in the United States as in Germany and Japan. U.S. management structures, many analysts claimed, were top-heavy, flabby, and redundant.

Osterman (1996) concurs with Gordon that managerial ranks are not shrinking rapidly in the United States, but provides a more nuanced picture of changes in the terms of managers' employment prospects. Middle-level managers are experiencing distress from restructuring, he argues. His analyses show a fairly dramatic decrease in rates of management retention, greater than that experienced by blue-collar employees with comparable job tenure (Osterman 1996,

9). In an excellent study of the insurance industry, Elizabeth Scott et al. (1996) finds a substantial flattening of the structure of firms. This "delayering" is accomplished by cutting several levels of middle to lower management, and greatly upgrading and expanding the role of claims adjusters through the use of expert systems and intensive monitoring. In a careful analysis of a nationwide survey of displaced workers, Farber (1996, 33) documents that "older and more educated workers, while continuing to have lower rates of job loss than younger, have seen their rates of job loss increase more than those of other groups." Moreover, he finds that job loss due to position-abolished reasons, as opposed to layoffs or plant closings, has increased, largely among more educated workers. Thus the number of management jobs may not be declining, but job security clearly has lessened.

Similar complications abound concerning contingent employment, and much of the debate turns on what is meant by routine and nonstandard work, and whether labor-market circumstances are voluntary or involuntary.[4] Standard work has long been thought to be continuous, secure, on a preset schedule, and full-time. In return for satisfactory performance and loyalty, the

---

[4] Indeed, estimates of the size of the contingent workforce vary widely. In 1995 the Bureau of Labor Statistics reported that "contingent and alternative" employment represented five percent of the U.S. work force. The National Association of Part-Time and Temporary Employees, taking a very broad view and including full-time workers employed by temporary agencies and permanent part-time workers, estimates that twenty-four percent of the work force is contingent. (Reported in Elena Bianco, "Temporary Workers Gaining Market Share, Statistics Show," *Los Angeles Times,* 31 December 1996, p. A5.) And whatever the "correct" size of the contingent labor force, there has been another key change: many more workers now pass through temporary agencies on their way to permanent jobs.

employer provided benefits and abided by government regulations of employment, in particular protection from hazardous conditions and unfair discrimination, and provided some array of benefits for retirement and health care. These benefits in turn are buttressed by government through social security and unemployment insurance. Nonstandard work, which was the most typical form of work probably until the middle of this past century, comes in many guises, ranging from independent contractors (e.g., plumber, storefront lawyer, seamstress, or computer consultant) to part-time shift workers to temporary employees. All such arrangements purportedly involved weak attachment between a worker and a firm.

The basic analytical problem is whether such agreements are voluntary or involuntary, and whether weak attachment is an apt description. Clearly the labor force includes some people who do not choose to seek full-time jobs and others who would prefer them but can find only contingent work. Has the recent surge in downsizing increased the number of people with involuntary contingent work? The available evidence suggests yes, with women and minorities most likely to be rendered worse off by these new circumstances. . . .

We need to be careful, however, that we do not remain fixed on an image of a mythical workplace. Harriet Presser's (1995) work reminds us that the stylized model of the standard workday no longer holds: less than one third of employed Americans over age eighteen worked the "traditional" Monday-through-Friday, nine-to-five workweek in 1991. Consider too that not all temporary work is low wage. Contingent employment now covers every position up to chief executive. Manpower Incorporated placed 750,000 people in temporary jobs in 1995; high-technology was their fastest growing segment. The growth is fueled by a thirst for high-tech specialists whose wages range from $15–50 an hour and who work on short-term projects averaging thirty-six months. Moreover, whose situation is more contingent—an employee who does the same job but over the course of several years sees considerable turnover in her coworkers and supervisors, or an independent contractor or temporary worker with a long-term, stable clientele?

In a poignant series on "The Downsizing of America," the *New York Times* (3–9 March 1996) emphasized the dislocation and sacrifice that has resulted from this profound remaking of employment. In a segment on the job losses accompanying the merger of Chase Manhattan and Chemical Bank, entitled "Farewell, Mother Chase," the reporters described a thirty-five-year-old bank employee who had previously spent several years as an itinerant pianist in New York:

> He never sought security in corporate work, and thus the merger doesn't especially throw him. He has embraced Chase's career assistance and thinks he has sharpened his abilities, become a resilient worker. His background has given him an emphatically 90s outlook on work. "I feel my job is to do the best that I possibly can, but my whole area could look totally different in five years through no fault of Chase. I can't imagine any corporate entity owes anyone a career.

> By virtue of his background, Matt Hoffman is perhaps the archetypal corporate man of the future. His introduction to the world of work was a terrain where his paycheck depended on how well he sold himself each day. Nothing was guaranteed past tomorrow.

> He has imported that mindset into banking and currently, into Chase, and he has found the fit to be all too perfect.

For an odd reality of the new work environment is that the turbulent world of the freelance classical pianist is more like than unlike the world of the corporate employee. He, too, has to sell himself every day, and he, too, doesn't know if the gig will be there tomorrow. (New York Times, 4 March 1996).

The reporter conceptualized this new form of employment as a game of musical chairs, an aberrant alternative to a steady, life-long job with clear career prospects. But perhaps the fact that working for a bank now resembles the challenges of "gigging" practiced by freelance musicians is no longer aberrant and instead represents a labor practice that is becoming the norm. Sociologists have long studied "craft-based work" in which workers labored on short-term projects and were paid for specific performances (Stinchcombe 1959; Eccles 1981; Faulkner and Anderson 1987—see the review of this literature in Powell 1990, 306–9). But we treated work in such fields as construction and the film industries as exceptions to a more "standard" organizational structure in which jobs and careers were tied to a single organization. I next argue that the set of social arrangements we label a job are fast disappearing as work is being packaged in a different form and the conditions that once gave rise to a career of performing repeated tasks for a single employer are now disappearing.

For now, three observations seem salient. First, if jobs as a way of organizing work are no longer adaptive, then cutting jobs is not necessarily an effective response. Downsizing reduces head count and creates turmoil, but seldom addresses the idea that work no longer needs to be organized into neat packages called jobs. Consequently, downsizing efforts fail to deliver on expectations, often leading to even further cuts, which in turn leave gaps in corporate memory, diminished reputation, and dissatisfied customers. The American Management Association's survey of downsized companies reports few productivity enhancements in the wake of cutbacks and a host of problems; a *Wall Street Journal* cover story dubbed the trend "dumbsizing."[5]

Second, in companies where rapid technological change is commonplace and tightly defined job ladders are not viable, a project-based model for organizing work has evolved. These companies have the advantage of having never developed career structures and management systems that defined work as a steep vertical ladder, hence there are fewer transition costs to a new form of organizing. At Intel, the largest maker of microchips for computers, the corporate hierarchy is so flat that there are few upper positions to vie for. A horizontal employment model makes sense in areas of semiconductors where each new generation of microprocessors requires a different mix of skills. Intel invests more than $120 million a year on training, or nearly $3,000 per worker, with a goal to redeploy employees as fast as a new generation of chips emerges. The expectation is that workers will redeploy themselves, finding new jobs within the company. But if they are not successful, they are out of work.

Third, by holding fast to the idea of work organized around well-defined jobs and lamenting the loss of job security, we neglect to evaluate the range of options necessary in a world in which the focus should be more on employability and less on preserving dead-end jobs. Access to universal health coverage, portable pension plans, and a form of unemployment benefits for independent contractors and contingent workers are much-needed steps in an environment where work is more likely to consist of short-term projects. A focus only on job preservation leaves workers alone to grapple with the risks of the new workplace. In the labor movement there are clear signs of recognition of these new circumstances. The Justice for Janitors campaigns in Silicon Valley reflect the development of new multi-employer collective bargaining strategies. Benner (1996) points to the Alliance of Motion Picture and Television Producers as one collective response to an industry based on flexible production, craft and technical work, and short-term contracts. The alliance takes on administrative functions formerly done by management and protects the income of "members" directly without necessarily protecting their jobs. Similar innovations are underway in the building and garment trades, where new efforts are afoot to respond to the competitive success of the industry as a whole. In sum, we need more creative responses to the fluidity of project-based work, arrangements possibly like guilds for independent contractors that provide opportunities for professional community and learning, as well as financial security.

Globalization

In the minds of many people, global competition costs workers in advanced industrial nations their jobs and contributes to financial uncertainty as capital flows freely around the globe. Citizens and politicians alike contend that foreign competition robs jobs at home. Corporations now locate their activities according to the logic of a global market. Moreover, fickle international financial markets have become the judge and jury of policymaking, and central banks no longer have the capacity to intervene and stabilize currencies. But is global economic interdependence actually responsible for job

---

[5]See "Fire and Forget?" *The Economist,* 20 April 1996: 51–52 for discussion of AMA survey; see "Call It Dumbsizing: Why Some Companies Regret Cost-Cutting," *Wall Street Journal,* 14 May 1996, pp. A1, A8.

loss, declining wages, and changes in the organization of work? The evidence is much less compelling than the heated rhetoric suggests.

The great bulk of our trade imbalance is with Japan (about two-fifths of the total trade deficit) and with Western Europe. In both cases, hourly wages in manufacturing are higher than ours, in Japan by 25 percent and in much of Europe by 10 to 15 percent.[6] The sharpest impact of import competition is in manufacturing, but there has not been a steep decline in wages in this sector. In his analysis of wage decline between 1979 and 1994, Gordon (1996, 191) shows that production-worker wages fell most rapidly in mining, construction, transportation, public utilities, and retail trade—sectors not heavily exposed to competition from abroad. Indeed, immigration into the United States may be more responsible than global competition for wage stagnation in these sectors.

Viewed broadly, today's global economy is not even particularly new. Economic historians remind us that the half century before World War I was roughly comparable in economic integration (J. Williamson 1995, 1996; O'Rourke, Taylor, and Williamson 1996). Trade in goods and services is only slightly larger now, as a fraction of gross world product, than it was in 1914. Measured against GDP, United States imports are somewhat bigger now (11 percent) than they were in 1880 (8 percent). But labor mobility was probably higher in the late nineteenth century. Migrants left Europe for Australia and the United States in extraordinary numbers and investment from the "Old World" followed labor into the New. We also forget that a substantial foreign corporate presence in the United States is not novel either. In 1913 the United States pharmaceutical business was largely German-dominated, and Bayer aspirin the most common medicine of the day. On the other hand, there was scant manufacturing located in the less developed world, and product markets were not global in the pre–World War I period.

What is different today, dramatically so, is the speed with which massive amounts of information can be transmitted and received, making it possible to react to shifts in demand faster. And the content of much of what is traded internationally has high value. The fields most influenced by global competition—accounting, banking, computers, construction, consulting, legal services, semiconductors—are high-wage industries. Thus, globalization does not appear to be the chief culprit for wage decline and job loss in the United States. In a survey of the impact of globalization of wages, labor economist Richard Freeman (1995, 30) concluded that "we lack compelling evidence that trade underlies the problem of the less skilled."

Global economic interdependence is fundamental in an altogether novel respect, however. The speed with which information and certain commodities move around the globe reshapes production in powerful ways. A decade or two ago, new pharmaceutical drugs were initially released in the United States and Western Europe, and after a five- to even 10-year period of sales in the home market, they were sold abroad in less developed countries at cost, while newer medicines were released at home. Now there is demand for new medical interventions from all corners of the globe. Similar product life-cycle stories, with different time lines, could be told for such diverse industries as autos, electronics, or movies. Today, development times are vastly speeded up

---

[6]According to the United States Bureau of Labor Statistics, in 1994 dollars, manufacturing employees in the United States averaged $17.10 an hour, $27.31 in Germany, and $21.42 in Japan. The industrial nations with appreciably lower wages than the United States were Canada at $15.68 and the United Kingdom at $13.62 (Gordon, 1996, 29).

for almost every product, but especially for these regarded as innovative or fashionable. Whether we are talking about a new CD, cell phone, computer, or clothing, consumers in Mexico City, Helsinki, or Singapore want it at the same time. Sun Microsystems offers round-the-clock technical services at a single phone number, drawing on staffers around the globe who electronically hand work off as each shift comes on line. Such changes in demand press firms to recast their internal organization in a manner that stresses speed and learning. And when competition is based on ideas, the costs of creating additional copies of a conceptual product are low. The advantages of selling in many countries are considerable, provided that the firm is first to market.

The traditional multinational firm's strengths were its wealth and concomitant influence and the economies of scale it reaped in global production. But high tariffs, transportation costs, and local politics often necessitated that a multinational firm set up redundant "full-service" operations in most of the countries in which they sold products. Thus the economies of production were greatly offset by costs of administration. In contrast, an emerging focus on faster product development, combined with sensitivity to local tastes, rewards speed rather than sheer size. The model transnational firm today is no longer Coca-Cola, IBM, or Royal Dutch Shell, but Asea Brown Boveri (ABB), the Swiss-Swedish energy and engineering firm, organized as a "constellation" with more than 65 business areas, 1,100 companies, and 4,500 profit centers, coordinated by a corporate staff in Zurich of less than 200 (Taylor 1991; Bartlett and Ghoshal 1993).

In the United States, General Electric has evolved to a radically decentralized organization with thousands of parts connected not by centralized control but by a passionate commitment to organizational learning. Rather than standardization, GE relies on

relentless efforts at knowledge transfer, of moving successful organizational practices and processes across highly disparate units. The aim, then, is diversification and local experimentation, complemented by rapid diffusion of new ideas.[7] These radically decentralized corporations are remaking both the geography of production and the administration of large-scale organization.

But ABB or GE are not here, there, and everywhere at once. They do not shift operations from one site to another in search of lower labor costs as do smaller global firms such as Nike. The United Nations Conference on Trade and Development, which keeps a watchful eye on multinational firms, distinguishes between simple and complex integration. The Nike strategy of chasing cheap labor and switching production exemplifies the simple strategy. In contrast, firms like ABB or GE, which pursue the complex strategy, must rethink all of the activities and strategies that multinationals have long pursued. In trying to be both global and local simultaneously, these firms find that region matters more than ever before. To begin with, subsidiaries are no longer regarded as distant back offices, but may have responsibility for global functions or products. Thus, if the Canadian subsidiary masters cost competitiveness best, it is given the reins of that program throughout a firm's global operations. Or if Hewlett Packard decides the office products market is most appealing in Europe, it relocates responsibility for that business unit in France and serves the United States from abroad. In turn, European firms like Glaxo, Thomson, and Unilever migrate to the United States and set up primary operations here. Far from being oblivious to locale and in search

---

[7]Remarks of Steve Kerr, Chief Knowledge Officer, General Electric, at "fireside chat," Organization Science Winter Conference, Keystone, Colorado, 12 February 2000.

Region is significant for complex MNCs (as opposed to 'simple' ones like Nike)

MNCs w/ internally competing parts

only of low-cost labor, most multinationals are reorganizing into complex internal networks that compete with one another.

Region → v. imp!

Region looms large in several other respects as well. Many of the recognized centers of excellence around the world are found in industrial districts—the Prato region in northern Italy for fashion and design, Seattle for software, Japan for electronics miniaturization, Hollywood for film-making, to name only a few. Companies in these industries have no choice but to locate in or have access to these centers in order to stay abreast and draw upon the best talent. Finally, most foreign investment still clusters around the home country—Western Europe moves into Eastern Europe, Japan into Southeast Asia, the United States, into Canada, Mexico, and South America. And the huge growth in many service industries, such as health care, day care, financial services, and the like, represent sectors that are not moveable. These fields must locate where the customers are . . .

Location still matters

. . . Thus, despite much popular talk about globalization location still matters a great deal.

→ But to whom? Workers?! or are they moved around?

Technological Change

Another common explanation for recent workplace changes is that technological innovations have failed to deliver dramatic increases in productivity and instead have replaced workers rather than enlarged their skills. In this respect, 1990 was a watershed year—one in which, according to the U.S. Department of Commerce, capital spending on the information economy (i.e, computers and telecommunications equipment) was greater than on all other aspects of the country's industrial infrastructure (Zuboff 1995, 202). By 1996 the information technology sector—defined as including computing and telecommunications but not semiconductors or electronic games—was the largest industry

Asks! Has technological skill reduced need for labor?

in the United States, according to Commerce Department data, employing 4.3 million people and generating 6.2 percent of the nation's output.[8] Has there been a related substitution of machines for hands and minds? Chrysler, for example, produced 1.72 million cars in 1995, the same number as in 1988, but with seven thousand fewer workers. Former Secretary of Labor Robert Reich frequently argued that there is a mismatch between the skills Americans have and the skills the economy requires. Wages are falling for various categories of workers, so the argument goes, because they have become technologically obsolete. Obviously, computing capability once viewed as astounding is now trivial. My son's Nintendo 64 runs on a higher performance processor than the original 1976 Cray supercomputer, which was accessible back then only to an elite team of physicists. Surely, then, one answer to why organizations are restructuring is that there is a mismatch between worker skills and organizational needs.

But not so fast, Hasn't the increase in computing power also allowed workers to produce more? Bound and Johnson (1995), two influential proponents of the skills mismatch view, recognize that evidence in favor of the argument that technology has rendered classes of workers obsolete is "largely circumstantial." Perhaps, then, the explanation is not a misfit in worker skills but a disconnect between organizational form and the new technologies. The canonical twentieth-century bureaucracy was designed to meet the business needs of increasing throughput and lowering unit costs. As Alfred Chandler (1962, 1977) has shown in his magisterial studies of the rise

[8]The study, "Cybernation: The Importance of the High-Technology Industry to the American Economy," was reported in Steve Lohr, "Information Technology Field Is Rated Largest U.S. Industry, *New York Times,* 18 November 1997.

of first a functional hierarchy, then a multi-divisional structure, the proliferation of mass production entailed a detailed division of labor and the simplification and delegation of administrative tasks. The role of a manager "evolved as guardian of the organization's centralized knowledge base" (Zuboff 1995, 202). Dramatic gains in computing power were initially harnessed to reinforce hierarchical, centrally controlled organizational structures—to watch, control, detect, and duplicate. Managers fought hard to hold onto the information on which their power rested, even as the new information technologies opened up novel possibilities for broad distribution of information. The organization of General Motors in the 1960s was a complicated analog of a mainframe computer. But, as I later argue, the economy today resembles a web, not a hierarchy, and to force technologies that enhance "networking" into a pyramidal form serves only to constrain their effectiveness. If there is a mismatch, then, I contend it is between the capabilities of information technology to handle information and problems whenever and wherever necessary, and the older organizational arrangements that force decisions to be made by a central managerial hierarchy (see also C. Freeman 1994; Zuboff 1995).

The coevolutionary process by which technologies and institutions adapt to one another entails experimentation and learning, therefore it takes time for fundamentally new technologies to be debugged, widely diffused, and become productive. Thus the long-expected gains in productivity from information technology do not flower until older, centralized organizational arrangements are abandoned and new ways of organizing are institutionalized, and until new methods of measuring productivity, which capture gains in speed and innovation, are developed. Consider how slowly we are adjusting to a world in which companies low on physical capital but extraordinarily high on intellectual capital are in ascendance. We still measure the economy with indicators created for a mass production era. Intellectual assets do not appear anywhere on a balance sheet. The ability to generate new discoveries, to make dramatic improvements in design, service, or customization are not easily measured. But we are moving to a regime where the speed at which individuals and organizations learn may prove to be the only sustainable advantage. The evolution and spread of new information technologies that enhance collaborative work hold the possibility for remaking work practices in radical ways (Brynjolfsson et al. 1994). Achieving results from investments in intellectual capital, that is, winning in a learning race, requires new organization arrangements that allow information to flow freely.

A "Winner-Take-All" System?

There is considerable evidence of a growing disparity in income, in which people in the top one-fifth of the income distribution have grown much wealthier, while those in the lowest fifth have become poorer, and those in between have largely failed to keep pace with inflation. Moreover, the real wages of many blue- and pink-collar workers did not increase in tandem with the economy's resurgence in the 1990s. Thus, to many, capitalism has grown both leaner and meaner, exacerbating social inequality. Wall Street investment banker Felix Rohatyn puts the case vividly, arguing that "advanced capitalism" and its harsh and cruel climate "imposes stringent discipline on its participants." "What is occurring," he claims, "is a huge transfer of wealth from lower skilled, middle-class American workers to the owners of capital assets and to a new technological aristocracy with a

Asks: Are corps concentrating wealth & power despite decentralization?

large element of compensation tied to stock values."[9]

Bennett Harrison (1994) is more direct, arguing that the global economy is increasingly dominated by large firms that have become skilled in "lean production," which utilize cross-border alliances and extensive networks of subcontracting to maximize their advantage. "Dressed in new costumes— and armed with new techniques for combining control over capital allocation, technology, government relations, and the deployment of labor with a dramatic decentralization of the location of actual production—the world's largest companies, their allies, and their suppliers have found a way to remain at the center of the world stage" (Harrison 1994, 12). Dubbing the process "concentration without centralization," Harrison argues that firms that have mastered global network production have four key components: (1) core-ring structures, typified by the auto industry's lean manufacturing process, in which there is a center of high-paid, high-skill employees and the rest of production is relegated to a lower-paid periphery; (2) new uses of computerized manufacturing and information management to coordinate far-flung activities according to principles of "just-in-time" production; (3) extensive use of subcontracting and strategic alliances, especially across national borders; and (4) attempts by management to elicit more active collaboration on the part of their most expensive-to-replace employees. Harrison is deeply concerned that these practices exacerbate labor market inequality and free firms from oversight and regulation by national governments.

Critics agree that a new and more flexible mode of organizing has been adopted by many capitalist firms, but they maintain that this new form is a concerted effort to differentiate sharply workers and managers with different levels and types of skills. The much-vaunted lean production system, developed by Japanese automakers, "dramatically lowers the amount of high-wage effort needed to produce a product . . . , and it keeps reducing it through continuous incremental improvement" (Womack et al. 1990, 260). In a similar vein, Vallas and Beck's (1996) research on the introduction of programmable control systems and new process technologies in the paper-making industry shows that these innovations undercut the experience of established manual workers and contributed to the hegemony of well-educated engineers as production decisions came to be based on engineering criteria. More broadly, the massive upsurge in reengineering efforts places considerable power in the hands of those who control the relevant software and computer technologies that guide workplace reorganization.

Changes in the design of work, in tandem with growing reliance on outsourcing and contract manufacturing, have indeed altered the landscape of work. Semi-skilled, decent-paying jobs in manufacturing and transportation have fallen sharply, and this decline has been especially devastating for low-skilled African-American men at the end of the employment queue (Bound and Freeman 1992; Kassarda 1995; Wilson 1996). Combined with the shrinkage in the size and clout of organized labor in manufacturing and the overall evaporation of job security, there has been an erosion in the kind of jobs for blue-collar workers that used to provide a steady, reliable income. Employees who have fallen from semi-skilled positions into low-wage and/or temporary jobs find not only that their incomes and benefits have dropped, but that their work conditions have worsened as well. No longer is work predictable and routine. Even those who secure employment find themselves treated

Real-life conseqs. of chng in work & corp. employment levels

[9]In a speech entitled "Requiem for a Democrat," delivered at Wake Forest University, 17 March 1995, quoted in Simon Head (1996, 47).

like yo-yos, yanked from part-time work to full-time and back, from the day shift to the night shift.

BUT - it's ok bc others do it?

But treating the labor supply like a spigot to be turned on and off as market conditions dictate is by no means unique to the United States. In West European nations, where the greater power of labor unions makes wholesale restructuring less of an option for employers, more and more manufacturing has moved to the model of the "breathing factory," in which work and hours expand to meet rising demand and contract when conditions slacken. The trans-

Yet they have ↓ ≠

formation of production to a system that responds much more rapidly to changes in markets is a global phenomenon. Why, then, is growing income-polarization more pronounced in the United States?

Why?

The answer turns on a combination of political, institutional, and technological factors. The comparative weakness and decline of the United States labor movement vis-à-vis its relative strength in West European nations (and the broadly diffused system of seniority-based wages in Japan) means that in those industries most affected by economic changes, managers in the United States dominate labor to an extent unprecedented in the latter half of the twentieth century. Moreover, wage inequality is but one key component of overall inequality. The sparseness of the U.S. social safety net—unemployment, retraining, and welfare—and the more general reliance on the private sector rather than on government for health care and pensions means that changes in the private sector exacerbate inequalities.

But there is a reverse side to the structural change that the United States is undergoing. The United States has been in the forefront of economies creating new jobs and making the shift in its industrial structure to a high-tech, knowledge-based economy. The very dynamism and flexibility that creates volatility and renders groups of

workers less employable also fosters the development of new industries and new companies that spur job growth. In many of these new fields, pay and other benefits are tied directly to company performance, and so successes result in even greater rewards. The very success of the high-tech sector, however, generates inequality by widening the gap between winners and losers, by closing off opportunities to those experienced in the older system and who are unable to make the transition, and by narrowing the points of entry for unskilled workers.

Wide view of problem (structural)

The shift to the so-called "new economy" widens polarization in several other respects as well. There is, clearly, a dramatic difference between the extraordinary success of a relatively small number of employees at a firm like Microsoft, who are millionaires many times over from their gains on stock options, and the larger number of workers left with only low-wage options. Successes at Microsoft or throughout Silicon Valley contribute to a growing winner-take-all ethic (Frank and Cook 1995), in which success creates increasing returns; that is, the capabilities, skills, and experiences of those who have prospered rebound such that they are vastly better positioned and qualified than those left behind. This reinforcing cycle is virtuous for the winners, vicious for the losers. Moreover, an added consequence of this transformation is that labor conflict has been altered. Unlike the traditional antagonisms between management and labor, conflicts generated by new forms of production disperse laterally: between full-time and part-time workers, between insiders and outsiders, and between knowledge workers and the unskilled. But it is wrong, I believe, to argue that the new system is just a kind of decentralized Fordism or a wolf in sheep's clothing. We are undergoing a period of "creative destruction," in which the established practices of one regime are being replaced by new ones.

Winner-take-all ethic

& labor conflict "altered"

BRILLIANT - Conflict disperses laterally

Thesis

Income polarization is a clear outcome of the turbulent transition from one system to another, but it is not at all clear that these inequalities are a necessary component of the new form. I have argued previously that the contradictory pulls of integration and disintegration, of collaboration and cut-throat competition, are built into the very nature of how network forms of organization grow and develop (Powell 1990). How these combinatory possibilities are realized depends largely on social and political relations and on the trajectories inherent in particular technologies. . . .

Summary and Conclusion

I have argued that a series of changes are well underway in how work is constituted, organizations are structured, and competition is conducted. These changes are responses to different pressures, and stem from experimentation with divergent ideas. But I contend that they are converging to produce a distinctive and novel logic of organizing that is built around project-based work and team organization; flatter, more horizontal organizations that rely on long-term interdependent relations with external parties; and extensive efforts to leverage capabilities across a wide range of activities. One consequence is that the activities of many organizations are now more interdependent, and selection increasingly operates at the network level as rivalry shifts from firm-versus-firm to coalition-versus-collaboration. This system seems to combine the give and take of long-term relational contracting with a short-term focus on results and market discipline. The transition to this new system is rocky, and there are both considerable gains for the winners and steep losses for the losers. At present, it appears the flexibility of the new model is well suited to an era of rapid technological change. Whether the

new system will prove adaptive for the long haul, or be as robust as the post–World War II system was for nearly four decades, is not clear. But what is apparent is how rapidly the social technology for organizing work has changed. Our shared understandings about how work and organization are to be carried out now involve fundamentally different recipes than existed previously.

We need, I suggest, to think much more deeply about the social and political consequences of this transformation. Richard Sennett (1998) has argued that there are considerable costs to individuals when attachment and loyalty are replaced by flexibility and constant change. Although he provides evidence mostly from older workers, he shows poignantly that connection to a larger purpose is hard to sustain in a world of projects and perpetual change. We need to ask who has been harmed the most by this transition, and what social policies might ease the burdens of the shift? What kinds of institutional supports—public, private, and civic—are needed both to cushion and sustain new forms of organizing? What actions might push more organizations to follow the high road of continuous learning for their employees rather than the low road of intensified and insecure work? A key transition is underway, and organizations have, in many respects, become much more productive and responsive. We now know a good deal about the organizational consequences of this transformation; but our understanding of its social ramifications is murky. This chapter is an effort to start these conversations by sketching the outline of the new system and arguing that our current thinking has not kept pace.

REFERENCES

Barker, Kathleen, and Kathleen Christensen, eds. 1998. *Contingent Work: American Employment Relations in Transition.* Ithaca, N.Y.: ILR Press.

Upshot: The economy is changing due to ↑ technology & speed (which info can be shared.
• Workplaces/orgs. are restructuring, resulting in
The Capitalist Firm in the Twenty-First Century **93**
↑ ≠
• Examine nature of Chng &

Bartlett, Christopher, and Sumantra Ghoshal. 1993. "Beyond the M-Form." *Strategic Management Review* 14:23–46.

Benner, Chris. 1996. "Shock Absorbers in the Flexible Economy: The Rise of Contingent Employment in Silicon Valley." Manuscript, Deptartment of City and Regional Planning, University of California, Berkeley.

Bernhardt, Annette, Martina Morris, Mark Handcock, and March Scott. 1998. "Summary of Findings: Work and Opportunity in the Post-Industrial Labor Market." Report to the Russell Sage and Rockefeller Foundations, New York.

Bound, John, and Richard B. Freeman. 1992. "What Went Wrong? The Erosion of the Relative Earnings of Young Black Men in the 1980s." *Quarterly Journal of Economics* 107: 201–33.

Bound, John, and George Johnson. 1995. "What Are the Causes of Rising Wage Inequality in the United States?" Federal Reserve *Bank of New York Economic Policy Review* (January).

Brynjolfsson, Erik, Thomas Malone, Vilay Gurbaxani, Ajit Kambil. 1994. "Does Information Technology Lead to Smaller Firms?" *Management Science* 40, 12:1628–44.

Capelli, Peter, with L. Bassi, H. Katz, D. Knoke, P. Osterman, and M. Useem. 1997. *Change at Work.* New York: Oxford University Press.

Carnoy, Martin, Manuel Castells, and Chris Benner. 1997. "Labor Markets and Employment Practices in the Age of Flexibility: A Case Study of Silicon Valley." *International Labour Review* 136 (1): 27–48.

Chandler, Alfred A., Jr. 1962. *Strategy and Structure: Chapters in the History of the American Industrial Enterprise.* Cambridge: MIT Press.

———. 1977. *The Visible Hand: The Managerial Revolution in American Business.* Cambridge: Harvard University Press.

Eccles, Robert. 1981. "The Quasifirm in the Construction Industry." *Journal of Economic Behavior and Organization* 2:335–57.

Farber, Henry S. 1996. "The Changing Face of Job Loss in the United States." Working paper 5596, National Bureau of Economic Research.

Faulkner, Robert R., and Andy Anderson. 1987. "Short-Term Projects and Emergent Careers: Evidence from Hollywood." *American Journal of Sociology* 92:879–909.

Frank, Robert H., and Phillip J. Cook. 1995. *The Winner-Take-All Society.* New York: Free Press.

Freeman, Christopher. 1994. "The Economics of Technical Change." *Cambridge Journal of Economics* 18:463–514.

———. 1995. "The National System of Innovation in Historical Perspective." *Cambridge Journal of Economics* 19:5–24.

Gordon, David M. 1996. *Fat and Mean: The Corporate Squeeze of Working Americans and the Myth of Managerial Downsizing.* New York: Free Press.

Harrison, Bennett. 1994. *Lean and Mean: The Changing Landscape of Corporate Power in an Age of Flexibility.* New York: Basic Books.

Head, Simon. 1996. "The New, Ruthless Economy." *New York Review of Books,* 29 February: pp. 47–52.

Kassarda, John D. 1995. "Industrial Restructuring and the Changing Location of Jobs." In *State of the Union: America in the 1990s,* vol. 7, edited by Reynolds Farley. New York: Russell Sage Foundation.

O'Rourke, Kevin, Alan Taylor, and Jeffrey Williamson. 1996. "Factor Price Convergence in the Late 19th Century." *International Economic Review* 37 (3): 499–530.

Osterman, Paul. 1999. *Securing Prosperity.* Princeton N.J.: Princeton University Press.

———, ed. 1996. *Broken Ladders: Managerial Careers in the New Economy.* New York; Oxford University Press.

Powell, Walter W. 1990. "Neither Market nor Hierarchy: Network Forms of Organization." In *Research in Organizational Behavior,* edited by Barry Staw and Lawrence L. Cummings, 295–336. Greenwich, Conn.: JAI Press.

Presser, Harriet B. 1995. "Job, Family, and Gender: Determinants of Nonstandard Work Schedules Among Employed Americans in 1991." *Demography* 32 (4): 577–98.

Schumpeter, Joseph. 1934. *The Theory of Economic Development.* Cambridge: Harvard University Press.

Scott, Elizabeth D., K. C. O'Shaughnessy, and P. Capelli. 1996. "Management Jobs in the Insurance Industry: Organizational Deskilling and Rising Pay Inequity." In *Broken Ladders,* edited by P. Osterman, 124–54. New York: Oxford University Press.

Sennett, Richard. 1998. *The Corrosion of Character.* New York: Knopf.

Stinchcombe, Arthur L. 1959. "Bureaucratic and Craft Administration of Production." *Administrative Science Quarterly* 4:194–208.

Taylor, William. 1991. "The Logic of Global Business: An Interview with ABB's Percy Bavenick." *Harvard Business Review* 69 (2): 91–105.

Vallas, Stephen Y., and John P. Beck. 1996. "The Transformation of Work Revisited: The Limits of Flexibility in American Manufacturing." *Social Problems* 43 (3): 339–61.

Williamson, Jeffrey. 1995. "The Evolution of Global Labor Markets Since 1830: Background Evidence and Hypotheses." *Explorations in Economic History* 32:141–96.

Wilson, William Julius. 1996. *When Work Disappears.* New York: Knopf.

Womack, James P., Daniel T. Jones, and Daniel Roos. 1990. *The Machine That Changed the World: The Story of Lean Production.* New York: Harper and Row.

Zuboff, Shoshana. 1995. "The Emperor's New Workplace." *Scientific American* 273:202–204.

❧ READING 10 ❧

Structural Unemployment and the Reconstruction of the Self in the Turbulent Economy

Vicki Smith

Hi, my name is Harvey Dixon. I specialize in human resources management and have extensive experience working in the telecommunications industry. I've been responsible for up to 750 people. I'm credentialed in teamwork and want to work in a professional environment that values working with others. I especially seek challenges, change, and opportunities for making innovations. So if you know anyone seeking a person with my skills, tell them to call Harvey Dixon.

A professional introduction, scripted and delivered by Harvey Dixon (a pseudonym) at the general membership meeting of Experience Unlimited, a job club for unemployed professionals and managers.

Being a Manager, Being a Professional, Being Unemployed

How do . . . unemployed managers and professionals, once untouched by layoffs, displacement, and corporate restructuring, interpret the new rules of the employment relationship or feel about having to reevaluate and put a new gloss on their employment identities? How do labor-market intermediaries, such as job training agencies and job and career search organizations, insert themselves into these processes? What kinds of signals do they give the unemployed about corporate restructuring and impermanency? In short, what messages are being transmitted to people who have fallen into an abyss, who are stuck in the great divide itself and striving to reach the more promising terrain of the new economy?

Lack of a job in the latter years of the 1990s has had humiliating implications for unemployed professionals and managers. Many of the individuals whom I interviewed and observed at a job search organization, who were experiencing in blunt form the dynamism of the labor market, understood that they were up against challenging institutional changes: the decline of the permanent job model, erosion of internal labor markets, and the pervasiveness of employment insecurity. They were deeply discouraged by their sense—often grounded in protracted, painful experience—that emergent structures were impenetrable to them, that the rules of getting and keeping a good job were increasingly indecipherable.

Unemployed professionals and managers labored to learn new job-search, interviewing, and negotiating tactics that they believed would position them advantageously in the turbulent economy. Desiring respectable employment that would offer a modicum of security and opportunities for mobility, dignity, and a reasonable wage, they craved the chance to demonstrate to employers that they could learn new skills and would be committed employees. They articulated well the master narrative of the new, destabilized economy: a story with subplots including routine corporate downsizing, employers' preference for adaptable workers with general rather than firm-specific skills, employers' desire to depress wages by downsizing older, long-term workforces, and the growth of contingent employment. It is a story that reassured them that their personal problems were structural in nature.

Yet, in counterbalance to this version of economic change, they read of astonishingly low unemployment rates. They read newspaper articles citing the leading employers in the area, who lament the shortage of available skilled labor. The skills employers say they can't find are the skills that unemployed managers and professionals are willing to learn, and they believe they have the organizational and cultural capital to do so from their previous employment experiences. They also read of the so-called work revolution, the dazzling range of income and work opportunities, seemingly just out of their reach in the information- and communications-based dot.com economy. These labor-market facts don't add up, but they do create a deep sense of personal insecurity and failure. Interpreting and being at the epicenter of these contradictory trends constitute the daily experiences of the experienced but unemployed professional or manager.

Studying lived experience in intermediary labor-market organizations yields much sociological data about these questions and issues. . . . In this chapter I focus on how an organization for the un- and underemployed—a professional and managerial job search club organized under the auspices of the California Employment Development Department (EDD)—framed the dynamics of job searching and labor markets to its clientele, and how members of the organization responded to this framework. It is within such organizations that people learn about and map out the dynamics of labor-market processes and job acquisition procedures, identify particular career paths or occupational fields, strategize to identify, build, and improve their job skills, and come to grips with unemployed comrades, with rejections from employers and with discouraging holding patterns such as long periods of temporary employment. . . .

Labor-Market Organizations and Their Role in Constructing the Terms of the Great Divide

Labor-market organizations such as state-sponsored training or job search agencies play a vital role in smoothing the uneven interface between shifting labor markets and people looking for work. Agencies for the unemployed present a selective view of how labor markets work, propel particular groups of people toward particular types of opportunities, and act as a link between formal institutions and an aggregate of individuals who desire employment. The type of organization I studied—going by the names of both Experience Unlimited (EU) and the Sacramento Professional Network (SPN)—is part of a population of organizations that has been researched and analyzed by others in a search to understand how displaced managers and professionals navigate through the labor market. . . .

Experience Unlimited: A State-Sponsored Job Search Club for Professionals, Managers, and Technical Workers

In 1959 the California EDD established Experience Unlimited because the department felt that it could not adequately serve the needs of the managerial and professional unemployed. Correctly, EDD pointed out that employers typically didn't list announcements with them about professional and managerial job openings, and that the managerial and professional job market tended to operate more through networks and connections than through formal job listings of open positions. EDD also believed that unemployed professionals and managers needed to be actively involved in their searches to a degree that was not possible in the traditional bureaucratic and hierarchical organization of EDD. Utilization of Experience Unlimited declined dramatically in the 1970s but began to pick up in the late 1980s and exploded in the 1990s.[1] When I conducted my research, EU paid the salary of one full-time staff person (Karen) and provided resources such as computers, telephones, furniture, and office space.

Following on the principle that different conditions and resources were required to facilitate unemployed managers' and professionals' quest for jobs, the EDD designed an autonomous professional space for their use. The physical layout of the Employment Development Department architecturally stratified the job seekers using its services from the unemployed of other classes. When other unemployed people went to file for unemployment benefits or obtain information about available jobs, they entered through the main door of the EDD into a large impersonal waiting area. These "regular" unemployed—the large numbers of people looking for entry-level service, production, or construction jobs, mostly people of color, people who dressed casually and informally, some sprawled out and fast asleep, others who didn't have the "luxury" of napping because of small, impatient children—were separated from and ranked below the agency workers by a thick wall of Plexiglass. Standing in front of the tiny opening in the Plexiglass, individuals were fed narrow bits of information from the frontline workers. Until then, they sat in rows of hard plastic chairs, waiting for their names to be called, for the "privilege" of being grilled and processed by the EDD employees.

The members of EU, however, were cushioned from the stigma and the experience of unemployment in various ways. The unemployed managers and professionals had a separate entrance that led into a large and comfortable suite. It was fully equipped for members to conduct job searches with comparative privacy and autonomy. Their hours and days at EU were self-organized, often filled with friendly and supportive interactions with their unemployed colleagues. They were free to explore reams of information at their leisure. Here, there were no spatial or administrative hierarchies inscribed in the everyday arrangements of the organization: no bulletproof Plexiglass repelled and reminded them that they were to be managed with apprehension, if not contempt; no bureaucratic cadre suggested that the professionals and managers were in an organizationally subordinate or socially stigmatized position. Although Karen, the paid staff member, was responsible for the general functioning of the center, EU was otherwise completely coordinated and governed by volunteer participants themselves.

The stigmatizing label of "unemployed" was obscured by the name always cited by any volunteer answering the main telephone: "Sacramento Professional Network." Members often gave this telephone number to potential employers so that when an employer needed to contact a member about an interview or a job offer, they left their message at what sounded like a professional answering service. On its surface EU had the feel of a friendly professional club.

In separating the unemployed professionals and managers from and privileging them in comparison to the unemployed from the ranks of those who are working-class or lack skills and education, EDD also spun a class-specific rhetoric about the unique needs of the former groups. In the EDD's *Fact Sheet* describing the rationale for EU, the department connected the goals of the organization directly to the currents of the 1990s economy, noting that "many professional, managerial, and technical workers . . . have unexpectedly found themselves out of work" and that the organization's services are "a response to the needs of communities faced with an increase in corporate mergers, relocations and downsizing, or an increased number of people forced to change jobs due to technological shifts."

———

A Profile of the Membership. The membership of Experience Unlimited was predominately male. Karen, the staff member, estimated that the ratio of women to men was approx-imately thirty-five to sixty-five, and that the racial and ethnic ratio was approximately 20 percent nonwhite to 80 percent white. The membership was also mature. A quick gaze across the room at any time suggested a group with enormous collective experience, with many people, both men and women, looking to be in their late thirties, forties, or fifties. The sixteen members who were in my introductory workshop averaged in age forty-five years, while the seventeen individuals in my interview sample averaged forty-four years of age.[2] For individuals who had had what could be called long-term, permanent jobs prior to coming to EU, the average length of time they spent in their job was fourteen years. This group constituted about one-third of the total in my workshop and interview sample; the remaining two-thirds had had shorter tenure at a greater number of jobs.

The occupational status of nearly all EU members was professional and managerial, broadly defined. Previously, most of them had held lower-to-middle staff and line management positions or belonged to less specialized professions and semi-professions. I met no doctors or lawyers, although I did interview a woman who had a law degree but had never practiced law and was seeking a new career line. In fact, only four individuals held higher degrees: the woman with a law degree, a man with master's degrees in engineering and in business; a woman with a Ph.D. in chemistry; and a woman with a master's in public health. What is important here is that these individuals were in a position where personal/ professional networks were failing them, where demand for their labor was weak, either because of their limited skills, age, and seniority or because they were handicapped by previous employment experiences, a matter I discuss later in this chapter.

Many of the people I studied had had direct experience with temporary employment, in several ways. Eleven of the seventeen people in my interview sample had worked as a temporary or contract worker. Nearly every one of the eleven had been employed by an agency, not directly by the company. Of those who had worked on a temporary basis, five were what I would call "serial temps": they regularly held temporary jobs, ranging from a period of months to several years, and had used EU when they could afford to devote their energy toward hunting for more regular employment.

Three others had worked on the *staff* of temporary firms. Their labor had, in small but nevertheless significant ways, contributed to the destabilization of the employment structure. For example, one woman helped her employer—who owned a legal-services temporary help agency—to market, sell, and set up franchises of that agency, thus building the temporary-help service industry. Another individual, employed by a temporary agency and working for a large regional utility company, had conducted "Activity Value Analysis," wherein he analyzed detailed company data to conduct a cost assessment of various companywide functions. The company needed this information to determine what functions were most suitable for outsourcing to vendors. Thus, he, as a temporary worker, was collecting and analyzing the data that would allow this company to downsize *its* permanent workforce.

Seven of the individuals in my interview sample had acquired additional degrees, credentials, and certificates in their quest to expand their options and make themselves more marketable. For example, two individuals had gone through the career search program at a national company called Haldane, paying approximately three thousand dollars of their own money to do so. Three other people I interviewed had considered using Haldane, had attended Haldane's preliminary workshop to determine whether they wanted to go through the whole program, and had decided against it. They were discouraged by Haldane's steep price and the program's vague promises of actually landing a job. One man had obtained an MBA, and one woman working in the field of insurance and investment service had acquired four licenses and had paid four thousand dollars to complete yet another career evaluation and search program. Others had obtained certificates (in quality management programs and professional conference and meeting planning, for example), while yet others had taken various courses to hone their computer skills, such as word processing, web page design, desktop publishing, and database management.

Finally, nine of the people I interviewed, and an indeterminate number of people in my workshop, were compelled to use EU after they had been caught in the cross fire of corporate restructuring. That is, the direct causes of unemployment were widespread layoffs in a single company (in some cases, people had experienced multiple layoffs) or layoffs caused by their company's merger with another company or by technological/organizational restructuring and displacement.

While a slim majority of people I discuss here lost their jobs through corporate restructuring or downsizing, some of the remaining group had been fired for what appeared to have been poor performance or personality conflicts. I make no effort to compare the two groups or to suggest that one group was structurally victimized while the others were "losers," the latter a negative stereotype held even by some of the unemployed themselves. (One woman's comments typify an ambivalence I heard in many interviews. "I know this is very bad of me to say but I felt, I looked around, and you heard of everybody's personal needs, and it was like, Why can't these people get jobs? I mean, if they are this skilled and qualified, why can't they get jobs, and why can't I get a job? On the one hand, I understand it because I was having trouble too, but on the other hand, I didn't get it.") . . .

Professionalizing Unemployment or, Daily Life at Experience Unlimited, aka the Sacramento Professional Network

On the sweltering summer morning on which I am supposed to make a pitch to recruit interviewees for my project, I drive to Sacramento, park my car in the vast, steamy parking lot of the California Employment Development Department, and go through an unmarked door to present "proof" to the volunteer at the front desk that I am authorized to attend the EU general meeting. Not just anyone can enter the EU facility. As if to continually remind themselves of their professional norms and identity, members have erected administrative and symbolic shields around their premises, barriers of entry to any casual or inappropriate visitor to the center. In so doing, they recreate professionalism: they define the boundaries of their professional field and apply well-defined criteria to determine admission to their ranks.

First, anyone not authorized is not admitted. EU members jealously guard their resources and their turf. While I am filling out information for my visitor's pass, I hear Ramon, the sentry, deny one man entry and explain to him what he has to do to gain entrance. Obtaining authorization either means having the permission of the single EDD staff member or filling out extensive paperwork enumerating work history, personal data, and career goals. Even when a potential member completes the required paperwork, he or she is only allowed to initiate participation at an appointed date specified by the sentry. Each prospective

member must take their place on a lengthy waiting list.

Other measures create the aura of professionalism and reinforce the professional shield. If a member is inappropriately dressed—that is, not dressed professionally as defined in the manual of rules—he or she is not allowed to enter. The exception is if the dress-code violator agrees to don an article of clothing from the surplus professional clothing supply, a coat-rack hung with men's ties and sports jackets and women's linen jackets. Bare legs on women are frowned upon, as are slacks. The dress with nylons is uniquely considered the evidence of women's professionalism, as the tie is for men.

The center hums as members perform the work they believe is necessary to find a job. Searching for a job, I come to see, is a job itself. As I learn in the following weeks of workshops, job searching is taught as a near-scientific process (represented as a pyramid of ten ascending steps one must follow to get a job), with specified tasks, a prescribed and systematic methodology, schedules for meetings, and collective expectations for performance. To conduct this work, EU has a significant amount of open, communal space for large meetings and cozier cubicles and work areas for small group meetings, individual tasks, and one-on-one conversations between members. When I arrive at 8:45 A.M., some members are setting up folding chairs for the mandatory weekly general meeting. Although some people jovially share stories about their weekends with fellow members, most seem to be carrying out tasks that are part of the daily and weekly work in the organization. Several sets of people confer about their plans for workshops to be held that week.

Some individuals thumb through job announcement binders and clipboards, while some work on their personal organizers. Others station themselves at one of many computers available for on-line job search activities, make calls at the bank of phones to schedule appointments or inquire about openings, or read informational and inspirational news stories on the bulletin board. Articles with headlines such as "Understanding the Hidden Job Market," "Job Search Stress," "Changing Careers," "Fatal Mistakes in Interviews," "Should You Lie to Land a Job?" "Creating a Better Life after Topping Out Early," and "Mantras to Make Yourself Feel Positive" confirm the realities of the treacherous job market but suggest that the reader can minimize or overcome such treachery. By engaging in these activities, EU members sustain a sense of autonomy, industriousness, and professionalism, but the activities also serve as vivid testimony to the hard realities of why people are members in the first place.

Regular attendance at EU provides members with a salient connection to a stable institution. They find the resources they need to do their work—the job search. They learn skills that for some are new: how to facilitate meetings, write newsletters and reports, improve their public speaking skills, network, and learn the theory behind cross-training and multitasking. They engage in regular events and rituals; they are part of an organization with a history; and they are embedded in a set of ongoing social relationships. The faces of those with whom they interact may change (and in fact, everyone hopes they will change, since it is inspiring evidence that people do find jobs), but there is a general stability to EU's population. Hence, joining EU confers membership in an ongoing social and professional unit, while the work the unemployed do there affords them a sense of control and efficacy under circumstances in which they have little control. Coming to EU everyday, as the leadership of the organization advocates, anchors people who have no active relationship to any other stable, collective entity or project.

As one woman said to me, EU "kept me going through a time when I was kind of like searching for some kind of identity" after working for AT&T for nine years. Unemployed people who have invested much time and effort to carve out their professional niches face enormous challenges to their sense of identity. . . .

I have arrived for the weekly general meeting, at which new members introduce themselves and all members share information about job announcements, job placements of former members, and upcoming skills workshops in which members might want to participate. Items on the agenda impart many lessons about what is happening to people searching for employment, as well as how members of the organization view the nature of the 1990s economy. Karen begins by announcing messages sent to her by former members who have let her know why they're no longer coming to EU. The reasons cited make clear that few people are landing desirable professional jobs, but Karen couches the news in a way that softens impact.

The majority of people who sent in an update have obtained "bread-and-butter" jobs, not their dream jobs. A bread-and-butter job is the organization's standard lexicon for an entry-level job or a job that otherwise represents downward mobility to the job holder. Bread-and-butter jobs, de facto, are temporary jobs in Karen's eyes. Karen reports the bread-and-butter news optimistically, emphasizing the importance of even having a job, as well as her belief that everyone, at one point or another, has to compromise their dreams. She stresses that their job outcomes are either temporary or are bridges to more desirable employment and she is stern about the fact that no one should interpret such a job in negative terms.

Not far behind individuals with bread-and-butter jobs are those who have accepted de jure temporary jobs, a type of employment that Karen frames in similarly optimistic terms. Before she announces where each individual has landed, Karen recommends that *everyone* should sign up with a temporary agency, because, she says, the temp-to-regular job route has become a routine method for landing a stable job. Some of the benefits of working on a temporary basis, she adds, include gaining new opportunities for networking, learning new skills and gaining experiences in new industries, and gathering information crucial to developing a job search plan.

Her words represent an institutionalized opinion about the virtues of temporary work that . . . are real for many workers. . . . Yet I can well understand why EU members don't take comfort in the examples that Karen regales us with from former members. She mentions a temporary clerical position with a law firm; a one-month job doing administrative work for the Sacramento County fair organizers; a temporary data entry job; a temp job as a "beauty consultant" at the perfume counter at K-mart; and a subcontracted position "consulting" for an organization called the American Productivity and Quality Center.

The audience nods as she lists the benefits of temporary employment but, as I learn later in one-on-one interviews and in small workshops, they are painfully aware that her perspective makes a virtue out of a necessity. Every single one of my interviewees, and many of my workshop comrades, has been stationed at some point along the temporary employment circuit, having either worked on a temporary basis or having worked for short periods of time as staff members in temporary placement firms. A small number worked as well-paid contract workers, as programmers and systems analysts; the vast majority worked as administrative assistants and clerical workers, and a few worked as assemblers and inventory

controllers at local high-tech firms. Despite substantial evidence about the pervasiveness of temporary employment, and although the organization overflows with reminders that the stability of the past has disappeared, EU members' long-range goal is to land full-time, permanent employment.

Members view the temporary job as no more and no less than a temporary strategy, evidenced in Sam's comment that the temp jobs he'd had were "gigs, not jobs." Yet temporary work was a trap for some who were stuck in a cycle of temporary employment. Having been forced to accept a temporary job to make ends meet, they then found it difficult to muster the effort and the time to find a full-time, permanent job. Elana, for example, when first unemployed, had taken a series of clerical and technical temporary jobs, viewing this as a holding pattern until she could land her "dream job." This had ensnared her. She told me: "I haven't the time now to take to look for a permanent job. I made, I think, what my pastor called a short-term favorable decision with long-term negative consequences."

Three individuals had returned to their previous employers, while one appeared to have obtained a well-paying management position. At any given time at EU, there are various individuals who have left to accept temporary positions but have returned to the club to continue their job search. "Retreads," as members wryly call themselves, tell me in interviews that they do accrue some of the benefits that Karen mentions, but that, bottom line, they wish to leave the cycle of temporariness and land a "permanent" job. How normative this range of potential job outcomes is is revealed in the "New Job Information Sheet," an exit survey that newly employed EU members fill out. One can check off "Permanent, 40 hours/week," "Temporary, 40 hours/week," "Permanent, part-time," "Temporary, part-time," "Permanent but not dream job," or "Job is part-time, I wish to continue in program."

Karen also reads off information about new job openings, some of which she's just received in the mail, others from members. Her language reveals her belief that EU members may have to settle for less, but it also reveals her appreciation for members' professional aspirations and concerns. Members at the meeting furiously take notes, writing down names and phone numbers as she informs them of a truck-driving position "with professional-level salary"; bacteriologist; quality assurance supervisor; administrative assistant; cabinetmaker and cabinet finisher, both at "professional wages"; inventory scheduler. As I observe people taking down the details, I find the limits inherent in these job announcements to be both evident and painful. They're either highly specialized (a commercial truck driver, a bacteriologist, a cabinetmaker); or they're low-level and quite likely low-paid (administrative assistant or inventory scheduler). Karen ends this portion of the meeting by asking members whether they'd like to announce jobs that they know about but won't take, hardly an upbeat conclusion to an agenda item that in itself was sobering. . . .

Mantras for the Job Seeker: How to Reinvent the Self for Desirable Employment Outcomes

EU participants receive a recurrent and integrated set of lessons about how best to combat unemployment. The lessons are encoded in the content of general meetings, in the introductory training sessions, in specialized workshops, in the bylaws of the organization, in the literature and documents used to educate members, and in one-on-one pep talks delivered by the staff coordinator. All these sources consistently emphasize that employment and labor markets have changed. Members are told that they shouldn't expect to find "permanent" jobs.

Due to the shaking and rumbling of labor markets, they should brace themselves for possible downward mobility: the optimistic discourse about the "bread-and-butter job" and the admission that temp jobs may be the only available jobs for the time being both normalize this possibility. Stability and tenure—either of past job experience or of future job expectations—is to be deemphasized and even hidden; adaptability is crucial and, although unemployment may have structural causes, it can only be resolved by individual solutions.

A core mission of EU is to shake up and dissolve members' aspirations for predictability and continuity. At the same time, organizational discourse and logic are premised on getting the unemployed to construe uncertainty and risk as an opportunity to grow personally and professionally. There are several tactics through which members can develop new personae to present to potential employers.

————

Recrafting One's Employment Profile: The Resume and the Thirty-Second Me. Socialization into the goals and the norms of Experience Unlimited, preparing oneself for entering the rocky terrain of the job market, entails a process of self-reconstruction on several levels. This process aims to reconfigure a self that, for many participants, has held steady over many years of employment. Creating a new professional profile takes place primarily in two venues: writing resumes and scripting professional introductions. EU participants call the latter the "Thirty-Second Me." Using a three-page set of guidelines for a Thirty-Second Me, participants compose concise statements to impress themselves on anyone who might employ them. Each Thirty-Second Me starts with "Hi, my name is . . ." and ends with "if you know anyone looking for a person with my skills, tell them to contact . . ." as exemplified in Harvey Dixon's Thirty-Second Me presented at the beginning of the chapter. Both venues supply messages about the self, and participants craft each one seriously, always feeling that their futures are limited if their craftsmanship is shoddy. The information that finds its way into the resume and the Thirty-Second Me constitutes the creative work that individuals engage in as they strive to position themselves for the demands and the peculiarities of emerging employment practices.

Certain principles of resume production are well-known to anyone trying to get a job in the postindustrial economy. Some of the advice EU participants receive about putting together a successful resume mirrors the advice that career counselors and placement officers give students in colleges and universities. An effective resume shouldn't be too long (EU workshop leaders stress that a resume should never exceed two pages; one page is ideal); material should be presented simply and accessibly; and the document should look professional and be printed on high-quality paper. It should highlight key experiences, skills, and competencies and should state job and professional goals. On the first day of our weeklong training, my cohort debated the advantages and disadvantages of differing type sizes, fonts (proportional vs. nonproportional, serious vs. humorous, clear vs. bizarre), the faxability or scannability of different qualities and weights of resume paper, and other elements of resume production that we believed would give us greater control and efficacy in finding a job.

Unemployed professionals and managers at EU, however, face additional, unique dilemmas in trying to land a job. Karen and the workshop leaders stress to us that not only must we find a job, we also face the painful exercise of having to hide, even erase employment histories that will be viewed as undesirable and dysfunctional, that render us uncompetitive for positions in

the turn-of-the-century economy. For all intents and purposes we are encouraged to hide our human capital, that bundle of job and training experiences and educational backgrounds that make up our unique occupational autobiographies. The leaders continually point out that employers don't want to hire people who have developed a sense of entitlement forged in previous long-term employment in paternalistic firms, people who might wish to settle into one position for the long haul, or people who have worked in stodgy industrial or military sectors where they have not been forced to be innovative or to change.

This advice guides the reconstruction of the self in the resume. My cohort members, many of whom have not written a resume in years, attempt to repackage themselves to convince classmates and future employers that their skills are transferable across different industrial/sectoral contexts. They strive to demonstrate that they are multitaskers, people who thrive on conducting several lines of activities at once. They endeavor to avoid the impression that they are looking to stay with one company for a protracted period of time. In the resume, the reinvented version of themselves, revealing nothing fixed about who they are or what they do, is ironclad.

There is no such thing, for example, as "a" resume. Our leader advocates writing multiple resumes, versions and revisions of who we are that are adaptable to the diverse organizational and employment settings that we can encounter in looking for a job. Indeed, she boasts that she has produced "hundreds" of resumes, each one carefully crafted to adjust to various positions. No one dares voice the obvious illogic in her point: the fact that *she* is here, still at EU, implicitly sends the message that the high-volume approach to resume production isn't especially effective. The leaders do not suggest that we present ourselves dishonestly

but that we package ourselves in less traditional, more creative terms that are consistent with expectations in the new economy.
For those who have difficulty pinning down
what their skills are, they can read the "skill
clusters" list for appropriate and marketable
terms.

Exactly how can my unemployed colleagues reconstruct themselves with these
lessons in mind? First, "students" recom-
pose themselves temporally by removing
evidence of extended job tenure or gaps in
employment, both of which are viewed as
handicaps. For example, they obliterate
dates, from resumes and personal introductions, that indicate lengthy tenure at previous jobs. They also downplay references to
companies at which they worked that might
sound the alarm to human resources personnel that they were accustomed to traditional,
stable work environments. For example,
Bruce had worked at IBM for twenty-two
years and Ron had worked for the telecommunications giant, GTE, for twenty-one
years. Both are strongly cautioned to remove
those signifying facts from their resumes.
The alternate phrasing that workshop participants come up with, under the prodding
of the workshop leaders, is that each has
"extensive experience" in the "high-tech"
and "communications" industries. Several
men and one woman in the introductory
workshop I attend have lengthy experiences
in the military. After heated discussion they
agree that they should deemphasize the fact
that they were in the armed forces for twelve
or fifteen or twenty years, and they put in
the foreground the skills they acquired, such
as "experience with international cultures,"
leadership, delegation, inventory procurement, multilanguage fluency, and so forth
(deemphasis on the military itself is achieved
by writing it in small type *after* listing their
skills).

As another element of such an evasive
approach, workshop participants are given a

sheet with "red light" answers and "green
light" answers that they can offer in response to an employer asking, "Why did
you leave your previous job?" An answer
that shouldn't be given—a "red light"
term—would be "left town" or "fired for
tardiness or late to work," while "green
light" answers—legitimate explanations—
include "forced reorganization or merger,"
or "contract successfully completed."

Logically following the principle of
erasing indicators of lengthy job tenure from
one's record, participants are cautioned that
they undermine themselves if, in a brief resume section stating professional goals, they
say anything revealing a desire for a permanent, long-term job. Instead, they should
stress their desire for change, for new and
challenging work environments, and for
gaining experience in a specific company or
industry, rather than for a particular job.
Further straining the self-reconstruction
process, unemployed participants are supposed to obscure any information that reveals gaps in their employment histories.
For this reason, many individuals in the
organization mention skills gained through
participation in EU, and some cite positions
that they have held at EU while unemployed,
listing "President" or "Vice President" of
"Sacramento Professional Network" as evidence of professional activity.

Others with advanced educational degrees and credentials are advised to leave
these off their resumes in situations where
they might be handicapped if seen as
overqualified or overly experienced. Across
the board, men and women are urged to
compress lifetimes of work experience into
two or three essential skill or competency
categories. Great premium is placed on leadership skills, innovations, general rather
than firm-specific skills, and all experiences
and competencies that would be applied to a
variety of situations. We help individual
after individual come up with the language

that allows them to emphasize general employability rather than specific employment. Although we don't name the process as such, the effect is that we all participate in devaluing and degrading members' past work contributions and histories. Each person has to disassemble his or her own history and repackage it to increase marketability in an economy with transformed institutions and norms. In other words, uncertainty and insecurity force them to rewrite the *representation* of the self, to jettison pieces that may handicap them in the job market, to erase some skills, experiences, and competencies while coming up with new categories to capture their strengths and contributions.

Participants are encouraged to downplay or erase numbers when it comes to years of employment, but at the same time they are encouraged to deploy numbers that underscore their readiness, creativity, and initiative. In reconstructing themselves as multitalented individuals who are ready and willing to take on any challenge future employers might present to them, to display themselves as people who are bold and forward-thinking enough to introduce innovations and change, EU students also add what I call "mythical statistics" to their package of "assets." In a process I call "strategic quantification" students throw around mythical statistics—memorable sound bites—easily and frequently, both in the resume and in their Thirty-Second Mes. The statistics are socially constructed and fantastic, yet consistent enough with common parlance about business practices that they don't initially raise an eyebrow. These statistics, as I ponder them, seem to me to defy reconstruction or validation by any outside party. Indeed, some of the measures seem to defy quantification, period. Ironically, as one interviewee noted, by quantifying their achievements, EU participants are commodifying themselves.

At one general meeting three women deliver their Thirty-Second Mes, announcing, respectively, that they had "improved customer satisfaction rates by 700 percent," "improved customer satisfaction rates by 250 percent," and "supervised five thousand people." In all three cases the statistics are cited without reference to a specific job, employer, or industry. A fourth woman calls attention to the fact that she had "improved sales in her previous job by 3,000 percent," while one man had "handled a five-million-dollar purchase order." A man who had been in management for a fast-food chain claims to have been responsible for "twenty-five thousand dollars savings per fast-food unit."

Others offer not statistics but less obvious, difficult-to-pin-down achievements such as "decreasing the number of lawsuits brought against my company," "saving my company thousands of dollars in insurance costs," and "minimizing waste levels in my company unit." Such statements of accomplishment are not fabrications, but the result of complex and creative calculations deemed desirable and appropriate in EU philosophy. Organizational literature about preparing general yet impressive summaries of skills and experiences encourage [s] this approach, offering up boilerplate examples such as "Supervised branch staff of sixteen on work performance, goal setting, and success measurement, reducing turnover by 20 percent and improving productivity by 8 percent," or "Maintained overview of projects identifying and correcting problems at early stage of development, ensuring on-schedule completion."

This overly general approach to the reconstruction of the individual can be problematic and painful to the individuals involved. In his Thirty-Second Me, an African American man describes himself as an architect who specializes in "management and city building," and works with "multimillion-dollar projects." In the evaluation session that follows his presentation, we struggle to figure out what he actually had done or could do, because the language in his self-description is so broad. The goal is to help him figure out a way to make his accomplishments more concrete so he can present himself more effectively. We fear that he is doing himself a disservice by claiming expertise that is so broadly formulated as to be indecipherable. Increasingly distressed by the pressure, he rephrases, saying he is a "city builder, a team player." He finally refuses to talk, asking fellow participants to back off, saying that "this just isn't the time" to try to pin all this down. The stress level in the group is pretty high at that moment.

Piecing together a Thirty-Second Me isn't always this excruciating, but the more typical efforts to script one do reflect a struggle to find the magical wording that will enable an individual to say the right thing at precisely the right moment. "Perfect" is a Thirty-Second Me that includes buzz words of the new economy and that also conveys some general information about one's skills. This, however, is a difficult balance to maintain. Marianne's struggle to reframe herself compellingly, for example, came out when I asked her what kind of job she was looking for, how specific, how general, and what kind of work she desired. Her answer—which touches on some "hot" areas of expertise such as total quality management, training, and education—is extremely vague, to the point where it is difficult to discern a specific field she has worked in or position that she desires. It illustrates the difficulty of packaging oneself as the multivalent, all-purpose person who can step into any situation but preferably into one that is consistent with her own aspirations.

> I'm concentrating more on teaching and training positions. This is where my Thirty-Second Me comes in. What I'm trying to do is identify a training position, preferably in a large corporation, where I can utilize my communication skills and my teaching abilities, my educational experiences, my management background. And what I want to do is train in management-oriented issues. Because of my experience in total quality management [she had received a certificate in total quality management at her local community college—V.S.], I have a real interest there in using quality tools to try to make the workplace better. And so that's really an interest of mine.

In an interview Anthony, the former nuclear engineer, touched on why it was so difficult to buy into the mechanisms for rewriting one's occupational self in the ways that facilitators were prescribing. For him, retooling, transitioning, and transforming himself into a more broadly marketable person had been difficult. He believed that the essential facts of who he was as a professional were indisputable, not general stories that could be easily manipulated, with plots that he could just change and embellish depending on the audience. As he noted,

> Probably in about one-third of my interviews, I get a question like, "Why does a nuclear engineer want to work for Packard Bell? Or Hewlett Packard?" That's their first question, because when they look at my resume there's one line that says MBA. Then there's three-quarters of my resume that says "Nuclear Engineer." That's the way they see me . . . that's the hurdle I have to get over in the beginning, to prove that I'm not just a nuclear engineer. I have an MBA. So that's the first hurdle I have to clear.

Anthony's point highlights how important it is to have institutional connections prior to retooling and recrafting oneself. An individual can have the most reasonable, even rational goal—to obtain an MBA, in Anthony's case, or, in the case of another man, a credential in professional meeting and conference planning—but if one does not have connections to the people and the organizations where one gets hands-on experience, a degree or credential doesn't automatically open the doors to getting a job. Neither individual had, at the time of our interview, found a job in his desired field.

Madeline Cox, whom I quoted at the outset of this book, detested the advice to reduce her work life to one dimension, to sound bites and snippets. For her, who she was as a professional consisted of much more than statistics about productivity achievements or cost savings, and vastly more than what she contributed to the world when she was "on the job." Her objections are interesting because she doesn't challenge the organizational rhetoric of a "Me" or the concept of repackaging oneself for future employers, but nevertheless talked about pushing the boundaries to present a more well-rounded, multi-dimensional "Me." She argued,

> We need to broaden a Thirty-Second to a Sixty-Second Me. And not only do you need a *work* Thirty-Second Me, you need a *personal life* Thirty-Second Me. You know, we're many facets, and if you can learn how to pull out and talk about yours, about the appropriate qualifications for whatever it is you're doing, it's gonna make your Thirty-Second Me that much better to any employer.

> You know, it's ok to try to tailor yourself quickly on your feet and to get comfortable at that takes practice. But we need to be able to incorporate even the personal side of things, where you bring in your church and your community groups and, you know, some of your social activities, and volunteer work. . . .

I would like to see it that we get people to think about all these things.

Her criticism of the process of occupational transformation went even further. She was advised to package herself as someone with general skills and interests, yet her bachelor's degree was in environmental science; she had spent her career working in this field in the private sector, and she desperately wanted to stay in the field. Put simply, she loved her work. She didn't want to reinvent herself: she wanted a job in hazardous waste management and rarely found job announcements for such positions. Facilitators in her workshops had advised her to think and plan more broadly, but it was difficult for her to make the leap, in her mind and in her repackaged self. "Part of what I'm havin' trouble with is, 'Well, if I do have to leave the environmental field, what do I call what I want? How do I package me?' Everybody just says, 'Geez, your skills are so great.' Well, if they're so great, how come I don't have a job?" Mike Daly, in contrast, *did* resist the notion of packaging and marketing the self, saying it was his belief that "it is contrary to human nature for many of us to sell ourselves."

———

Be Instrumental and Attentive at All Times: Working on Self-presentation. The unemployed at EU try to maximize their options by working on formal and scriptable venues such as the resume and the Thirty-Second Me. Increasing the pressure to seize any and all opportunities, organizational literature and workshop facilitators also exhort the unemployed to be prepared for all informal, unscriptable, spontaneous encounters as well. There are many points in everyday life and in the job search process during which an unemployed manager or professional has a chance to present him or herself in the best possible light to someone who might offer him or her a job. Part of EU's mission is to educate participants about such events and occurrences and to raise their sensitivity about all situations where they might unknowingly be auditioning for a job. Members are expected to map out a systematic search strategy for themselves, but they are encouraged at the same time to rationalize casual and leisure time: to poise themselves to jump on unanticipated opportunities, to be constantly vigilant, to view any social situation or relationship as possibly consequential for their career outcomes, and to never drop their regimen of looking for work. The core elements of this philosophy mirror the emphasis on flexibility, adaptability, and unpredictability that workers *with* jobs face to an increasing degree. But in Panopticonic fashion, EU participants anticipate that the gaze of future employers can fall on them at any time, demanding constant self-discipline.

For the unemployed, time when they might ordinarily be able to relax from the pressures of job hunting becomes time where every second contains the possibility for scrutiny, observation, and evaluation. In out job workshop, in a module on "cold-call networking," we are encouraged by the workshop literature to:

> Seek every opportunity to meet people. Don't wait until you actually walk into the meeting room to begin networking. If you arrive at the meeting place by car and notice a group of women in the parking lot, take the opportunity to strike up a conversation. "Are you going to the women's network meeting? Did you run into that traffic on the freeway?" *Whether you are in the elevator, the ladies room, or waiting at the bar, start talking.* [Emphasis in the original—V. S.]

Thus, personal time, regarded as casual and unrationalized, should be saturated with continual sensitivity to unpredictable labor-market patterns and dynamics. This advice also points to the belief in a "hidden market," the notion that most professional jobs aren't obtained as a result of reading and pursuing advertisements in the newspaper or in announcements sent to EU but through connections, networks, or random occurrences. In this hidden job terrain, EU facilitators claim, it is possible for the unemployed to create their own jobs, to present themselves as people capable of identifying a need and a niche in a company, and to persuade the employer that they are indispensable. Despite the many structural causes of professional and managerial unemployment and displacement, all these "tips" about how the hidden job market works put the responsibility for success and failure soundly on the shoulders of each unemployed individual. Being poised and ready calls for individual strategic attentiveness at all times.

Two examples illustrate how central this point is to the everyday rhetoric of EU. First, a recurrent narrative, espoused in both the general meetings and in the workshops of the introductory training week, highlights the need to be prepared by way of negative examples demonstrating the consequences of *not* always being prepared. Significant because it provides a vivid contrast to the mental stance EU members are encouraged to cultivate, the narrative of the "lazy unemployed" is evoked on many occasions, each time containing nearly exactly the same "plot elements."

Karen frequently congratulates attendees for "getting out of the house," not falling back into the "pity pit" and isolating themselves in the privacy of home. According to her, attendees need to do all they can at all times to take action, follow leads, engage in impression management, and be opportunistic in unforeseen encounters. Who knows when one might be asked to come for a job interview in thirty minutes, or just spontaneously accept an invitation to step into someone's office for an informal interview? If a person is not ready at all times to leap into action or isn't dressed professionally or hasn't adopted the professional mind-set, they simply aren't going to be able to roll with the rapid and unpredictable punches that life in the world of employment could deal them.

Karen and others hold up the scenario of the "lazy unemployed" to reinforce this view. Details of this stereotypical individual vary slightly from telling to telling, but certain core elements are consistent. A lazy unemployed person is someone who isn't on the alert, isn't constantly in the job search mode. We would find this person slouched on a couch at home, drinking Pepsi or beer, watching television with the volume blasting, whether it's soap operas or football games. He or she is always dressed in worn, tattered T-shirts or oversized sweatshirts. The women lack makeup and well-tended hairstyles, and the men sport hair on their faces, evidence not of beards but of failure to shave. Everyone has put on extra pounds as a result of their slovenliness. No matter the gender of the unemployed, undisciplined children run screaming in the background, signaling to anyone who calls that they've contacted a highly unprofessional environment. To top it off, the guilty individual can never find his or her appointment book to schedule possible appointments. This individual, according to organizational lore, stands little chance of being viewed positively by employers and would not be able to compete with others who can drop things in an instant and who can, given the opportunity, change their plans without batting an eye.

A milder example sees the unemployed individual as being more professional but still lacking the attentiveness to ubiquitous opportunities. Marvin, a leader, recites the purportedly true story of Ray. Ray drove to an appointment for a job interview. Arriving early, he parked his dirty, messy car right in front of the building where the interview

was to take place. As he approached a man leaning against the front of the building, Ray asked him if he had a light for his cigarette. The man replied negatively; Ray asked one or two other people entering the building if they had a light, finally finding one, smoking his cigarette, and entering for his appointment. He discovered that the interviewer was the first man be had asked for a light, the same man who had witnessed the condition of Ray's car, and seen Ray indiscriminately halting people in his search for a good smoke. The leader asks the workshop participants: When did Ray's interview start? Because we've been following the facilitators' logic about the ubiquity of opportunity the point is obvious to all of us: it started when Ray drove into the parking lot. The message to participants is: never relax, never assume you are unobserved, and never take for granted—moreover, take control of—any social interaction.

————

Don't let your bitterness and frustration defeat you: emotion work of the unemployed.

> Body language! When shaking hands, offer a firm handshake. Erect posture shows confidence. Sit down only after offered a chair. Lean forward in your chair and relax. Do not fidget.

> Enthusiasm! Bring a positive attitude into the interview without being too familiar. Avoid being negative. Find something you like about the interviewer. Sell yourself. Remember, the difference between bragging and self-confidence is enthusiasm.

While conducting the work of finding a job, EU members have to hold themselves together mentally and emotionally. Facilitators call on participants to self-consciously perform emotion work on themselves in order to leave unemployment, with its angst and its financial insecurity behind. Yet the unemployed find it difficult to uphold these principles when they are awash in uncertainty and anxiety about employment futures. When Karen speaks of "the pity pit," she names what many members fear: that their negative attitudes can hold them back from improving their situations. People in workshops and in in-depth interviews express their fear that their own negative frame of mind has the power to hex their job search or block their ability to present themselves as a desirable potential employee. Participants fear sabotaging themselves and continually talk about suppressing their fear and anger, trying to remain emotionally detached from the labor-market turbulence surrounding them.

Esther, an African American woman who lost her job as a supervisor in the banking industry, remarked, over and over in our interview, how much she feared blocking herself because of her anxiety. Esther was emotionally scarred from the institutional and technological transformations that had buffeted her. Over the course of twenty years Esther has been steadily pushed out of her work, supervising backroom production operations for various banks, as a result of corporate centralization and automation. Unemployed at the time of her interview, she had sold her house and had had to rely on some money from her son: "I'm looking around and now I'm scared. I can't figure out what's going on. For the salary I'm used to, people have degrees. I'm a dinosaur now. My type of position doesn't exist anymore. Business is changing; it keeps shrinking and places keep getting bigger. And so, for instance, there used to be perhaps a hundred places in the state that did what I did, like, twenty years ago . . . now, there's maybe ten."

She claimed that she did active work on her attitude to maintain a positive mental outlook on her situation. It was as if she believed that she had to quash her anger or it would follow her through her interviews, contaminating her presentation of self.

> I've had to work so hard at not being bitter and hateful. There's so many people at work who are. I wanted to make sure I had my act together because nobody will hire somebody who's bitter or hateful or anything. So I decided, well, I'm going to see a therapist to make sure I keep balanced on this.
>
> I mean, how can I get a job if I go to an interview and I'm bitter about my last company and I'm scared of my future? I mean, how could I get a job based on who I am? Because no matter what your qualifications are, hiring managers still go by personality, gut feelings about who you are. Whether you are going to be a match or not.

Anthony, who had a fairly realistic understanding of the difficulty of repositioning himself with his MBA in the business world after working many years as a nuclear engineer, actively worked to change his inner sense of who and what he was. He would visualize himself in the role of a business manager rather than in the role of nuclear engineer. His visualization work hadn't yet yielded any gains, and he feared that he hadn't sufficiently aligned his image of his old self—nuclear engineer—with his new skills and capacities. His own analysis was: "I don't want anyone to think that I'm just a nuclear engineer. That's probably what's holding me back."

One woman stressed that she experienced "two kinds of hard" in her current circumstances, explaining that she tackled them at two levels. One was what she called the "technical" part, knowing where and how to look for a job, learning how to maximize personal connections, and how to put on the best professional face. The other, though, was the "personal hard," the emotional labor of simply maintaining oneself, day in and day out, feeling humiliated at one level but participating in an organization where, in the public presentation of self, expressions of humiliation and anger were not tolerated. She felt challenged, in particular, by the work that she had to do on her confidence when interacting with her EU peers.

> The thing that is personally hard for me is I actually know that though I have some inventiveness about me and I've done well within my field or within my skill level or accomplishment level, at SPN I meet people who are more qualified than me. And sometimes I find myself almost marketing myself almost as if I'm as capable or experienced as them. And underneath I feel kind of a little embarrassed or ashamed. The hard part comes when I give my Thirty-Second Me in the class and I see other people and they're basically sizing me up. It's a little humbling, it hurts a little.

Emotion work has limits, however. At many points, participants are unable to maintain the positive attitude "necessary" for playing by the rules of the organization. The tension in their situations pops up for the facilitators, the unemployed who promulgate the culture and the activities of EU. While facilitators and leaders teach new members and lead workshops, they must often grapple with their own distress and ambivalence. Mike designed and regularly offers a successful, well-attended workshop on improving self-esteem while searching for a job: "This was a problem for me. I developed the curriculum for this particular class, and I'm really an inappropriate person to do that because my esteem right now is as low as it could possibly get because of the experiences that I've had. They want me to teach it again and I came up with an excuse why I couldn't do it. I just can't do it anymore." Nevertheless, other members were eager to step in and take over the workshop.

Conclusion

Stay vigilant and alert, relinquish the trappings of the traditional employment model, transform oneself into the flexible professional employee of the turbulent economy, and maintain a modicum of control under unpredictable circumstances. These messages constituted the optimistic perspective imparted by the EU curriculum and rhetoric to empower its unemployed participants. Yet it was impossible to shield the unemployed from the intractable contradictions of their situations or from their fundamental disempowerment. A "scientifically based" job search rarely allows anyone to maintain the kind of control they are desperate to gain. Members were advised to keep their cars clean and well-maintained, because a person with the power to hire them might observe their vehicles and pass judgment accordingly. But their cars were funky because they lacked the money to repair and clean them or to buy a more updated model. Members were to wear tasteful, pressed, professional clothes and avoid wearing clothes that were frayed or out-of-fashion. Yet often they lacked the money to purchase, dry-clean, and otherwise maintain clothes, rarely a problem when they held a job. They were to produce high-quality resumes and should send them out by the hundreds, but producing such resumes (particularly producing multiple versions) and mailing them out in such high volume was often unaffordable.

If given an opportunity for a job interview, an EU member was encouraged to approach it as a fifty-fifty partnership. Don't let the interviewer take the upper hand; exploit the interview as a time where you, the interviewee, can obtain information about the company; act as though you, the interviewee, are going to the interview to let the potential hirer *persuade you* that their company is a place you would like to work. The interviewee should control his or her body language, avoid slumping or giving off any signals of desperation. But many EU participants were worn down and found it difficult to hold back from employers their genuine desire for the job. They also would accept a reasonable job offer in a heartbeat and feared playing the negotiating game because they didn't want the interviewer to call their bluff.

Such elements of a positive mental framework resonated only weakly with the people I observed in workshops and with whom I spoke at length in interviews. The rules of the new economy have changed, and they felt they had little choice but to go along with advice and strategies that presented at least some alternative for improving their circumstances. At the same time, as previous quotes have illustrated, EU members did not engage in occupational reconstruction uncritically. Throughout this chapter we heard of different participants doing what they could to successfully reposition themselves, all the while resenting employers for changing the rules, regretting the loss of a more stable occupational base, and fearing an unpredictable future. . . .

Ironically, this whole process can also be a time for personal reflection that leads to new ways of thinking about what one really wants from work. I conclude with the comments of a white woman named Caroline, who was trained and had experience working in the field as a geologist. After traveling around the United States to follow different jobs in the private sector, Caroline had settled in Sacramento with her husband but had been unable to find a job in her field. Few jobs were posted, and her interviews had not netted her any offers of a regular job. She had, instead, held several temporary clerical jobs. When I asked her about her dream job, I was struck by the fact that she didn't mention a particular industry or occupation. Although during "public" sessions at EU members usually refrained from citing

specific positions, firms, or industries they hope to work in, in private interviewees usually "confessed" to highly specific situations they were seeking. In contrast, Caroline lists the qualities of work and employment that appeal to her so much in comparison to the temp jobs she's been able to find:

> Well, it would probably be like a twenty- to thirty-hour work week with the state. I really like the idea of not having to worry about marketing myself and chasing down work all the time. I like the idea of being involved with projects where you're involved with them from when you start until it's over. Once there, when you're there, you're the one involved with the final decision. Has enough work been done? Is the outcome good enough? So you're part of a team. You're part of making those decisions.

Being valued for your skills, not your success in packaging yourself; being involved in work holistically, seeing projects through from beginning to end; working with others collaboratively—such are the characteristics of jobs, both finding one and keeping one, that many people at the turn of the century would view as ideal.

NOTES

1. Unless otherwise noted, all quotations from printed material are from documents prepared by EU participants, for the in-house use of members only. That is, they are original organizational artifacts. Much of the material was written several years before I appeared on the scene and was faithfully used as a set of guidelines for new members. I have assigned pseudonyms to all the members, including the one paid staff member, that I discuss and quote.

2. Of the seventeen people in my interview sample, nine were women and eight were men. Three were people of color (two African Americans and one Hispanic).

▨▨▨ **TECHNOLOGY AND FLEXIBILITY ON THE JOB** ▨▨▨

ↂ **READING 11** ↂ

In the Age of the Smart Machine

Shoshana Zuboff

Without a doubt, the part of mankind which has advanced intellectually is quite under the spell of technology. Its charms are twofold. On the one hand, there is the enticement of increasingly comfortable living standards; on the other, there is a reduction in the amount of work which is necessary to do. . . . The irresistible pull toward technological development . . . is caused, we should remember, by the unconscious and deep-rooted desire to free ourselves from the material oppression of the material world.

—Folkert Wilken, *The Liberation of Capital*

The Body's Virtuosity at Work

In the older pulp and paper mills of Piney Wood and Tiger Creek, where a highly experienced work force was making the transition to a new computer-based technology, operators had many ways of using their bodies to achieve precise knowledge. One man judged the condition of paper coming off a dry roller by the sensitivity of his hair to electricity in the atmosphere around the machine. Another could judge the moisture content of a roll of pulp by a quick slap of his hand. Immediacy was the mode in which things were known; it provided a feeling of certainty, of knowing "what's going on." One worker in Piney Wood described how it felt to be removed from the physical presence of the process equipment and asked to

Excerpts from *In the Age of the Smart Machine: The Future of Work and Power,* by Shoshana Zuboff. Copyright © 1988 by BasicBooks, Inc. Reprinted by permission of BasicBooks, a division of Perseus Books, LLC.

perform his tasks from a computerized control room:

> It is very different now. . . . It is hard to get used to not being out there with the process. I miss it a lot. I miss being able to see it. You can see when the pulp runs over a vat. You know what's happening.

The worker's capacity "to know" has been lodged in sentience and displayed in action. The physical presence of the process equipment has been the setting that corresponded to this knowledge, which could, in turn, be displayed only in that context. As long as the action context remained intact, it was possible for knowledge to remain implicit. In this sense, the worker knew a great deal, but very little of that knowledge was ever articulated, written down, or made explicit in any fashion. Instead, operators went about their business, displaying their know-how and rarely attempting to translate that knowledge into terms that were publicly accessible. This is what managers mean when they speak of the "art" involved in operating these plants. As one manager at Piney Wood described it:

> There are a lot of operators working here who cannot verbally give a description of some piece of the process. I can ask them what is going on at the far end of the plant, and they can't tell me, but they can draw it for me. By taking away this physical contact that he understands, it's like we have taken away his blueprint. He can't verbalize his way around the process.

In this regard, the pulp and paper mills embody a historical sweep that is unavailable in many other forms of work. Unlike other continuous-process industries, such as oil refining or chemical production, the pulp-and-paper-making process has not yet yielded a full scientific explication. This has retarded the spread of automation and also has worked to preserve the integrity of a certain amount of craft know-how among those operators with lengthy experience in the industry. Like other continuous-process operations, the technological environment in these mills has created work that was more mediated by equipment and dependent upon indirect data than, say, work on an assembly line. However, discrete instrumentation typically was located on or close to the actual operating equipment, allowing the operator to combine data from an instrument reading with data from his or her own senses. Most workers believed that they "knew" what was going on at any particular moment because of what they saw and felt, and they used past experience to relate these perceptions to a set of likely consequences. The required sequences and routines necessary to control certain parts of the process and to make proper adjustments for achieving the best results represented a form of knowledge that the worker displayed in action as a continual reflection of this sentient involvement. Acquired experience made it possible to relate current conditions to

past events; thus, an operator's competence increased as the passing of time enabled him or her to experience the action possibilities of a wide variety of operating conditions.

In Piney Wood and Tiger Creek, the technology change did not mean simply trading one form of instrumentation for another. Because the traditional basis of competence, like skilled work in most industries, was still heavily dependent upon sentient involvement, information technology was experienced as a radical departure from the taken-for-granted approach to daily work. In this sense, workers' experiences in these mills bridge two manufacturing domains. They not only illustrate the next phase of technological change within the continuous-process industries but also foreshadow the dilemmas that will emerge in other industrial organizations (for example, batch and assembly-line production) with the transition from machine to computer mediation.

When a process engineer attempts to construct a set of algorithms that will be the basis for automating some portion of the production process, he or she first interviews those individuals who currently perform the tasks that will be automated. The process engineer must learn the detail of their actions in order to translate their practice into the terms of a mathematical model. The algorithms in such a model explicate, rationalize, and institutionalize know-how. In the course of these interviews, the process engineer is likely to run up against the limits of implicit knowledge. A worker may perform competently yet be unable to communicate the structure of his or her actions. As one engineer discovered:

> There are operators who can run the paper machine with tremendous efficiency, but they cannot describe to you how they do it. They have built-in actions and senses that they are not aware of. One operation required pulling two

levers simultaneously, and they were not conscious of the fact that they were pulling two levers. They said they were pulling one. The operators run the mill, but they don't understand how. There are operators who know exactly what to do, but they cannot tell you how they do it.

Though every operator with similar responsibilities performs the same functions, each will perform them in a unique way, fashioned according to a personal interpretation of what works best. A process engineer contrasted the personal rendering of skill with the impersonal but consistently optimal performance of the computer:

> There is no question that the computer takes the human factor out of running the machine. Each new person who comes on shift will make their own distinct changes, according to their sense of what is the best setting. In contrast, the computer runs exactly the same way all the time. Each operator thinks he does a better job, each one thinks he has a better intimate understanding of the equipment than another operator. But none of them can compete with the computer.

These comments describe a particular quality of skill that I refer to as *action-centered*. Four components of action-centered skill are highlighted in the experiences of these workers:

1. *Sentience.* Action-centered skill is based upon sentient information derived from physical cues.
2. *Action-dependence.* Action-centered skill is developed in physical performance. Although in principle it may be made explicit in language, it typically remains unexplicated—implicit in action.
3. *Context-dependence.* Action-centered skill only has meaning within the context in which its associated physical activities can occur.

4. *Personalism.* It is the individual body that takes in the situation and an individual's actions that display the required competence. There is a felt linkage between the knower and the known. The implicit quality of knowledge provides it with a sense of interiority, much like physical experience.

The Dissociation of Sentience and Knowledge

Computerization brings about an essential change in the way the worker can know the world and, with it, a crisis of confidence in the possibility of certain knowledge. For the workers of Piney Wood and Tiger Creek, achieving a sense of knowing the world was rarely problematical in their conventional environments. Certain knowledge was conveyed through the immediacy of their sensory experience. Instead of Descartes's "I think, therefore I am," these workers might say, "I see, I touch, I smell, I hear; therefore, I know." Their capacity to trust their knowledge was reflected in the assumption of its validity. In the precomputerized environment, belief was a seamless extension of sensory experience.

As the medium of knowing was transformed by computerization, the placid unity of experience and knowledge was disturbed. Accomplishing work depended upon the ability to manipulate symbolic, electronically presented data. Instead of using their bodies as instruments of *acting-on* equipment and materials, the task relationship became mediated by the information system. Operators had to work through the medium of what I will call the "data interface," represented most visibly by the computer terminals they monitored from central control rooms. The workers in this transition were at first overwhelmed with the feeling that they could no longer see or touch their work, as if it has been made both invisible and intangible by computer mediation.

> It's just different getting this information in the control room. The man in here can't see. Out there you can look around until you find something.

> The chlorine has overflowed, and it's all over the third floor. You see, this is what I mean . . . it's all over the floor, but you can't see it. You have to remember how to get into the system to do something about it. Before you could see it and you knew what was happening—you just knew.

> The hardest thing for us operators is not to have the physical part. I can chew pulp and tell you its physical properties. We knew things from experience. Now we have to try and figure out what is happening. The hardest part is to give up that physical control.

In a world in which skills were honed over long years of physical experience, work was associated with concrete objects and the cues they provided. A worker's sense of occupational identity was deeply marked by his or her understanding of and attachment to discrete tangible entities, such as a piece of operating equipment. Years of service meant continued opportunities to master new objects. It was the immediate knowledge one could gain of these tangible objects that engendered feelings of competence and control. For workers, the new computer-mediated relationship to work often felt like being yanked away from a world that could be known because it could be sensed.

> Our operators did their job by feeling a pipe— "Is it hot?" We can't just tell them it's 150 degrees. They have to believe it.

> With computerization I am further away from my job than I have ever been before. I used to listen to the sounds the boiler makes and know just how it was running. I could look at the fire in the furnace and tell by its color how it was burning. I knew what kinds of adjustments were needed by the shades of color I saw. A lot of the men also said that there were smells that told you different things about how it was running. I feel uncomfortable being away from these sights and smells. Now I only have numbers to go by. I am scared of that boiler, and I feel that I should be closer to it in order to control it.

It is as if one's job had vanished into a two-dimensional space of abstractions, where digital symbols replace a concrete reality. Workers reiterated a spontaneous emotional response countless times—defined by feelings of loss of control, of vulnerability, and of frustration. It was sharpened with a sense of crisis and a need for steeling oneself with courage and not a little adrenaline in order to meet the challenge. It was shot through with the bewilderment of a man suddenly blind, groping with his hands outstretched in a vast, unfamiliar space. "We are in uncharted water now," they said. "We have to control our operations blind." This oft-repeated metaphor spoke of being robbed of one's senses and plunged into darkness. The tangible world had always been thick with landmarks; it was difficult to cast off from these familiar moorings with only abstractions as guides.

One operator described learning to work with the new computer system in Tiger Creek's pulping area. "The difficulty," he said, "is not being able to touch things." As he spoke, his hands shot out before him and he wiggled all his fingers, as if to emphasize the sense of incompleteness and loss. He continued:

> When I go out and touch something, I know what will happen. There is a fear of not being out on the floor watching things. It is like turning your back in a

dark alley. You don't know what is behind you; you don't know what might be happening. It all becomes remote from you, and it makes you feel vulnerable. It was like being a new operator all over again. Today I push buttons instead of opening valves on the digester. If I push the wrong button, will I screw up? Will anything happen?

Many other descriptions conveyed a similar feeling:

With the change to the computer it's like driving down the highway with your lights out and someone else pushing the accelerator.

It's like flying an airplane and taking all the instruments out so you can't see. It's like if you had an airplane and you put pieces over each instrument to hide it. Then, if something went wrong, you have to uncover the right one in a split second.

Doing my job through the computer, it feels different. It is like you are riding a big, powerful horse, but someone is sitting behind you on the saddle holding the reins, and you just have to be on that ride and hold on. You see what is coming, but you can't do anything to control it. You can't steer yourself left and right; you can't control that horse that you are on. You have got to do whatever the guy behind you holding the reins wants you to do. Well, I would rather be holding the reins than have someone behind me holding the reins.

The feeling of being in control and the willingness to be held accountable require a reservoir of critical judgment with which to initiate informed action. In the past, operators like those at Piney Wood derived their critical judgment from their "gut feel" of the production process. Becoming a "good" operator—the kind that workers and managers alike refer to as an "artist" and invest with the authority of expertise—required the years of experience to develop a finely nuanced, felt sense of the equipment, the product, and the overall process. With computerization, many managers acknowledged that operators had lost their ability "to feel the machine." Without considering the new skill implications of this loss, many managers feared it would eliminate the kind of critical judgment that would have allowed operators to take action based upon an understanding that reached beyond the computer system.

Piney Wood's plant manager, as he presided over the massive technology conversion, asked himself what the loss of such art might mean:

In the digester area, we used to have guys doing it who had an art. After we put the computer in, when they went down we could go to manual backup. People remembered how to run the digesters. Now if we try to go back, they can't remember what to do. They have lost the feel for it. We are really stuck now without the computer; we can't successfully operate that unit without it. If you are watching a screen, do you see the same things you would if you were there, face-to-face with the process and the equipment? I am concerned we are losing the art and skills that are not replenishable.

There were many operators who agreed. In one area of Piney Wood, the crew leader explained it this way:

The new people are not going to understand, see, or feel as well as the old guys. Something is wrong with this fan, for example. You may not know what; you just feel it in your feet. The sound, the tone, the volume, the vibrations . . . the computer will control it, but you will have lost something, too. It's a trade-off. The computer can't feel what is going on out there. The new operators will need to have more written down, because they will not know it in their guts. I can't understand how new people coming in are ever going to learn how to run a pulp mill. They are not going to know what is going on. They will only learn what these computers tell them.

Sam Gimbel was a young production co-ordinator in Piney Wood. Though trained as a chemical engineer, he had been particularly close to the operators whom he managed. He had shepherded them through the technology conversion and construction of the new control room, and worked closely with them as they grappled with new ways of operating:

> We are losing the context where hands-on experience makes sense. If you don't have actual experience, you have to believe everything the computer says, and you can't beat it at its own game. You can't stand up to it. And yet who will have the experience to make these kinds of judgments? It will surely be a different world. You lose the checkpoints in reality to know if you are doing it right; therefore, how will anyone be able to confront the computer information?

Piney Wood's management had approached the technology conversion with the following message: "We are simply providing you with new tools to do your job. Your job is to operate the equipment, and this is a new tool to operate the equipment with." Managers repeatedly made statements such as, "We told them this was a tool just like a hammer or a wrench." One manager even went so far as to say, "We hoped they wouldn't figure out that the terminal we were giving them was really a computer."

As experience with the new operating conditions began to accumulate, many managers began to see that treating the computer system like a physical object, "just another tool," could lead to chronic suboptimization of the technology's potential. A power house worker with over twenty-five years of experience had developed a special way of kicking the boiler in order to make it function smoothly. He used the same approach with the terminal; if he hit a certain button on the keyboard, a particular reading would change in the desired direction, but he did not know why or how. Piney Wood's powerhouse manager put it this way:

> The guy who kicks the boiler is the same guy who mashes the button a certain way just to make the line go down. This person will never optimize the process. He will use too much chemical and too high pressure. He will never make you money because he doesn't understand the problem.

Just as the digester operators had lost their ability to cook manually, other workers throughout the mill felt equally powerless:

> In the old way, you had control over the job. The computer now tells you what to do. There is more responsibility but less control. We lost a boiler that was on computer control. We just had to sit there and stare. We were all shook up.

> Sometimes I am amazed when I realize that we stare at the screen even when it has gone down. You get in the habit and you just keep staring even if there is nothing there.

Ironically, as managers and operators across the mill watched the level of artistry decline, the senior technical designers continued to assume that manual skills would provide the necessary backup to their systems.

The problem was even more acute in Cedar Bluff, where most of the work force lacked the experience base from which felt sense and critical judgment are developed.

Managers at Cedar Bluff engaged in a quiet debate as to how much of a problem this lack of experience would ultimately be. On one side of the argument were the "old-timers"—managers with years of experience in the industry:

> I like to smell and feel the pulp sometimes. It can be slick, it can be slimy, it can be all different consistencies. These are the artistic aspects of making pulp that the computer doesn't know about. Some of the operators have been picking up these aspects, but there are so many numbers so readily accessible, we have to shortcut it at times and solve more problems from the office. The information is so good and rapid we have to use it. . . . You have got to be able to recognize when you can run things from the office and when you have to go and look. Yet, I recognize that I am not as good a pulp maker as the people who trained me, and the new operators are not as good as I am. They are better managers and planners. I am very happy with the new managers, but not with the new pulp makers.

The younger engineers, schooled in computer-based analytic techniques, had little patience with anxious laments over the loss of the art of pulp making. They were relentlessly confident that a good computer model could reproduce anything that operators knew from experience—only better. Here is how the process engineers articulated the argument:

> Computer analysis lets us see the effects of many variables and their interactions. This is a picture of truth that we could not have achieved before. It is superior to the experience-based knowledge of an operator. You might say that truth replaces knowledge.

> People who have this analytic power do not need to have been around to know

what is going on. All you need is to be able to formulate a model and perform the necessary confirmation checks. With the right model you can manage the system just fine.

Most Cedar Bluff managers agreed that the computer system made it possible to do a better job running the plant with an inexperienced work force than otherwise would have been possible, though some wondered whether the levels of expertise would ever be as high as among workers with hands-on exposure to the pulping process. Yet even as managers argued over the essentiality of action-centered skill, technology was irreversibly altering the context in which the operators performed. The opportunities to develop such skills were becoming increasingly rare as the action context was paved over by the data highway.

Many of Cedar Bluff's managers believed that the traditional knowledge of the pulp mill worker would actually inhibit the development of creativity and flexibility. Under the new technological conditions, the young operators would develop their capacity to "know better" than the systems with which they worked as they struggled with the complexities of the new technology and the data it provided. The data interface would replace the physical equipment as the primary arena for learning.

Yet as months passed, other managers observed a disturbing pattern of interactions between the operators and the computer system. Some believed that the highly computerized task environment resulted in a greater than usual bifurcation of skills. One group of operators would use the information systems to learn an extraordinary amount about the process, while another group would make itself an appendage to the system, mechanically carrying out the computer's directives. These managers complained that the computer system was becoming a crutch that prevented many operators from developing a superior knowledge of the process. One "old-timer" provided an example:

> When there is a shift change and new operators come on, the good operator will take the process from the computer, put it on manual, make certain changes that the operator thinks are necessary, and then give it back to the computer. The average operator will come in, see this thing on automatic control, and leave it with the computer. Sometimes that operator won't even realize that things are getting bad or getting worse. They should have known better, but they didn't.

Most Cedar Bluff operators spoke enthusiastically about the convenience of the computer interface, and some freely admitted what they perceived to be a dependence on the computer system:

> The computer provides your hands. I don't think I could work in a conventional mill. This is so much more convenient. You have so much control without having to go out to the equipment and adjust things.

> We can't run this mill manually. There are too many controls, and it is too complex. The average person can only run four or five variables at once in a manual mode, and the automatic system runs it all. If the computer goes down, we have to sit back and wait. We sit and we stare at the screens and we hope something pipes in.

Many managers observed with growing alarm the things that occurred when operators neither enjoyed the traditional sources of critical judgment nor had developed enough new knowledge for informed action.

> In a conventional mill, you have to go and look at the equipment because you cannot get enough data in the control room. Here, you get all the data you need. The computer becomes a substitute tool. It replaces all the sensual data instead of being an addition. We had another experience with the feedwater pumps, which supply water to the boiler to make steam. There was a power outage. Something in the computer canceled the alarm. The operator had a lot of trouble and did not look at the readout of the water level and never got an alarm. The tank ran empty, the pumps tripped. The pump finally tore up because there was no water feeding it.

> We have so much data from the computer, I find that hard drives out soft. Operators are tempted not to tour the plant. They just sit at the computer and watch for alarms. One weekend I found a tank overflowing in digesting. I went to the operator and told him, and he said, "It can't be; the computer says my level is fine." I am afraid of what happens if we trust the computer too much.

At least since the introduction of the moving assembly line in Ford's Highland Park plant, it has been second nature for managers to use technology to delimit worker discretion and, in this process, to concentrate knowledge within the managerial domain. The special dilemmas raised by information technology require managers to reconsider these assumptions. When information and control technology is used to turn the worker into "just another mechanical variable," one immediate result is the withdrawal of the worker's commitment to and accountability for the work. This lack of care requires additional managerial vigilance and leads to a need for increased automatic control. As this dynamic unfolds, it no longer seems shocking to contemplate an image of work laced with stupefaction and passivity, in which the human being is a hapless bystander at the margins of productive activity. One young operator in Cedar Bluff discussed his prior job as a bank clerk. I asked him if his two employment experiences had anything in common. "Yes," he said, "in both cases you punch the buttons and watch it happen."

As automation intensifies, information technology becomes the receptacle for larger and larger portions of the organization's operating intelligence. Algorithms become the functional equivalent of a once diffuse know-how, and the action context in which know-how can be developed and sustained vanishes. Because many managers assume that more technology means a diminished need for human operating skill, they may recognize the waning of worker know-how without becoming concerned enough to chart a different course. Left unchallenged, these systems become more potent, as they are invested with an escalating degree of authority. Technical experts temporarily serve as resources, but once their knowledge has been depleted, and converted into systematic rules for decision making, their usefulness is attenuated. The analysts and engineers, who construct programs and models, have the capacity to manipulate data and, presumably, to make discoveries. Ultimately, they will become the most important human presence to offer any counterpoint to the growing density and opacity of the automated systems.

There is an alternative, one that involves understanding this technological change as an occasion for developing a new set of skills—skills that are able to exploit the information capacity of the technology and to become a new source of critical judgment. In order to assess the likelihood of this alternative—the forces that will drive organizations in this direction and those that will impede them—we first have to understand the nature of these new skills. What can the experiences of workers in these three mills teach us about the emerging requirements for competence at the data interface?

From Action-Centered to Intellective Skill

The pulp and paper mills reveal the shift in the grounds of knowledge associated with a technology that informates. Men and women accustomed to an intimate physical association with the production process found themselves removed from the action. Now they had to know and to do based upon their ability to understand and manipulate electronic data. In Piney Wood, a $200 million investment in technology was radically altering every phase of mill life. Managers believed they were merely "upgrading" in order to modernize production and to improve productivity. Tiger Creek was undergoing a similar modernization process. In both cases, informating dynamics tended to unfold as an unintended and undermanaged consequence of these efforts. Cedar Bluff had been designed with a technological infrastructure based on integrated information and control systems. In that organization, managers were somewhat more self-conscious about using the informating capacity of the technology as the basis for developing new operating skills.

The experiences of the skilled workers in these mills provide a frame of reference for a general appraisal of the forms of knowledge that are required in an informated environment. My contention is that the skill demands that can be deciphered from their experiences have relevance for a wider range of organizational settings in both manufacturing and service sectors. Later chapters will compare the experiences of clerks and managers to those of the mill operators. This joint appraisal will help to unravel the intrinsic and the contingent aspects of change and to gauge the generalizations that follow from the dilemmas of transformation described here.

A fundamental quality of this technological transformation, as it is experienced by workers and observed by their managers, involves a reorientation of the means by which one can have a palpable effect upon the world. Immediate physical responses must be replaced by an abstract thought process in which options are considered, and choices are made and then translated into the terms of the information system. For many, physical action is restricted to the play of fingers on the terminal keyboard. As one operator put it, "Your past physical mobility must be translated into a mental thought process." A Cedar Bluff manager with prior experience in pulping contemplates the distinct capacities that had become necessary in a highly computerized environment:

> In 1953 we put operation and control as close together as possible. We did a lot of localizing so that when you made a change you could watch the change, actually see the motor start up. With the evolution of computer technology, you centralize controls and move away from the actual physical process. If you don't have an understanding of what is happening and how all the pieces interact, it is more difficult. You need a new learning capability, because when you operate with the computer, you can't see what is happening. There is a difference in the mental and conceptual capabilities you need— you have to do things in your mind.

When operators in Piney Wood and Tiger Creek discuss their traditional skills, they speak of knowing things by habit and association. They talk about "cause-and-effect" knowledge and being able to see the things to which they must respond. They refer to "folk medicine" and knowledge that you don't even know you have until it is suddenly displayed in the ability to take a decisive action and make something work.

In plants like Piney Wood and Tiger Creek, where operators have relied upon action-centered skill, management must convince the operator to leave behind a world in which things were immediately known, comprehensively sensed, and able to be acted upon directly, in order to embrace a world that is dominated by objective data, is removed from the action context, and requires a qualitatively different kind of response. In this new world, personal interpretations of how to make things happen count for little. The worker who has relied upon an intimate knowledge of a piece of equipment—the operators talk about having "pet knobs" or knowing just where to kick a machine to make it hum—feels adrift. To be effective, he or she must now trade immediate knowledge for a more explicit understanding of the science that undergirds the operation. One Piney Wood manager described it this way:

> The workers have an intuitive feel of what the process needs to be. Someone in the process will listen to things, and that is their information. All of their senses are supplying data. But once they are in the control room, all they have to do is look at the screen. Things are concentrated right in front of you. You don't have sensory feedback. You have to draw inferences by watching the data, so you must understand the theory behind it. In the long run, you would like people who can take data and draw broad conclusions from it. They must be more scientific.

Many managers are not optimistic about the ability of experienced workers to trade their embodied knowledge for a more explicit, "scientific" inference.

> The operators today know if I do "x," then "y" will happen. But they don't understand the real logic of the system.

Their cause-and-effect reasoning comes from their experience. Once we put things under automatic control and ask them to relate to the process using the computer, their personal judgments about how to relate to equipment go by the wayside. We are saying your intuition is no longer valuable. Now you must understand the whole process and the theory behind it.

Now a new kind of learning must begin. It is slow and scary, and many workers are timid, not wanting to appear foolish and incompetent. Hammers and wrenches have been replaced by numbers and buttons. An operator with thirty years of service in the Piney Wood Mill described his experience in the computer-mediated environment:

> Anytime you mash a button you should have in mind exactly what is going to happen. You need to have in your mind where it is at, what it is doing, and why it is doing it. Out there in the plant, you can know things just by habit. You can know them without knowing that you know them. In here you have to watch the numbers, whereas out there you have to watch the actual process.

"You need to have in your mind where it is at"—it is a simple phrase, but deceptive. What it takes to have things "in your mind" is far different from the knowledge associated with action-centered skill.

This does not imply that action-centered skills exist independent of cognitive activity. Rather, it means that the process of learning, remembering, and displaying action-centered skills do[es] not necessarily require that the knowledge they contain be made explicit. Physical cues do not require inference; learning in an action-centered context is more likely to be analogical than analytical. In contrast, the abstract cues available through the data interface do require explicit

inferential reasoning, particularly in the early phases of the learning process. It is necessary to reason out the meaning of those cues—what is their relation to each other and to the world "out there"?

It is also necessary to understand the procedures according to which these abstract cues can be manipulated to result in the desired effects. Procedural reasoning means having an understanding of the internal structure of the information system and its functional capacities. This makes it possible both to operate skillfully through the system and to use the system as a source of learning and feedback. For example, one operation might require sixteen control actions spread across four groups of variables. The operator must first think about what has to be done. Second, he or she must know how data elements (abstract cues) correspond to actual processes and their systemic relations. Third, the operator must have a conception of the information system itself, in order to know how actions taken at the information interface can result in appropriate outcomes. Fourth, having decided what to do and executed that command, he or she must scan new data and check for results. Each of these processes folds back upon a kind of thinking that can stand independent from the physical context. An operator summed it up this way:

> Before computers, we didn't have to think as much, just react. You just knew what to do because it was physically there. Now, the most important thing to learn is to think before you do something, to think about what you are planning to do. You have to know which variables are the most critical and therefore what to be the most cautious about, what to spend time thinking about before you take action.

The vital element here is that these workers feel a stark difference in the forms of knowledge they must now use. Their experience of competence has been radically altered. "We never got paid to have ideas," said one Tiger Creek worker. "We got paid to work." Work was the exertion that could be known by its material results. The fact that a material world must be created required physical exertion. Most of the operators believed that some people in society are paid to "think," but they were not among them. They knew themselves to be the ones who gave their bodies in effort and skill, and through their bodies, they made things. Accustomed to gauging their integrity in intimate measures of strain and sweat, these workers find that information technology has challenged their assumptions and thrown them into turmoil. There was a gradual dawning that the rules of the game had changed. For some, this created panic; they did not believe in their ability to think in this new way and were afraid of being revealed as incompetent.

Such feelings are no mere accident of personality, but the sedimentation of long years of conditioned learning about who does the "thinking"—a boundary that is not meant to be crossed. As a Tiger Creek manager observed:

> Currently, managers make all the decisions. . . . Operators don't want to hear about alternatives. They have been trained to *do,* not to *think.* There is a fear of being punished if you think. This translates into a fear of the new technology.

In each control room, a tale is told about one or two old-timers who, though they knew more about the process than anyone else, "just up and quit" when they heard the new technology was coming. From one plant to another, reports of these cases were remarkably similar:

> He felt that because he had never graduated high school, he would never be able to keep up with this new stuff. We tried to tell him different, but he just wouldn't listen.

Despite the anxiety of change, those who left were not the majority. Most men and women need their jobs and will do whatever it takes to keep them. Beyond this, there were many who were honestly intrigued with the opportunity this change offered. They seemed to get pulled in gradually, observing their own experiences and savoring with secret surprise each new bit of evidence of their unexpected abilities. They discussed the newness and strangeness of having to act upon the world by exerting a more strictly intellectual effort. Under the gentle stimulus of a researcher's questions, they thought about this new kind of thinking. What does it feel like? Here are the observations of an operator who spent twenty years in one of the most manually intensive parts of the Tiger Creek Mill, which has recently been computerized:

> If something is happening, if something is going wrong, you don't go down and fix it. Instead, you stay up here and think about the sequence, and you think about how you want to affect the sequence. You get it done through your thinking. But dealing with information instead of things is very . . . well, very intriguing. I am very aware of the need for my mental involvement now. I am always wondering: Where am I at? What is happening? It all occurs in your mind now.

Another operator discussed the same experience but added an additional dimension. After describing the demand for thinking and mental involvement, he observed:

> Things occur to me now that never would have occurred to me before. With all of this information in front of me, I begin to think about how to do the job better. And, being freed from all that

manual activity, you really have time to look at things, to think about them, and to anticipate.

As information technology restructures the work situation, it abstracts thought from action. Absorption, immediacy, and organic responsiveness are superseded by distance, coolness, and remoteness. Such distance brings an opportunity for reflection. There was little doubt in these workers' minds that the logic of their jobs had been fundamentally altered. As another worker from Tiger Creek summed it up, "Sitting in this room and just thinking has become part of my job. It's the technology that lets me do these things."

The thinking this operator refers to is of a different quality from the thinking that attended the display of action-centered skills. It combines abstraction, explicit inference, and procedural reasoning. Taken together, these elements make possible a new set of competencies that I call *intellective skills*. As long as the new technology signals only deskilling—the diminished importance of action-centered skills—there will be little probability of developing critical judgment at the data interface. To rekindle such judgment, though on a new, more abstract footing, a reskilling process is required. Mastery in a computer-mediated environment depends upon developing intellective skills. . . .

⌘ **READING** **12** ⌘

On the Digital Assembly Line

Simon Head

In the summer of 1999, I met with a dozen call center employees who wanted the Communication Workers of America (CWA) to organize their plant, a workplace of about 200 employees located in a small Iowa town. We met in the bland yet reassuring setting of a Baptist meetinghouse, but as our meeting progressed it was the call center's physical and psychological aspects were predominant: its cramped geography; the bilious colors of its ceilings, walls, and carpets; the personalities and habits of its managers; its fraught, harassed routines; and above all, the constant efforts of employees to carve out moments of privacy, however modest, for themselves. A CWA organizer was also present, and this was the employees' first meeting with someone from the union. As often happens on such occasions, the accumulated resentments of the years came pouring out.

The first complaints were about the call center's layout. In each of the call center's five departments the employees' cubicles were organized around a central platform at which supervisors presided, surrounded by banks of computer screens. These platforms were slightly elevated so that supervisors could see directly into the agents' cubicles; for the employees, management's ability to keep them under direct observation was particularly burdensome. Rick Hamsen (name changed), a leader of the organizing effort, described the technology at the disposal of the supervisors as "awesome"; the software bundled together all the powers of analysis, surveillance, and control. . .

The hyperefficiency of the software encouraged managers to micromanage employees' work. Since the software performed all the substantive tasks of data gathering and analysis, supervisors had to spend much of their time gazing at their screens, waiting for the system to tell them when an employee was falling short in any one of the myriad ways defined by managers themselves and then embedded in the software. Once this happened and the red light flashed, the upbraiding of the employee at the next work break was for managers both a means of exercising their powers and of relieving their boredom. The call center's work regime guaranteed that there would be a steady supply of such incidents and so a steady demand for managerial intervention.

This regime was a service sector variant of what Mike Parker and Jane Slaughter, in their studies of Japanese auto plants, have called "management by stress."[1] Many Japanese plants equip their assembly line workers with a light that flashes green or red according to whether they are performing their tasks within the allotted tac.[2] For scientific managers, counterintuitively, it is not necessarily a positive sign if all the lights along the line are flashing green. It may mean that tacs are too lax and need to be shortened. The ideal situation is one in which a significant minority of workers are operating at the margin of inefficiency, so that supervisors can then bear down on these workers and get them to work faster. Once this is done, and all lights are flashing green, then the next round of speed up can begin.

At the Iowa call center, managers would speed up the line by throwing a digital switch and reprogramming the software, much as Henry Ford had done at his Highland Park plant in 1915. Managers would do this without any prior discussion, let alone negotiation, with employees. The latest tacs would simply be announced at the beginning of the work week. At any given time, between 15 and 20 percent of the workforce would have trouble meeting their target times, and these workers then became the special concern of their supervisors. More than any other workplace issue—pay, benefits, workings hours, shrinking tacs—it was the arbitrary treatment of these faltering workers by supervisors that had enraged the employees at the CWA meeting and convinced them of the need for a union.

This corrective treatment followed no coherent pattern and varied according to the whims of the supervisor. Some employees were given special coaching so that they could meet their target times. Others were threatened with immediate dismissal unless they improved. Employees supporting the union drive almost invariably found themselves at the receiving end of management's harsh side. The moment an employee wore the union label, management was ready with every manner of harassment, even though such behavior was wholly illegal under the terms of the National Labor Relations Act (NLRA), the toothless federal law that regulates labor-management relations.

The case of Rick Hamsen himself is particularly revealing. Most of those at the CWA meeting saw the relationship between management and employees as inherently adversarial and believed that the best a union could do was to blunt some of management's more egregious practices. Hamsen's view was different and reminded me of a certain kind of Soviet dissident found during the declining years of the Brezhnev regime, who later became a strong supporter of Mikhael Gorbachev. These dissidents, still party members, continued to believe that a store of Leninist idealism remained buried under the corruption and inertia of the Brezhnevian officialdom and that it was the task of party reformers to bring this idealism to the fore before it was too late (which of course it was).

This was Hamsen's approach to the politics of the call center. Hamsen viewed his work as a vocation, and according to coworkers, he was one of the center's best performers. He was very respectful of management and invariably referred to his supervisors as "Mr. Schulz" or "Mr. Kelley," as opposed to his coworkers' usual "that asshole Schulz." Although often disappointed by management's performance, Hamsen viewed their shortcomings as a reflection of their lack of proper training; managers could not understand where their true interests lay. The union would join with the more enlightened managers and persuade their dimmer colleagues that the success of the business depended on a cooperative relationship between management and the workforce, represented by the union.

The Iowa managers should have realized that an employee like Hamsen could be a big asset for any business, whether as head of a union local or of a less formal body representing employee interests. But once the Iowa managers realized that Hamsen was a leader of the union drive, they began to harass him relentlessly. Supervisors started following him into the canteen, staring at him as he had his meals. Hamsen found that his cubicle was being regularly searched. Senior managers interrogated him at length about his pro-union activities. Finally, his supervisor accosted him in the center's parking lot and, falsifying the evidence, warned that Hamsen's perfor-mance was unsatisfactory and that he would be fired unless it improved. All these acts were illegal under the terms of the NLRA, but they had the desired effect. Stress took its toll on Hamsen's health, and although he

still believes strongly in the need for a union, he has stopped campaigning for one.

————

The Great Plains states of Iowa, Nebraska, and South Dakota are all strongholds of the call center industry. So, too, are the Sunbelt states of Arizona and New Mexico, which now rank with the Deep South as among the nation's poorest regions. Some of the best reporting on call centers in the Sunbelt has been done by RuthAnn Hogue, a reporter at the Tucson, Arizona, *Daily Star*. In a thirty-part series on Tucson's call center industry that ran in the *Star* in October and November 1998, Hogue showed how the call center industry can play a leading role in the economy of a booming Sunbelt community such as Tucson. Tucson is rated one of the "hot cities" for the industry, along with Phoenix, Arizona; Albuquerque, New Mexico; Omaha, Nebraska; and Sioux Falls, South Dakota. Among the factors that have made these cities "hot" for the call center industry are a plentiful supply of low-wage, predominantly high school–educated workers; the absence of unions; the presence of the phonetically neutral and so "acceptable" midwestern or Rocky Mountain dialect; and, in Hogue's words, "a reduced likelihood that people in a particular region will file law suits."[3]

Hogue comes up with evidence showing that, in the Sunbelt, the treatment of call center employees by their managers is very similar to what I came across in Iowa, and can only be described as harsh. A woman identified only as S. Sullivan worked as a call center agent for Intergroup of Arizona, a company employing 250 workers in Tucson. When Sullivan became pregnant she was criticized by her supervisors because she often had to go to the bathroom to throw up. They told her she should throw up in the trash can at her desk.[4] Paula Dabbart, an employee at an American Airlines reservations center in Tucson, said that she wore a stopwatch on a string around her neck to time each break. She felt that, for her own protection, she had to log all her movements.[5] Chuck Irvin, a fellow employee at the facility, explained Dabbart's precautions: "They tend to treat us like a machine for the eight hours you are plugged in . . . every time your butt leaves the chair you can hear the clock ticking."[6]

Hogue interviewed a middle-aged couple, Vivienne and Douglas Farrow, who were in danger of falling victim to an involuntary nomadism. Neither could satisfy the "average talk time" (ATT) set by their respective supervisors. At American Airlines' Tucson reservations center, Vivienne Farrow could not meet an ATT of two minutes and thirty seconds and was fired. At Greyhound's Tucson call center, Douglas Farrow was struggling to meet an ATT of 1 minute and 30 seconds. Farrow told Hogue that he had got his ATT down from 1 minute 95 seconds to 1 minute and 55 seconds, but the last 25 seconds were a problem: "I don't know how to get it down to one minute thirty. . . . I'm trying, but I can't do it."[7]

One of Hogue's more bizarre findings was that many of Tucson's call centers had drawn up strict dress codes for their employees. This was puzzling since call center employees never come into physical contact with their customers and the dress habits of the Southwest are notably relaxed. But by drawing up and enforcing strict dress codes, call center managers could open up a whole new field of employee activity that they could bring under their control, thus adding to an already draconian regime of regulation and surveillance. Managers at one leading telemarketing company, Teletech, were notable sticklers for sartorial conformity. Carolyn Grogg, a Tucson resident who worked for Teletech for a year, failed to comply with the company's footwear regulations. Suffering from a swollen toe, Grogg came to work with a closed-toe shoe on her healthy foot, and a matching sock and sandal on her injured foot. Sandals, however, were against regulations, and Teletech's managers

were going to send her home, an "occurrence" or demerit that would have been entered onto her employment record. Grogg had to take off her sandal and sock "and show them my toe was black and blue."[8] Hogue also found that managers frequently fired employees for tardiness, even when it was due to illness or a family emergency confirmed in writing by a doctor or teacher.

Kindra Frazier worked at Teletech's Tucson call center, helping United Parcel Service (UPS) customers keep track of their packages.[9] Frazier was highly rated by her supervisors, who described her as a "team player" with a "positive team spirit." In August 1997 her annual employment review described her as "very polite, courteous, and works well with others." She was also "effective and efficient when helping customers track their UPS packages." However, in November 1997 Frazier tripped in the company cafeteria and injured her back. For the next two months, Frazier continued to work, even though she had not fully recovered from her injury and often had to walk on crutches.

In this condition she found it hard to meet the company's draconian punctuality requirements: "It seemed like no matter what I did at work, if I went on crutches, I would get back a minute late." Company memos seen by Hogue reveal that when Frazier tried to take breaks at her desk to avoid being late, she was reprimanded. Despite her injury and her good record, in February 1998 Teletech fired Frazier for tardiness. Her life then went into a downward spiral. She was treated for depression and had to spend time in a mental hospital. In October 1998 she and her husband lost their house when the bank foreclosed, and they went bankrupt.

All the case histories recounted by Hogue were from call centers in which there was no union representation, and in which employees could do little to resist the kind of management practices she describes. But an estimated 7 percent of the call center work-force does belong to a union, mostly in call centers run by AT&T or its offshoots— Lucent Technology, and the now not-so "Baby Bells." Most of this unionized work-force is represented by the Communication Workers of America (CWA). However, the case of Gayle Brown (name changed), a for-mer employee of AT&T's call center at Fairhaven, Massachusetts, shows that, un-der present labor law, even a relatively strong union like the CWA has limited power to resist the call center industry's harsh employment practices.

Agents at AT&T's Fairhaven call center are direct employees of the corporation, and not of a call center "middleman" such as Teletech or Apac. At the time that Gayle Brown worked there (1997–1998), the chief task of the Fairhaven workforce was to win back AT&T customers who had deserted to other long-distance carriers. Gayle Brown began work as an AT&T trainee early in 1997.[10] On March 7, Brown's mother, with whom she lived, had to undergo surgery for the removal of a malignant tumor in her breast. When Brown told her supervisor that she would have to accompany her mother to the hospital and would miss part of her shift, Brown was told that she should "do what she had to do" but that her absence would count as an "occurrence," or demerit, to be entered into her employment record. At Fairhaven, AT&T's policy on "occur-rences" was and is "four strikes and you're out"—fired.

Early in the summer, Brown herself be-gan to experience internal bleeding, and in mid-June this became so bad that she had to see a doctor, who recommended surgery. Once again, she had to take time off from her shift, and once again her supervisor warned "do what you have to do but it'll be occur-rence no. 2." At the end of June, Brown underwent surgery, and a number of non-malignant tumors, cysts, and polyps were discovered behind her ovaries. Brown re-ceived her third "occurrence" when, in the opinion of her supervisors, she did not re-turn to work sufficiently soon after her sur-gery. Then, in July, Brown was injured in a car accident, and although she went to work later that day, she was experiencing the de-layed effects of concussion, as well as a loss of reflexes in her right leg.

It was not until January 12, 1998, that she was told by her doctor that she could re-turn to work. But when she contacted AT&T's management at the Fairhaven plant, she was told that she had been fired for her "poor overall attendance record." Gary Johnson, then a steward at the CWA's Fairhaven local, and now president of the local, told me that he had had to deal with many cases of what he regarded as unfair dismissals at Fairhaven, but that the Brown case was the one that troubled him most. He had fought hard for Brown but had failed to get her reinstated. I spoke to Brown soon after her dismissal. She was distraught at her treatment by AT&T, and has not worked since.

There is substantial research showing that these examples of the harshness of working life at call centers are not isolated incidents but form part of a work culture characteris-tic of the industry as a whole. In 1999 the Radclyffe Group, business consultants whose clients have included CIGNA, Coca-Cola, and New York Life, undertook a sur-vey of the call center industry and identified four factors that drove what it calls a "nega-tive call center culture." With the detached, modular language of the business consult-ant, Radclyffe describes a work regime very similar to the one that RuthAnn Hogue and I came across in Arizona and Iowa. The first of Radclyffe's four negative factors is the call center industry's "stringent and inflexible rules," particularly the demand that "agents subordinate their psychological, emotional and even physical needs" to the tasks of "consistently handling fluctuating call volumes."[11]

Radclyffe's second negative factor is the "stressful nature of the work": "worried about not meeting their standards . . . representatives can become anxious about going to lunch or sometimes even to the bathroom when they wish. . . . this can lead to their feeling trapped at the phone and out of control."[12] Radclyffe's third and fourth "negative factors" are both bound up with management's focus on "quantitive measurement." In almost all call centers," Radclyffe reports, "the availability of representatives is monitored on a real time basis, and reports can be reviewed in half hour intervals." A drop in performance levels can lead to a "concerned reaction from managers who are held accountable for a specific service level." This "adds fear to an environment already laden with negative emotion." This management approach, along with the relentless demand for call volume, "means representatives often become entrenched in feelings of victimization, hostility and resentment."[13]

Of all the ingredients that make up Radclyffe's "negative call center culture," it is perhaps the monitoring of employees by their managers that has most contributed to the employees' feelings of "victimization, hostility and resentment." In 1989 the Massachusetts Coalition on New Office Technology carried out a survey on employee attitudes toward monitoring, based on interviews with seven hundred employees, working for forty-nine companies, in a dozen different industries. Although the report is now fourteen years old, monitoring technology has grown ever more detailed and intrusive during these years and is today more burdensome for employees than it was in 1989. In 1989, 80 percent of those interviewed said that monitoring made their job more stressful, 65 percent said that they could not do a quality job because monitoring and the quotas it enforced obliged them to work too fast, and 68 percent said that employers used the results of monitoring as grounds for disciplinary measures. Sixty-four percent said that monitoring made it hard to get up for a break, even to go to the bathroom.[14]

Still another telling category of evidence supports the Radclyffe Group's findings about the "negative call center culture." Job turnover at call centers is exceptionally high as employees vote with their feet and leave the digital assembly lines in droves. At the sixty-two call centers surveyed in 1998 by the consultants Omnitech, the mean annual rate of employee turnover was 24 percent.[15] Dina Vance of the consultancy FTR Inc., and a leading expert on the call center operations of the financial services industry, estimated the annual turnover rates at her industry's call centers to be around 39 percent.[16] Mike McGrath, chief organizer for Local 1026 of the CWA in Tucson, puts annual turnover at some of the city's call centers even higher, at between 50 and 60 percent.[17] Contributors to *CCS* often remind readers about the industry's very high rates of employee turnover. In 1999 Rodney Kuh, president of Envision Telephony of Seattle, told *CCS* readers that "more than 25 percent of your call center staff could seek employment elsewhere this year."[18]

The call center industry and its work practices provide near-textbook examples of what I have called the new ruthless economy. Possessed of overwhelming power, unconstrained by organized labor or by effective workplace regulation, management drive their employees as hard as they can, and usually get away with it. This is exploitation in the classic manner of the nineteenth and early twentieth centuries, but there is also a basic difference between these contemporary practices and those of a century ago. Ford and Taylor were mostly intent on controlling the bodily movements of workers tied to machine shops and assembly lines. But today's scientific managers are trying also to control the minds of their white-collar employees. That is what the whole superstructure of control, scripting, and surveillance along the digital assembly lines is designed to achieve.

Here are the outlines of a project truly Orwellian in its ambitions. The project is to develop technologies that are essentially human-proof in their operation, technologies whose control over employee behavior is so powerful that, no matter how ill trained, alienated, or transient a workforce may be, technology can still be relied upon to deliver strong and improving levels of employee productivity. No other hypothesis can account for the call center industry's surreal and chilling combination of employee exploitation combined with hyperimmersion in information technology. With this technology the employee's managers apparently believe that they can keep employees working flat out, pushing aside the employee's knowledge in favor of scripts and databases, and relying on technology's all-seeing eye to detect and contain manifestations of employee discontent.

But can this project really work? Can technology be relied upon to neutralize the effects of an employee's alienation and lack of training? In their paper, "Diagnosis Document Machine Problems over the Telephone," Jack Whalen and Erik Vinkhuyzen show in detail what happens when a corporation uses undertrained workers to perform complex tasks, while relying on information technology to make up for the employee's deficiencies.[19] For example, consider what MMR Corporation, a thinly disguised Xerox, hoped to achieve with Case-Point, an expert system that provides solutions for customers whose copying machines are malfunctioning. MMR Corporation

wanted customer service agents to become passive conduits relaying the customer's testimony to CasePoint, and then CasePoint's recommendations back to the customer. Whalen and Vinkhuyzen stayed around to see how the system actually worked. Their findings are based on transcripts of recorded conversations between agents and customers.

Whalen and Vinkhuyzen found that CasePoint did not deliver. The system's deficiencies were bound up with the difficulties of reconciling the two languages used in the transactions between customer, agent, and system: the language used by customers to describe the symptoms of their faulty machines, and the language that the expert system was programmed to understand. CasePoint's designers assumed that no such problem of reconciliation existed, which is why agents could simply pass along the customers' descriptions to the system. But the MMR tapes show that problems of reconciling the two languages permeate the interactions between customer, agent, and system. These problems arose for three reasons.

CasePoint's designers had programmed the system to recognize a vocabulary of machine error that they and their management colleagues used, and that they assumed the customer would use as well. But customers frequently used "unauthorized" words of their own. When this happened, it was the inescapable task of the agent to try to establish which of the designer's authorized words best corresponded to the customer's rogue word. But agents were not trained to carry out this kind of interrogation and had to do the translations on a hit-or-miss basis. When agents got the translation wrong, CasePoint would take off on an irrelevant line of questioning and end up making a faulty diagnosis.[20]

A second and even less realistic assumption of the software designers was that customers would provide a description of a faulty machine's symptoms which, in its logical structure, would conform naturally to the structure the system was programmed to understand. But customers often came up with rambling, incoherent descriptions that CasePoint could not possibly digest, and agents then had to make sense of the customer's raw utterances. The transcripts show agents trying to perform this editorial task but finding themselves severely handicapped by a lack of training, a lack of confidence, and the pressure of time. More often than not, agents would abandon the struggle and arrange for a technician to visit the customer's offices—the very outcome the expert system was designed to head off.

A third error of the software engineers was their assumption that a digestible account of a machine's symptoms could be put together at the very outset of a conversation between agent and customer. But customers had the inconvenient habit of failing to provide all the relevant information up front, with vital bits of information instead dribbling out when a conversation was already under way. But for a new description of a problem to be considered by CasePoint, the system had to be reset and questioning started anew. There were strong pressures on the agent not to do this. Coming up with a new problem description took time, and agents were always under pressure to fulfill their quota of calls per day. With more than one problem description now on offer, agents also had to choose between them, again something the agents were not trained to do.

After observing CasePoint for twenty months, Whalen and Vinkhuyzen found the systems deeply flawed. Less a substitute for skill, CasePoint created a demand for new skills, those needed to cope with CasePoint itself. The system ran like an aging machine tool whose eccentricities had to be offset by expert handling, an expertise its handlers did not possess. Whalen and Vinkhuyzen do not try to estimate CasePoint's effect on the productivity of MMR Corporation's customer service workforce. But in their paper, they do not come up with a single example in which CasePoint worked as it should have, with the system providing a correct solution to a customer's problem based on information relayed by the agent.

CasePoint is just one expert system and MMR/Xerox just one corporation. But there is also major research evidence showing that the call center industry, and indeed service industries generally, pay a high price in increased costs and lost output for their reliance on an underskilled and transient workforce, and despite an ever greater reliance on information technology. Frederick Reichheld of Bain and Company, the Boston consultancy, has broken new ground in estimating these costs. A maverick thinker in the world of business consultants, Reichheld sees the industrialization of service industries as a ubiquitous phenomenon: "Most business people," he wrote in 1990, "without knowing it, see the service world through the lenses of manufacturing goggles. . . . They are influenced by historical traditions in business training, strategy techniques and organizational theory, all rooted in manufacturing."[21]

Symptomatic of this industrial mindset has been the way in which most service companies "focus their cost reduction efforts on process reengineering and layoffs," which appear to lower costs "but in fact lower employee motivation and retention, leading to lower customer retention, which increases costs."[22] Much of Reichheld's research has been about the impact of customer loyalty on company revenues and profits. But he also shows how the loyalties of customers and employees are closely linked, and so extends his analysis to include the revenue and profit effects of differing levels of employee turnover. His research is focused on service industries such as banking and insurance, and while he does not single out call center agents as special subjects of research, nonetheless, as the company's front line in the battle for customers, call center agents clearly have a major role to play in his scheme.

Reichheld describes the many ways in which loyal, long-term customers are good for company profits: such customers spend more, they tolerate higher prices, they do not have to be paid for with special discounts and offers, and they bring in new customers. Pulling all these factors together, Reichheld shows how even marginal changes in customer retention rates can have a spectacular impact on the value of a customer to a business. In the case of a credit card company that was also a Bain client, Reichheld found that an increase in its annual rate of customer retention, from 80 to 90 percent, increased the value of each new customer from $134 to $300.[23] However, Reichheld also found that customer loyalty and employee loyalty were inextricably bound, so that these rewards could not be harvested unless companies found ways of reducing their rates of employee turnover, and here Reichheld does mention the call center agent:

> Those employees who deal directly with customers day after day have a powerful effect on customer loyalty. Long-term employees can serve customers better than newcomers; after all a customer's contact with a company is through employees, not the top executives. It is with employees that the customer builds a bond of trust and expectations, and when those people leave, the bond is broken.[24]

Reichheld has found that a strengthening of employee loyalty, and the accompanying reduction of employee turnover, can have as positive an impact on company earnings as a reduction of customer turnover.

In his book *The Loyalty Effect* (1996) Reichheld describes in detail how reduction in employee defection rates can benefit company revenues and profits.[25] When an employee stays with a company years rather than months, recruitment and training costs are not wasted and can instead be amortized over the entire period of an employee's stay with the company. Longer-term employees are also more efficient.

"As a general rule," Reichheld writes, "employees who stay with the company because they're proud of the value they create for themselves, are more motivated and work harder." Experienced employees cement higher customer loyalty and are skilled at finding and recruiting the best customer. They can also generate the "best flow of high caliber job applicants," which not only raises the quality of new employees but also reduces a company's recruitment costs. Reichheld notes that companies with the highest level of employee retention "consistently hire the vast majority of their recruits through employee referrals."[26]

As with his analysis of customer loyalty, Reichheld pulls these factors together and shows how an employee's value to a company increases dramatically with his tenure.[27] Bain has developed a model showing the results over time of seven economic effects of employee loyalty. The model is based on a ten-year study of a range of service industries. Bain found that the per-annum value of an employee who stays with a company seven years is three times the value of one who stays for only three years; the annual value contributed by this three-year employee is in turn double the value contributed by an employee who stays only a year. The value of an employee who stays less than a year is negative. His recruitment and training are not offset by any gains in efficiency, customer retention, or customer referral.

In their paper, Whalen and Vinkhuyzen show what can be achieved with the kind of experienced and committed employee whom Reichheld writes about. In one of the MMR transcripts, an agent pushes aside the expert system and decides to solve the customer's problem himself.[28] The agent begins by listening to the customer's rambling account of the faulty machine. The agent then starts his own line of questioning, which elicits a fuller and more complex description of the machine's symptoms. The agent makes a number of deductive leaps from one symptom to another and finally comes up with a description that CasePoint can digest and understand. But in this case the agent would not need to give CasePoint his description, for the obvious reason that the expertise that is advanced enough for the agent to formulate his description is also advanced enough for the agent to bypass CasePoint altogether.

Drawing on this example, Whalen and Vinkhuyzen come up with a bold suggestion about how the productivity of a system such as CasePoint could be improved, and in a way that enhances rather than diminishes the role of employee skills. They propose that this expert system and others like it become "systems for experts."[29] At the heart of a conventional expert system such as Case-Point are the judgments of senior engineers and managers about all the possible ways in which a machine can go wrong, with an appropriate remedy attached to each problem. Both kinds of judgment then become embedded in the software. But with a system for an expert, the expertise of the agent is equal in importance to the engineer's and manager's expertise that is already built into the system.

With a system for experts, whenever an agent comes across an unusual case of machine failure, or whenever the agent himself finds a new way of dealing with a faulty machine, this knowledge is entered into the database, alongside the knowledge of managers and engineers. The system's database

therefore loses its closed, canonical status and becomes instead an open, expanding resource that any agent can use and renew. When such a system for experts was introduced for MMR-Xerox's field technicians, their productivity quickly rose by between 10 and 15 percent. However, with the field technicians the introduction of a system for experts did not require a major change in their status and pay. They were already skilled workers, and the new system simply required them to exercise their skills in a somewhat different way.

But for call center agents a system for experts would change significantly both their status and their methods of work. Agents would have to be properly trained in the operations of copying machines and, as newly skilled workers, they would have to be better paid. Reform would therefore come with a price tag. These bottom-line issues may explain why senior managers' tolerance of a system for experts did not extend from the field technician in the pickup truck to the call center agent in the cubicle. When Whalen and Vinkhuyzen presented their diagnoses and remedies to MMR-Xerox's senior management, they came up against managers' "unshakable commitment" to the status quo. Managers did not "want to invest in any modification in the design and deployment of the system." They were backed up by CasePoint's software designers, who were still interested in seeing how far they could go in relying "exclusively on machine expertise as a substitute for agent knowledge."[30]

A technical support center such as Xerox's stands at the higher end of the call center industry, but the high-performance model can be extended to the entire industry, even to the present-day wastelands of sales and marketing that are so heavily represented in the pages of *Call Center Solutions*. But this cannot happen until the call center industry rids itself of its whole oppressive superstructure of digital surveillance and control. Employees cannot exercise skills in a workplace heavy with scripts and pre-scribed action responses. Nor can they do so in a workplace ruled by the grim vehicles of classic Taylorism: active talk time, time between calls, calls per half hour, length of calls, time unplugged, time spent going to the bathroom.

The unwillingness of managers to dis-mantle this apparatus testifies to the still-dominant influence of scientific manage-ment and its industrial model. Moreover, the constant flow of new and upgraded soft-ware products encourages managers to believe that the faults of a system such as CasePoint can always be patched with the latest high-tech fix. MMR/Xerox's software designers had the spirit of the times on their side when they opposed Whalen and Vinkhuyzen's plans for a high-performance call center, urging management to continue "relying exclusively on machine expertise as a substitute for agent knowledge." This the corporation has been doing, employing more and more temporary workers in its call centers and tolerating high rates of em-ployee turnover.[31]

The call center industry is in need of renewal because it is, despite its present condition, an industry emblematic of the digital economy. It is fast-growing and in-tensive in its use of technology, the chief means by which a company reaches its cus-tomers, as Bill Gates, Tom Peters, and the reengineers have all pointed out. With its huge workforce, the industry is also an im-portant employer of Americans who have not been to college, and with the decline of the blue-collar middle class of unionized factory workers, there is a need to create good jobs for the non-college educated—jobs that are skilled, pay well, and offer the prospects of a career. High-performance call centers can provide such opportuni-ties. But the industry has first to rid itself

of the all-pervading legacy of Fredrick Winslow Taylor and William Henry Leffingwell.

NOTES

1. See Mike Parker and Jane Slaughter, "Choos-ing Sides: Unions and the Team Concept," *Labour Notes* (Detroit, 1998); see also Mike Parker and Jane Slaughter, "Working Smart, A Union Guide to Participation Programs and Reengineering," *Labor Notes* (Detroit, 1994).
2. "Tac" is Japanese industrial parlance for a target time set by management for the per-formance of a task. . . .
3. RuthAnn Hogue, "Why Do They Come?" *Arizona Daily Star* (hereafter *ADS*), November 17, 1998: available at www.azstarnet.com/growingpains/tues02.htm, p. 2; RuthAnne Hogue, "Tucson Poised for Growth," *ADS,* November 18, 1998: available at www.azstarnet.com/growingpains/plusminus.htm.
4. RuthAnn Hogue, "Your Feedback," *ADS,* November 16, 1998.
5. RuthAnn Hogue, "Centers a Target for Union Effort," *ADS,* November 17, 1998: available at www.azstarnet.com/growingpains/tues06.htm, p. 2.
6. Ibid.
7. RuthAnn Hogue, "Couple Fell into Call Jobs: It's a Way to Get By," *ADS* (November 15, 1998), pp. 1–3. Available at www.azstarnet.com/growingpains/8hours.htm.
8. Hogue, "Centers a Target for Union Efforts," pp. 1–2.
9. RuthAnn Hogue, "Fighting for Benefits, Workers Find It Hard to Get Help After Firing Injury," *ADS,* November 16, 1998.
10. Interviews with Gayle Brown and Gary John-son, Steward (now president) of Fairhaven CWA Local, January 29, 1998. AT&T refused my request for an interview to discuss the Gayle Brown case.
11. The Radclyffe Group, "Call Center Culture: The Hidden Success Factor—Achieving Service Excellence" (Fairfield, N.J., June 1998): 1–10. See also follow-up report, June 1999.
12. Ibid.
13. Ibid.
14. 9–5, "Stories of Mistrust and Manipulation: The Electronic Monitoring of America," February

1990, p. 11. 9–5 is a lobbying group for working women, now based in Milwaukee, Wisconsin.

15. Arnold and Hoffman, "Training Drivers and Opportunities in Call Centers," p. 11.

16. Dina Vance, "Call Centers Lead the Wave of Banking's Future," *CCS* (February 1999): 3. Available at www.tmcnet.com/articles/ccsmag/0299/0299hr.htm.

17. Author's telephone interview with Mike McGrath, January 14, 2000.

18. Rodney Kuhn, "Using Quality Monitoring to Enhance Performance and Improve Morale," *CCS* (June 1999): 116.

19. Whalen and Vinkhuyzen, "Expert Systems in (Inter)Action," pp. 92–140.

20. Ibid., pp. 96–126, for Whalen and Vinkhuyzen's discussions of Case-Point's shortcomings.

21. Frederick Reichheld and Robert G. Markey Jr., "Loyalty and Learning; Overcoming Corporate Learning Disabilities," *Bain and Company Essays: The Relations Between Loyalty and Profits # 1* (Boston, undated), p. 1.

22. Frederick Reichheld, "Loyalty-Based Management," *Harvard Business Review*, Reprint 93210 (March–April 1993): 71.

23. Frederick Reichheld and W. Earl Sasser Jr., "Zero Defections: Quality Comes to Services," *Harvard Business Review*, Reprint 905081 (September–October 1990): 107.

24. Reichheld, "Loyalty-Based Management," p. 68.

25. Frederick Reichheld, *The Loyalty Effect: The Hidden Force Behind Growth, Profits, and Lasting Value* (Cambridge, Mass., 1996), pp. 1–21, 91–116.

26. Ibid., pp. 101–2.

27. Ibid., pp. 100–105.

28. Whalen and Vinkhuyzen, "Expert Systems in (Inter)Action," pp. 126–32.

29. Ibid., pp. 132–38.

30. Ibid., p. 137.

31. Author's telephone interview with Jack Whalen, January 8, 2003.

⤚ READING 13 ⤙

The Transformation of Work Revisited

The Limits of Flexibility in American Manufacturing

Steven P. Vallas and John P. Beck

Introduction

In recent years social scientists concerned with the nature of work have increasingly spoken of an emerging "post-Fordist" pattern of work organization within the industrial capitalist nations. Advocates of this view typically argue that as large-scale shifts have occurred in both product markets and process technologies, large corporations have begun to shed their traditional reliance on centralized bureaucracy and standardized tasks, adopting a new set of work arrangements that answers to many names: "flexible specialization" (Piore and Sabel 1984; Sabel 1991), "the post-hierarchical workplace" (Zuboff 1988), and the "learning

Excerpts from "The Transformation of Work Revisited: The Limits of Flexibility in American Manufacturing" by Steven P. Vallas and John P. Beck reprinted from *Social Problems*, Vol. 43, No. 3, August 1996: pp. 339–361. Copyright © 1996 by The Society for the Study of Social Problems. Reprinted with permission of The University of California Press, Journals Division, via the Copyright Clearance Center and the authors.

organization" (Senker 1992), to cite a few. Regardless of the precise formulation, the general argument has been that the organizational models appropriate to mechanized, mass production processes can no longer suffice in a technologically advanced, post-industrial economy.

Such bold assertions have succeeded in winning the ears of managerial personnel, public policy analysts, trade union officials, and others concerned with the changing structure of work. Yet despite its sweeping claims of the obsolescence of mass production techniques, post-Fordist theory remains afflicted by abiding ambiguities and conflicting formulations. Disagreements persist as to which factors seem to drive organizational change, with some theorists stressing factors exogenous to the work organization (such as volatile product demand), while others fasten on factors endogenous to the workplace (mainly, the dynamics of technological change). There is also significant uncertainty regarding the coordinates of the post-Fordist work organization: Some theorists anticipate a rehabilitation of the craft tradition within new economic contexts (Piore and Sabel 1984), while others speak of entirely "new production concepts" that synthesize mental and manual skills (Kern and Schumann 1992). Moreover, few accounts have shown how large, bureaucratic firms can shed their traditionally rigid modes of operation and embrace the new post-Fordist arrangements (see Kelley 1990). Mindful of these and other difficulties we will discuss further, many commentators have remained sharply critical of the degree to which post-Fordist theory can provide an empirically useful guide to workplace transformation in the advanced capitalist world today (Hyman 1988; Penn and Sleightholme 1995; Taplin 1995).

This [article] addresses the continuing debate over post-Fordism by exploring the transformation of work at four large manufacturing plants in the U.S. pulp and paper industry, all of which are owned by the same multinational corporation. The study's goal is two-fold: first, to contribute to the larger task of assessing the empirical validity of post-Fordist claims; and second, to open up for discussion aspects of workplace change that advocates of post-Fordism have tended to neglect. Our research strategy is to focus upon a small number of establishments in one industry, in effect trading breadth of analysis for greater depth (see Wilkinson 1983; Child 1972; Child et al. 1984; Thomas 1994). Although this paper involves merely one dimension of a larger research project, it does point toward an important aspect of the current work restructuring that has gone largely unnoticed—the often-conflictual relations between technical experts and manual workers—and that calls for important qualifications within post-Fordist theory as typically construed. . . .

Post-Fordism Re-Examined

While sociologists of work have long studied the relationship between organizations and technologies, the area has gained greater prominence in recent years with the spread of what many refer to as a new scientific-technological revolution, often compared in magnitude to the first industrial revolution unleashed in late 18th-century England. Most analysts agree that massive changes are under way in the organization of manufacturing, but sharp differences remain as to which facets of work are likely to be recast, precisely how the structure of work (especially the management function) is likely to change, and why.

Adler (1992) usefully distinguishes four generations of post-war thinking about the relation between technological change and the structure of work. The first, "upgrading" approach is associated in the United States with the work of Blauner (1964), and in

England with that of Joan Woodward (1958). Reflecting broader theories of modernization and the logic of industrial society, this generation of analysts concluded that the automation of manufacturing tended to free workers from highly standardized tasks and to give them a fuller, more integrated view of the work process, thus easing capitalism's endemic problems of alienation and industrial conflict. The second, "deskilling" approach of Braverman (1974) and his followers contested these upgrading claims and in some respects stood them on their head. For this second generation of scholars, the pressures of capital accumulation relentlessly forced employers to simplify the labor of skilled manual and "mental" occupations, using new technologies to place production knowledge into the hands of managerial employees.

The conflict between these two perspectives until recently has occupied much of the existing research, as analysts have sought to adjudicate their competing claims (see Spenner 1983, 1990; Vallas 1990, 1993; Smith 1994). Yet by the early 1980s, a third generation of theorists had explicitly renounced the search for a single dominant tendency in the evolution of work, arguing instead that "the quest for general trends about the development of skill levels, or general conclusions about the impact of technologies, is likely to be in vain and misleading" (Wood 1989:4). This third, "contingent" view has more modestly sought to identify the social conditions that help account for the varied consequences of technological change (e.g., Cornfield 1987; Kelley 1990; Child et al. 1984; Barley 1986; Form et al. 1988).

Frustrated with this contingent view of technological change, a loose assemblage of theorists (including Adler himself) has sought to articulate the elements of a fourth approach. Despite variations in its precise formulation, proponents of this last school of thought broadly agree on the contemporary emergence and spread of a "post-Taylorist" or post-Fordist model of work (e.g., Sabel and Zeitlin 1985; Piore and Sabel 1984; Sabel 1991; Hirschhorn 1984; Kern and Schumann, 1992). Their claims can quickly be recited. During an earlier period of capitalism, machine designs were largely consonant with rigid, standardized job structures that accorded workers little responsibility and demanded of them few skills. Organizational structures under this regime reflected a sharp division between managers and the "managed," as the former sought to rule by command. Steady growth in mass consumption, stabilized by Keynesian economic policies, undergirded the Fordist paradigm. Yet now, dramatic shifts in process technologies and consumer markets have combined to generate a crisis of mass production throughout the advanced capitalist nations. To begin with, information technologies have transformed the structure of production in at least two respects: the spread of microprocessor technologies has made small-batch production more economically feasible than before, while at the same time requiring the use of greater analytic or "intellective" skills for the best use of new machines. Equally important, consumption patterns are more subject to rapid and volatile change, inducing firms to favor more flexible, general-purpose production systems over highly specialized (and therefore rigid) ones. What transpires, say post-Fordists, is a heightened level of skills required of manual workers; more generally, an expansion of craft discretion, presaging a synthesis of "mental" and manual functions within the automated plant; and a broader shift from bureaucratic "control" to organizational "commitment" as the principle that undergirds the new structure of work (R. Walton 1986; Zuboff 1988). Ironically, some theorists contend, the "project of liberated, fulfilling work, originally interpreted as an *anti*-capitalist project," is now "likely to be staged by capitalist management itself" (Kern and Schumann 1992: 111). . . .

The Study

[handwritten: The why, how, & what]

. . . We conducted an intensive study of a single branch of production: the pulp and paper industry. This branch of production has historically made widespread use of continuous-process work methods, which have figured so prominently in the debate over the evolution of industrial work that one flexibility theorist has termed them "the paradigmatic settings of post-industrial manufacturing" (Hirschhorn 1984:99; cf. Blauner 1964; Nichols and Beynon 1977; Halle 1984; and Zuboff 1988). Because the industry relies heavily on workers employed as control room operators called "machine tenders"— highly skilled jobs at the center of production control systems—it provides an especially good terrain on which to apply Kern and Schumann's (1992) expectations about the role of the "systems controller" (a position they believe epitomizes the emerging synthesis of theoretical and practical knowledge).

[handwritten left margin: their study]
[handwritten left margin: the "why"]

Equally important, the major corporations in this industry have witnessed a massive wave of organizational and technological changes, beginning in the late 1970s and early '80s, which has only now begun to recede. In less than a single decade, microelectronic controls and mill-wide information systems have transformed this terrain from a traditionally organized craft industry into a major outpost of automated manufacturing. Moreover, as the leading corporations in this industry have embraced the "quality movement" in general, and Total Quality Management (TQM) approaches in particular, new organizational principles have rippled throughout the industry, with many suppliers and contractors now formally constrained to demonstrate their application of TQM

principles. Because the industry has been marked by the rapid adoption of these and other process innovations, then, it provides an especially opportune site for research on the transformation of work in U.S. industry (cf. Penn and Scattergood 1988; Penn, Lilja, and Scattergood 1992).

The evidence we present has been gathered from four pulp and paper mills located in different regions of the United States, all of which have been acquired in the last 10 years by the same multinational corporation with a reputation for its relatively cooperative labor relations policies. While not a leader in the implementation of team systems, the firm has sought to incorporate such principles into its labor management approach, providing each mill with resources and support toward this end. Our focus on a relatively progressive, forward-looking firm should provide a research context that is relatively favorable to the newer and more flexible production concepts that are so commonly discussed in the literature.

[handwritten right margin: Details on mills; 4 - owned by 1 single mnc (but ~ progressive)]

The selection of mills for inclusion in the study was guided by two considerations: the desire to include a broadly representative mix of plants that vary in their size, age, product mix, and locale; and our interest in plants that have adopted the most recent generation of information technologies and process controls. During the early stages of our fieldwork at a large southeastern mill, we encountered job training seminars that were part of the company's plan to introduce new mill-wide information systems at several of its plants. Inasmuch as we were particularly eager to explore workplace relations within technologically advanced settings, we sought and received research access at three other plants that had recently introduced the new systems (although in a slightly different form). The four mills we ultimately selected are broadly representative of the company's production facilities and employ methods that are parallel to the pulp and paper establishments we have toured within the industry at large. The smallest of the mills in our research employs 700 workers in all positions, while the largest employs in excess of 2,000. Two of the mills are in the Southeast and two are in the Northwest. Two are located near urban areas, while two are in outlying rural areas. The oldest of the four mills was built in 1882 and has been repeatedly expanded and modernized; the other three (including both Southern mills) are more modern establishments, built in the late 1950s. All four mills produce a mixture of consumer products such as tissue and paper towels, combined with commercial products such as photocopying paper and coated paper for magazines. Hourly workers at all four mills are unionized, as is the great majority of workers in the industry.

The remarks reported here are based on two periods of study conducted between 1992 and 1995. An initial phase of the research grew out of an exploratory study of work commitment and job satisfaction at one of the mills; this pilot phase of the research ultimately included semistructured interviews with a strategic sample of 50 managers and workers. An additional wave of data collection was then conducted by the first author, who conducted approximately 200 hours of fieldwork and an additional 65 open-ended interviews with roughly equal proportions of process engineers, manual workers, and plant managers. During both waves of research, the authors were granted free rein to sit in with production crews during their shifts, observing their routine activities and work culture while participating in their ongoing conversations. Interviews were conducted under conditions deemed least inhibiting to respondents: for manual workers, in their control rooms, as the rhythm of production allowed; for engineers and managers, in their offices. Finally, for purposes of comparison, we jointly conducted a

small number of interviews and observations at three older mills in New England and the South, to understand the nature of the traditional methods of production that predominated during the manual era of production. In many respects these traditional mills served as living museums, showcasing craft-based tricks of the trade that have all but faded from human memory.

The Case of Pulp and Paper

The Labor Process Before Automation

The pulp and paper mills we studied are massive industrial complexes that daily ingest tons of logs, wood chips, water, and chemicals at one end and spew out truckloads of packaged paper products at the other. The process begins when trucks (sometimes railroad cars or river barges) deliver wood and chemicals to the mill. The wood is mechanically debarked and reduced to chips that are then automatically fed into the mill's digesters. These are vertical towers that use either chemical compounds ("white liquor") or mechanical grinding stones to produce liquid pulp, called brown stock. Workers in chemical processing areas are responsible for producing white liquor, other caustic agents, and bleaching compounds used in the pulping stages of production. Other workers oversee the bleaching, washing, and refining of the brown stock and add any necessary dyes or additives before furnishing the pulp to the appropriate paper machines—huge mechanical complexes in their own right. At the wet end of a paper machine, the pulp moves first to a head box, which evenly disperses it onto flat screens called "wires," which press and heat the stock to reduce its moisture content, until it rolls out as a continuous paper sheet at the dry end of the machine. Workers routinely oversee the accumulation

Before Automation: — Skilled, sensory labor — Hierarchical structure but w/ knowledge workers @ pinnacle

of paper onto large, 10-foot-wide reels that often weigh more than 20 tons each. At this point, the process enters a number of final stages, which may include the coating, supercalendering (receiving a glossy finish), and eventual conversion into a shippable, packaged product by being cut into smaller rolls or sheets. Up until the dry end of the paper machine, the process is essentially a chemical production process. At the dry end, however, where the paper is formed, the process becomes a mechanical one, with more immediate contact between workers, product, and machines.

Each of the production areas we studied was closely dependent upon the others in the mill. As workers at a paper machine know only too well, slight variations in the bleaching and digesting process "upstream" from their work can and often do have huge effects on the quality of their output and even on the intensity of their work effort: slight variations in fiber length, for example, may result in frequent "breaks" on the paper machine, forcing workers to engage in arduous and sometimes dangerous efforts to rethread the machines and bring production back on line. Conversely, variations in the behavior of the paper machines can ripple upward, affecting work in bleaching and digesting areas. Frequently, we watched failures on a paper machine force workers in the bleaching and brown stock area to slow down the chemical reactions they controlled, only to have to speed them back up again once their co-workers brought the paper machines back on line. These changes are difficult and sometimes dangerous to control and can result in major spills and wastage of costly stock or white liquor. Such tight coupling among different production areas requires frequent communication among workers in different areas of the mill who must learn to anticipate the decisions made by their co-workers in other departments. Despite the spread of portable

Workers & interdep. process must be uniform throughout

phones, digital pagers, and radio intercoms, communication across production areas, shifts, and organizational ranks is often difficult. Seemingly minor changes in production methods—for example, adjustments in the specifications for particular grades of paper—are often not effectively transmitted. Intensifying this problem among workers in the mill is the fact that seniority rules and promotion sequences are typically intradepartmental. On the one hand, this rewards workers for the slow and patient accumulation of knowledge concerning their area's processes and machines. But on the other hand it has important social effects: It isolates hourly workers from their counterparts in other production areas and spawns departmental allegiances and identities that limit broader forms of cohesion among workers. Despite claims made by Blauner (1964) and some flexibility theorists, the organization of the production process provides little opportunity for workers to glimpse the production process as a whole.

Difficulty of communication

Fx of intradept. promotion

Major effect: worker has no prod. "big picture"

Until the early 1980s, the consoles of most control rooms were equipped with pneumatic controls that provided workers with only a limited set of readings and process control capabilities. Typically, control rooms also contained panel boards—essentially, wall-mounted maps of each production area located above the pneumatic consoles and equipped with flashing indicators that displayed the status of valves, pumps, and tanks out on the shopfloor. Given the paucity of information these process controls provided, workers had to rely on direct physical or sensate means of collecting information about the process, much as Zuboff (1988) has described. Thus the workers we interviewed recalled spitting tobacco juice onto the winder (to gauge its take-up speed), and using wooden sticks to bang on the logs of the finished product (listening for signs of variation in their product's weight). Several recalled having to run

Worker innovation in earlier process

their hands over the stock at the dry end of the mill (too much dust or static electricity told workers that their output was too dry). In pulping areas, workers would often take samples of bleached pulp directly from their dryers, judging the fiber length and acidity of the stock on the basis of its look, feel, and even taste. Reflecting the primacy of sensory knowledge during the manual era, respondents often could not describe older forms of production knowledge without referring to one or more of the human senses: Thus workers and supervisors routinely recalled the workers' need to have a good "feel for the machinery," "an eye for the process," and a "nose for trouble."

To accumulate the repertoire of manual skills they needed to perform their jobs, operators had to serve long years of a *de facto* apprenticeship, moving from jobs as fifth or fourth hands to backtender, and (perhaps) even to the most senior job on a paper machine, the machine tender. During the years needed to move through this career progression, workers amassed a stock of knowledge that became an important form of intellectual property, qualifying them for promotion into more rewarding positions and giving them a critical source of power in relation to their supervisors and fellow workers (Halle 1984; Kusterer 1978). One worker we interviewed recalled a machine tender who stopped work whenever his fourth hand was nearby, explaining that such guarding of work knowledge "was his personal job security program." Even today, some workers carefully record vital information gained while making particular grades of paper, rarely offering to share the content of their "black books" with others in the mill.

Remaking the Labor Process

This portrait of paper making would be familiar to virtually all the workers in the mills we studied, but increasingly as an historical representation. For since the early 1980s, craft control over the production process has experienced a profound transformation, brought about by three distinct but interrelated changes in both the technology and the organization of production: Chronologically, these include (1) the introduction of Distributed Control Systems (DCS)—automated process controls that interpose symbolic, computer-mediated representations between machine tenders and the production process; (2) the adoption of Total Quality Management principles, which have dramatically altered decision-making methods and procedures within production areas; and (3) the introduction of a mill-wide information system that supplements the automated process controls with an array of analytic and communications tools. In the following pages we briefly describe these changes, and then analyze their effects on the structure and culture of shopfloor life.

Distributed Control Systems   Beginning in the late 1970s, the company began to follow an economic strategy based on the acquisition of undervalued capital assets. By the early 1980s it had accumulated significant numbers of older mills and began to modernize many of its key production facilities with an eye toward achieving greater stability in its operations and appreciable reductions in crew sizes. With these ends in mind, top management elected to introduce new, automated process controls—especially within the larger mills producing consumer goods. The result has involved massive changes in operators' working lives.

Especially in their most advanced incarnations, Distributed Control Systems employ computer terminals to provide visual depictions of the production process, using diagrams, graphs, and maps to represent the functioning of myriad pipes, valves, and pumps operators must oversee. In some respects, it is as if the old panel boards had sprung to electronic life. By using computer keyboards and touchscreen monitors, workers can peer into and adjust the most remote details of the process. Patiently moving through dozens of computerized screens of graphical maps and data, workers track key process variables—the acidity, fiber length, and brightness of the pulp, or the thickness, weight, and tensile strength of the paper—monitoring even minor changes during the course of their shifts. It is true that workers can sometimes put their systems on "cascade"—an automatic state of functioning in which the process controls become self-adjusting, and change in one variable triggers appropriate actions in other process variables. Yet even when workers leave the process on cascade, they must continue to track the state of their operations, lest the machine make inappropriate changes with potentially costly or even disastrous results.

The coming of DCS has granted operators access to a wealth of production data, but it has also placed workers at much greater distance from the process they control. Time on the floor checking the process has been replaced with time in the control room tending DCS controls and video monitors showing key bottlenecks in the process outside. Now, workers directly engage the machines only when they are down—e.g., during scheduled maintenance or when a "break" occurs in the flow of paper coming off the machines. In the latter case, workers must hurriedly intervene, feverishly cooperating to bring production back up. During "normal" periods of their working day, however, workers are now largely isolated from the material objects of their labor and work mainly with symbolic representations of the production process: a development that Zuboff (1988:58–96) has appropriately termed the increasing "abstraction" of industrial work.

Most workers recall having great difficulty in adapting to the new work methods.

The new processes intimidated many workers, especially those with less education, and left them fearful of the consequences of a personal failure to master them. In one mill where trade union consciousness is fairly well developed, the introduction of DCS in the mid-1980s prompted workers to slash the tires of an engineer's car and to ostracize the technical implementation team. Workers remain wary even now, checking and double-checking the truth of computer-mediated data—as one worker put it, "to make sure the machine ain't lyin' to you." Workers often experience an enduring tension between two conflicting dispositions toward the machines: *hope* that they are correct (reflecting the workers' concern for the product, and their wish to avoid hard physical labor), and *fear* that the machines (and therefore a process that had relied on their personal skills) have grown beyond their control. Most find that the capacities of the new machines—their ability to enhance the system's stability—gain for the whole system (and therefore for management) a greater control at the expense of individual workers who must accept an end to their craft knowledge in the process. Many workers seem to have reconciled themselves to the loss of individual creativity and discretion in their jobs by focusing on the material benefits of the new technologies, such as the reduction of physical labor. This trade-off is perfectly expressed in one worker's comment that "I'd rather be bored to death than worked to death."

Total Quality Management. As top management began to introduce DCS technology into the company's larger mills, it also set about rethinking its organizational strategies. After having experimented with other innovations, by the mid-1980s it elected to incorporate many of the principles of Total Quality Management into its operations (for discussion see Appelbaum and

Batt 1994; Hill 1991; Walton 1986). Viewing TQM against the background of previous management efforts at reform, many of which were both superficial and short-lived, production workers have commonly adopted a cynical view of TQM as the latest "program of the month." Yet TQM seems to comprise more than just another managerial fad. Unlike earlier forms of workplace reform, TQM is directly tied to the technical methods and procedures of the work process itself (Hill 1991). Indeed, subsequent developments in process technology that we will discuss have begun to build TQM principles into their very design.

One of the key elements of TQM is its emphasis on Statistical Process Control (SPC), a heavily quantitative system of interpreting fluctuations in production outcomes that uses probability theory to distinguish between random and systematic variations. Production areas, led by engineers, have established target values (called "centerlines") for each critical process variable and have defined confidence intervals at given distances above and below these centerlines. Managers have directed the workers on each shift to take scheduled readings of key measures, plot the datapoints on control charts, and inspect the resulting patterns of deviation from the centerline value. Workers are trained to alter key process variables only when the observed pattern violates a rule, indicating that a "special" (or non-random) cause of variation has upset the equilibrium of the production process. Management has posted the rules governing centerlining on the walls of most control rooms, and workers who defy the rules must justify their actions. Although workers often comply in a ritualistic fashion (completing control charts only at the end of their shifts, rather than as an active tool during the work itself), the effect of centerlining and SPC has been to standardize production methods,

removing a considerable degree of autonomy from workers' hands (Klein 1994).

Most of the managers we interviewed seemed quite aware of the potentially alienating effects that SPC can have and are often at pains to remind workers that they drew on workers' knowledge when defining centerline values. Moreover, in training sessions many technical staff have tried to translate quantitative concepts into more colloquial language that will be less off-putting from the workers' point of view. Thus one engineer liked to use a highway metaphor to explain centerlining and confidence intervals:

> Imagine you're riding down the highway on a motorcycle. If you get too far from the center stripe, you're gonna wind up in the ditch, right?

Regardless of the rhetorical devices managers employ, the reality is that centerlining has constrained workers' customary methods of process control. One departmental manager who had previously been a process engineer observed:

> It's tightened output up around the standard deviation, but it's eliminated a lot of individuality. Workers used to set things the way they liked to, with lots of variability. That's gone now.

In addition to the introduction of SPC methods, the shift toward Total Quality has also involved an increasing reliance on team systems of management, which the company hopes will foster greater cooperation across departments and levels in the organizational hierarchy. Often composed of both workers and supervisory personnel, teams vary widely in the breadth of their mission. One relatively pedestrian example concerned an *ad hoc* team composed of maintenance craftworkers, whom management had charged with designing a system for the storage of technical manuals and documents that are vital to expeditious machine repair.

[margin note: Still v. bureaucratic]

A somewhat more substantively important case was that of a small group of senior craftworkers who were invited to design a training and certification program for highly skilled operators. Regardless of the particular task that teams have been assigned, their effects have been fairly limited: Decisions to authorize the work of each team remain in the hands of departmental managers; the hierarchical chain of command has remained in place; and production standards continue to distinguish between the performance of each bureaucratic unit. In short, despite an overlay of cross-functional teams, the logic of bureaucratic hierarchy has been left largely intact.

[margin note: 3)]

Information Systems A last and most recent set of changes began during the late 1980s, when process engineers in the company's technical center developed a generation of information systems that have been introduced into several key plants, including all four of the mills in our study. The most important of these is the Mill-wide Information Network on Economics (MINE). Initially intended as a tool for middle managers to control production costs, it was designed for use on minicomputer systems and incorporated few user-friendly features. Since then, the company's development team has rewritten the system's software, incorporating a graphical user-interface and PC compatibility to make it more accessible to non-technical employees. MINE does not have operational functions: The task of controlling production remains the province of the DCS equipment. Instead, MINE provides a set of communications and analytic functions that even the most advanced DCS controls lack. The new information system provides for on-line bulletin boards, e-mail systems, and shift reports, all of which can now be accessed from any work station in the mill. Moreover, MINE enables workers to "see" into remote production areas—even

[margin note: Communication fxns]

into areas at mills elsewhere in the country— thus providing information that may have bearing on their own operations. The intent of the designers has clearly been to break down the pattern of departmental isolation that characterizes even the most advanced DCS-equipped production area. In so doing, MINE provides a broader, more inclusive overview of the mills' operations, rendering the process more transparent, both to workers and to managers, than was possible before.

[margin note: Now workers can see big pic- not so deptmntl.]

MINE also provides an array of programs that support the analysis of data on the causes of downtime, variations in quality, and fluctuations in production costs, most of which make explicit use of SPC terminology. In theory, operators who want to understand why significant deviations from certain centerline values have occurred in the past can access MINE's database and construct bivariate bar charts that show the proportion of such deviations attributable to each cause. Although many mill managers expressed the hope that not only technical personnel but also manual workers would share in the use of MINE, participation has been almost entirely limited to managerial and engineering personnel, for reasons that will be discussed.

[margin note: For ↑ control of process (& worked) BUT much used by mgmt]

The Changing Nature of Shopfloor Life

The changes just described make clear that there has indeed been ample opportunity for the transcendence of Fordist work structures. The profusion of information about the work process, the spread of team systems, and the availability of analytic tools like MINE render post-Fordist work structures more conceivable than ever before. The question to be addressed is how these technological and organizational developments have combined to reconfigure the structure and culture of the shopfloor. The answer that emerges from our research centers on

[margin note: Do we see a post-Fordist work structure out of post-Fordist techn?]

three decisive shifts: the increasing centrality of process engineers within the production process; the redefinition of what constitutes legitimate work knowledge; and the growing standardization of decisions made by non-expert workers, in accordance with quantitative expertise. We discuss these shifts in turn.

Process Engineers   The first and most obvious change in shopfloor life is the increasingly decisive role played by process engineers in the day-to-day operations of the mill. The simplest manifestation of this trend is the disproportionate growth in the number of process engineers now directly involved in each mill's production process. This growth partly is due to the hiring of engineers into newly created positions such as that of the "shift engineer"—technical employees assigned to work alongside production crews more closely than before. It also stems from the creation of new technical positions that center on the monitoring of production standards in various departments. A final and perhaps most important source of growth in the ranks of the process engineers has stemmed from their increasing representation in supervisory and second-line management jobs that had traditionally been filled from the ranks of hourly personnel. The experience of one of the mills is representative of this latter development. As recently as 1986, 48 percent of all first- and second-level supervisors at this mill held B.S. degrees in an engineering field; only nine years later this proportion had increased by more than a third, rising to 62 percent. The superintendent of this mill has since declared that *all* supervisory openings will be filled with applicants with engineering degrees. When we inquired into this decision, the mill manager articulated an organizational strategy predicated on the expansion of technically qualified expertise. To hammer his point home he held up an

organizational chart with the names of all salaried personnel. The names of degree-holding engineers had been marked with a yellow highlighter, indicating each department's relative strength at a glance.

The increasingly prominent role played by process engineers has had important effects on the structure of opportunity within the mills, as many manual employees have experienced a narrowing of their promotion prospects. For one thing, supervisors who have come up through the ranks no longer enjoy reasonable chances of promotion into jobs as second-line managers. Because these supervisors find themselves stuck in their present positions, and because technical education is increasingly required for even first-line supervisory jobs, hourly workers too find their opportunities reduced. These changes have erected or (in some cases) solidified a credential barrier between expert and non-expert labor (see Burris 1993).

Legitimate Work Knowledge   As technically trained personnel have grown more prominent, more subtle changes have occurred in the social context in which manual workers are employed. Especially during day shifts, when salaried employees are most strongly represented, the numbers of engineers sometimes begins to approach those of the hourly personnel, especially when grade changes are introduced. This has brought engineers and hourly workers into much closer contact, as Blauner (1964) anticipated some decades ago; the results, however, have been at odds with what Blauner expected.

Bolstered by their increasing prominence in the mill and by the spread of sensors and other instruments that displace manual functions, engineers have set in motion a process that might be termed an "epistemological revolution" within mill life: an inversion in the criteria that define legitimate knowledge of the work process.

Implied here is an overturning of traditional craft methods for generating knowledge about production and their replacement by a newer set based on scientific and engineering discourse—a process that has symbolically devalued craft expertise. In lunchroom discussions or meetings now, one sometimes hears engineers portray workers' knowledge in derisive terms: as either amateurish ("sandlot baseball") or else as a form of superstition ("black magic" or "voodoo"). The general thrust of such portrayals is that craft knowledge is indicative of a backward, pre-scientific approach toward work that is steeped in the dogma of tradition. As one process engineer told us:

> It drives me *crazy* when operators say you can't control the whole process with the computers. They'll stand there and scrape the stock with their thumbnail, and say they can tell me more about the stock than the $40 million Accuray nuclear instruments we just installed! They're just feeling threatened by us, like all their secrets are being taken away, and they don't like that at all.

This engineer is convinced of the inherent superiority of the new equipment; he rejects the argument that craft knowledge might perceive things that sophisticated measurement instruments cannot detect. In this respect, his views are shared by many of his fellow process engineers. Another engineer said:

> I get frustrated whenever people talk about the "art" of papermaking... From my standpoint, it's a lot better if I put another control loop and some calibrated instrumentation on a paper machine, and just put out a memo telling the operators to leave the system on cascade, not to touch it. I'd rather have things that way than depend on a 50-year-old man filling out control charts and applying complex rules by himself.

The dominant view, as expressed here, is that nothing makes it harder to achieve consistency in the quality of output than workers who feel they must change production values on the basis of their own experience. This is precisely why control loops are often installed: to overcome what we have termed the "surplus creativity" of the operators.

In most of the production areas we studied, this shift in mill epistemology unfolded gradually. Yet, in a few cases, the process found expression in a single defining event, as occurred in the brown-stock area of one mill in the South. The following incident was related by a widely respected machine tender whose experience is especially noteworthy, for he has been extremely accommodating toward management during the restructuring of mill operations.

> I used to put my hands in and take out a handful of brown stock, squeeze it, tell you whether it was good quality Kraft [pulp], good pine stock or what. I'd tell you about fiber lengths. But then they started bringing in these sensors and machines and whatnot. I still used to put my hands in the dryer, see what I could tell. One day when I did, I said to myself, "that's not right, that's not good quality Kraft." So I told my superintendent. They got the lab testers to work and got the engineers down here. But the lab tests came out OK. So the question was, who they gonna go with? This went on for some time, until finally, this was two years ago, my superintendent said, "J.W., we're gonna go with the lab tests." See, they didn't trust my way of knowin' anymore.

It later turned out that J.W. was right: He had detected an impurity in the white liquor used to digest the wood that had gone unnoticed by the laboratory tests. In this case the result was not serious, but the event was significant in J.W.'s eyes; for to him it symbolized the end of an era. Asked how he

[Handwritten margin notes: "Engineers' knowledge symbolically replaces trad. craft knowledge"; "Animosity b/w engineers & craft knowl."; "Engineers 'annoyed' by workers"; "Usually gradual but"]

felt, he said simply, "I don't put my hands in the brown stock anymore." At this point, he knew that the language of engineering had gained hegemony over its craft equivalent.

Despite these shifts in the definition of legitimate production knowledge, one sometimes hears evidence of a dissenting world view among engineers that breaks with the newly dominant epistemology and seeks to acknowledge the legitimacy of craft knowledge. Such engineers sometimes become defenders of traditional forms of working knowledge within highly automated control rooms. Consider for example the words of one process engineer in his early 20s, born and raised near the Southern mill at which he now worked:

> I've been told to idiot-proof things, to lock people out. I've been told to put in [automatic feedback] loops that locked people out. But I'm not comfortable with people sitting back in their chairs, waiting for an alarm.

The same sentiments were put even more clearly by an engineer in one of the Northwestern mills, who explicitly challenged his peers' emphasis on electronic sensors and computer-mediated process controls.

> Some of our engineers think everything can be characterized in technical terms, and that if it can't, then it doesn't make sense. They just aren't able to listen to an hourly person talk about paper making. I mean, sometimes I think we get hooked on control rooms. It helps from the process point of view. It's quiet, so we can talk and use the computers to play "what if" games. But it takes you away from the process, isolates you. Out there, you can smell it, hear it, taste it. We have lots of sensors, but there's a lot of things that we don't have sensors for, and some of them can be extremely important for keeping the process on line.

Engineers who subscribe to this latter, more worker-centered view are in the minority. Yet they play an important role in shopfloor relations, often serving to maintain the fabric of trust among occupational groups that would otherwise be at odds.

Standardization of Decisions   A further way in which shopfloor life has been reconfigured centers on the ways in which analytic functions and decision-making powers have been distributed. Recall that post-Fordist theory expects the process of work restructuring to reallocate a portion of these tasks downward, blurring or even transcending the traditional division between mental and manual labor. We find little evidence of such a trend. Instead, our research indicates that the dominant tendency has involved a pattern of *tightened* constraints upon manual workers' judgment rather than the "*relaxation* of constraints" that flexibility theory foresees (Hirschhorn 1984).

The point is clearly manifest in the workings of Statistical Process Control. In essence, SPC involves the effort to define expected values for key process variables and to formulate detailed rules that govern how workers respond to deviations from centerline values. A key issue here, which managers and engineers have rarely considered in any depth, concerns the process through which centerline values themselves are established. When we asked managers and engineers to explain how particular centerlines were chosen, many referred somewhat vaguely to "collective experimentation" or "inherited wisdom"—as if the target values were a consensual product of shopfloor history. Occasionally, managers would sense a contradiction here, even stopping in mid-sentence to reformulate their thoughts, as in the case of one quality engineer who oversaw tissue production. After he spoke somewhat critically of top management's effort to direct his *own* behavior, we asked him whether he thought that workers ever resented the imposition of centerlines on *their* routines:

> Yeah. And I can understand that. It's the same thing as we're being told [by headquarters] what starch we should use. *We're* telling *them* [hourly workers] . . . [Pauses]. We're not . . . I mean, it can come across that way, that we're telling them how we want them to run the machine, and to a certain point that's true. But actually, if we do our job right, we should be able to explain to them that we're *not* telling them how to run the machines, but rather, this is where we *want* them to run it, and if they can't run it there, they need to understand why they can't and be able to explain that.

Displeased with the imposition of rigid, centralized patterns of authority on his own work situation, this man was reluctant to acknowledge participating in the standardization of craftworkers' jobs. Other respondents spoke more bluntly. Asked if the practice of centerlining made operators feel they were being told how to run their machines, a young engineer replied:

> Sure. That's natural. And you *are* telling them how to run. You're saying, in the collective opinion of the people who are good at running this process, it runs best at X. Therefore, we're gonna run it at X. When we deviate from X, it'll be under experimental, controlled conditions, and *we'll* determine if the deviation is in fact better than the old one. If it is better, we're gonna move to that one. So you *are* in fact telling them how to run.

This statement accords quite closely with our own field observations: The definition of centerline values has typically been defined as a technical question best left to the judgement of formally trained engineers.

There were of course dissenting voices among managers and engineers. Asked whether workers might play a more active role in establishing parameters for the process, some engineers felt that it would be both possible and desirable. Said one business manager with long experience as a mill engineer:

> We just don't . . . We tend to think only technically trained people can understand SPC. We're missing the boat in the formation of centerlines.

Other engineers acknowledge that centerlining was "largely a management program," expressing their regret at this turn of events. But again, such dissent was exceptional. Most engineers felt that workers had sufficient powers of consultation, and that any efforts to involve workers more fully would only magnify the problem of inconsistency and instability (surplus creativity) they had long sought to transcend. A high-ranking engineer in the company's technical center who himself oversaw the design of the new information systems said:

> We've got to get over *to* the boring stage. *We've got to make workers' jobs more boring.* We have to go from the chaos we have now to the stability that makes us money. I don't know how to deal with that [the social consequences of boredom]. Teams, or whatever. But this is where we have to go.

In this view, workers' discretion is equivalent to "chaos." Only a standardized work regime, achieved via the coupling of SPC and automation, can deliver the stability the company needs.

Discussion

It is clear that the structure of work in these mills has been evolving in a direction that departs in certain important respects from the expectations of post-Fordist theory. It is true that, with respect purely to skill requirements, manual workers have indeed encountered a rising set of skill demands, as they have had to learn the use of DCS equipment and to cope with the wealth of process information it makes available. In addition, workers have had to learn when to accept computer-provided directions, and when to intervene. Yet even as workers' *skill* requirements have apparently increased, we find little evidence of any expansion of craft *discretion* or *autonomy*, or any imminent synthesis of mental and manual labor, as post-Fordists predict. Before we can address the larger implications of this finding, however, the question must be asked: Why has the hierarchical, Fordist structure of work proved so tenacious throughout the mills in our research?

Advocates of post-Fordist theory might point to the external market environments of these plants, and suggest that the structure of product demand has limited the development of alternative work structures. The argument here is that since much of the demand for pulp and paper products involves mass consumer markets for towel and tissue products—commodity items most economically produced through standardized work structures—the ingredients necessary for the cultivation of flexibility are largely absent from this case. While this thesis is plausible, we are compelled to reject it on a number of empirical grounds.

To begin, all of the mills in our study are complex, multi-product mills supplying heterogeneous markets that range from mass consumer products (towel and tissue, napkins) to smaller, specialty niches (unbleached coffee filters, specialty coated papers). There was no difference in work organization across mills or production areas oriented toward one or another product type. Smaller, specialty product lines whose paper machines undergo more frequent grade changes were no more disposed to adopt flexible work methods than their counterparts supplying larger, commodity markets. Indeed, of the company's two major product divisions—consumer products and communications paper (which includes such items as coated paper)—support for self-directed teams was appreciably stronger in the former division, which is more fully oriented toward mass production for commodity markets. We therefore doubt that the structure of product markets can suffice to explain the limits of flexibility in these mills.

While our observations are somewhat tentative, we believe that the limits of flexibility can be traced to two alternative influences. First, and at a macrosocial level of analysis, is the nature of the wider culture and society, whose institutional structure confers relatively little legitimacy on craft knowledge and provides relatively few resources for vocational training, certification, or recruitment (Lane 1988). Although we have not interviewed corporate managers, indirect evidence (such as directives expressing their desire to "catch up" with rival firms' technical strengths) indicates that corporate managers view the engineering composition of each mill's personnel as a symbol of its modernity. A second set of influences operates on the shopfloor itself, involving the distribution of resources among engineers and manual workers, affecting which groups are able to benefit from the restructuring of work. The following remarks are confined to the latter, organizational influences.

Recall that manual workers are typically embedded within intra-departmental seniority systems and progression ladders that anchor them within particular production areas. This system, codified in collective bargaining agreements, serves important functions for the company and its workers alike: It encourages workers to accumulate specialized knowledge of their immediate production locale, while it establishes a system of job security that protects the position of skilled workers in particular. At the same time, however, it perpetuates a pattern of local identification and occupational rivalry that often constrains workers' capacity to view the production process as a whole. Thus, one worker on a paper machine had been employed at the same Northwestern mill for more than 30 years, but he had never set foot in the pulping area that furnished his machines with its raw materials—a situation that leads pulp workers to comment that "it's like they think their furnish arrives through a magic pipe in the wall." Moreover, the use of computerized process-controls has meant a shift toward fewer control rooms and sharp reductions in crew sizes, expanding the production areas that workers must oversee, increasing the pressure they feel to keep production on-line. Workers thus find themselves even more tightly confined within their traditionally defined job duties than before. Finally, although many workers are critical of formal, theoretically based knowledge and expertise, which they sometimes view as a tool of self-aggrandizement, they typically lack more than the rudiments of formal education and often seem intimidated by the cultural capital their superiors can wield (Bourdieu and Passeron 1977; Lamont and Lareau 1988). All these factors combine to limit craftworkers' capacity to compete for larger, more autonomous roles within the mills.

It is important to point out that despite the new-found dominance that engineering discourse enjoys, manual workers have nonetheless preserved a residue of informal, experiential knowledge that remains vital to production. As one worker on a paper machine admitted, "the knowledge stays, but in the cracks. We like to keep it hidden" (cf. Halle 1984; cf. Hodson 1991a, b). The question thus arises: If workers' knowledge has in effect been driven underground, can they not use this hidden knowledge as a strategic resource with which to weaken the hegemony of the engineers? At times, the workers we have studied did indeed employ their knowledge as a weapon, typically to retaliate against assaults upon their own dignity. In one representative case, workers suffered a series of insults at the hands of the same engineer. Led by their machine tender, they withheld their knowledge during a production change, rendering the engineer helpless as pulp eventually began to spill out (as one worker recalled), "looking like oatmeal all over the shopfloor." Workers refused to intervene until the engineer had retreated to his office, enabling them publicly to reaffirm their own competence.

Such instances prompt two observations. First and most obvious is the fact that open resistance like this is quite rare, in no small part because it represents a double-edged sword: it involves costly and often laborious disruptions in production, and it can damage workers' own performance records. Second and more important is the fact that even when such resistance occurs, it is almost always aimed at the "*abuse*" of engineering authority—as in the above example, an assault upon their dignity—leaving untouched the engineers' normal claim to superior expertise. We believe that such acts of resistance represent part of a broader process of informal negotiation, through which workers impose certain limits on engineers' interpersonal practices. Such tactics enable workers to exact a modicum of respect from their superiors—in workers' terms, ensuring that engineers "learn to play ball"—but in ways that rarely if ever challenge the hegemony of engineering knowledge itself.

Process engineers, for their part, are far better situated to benefit from the process of workplace change. Although they are also divided by their engineering specialties and their attendant levels of prestige—electrical engineers are "top dog," while civil engineers are merely "the concrete guys"—these differences seem to have little material effect. For the most part, process engineers constitute a relatively cohesive occupational group whose members spontaneously feel a shared sense of mission in relation to the production process. One major reason, we surmise, lies in the structure of mobility established for technical personnel within all of the mills. In contrast to the situation of hourly employees, engineers are expected to progress through a number of distinct positions within far-flung areas of the mill. (A newly hired engineer might be assigned to a technical group in a given department, to gain hands-on experience in technical support. After a few years, he or she commonly moves into a job as a technical specialist on a paper machine, and then into a position as a first-line supervisor in production. He or she would then be poised to assume a position with substantial authority within an engineering department.) Such mobility patterns make possible the accumulation of knowledge regarding the production process as a whole, which management increasingly values. These patterns also equip engineers with shared organizational experiences, enabling them to sustain a common sense of purpose in relation to the mill as a whole. Coupled with the generalized authority conferred on technical expertise by the wider culture and organizational environment and the traditional presumption that analytic functions are properly lodged in the engineers' hands, these factors quite naturally position engineers to reap the benefits of workplace change (cf. Wilkinson 1983; Child et al. 1984).

Conclusion

This [reading] has explored the transformation of work under conditions that should be relatively favorable to the flexibility thesis.

These mills all employ continuous-process methods of production that make widespread use of programmable control systems and sophisticated information technologies. All four mills are owned by a large multinational corporation with a reputation as an innovative, forward-looking firm. Opportunities for the adoption of flexible, post-Fordist structures are therefore present in abundance. Yet our research has uncovered only partial support for the flexibility thesis. Indeed, the thrust of this paper has drawn attention to a set of obstacles to flexibility—centering on the power of engineering knowledge and its symbolic devaluation of skilled manual labor—that post-Fordist theory has ignored.

We do indeed find some halting developments that lead beyond the rigid bureaucratic structure of industrial organization. For one, management has sought to cultivate workers' normative commitment to the mill, especially through the articulation of cross-functional teams in all of the mills. Moreover, the evidence does indeed suggest that the complexities of new process technologies brought about an increasing level of skill requirements among manual employees, who must learn to master an increasing array of data generated by the computerized machine. This latter point effectively refutes Braverman's (1974:224) characterization of continuous-process work as involving little more complexity than "learning to tell time." Finally, a number of managers have expressed the hope that new methods of skill deployment could take root and would empower production workers as full citizens within the labor process. Yet these tendencies have been overwhelmed by a different set of influences that have imposed a rigid, hierarchical pattern founded on the language of technical expertise. As we have seen, process engineers play an increasingly salient role within mill operations, multiplying in relative numbers and importance, and by implication placing limits on manual workers' career opportunities. The definition of legitimate knowledge at work has shifted in ways that increasingly favor scientific discourse over local or experiential knowledge, rendering craft skill a frequent object of derision among salaried personnel. Finally, as management has introduced Statistical Process Control and other elements of Total Quality Management, work methods have been subject to increasing levels of standardization, as centerline values have come to be defined on the basis of formal expertise. These developments, it seems clear, are not easily reconciled with the concept of post-Fordism. Indeed, there may be some virtue in speaking of the prevalence of important *neo*-Fordist tendencies in these mills, or of a neo-Taylorist search for the "one best way" to run the production process. . . .

REFERENCES

Adler, Paul. 1992. "Introduction." In *Technology and the Future of Work,* ed. Paul Adler. New York: Oxford.

Appelbaum, Eileen and Rosemary Batt. 1994. *The New American Workplace: Transforming Work Systems in the United States.* Ithaca, NY: ILR Press.

Barley, Steven. 1986. "Technology as an Occasion for Structuring." *Administrative Science Quarterly* 31:78–108.

Blauner, Robert. 1964. *Alienation and Freedom: The Factory Worker and His Job.* Chicago: University of Chicago Press.

Bourdieu, Pierre and Jean-Claude Passeron. 1977. *Reproduction: In Education, Society and Culture.* Thousand Oaks, CA: Sage.

Braverman, Harry. 1974. *Labor and Monopoly Capital: The Degradation of Work in the Twentieth Century.* New York: Monthly Review.

Burris, Beverly. 1993. *Technocracy at Work.* Albany, NY: SUNY Press.

Child, John. 1972. "Organizational Structure, Environment and Performance: The Role of Strategic Choice." *Sociology* 6:2–22.

Child, John, R. Loveridge, J. Harvey, and A. Spencer. 1984. "Microelectronics and the Quality of Employment in Services." Pp. 163–190 in *New Technology and the Future of Work and Skills,* ed. P. Marstrand. London: Pinter.

Cornfield, Daniel. 1987. *Workers, Managers and Technological Change: Emerging Patterns of Labor Relations.* New York: Plenum.

Form, William, Robert L. Kaufman, Toby Parcel, and Michael Wallace. 1988. "The Impact of Technology on Work Organization and Work Outcomes: A Conceptual Framework and Research Agenda." Pp. 303–330 in *Industries, Firms and Jobs: Sociological and Economic Approaches,* eds. G. Farkas and P. England. New York: Plenum.

Halle, David. 1984. *America's Working Man.* Chicago: University of Chicago Press.

Hill, Stephen J. 1991. "Why Quality Circles Failed, but Total Quality Management Might Succeed." *British Journal of Industrial Relations* 29:4.

Hirschhorn, Larry. 1984. *Beyond Mechanization.* Cambridge, MA: MIT Press.

Hodson, Randy. 1991a. "The Active Worker: Compliance and Autonomy at the Workplace." *Journal of Contemporary Ethnography* 20:47–78.

———. 1991b. "Workplace Behaviors: Good Soldiers, Smooth Operators, and Saboteurs." *Work and Occupations* 18:271–290.

Hyman, Richard. 1988. "Flexible Specialization: Miracle or Myth?" Pp. 48–60 in *New Technology and Industrial Relations,* eds. R. Hyman and W. Streeck. Oxford: Basil Blackwell.

Kelley, Maryellen. 1990. "New Process Technology, Job Design and Work Organization: A Contingency Model." *American Sociological Review* 55:191–208.

Kern, Horst and Michael Schumann. 1992. "New Concepts of Production and the Emergence of the Systems Controller." Pp. 111–148 in *Technology and the Future of Work,* ed. Paul Adler. New York: Oxford.

Klein, Janice. 1994. "The Paradox of Quality Management: Commitment, Ownership, and Control." Pp. 178–194. In *The Post-Bureaucratic Organization: New Perspectives on Organizational Change,* eds. C. Heckscher and A. Donnellon. Thousand Oaks CA: Sage.

Kusterer, Kenneth. 1978. *Know-How on the Job: The Important Working Knowledge of Unskilled Workers.* Boulder, CO: Westview.

Lamont, Michele and Annette Lareau. 1988. "Cultural Capital: Allusions, Gaps and Glissandos in Recent Theoretical Developments." *Sociological Theory* 6:153–168.

Lane, Christel. 1988. "Industrial Change in Europe: The Pursuit of Flexible Specialization in Britain and West Germany." *Work, Employment and Society,* 2:141–168.

Nichols, T. and H. Beynon. 1977. *Working for Capitalism.* London: RKP.

Penn, Roger and Hilda Scattergood. 1988. "Continuities and Change in Skilled Work: A Comparison of Five Paper Manufacturing Plants in the UK, Australia and the USA." *British Journal of Sociology* 39:69–81.

Penn, Roger, Kari Lilja, and Hilda Scattergood. 1992. "Flexibility and Employment Patterns in the Contemporary Paper Industry: A Comparative Analysis of Mills in Britain and Finland." *Industrial Relations Journal* 23:214–223.

Penn, Roger and David Sleightholme. 1995. "Skilled Work in Contemporary Europe: A Journey into the Dark." Pp. 187–202 in *Industrial Transformation in Europe: Process and Contexts,* eds. E. J. Dittrich, G. Schmidt, and R. Whitley. London: Sage.

Piore, Michael and Charles F. Sabel. 1984. *The Second Industrial Divide: Possibilities for Prosperity.* New York: Basic.

Sabel, Charles. 1991. "Moebius-Strip Organizations and Open Labor Markets: Consequences of the Reintegration of Conception and Execution in a Volatile Economy." Pp. 23–53 in *Social Theory for a Changing Society,* eds. P. Bourdieu and J. Coleman. New York: Russell Sage.

Sabel, Charles and Jonathan Zeitlin. 1985. "Historical Alternatives to Mass Production: Politics, Markets and Technology in Nineteenth Century Industrialization." *Past and Present* 108:133–176.

Senker, Peter. 1992. "Automation and Work in Great Britain." Pp. 89–110 in *Technology and the Future of Work,* ed. Paul Adler. New York: Oxford University Press.

Smith, Vicki. 1994. "Braverman's Legacy: The Labor Process Tradition at 20." *Work and Occupations* 21:403–421.

Spenner, Kenneth. 1983. "Deciphering Prometheus: Temporal Change in the Skill Level of Work." *American Sociological Review* 48:824–837.

———. 1990. "Skill: Meanings, Methods and Measures." *Work and Occupations* 17:399–421.

Taplin, I. 1995. "Flexible Production, Rigid Jobs: Lessons from the Clothing Industry." *Work and Occupations* 22:412–438.

Thomas, Robert J. 1994. *What Machines Can't Do: Politics and Technology in the Industrial Enterprise.* Berkeley: University of California Press.

Vallas, Steven. 1990. "The Concept of Skill: A Critical Review." *Work and Occupations* 17:379–398.

———. 1993. *Power in the Workplace: The Politics of Production at AT&T.* Albany: State University of New York Press.

Walton, Mary. 1986. *The Deming Management Method.* New York: Perigee.

Walton, R. E. 1986. "From Control to Commitment in the Workplace." *Harvard Business Review* 63:77–84.

Wilkinson, Barry. 1983. *The Shopfloor Politics of New Technology.* London: Gower.

Wood, Stephen. 1989. "Introduction." In *The Transformation of Work? Skill, Flexibility and the Labour Process,* ed. Stephen Wood. London: Unwin Hyman.

Woodward, Joan. 1958. *Management and Technology.* London: HMSO.

Zuboff, Shoshana. 1988. *In the Age of the Smart Machine.* New York: Basic.

⬯ READING 14 ⬯

Employee Involvement, Involved Employees

Participative Work Arrangements in a White-Collar Service Occupation

Vicki Smith

Throughout the U.S. economy, employers and managers are promoting a new ethos of participation for their workers. The spread of a paradigm of participation—comprised of extensive discussion about the merits of worker involvement as well as actual transformation of production methods and staffing practices—may indeed be one of the most significant trends sweeping across postindustrial, late twentieth-century workplaces (Appelbaum and Batt 1994; Harrison 1994; Heckscher 1988; Hodson 1995; U.S. Department of Labor 1994). As Appelbaum and Batt (1994:5) note in their exhaustive study of emergent U.S. work systems, "In the 1990s, a new *vision* of what constitutes an effective production system appears to dominate management's views, if not yet its actions."

Sociologists, industrial relations researchers, organizational scientists, and policymakers who have studied this trend agree that leaders and managers of U.S. companies are climbing aboard the bandwagon of worker participation in their urgent attempts to maintain competitiveness under changing economic circumstances. Employers believe that when workers participate in making decisions, when they gain opportunities to apply their tacit knowledge to problem solving, and when they acquire responsibility for designing and directing production processes, they feed into an infrastructure enabling firms to respond to shifting market and product demands in a rapid and timely way.

The introduction of management-initiated employee involvement programs (EIPs) has inspired a significant body of research by sociologists who study work, the labor process, organizations, and industrial relations. By and large, these researchers have been skeptical about workers' commitments and consent to such participative programs, suggesting that demands for participation thinly veil a reality of harder work with fewer resources, leaving workers themselves suspicious of such reform (Hodson 1995). Yet, as I will discuss, most research has focused on participative arrangements that are subject to collective bargaining in unionized, industrial work settings that employ a homogeneous and declining fraction of the U.S. labor force. As a result, our knowledge about the causes of, negotiations over, and outcomes associated with EIPs does not extend to the white-collar service work settings in which a vast number of Americans are employed in the late twentieth-century postindustrial U.S. . . .

Abridgment of "Employee Involvement, Involved Employees: Participative Work Arrangements in a White-Collar Service Occupation" by Vicki Smith, reprinted from *Social Problems*, Vol. 43, No. 2, May 1996: pp. 166–179. Copyright © 1996 by The Society for the Study of Social Problems. Reprinted with permission of The University of California Press, Journals Division, via the Copyright Clearance Center and the author.

Employee Involvement Programs in the U.S. Economy

The data on employee involvement or participation programs in the United States are overlapping, murky, sometimes contradictory, occasionally reported to be scientific but generally believed not to be entirely reliable. Thus, estimates vary about how extensively employers have adopted such programs, ranging from claims that the proportion of Fortune 1000 companies with at least one employee involvement practice had reached about 85 percent in 1990 (Appelbaum and Batt 1994:60), to more cautious projections that a smaller number (37 percent) have "*significant* (my emphasis) involvement . . . (in which) a majority of core employees (are) covered by two or more forms of workplace innovation" (U.S. Department of Labor 1994:34–35).

As Fantasia, Clawson, and Graham (1988:469) point out, "Everything from a suggestion box to a worker-controlled economy has been included under the rubric" of worker participation. Despite the wide-ranging nature of these data, few sociologists who study work dispute that at the very least a *discourse* of involvement, but very often its practice, has become a common approach to work in the postindustrial workplace.

Part of the difficulty in pinning down precisely what employee involvement is and how far it has entered the corporate workplace is that many different participative schemes are included in the definition. Nevertheless, it is possible to categorize these schemes into two clusters, one geared toward the macro-level, power structure of the firm, and one geared toward micro-level work systems, toward improving and changing the way goods and services are produced.

In the first cluster of EIPs, workers negotiate and shape firm-level policies. Including representation on boards of directors (Stern 1988), joint labor/management committees (Bate and Murphy 1981); and ownership by workers (Tucker, Nock, and Toscano 1989), these organizational modes of participation are formal, structured, and nearly completely pertain to goods-producing, manufacturing workers who are represented by unions.

The second cluster contains participative approaches, varied in their depth, duration, and transformative potential, that oversee, coordinate, direct, and manage work systems. Some *consultative* practices, such as intermittently organized quality circles, or daily, weekly or monthly problem-solving and communicational meetings involving workers and managers, exist apart from everyday work routines.

Other participative innovations are comparatively more integrated into the labor process, enabling workers to participate on a permanent rather than sporadic, consultative basis. In theory, they reorganize how workers produce goods and services. They create opportunities for workers to learn new skills, acquire greater amounts of organizational/production information, use their judgement, provide meaningful input, and to make on-the-spot decisions. Particular innovations include job rotation, job enrichment, and self-managed teams and can be found across the occupational and industrial spectrum.

This paper addresses the latter cluster of EIPs—involvement at the point of production—but looks at a work setting that is different from those typically studied. Although all evidence suggests that these programs can be found across the spectrum of occupations and industries, to date we know much more about how they work in unionized, goods-producing firms (Appelbaum and Batt 1994; Fantasia, Clawson, and Graham 1988; Harrison 1994; Heckscher 1988; Hodson et al. 1993; Kochan, Katz, and McKersie 1986;

Wells 1987). This limited framework universalizes the experiences of a relatively small proportion of the U.S. workforce, and implicitly suggests that innovations reshaping unionized, blue-collar workplaces are a harbinger of things to come for all U.S. workers.

Because we lack a well-developed body of research about participative forms in white-collar, service, non-union firms, our model of worker participation in the U.S. economy, and our knowledge about control, skill, and autonomy, is incomplete. Moreover, our explanation for why workers' responses to EIPs range from "cynicism and active resistance to grudging acceptance and even enthusiasm" (Hodson 1995:101) is partial. Most studies focus on the cynicism, resistance, or grudging acceptance that follows when workers feel they have no choice but to participate. They either have to comply with management's request for worker involvement and intensified effort or they lose their jobs and perhaps their plant. Sociologists and industrial relations researchers have well documented U.S. workers' weakened bargaining power as employers have shipped their jobs overseas, have downsized and laid off workers, forcing workers to accept management's terms for greater involvement. Such disadvantageous conditions can well explain why much of the labor movement has resisted or only grudgingly gone along with the new participatory agenda.

But those conclusions apply to a limited set of historically specific institutional work settings. Firms that are restructuring both entrenched production processes and industrial relations systems presumably will vary significantly from firms in which labor processes have not been as firmly institutionalized and bound by rules, which have never been characterized by adversarial labor/management relations, and whose workers demographically are comparatively

new to core-sector, white-collar employment. We must ask whether, under the latter set of conditions, workers might be less likely to resist and will perhaps even embrace work reforms. And, if they embrace them, is it because they are uncritical dupes of managerial control, or is their endorsement linked in some fundamental way to the demands, constraints, and opportunities presented in their work? One purpose of the following analysis is to demonstrate that production workers' "enthusiastic effort" was explained by their belief that EI gave them new competencies in simultaneously handling and deflecting stressful work relations.

A secondary claim here is that endorsement was conditioned by the prevailing class, gender, and race hierarchy in the postindustrial United States. What we *do* know about why workers have appropriated or struggled over participation programs is limited to the experiences of male, primarily white workers, workers who have held historically secure positions in the labor market and who make up the overwhelming majority of the industrial, unionized workforce. Their institutionalized interests in regulating work, their definition of advantages gained and privileges lost, their willingness to adopt a new ethos of production, will most likely differ from the interests of relatively new workforce entrants, white women, and men and women of color who have struggled recently to make strides in an expanding, white-collar service economy.

Case Study Participants and Methods

The data analyzed here, drawn from interviews with and observations of white-collar service workers, were gathered in the course of studying an employee involvement program in a division of a large U.S. service firm: Reproco, a pseudonym for a company that manufactures photocopy and computer equipment and sells copying and other business services. These data illuminate the subjective side of a structural innovation as experienced by nonmanagerial employees.

I observed (in 10 of 40 worksites in this division), used company and business publications to do archival research, and conducted 26 in-depth, semistructured interviews (ranging from 1 to 2½ hours) with 10 supervisors and managers and 16 nonmanagerial employees. Of the managers and supervisors, 5 were men and 5 were women (8 white women and men, 2 women of color); of the nonmanagerial employees 11 were women and 5 were men (6 white, 10 nonwhite [African American and Hispanic]).

I interviewed Reproco employees about the programmatic aspects of employee involvement and explored their work biographies, job requirements, and experiences with the program. In particular, I explored their interpretations of employee involvement and their organizational interests in participation. Interview data were then coded to mine the subjective experiences of corporate workers at different organizational levels. This paper focuses on an unsolicited, serendipitous finding, in which workers delved at length into personal transformations that they felt had occurred as a result of training and participation. Finally, I distributed a survey to everyone I interviewed that collected data on salary, job experience, educational background, age, and family status.

The Jobs and the Workers: Skill, Compensation, Training

Reproco's employee involvement scheme was introduced to white-collar service workers who labored in an unpredictable, continually changing, low-status, and socially variegated job environment. To understand

the meaning of employee involvement to workers, then, requires understanding the work conditions, job rewards, and human capital of the job holders; and how the EIP attempted to smooth possible friction between these features.

First, this division of Reproco had successfully marketed a flexible service by subcontracting out business-service workers to perform photocopy work in "facilities" on the premises of other companies. Taking advantage of an economic climate in which an increasing number of U.S. firms are downsizing the total number of their permanent employees and hiring others to work for a delimited period of time (Callaghan and Hartmann 1992; Harrison 1994), Reproco subcontracted the photocopy function to companies that no longer wished to organize and manage this service themselves. Reproco employees set up photocopy rooms in other companies, staffing them with two to five machine operators; company managers trained the photocopiers and provided, in Reproco's own centralized office, backup staff and machines to accommodate changing, unpredictable photocopy loads.

This arrangement meant that while employed by Reproco, machine operators performed their work in diverse organizational settings; they were "organizational boundary spanning" workers (Wharton 1993) who continually and simultaneously had to be cognizant of their own employers' demands (Reproco) and those of the employing company in which they physically worked. They were accountable to diverse sets of "corporate clients" (who differed with respect to professional and industry status, and race and gender) as well as to their off-site supervisors.

They moved from one type of organizational setting to another over time, receiving little forewarning about when and where they would work when a contract expired. They could perform quite routine photocopy work (photocopying 8.5" × 11"

An unusually engaged occup.

documents day in and day out for an insurance company) or they could perform highly complex photocopy work, quality production of which could be urgent (photocopying plant blueprints for trouble-shooting engineers in a nuclear power facility, for example). They learned the specifications for each organization on the job.

During any given day, the machine operators' work load was unpredictable and potentially stressful: "Corporate clients," those employees bringing jobs to the machine operators, rarely knew in advance when they would need something photocopied, and they felt no compunction to try and coordinate with or subordinate their needs to the needs of others, often demanding immediate turnaround for their job. The machine operators had to use their own judgement continually, whether about scheduling copy jobs, deciding upon specifications they could provide for a client, or sending jobs they couldn't accommodate to the divisional center.

The tone of these "unscriptable" interactions could be problematic because corporate clients often viewed Reproco machine operators as low-status workers: "just button pushers," or "just copiers" (epithets reported by copiers). In this highly uncertain, social-relationally complex environment, machine operators had no official supervisor or managers; a lead operator, designated as head worker without formal managerial status or compensation, took informal responsibility for coordinating the group as a whole. This reflected Reproco's agenda to cut back layers of management (typical of many large firms [Smith 1990]); supervisors and managers from the division's center periodically visited the facilities to gather information and evaluate work performance. In significant ways, corporate clients were as much agents of control as were Reproco managers.

The job carried with it a bundle of characteristics typical of white-collar service sector jobs in the U.S. postindustrial occupational structure (Sullivan 1989). Like other white-collar working-class jobs, it offered modest pay (the typical income category checked off by machine operators on a survey was the $15,000–$19,000 category), low status in the organizational hierarchy, required only a high school degree (only one machine operator of the 16 I interviewed possessed a college degree), offered limited mobility to management, and did not demand or develop complex technical skills. But it also had characteristics of a white-collar middle-class job: Job holders developed social-relational skills and unique kinds of organizational knowledge, the work was unpredictable rather than routine, and semi-autonomous rather than directed by others.

The machine operator position was highly race stratified although surprisingly gender balanced. Nearly 40 percent of the machine operators were African American and Hispanic, and these aggregate company statistics covered up much deeper regional stratification—in urban facilities there was much higher representation of men and women of color. Most men in machine operator positions were African American and Hispanic, while white men were found primarily in supervisory and management positions.

Like many other U.S. companies, Reproco's top management had formulated a new work system to increase the ability of its workforce to handle both the complexities of decentralized production and occupationally and demographically diverse work relations. To level its own organizational hierarchy, to iron out disparate work conditions and the potential tensions that might occur at their intersection, corporate-level management had implemented an employee involvement program. Reproco was attempting to manage the unpredictable work environment and to equip new workers to accommodate this unpredictability.

Reproco's EIP taught an in-depth approach to understanding the social relations

Job chars. / reqs.

+s

+s

RCG chars.

↑ racially stratified

Reasons for ⊗ EIP

Reacting to unpredictability

↓ human cop in various offices

little support

of work, couched in conventional individualistic and psychologistic terms. Employees learned new communication techniques, taking turns, for example, playing different roles, simulating attack and defend situations, and learning to identify different kinds of statements and types of dialogues. They learned how to respond to aggressive and/or hostile individuals in an "appropriate" manner, in a way that supported the adage that "the customer is always right" but that allowed the worker to remain self-possessed.

The communications skills tied into the techniques they learned for determining the production of services independently of management. Employees were trained to initiate and lead problem-solving groups, for example, using their newfound communications skills to facilitate them. They learned group process procedures, such as running the meetings, identifying, describing, analyzing, and solving problems. Round-robin techniques, which gave everyone a chance to talk and which enabled the suppression of constant talkers, formally opened up the opportunity for all to participate.

Communications, problem solving, and group process techniques were used for myriad purposes. Workers and managers used them, casually and more formally, to figure out how to work more cost effectively, to open up bottlenecks in production processes, and adjudicate conflicts between fellow employees, or between Reproco employees and clients. The whole package of techniques was designed to enhance flexibility at work, to give company employees a chance to act on their own accumulated knowledge about the best way to conduct work tasks, to depend on co-workers to get them through difficult and unanticipated situations in the absence of formal management: in other words, to self-manage through the often choppy waters of flexible work life. Thus, despite the low level of these jobs in the overall

hierarchy, there was a structural basis for involvement, for autonomous decision making, job planning, and limited self-management albeit under conditions clearly established by management.

Participating in Participation: Workers' Perceptions

Machine operators were expected to accommodate to shifting work loads and organizational contexts and to assume responsibility for basic supervisorial tasks without the formal recognition and compensation for being a manager. I anticipated, when I started interviewing the service workers in these settings, to find significant evidence of stress, noncompliance, or at least, cynicism about the conditions under which they worked. But I found instead something quite unanticipated: workers' expression of what Hodson (1991) calls "enthusiastic effort," wherein workers not only were willing to fine tune their efforts to unpredictable work loads, but they routinely praised the EIP, articulating their perceptions of benefits they received from their preparation and training for EI.

I argue that white-collar business-service workers in Reproco endorsed employee involvement because they saw it as providing a set of interpretive skills that enabled them to negotiate complex social relations in a decentralized organizational context. Working autonomously, building and using tacit knowledge, and working across the boundaries of multiple organizations implicated them in exacting and stressful work encounters. The EIP, according to my informants, had offered a means for reflecting on these encounters and to interpret them, thus increasing workers' feelings of efficacy in controlling them. In other words, workers viewed the EIP as critical to on-the-job survival.

Their interpretations of these advantages are situated within a larger context of class and race stratification. Most people hired as machine operators had limited educational backgrounds and occupational histories and had experienced rocky transitions into even this low level of the corporate work world. Their chances for upward mobility into professional and managerial occupations were statistically narrow. I argue that their responses to Reproco's EIP were thus conditioned by the prevailing institutional sources of race, class, and gender inequality constraining their labor market choices. The EIP training and skills positioned them with a new cultural capital (Lamont and Lareau 1988), a body of knowledge about and awareness of interactions in the corporate world; workers believed this would help them succeed in their current position but also with long-term professional goals.

It is impossible to say with certainty that what workers identify as a new set of skills would genuinely lead to new opportunity, or that their perceptions of control translate into real control over interactions; nevertheless their impression of opportunity and advantage is an important ingredient in their willingness to accommodate themselves to the chaotic job of machine operator.

Building the Self, Learning Interaction

Machine operators repeatedly emphasized the sharpening of four skills: interpreting others' actions and meaning; taking the role of others; "depersonalizing" or transcending particular conflicts; and gaining confidence to participate to a greater degree.

Anita, a pseudonym for a 33-year-old African American woman who had worked for Reproco as a machine operator in various sites for 11 years, described her experiences and thoughts in painstaking terms that were echoed by many of the machine operators. Anita started working for Reproco as a temporary worker when, after a year of college,

she was told that she would not be allowed to return due to poor grades.

Reproco's EIP had required her to participate in meetings and problem-solving groups for the first time in her life, a process that appeared to have been personally difficult. She said she had had to become involved:

> One step at a time. It's, ah, 'cause I don't want to get out there and fall flat on my face. But people are like taking numbers. "Oh god, there she is. She was never here before. What's she doing back there?" 'Cause you're seen, you know, you become more focused, you know, they can see it. "Gosh, she's in view."

Even though major life experiences such as having children and raising them as a single parent had forced her to be a "leader" (her word) in her family, it was only recently, in the course of participating in a few problem-solving groups, that she felt other people had "brought her into focus," recognizing about her, "Oh, she *does* have a mouth, and, oh, she *does* have thought."

When I asked Anita how EI might be useful to her in the way she performed her job—serving professional "clients" in a facility in a large architectural firm—she reflected that:

> There's a way that you want to be perceived. There's a way that you want people to respond to you. You don't want people snapping at you. You don't want people, ah, just tuning you out. You want people to try and understand what's going on with you and where you're coming from.
>
> I have to try and understand what the other person's point is. And to understand the other person's point you have to step out of your shoes for a moment and step in theirs. What they want. What they require . . . I come to work, put myself in the customer's position. Well,

you don't want nobody snapping at you. Because if you snap at someone too much, it's a snap back attitude. But you have to remove yourself and think about the other person. So, yes, I've taken it and put it into everyday life.

Learning to detect and gaining the ability to deflect the "snap back attitude" of other people had been eye opening for Anita; she spoke of becoming "voiced" (her word) and visible in her facility work group when she gained the ability to interpret the needs of clients and co-workers, and to more successfully manage perceptions of herself.

The notion of stepping into someone else's shoes was echoed by Sally, a white re-entry woman in her fifties, who commented that she had learned new tools to

> . . . look at their [her clients'] perspective as well as your own and how you're trying to solve the problem. So, I try to . . . get their perspective of it and see if I can work around it.

This growing awareness of interpersonal dynamics and their implications for work was reported by men as well, who noted similar processes that had occurred in both training and in on-the-job deployment of new communications skills at Reproco. Ralph, for example, emphasized how he felt his ability to interpret others' behavior, to gain some control over interactions with others, had grown and that he felt mentally better equipped to control his reactions to others' behavior.

Ralph was an ex-Marine and Vietnam veteran, one of 10 children raised in a Hispanic family in the Bronx who had moved through a series of working-class, white-collar jobs, and had unsuccessfully tried to establish a small business, before working for Reproco. He emphasized that he had never had professional role models in his family and that he ultimately wished to run his own small business (a goal he felt he was

getting closer to because of his experience with Reproco as a machine operator in the engineering division of a nuclear power plant facility). When I asked Ralph whether EIP had assisted him in any way he answered:

> Yeah, the communicative skills impressed me. They showed me how I could get information from the customer in a clear way, *taught me how to read body language.* I used to say "Here's your copies, now get out of here." Now I have to make sure I'm communicating, *to understand their needs.* The customer is important and I have to figure out what they need and I'm trying to have more sensitivity to their needs.

In Ralph's eyes, the ability to interpret others' needs and to avoid overreacting to people had enabled him to master his ability to avoid and/or manage crisis, an ability he claimed was newfound. He spoke of avoiding "chain reactions and repetition of problems" (referring to business misfortunes in the past), and how the problem identifying and solving process had "organized his problem solving" ability (as did a number of other respondents, he elaborated in some detail how he used this in church and family affairs). In his thinking, these skills had very tangible outcomes: he saw them as necessary for eventually having his own business. He remarked:

> I don't want to reach the point where I'll have multiples of problems. I don't want to make the mistakes others have made. I want to be able to identify and solve before problems turn into a big crisis. I always wanted to have my own business but I've always been insecure *about my knowledge of people,* customers.

Having dropped out of Howard University and then community college for financial reasons, and having worked at two temporary clerical positions before joining Reproco, James, a 29-year-old African American man, was understandably committed to the company: The job security, the benefits package, the training he had undergone, and prospects for diverse job opportunities, were attractive even if limited. He started as a machine operator and at the time of our interview was working as a lead operator, coordinating seven operators. James's facility was one of the few that was not located inside another company; it was in a regional center and accepted copy jobs from firms in the area. This entailed a more complex set of negotiations with people from a range of diverse organizations.

He felt that training in group process and communications had changed his work life and his ability to effectively work in a job that was de facto a supervisorial job. Moreover, he emphasized that he had imported the tools and insights into other realms of his life, a claim mentioned by nearly all of my respondents. He spontaneously described his feeling that clear and undefensive communication enabled him to coordinate the work of the machine operators and deal with clients more authoritatively:

> . . . like I said, what I've learned here and dealing with people, I've taken outside. And I transfer what I learned and put it into my daily life and it helped me to, I learned how to, like I said before, *how to listen, and how to make sure that I understand exactly what someone is telling me. . .* just to listen and see if I'm able to do as someone is instructing me to do or if I'm able to do that . . .

Using the technique of getting people to clarify their statements, confusion about which could evoke the wrath of customers (and had, on occasion), enabled him to

> . . . test my understanding, make sure I understand exactly what someone was telling me. (I get them) to repeat it, to clarify it. That way, you won't cause any

problems at the end because I . . . if I asked you again to repeat it, to clarify, then we won't have any problems at the end. I find that it helps me to avoid conflict, helps me to resolve conflict . . . I find I help a lot of other people resolve conflicts and issues in their lives . . . It gives me a way of helping them see things from another perspective and in a non-threatening way, it's kinda weird.

New to him, learning to pay attention to the dynamics of conversation and interaction added to his belief that he was better able to organize and accomplish complex jobs. In one recent job for which he could take credit, a leading chemical company had contracted the services of this facility to photocopy volumes of material for a federal investigation. James had not only had to organize the entire production process, but he also had to coordinate dozens of temporary workers brought in solely for this purpose and negotiate extensively with Reproco divisional-level management and with representatives of the federal government.

Being trained in communication and involvement, acquiring knowledge about work relations, I argue, built workers' perception of greater efficacy in interaction. The formal techniques of EI also provided openings for people to experience validation of different kinds of verbal participation by the organization. Gaining the confidence to talk, and thus not feeling completely at the mercy of others who could monopolize interaction, was another outcome of the EIP identified by nearly all my respondents.

For example, linguistic competence itself can be an important barrier for individuals who wish to deal effectively with co-workers and clients. For one Hispanic woman—for whom English was her second, extremely well-spoken language—differences in language competency translated, in her mind, to inferior thought itself.

Hilda's experience shows how one of the techniques followed in EI groups—the round-robin approach, wherein everyone around the room has to verbally contribute—helped her overcome genuine terror over language inadequacies and to place her own insights and contributions on a par with those she perceived as being "smarter," "more impressive" (who happened to be experienced male co-workers). She described her introduction to an EI group in the following way:

> I remember when we were first trained in leadership through quality, that you do the meetings and we were learning the lingo—seeking information, giving information—normally in a crowd full of people I would not talk because I'd figure—I would feel—the barrier of language would come up, the barriers of, well, these are men that have been doing this for years, maybe they know better than I do so let me shut up and not get involved . . .
>
> *They were more impressive.* And then once the employee involvement makes everybody get involved and the best thing about it, which I loved was that nobody is—when you're brainstorming, no one is allowed to criticize your idea. Even if it's weird, even if it's the worst idea you could ever make and you know it and it sorta comes out of your lips—nobody is allowed to make a comment because that's what brainstorming is. *Free ideas without an evaluation on them.* So the facilitator was, "No, no, no, you can't make a comment" (Author's note: Her facilitator stopped people from interrupting her). And he makes you feel better because you can say anything and you don't feel like, intimidated by the boys network.

Her insights about how public involvement and visibility rattled her were vivid in equating language mastery with competency itself:

. . . in meetings, as soon as you said a meeting—I would have a fit. My palms would sweat. I would start sweating and I would be like, "Please God, don't let them ask me anything." *Because my accent would automatically get very heavy and my brain was not translating at the pace that it normally does.* So my thoughts were coming in two languages . . . You know that I had a stomach ache. But I had to think real good because I wanted to say something that was intelligent. But it made me say something and it made me open up a little bit more in meetings and things like that.

These insights and experiences were seconded by others. Hillary, a 48-year-old African American woman, identified the importance of understanding hidden principles of communication, which she learned in her in-depth training session, for independently organizing cooperative relations in the course of working. She appreciated the participative approach to problem solving because it meant that groups had to "acknowledge that a person has made a proposal instead of *just ignoring it and going on,*" a kind of silencing process in which she felt herself to have been on the receiving end.

Speaking especially of one communication technique (learning how to clarify statements and requests) she pointed out the virtues of using this technique for helping people better understand cultural complexity and smoothing out tensions incurred in the process of accomplishing work tasks:

> These are all behaviors that this training helped us to identify, and that's part of the first step of being able to change anybody's behavior, *is to recognize it.* And once you are aware of it then you can begin to change it, address it. One of the areas that they taught and I was unaware of this until this training so this is very key for me, was the—what they

call, clarifying, the clarifying behavior. To ask a clarifying question as opposed to making an assumption that is wrong. Because our language can be very, ah, ah, *can have many meanings,* depending on voice inflection and ah, you know, a person can say something and they can mean something totally different from what you understand.

Pondering meaning, interpreting action, and taking the perspective of others; using the communication tools and an interpretive framework to strengthen one's voice and efficacy in a complex work setting; to become more involved in group processes and decision making, were themes raised over and over and spontaneously in interviews with machine operators. The perceived benefits that service workers identified cemented their commitments to Reproco, even when it was questionable whether these benefits lent themselves to meaningful upward mobility or wage improvement. In these informants' minds, new interactional insights and skills were meaningful if intangible assets.

"Procedural Resistance": Using Employee Involvement Techniques to Resist Clients

Workers' beliefs about how they benefited were bolstered in additional and comparatively concrete ways by the EI training. The EIP provided the techniques for "procedural resistance," a means for machine operators to coopt unreasonably insistent, contemptuous and otherwise difficult corporate clients, many of them professionals who could be a more immediate, intense, and stressful source of control than off-site supervisors or managers. Machine operators appropriated these simple techniques to enlist clients themselves as partners in the participative agenda and to set limits on their demands.

Machine operators reported having talked clients into helping finish copy jobs that operators couldn't complete themselves (for example, collating particularly complex documents); drawing clients into the process of planning the work flow; getting clients to take joint responsibility for decisions about working overtime to complete urgently needed jobs; and using simple surveys to solicit feedback about machine operators' job performance as well as ideas about improving the service.

Using communications skills with the goal of sharing information with clients, encouraging them to participate in brainstorming about techniques for completing work, and eliciting feedback about service production and improvement of service delivery gave machine operators a way to negotiate competing demands and defuse potentially hostile client-operator interactions within the terms of the new participative program. This ability to use authorized procedures as tools of resistance, to establish parameters on their work loads, was an important defense mechanism for the operators. Importantly, workers didn't resist new techniques themselves, but they used the techniques to resist and co-opt negative, antagonistic clients.

Conclusion

In many ways, Reproco's EIP is a stunning example of how contemporary managers draw on prevailing popular ideologies about participation to extract greater effort from workers. The machine operators in this study willingly directed their own work efforts day in and day out, engaged in group decision making, took risks in using their own judgement for production decisions, and represented the interests of Reproco by absorbing conflict and dispute in relations with corporate clients. In other words, this

Social-relational skills most useful for low-class workers

program coordinated workers' and management's goals, a participative system of control (Dickson 1981) highly successful in "securing yet obscuring" (Burawoy 1979:30) workers' consent.

Living up to the gravest concerns that observers have about EIP in U.S. workplaces, Reproco's system has intensified everyday work life for poorly compensated workers. The findings presented here confirm one pessimistic claim that has been made by those studying EIP: that these innovations may strengthen management's capacity to extract additional effort from workers by concealing job speedups and work intensification behind the language of enrichment (cf. O'Reilly 1994).

one main crit of such EIP → 1 more!

But what this research makes clear is that some workers have compelling reasons to participate in new systems and may consent to the conditions described throughout this paper because they perceive unanticipated payoffs and opportunities. For one thing, low-level, white-collar service workers endorsed Reproco's EIP precisely because the program and its micro-level techniques, in their eyes, heightened their sense of greater efficacy in managing those conditions. Their endorsement, then, was conditioned by the structural arrangements and the social relations of their jobs.

For another, workers saw these new skills as part of a process of career building. They envisioned taking these skills and applying them to their own small businesses, to different positions in other large corporations, and to higher level positions inside Reproco. Thus, while Reproco's participative arrangements entailed significant intensity of work effort and commitment, they also created a context for workers to develop new skills, seen by workers as relevant to future opportunity. They were not technological skills, much emphasized by the literature on involvement and worker participation; rather they

were social-relational skills that were potentially transferable to other white-collar, service contexts, and perhaps to low levels of supervision and management. Participation in participation, then, ostensibly represented a new step on a constrained mobility ladder.

Broadly, the acquisition of these skills is important for workers who have historically been excluded from core-sector, permanent job opportunities. Much research has been done on the difficulty African American and Hispanic youth, for example, have in making the transition from school to paid work (see Powers, forthcoming, for an overview of this transition). Neckerman and Kirshenman's (1991) important article on the way racist assumptions circumscribe employers' recruitment, selection, and hiring practices similarly underscores the achievement of those African Americans and Hispanics who have made it into the secure, albeit lowest employed, ranks of large, urban, white-collar firms. Neckerman and Kirschenman emphasize the significance of the very skills, identified by my informants, that employers use to screen out many people of color in the hiring process: Employers look for "appropriate interaction and conversational style—in short, shared culture" (1991:442); "job applicants must be sensitive to verbal and nonverbal cues and to the hidden agenda underlying interviewers' questions" (1991:442). These "social skills and cultural compatibility" are used to make future promotion decisions.

These conclusions are echoed by Moss and Tilly (1995), who analyze the way employers discriminate against African American men in their hiring practices. Employers feel that African American men lack the appropriate "soft" skills (communication and people skills, teamwork skills, demeanor and so forth) that are crucial to successful outcomes in the post-industrial workplace.

My respondents have made it past this screening process, laden with negative assumptions about race and class, and are now struggling to survive—to do their jobs on terms acceptable to the corporation, to achieve some degree of personal and occupational efficacy in order to work with others. They have found success in Reproco's white-collar ranks, doing work that is unskilled technically, but that builds white-collar interpersonal skills that can be transferred to other corporate contexts; in a position that pays low wages but offers a benefits package and secure employment; working in demographically and occupationally heterogeneous settings that build their interactional skill set.

Even if these new skills don't lead directly to upward mobility, even if structural reorganization flattens hierarchies and runs counter to the expansion of vertical opportunities (a structural trend affecting workers across the occupational spectrum [Smith 1993]), lower-level workers can compete for new lateral opportunities and learn to more effectively manipulate their work environments to defend their own interests and existing status, an important skill noted recently by sociologists studying other work settings (Paules 1991). They can learn to better negotiate the day-to-day operations of workplaces and to exercise authority in relations with co-workers. Although a beginning, such individual paths of change may have the long-term effect of transforming the workplace hierarchies that have consolidated around race, gender, and class.

REFERENCES

Appelbaum, Eileen and Rosemary Batt. 1994. *The New American Workplace*. Ithaca: ILR Press.

Bate, S. P. and J. Murphy. 1981. "Can Joint Consultation Become Employee Participation?" *Journal of Management Studies* 18:389–409.

Burawoy, Michael. 1979. *Manufacturing Consent.* Chicago: University of Chicago Press.

Callaghan, Polly and Heidi Hartmann. 1992. *Contingent Work: A Chart Book on Parttime and Temporary Employment.* Washington, D.C.: Institute for Women's Policy Research/ Economic Policy Institute.

Dickson, John. 1981. "Participation as a Means of Organizational Control." *Journal of Management Studies* 18:159–176.

Edwards, Richards. 1979. *Contested Terrain.* New York: Basic Books.

Fantasia, Rick, Dan Clawson, and Gregory Graham. 1988. "A Critical View of Worker Participation in American Industry." *Work and Occupations* 15:468–488.

Harrison, Bennett. 1994. *Lean and Mean.* New York: Basic Books.

Heckscher, Charles. 1988. *The New Unionism.* New York: Basic Books.

Hodson, Randy. 1991. "The Active Worker: Compliance and Autonomy at the Workplace." *Journal of Contemporary Ethnography* 20:47–78.

———. 1995. "Worker Resistance: An Underdeveloped Concept in the Sociology of Work." *Economic and Industrial Democracy* 16:79–110.

Hodson, Randy, Sean Creighton, Cheryl Jamison, Sabine Rieble, and Sandy Welsh. 1993. "Is Worker Solidarity Undermined by Autonomy and Participation? Patterns from the Ethnographic Literature." *American Sociological Review* 58:398–416.

Kochan, Thomas, Harry Katz, and Robert McKersie. 1986. *The Transformation of American Industrial Relations.* New York: Basic Books.

Lamont, Michelle and Annette Lareau. 1988. "Cultural Capital: Allusions, Gaps, and Glissandos in Recent Theoretical Developments." *Sociological Theory* 6:153–168.

Leidner, Robin. 1993. *Fast Food, Fast Talk.* Berkeley: University of California Press.

Moss, Philip, and Chris Tilly. 1995. "'Soft' Skills and Race: An Investigation of Black Men's Employment Problems." *Russell Sage Foundation* Working Paper #80.

Neckerman, Kathryn and Joleen Kirschenman. 1991. "Hiring Strategies, Racial Bias, and Inner-City Workers." *Social Problems* 38:433–447.

O'Reilly, Jacqueline. 1994. *Banking on Flexibility.* Aldershot: Avebury.

Paules, Greta. 1991. *Dishing It Out*. Philadelphia: Temple University Press.

Powers, Brian. Forthcoming. *Shadowed Passages: Remaking Inequality from High School to the Workplace*.

Smith, Vicki. 1990. *Managing in the Corporate Interest*. Berkeley: University of California Press.

———. 1993. "Flexibility in Work and Employment: The Impact on Women." *Research in the Sociology of Organizations* 11:195–216.

Stern, Robert. 1988. "Participation by Representation: Workers on Boards of Directors in the United States and Abroad." *Work and Occupations* 15:396–422.

Sullivan, Teresa. 1989. "Women and Minority Workers in the New Economy." *Work and Occupations* 16:393–415.

Tausky, Curt and Anthony Chelte. 1988. "Workers' Participation." *Work and Occupations* 15:363–373.

Tucker, James, Steven Nock, and David Toscano. 1989. "Employee Ownership and Perceptions of Work: The Effect of an Employee Stock Ownership Plan." *Work and Occupations* 16:26–42.

U.S. Department of Labor. 1994. *Fact Finding Report: Commission on the Future of Worker-Management Relations*.

Wells, Donald. 1987. *Empty Promises: Quality of Working Life Programs and the Labor Movement*. New York: Monthly Review Press.

Wharton, Amy. 1993. "The Affective Consequences of Service Work: Managing Emotions on the Job." *Work and Occupations* 20: 205–232.

Discussion Questions for Part II

1. Powell (Reading 9) suggests that we are in the midst of a "fundamental change in the way work is organized, structured, and governed." In what ways does the new system he describes differ from the Fordist model described in previous readings?

2. Powell wants us to consider "who has been harmed the most by this transition, and what social policies might ease the burdens of this shift?" How would you answer these questions?

3. Smith describes professionals' and managers' experience of unemployment in the new economy. How might these experiences differ for other types of workers (e.g, blue-collar workers, service workers)?

4. In light of the information contained in Reading 9 (Powell), how would you evaluate the advice given the unemployed professionals and managers in Smith's study?

5. What are the implications of the changes Powell and Smith describe for today's college graduates?

6. What are the most important skills required to work on the digital assembly line? Are these "action-centered" or "intellective" skills?

7. According to the readings in Part II, in what respects (if any) have computerization and automation improved the jobs of lower-level (i.e., nonprofessional, nonmanagerial) workers? In what ways have these jobs been made worse?

8. Discuss the concept of "flexibility" as it is used by the authors in this part and as it applies to the 21st-century workplace. What are the advantages and disadvantages of a more flexible workplace for workers? Employers? Consumers?

PART III

Work and Inequality

████   **WORK WAGES AND INEQUALITY**   ████

∞ **READING 15** ∞

The New Geography of Global Income Inequality

Glenn Firebaugh

A t the time of the first Industrial Revolution, Thomas Malthus (1960 [1798]) and other classical economists feared that humans might be doomed to near-subsistence levels of living. A century earlier Thomas Hobbes had warned that a powerful sovereign was needed lest life be "solitary, poor, nasty, brutish, and short" (Hobbes 1962 [1651], p. 100). Malthus was even more pessimistic, warning that poverty is the likely human lot with or without a powerful ruler. Malthus's fear was based on a population-trap model positing that economic growth is unlikely to outpace population growth over the long run. In this model, economic gains are short-lived, because the geometric growth of population inevitably catches up with linear economic gains. Unless there are other checks on population growth, income per person will inevitably return to a low equilibrium level. A new round of economic expansion will upset that equilibrium in the short run, but in the long run income per capita will track back down to its preexpansion level. In other words, economic growth will serve to increase the size of the human population, but it will not boost living standards over the long run.

The Growing World Income Pie

The pace of population growth and economic growth over the last two centuries has proved Malthus right about the expansion of the human population but wrong about the population trap. In line with Malthus, the productivity gains of the Industrial Revolution were accompanied by an era of unprecedented population growth. In 1820 the world's population was about 1.1 billion (Maddison 1995, table 1.1a). Today the world's population has surpassed 6 billion. But contrary to Malthus's warning that rapid population growth will undermine economic growth, the quintupling of the world's population has not resulted in stagnant incomes and living standards. The economic historian Richard Easterlin recently wrote that "a revolution in the human condition is sweeping the world. Most people today are better fed, clothed, and housed than their predecessors two centuries ago. . . . Although the picture is not one of universal progress, it is the greatest advance in the condition of the world's population ever achieved in such a brief span of time" (Easterlin 2000, p. 7). In the face of unprecedented growth in world population, world income has grown even faster. In fact economic growth over the past two centuries has so greatly outpaced population growth that, according to the standard source for such historical comparisons, income per capita for the world as a whole has, in constant dollars, increased roughly eight-fold since 1820 (Maddison 1995, table 1.1a).

So over the past two centuries a world population explosion has been outdone by a world income explosion. The world income pie has expanded not only in an absolute sense, but also in a per capita sense, as most people today enjoy a much higher standard of living than their ancestors had in the preindustrial world. Although scholars have tended to pay more attention to the population explosion than to the income explosion, the growth in per capita income is the defining feature of our historical epoch. Moreover, the remarkable growth in world per capita income has shown no signs of leveling off in recent decades. As Robert Lucas (2000, p. 159) notes, "The real income of an average person has more than doubled since World War II and the end of the European colonial age." Before that time, during the first half of the twentieth century and during the nineteenth century, there is strong evidence (despite the fact that income estimates before 1950 tend to be less reliable than those after 1950) that world income growth was not doubling as rapidly (see Maddison 1995, table G-3).

The best estimates of world and regional incomes over the last two centuries are from the economic historian Angus Maddison. Maddison's (1995) monumental income series begins with 1820, and Figure 1 depicts Maddison's estimates of per capita income for the whole world for 1820, 1950, and 1990. The figures are in 1990 U.S. dollars, so the observed growth is not due to inflation. Although the estimates for the nineteenth century in particular are based on gross approximations for many nations, the general pattern of sustained growth is unmistakable. As these figures indicate, recent growth has been especially remarkable. In terms of absolute change, average income in the world increased twice as much over the 40-year period 1950–1990 as it did over the previous 130 years combined (an increase of $3,066 from 1950 to 1990 versus an increase of $1,487 from 1820 to 1950).

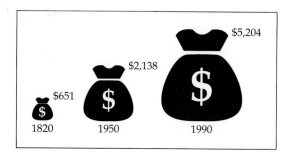

FIGURE 1 World Average Income in 1990 U.S. Dollars: 1820, 1950, and 1990 Based on Maddison 1995.

The 1950–1990 interval also exhibits a faster growth rate, as average income increased by a factor of 2.4 over the 40 years from 1950 to 1990 after increasing by a factor of 3.3 over the much longer period of 1820 to 1950.

Other Welfare Changes

In addition to rising incomes over the past two centuries, there are two other significant changes that bear on the issue of changing human welfare. The first is that we tend to live longer now than before. Life expectancy today is estimated to be sixty-six years at birth for the world as a whole (World Almanac 2001), which is likely almost double what it was at the beginning of the twentieth century.[1] This dramatic increase in life expectancy is one of the singular features of the past hundred years. Not only do people live better than before, they also live much longer—a fact not captured by statistics on income growth per se. No doubt most people agree with C. P. Snow's (1963, p. 78) statement that "it seems to me better that people should live rather than die . . . [and] that they shouldn't have to watch their children die." Although it is difficult to place a dollar value on longer life, most would agree that length of life is part of human welfare. Because the analysis in this [chapter] focuses on change in per capita income without also factoring in rising life expectancy, one could argue that I in fact understate the rise in human welfare since the early nineteenth century. Moreover, the change in average income fails to capture the increased welfare that results from the new choices that we have in the twenty-first century that were not available earlier. Our ancestors in the early nineteenth century knew nothing of automobiles, computers, telephones, air travel, and other inventions of the past two centuries. So if human welfare is largely about options and freedom—as Amartya Sen (1999) has argued—then on that basis the estimated rates of income growth given above most likely understate the rise in material welfare over the last century, since they fail to factor in the new choices available to many today.

The Rise in Income Disparities over the Nineteenth and Twentieth Centuries

There are two big stories about world income trends over the past two centuries. The first story is the remarkable growth in the world's average income, just described. The second story is that the growth has disproportionately benefited different regions of the world, with richer regions generally benefiting much more than poorer regions. As a result global income inequality has worsened dramatically since the early nineteenth century. (In this [chapter] the terms "global income inequality" and "world income inequality" are used as synonyms to refer to the total level of income inequality across all the world's people.) A central message of this [chapter] is that the enormous growth in global inequality occurred during the period of Western industrialization, that is, during the nineteenth century and the first half of the twentieth century. Today, during the period of Asian industrialization, global inequality is no longer growing. (A note on terminology: "Period of Western industrialization" is shorthand for the era when industrialization was led by Western nations. Not all industrialization occurred in the West during this era, of course, but Western nations took the lead in industrializing during this period. Similarly, Asian nations have been industrializing the most aggressively in recent decades, so I use the term "period of Asian industrialization," even though recent industrialization obviously has not been restricted to Asia. Historians sometimes distinguish a "first Industrial Revolution"—about 1760 to 1830, centered in England—from a "second Industrial Revolution"—about 1860 to 1900, occurring simultaneously in the United States and Europe—but in the case of global inequality, the distinction between the first and second Industrial Revolutions is much less significant than the distinction between the Western and Asian periods of industrialization. . . .

This [chapter] focuses on the second story, the unevenness of the income growth. The remarkable rise in average income over the past two centuries has produced massive global income inequality, as income growth in the world's richer regions and nations has outpaced growth in poorer regions and nations. The practical implication for individuals is that in today's world, one's income is determined largely by one's residence. Figure 2 shows the magnitude of the regional disparity in incomes by disaggregating the world averages for 1820 and 1990 and mapping the regional averages with China and India separated out from the rest of Asia. These maps, based on the data in Table 1 below, reveal at a glance not only the striking growth in world per capita income over the past two centuries but also the striking unevenness of that growth across space. Incomes have surged ahead in Europe and lagged behind in Africa and (until recently) in Asia. So the eightfold increase in average world income since 1820 is easy to misinterpret, because it masks huge differences in income growth across the world's major regions.

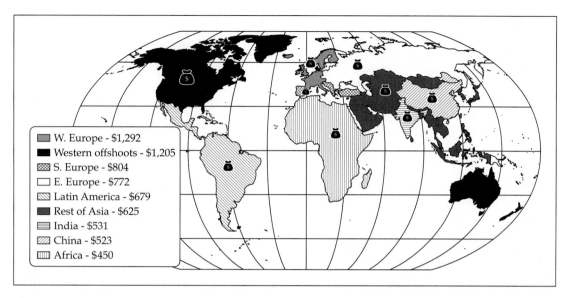

FIGURE 2a Average Incomes in Major Regions of the World, 1820 (in 1990 U.S. Dollars) Based on Table 1. "Rest of Asia" refers to Asia outside China and India; "E. Europe" includes Russia.

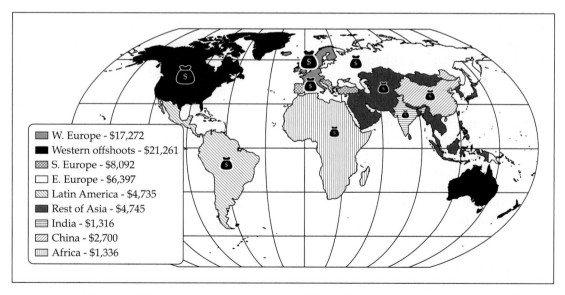

FIGURE 2b Average Incomes in Major Regions of the World, 1990 (in 1990 U.S. Dollars) Based on Table 1. "Rest of Asia" refers to Asia outside China and India; "E. Europe" includes the Soviet Union.

TABLE 1   World "Trifurcation" Since 1820: Average Income in Major Regions of the World in 1820, 1950, and 1990

Region	Income per Capita			Income Growth	
	1820	1950	1990	1950/1820	1990/1950
High-income group					
Western Europe (23 nations)	$1,292	$5,126	$17,272	4.0	3.4
Western offshoots (4 nations)	1,205	9,255	21,261	7.7	2.3
Middle-income group					
Southern Europe (7 nations)	804	2,021	8,092	2.5	4.0
Eastern Europe (9 nations)	772	2,631	6,397	3.4	2.4
Latin America (44 nations)	679	2,487	4,735	3.7	1.9
Low-income group					
Asia (56 nations)					
China	523	614	2,700	1.2	4.4
India	531	597	1,316	1.1	2.2
Rest of Asia	625	1,081	4,745	1.7	4.4
Africa (56 nations)	450	830	1,336	1.8	1.6
World totals	651	2,138	5,204	3.3	2.4

Source: Calculated from Maddison (1995), tables G-l and G-3 for regional data; tables A-3e and D-le for data for China and India.
Note: Regional incomes are population-weighted averages, in 1990 U.S. dollars. The ratios 1950/1820 and 1990/1950 are calculated from the income data. "Western offshoots" refers to Australia, Canada, New Zealand, and the United States. "Asia" includes Oceania.

An important part of the global inequality story is that the world has divided into three income camps. As Table 1 shows, although the three camps were discernible in 1820, the divisions are much sharper today. It is important to note, however, that the divisions are no longer becoming more and more distinct, because the era of global "trifurcation" in income occurred during the period of Western industrialization and now appears to be behind us. Compare the two columns under Income Growth in Table 1. If we rank regions on the basis of their estimated income levels in 1820, we find that over the course of the nineteenth century and first half of the twentieth century the initially richer regions got richer much faster than the poorer regions did (first column under Income Growth). From 1820 to 1950—the period of Western industrialization—per

capita income increased by a multiple of 4.0–7.7 for the initially higher-income regions, by a multiple of 2.5–3.7 for the middle-income regions, and by a multiple of 1.8 or less for the lower-income regions. Since 1950—the period of Asian industrialization—income growth rates no longer line up with initial incomes. Some regions in the low-income group have been growing faster than some regions in the high-income group. These results point to the possibility that the era of big-time growth in global income inequality may be ending.

In the meantime the legacy of the big-time growth in inequality remains. To appreciate the unevenness of the income growth across regions during the period of Western industrialization, compare income growth in the Western offshoots (Australia, Canada, New Zealand, and the United States) to income growth in Africa from 1820 to 1950. Average income is estimated to have been about $1,200 in the Western offshoots in 1820 compared with about $450 in Africa in 1820—a ratio of less than 3 to 1 at the early stages of Western industrialization. By 1950 the ratio had ballooned to about 11 to 1 ($9,255 versus $830). Unless income estimates are wildly off the mark, . . . regional differences in average incomes are profound.

In sum, the world income pie has expanded greatly over the past two centuries, but not everyone's piece has expanded at the same rate. Because incomes tended to grow more rapidly in the richer regions in the nineteenth and early twentieth centuries, income inequality has increased across the world's major regions. . . .

Why Nations?

There are two answers to the question of why nations are strategic in the study of global income inequality. The simple answer is that one uses nations because the income data come that way, packaged in national chunks. Nations have national accounting offices charged with collecting data on the nation's annual productivity, and these data are combined with price data, aggregated, and combined with demographic data to estimate national per capita income. The United Nations, the World Bank, and other international agencies assemble these data and make them readily available.

Yet there is much more than convenience involved in the choice of nations as the unit of analysis for a study of world income inequality. To appreciate why the nation is a strategic unit for studying world income inequality, consider the following thought experiment: Suppose we had income data for every individual in the world (unfortunately, we do not have such data)—over six billion cases in all. Then with a powerful enough

computer we could summarize the level of income inequality for the whole world by calculating some standard summary inequality measure. . . . Now suppose that we were required to aggregate the data to reduce the cases by a factor of 50 million, that is, from 6 billion cases down to 120 cases. One strategy would be to aggregate by assigning individuals the mean income for the nation where they live. This strategy would pare the 6 billion cases to 120 cases since there are about 120 nations with significant populations. In effect we would be replacing six billion cases with 120, and we would calculate the inequality in income across nations instead of across individuals.

How much information about world income inequality would be lost by collapsing 6 billion cases down to 120 nations? Not as much as one would expect for such a drastic reduction in cases. By assigning each individual the national mean on income, we ignore all the variance in income within nations—so within each nation the rich and the poor are assigned the same income. In short, our method of aggregation discards all the within-nation income inequality. But within-nation income inequality accounts for only about one-fourth to one-third of the world's total income inequality (Schultz 1998; Goesling 2001; Milanovic 2002), so if we magically eliminated all income inequality within nations, the world's total income inequality would shrink by only one-third at most. . . .

The central point here is that nations are key in the production and distribution of the world's income. By knowing only one piece of information about individuals—where they live (nation)—we can explain about 70 percent of the variance in individuals' incomes worldwide. The link between national residence and income is strong not because within-nation income inequality is so small, but because the disparity in income across nations is so large. To understand global income inequality, then, we begin with income inequality across nations.

Why Not Focus on Poverty Rather Than on Inequality?

As we have just seen, between-nation income inequality matters because it constitutes the major portion of global income inequality. But why should we care about income inequality in the first place—isn't it poverty that we should really be concerned about, not inequality? Why should we care if some are rich, so long as no one is poor? Aside from ethical arguments about equality and justice there are two compelling reasons for studying world inequality. The first reason is to understand world poverty. As this book will make clear, if we were to study world poverty without also studying world inequality then we would miss an essential element of the story about world poverty: that the poverty problem changed from a production problem to a distribution problem over the course of the Industrial Revolution of the nineteenth and twentieth centuries. Hence the study of global inequality is critical to the study of global poverty. By examining the big picture on global inequality we understand the changing roots of global poverty.

Second, the study of global inequality is critical to major theoretical traditions in sociology and economics (to cite a familiar example, the assumption of income bifurcation is a key component of Marx's theory of history). Here we examine inequality and poverty. . . .

Inequality and Poverty

Income inequality matters because poverty in the world today is largely a problem of distribution, not production. As shown in Figure 1, the growth in total world production has outpaced the growth in world population over the past two centuries. So the average person today is much richer than the average person in the past.

With respect to the trend in the world's *average* income, then, the news has been encouraging over the past two centuries. Although the rise in world incomes does not appear to be accompanied by rising human happiness or contentment, . . . at the least it can be said that at this juncture in history there is greater potential than there was in earlier eras for meeting the essential human needs for food, shelter, clothing, and medical attention. The central economic issue in Malthus's era was whether or not there was enough to go around, so the problem of poverty was primarily a problem of insufficient production. According to the estimates of François Bourguignon and Christian Morrisson (1999, p. 8), in the early nineteenth century about three-fourths of the world's people were poor when poverty is defined as a consumption level of less than $1 per day (in constant 1985 U.S. dollars), and 90 percent were poor if a threshold of $2 per day is used. Adjusting for inflation between 1985 and 1990 and for investment's share of gross domestic product (GDP), $1 per day in 1985 equals an annual income of roughly $625 in 1990 dollars and $2 per day equals an annual income of roughly $1,250 (Bourguignon and Morrisson 1999). Note that $625 is just below the estimated 1820 world *average* income of $651 in Figure 1. Because both income figures are in the same unit (1990 U.S. dollars), they imply that the average person in 1820 was close to the poverty line using the severe standard of $1 consumption per day (in 1985 dollars) and well below the poverty line using the standard of $2 per day (both standards based on the World Bank 1990). In short, as recently as two centuries ago the vast majority of our ancestors were poor, and the cause of that poverty was not income concentration, since according to the $2 per day standard *all* would have been poor if incomes had been distributed equally. For our ancestors the poverty problem was primarily a production problem, not a distribution problem.

Today the situation is quite different. According to the Bourguignon-Morrisson (1999, p. 8) estimates, about 40 percent of the world's people are poor today if we use the $2 per day threshold and about 16 percent are poor if we use the $1 per day threshold. These declines—from 75 percent down to 16 percent poor according to the $1 per day criterion, and from 90 percent down to 40 percent poor according to the $2 per day criterion—certainly provide historical support for the argument of David Dollar and Aart Kraay (2000) that income growth *is* good for the poor. Also note, however, that in 1990 the world's average income in 1990 dollars was about $5,200 (Figure 1), more than four times the poverty threshold of $1,250 (in 1990 dollars) if the higher poverty threshold is used. So if incomes were distributed equally across the world today, all would have incomes well above the World Bank's poverty thresholds. In today's world, then, absolute poverty is primarily a problem of distribution, not production. Today there is more to go around than ever before and, with regard to poverty, the issue is not whether we are producing enough, but how evenly the total product is being distributed.

World poverty evolved from a production problem into a distribution problem during the period of Western industrialization. As we have seen, Western industrialization brought growing global income inequality along with growing global income, as the world divided into three income camps, with Western Europe and its offshoots at the high end and Asia and Africa at the low end. So if you live in Germany or Switzerland or the United States, you are probably enjoying a standard of material comfort that your ancestors could scarcely imagine. If you live in Nepal or Ethiopia or Chad, your standard of living might differ little from that of your ancestors. In short, some populations benefited much more than others from the increased bounty of the Industrial Revolution, and the demarcation between winners and losers over the past two hundred years has largely coincided with regional and national boundaries. The distribution of income at the beginning of the twenty-first century is highly spatially based. Can we expect to see a reduction in the spatial basis of income over the next decades? Although no one expects a sudden change in the world income distribution, there is much talk in the globalization literature of a new global economy where nations diminish in importance. If so, then as national forces yield to global forces in the production of income, we might expect the association of income and nation to diminish over time. . . .

NOTES

1. For most nations of the world we lack good estimates on life expectancy for the first half of the twentieth century. Life expectancy for female babies was 43.7 years in Japan in 1899, 43.7 in Italy and 49.4 in England and Wales in 1901, and 32.5 in Chile in 1909, with males having a life expectancy about 3–4 years less (Preston, Keyfitz, and Schoen 1972). Of these nations, probably life expectancy in Chile was the nearest to that for the world as a whole at the turn of the century. If so, then life expectancy virtually doubled in the twentieth century.

REFERENCES

Bourguignon, François, and Christian Morrisson. 1999. "The size distribution of income among world citizens: 1820–1990." Draft. June.

Dollar, David, and Aart Kraay. 2000. "Growth *is* good for the poor." Draft. March. Retrieved January 2001 from www.worldbank.org/research.

Easterlin, Richard A. 2000. "The Worldwide Standard of Living since 1800." *Journal of Economic Perspectives* 14:7–26.

Goesling, Brian. 2001. "Changing income inequalities within and between nations: New evidence." *American Sociological Review* 66:745–761.

Hobbes, Thomas. 1962 [1651]. *Leviathan: Or, the Matter, Forme, and Power of a Commonwealth, Ecclesiasticall and Civil.* New York: Simon and Schuster.

Lucas, Robert E., Jr. 2000. "Some macroeconomics for the twenty-first century." *Journal of Economic Perspectives* 14:159–168.

Maddison, Angus. 1995. *Monitoring the World Economy, 1820–1992.* Paris: OECD.

Malthus, Thomas R. 1960 [1798]. *On Population.* New York: Modern Library.

Milanovic, Branko. 2002. "True world income distribution, 1988 and 1993: First calculation based on household surveys alone." *Economic Journal* 112:51–92.

Schultz, T. Paul. 1998. "Inequality in the distribution of personal income in the world: How it is changing and why." *Journal of Population Economics* 11:307–344.

Sen, Amartya. 1999. *Development as Freedom.* New York: Knopf.

Snow, Charles Percy. 1963. *The Two Cultures: And a Second Look.* New York: Mentor.

World Almanac. 2001. *The World Almanac and Book of Facts.* Mahwah, N.J.: World Almanac Education Group.

World Bank. 1990. *World Development Report 1990.* Oxford: Oxford University Press.

∽ READING 16 ∽

Jobless Poverty

A New Form of Social Dislocation in the Inner-City Ghetto

William Julius Wilson

In September 1996 my book, *When Work Disappears: The World of the New Urban Poor,* was published. In this chapter, I integrate some of the main arguments and conclusions presented in that book with social policy research in order to address current issues of welfare reform.

When Work Disappears describes a new type of poverty in our nation's metropolises: poor, segregated neighborhoods in which a majority of adults are either unemployed or have dropped out of the labor force altogether. What is the effect of these "jobless ghettos" on individuals, families, and neighborhoods? What accounts for their existence? I suggest several factors and conclude with policy recommendations: a mix of public and private sector projects is more effective than relying on a strategy of employer subsidies.

The Research Studies

When Work Disappears was based mainly on three research studies conducted in Chicago between 1986 and 1993. The first of these three studies included a variety of data: a random survey of nearly 2,500 poor and nonpoor African American, Latino, and white residents in Chicago's poor neighborhoods; a more focused survey of 175 participants who were reinterviewed and answered open-ended questions; a survey of 179 employers selected to reflect distribution of employment across industry and firm size in the Chicago metropolitan areas; and comprehensive ethnographic research, including participant-observation research and life-history interviews by ten research assistants in a representative sample of inner-city neighborhoods.

The first of the two remaining projects also included extensive data: a survey of a representative sample of 546 black mothers and up to two of their adolescent children (aged eleven to sixteen—or 887 adolescents) in working-class, middle-class, and high-poverty neighborhoods; a survey of a representative sample of 500 respondents from two high-joblessness neighborhoods on the South Side of Chicago; and six focus-group discussions involving the residents and former residents of these neighborhoods.

Jobless Ghettos

The jobless poverty of today stands in sharp contrast to previous periods. In 1950, a substantial portion of the urban black population was poor but they were working. Urban poverty was quite extensive but people held jobs. However, as we entered the 1990s most adults in many inner-city ghetto neighborhoods were not working. For example, in 1950 a significant majority of adults held jobs in a typical week in the three neighborhoods that represent the historic core of the Black Belt in Chicago—Douglas, Grand Boulevard, and Washington Park. But by 1990, only four in ten in Douglas worked in a typical week, one in three in Washington Park, and one in four in Grand Boulevard.[1]

In 1950, 69 percent of all males aged fourteen and older who lived in these three neighborhoods worked in a typical week, and in 1960, 64 percent of this group were so employed. However, by 1990 only 37 percent of all males aged sixteen and over held jobs in a typical week in these three neighborhoods.

The disappearance of work has had negative effects not only on individuals and families, but on the social life of neighborhoods as well. Inner-city joblessness is a severe problem that is often overlooked or obscured when the focus is mainly on poverty and its consequences. Despite increases in the concentration of poverty since 1970, inner cities have always featured high levels of poverty. But the levels of inner-city joblessness reached during the first half of the 1990s were unprecedented.

Joblessness Versus Informal Work Activity

I should note that when I speak of "joblessness" I am not solely referring to official unemployment. The unemployment rate represents only the percentage of workers in the *official* labor force—that is, those who are *actively* looking for work. It does not include those who are outside of or have dropped out of the labor market, including the nearly six million males aged twenty-five to sixty who appeared in the census statistics but were not recorded in the labor market statistics in 1990 (Thurow 1990).

These uncounted males in the labor market are disproportionately represented in the inner-city ghettos. Accordingly, in *When Work Disappears*, I use a more appropriate measure of joblessness, a measure that takes into account both official unemployment and non–labor-force participation. That measure is the employment-to-population ratio, which corresponds to the percentage of adults aged sixteen and older who are working. Using the employment-to-population ratio we find, for example, that in 1990 only one in three adults aged sixteen and older held a job in the ghetto poverty areas of Chicago, areas representing roughly 425,000 men, women, and children. And in the ghetto tracts of the nation's one hundred largest cities, for every ten adults who did not hold a job in a typical week in 1990 there were only six employed persons (Kasarda 1993).

The consequences of high neighborhood joblessness are more devastating than those of high neighborhood poverty. A neighborhood in which people are poor but employed is much different than a neighborhood in which people are poor and jobless. *When Work Disappears* shows that many of today's problems in the inner-city ghetto neighborhoods—crime, family dissolution, welfare, low levels of social organization, and so on—are fundamentally a consequence of the disappearance of work.

It should be clear that when I speak of the disappearance of work, I am referring to the declining involvement in or lack of attachment to the formal labor market. It could be argued that, in the general sense of the term, "joblessness" does not necessarily mean "nonwork." In other words, to be officially unemployed or officially outside the labor market does not mean that one is totally removed from all forms of work activity. Many people who are officially jobless are nonetheless involved in informal kinds of work activity, ranging from unpaid housework to work that draws income from the informal or illegal economies.

Housework is work, baby-sitting is work, even drug dealing is work. However, what contrasts work in the formal economy with work activity in the informal and illegal economies is that work in the formal economy is characterized by, indeed calls for, greater regularity and consistency in schedules and hours. Work schedules and hours are formalized. The demands for

discipline are greater. It is true that some work activities outside the formal economy also call for discipline and regular schedules. Several studies reveal that the social organization of the drug industry is driven by discipline and a work ethic, however perverse. However, as a general rule, work in the informal and illegal economies is far less governed by norms or expectations that place a premium on discipline and regularity. For all these reasons, when I speak of the disappearance of work, I mean work in the formal economy, work that provides a framework for daily behavior because of the discipline, regularity, and stability that it imposes.

Effect of Joblessness on Routine and Discipline

In the absence of regular employment, a person lacks not only a place in which to work and the receipt of regular income but also a coherent organization of the present—that is, a system of concrete expectations and goals. Regular employment provides the anchor for the spatial and temporal aspects of daily life. It determines where you are going to be and when you are going to be there. In the absence of regular employment, life, including family life, becomes less coherent. Persistent unemployment and irregular employment hinder rational planning in daily life, a necessary condition of adaptation to an industrial economy (Bourdieu 1965).

Thus, a youngster who grows up in a family with a steady breadwinner and in a neighborhood in which most of the adults are employed will tend to develop some of the disciplined habits associated with stable or steady employment—habits that are reflected in the behavior of his or her parents and of other neighborhood adults. These might include attachment to a routine, a recognition of the hierarchy found in most work situations, a sense of personal efficacy

Handwritten annotations at top:
W.J.O. — ~~Loss of work~~ Theoretically, this could just be an outcome of ~~loss of work~~ but in context of US this becomes wrong/highly deviant. → Hegemonic view.

Left margin handwritten: changing econ. structure & rigid class strat. seg.

attained through the routine management of financial affairs, endorsement of a system of personal and material rewards associated with dependability and responsibility, and so on. Accordingly, when this youngster enters the labor market, he or she has a distinct advantage over the youngsters who grow up in households without a steady bread-winner and in neighborhoods that are not organized around work—in other words, a milieu in which one is more exposed to the less disciplined habits associated with casual or infrequent work.

With the sharp recent rise of solo-parent families, black children who live in inner-city households are less likely to be socialized in a work environment for two main reasons. Their mothers, saddled with child-care responsibilities, can prevent a slide deeper into poverty by accepting welfare. Their fathers, removed from family responsibilities and obligations, are more likely to become idle as a response to restricted employment opportunities, which further weakens their influence in the household and attenuates their contact with the family. In short, the social and cultural responses to joblessness are reflected in the organization of family life and patterns of family formation; there they have implications for labor-force attachment as well.

Left margin handwritten: Young inner-city blacks are not socialized in a work env.

Given the current policy debates that assign blame to the personal shortcomings of the jobless, we need to understand their behavior as responses and adaptations to chronic subordination, including behaviors that have evolved into cultural patterns. The social actions of the jobless—including their behavior, habits, skills, styles, orientations, attitudes—ought not to be analyzed as if they are unrelated to the broader structure of their opportunities and constraints that have evolved over time. This is not to argue that individuals and groups lack the freedom to make their own choices, engage in certain conduct, and develop certain styles and orientations; but I maintain that their decisions and actions occur within a context of constraints and opportunities that are drastically different from those in middle-class society.

Explanations of the Growth of Jobless Ghettos

What accounts for the growing proportion of jobless adults in inner-city communities? An easy explanation would be racial segregation. However, a race-specific argument is not sufficient to explain recent changes in such neighborhoods. After all, these historical Black Belt neighborhoods were *just as segregated by skin color in 1950* as they are today, yet the level of employment was much higher then. One has to account for the ways in which racial segregation interacts with other changes in society to produce the recent escalating rates of joblessness. Several factors stand out: the decreasing demand for low-skilled labor, the suburbanization of jobs, the social deterioration of ghetto neighborhoods, and negative employer attitudes. I discuss each of these factors next.

Right margin handwritten: RQ — goes against D. Massey — Interaction

Decreasing Demand for Low-Skilled Labor

The disappearance of work in many inner-city neighborhoods is in part related to the nationwide decline in the fortunes of low-skilled workers. The sharp decline in the relative demand for unskilled labor has had a more adverse effect on blacks than on whites because a substantially larger proportion of African Americans are unskilled. Although the number of skilled blacks (including managers, professionals, and technicians) has increased sharply in the last several years, the proportion of those who are unskilled remains large, because the black population, burdened by cumulative experiences of racial restrictions, was overwhelmingly unskilled just several decades ago (Schwartzman 1997).[2]

The factors involved in the decreased relative demand for unskilled labor include changes in skilled-based technology, the rapid growth in college enrollment that increased the supply and reduced the relative cost of skilled labor, and the growing internationalization of economic activity, including trade liberalization policies, which reduced the price of imports and raised the output of export industries (Schwartzman 1997). The increased output of export industries aids skilled workers, simply because they are heavily represented in export industries. But increasing imports, especially those from developing countries that compete with labor-intensive industries (for example, apparel, textile, toy, footwear, and some manufacturing industries), hurts unskilled labor (Schwartzman 1997).

Accordingly, inner-city blacks are experiencing a more extreme form of the economic marginality that has affected most unskilled workers in America since 1980. Unfortunately, there is a tendency among policy makers, black leaders, and scholars alike to separate the economic problems of the ghetto from the national and international trends affecting American families and neighborhoods. If the economic problems of the ghetto are defined solely in racial terms they can be isolated and viewed as only requiring race-based solutions as proposed by those on the left, or as only requiring narrow political solutions with subtle racial connotations (such as welfare reform), as strongly proposed by those on the right.

Overemphasis on Racial Factors

Race continues to be a factor that aggravates inner-city black employment problems as we shall soon see. But the tendency to overemphasize the racial factors obscures other more fundamental forces that have sharply

increased inner-city black joblessness. As the late black economist Vivian Henderson put it several years ago, "[I]t is as if racism having put blacks in their economic place steps aside to watch changes in the economy destroy that place" (Henderson 1975, 54). To repeat, the concentrated joblessness of the inner-city poor represents the most dramatic form of the growing economic dislocations among the unskilled stemming in large measure from changes in the organization of the economy, including the global economy.

Suburbanization of Jobs

But inner-city workers face an additional problem: the growing suburbanization of jobs. Most ghetto residents cannot afford an automobile and therefore have to rely on public transit systems that make the connection between inner-city neighborhoods and suburban job locations difficult and time consuming.

Although studies based on data collected before 1970 showed no consistent or convincing effects on black employment as a consequence of this spatial mismatch, the employment of inner-city blacks relative to suburban blacks has clearly deteriorated since then. Recent research (conducted mainly by urban labor economists) strongly shows that the decentralization of employment is continuing and that employment in manufacturing, most of which is already suburbanized, has decreased in central cities, particularly in the Northeast and Midwest (Holzer 1996).

Blacks living in central cities have less access to employment (as measured by the ratio of jobs to people and the average travel time to and from work) than do central-city whites. Moreover, unlike most other groups of workers across the urban-suburban divide, less-educated central-city blacks receive lower wages than suburban blacks who have similar levels of education. And the decline in

W.U. → Flipside of Hays' welfare chapter

earnings of central-city blacks is related to the decentralization of employment—that is, the movement of jobs from the cities to the suburbs—in metropolitan areas (Holzer 1996).

Social Deterioration of Ghetto Neighborhoods

Changes in the class, racial, and demographic composition of inner-city neighborhoods have also contributed to the high percentage of jobless adults in these neighborhoods. Because of the steady out-migration of more advantaged families, the proportion of nonpoor families and prime-age working adults has decreased sharply in the typical inner-city ghetto since 1970 (Wilson 1987). In the face of increasing and prolonged joblessness, the declining proportion of nonpoor families and the overall depopulation ha[ve] made it increasingly difficult to sustain basic neighborhood institutions or to achieve adequate levels of social organization. The declining presence of working- and middle-class blacks has also deprived ghetto neighborhoods of key structural and cultural resources. Structural resources include residents with income high enough to sustain neighborhood services, and cultural resources include conventional role models for neighborhood children.

On the basis of our research in Chicago, it appears that what many high jobless neighborhoods have in common is a relatively high degree of social integration (high levels of local neighboring while being relatively isolated from contacts in the broader mainstream society) and low levels of informal social control (feelings that they have little control over their immediate environment, including the environment's negative influences on their children). In such areas, not only are children at risk because of the lack of informal social controls, they are also disadvantaged because the social interaction among neighbors tends to be confined to those whose skills, styles, orientations, and habits are not as conducive to promoting positive social outcomes (academic success, pro-social behavior, employment in the formal labor market, etc.) as those in more stable neighborhoods. Although the close interaction among neighbors in such areas may be useful in devising strategies, disseminating information, and developing styles of behavior that are helpful in a ghetto milieu (teaching children to avoid eye-to-eye contact with strangers and to develop a tough demeanor in the public sphere for self-protection), they may be less effective in promoting the welfare of children in society at large.

Despite being socially integrated, the residents in Chicago's ghetto neighborhoods shared a feeling that they had little informal social control over the children in their environment. A primary reason is the absence of a strong organizational capacity or an institutional resource base that would provide an extra layer of social organization in their neighborhoods. It is easier for parents to control the behavior of the children in their neighborhoods when a strong institutional resource base exists and when the links between community institutions such as churches, schools, political organizations, businesses, and civic clubs are strong or secure. The higher the density and stability of formal organizations, the less illicit activities such as drug trafficking, crime, prostitution, and the formation of gangs can take root in the neighborhood.

Few Community Institutions

A weak institutional resource base is what distinguishes high jobless inner-city neighborhoods from stable middle-class and working-class areas. As one resident of a high jobless neighborhood on the South Side of Chicago put it, "Our children, you know, seems to be more at risk than any other children there is, because there's no library for them to go to. There's not a center they can go

[margin note: Families really disintegrate bc they are not functioning — W.W.]

to, there's no field house that they can go into. There's nothing. There's nothing. There's nothing at all." Parents in high jobless neighborhoods have a much more difficult task controlling the behavior of their adolescents and preventing them from getting involved in activities detrimental to pro-social development. Given the lack of organizational capacity and a weak institutional base, some parents choose to protect their children by isolating them from activities in the neighborhood, including avoiding contact and interaction with neighborhood families. Wherever possible, and often with great difficulty when one considers the problems of transportation and limited financial resources, they attempt to establish contacts and cultivate relations with individuals, families, and institutions, such as church groups, schools, and community recreation programs, outside their neighborhood. A note of caution is necessary, though. It is just as indefensible to treat inner-city residents as super heroes who overcome racist oppression as it is to view them as helpless victims. We should, however, appreciate the range of choices, including choices representing cultural influences, that are available to inner-city residents who live under constraints that most people in the larger society do not experience.

[margin note: Isolation]

Effect of Joblessness on Marriage and Family

[margin note: W.W.]

It is within the context of labor-force attachment that the public policy discussion on welfare reform and family values should be couched. The research that we have conducted in Chicago suggests that as employment prospects recede, the foundation for stable relationships becomes weaker over time. More permanent relationships such as marriage give way to temporary liaisons that result in broken unions, out-of-wedlock pregnancies, and, to a lesser extent, separation

and divorce. The changing norms concerning marriage in the larger society reinforce the movement toward temporary liaisons in the inner city, and therefore economic considerations in marital decisions take on even greater weight. Many inner-city residents have negative outlooks toward marriage, outlooks that are developed in and influenced by an environment featuring persistent joblessness.

The disrupting effect of joblessness on marriage and family causes poor inner-city blacks to be even more disconnected from the job market and discouraged about their role in the labor force. The economic marginality of the ghetto poor is cruelly reinforced, therefore, by conditions in the neighborhoods in which they live.

Negative Employer Attitudes

[margin note: Negative opinions of work ethic]

In the eyes of employers in metropolitan Chicago, the social conditions in the ghetto render inner-city blacks less desirable as workers, and therefore many are reluctant to hire them. One of the three studies that provided the empirical foundation for *When Work Disappears* included a representative sample of employers in the greater Chicago area who provided entry-level jobs. An overwhelming majority of these employers, both white and black, expressed negative views about inner-city ghetto workers, and many stated that they were reluctant to hire them. For example, a president of an inner-city manufacturing firm expressed a concern about employing residents from certain inner-city neighborhoods:

> If somebody gave me their address, uh, Cabrini Green I might unavoidably have some concerns. *Interviewer:* What would your concerns be? *Respondent:* That the poor guy probably would be frequently unable to get to work and . . . I probably would watch him more carefully even if it wasn't fair, than I would with somebody

As econ. assets any longer.
Diff. types of relationships evolve.

else. I know what I should do though is recognize that here's a guy that is trying to get out of his situation and probably will work harder than somebody else who's already out of there and he might be the best one around here. But I, I think I would have to struggle accepting that premise at the beginning. (Wilson 1996, field notes)

Main emplr. concerns

In addition to qualms about the neighborhood milieu of inner-city residents, the employers frequently mentioned concerns about applicants' language skills and educational training. An employer from a computer software firm in Chicago expressed the view "that in many businesses the ability to meet the public is paramount and you do not talk street talk to the buying public. Almost all your black welfare people talk street talk. And who's going to sit them down and change their speech patterns?" (Wilson 1996, field notes). A Chicago real estate broker made a similar point:

w/o ↓ It's all cap..

long

A lot of times I will interview applicants who are black, who are sort of lower class. . . . They'll come to me and I cannot hire them because their language skills are so poor. Their speaking voice for one thing is poor . . . they have no verbal facility with the language . . . and these . . . you know, they just don't know how to speak and they'll say "salesmens" instead of "salesmen" and that's a problem. . . . They don't know punctuation, they don't know how to use correct grammar, and they cannot spell. And I can't hire them. And I feel bad about that and I think they're being very disadvantaged by the Chicago Public School system. (Wilson 1996, field notes)

Another respondent defended his method of screening out most job applicants on the telephone on the basis of their use of "grammar and English":

I have every right to say that that's a requirement for this job. I don't care if you're pink, black, green, yellow or orange, I demand someone who speaks well. You want to tell me that I'm a bigot, fine, call me a bigot. I know blacks, you don't even know they're black. (Wilson 1996, field notes)

Finally, an inner-city banker claimed that many blacks in the ghetto "simply cannot read. When you're talking our type of business, that disqualifies them immediately, we don't have a job here that doesn't require that somebody have minimum reading and writing skills" (Wilson 1996, field notes).

How should we interpret the negative attitudes and actions of employers? To what extent do they represent an aversion to blacks *per se* and to what degree do they reflect judgments based on the job-related skills and training of inner-city blacks in a changing labor market? I should point out that the statements made by the African American employers concerning the qualifications of inner-city black workers did not differ significantly from those of the white employers. Whereas 74 percent of all the white employers who responded to the open-ended questions expressed negative views of the job-related traits of inner-city blacks, 80 percent of the black employers did so as well.

meaning of race?

This raises a question about the meaning and significance of race in certain situations—in other words, how race intersects with other factors. A key hypothesis in this connection is that given the recent shifts in the economy, employers are looking for workers with a broad range of abilities: "hard" skills (literacy, numerical ability, basic mechanical ability, and other testable attributes) and "soft" skills (personalities suitable to the work environment, good grooming, group-oriented work behaviors, etc.). While hard skills are the product of education and training—benefits that are apparently in short supply in inner-city schools—soft skills are strongly tied to culture, and are therefore shaped by the harsh environment of the inner-city ghetto. For example, our research revealed that many parents in the inner-city ghetto neighborhoods of Chicago wanted their children not to make eye-to-eye contact with strangers and to develop a tough demeanor when interacting with people on the streets. While such behaviors are helpful for survival in the ghetto, they hinder successful interaction in mainstream society.

Statistical Discrimination

If employers are indeed reacting to the difference in skills between white and black applicants, it becomes increasingly difficult to discuss the motives of employers: are they rejecting inner-city black applicants out of overt racial discrimination or on the basis of qualifications?

Nonetheless, many of the selective recruitment practices do represent what economists call "statistical discrimination": employers make assumptions about the inner-city black workers *in general* and reach decisions based on those assumptions before they have had a chance to review systematically the qualifications of an individual applicant. The net effect is that many black inner-city applicants are never given the chance to prove their qualifications on an individual level because they are systematically screened out by the selective recruitment process.

Statistical discrimination, although representing elements of class bias against poor workers in the inner city, is clearly a matter of race both directly and indirectly. Directly, the selective recruitment patterns effectively screen out far more black workers from the inner city than Hispanic or white workers from the same types of backgrounds. But indirectly, race is also a factor, even in those decisions to deny employment to inner-city black workers on the basis of objective and thorough evaluations of their qualifications. The hard and soft skills among inner-city blacks that do not match the current needs of the labor market are products of racially segregated communities, communities that have historically featured widespread social constraints and restricted opportunities.

Thus the job prospects of inner-city workers have diminished not only because of the decreasing relative demand for low-skilled labor in the United States economy, the suburbanization of jobs, and the social deterioration of ghetto neighborhoods, but also because of negative employer attitudes. This combination of factors presents a real challenge to policy makers. Indeed, considering the narrow range of social policy options in the "balance-the-budget" political climate, how can we immediately alleviate the inner-city jobs problem—a problem which will undoubtedly grow when the new welfare reform bill takes full effect and creates a situation that will be even more harmful to inner-city children and adolescents?

Public Policy Dilemmas

What are the implications of these studies on public policy? A key issue is public-sector employment. If firms in the private sector cannot hire or refuse to hire low-skilled adults who are willing to take minimum-wage jobs, then policy makers should consider a policy of public-sector employment-of-last-resort. Indeed, until current changes in the labor market are reversed or until the skills of the next generation of workers can be upgraded before they enter the labor market, many workers, especially those who are not in the official labor force, will not be able to find jobs unless the government becomes an employer-of-last-resort (Danziger and Gottschalk 1995). This argument applies especially to low-skilled inner-city black workers. It is bad enough that they face the problem of shifts in labor-market demand shared by all low-skilled workers; it is even worse that they confront negative employer perceptions about their work-related skills and attitudes.

For all these reasons, the passage of the 1996 welfare reform bill, which did not include a program of job creation, could have very negative social consequences in the inner city. Unless something is done to enhance the employment opportunities of inner-city welfare recipients who reach the time limit for the receipt of welfare, they will flood a pool already filled with low-skilled, jobless workers. . . .

The Need for Action

At the same time that the new welfare law has generated a greater need for work opportunities, high jobless urban and rural areas will experience more difficulty in placing individuals in private-sector jobs. To create work opportunities for welfare recipients, these areas will therefore have to "rely more heavily upon job creation strategies in the public and private non-profit sectors" (Center on Budget and Policy Priorities 1996, 4). Although the placement of disadvantaged workers in private-sector jobs can help contain the overall costs in some communities (including many jobless ghetto areas and depressed rural areas) a mainly private-sector initiative will not be sufficient to generate enough jobs to accommodate the large oversupply of low-skilled individuals.

West Virginia, a state that has been plagued with a severe shortage of work opportunities, has provided community service jobs to recipients of welfare for several years. In Wisconsin, Governor Thompson's welfare reform plan envisions community service jobs for many parents in the more depressed areas of the state, and the New Hope program in Milwaukee provides community service jobs for those unable to find employment in the private sector (Center on Budget and Policy Priorities 1996). It is especially important that this mixed strategy include a plan to make *adequate* monies available to localities or communities with high jobless and welfare dependency rates. Three billion dollars for this purpose is hardly sufficient.

Obviously, as more people become employed and gain work experience, they will have a better chance of finding jobs in the private sector when jobs become available. The attitudes of employers toward inner-city workers could change, in part because they would be dealing with job applicants who have steady work experience and who could furnish references from their previous supervisors. Children are more likely to be socialized in a work-oriented environment and to develop the job readiness skills that are seen as important even for entry-level jobs.

Thus, given the recent welfare reform legislation, *adequate* strategies to enhance the employment opportunities of inner-city residents should be contemplated, strategies that would be adequately financed and designed to address the employment problems of low-skilled workers not only in periods of tight labor markets, but, even more important, in periods when the labor market is slack. With the sharp reduction in the federal deficit and the talk about an economic surplus in the near future, now is an ideal time to urge the president and to press Congress to develop such strategies. If steps are not taken soon to enhance the job prospects of hundreds of thousands of inner-city residents, including welfare recipients who reach their time limit for receipt of welfare, we could be facing major social dislocations in many urban areas, especially if the current economic recovery ends in the near future.

NOTES

1. The figures on adult employment are based on calculations from data provided by the 1990 U.S. Bureau of the Census (1993) and the *Local Community Fact Book for Chicago—1950* (1953) and the *Local Community Fact Book for Chicago—1960* (1963). The adult employment rates represent the number of employed individuals (aged fourteen and older in 1950 and sixteen and older in 1990) among the total number of adults in a given area. Those who are not employed include both the individuals who are members of the labor force but are not working and those who have dropped out or are not part of the labor force.

2. The economist David Schwartzman defines "unskilled workers to include operators, fabricators, and laborers, and those in service occupations, including private household workers, those working in protective service occupations, food service, and cleaning and building service." On the basis of this definition he estimates that 80 percent of all black workers and 38 percent of all white workers were unskilled in 1950. By 1990, 46 percent of black workers and 27 percent of white workers were employed in unskilled occupations (Schwartzman 1997).

REFERENCES

Bourdieu, Pierre. 1965. *Travail et Travailleurs en Algerie.* Paris: Editions Mouton.

Center on Budget and Policy Priorities. 1996. *The Administration's $3 Billion Jobs Proposal.* Washington, DC: Center on Budget and Policy Priorities.

Danziger, Sheldon H., and Peter Gottschalk. 1995. *America Unequal.* Cambridge, MA: Harvard University Press.

Henderson, Vivian. 1975. "Race, Economics, and Public Policy." *Crisis* 83(Fall):50–55.

Holzer, Harry J. 1987. "Informal Job Search and Black Youth Unemployment." *American Economic Review* 77:446–52.

———. 1996. *What Employers Want: Job Prospects for Less-Educated Workers.* New York: Russell Sage.

Kasarda, John D. 1993. "Inner-City Concentrated Poverty and Neighborhood Distress: 1970–1990." *Housing Policy Debate* 4(3):253–302.

Local Community Fact Book for Chicago—1950. 1953. Chicago: Community Inventory, University of Chicago.

Local Community Fact Book for Chicago—1960. 1963. Chicago: Community Inventory, University of Chicago.

Schwartzman, David. 1997. *Black Unemployment: Part of Unskilled Unemployment.* Westport, CT: Greenwood.

Thurow, Lester. 1990. "The Crusade That's Killing Prosperity." *American Prospect* March/April:54–59.

U.S. Bureau of the Census. 1993. *Census of Population: Detailed Characteristics of the Population.* Washington, DC: U.S. Government Printing Office.

Wilson, William Julius. 1987. *The Truly Disadvantaged: The Inner City, the Underclass, and Public Policy.* Chicago: University of Chicago Press.

———. 1996. *When Work Disappears: The World of the New Urban Poor.* New York: Alfred A. Knopf.

[Handwritten notes:]

Impacts

Upshot: - A changing global econ. (deindus.) in inner-cities, where it has led to an epidemic of joblessness (& ↑ poverty)

- This is caused also / perpetuated by racial stereotypes of employers & ↓ education etc. due to racial segreg., suburbanization of jobs, & weak institutions

Joblessness - Causes ↑ social dislocation, dissolution of families, ↑ crime rates, ↓ social organization

Policy: needs to create jobs in inner-cities! Govt needs to be public-sector employer-of-last-resort

∽ **READING 17** ∽

Gender Inequality at Work

David A. Cotter, Joan M. Hermsen, and Reeve Vanneman

A cigarette advertising slogan of the 1980s targeting women proclaimed: "You've come a long way, baby." By all accounts, this slogan is true. The transformation of men's and women's work roles stands out among the many technological, economic, social, and cultural changes in the last half of the 20th century. In 1950, only a small number of women (29 percent) worked outside the home; but in 2000, nearly three-quarters of women did. In 1950, women who were employed worked in a relative handful of nearly exclusively female occupations; but by 2000, women worked in nearly the entire spectrum of occupations. On average, a woman in 1950 earned 59 cents for every dollar earned by a man, while in 2000, she earned 73 cents. The scale of this change is indeed monumental, and its momentum has made it in retrospect seem almost inevitable.

Despite this progress, however, inequality remains between men and women. In 2000, men were still more likely than women to have access to paid employment, to be employed in better jobs, and to be better paid in those jobs. Additionally, across three main dimensions—work outside the home, kind of job, and pay—progress for women slowed and even reversed in the last decade of the century.

This report tracks changes in work-related gender inequality in the 1990s, placing these changes in the context of trends over the last 50 years in educational attainment, work experience, politics, and attitudes. The report also examines variations in inequality across race and ethnic groups, education levels, and age cohorts. The analysis contained in the report relies on data from the 1950 to 2000 censuses as well as from Current Population Surveys (CPS) from 1963 to 2002.

For the most part, the report focuses on the working-age population, people between the ages of 25 and 54. These people can be expected to have finished their education, but they are not likely to have begun to retire.

Three central conclusions emerge from our analysis of changes in gender inequality over time:

- Gender inequality in the labor market persists. While nearly nine of every 10 men are in the labor force, only three of four women are working. In addition, women and men continue to be highly concentrated in typically female and typically male jobs, respectively. Women continue to earn substantially less than men.

- The declines in gender inequality in the labor market that have been evident since at least 1950 have essentially stalled. The 1990s were a time of stability and possibly even retrenchment with regard to gender inequality. This decade may mark the end of an era of profound changes in women's labor market position. For each of the primary outcomes examined—labor force participation, occupational segregation, and earnings—the end of the 1990s closely resembled the beginning of the 1990s: a pattern of stability not seen in over 50 years.

- Notable variation exists across demographic groups in the pattern and degree of inequality experienced. For example, blacks and Hispanics lag behind whites in rates of labor force participation, the degree of occupational integration, and the level of earnings; and important differences in labor force participation and earnings have become more pronounced when comparing female high school dropouts with female college graduates.

Thus, our findings suggest that while both women and men have "come a long way," there is still a long way to go, and progress in the United States on gender equality seems to be slowing. . . .

Trends and Patterns in Men's and Women's Occupations

Women and men in the labor force do very different kinds of work. In general, the differences in women's and men's work persist, but are much reduced from a half-century ago. The integration of work marks another aspect of stunning change. Little more than 30 years ago, the idea of women becoming doctors, clergy, bartenders, or bus drivers in numbers equal to men would have seemed naive. But, as the data reveal, this equalization is precisely what has happened. However, as with labor force participation, there is still a considerable gap in the occupations that men and women hold. Many have remained decidedly male or female and, as with labor force participation, there is good evidence that integration has stopped in recent years.

Census 2000 Findings

Despite the fact that women make up nearly half of the labor force, men and women work in very distinct occupations. An occupation is a convenient way of categorizing the many different kinds of work that people do, grouping similar kinds of work performed in different settings. For instance, people who examine other people's physical and psychological condition and make recommendations about their treatment (doctors, psychiatrists, psychoanalysts, chiropractors, and nurses) are all "health diagnosing and treating practitioners." Similarly, people who sell things, such as art dealers, insurance agents, or gas station attendants, are all in sales and related occupations. Different coding systems categorize occupations into greater or lesser degrees of detail and make gross or fine distinctions among the types of work done.

The level of occupational detail is important for understanding gender differences, since the more detailed the coding system, the more segregated men's and women's work will appear. This can be illustrated by the difference between "teachers" at various levels. If all teachers are grouped, 74 percent of them are women. But if this group of teachers is disaggregated by grade level, 97 percent of preschool, 78 percent of elementary and middle school, 58 percent of secondary school, and 46 percent of college teachers are women. Thus, greater detail allows a more accurate estimate of how much segregation there is. In fact, some researchers have analyzed cross-classifications of industries and occupations or even organization-level data on job titles, and each analysis results in higher estimates of the "true" degree of gender segregation.

The Census Bureau uses several occupational coding systems with varied degrees of detail. In 2000, there were 505 categories, but the microdata file collapses that number slightly to 475. The percentage of women in each of these occupations ranges from 98 percent for preschool teachers to 1 percent for heavy-vehicle mechanics.

Scholars examining gender segregation have commonly treated occupations in which more than 70 percent of the workers are of one sex as "sex-typed" occupations. By this standard, more than half (52 percent) of all women work in occupations that are more than 70 percent female, and 57 percent of men work in occupations that are more than 70 percent male. Conversely, only 11 percent of women work in "male" occupations, while 7 percent of men work in "female" occupations. That leaves less than half of men (41 percent) and women (37 percent) working in "mixed" occupations (those between 31 percent and 69 percent female). Among the most heavily female occupations in 2000 were secretaries, cashiers, and elementary- and middle-school teachers; while the overwhelmingly male occupations were truck drivers, laborers and material movers, and janitors and building cleaners. The predominantly mixed occupations were retail sales workers, supervisors of retail sales workers, and miscellaneous managers.

A principal tool that scholars use to describe patterns of gender segregation is the dissimilarity index. This measure can be interpreted as the percentage of women or men who would have to change occupations in order for each occupation to be evenly female—that is, to match the gender distribution in the labor force as a whole. Using this set of occupations, more than half (52.0 percent) of all women or men would have to change occupations in order for all occupations to match the 46.5 percent female rate found in the labor force as a whole.

Long-Term Trends

The Census Bureau has changed the occupational classification system almost every decade. The 2000 Census was no exception. These changes reflect, in part, changes in the type of work we do, but also changes in our understanding of that work. These changes in classification cause problems for comparing changes in the kinds of work that women and men do. To have comparable occupations over these 50 years, it was necessary to recode all the occupations into a standard set of 179 occupations. This smaller set, however, limits the detail about the types of occupations, resulting in underestimates of the levels of segregation.

The rapid entry of women into the labor market in the 1960s, 1970s, and 1980s had consequences for the types of jobs they held. During these decades, women gained access to many occupations that had previously (whether formally or informally) been closed to them. But women's entry into occupations was uneven. Many occupations remain nearly as heavily male or female as they were in the 1950s. Some occupations have even *become* predominantly female since the 1950s (see Table 1). For example, while women have made some inroads into the skilled trades, women are only slightly more likely to be electricians or mechanics today than in 1950. Similarly, despite much popular attention to the phenomenon of the male nurse, a patient is nearly as likely today to have a female nurse as in 1950, children are equally likely to have a female teacher in 2000 as in 1950, and the office secretary is just as likely to be a woman today as in 1950.

In other occupations, though, changes have been far more substantial. For instance, in 1950 it was extremely unlikely to find a woman driving a bus or mixing drinks in a bar—but by 2000, the probability was more than 50 percent. Much the same can be said about real estate agents, accountants, and bill collectors; each of those occupations had female majorities by 2000. Finally, some occupations that in 1950 were fairly evenly split between women and men have now

TABLE 1   Women's Share of Selected Occupations, 1950–2000

Occupation	Percent of Workers Who Are Women			
	1950	1980	1990	2000
Male occupations				
Electricians	1	2	3	3
Firefighters	0	1	2	4
Airplane pilots	0	1	4	4
Truck drivers	1	3	6	6
Electrical engineers	1	5	10	9
Clergy	4	5	11	15
Police	2	5	13	16
Architects	2	9	16	21
Mixed occupations				
Physicians	6	15	23	30
Lawyers	4	15	26	33
Mail carriers	1	14	28	34
Managers	13	25	34	36
Real estate agents	16	50	53	52
Bartenders	8	47	55	57
Bus drivers	4	53	55	57
Accountants and bookkeepers	13	37	53	60
Female occupations				
Bill collectors	17	62	68	72
Medical and dental technicians	41	67	73	73
Teachers	73	67	74	75
Waiters and waitresses	83	88	82	76
Librarians	91	84	85	80
Nurses (professional)	97	91	91	92
Bank tellers	43	94	94	94
Secretaries and typists	94	99	98	97

Note: Labor force participation calculated for men and women ages 25–54.
Source: Authors' calculations using the Integrated Public Use Micro-data Series (IPUMS), 2003.

become predominantly female. Both medical and dental technicians and bank tellers went from being just under half female in 1950 to being predominantly female by 2000.

Again, the dissimilarity index is useful for summarizing the changes throughout the occupational structure. Based on the smaller set of 179 occupations, the dissimilarity index was 46.6 for 2000 (see Table 2). This figure represents a total decline of 14.2 points in the index of dissimilarity between 1950 and 2000—just under one-third of a point each year for 50 years. At that rate, occupational segregation would disappear by the year 2150. The decline, however, has not been evenly paced over the period. Most of the change occurred from 1960 to 1990; both the 1990s (1.8 point decline) and 1950s (1.2 point increase) experienced much lower levels of change.

TABLE 2   Changes in Gender Segregation in Occupations, 1950–2000

Source of Change	1950	1960	1970	1980	1990	2000
Occupational segregation	60.8	62.0	56.8	53.1	48.4	46.6
Actual change from previous decade	——	+1.2	−5.2	−3.7	−4.7	−1.8
Change from integration of occupations	——	+1.8	−3.3	−4.6	−3.4	+0.7
Change from shifts in the occupational structure	——	−1.0	−1.7	+1.6	−1.2	−2.1

—— Not applicable.

Note: Includes men and women ages 25–54. The dissimilarity index is the percentage of men or women who would have to change occupations for each occupation to be evenly female—that is, to match the gender distribution in the general labor force.

Source: Authors' calculations using the Integrated Public Use Micro-data Series (IPUMS), 2003.

Declines in segregation come from two main sources. The most obvious type of change is the integration of previously segregated jobs—for example, women becoming doctors and men becoming nurses. Less obvious is the more rapid growth of already-integrated occupations (the growth of the number of cooks) or the decline of segregated ones (declining numbers of miners since 1950 or of telephone operators and secretaries since 1970). Tools to decompose the changes in occupational segregation into these two components have been developed. Table 2 identifies what portion of each decade's changes represents changes in the gender composition of occupations and what percentage is just the consequence of differential occupational growth and decline. The declines in segregation seen in censuses from 1960 to 1990 resulted mostly from occupational integration, although in the 1960s and the 1980s, the more rapid growth of integrated occupations also contributed. All of the rather small decrease between 1990 and 2000 can be attributed to the growth of integrated occupations. In fact, without changes in the occupational structure, the 2000 Census would have registered an increase in occupational segregation. This reversal is consistent with the labor force participation trends that also identified the 1990s as a break from the previous decades.

Another question frequently asked about integration is how much of the change stems from women entering occupations that had been male-dominated and how much from men entering occupations that had been female-dominated. That is, are women becoming carpenters and clergy, or are men becoming librarians and nurses? The specific occupational changes summarized in Table 1 suggest that most of the change came from women entering previously male occupations. More detailed calculations confirm this conclusion. If we look at the 13.6 point drop between 1960 and 1990, about 6.3 points of that drop are the result of women's changes (women's 1990 occupational distribution looking more like men's in 1960 than women's did in 1960). None of the drop is due to changes in men's occupations: Men's occupations in 1990 looked less like women's 1960 occupations than was the case 30 years earlier. A large portion of the declining segregation is due to the simultaneous changes in men's and women's occupations to look more like each other. So, however interesting the phenomena of male nurses and librarians may be, these phenomena do not account for much of the occupational integration. The changes in the middle portion of Table 1, occupations that shifted from male-dominated to integrated, drove the decline in occupational segregation. . . .

TABLE 3   Occupational Segregation by Gender and by Race and Ethnicity, 2000

Race/Ethnicity	Gender Segregation (Women vs. Men)		Racial Segregation (from Whites of Same Gender)	
	Within Race/Ethnicity	Versus White Men	Women	Men
White (only)	52.7	52.7	———	———
African American	47.7	57.4	21.7	26.5
Hispanic (any)	51.4	55.9	23.5	28.3
Mexican	52.1	57.5	28.3	34.7
Puerto Rican	47.0	53.9	17.1	23.2
Central American	47.7	58.1	37.9	37.3
South American	42.6	50.8	21.1	20.4
Cuban	44.7	48.5	10.5	13.6
Dominican	46.4	56.8	31.3	31.8
Asian (any)	39.6	51.7	23.4	30.2
Chinese	34.4	49.8	30.7	38.1
South Asian	36.6	52.0	28.7	41.8
Filipina	40.9	56.6	24.5	28.5
Southeast Asian	37.3	55.3	40.8	35.8
Korean	38.3	48.3	28.6	30.5
Japanese	39.5	48.9	15.5	22.9
American Indian	48.3	50.7	13.7	16.3
Pacific Islander	45.4	50.1	15.3	17.1

——— Not applicable.

Note: Occupations for men and women ages 25–54. The dissimilarity index is the percentage of men or women who would have to change occupations for each occupation to be evenly female—that is, to match the gender distribution in the general labor force. Racial segregation is measured by a dissimilarity index defined as the percentage of same gender whites or other races (such as African American or Hispanic) that would have to change occupations for each occupation to be evenly white—that is, to match the racial distribution in the labor force for each gender group.
Source: Authors' calculations using Census 2000 5% Public Use Micro-data Sample (PUMS).

Occupational Segregation by Race and Ethnicity

Census 2000 Findings   As with labor force participation, occupational segregation varies by race and ethnicity as well as by gender. Not only are occupations racially segregated, but levels of gender segregation also may vary by race. Separate gender segregation indices can be calculated within each racial and ethnic group, and racial segregation indices can be calculated within each gender (see Table 3).

Two conclusions emerge from these calculations. First, women of color are generally far less segregated from white women (column 3) than from men of their own race or ethnicity (column 1). Asian women are an exception: Their racial segregation levels often approach the levels of gender segregation.

Second, levels of occupational gender segregation are quite similar across all racial and ethnic groups, except for Asians, who have substantially lower levels of gender segregation. Other groups also have lower gender segregation than whites, but the differences are small. Hispanics are about 1 percentage point below whites; African Americans and American Indians, 5 percentage points below. The lower levels of gender segregation among people of color are not the result of any privileged position of minority women. Rather, the lower segregation results because minority men are less privileged than white men. Segregation based on race and ethnicity is greater among men (column 4) than among women (column 3).

Long-Term Changes   Changes in occupational gender segregation over the last half-century roughly parallel the general gender story: limited change in the 1950s, followed by declines from the 1960s through the 1990s, when declines slowed or ended. Like labor force participation, the changes over the last 50 years cross racial and ethnic divisions fairly consistently. Indeed, changes over time within any one racial or ethnic group are greater than the differences across these same groups (with the exception of Asians). Even Asians have experienced the same changes as other groups since 1970, although at a lower level. African Americans have seen the largest drop: In the 1950s and 1960s, their gender segregation was greater than for whites or any other group. Only since 1970 have whites had more occupational gender segregation than other racial or ethnic groups. . . .

Changing Work

The trends and patterns outlined in this section indicate a considerable integration of men's and women's work, but a substantial amount of segregation persists. Whether one looks at individual occupations, overall distributions, or summary statistics, it is clear that the barriers that kept women from certain occupations and trapped them in others have been lowered. But it is also clear that men and women continue to occupy separate spheres in the world of work. It also appears from this data that the pace of change has slowed. For almost all groups, there was less change in integration in the 1990s than in any decade since the 1950s. Again, it remains to be seen if this is a temporary slowing or the beginning of a reversal of the trends of the 1960s, 1970s, and 1980s.

Earnings

To some extent, changes in both labor force participation and occupational segregation over time are easily observable. We see more women working today and working in a wider variety of occupations than in the past. In fact, the sight of women in large numbers in previously male occupations, such as police officers and politicians, can sometimes mask the persistence of inequality. While perhaps the least directly visible of the three dimensions of work-related gender inequality, differences in men's and women's pay may have garnered the most public attention. Each year, when the U.S. Bureau of Labor Statistics releases results from the March Current Population Survey, a spate of newspaper stories appear on the gender gap in earnings. These stories tell both good news (a narrowing gap) or bad (a widening gap). Cumulatively, as we will see, the last 50 years have brought good news—but the differences remain large, and the gap between men's and women's earnings widened again in the last half of the 1990s. Women still earn less than men. The average woman age 25 to 54 who worked full-time/year-round in 1999 reported earnings of $28,100. That is only 73 percent of the $38,700 reported by the average man age 25 to 54. The ratio is somewhat better if hourly wages for all workers are estimated by adjusting annual earnings for the reported usual hours worked and the number of weeks worked last year. Women's average hourly wage of $12.44 is 79 percent of men's $15.72.

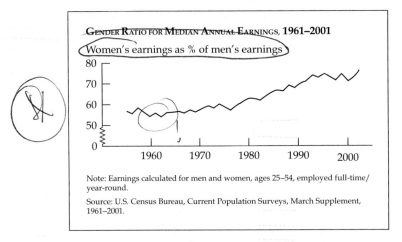

FIGURE 1 Gender Ratio for Median Annual Earnings, 1961–2001

The gender gap in earnings declined during much of the last quarter of the 20th century. That advance appears to have ended in the mid-1990s. Census data from 1950 through 2000 show the ratio of women's to men's earnings to have hit bottom in 1969 and 1979 at 56 percent (the higher the ratio, the smaller the gender gap). In 1989, the ratio jumped to 66 percent, and it continued to improve to 71 percent in 1999. (Because the census collects data about last year's earnings, the 2000 Census yields estimates for 1999 earnings, the 1990 Census for 1989 earnings, etc.) More detailed annual data from the Current Population Survey (see Figure 1) suggest that the increase in the 1990s occurred entirely in the first half of that decade. Since the mid-1990s there has been little improvement in the gender earnings ratio.

FIGURE 2 Median Annual Earnings for U.S. Men and Women, 1961–2001

TABLE 4   Median Earnings for U.S. Women and Men by Race and Ethnicity, 1999

Race/Ethnicity	Women	Men	Women's Earnings as % of Men's	
			Same Race/ Ethnicity	White Men
White (only)	$28,000	$40,000	70	70
African American	$25,000	$30,000	83	63
Hispanic (any)	$21,000	$25,000	84	53
Mexican	$20,000	$23,900	84	50
Puerto Rican	$25,000	$30,000	83	63
Central American	$18,000	$22,500	80	45
South American	$24,000	$30,000	80	60
Cuban	$26,000	$31,000	84	65
Dominican	$20,000	$24,700	81	50
Asian (any)	$30,000	$40,000	75	75
Chinese	$34,000	$43,000	79	85
South Asian	$30,300	$35,000	87	76
Filipina	$32,300	$50,000	65	81
Southeast Asian	$23,100	$30,000	77	58
Korean	$35,000	$48,500	72	88
Japanese	$27,700	$38,000	73	69
American Indian	$24,000	$30,000	80	60
Pacific Islander	$25,000	$30,000	83	63

Note: Earnings calculated for men and women ages 25–54, employed full-time/year-round.
Source: Authors' calculations using Census 2000 5% Public Use Micro-data Sample (PUMS).

Changes in men's earnings are more closely correlated with changes in the gender ratio than are changes in women's earnings (see Figure 2). Women's average earnings have increased steadily since the 1960s. Men's average earnings, on the other hand, increased in the 1960s through the early 1970s, but then plateaued and even declined somewhat until the mid-1990s. In the mid-1990s, men's earnings again began to increase after two decades of stagnation. Thus, over the last 40 years, when men's earnings have risen, the gender earnings gap has held constant or even grown. But when men's earnings have stagnated or declined, the gender earnings gap has closed. Times of progress in gender equality have come mainly when men's earnings have stagnated. . . .

Earnings by Race and Ethnicity

Gender gaps in earnings vary across racial and ethnic groups somewhat more than does occupational segregation. Again, gender inequality is somewhat stronger among whites. The earnings of white women were just 70 percent of white men. Women's earnings were several percentage points closer to men's earnings among African Americans (83 percent) and Hispanics (84 percent) (see Table 4 . . .). Although black and Hispanic women earned less than white women, black and Hispanic men were even further behind white men, so gender differences are smaller. The gender earnings ratios of Asian Americans, American Indians, and Pacific Islanders are also larger than that of whites, although there are substantial differences among Asian

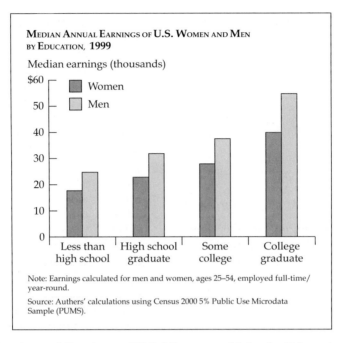

MEDIAN ANNUAL EARNINGS OF U.S. WOMEN AND MEN BY EDUCATION, **1999**

Median earnings (thousands)

Note: Earnings calculated for men and women, ages 25–54, employed full-time/ year-round.

Source: Authers' calculations using Census 2000 5% Public Use Microdata Sample (PUMS).

FIGURE 3   Median Annual Earnings of U.S. Women and Men by Education, 1999

groups as there are for occupational segregation and labor force participation.

The gender inequality trends from 1950 to 2000 for earnings were shared across most racial and ethnic groups. The gender earnings gap widened during the 1950s and 1960s, peaked or leveled off in the 1970s, and decreased in the 1980s and 1990s. The one exception was African Americans: Their gender earnings gap decreased substantially during the 1960s and 1970s, a period of little change or increased gaps for other racial and ethnic groups. Average earnings for African American women increased especially fast in the 1960s and 1970s as many women shifted from domestic service to higher-paying jobs that were newly open to them. As a result, by 1980, earnings by gender for African Americans had shifted from the most unequal of all racial and ethnic groups to the most equal. Equality continued in the 1980s and at a slightly reduced rate in the 1990s for African Americans.

Earnings by Education

The gender earnings ratio is quite uniform across education levels. High school dropouts have almost as large a gender ratio (72 percent) as college graduates (73 percent). Although more education means higher earnings for both women and men, more education makes almost no difference for the size of the gender ratio across education groups (see Figure 3). Moreover, the increase in the gender ratio over the last 25 years is quite similar at each level of education.

Unlike occupational integration, which has been primarily a middle-class trend, gender earnings equality improved among all levels of education. And the trends within education levels have followed an inverted U-shaped pattern similar to those for racial and ethnic groups. The gender earnings gap among college graduates was its largest in 1960, while for high school dropouts, high school graduates, and those

Even in heavily-♂ occups,, ♂ make more than ♀

with some college, the gender gap reached its highest point in the 1970s. There is some evidence that gender differences by education have narrowed since 1970, with the largest declines happening in the 1980s. Since 1950, the gender earnings gap has been smaller among college graduates than among high school graduates; that difference became negligible by 1999. Annual CPS data document the same convergence.

Earnings by Occupational Segregation

The segregation of women into female-dominated occupations has long been thought to be a principal cause of the gender earnings gap. Female-dominated occupations pay less, the argument goes, regardless of whether men or women work in those occupations. But because women more often work in these predominantly female occupations, they earn less on average. The association between occupation and earnings suggests two resolutions. If female occupations paid what male occupations paid, or if occupational segregation could be eliminated so that there were no predominantly female occupations, much of the gender earnings gap would be eliminated.

one resolution: get rid of occup. seg.

As in earlier decades, in 2000 women's occupations garnered lower earnings than men's. And regardless of occupation, men earned more than women. Median earnings for workers in men's occupations (30 percent female or less) averaged $38,240, while in mixed occupations (31 percent to 69 percent female) these earnings were slightly higher ($39,178). Across women's occupations (at least 70 percent female), the average was substantially lower ($27,219). But even within the same occupations, men earned more than women. An examination of the selected occupations presented in Table 5 shows that even where earnings were closest (nurses, librarians, mail carriers, and clergy), women earned less than men. For example, the average male

nurse working full-time/year-round earned $45,000, while his female counterpart earned $42,000. But there are also occupations where the differences are quite large (physicians and bus drivers), and these examples span the spectrum of occupations both in terms of gender composition and social class. So, the typical male physician earned $134,000, while the typical female physician's earnings were $86,000. Among male bus drivers, the median earnings were $32,000, compared with women's $21,000.

In fact, the connection between occupational gender segregation and the earnings gap is more complex than usually thought. Figure 4 shows median annual earnings for occupations along the full range of occupational gender composition. Although female-dominant occupations generally pay less than male-dominant occupations, there are two important exceptions. First, the most male-dominated occupations pay less than those occupations that are partially integrated. Second, the most female-dominated occupations pay at least as well if not better than those occupations with more men. These exceptions at the two ends of the gender composition scale mean that the relationship between the gender segregation of occupations and their earnings cannot be summarized by a straight line. This nonlinearity is not well recognized in the extensive research literature on occupational gender segregation and earnings. Some of the nonlinearity can be explained by other factors such as education, but even after extensive statistical controls for the personal characteristics of workers, the nonlinear shape of the relationship remains, although somewhat attenuated (results not shown).

♀-dominant occups. don't always pay less.

Upshot

The nonlinearity is not a new phenomenon; each census since 1950 shows a similar curve. Over this last half-century, both the maximum and the minimum median incomes have moved slightly to the right,

TABLE 5   Women's and Men's Median Annual Earnings in Selected Occupations, 1999

Earnings in 1999	Women	Men	Gender Ratio (%)
Male occupations			
Electricians	$33,000	$39,100	84
Firefighters	$40,000	$47,000	85
Airplane pilots	$44,000	$59,000	75
Truck drivers	$23,000	$32,400	71
Electrical engineers	$54,000	$64,000	84
Clergy	$29,000	$32,000	91
Police	$40,000	$45,600	88
Architects	$40,100	$52,000	77
Mixed occupations			
Physicians	$86,000	$134,000	64
Lawyers	$65,000	$88,000	74
Mail carriers	$36,700	$40,000	92
Managers	$36,000	$51,000	71
Real estate agents	$35,000	$50,000	70
Bartenders	$16,000	$22,000	73
Bus drivers	$21,000	$32,000	66
Accountants and bookkeepers	$36,000	$51,000	71
Female occupations			
Bill collectors	$25,700	$30,000	86
Medical and dental technicians	$30,000	$35,000	86
Teachers	$33,000	$40,300	82
Waiters and waitresses	$15,200	$21,000	72
Librarians	$35,000	$38,000	92
Nurses (professional)	$42,000	$45,000	93
Bank tellers	$19,000	$22,000	86
Secretaries and typists	$26,000	$32,000	81

Note: Earnings calculated for men and women, ages 25–54, employed full-time/year-round.
Source: Authors' calculations using the Integrated Public Use Micro-data Series (IPUMS), 2003.

toward the female end of the gender composition scale, but the general shape of the curve has not changed substantially.

A substantial gender earnings gap remains even at similar levels of the gender composition of occupations (see Figure 4). Men earn more than women even within the same occupation. This disparity is true among all occupations—those that are predominately male, predominately female, and integrated. For example, as shown in Table 5, the average female electrician earned $33,000 in 1999, while the average male electrician earned $39,100. Similarly, the average female secretary earned $26,000, while her male counterpart earned $32,000. The gap persists even among integrated occupations where, for example, the typical female lawyer earned $65,000 and the typical male lawyer earned $88,000.

But the fact that most men hold jobs on the left (high earnings) side of Figure 4 while most women hold jobs on the right (low earnings) side must explain some of the

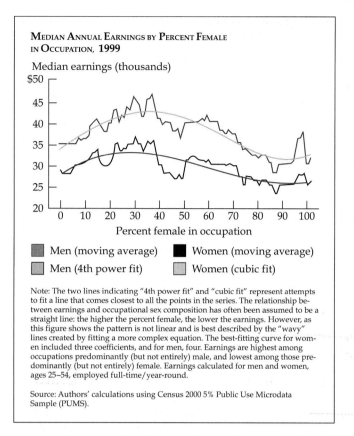

MEDIAN ANNUAL EARNINGS BY PERCENT FEMALE IN OCCUPATION, 1999

Note: The two lines indicating "4th power fit" and "cubic fit" represent attempts to fit a line that comes closest to all the points in the series. The relationship between earnings and occupational sex composition has often been assumed to be a straight line: the higher the percent female, the lower the earnings. However, as this figure shows the pattern is not linear and is best described by the "wavy" lines created by fitting a more complex equation. The best-fitting curve for women included three coefficients, and for men, four. Earnings are highest among occupations predominantly (but not entirely) male, and lowest among those predominantly (but not entirely) female. Earnings calculated for men and women, ages 25–54, employed full-time/year-round.

Source: Authors' calculations using Census 2000 5% Public Use Microdata Sample (PUMS).

FIGURE 4 Median Annual Earnings by Percent Female in Occupation, 1999

overall gender earnings gap. How much is due to this gender segregation of occupations? The nonlinearity of the gender segregation/earnings relationship creates difficulties for answering this question. Most prior research has evaluated this question using a linear approximation to the occupation-earnings relationship. The nonlinear shape of the relationship renders any such estimate suspect. Instead, we can use women's average earnings within each detailed occupation to estimate what would be the mean earnings of women if women had the same occupational distribution as men. If women worked in the same set of occupations as men, their mean earnings would in-

crease from $34,471 to $37,877; this would be 75 percent of men's mean earnings ($50,541) instead of the actual 68 percent. By these calculations, occupational segregation explains about 21 percent of the overall earnings gap. (A more realistic experiment of changing both men's and women's occupational distributions to match the overall occupational distribution reduces men's predicted earnings and raises women's predicted earnings to yield an expected earnings ratio of 74 percent—a gender gap about 18 percent smaller than the actual observed gap.) Thus, although most of the gender earnings gap occurs within occupations, about a fifth is directly attributable to gender segregation. . . .

RACE, GENDER, AND SEXUALITY
ON THE JOB

∝ READING 18 ∝

"Why Marcia You've Changed!"

Male Clerical Temporary Workers Doing
Masculinity in a Feminized Occupation

Kevin D. Henson and Jackie Krasas Rogers

To say that organizations are gendered has many meanings, from gender segregation at work to the part organizations play in the cultural reproduction of gender inequality (Acker 1990; Britton 2000). We know that "advantage and disadvantage, exploitation and control, action and emotion, meaning and identity are patterned through and in terms of a distinction between male and female, masculine and feminine" (Acker 1990, 146). Interaction and identity are but two means through which gender is constituted and reproduced in the workplace. Men and women "do gender" (West and Fenstermaker 1995; West and Zimmerman 1987) at work in organizations that are themselves gendered, and organizational imperatives shape interaction that "naturalizes" and essentializes cultural constructions of masculinity and femininity for men and women. This study provides a look at men doing gender in the highly feminized context of temporary clerical employment. . . .

"Why Marcia You've Changed! Male Temporary Clerical Workers Doing Masculinity in a Feminized Occupation" by Kevin D. Henson and Jackie Krasas Rogers from *Gender & Society*, Vol. 15, No. 2, April 2001: pp. 218–238. Copyright © 2001 Sociologists for Women in Society. Reprinted by permission of Sage Publications, Inc.

In this [chapter], we argue that although men's presence in temporary clerical work has the potential to challenge the "naturalness" of the gendered organization of work, in everyday practice it is assumed to say more about the essential nature of the individual men. Male clerical temporaries, as with other men who cross over into women's work, fall increasingly short of the ideals of hegemonic masculinity on at least two fronts. First, they face gender assessment through their lack of a "real" job (i.e., a full-time career in "men's work"). Second, their location in a feminized occupation that requires the performance of emphasized femininity, including deference and caretaking behaviors, calls into question their presumed heterosexuality. The resulting gender strategies (Hochschild 1989) these men adopt reveal how male clerical temporary workers "do masculinity" to reassert the feminine identification of the job while rejecting its application to them. In particular, we argue that men in clerical temporary work do masculinity through renaming and reframing the work, distancing themselves from the work with a cover story, and resisting the demands to perform deference. Paradoxically, rather than disrupting the gender order, the gender strategies adopted help reproduce and naturalize the gendered organization of work and reinvigorate hegemonic masculinity and its domination over women and subaltern men.

The Gendered Character of Temporary Clerical Employment

While temporary employment has increased dramatically in the past 15 years in response to employers' demands (Golden and Appelbaum 1992), researchers have only recently begun to systematically document the effects of this trend for workers and workplace relations. The rapid expansion of temporary employment is profoundly changing the experience, meaning, and conditions of work for temporaries who, like other contingent workers, fall through the cracks of existing workplace protections and provision of benefits (Henson 1996; Parker 1994; Rogers 2000; Rogers and Henson 1997).

The clerical sector of temporary employment, like the permanent clerical sector, is predominantly composed of women (Bureau of Labor Statistics 1995). Historically, this association of temporary work with women's work was reflected in the common inclusion of the infantilizing term *girl* in the names of the earliest temporary agencies (e.g., Kelly Girl). While temporary agencies have formally modernized their names (i.e., Kelly Girl became Kelly Services), the continued popular usage of the outdated names accurately reflects the gendered composition of the temporary clerical workforce. Indeed, a survey by the National Association of Temporary Services (1992) estimated that 80 percent of member agency temporaries were women. A recent government survey concluded that "workers employed by temporary help agencies in February 1997 were more likely than other workers to be young, female, Black or Hispanic" (Cohany 1998, 13).

Contemporary clerical temporary employment, like permanent clerical work, is so completely identified as women's work that until recently, it was considered inappropriate employment for a man, even by the temporary industry. Until the 1960s, in fact, it was common policy within the industry not to accept male applicants for clerical temporary work (Moore 1963, 35). Men, it was asserted, should be seeking a permanent, full-time career-type job—a "real job"—that would allow them to work hard, be financially successful, and take on the idealized (male) breadwinner role (Cheng 1996; Connell 1987, 1995).

Recently, however, men have come to constitute a greater proportion of temporary agency workers, although they are still more likely to be working as industrial than clerical temporaries (see Parker 1994). In fact, the continued numerical predominance of women in both the permanent and temporary clerical workforce often leads to the assumption that clerical temporary workers are women. Indeed, the job of clerical temporary worker is gendered—more specifically feminized—as women's work. Consequently, temporary work, clerical work, and especially temporary clerical work are perceived as women's work.

Given temporaries' low status and vulnerability to work deprivation, the expectations of temporary agencies and clients become de facto job requirements that shape temporary workers' interactions in such a way that one's gender and sexuality are prominently featured as aspects of the work (see Rogers and Henson 1997). For example, the demands of temporary agencies and client companies for particular (gendered or sexy) physical presentations, and the embedded expectations for deference and caretaking behaviors, highlight the gendered (feminized) and sexualized nature of temporary clerical work (Henson 1996; Rogers and Henson 1997). Indeed, the common association of temporary work with promiscuity, or "occupational sleeping around," highlights the ways in which clerical work and temporary work intersect to create a highly feminized job (see Rogers 2000 for a discussion of the gendering of temporary versus clerical work). In other words, temporary clerical work is a gendered (as well as raced, classed, aged, and heterosexualized) occupation that requires workers to do gender (and race, class, and so forth) in certain forms, recreating them and making them appear natural (see Acker 1990; West and Fenstermaker 1995; West and Zimmerman 1987). The type of gender one must "do" in clerical temporary work is primarily white, middle-class, heterosexual femininity. Consequently, while certain exceptions are made, it is nearly impossible to do this brand of femininity appropriately if you are a man or a woman of color. . . .

Method

This research is based on in-depth interviews and extensive participant observation from two broader studies on temporary clerical work we conducted in Chicago in 1990–91 (Henson 1996) and Los Angeles in 1993–94 (Rogers 2000). During the participant observation component of our studies, each of us worked as a clerical temporary worker for more than one year on a variety of assignments in many different types of organizations. We entered our temporary employment with many common characteristics such as relatively high educational attainment, whiteness, and youthfulness (Kevin was 26; Jackie was 28), yet our different respective genders affected our temporary work experiences in many dissimilar and revealing ways.

In addition to our participant-observation work, each of us conducted open-ended, semistructured interviews with temporaries and agency personnel, yielding 68 interviews in all (35 in Chicago and 33 in Los Angeles). Our interview participants included 10 temporary agency personnel and one client company representative, but the majority (57) were temporary clerical workers. We located participants of this highly fluid

and difficult-to-access workforce through a variety of methods—personal contacts made on assignment, responses to fliers placed at temporary agency offices, and personal referrals. We pursued a grounded theory approach in our research, including an emphasis on theoretical sampling (Glaser and Strauss 1965, 1967). Consequently, we sought out participants who maximized the range of temporary work experiences we studied rather than pursuing a strictly representative sample of the temporary workforce. In the end, our sample of temporary clerical workers included a relatively diverse group of participants, including 20 men and 37 women ranging in age from 20 to 60 (see Table 1).[1] Indeed, our sample approximates the age and race distribution of the general temporary workforce. However, our sample differs in at least one important way from the general clerical temporary workforce. We deliberately oversampled for men in this female-dominated occupation. Collectively, our interview participants had worked through more than 40 temporary agencies with individual tenure in temporary employment ranging from a few months to more than 10 years.

We followed flexible open-ended interview schedules, addressing themes that we had identified as salient during our participant-observation work and pursued new themes as they emerged. We both interviewed women and men in our respective locales, and although evidence of participants' negotiation of the "gendered context of the [interview] interaction" emerged (e.g., men talked directly about feeling "less manly" to Jackie but talked more abstractly about feeling like "failures" to Kevin), there was a remarkable overlap and consistency in the substance of participants' responses (see Williams and Heikes 1993). We tape-recorded, transcribed, and analyzed all of the interviews. Although at first we pursued an open coding process focusing on general concepts such

TABLE 1   Race/Ethnicity and Gender of Temporary Clerical Workers

Race/Ethnicity	Men	Women
White	13	28
African American	3	7
Asian	1	2
Latino/Latina	1	0
Other	2	0
Total	20	37

as stigmatization and coping strategies, eventually our analysis revealed consistent gendered patterns in our data. All names indicated in the body of the article are pseudonyms.

What's He Doing Here?

Male temporary clerical workers initially disrupt the gendered landscape of an organization since both the permanent and temporary clerical workforces are female dominated. This is reflected in the consistency with which token male clerical temporaries were met with surprise on the job. Indeed, the reaction to token men highlights the almost complete feminization of the work and the associated expectation that temporary workers will be women. The male temporaries we interviewed, for example, universally commented on their experiences as token men in women's work:

> There are areas where I felt that I did not fit in properly because I was a man on a temp assignment. (Michael Glenn, 26-year-old Asian American man)

> People are looking at me like, "What are you doing here?" Like they're thinking, "Gee, what's the deal? Shouldn't you be, I don't know, doing something else?" I mean it's like it's sort of fine if you're just out of school. They kind of expect well, you're doing this until you get a

regular job. (Harold Koenig, 29-year-old white man)

Similarly, Henson was conscious on more than one of his assignments of steady streams of chuckling female workers conspicuously moving past his workstation, (apparently) to see the male receptionist. While there might be socially acceptable reasons for a young man's location in temporary work (e.g., "just out of school" or "until you get a regular job"), for men, it is generally employment requiring an explanation.

In fact, the disruption of the taken-for-granted naturalness of workplace gender segregation by the presence of male temporaries was often a source of humor for permanent workers. For example, Henson repeatedly encountered variants of a joke that played on themes of gender and mistaken identity. Permanent workers, especially men, upon seeing him for the first time at a (female) permanent worker's desk, would declare with mock seriousness, "Why (Marcia, Faye, Lucy) you've changed!" The humor of this joke, apparently, derived from the mismatch between the expected gender of the worker and Henson's gender. Another widespread joke, playing on similar themes, was to knowingly misattribute ownership of a permanent female employee's personal (and feminine) belongings to a male temporary through a mock compliment such as, "Nice pumps." Jackie, however, experienced neither the need to explain her employment nor the jokes.

The feminized nature of the work was further highlighted when others failed to recognize a male temporary as the secretary, mistaking him for someone with higher organizational status. Jon Carter, for example, described the confusion callers experienced when they heard his masculine voice at the receptionist's desk: "I get a lot of people, you know, that are confused as to who I am because it's a male voice" (23-year-old gay white man). Henson also experienced being mistaken for a permanent (higher status) new hire. One coworker, realizing his error after warmly welcoming Kevin and introducing himself, quickly pulled back his extended hand and retreated in embarrassment.

Finally, the feminized nature of temporary work was revealed by the extent to which "male" continues to be the verbally marked category. Note, for example, Linda Schmidt's verbal marking of both "male secretaries" and "male temps":

> Roger Piderat. He was a male secretary. He was very good. And then we had a male temp come in. And he was English. He was a nice guy. And he did reception for a while. And he worked at Anne's desk for a while. But he was a very pleasant person too. So we've had male secretaries before. (Linda Schmidt, 38-year-old white woman)

As with women in nontraditional occupations (e.g., female doctors or female lawyers), men in nontraditional (secretarial and clerical) work are the marked category.

The expectation, indeed assumption, that (requested) temporary workers will be women sometimes is expressed as an overt preference for women—or aversion to men—in these positions. Although temporary agencies are legally required to operate under equal opportunity employer legislation (i.e., to hire workers without regard to race, sex, or age), temporaries are nevertheless often placed for non-skill-specific characteristics including their race, gender, age, and physical attractiveness (Henson 1996; Rogers 2000; Rogers and Henson 1997). Cindy Beitz, a temporary counselor, described how client companies sometimes explicitly, and quite illegally, requested female temporaries:

> You can call them and say, "We have a young gentleman who will be coming in there tomorrow for you." And sometimes they will say . . . they'll come out and say, "Well, I don't want him. I told you I wanted a woman." (Cindy Beitz, 33-year-old white woman)

Without prompting, approximately half of the agency representatives mentioned similar illegal requests. Similarly, temporary workers like Irene Pedersen, who were privy to client company-agency interactions, reported overhearing illegal requests:

> I worked on a temp assignment somewhere in the Personnel Department at this company, and the client wanted a temp receptionist. And he would come in and beat on the personnel manager, he didn't want a man. He didn't want anybody who was Black, he didn't want anybody who was this. (Irene Pedersen, 25-year-old white woman)

Temporary workers were often aware, or at least suspected, that personal characteristics such as gender determined their access to jobs. Arnold Finch, for example, hypothesized that he had lost a job because of his gender:

> I was working a temp job and I left there. I did really good work. They wouldn't call me back. The only reason why, I was a male. They only wanted females to work that job. . . . It's just that I guess companies that . . . when somebody comes in the door, they want a pretty, happy, smiling female face behind

the counter. (Arnold Finch, 23-year-old white man)

In addition, Henson lost at least one clerical assignment admittedly on the basis of his gender: "The client isn't sure if they want a male temporary or not. Whoever placed the order is going to check and see if it's okay" (Henson's field notes, 1990). Although Kevin had cross-trained in preparation at the agency's office on a specific word processing program (without pay), the assignment was withdrawn. Neither Rogers nor any of the women we interviewed experienced a negative gender screening similar to Henson's—they were the right gender.

Not only is clerical temporary work feminized, it is also heterosexualized, especially for women. Clients, for example, often included demands for particular feminized (even sexy) physical presentations when placing an order for temporary help:

> When we get a position like that in where they say, "She should wear this outfit" or "She should look like this." Whatever. We'll still recommend . . . we can still call men in too, but . . . (Cindy Beitz, 33-year-old white woman)
>
> They'll ask for blond and blue eyes and stuff like that. Always for the front office. We tell them that we'll send the best qualified. If we send a qualified person and they send 'em back because they're not blond, we obviously wouldn't be able to fill that order. They'll go to another agency that will. (Regina Mason, 44-year-old Latina agency manager)

Indeed, female temporary secretaries, like women serving higher status men in other traditional women's work (Hall 1993; MacKinnon 1979), were often expected to make an offering of their gender, including their sexual attractiveness, as part of the job. Since the agencies' interests are in pleasing clients,

even some of the more egregious requests for female temporary workers as sex objects (e.g., for a young, blond woman with great legs) are often honored (Henson 1996; Rogers 2000; Rogers and Henson 1997). Because temporary agencies depend on client companies for revenue, they are under considerable pressure to comply with these client requests. Agencies that assiduously follow the law risk losing their clients.

However, it would be inaccurate to describe the preference for women in temporary secretarial work as simply the desire to employ women as sexual objects. The employers' preference for women is partially explained by employers' essentialized understandings of gender as it relates to workers' capabilities. In other words, client companies and agencies often use a "gender logic" when matching workers with assignments (Hossfeld 1990). Women, in this logic, are often assumed to be innately superior at work calling for certain emotional and relational skills (Hochschild 1983; Leidner 1993; Pierce 1995). In fact, temporary secretaries, as part of the job, are expected to perform emotional labor—to be deferential and nurturing toward managers, coworkers, clients, and agency personnel (Henson 1996; Rogers and Henson 1997). As Pierce (1995, 89) has argued about another feminized occupation (paralegals), "The feminization of this occupation . . . is created not only by employer preference for women, but by the fact that the occupation itself—formally or not—calls for women to cater to men's emotional needs."

Challenges to Masculinity

Men who cross over to work in highly feminized occupations face institutionalized challenges to their sense of masculinity, that is, the extent to which they measure up to the dictates of hegemonic masculinity (Pierce 1995; Pringle 1993; Williams 1989, 1995).

Male clerical temporary workers, for example, face gender assessment—highlighting their failure to live up to the ideals of hegemonic masculinity—on at least two fronts. First, they are working temporary rather than permanent, higher paying, full-time jobs ("He should have a real job"), which limits their ability to assume the male breadwinner role. Second, they are doing clerical work (i.e., women's work), including demands for deference and caretaking, which challenges their presumed heterosexuality ("He could be gay"). Yet, unlike the situation of male nurses or elementary schoolteachers (Williams 1989, 1995), clerical temporary work is not a semiprofession with institutionalized room for upward mobility via the glass escalator.

He Should Have a Real Job

Male temporary clerical workers' individual failings, when faced with gender assessment, included questions about their drive, motivation, and competence for male career success (i.e., "Why doesn't he have a real job?"). Indeed, permanent work providing a sufficient financial base to assume the male breadwinner role is a core component of hegemonic masculine identity (Cheng 1996; Connell 1987, 1995; Kimmel 1994). Consequently, men who have jobs that do not allow them to assume the breadwinner role—such as those in part-time or temporary work—are perceived as "less manly" (Epstein et al. 1999; Rogers 2000).

Indeed, the assumption that men, but not women, should hold or desire permanent employment was widely shared by temporary workers, temporary agency staff, and client company supervisors. For example, Dorothy Brooke, a temporary worker, expressed the idea that temporary work was acceptable for women but that men should be striving to get real jobs. In other words, temporary jobs are unsatisfactory jobs that

no real man (i.e., white, heterosexual, and middle-class) would or should accept:

> I was surprised by how many older men were working as temporaries. I guess I expected to just see women. But I asked one of these guys if he was looking for full-time work. And he said he was just hoping that one of his temp jobs was going to turn into a full-time job. I thought you've got to have more spunk than that to get a job. (Henson's field notes, 1991)

Likewise, Regina Mason, a temporary agency manager, struggling to explain the anomalous presence of men in temporary work, tapped into gendered industry rhetoric portraying the work as good for women—a "flexible, secondary wage earning job"—but inadequate for men, except on a truly temporary basis (Henson 1996):

> I think that's the trend that men have never thought of working temporary. I mean that's a new thing to men to go work temp. It's the old attitude that men are breadwinners you know so they gotta have stability, permanency, a real job. But we still have a few men working. I think a lot of housewives don't want anything permanent. So they prefer to come in and just do temping so that they can take off when they want to. (Regina Mason, 44-year-old Latina agency manager)

Ironically, while men in temporary employment are curiosities to be pitied, the low-pay, impermanence, and dead-end nature of these jobs is seen as natural or unproblematic for women. Consequently, an agency manager can bemoan the difficulties she has telling men, but not women, "they'd only be getting maybe $8 an hour and not necessarily steady work" (Rogers's field notes, 1994).

The irregularity, uncertainty, and poor remuneration of clerical temporary work challenged male temporaries' abilities to live up to the breadwinner, and self-sufficiency, ideals contained in hegemonic masculinity. Without prompting, most men in the study detailed the challenges temping presented to their sense of masculinity. Kirk Stevens, for example, felt guilty and ashamed about his inability to take on the idealized (male) breadwinner role. An inadequate supply of assignments left Kirk financially dependent on his girlfriend:

> So far, this summer, Natalie, my girlfriend, has been supporting us both. I really can't stand it. She leaves at eight thirty and gets home at five thirty or six and she's totally exhausted. She can't stay up past eleven at night. And I feel really guilty 'cause she wouldn't have to be working quite so crazy if I were getting any money in at all. But it's difficult for both of us. (Kirk Stevens, 27-year-old white man)

While financial dependence is seen as an unproblematic aspect of low-wage temporary employment for women (i.e., the income is assumed to be secondary), this same dependence among men often challenges male temporary workers' sense of masculinity. In other words, not only is the male temporary worker unable to provide for others but he also finds himself in the painful position of dependence.

The lack of respect accorded to men who fail to live up to the career orientation ideals embodied in hegemonic masculinity was not lost on male temporary workers. Albert Baxter, for example, described his belief that male temporary workers received less respect than female temporaries:

> I think men get a little less respect if they're temping. There's that expectation that they should be like career oriented and like moving up in the world and being a businessman and moving himself forward in business. Where women can do that but it's not an expec-

tation. And so I think that, I think that's where that Kelly Girl image, that temporaries are women is. I have noticed that there is a certain amount, looking down upon. I think that's true of temps in general. They're somewhat looked down upon. I think the men maybe more. (Albert Baxter, 31-year-old white man)

Accordingly, male temporary workers sometimes experienced feelings of inferiority and inadequacy when recognized (and judged) as temporary secretaries by others. Denny Lincoln, for example, articulated feelings of inferiority when others assessed him on the basis of his low-wage, low-status temporary employment:

> Why are all these people taking $6.50 and $7.00 an hour jobs? Why? Why can't they go out and get a real job? And I think that's what goes through people's minds. Like you have a college degree! What the hell's going on here? There must be something wrong with this guy. He can't hold a job, he's working for 7 bucks an hour stuffing envelopes. (Denny Lincoln, 39-year-old white man)

Similarly, Bob Johnson described the embarrassment he felt when recognized on a temporary assignment by old college classmates:

> Where I work there's a lot of people who I graduated [from college] with on staff. And when they see me, you know, they go, "What are you doing? Why are you working as a secretary?" And you have to explain yourself. Well, I'm trying to find the ideal job. Maybe it's all in my mind because I feel sort of inferior to that because they're kind of established. I feel really inadequate. (Bob Johnson, 23-year-old gay white man)

Bob's reaction reveals his embarrassment about both the impermanence of his employment ("they're kind of established") and its feminization ("Why are you working as a secretary?").

He Could Be Gay

Male temporary workers' failing, when faced with gender assessment, does not stop with questioning their drive, motivation, and competence for male career success. Their location in a female-dominated occupation that requires and produces emphasized femininity, including deferential and nurturing behaviors, also calls into question their presumed heterosexuality, a core component of hegemonic masculinity. When men do deference and caretaking, they are popularly defined as feminine—like women—and therefore gay. As Donaldson (1993, 648) has noted, any type of powerlessness quickly becomes conflated with the popular stereotype of homosexuality. Male clerical temporaries, as with male secretaries (Pringle 1993), nurses (Williams 1989), elementary schoolteachers (Williams 1995), and paralegals (Pierce 1995), are regularly stereotyped as gay. Patsy Goodrich, for example, accepted the construction of male temporary clerical workers, but not male temporary industrial workers, as gay:

> But, yeah, I think most of the people [in temporary work] that I know have either been gay men or women. Or lesbian women. I don't really know. I can't think of a straight man that I know that's done it. Except for my brother. But he did the kind where it's like the industrial side. (Patsy Goodrich, 27-year-old white lesbian woman)

Similarly, in searching for an explanation for the presence of some men in temporary clerical work, Connie Young described the male temporary workers in her office as unmasculine or effeminate in appearance:

> We've had male temporaries come in to answer the phones and do whatever

typing jobs. And, for some reason, all the male temps we've gotten didn't have any masculine features. They're very longhaired, ponytailed, very artsy look. And the men in business suits would look at them and kind of not take them seriously actually. You know like, "Oh, he has an earring." (Connie Young, 25-year-old Asian American woman)

In addition, male temporary workers are feminized as they enter and interact in an organizational environment that requires the performance of emphasized femininity, including deference. Male temporaries' discomfort with the demands for deference, although more limited than the deferential demands made of female temporaries, revealed both the gendered nature of the work and its implicit threat to their sense of masculinity:

> It's a manly thing to be in charge. And men should want to be, supposedly in charge and delegating things. If you're a man and you're being delegated to, it somehow makes you less manly. You know what I'm saying? Whereas it seems to be okay for the person delegating to women. And the women, maybe they're just projecting that to get by. It seems that they're more okay with that than men are. I guess I'm saying that it makes me feel less of the manly kind of qualities, like I'm in charge, you know. And men should be like takin' meetings and barking orders instead of just being subservient. (Harold Koenig, 29-year-old heterosexual white man)

Several male temporary workers remarked that they were surprised by the deferential demands of temporary work—as men with male privilege, they had rarely experienced the requirement to enact deference.

Similarly, Kirk Stevens, was outraged when he was asked to perform the subservient work of cleaning bathrooms:

I got a phone call saying there was this company that needed me to go out and change the light bulbs And I met the guy and he gives me, you know, the obligatory tour. . . . And then he gives me a bucket and a mop, some rubber gloves, and he says, "Now what I'd really like you to do, just to start off, is clean, if you could, the bathrooms need cleaning. Could you clean this bathroom?" And it didn't even . . . I just . . . I just can't believe that I didn't just say, "Go to hell. I'm not going to clean your goddamn bathrooms." (Kirk Stevens, 27-year-old heterosexual white man)

While someone has to clean bathrooms (often work relegated to poor women of color), Kirk Stevens believed he was not the type of person (e.g., white, educated, and male) who should be asked to do so. The negative reactions to deferential demands were strongest (but not exclusive) among white, heterosexual, college-educated men who would fall closest to the cultural ideal of hegemonic masculinity (see Connell 1987, 1995).

Male temporary workers, heterosexual and gay, were aware of the construction of the male temporary as gay. A noted exception, Michael Glenn, positively rather than negatively framed and accepted an essentialized construction of temporary workers as gay:

> But temps usually are women or homosexual men. Um, it's not to say that some heterosexual men don't make good temps, but I think it's harder to find. And then you get into the whole psychology of heterosexual men I suppose. *Men [A]re from Mars* and all of that. But heterosexual men are not as great at being people-people. . . . you have to be flexible. And there's more of a rigidity to a heterosexual male. And then again in the gradations, I would say there's more rigidity for a homosexual male than for a woman. And I'm not even gonna try to place ho-

mosexual women. (Michael Glenn, 26-year-old Asian American gay man)

Note how Michael's assertion that gay men excel over heterosexual men at the emotional and relational demands of the job (being flexible and being "people-people") leads him to the conclusion that gay men are more suited to temporary clerical work. Ironically, while gay men come closer than straight men to naturally making good temps in his account, they still do not measure up to (real, i.e., heterosexual) women, leaving the natural gender order intact.

Gender Strategies/Hegemonic Bargains

The male temporaries we interviewed, faced with gender assessment, adopted three primary gender strategies—renaming and reframing the work, distancing themselves from the work with a cover story, as well as the more risky strategy of resisting demands for deference—to do masculinity in a feminized occupation. Ironically, rather than disrupting the gender order, each of these strategies "enables men to maintain a sense of themselves as different from and better than women—thus contributing to the gender system that divides men from women in a way that privileges men" (Williams 1995, 123). . . .

Doing Masculinity—Renaming and Reframing

One of the primary gender strategies male temporaries use to maintain their sense of masculinity is to distance themselves from the feminized aspects of the occupation by renaming or reframing the work. Male temporary secretaries, similar to men in other feminized occupations (Pierce 1995; Pringle 1993; Williams 1989, 1995), described their work in terms perceived to be more masculine, or at the very least, gender-neutral (e.g., word processor, administrative assistant, proofreader, bookkeeper). Steve Woodhead, a 35-year-old white gay man, for example, characterized his temporary work assignment as *bookkeeping*. Steve did not mention the temporary nature of his job, framing it more as an independent contracting arrangement. Indeed, male temporaries displayed an almost pathological avoidance of the term *secretarial*. In contrast, most of the female temporaries we interviewed described their work without hesitation as secretarial.

Occasionally, agency personnel and clients also participated in this project of renaming the work in more masculine terms. For example, on one of Henson's temporary assignments, the supervisor wondered aloud how to refer to the position in a more masculine or gender-neutral way: "Word processor? What should we call you? We're not going to call you secretary" (Henson's field notes, 1990). Whether this renaming was simply a courtesy to individual male temporary workers or a way of reconciling clients' discomfort in seeing men crossing over into women's work is unclear.

In addition, some male temporary workers attempted to reframe the work as masculine by focusing on the technical competencies required on their temporary assignments. Indeed, to be technically competent is to be masculine (Cockburn 1985; Messerschmidt 1996; Wright 1996). Bob Johnson, for example, described his work in terms of the computer environment or software he was required to use on his (secretarial) work assignments:

That was mostly work with IBM. You know, cause IBM is incredibly popular. So I used my WordPerfect a lot. And then when they didn't have any Word-Perfect, they sent me out on proofreading assignments. To proofread these books that no one would ever, ever read.

Basically, it's been a lot of word processing. (Bob Johnson, 23-year-old gay white man)

This focus on the technological aspects (computer) of the work, however, is not just a refusal to name the work. As Cynthia Cockburn (1985, 12) has noted, "Femininity is incompatible with technological competence; to feel technically competent is to feel manly." Therefore, focusing on the technological aspects of the work is part of a gender strategy that bolsters one's sense of power at the same time it reinforces segregation between men's and women's work.

Another reframing technique male temporaries use to maintain their masculinity is to borrow the prestige of the employing organization (Pierce 1995; Williams 1995) when describing their work to outsiders, especially other men. A male paralegal in Pierce's (1995) study of gender in law firms described how he used the name of the law firm rather than his job title to impress outsiders. Similarly, Bob Johnson described the unit he was assigned to at a consulting firm in elaborate detail rather than his specific work tasks when asked about his temporary job:

I work for six managers . . . in the change management services division. Companies hire them to do consulting work and they sort of do a lot of work with organizations that are going through organizational change. Implementing new systems. Both in the workforce and in terms of like information technology. Sort of reeducating them and reorganizing them around different responsibilities and different organizational hierarchies. And the other division I work for is integration services. And they're really technical experts. In terms of different [computer] hardware and software configuration systems. (Bob Johnson, 23-year-old gay white man)

Only in follow-up questions did he detail his more mundane day-to-day secretarial tasks: "I do support work. It's a lot of typing up correspondence between clients and interoffice correspondence. A lot of filing. A lot of typing. Answering phones a lot. Most of the time."

Doing Masculinity—Telling the Cover Story

Male temporaries, almost universally, invoked the "cover story" as a gender strategy to buttress their challenged sense of masculinity. The cover story, told to both self and others, invokes an alternative identity and defines one as truly temporary or occupationally transient (Henson 1996). Male clerical temporaries, through telling the cover story both on and off the job, provide an explanation for their apparent lack of drive or competence in obtaining a real (male) job. Steve Woodhead, for example, described how he strategically used his cover story on new assignments: "Oh, I always told them I was an actor. Immediately. Immediately. And they were, like, 'Great! This is wonderful.' So maybe that's what cut the ice, you know. They knew I wasn't just waiting to get a *real job*. 'Why doesn't this guy have a *real job* yet?'" (35-year-old gay white man). Likewise, Harold Koenig said, "I always wanna tell people that I'm just doing this because I'm a writer and I'm really here because of that. But they really don't want to know that. It's like to save your ego" (29-year-old white man). The cover story, then, explains why a man in clerical temporary employment does not have a real job and asserts a more valuable (masculine) social identity.

While permanent workers might also define themselves as occupationally transient (Garson 1994; Pierce 1995; Williams 1989), the organization of temporary work provided workers with the ready-made temporary label. For example, Pierce (1995, 170) noted that male paralegals frequently asserted their occupational transience despite their permanent, full-time status ("I'm planning to go to law school after working as a legal assistant for a few years"). The organization of their work as permanent, however, required that these workers simultaneously demonstrate commitment and noncommitment to their work.

The organization of temporary work, however, presupposes that male temporary workers are uncommitted and facilitates the assumption that there is an underlying reason to be revealed. Note, for example, Henson's failed use of his cover story, in response to direct questioning, in this field note excerpt:

> Someone asked me if I just temped all the time or what I did. And I said, "Well no. I'm a graduate student in Sociology at Northwestern." She asked what I was studying and I said, "Clerical temporary work." Which she thought was really funny. I saw her in the elevator today and she asked, "How's your little study going?" Like, "Sure. That's just your little story." And it is. Because I'm [also] doing it for money. So it is just my little story. But I felt really belittled because she just wasn't taking me seriously. (Henson's field notes, 1991)

Coworkers commonly elicited cover stories from men, but seldom from women. While some women did offer cover stories, their use appeared to be motivated by class rather than gender anxieties (i.e., "What am I doing here with a college degree?") In fact, since women's presence in clerical temporary employment is naturalized, coworkers rarely pressed them for explanations of any sort. On the few occasions when this happened, the question was precipitated by the temporary worker's efforts or exceptional work performance. During her fieldwork, for example, Rogers's presence in temporary clerical work was questioned only once when she was found to possess unusually detailed knowledge about insurance benefits.

Doing Masculinity—Refusing to Do Deference

Finally, men in clerical temporary work often adopted the risky gender strategy of resisting demands for deference in an effort to do masculinity. Deference, however, is part of being a "good" temporary worker for both male and female temporaries (Henson 1996; Rogers 1995; Rogers and Henson 1997). Temporaries must enact subservience and deference, for example, to continue getting assignments. While other researchers (Hochschild 1983; Pierce 1995; Williams 1995) have argued that men in women's work are not required to do deference (or at least in the same way), we believe that there are occupations in which men are required to do deference, including clerical temporary work. While the demands for deference may be different for women and men (and different within genders along dimensions of race, age, and sexual orientation), men were still expected to provide deferential services as clerical temporary workers.

While none of the men reported ever being asked to get coffee, a request many women reported with great irritation, they were still expected to provide deferential services—smiling, waiting, taking orders, and tolerating the bad moods of their supervisors. In other words, women were asked to provide more of the nurturing and caretaking components of deference than men, especially when working for older and more established men. Helen, for example, reported receiving (and resisting) a particularly egregious request for caretaking behavior on one of her assignments:

They had this glass candy jar this big. And like, "You're supposed to keep that filled with chocolate." Like, "Where do I get the chocolate from?" "Well, you know, just pick something up. Something cheap." Yeah. Like I'm supposed to go and buy a bag of Hershey's Kisses so that the executives can add to their waistlines. I'm like no. And it's been empty ever since I've been there. [Laughs]. (Helen Weinberg, 24-year-old white woman)

Helen, unlike many of the women we interviewed, resisted the most demeaning caretaking requests through a passive "forgetfulness" strategy. Although both female and male temporaries are generally passive in their resistance (Rogers 2000), the significance of deference in temporary employment for masculinity is heightened when we realize that most opportunities for resistance are passive ones.

The refusal to do deference, as doing masculinity, may be so important that male temporary workers risk losing the job rather than feel demeaned. Contrast Helen's forgetfulness strategy above with Bob's overt refusal to do deferential tasks, notably for a female superior:

At my long-term assignment, this one permanent secretary was out sick. I had my own desk and I had things that had to be done. And this woman comes up to me and she hands me a stack of photocopying to do. And I said, "Excuse me." And she said, "Well this is for you to do." And I said, "Well, thank you, but I have my own work to do. This work has to be done by 5." And she goes, "Well, you are just a temp and blah, blah, blah, blah." I said, "Wait a minute. I am a temporary worker, but I do have a desk and assigned work that has to be done. And she threw this little fit. And throughout the day she was really terse and really just a real bitch to me. . . . She was just awful. You know that whole mentality of "just a temp, just a temp." (Bob Johnson, 23-year-old gay white man)

Similarly, Pierce (1995, 92) reports a story of a male paralegal who did not successfully do deference and appropriately "manage his own anger" with an ill-behaved male attorney. He confronted the attorney on his abusive behavior, was removed from the case, and eventually pushed to a peripheral position within the firm.

Similarly, Henson discovered the risks in resisting demands for deference when he failed to adopt a submissive demeanor and was removed from an assignment. Near the end of his first week on a (scheduled) long-term assignment at a small medical college, Henson arrived to find a typed message from Shirley, his work-site supervisor, on his chair. The note clearly asserted the hierarchy of power and demanded deference and submission—especially since Shirley worked only a few feet from Henson's desk and could have easily communicated her request verbally:

"Kevin. RE: Lunch today (12/5). My plans are to be out of the office from about 11:45 AM to 1:00 PM. (If you get hungry early, I suggest you have a snack before I leave at 11:45 AM). Thanks. Shirl."

This annoys me: patronizing and hostile—at least that's the way I take it. So, I very casually and fully aware of the politics, walk to Shirley's door with the note in hand and say, "Oh, about lunch. . . . That's great! That works out fine with my plans too. No problem." I'm upbeat and polite, but I'm framing it as giving permission or at least as an interaction between equals. (Henson's field notes, 1990)

At the end of the day, Henson said good night to Shirley and left with every intention of returning in the morning. That evening, however, he received a call from his agency counselor: "Hi Kevin. This is Wendy. I don't know how to tell you this, but the college called us today and they said they just didn't think things were working out. They don't want you to come back tomorrow." While Henson had completed the formal work adequately, he had consciously resisted adopting the appropriate submissive demeanor. By refusing to perform deference and doing masculinity instead, he had lost the assignment.

Demands for deference seemed to be the breaking point for the male temporaries in this study. They were no longer able to reframe their way out of their feminized position. Male privilege no longer protected these men from the requirements of the job, including the performance of feminine styles of emotional labor and deference. While men do perform emotional labor and even deference on the job (Hochschild 1983; Pierce 1995), they typically do so in ways that are compatible with hegemonic notions of masculinity. In contrast, male temporaries were required to enact feminine modes of deference. Thus, men's refusals to do deference in temporary clerical work come to serve as proof that men are not suited for temporary clerical work.

Conclusion

Male clerical temporaries, as with other men who cross over into women's work, fail to conform to the dictates of hegemonic masculinity on at least two fronts. First, they are working temporary rather than permanent, higher paying, full-time jobs (i.e., a real job), which limits their ability to assume the male breadwinner role. Second, they are doing clerical work (i.e., women's work), including demands for deference and caretaking, which challenges their presumed heterosexuality.

At first glance, men's presence in a female-dominated job such as temporary clerical work might appear to disrupt the gendered landscape of the workplace. Unlike men in women's semiprofessions, however, these men cannot exercise their male privilege by riding the glass escalator to higher paying, more prestigious work. Work that is female dominated and very low status does not provide the credential system and internal labor market necessary for the operation of the glass escalator. Here, occupational specificity makes all the difference in understanding men's interactions in female-dominated work. The experience of male temporary clerical workers neither conforms wholly to Kanter's (1977) theory of tokenism nor to Williams's (1992) glass escalator theory. Rather, these men experience a gendered set of token-related problems that center on maintaining the ideals of hegemonic masculinity.

With little organizational opportunity for upward mobility, men do gender in such a way that they reassert the feminine identification of the job while rejecting its application to them. Through renaming and reframing their individual duties, men distance themselves from the most feminized aspects of the job. Through telling their cover story, men construct their presence in temporary work as truly transient while naturalizing women's numerical dominance in the job. While men's refusal to do female-typed deference places them at risk of job loss individually, the meanings attributed to those actions once again reproduce the gender order as men are confirmed as unsuited for temporary clerical work. Through their gender strategies, male temporary clerical workers strike a hegemonic

bargain, retracing the lines of occupational segregation and reinvigorating hegemonic masculinity and its domination over women and subaltern men.

NOTES

1. Although we did not systematically collect data on the sexual orientation of respondents, 2 women and 10 men in our sample self-identified as lesbian and gay. While we make no claims regarding generalizability on this front, we have marked sexual orientation of the interviewee where it is directly relevant as indicated by the respondents.

REFERENCES

Acker, Joan. 1990. Hierarchies, jobs, bodies: A theory of gendered organizations. *Gender & Society* 4:139–58.

Britton, Dana. M. 2000. The epistemology of the gendered organization. *Gender & Society* 14:418–34.

Bureau of Labor Statistics. 1995. *Handbook of labor statistics.* Washington, DC: Government Printing Office.

Cheng, Cliff. 1996. *Masculinities in organizations.* Thousand Oaks, CA: Sage.

Cockburn, Cynthia. 1985. *Machinery of dominance: Women, men, and technical know-how.* Boston: Northeastern University Press.

Cohany, Sharon R. 1998. Workers in alternative employment arrangements: A second look. *Monthly Labor Review* 121:3–21.

Connell, R. W. 1987. *Gender and power.* Stanford, CA: Stanford University Press.

———. 1995. *Masculinities.* Berkeley: University of California Press.

Donaldson, Mike. 1993. What is hegemonic masculinity? *Theory and Society* 22:643–57.

Epstein, C. F., C. Seron, B. Oglensky, and R. Saute. 1999. *The part-time paradox: Time norms, professional life, family and gender.* New York: Routledge.

Garson, Barbara. 1994. *All the livelong day: The meaning and demeaning of routine work.* Rev. 2d ed. New York: Penguin.

Glaser, Barney G., and Anselm L. Strauss. 1965. *Awareness of dying.* Chicago: Aldine.

———. 1967. *The discovery of grounded theory: Strategies for qualitative research.* Chicago: Aldine.

Golden, Lonnie, and Eileen Appelbaum. 1992. What was driving the 1982–88 boom in temporary employment: Preferences of workers or decisions and power of employers? *Journal of Economics and Society* 51:473–94.

Hall, Elaine. J. 1993. Smiling, deferring, and flirting: Doing gender by giving "good service." *Work & Occupations* 20:452–71.

Henson, Kevin. D. 1996. *Just a temp.* Philadelphia: Temple University Press.

Hochschild, Arlie R. 1983. *The managed heart: Commercialization of human feeling.* Berkeley: University of California Press.

———. 1989. *The second shift.* New York: Avon.

Hossfeld, Karen. 1990. Their logic against them: Contradictions in sex, race, and class in Silicon Valley. In *Women workers and global restructuring,* edited by K. Ward. Ithaca, NY: ILR Press.

Kanter, Rosabeth M. 1977. *Men and women of the corporation.* New York: Basic Books.

Kimmel, Michael S. 1994. Masculinity as homophobia: Fear, shame, and silence in the construction of gender identity. In *Theorizing masculinities,* edited by Harry Brod and Michael Kaufman. Thousand Oaks, CA: Sage.

Leidner, Robin. 1993. *Fast food, fast talk: Service work and the routinization of everyday life.* Berkeley: University of California Press.

MacKinnon, Catharine A. 1979. *Sexual harassment of working women: A case of sex discrimination.* New Haven, CT, and London: Yale University Press.

Messerschmidt, James W. 1996. Managing to kill: Masculinities and the space shuttle Challenger explosion. In *Masculinities in organizations,* edited by C. Cheng. Thousand Oaks, CA: Sage.

Moore, Mack. A. 1963. The role of temporary help-services in the clerical labor market. Ph.D. diss., University of Wisconsin–Madison.

National Association of Temporary Services. 1992. *Report on the temporary help services industry.* Alexandria, VA: DRI/McGraw-Hill.

Parker, Robert E. 1994. *Flesh peddlers and warm bodies: The temporary help industry and its workers.* New Brunswick, NJ: Rutgers University Press.

Pierce, Jennifer. 1995. *Gender trials: Emotional lives in contemporary law firms.* Berkeley: University of California Press.

Pringle, Rosemary. 1993. Male secretaries. In *Doing "women's work": Men in nontraditional occupations,* edited by C. L. Williams. Newbury Park, CA: Sage.

Rogers, Jackie K. 1995. Just a temp: Experience and structure of alienation in temporary clerical employment. *Work and Occupations* 22:137–66.

———. 2000. *Temps: The many faces of the changing workplace.* Ithaca, NY: Cornell University Press.

Rogers, Jackie K., and Kevin D. Henson. 1997. "Hey, why don't you wear a shorter skirt?" Structural vulnerability and the organization of sexual harassment in temporary clerical employment. *Gender & Society* 11:215–37.

West, Candace, and Sarah Fenstermaker. 1995. Doing difference. *Gender & Society* 1:8–37.

West, Candace, and Don H. Zimmerman. 1987. Doing gender. *Gender & Society* 1:125–51.

Williams, Christine L. 1989. *Gender differences at work: Women and men in nontraditional occupations.* Berkeley: University of California Press.

———. 1992. The glass escalator: Hidden advantages for men in the "female" professions. *Social Problems* 39:253–267.

———. 1995. *Still a man's world: Men who do women's work.* Berkeley: University of California Press.

Williams, Christine L., and Joel E. Heikes. 1993. The importance of researcher's gender in the in-depth interview: Evidence from two case studies of male nurses. *Gender & Society* 7:280–91.

Wright, Rosemary. 1996. The occupational masculinity of computing. In *Masculinities in organizations,* edited by C. Cheng. Thousand Oaks, CA: Sage.

∞ READING 19 ∞

The Locker Room and the Dorm Room

Workplace Norms and the Boundaries of Sexual Harassment
in Magazine Editing

Kirsten Dellinger and Christine L. Williams

Sexual behavior is common in workplaces, but for the most part sociologists have not paid attention to it unless sexual harassment is involved. Sexual harassment researchers have found that a large proportion of women workers have experienced behaviors that might fit the legal definition of sexual harassment—between 40 and 50 percent (Welsh 1999). But that does not mean that the women surveyed actually considered themselves to have been harassed. Even those who reported an offensive act against them, rarely answer "yes" to the survey question, "Have you ever been sexually harassed?" Why not?

At least part of the answer lies in the fact that sexual harassment is a feature of many jobs. Many women are employed in jobs where they are routinely subjected to deliberate or repeated sexual behavior that is unwelcome, as well as other sex-related behaviors that they consider hostile, offensive, or degrading. Studies of restaurant servers (Giuffre and Williams 1994; Allison 1994), amusement park attendants (Adkins 1995), nursing home aides (Foner 1994), and

maquiladora workers (Salzinger 2000) demonstrate that employees in a variety of fields encounter unwanted sexual behavior as a routine feature of their jobs. They rarely label their experiences sexual harassment, however, precisely because they are institutionalized as part their jobs. Those who refuse to put up with such requirements end up quitting or being fired, or never taking the job in the first place.

Yet not everyone who works in these jobs objects to their sexual aspects. Many people seek out and enjoy jobs that are highly sexualized. Meika Loe (1996), who studied the "Bazooms" restaurant chain, an establishment that requires waitresses to wear skimpy outfits and engage in sexual banter with customers, reported that 800 women applied for the job when she did. In a study of doctors and nurses in a teaching hospital, some high-ranking professional women claimed to enjoy the sexual elements of their jobs. A woman surgeon admitted that in the operating room, "[there's] teasing and joking and pinching and elbowing. It's fun. That's one reason people like being in that arena. That's part of the camaraderie" (Williams, Giuffre, and Dellinger 1999:86). Leslie Salzinger's (2000) study of a maquiladora plant found that women who initially resisted sexual objectification eventually became won over and gradually transformed themselves into sexual objects competing for the attentions of their male supervisors. But even in these cases, workers still draw boundary lines between sexual behaviors that they consider pleasurable, tolerable, and harassing.

In this paper, we compare two highly sexualized workplaces in the same industry, magazine publishing, to better understand how workers define sexual harassment and distinguish it from other, acceptable, forms of sexual expression. One of the organizations we studied publishes a men's pornographic magazine, and the other a feminist magazine. We use pseudonyms for each of the organizations to protect the identities of the individuals interviewed: the men's pornographic magazine is referred to as *Gentleman's Sophisticate* and the feminist magazine as *Womyn*. The editorial departments of the two magazines are our focus.

We chose these two organizations for comparison because they are both highly sexualized but in very different ways. The magazines produced by these organizations represent distinctive ideals of sexuality: one committed to feminism, and the other to what Robert W. Connell (1995) has called "hegemonic masculinity," the structural and cultural privileging of white, heterosexual male power. In this paper, we focus on the editorial departments at the two magazines because sexuality is an especially salient issue there. Editors are responsible for all of the written content published in their magazines (except for advertisements). Because members of these workplaces explicitly deal with sexuality as part of their jobs, we anticipated that editors at *Womyn* and *Gentleman's Sophisticate* would constantly have to draw boundary lines between acceptable and unacceptable expressions of sexuality.

The different values of feminism and hegemonic masculinity contained in the magazines are reflected in the organizational cultures of the two workplaces, but in complex ways. Organizational culture can be defined as the understandings, behaviors, and symbolic forms, including totems, rituals, taboos and myths, that are shared by members of a work organization (Reskin and Padavic 1994; Trice 1993). In these workplaces, the magazines themselves are among the most important symbols of the editors' shared organizational culture. Images from the magazines are posted throughout the workplaces, and copies of current and former issues are strewn about on desks. Although not all workers admire and identify with the magazines they edit—as we will see, this is especially the case at *Gentleman's Sophisticate*—the magazines, nevertheless, represent their collective effort and symbolize the values of the organization. Organizational culture also refers to the informal, emotional, and interpersonal dynamics of work, including the norms governing sexual interactions among workers (Gherardi 1995; Hearn and Parkin 1987). As we will show, editors consider these informal norms when drawing boundary lines between acceptable and unacceptable sexual behavior. While not all members of a workplace agree in every instance when a boundary has been crossed, we argue that understanding the process whereby workers make this determination requires taking organizational culture into account.

Although these two workplaces are in privately owned companies in the same industry, located in the same city, that employ people in the same occupations (editors, assistant editors, administrative assistants, secretaries, interns), there are several structural differences between them. Most importantly, all of the 18 members of the *Womyn* editorial staff are women, while six of the 12 editors at *Gentleman's Sophisticate,* including the top managers, are men. Overall, the occupation of editing is gender balanced (*Employment and Earnings,* January 1998, but it is not unusual for organizations committed to feminism to employ only women. Some might find the comparison of an all-women work site and a gender-balanced work site to be problematic because the assumption of most research has been that sexual harassment is solely a cross-sex phenomenon. A discussion of homophobia as sexual harassment has been limited (Williams 1997). We believe the comparison between *Gentleman's Sophisticate* and *Womyn* is useful in pointing out that the nature of occupational segregation in the workplace often finds women dealing with "male cultures" or working with other women in sex-segregated settings. We rarely find men who must negotiate a "female culture." The asymmetrical nature of these cases in regard to gender composition, actually allows us to examine the most common work experiences for women as they work in male dominated settings or as they work in women-only settings. If we are to understand women's experience with sexuality and sexual harassment at work, it is essential that we compare and contrast the workplace cultures that may develop in these different settings.

The ratio of men to women in a workplace is considered by some researchers to be an important predictor of the prevalence of sexual harassment (see Welsh 1999 for an overview of debates in this literature). Some researchers argue that the number of interactions between men and women at work is predictive of the likelihood of sexual harassment (Gruber 1998; Gutek, Cohen, and Konrad 1990). The findings from these studies would suggest that it is more likely that women editors would experience sexual harassment at *Gentleman's Sophisticate* than at *Womyn*, simply because there are more men employed at *Gentleman's Sophisticate*.

Other studies have endeavored to identify features of organizational culture that are conducive to sexual harassment. Pryor and his colleagues conducted a series of experiments that found that exposure to male supervisors and peers who sexually harass increases other men's likelihood of sexually harassing women (Hulin, Fitzgerald, and Drasgow 1996; Pryor, Giedd, and Williams 1995; Pryor, LaVite, and Stoller 1993). On the other side of the coin, Gruber (1998) found that workplaces with proactive methods of sexual harassment training were much more effective in reducing hostile environment harassment than workplaces that relied solely on less aggressive "get out the word" techniques.

These studies identify specific elements of organizational culture that are linked to the frequency and type of sexual harassment likely to occur in a workplace. But they do not address the meaning of sexual harassment, and how that meaning may be shaped by organizational context. In fact, these studies, like most quantitative studies of sexual harassment, assume that there is prior consensus regarding the meaning of sexual behaviors. As Welsh (1999:173) points out, "when using survey responses, it is common for researchers to define all unwanted sexual behaviors as sexual harassment, whether the respondent defines them as such (see Gruber 1998 for a notable exception)." Qualitative research is better suited to uncovering how the meaning of sexual behaviors varies in different organizational contexts. As Salzinger (2000) shows in her ethnography of a maquiladora, in certain workplace contexts, even egregious sexual behaviors on the part of management (ogling, demands for sexual access), may be accepted by workers as reasonable or inevitable conditions of their employment.

In addition to examining how organizational culture shapes workers' responses to sexual behavior, we explore the ambiguity that often surrounds sexuality for employees (Williams 1997; Williams, Giuffre, and Dellinger (1999). Unlike most studies that focus on the presence or absence of sexual harassment, our goal is to document the process whereby individuals decide whether a certain behavior is harassing, tolerable, or pleasurable. Finally, by focusing on a sexually diverse group of workers, we consider both heterosexual and nonheterosexual interactions, an element missing from most studies of sexual harassment.

Methods

In 1996, the first author conducted 65 in-depth interviews and 10 weeks of fieldwork at *Womyn* and *Gentleman's Sophisticate* in New York City as part of a larger study on the ways in which organizations are gendered and sexualized. *Gentleman's Sophisticate* is owned by Publisher's, Inc., which employs approximately 270 people, and Bradwell, Inc. is the publisher of *Womyn* and it employs about 170 workers. (The names of the publishers and the magazines are pseudonyms.) Interviews were conducted with editors, accountants, and administrative assistants who worked at the two magazines, including both current and former employees. The larger sample includes 45 women and 20 men. Of all the respondents, 11 are African American, six are Latina/o, two are Asian American, and 46 are white. The full sample includes 54 heterosexual men and women, two gay men, three lesbian women, three bisexual women, and three individuals who declined to give their sexual orientation.

In this article, we draw on the interviews conducted with 28 members of the editorial departments at the two magazines. The editor-in-chief at each magazine was initially interviewed and asked for permission to interview and observe in the respective editorial departments. All of the members of the editorial staff at *Womyn* (18) and all but two of the editorial staff at *Gentleman's Sophisticate* (10) agreed to be interviewed. (The two refusals were on vacation during the summer research.) Interviews were conducted in a semi-structured format, and were tape-recorded and transcribed for analysis. Most lasted one hour, and were conducted in a variety of locations: in private offices and conference rooms during the workday and in cafes or parks during lunch breaks.

These interviews were augmented by 10 weeks of participant observation at the two organizations. During August and September 1996, the first author was employed as a temporary filing clerk in the accounting department of *Womyn's* parent company, Bradwell Inc., where she worked for approximately 20 hours a week. The rest of the workday was spent conducting interviews or observing at both magazines. While filing, she observed the day-to-day workings of the accounting department at *Womyn*, and interacted frequently with members of the *Womyn* editorial staff, located in the same building down the hall. During this time, she received permission from the editor-in-chief to attend several editorial staff meetings. In November 1996, she was granted permission to observe full-time in the editorial offices for an additional two weeks. At *Gentleman's Sophisticate*, there are no regularly scheduled staff meetings, but the first author received permission from the editor-in-chief to observe the workings of the editorial department by "shadowing" the managing editor during two work days. She also attended formal and informal company gatherings including an evening art opening held at *Gentleman's Sophisticate* and two "happy hours" after work with members of the accounting department. Fieldnotes were recorded as soon as possible after observing and interviewing at each magazine.

The fieldwork portion of the study enables us to understand individuals' experiences, feelings, and expectations regarding sexual behavior in the context of the unstated, taken-for-granted rules of behavior that govern organizational life. The combination of in-depth interviews and participant observation at both workplaces provided valuable insights into the everyday work experiences of the editorial staffs.

Findings

Gentleman's Sophisticate

The editorial department at *Gentleman's Sophisticate* employs six women and six men. A primary component of editors' jobs is to make decisions about the written content of the magazine. Their jobs include editing sexual advice columns, writing and copyediting captions for the euphemistically called "pictorials" or "artwork," and editing and screening sexually graphic reader mail for potential publication. To illustrate one facet of her job, one of the editors produced a letter signed. "A Big Fan in Michigan," who writes to the magazine each month describing his sexual practices in detail and grading the photos to determine the one he thinks deserves his monthly "Big Fan Masturbation Award." This editor decides whether or not to publish these letters.

When asked to describe her everyday work, Margaret, the managing editor, explained that among other tasks, she engages in detailed conversations about copy style:

> Many of the conversations that we have are on when things should be capitalized or not or . . . is blow job one word or two . . . is it hyphenated or is it not hyphenated? Those are serious conversations and it's a copy style decision that needs to be made . . . and sometimes I'll just stop and say, "I cannot believe this is a discussion that we have at work!" (laughing).

Everyone at *Gentleman's Sophisticate* has to confront the sexually explicit nature of the magazine and, consequently, of their jobs. When describing her responsibility for writing the captions beneath the sexually explicit pictorials, Tina, another woman editor, said that you just have to get used to the material and you have to have a sense of humor to deal with it:

> It used to be so hard . . . It used to be like, torture. And now . . . you get used to what it's supposed to sound like. . . . You get used to it. So it's easier to write . . . I mean they're funny—you really have to have a sense of humor, that's the one requirement to work here. You gotta be able to have anything go off your back. Because there's just so much, you know. You gotta have a really open mind.

When Tina started working at *Gentleman's Sophisticate*, the sexual aspect of her job felt to her like "torture." Since she was subjected to a working environment that she considered offensive and that made her uncomfortable, her experience could be interpreted as sexual harassment. But instead of labeling it sexual harassment, she eventually learned to define it as "funny"—something not to be taken seriously. The transformation of the material from "torturous" to "funny" can be understood as a form of emotional labor required of many workers at *Gentleman's Sophisticate* (Hochschild 1983). This process of identity management may be more visible in settings where workers must manage a "legitimate" identity while creating a stigmatized product (Goffman 1963). Yet all workers probably engage in emotional labor to some extent (see Leidner 1993; Pierce 1995).

Emotional labor is shaped by workplace context. At least part of the reason for Tina's growing tolerance of her sexualized work environment might be attributed to the organizational policies at *Gentleman's Sophisticate*. Workers there are required to sign an acknowledgment that states that they are aware that they "will encounter and be called upon to work with pictures and written text that involve nudity and sexually explicit material." This measure was instituted, in part, to stave off the possibility of sexual harassment lawsuits. (Loe 1996 describes a similar policy in place at the "Bazooms" restaurant chain.) Margaret, the managing editor, explained the purpose of this requirement this way:

> I think that's more—not to eliminate the possibility that the company could be sued because a boss is harassing a single employee, but just in general, saying that you understand this is what you are going to work on when you are here. . . . So, that's something that we really do stress to people and we send them home with copies of the magazines and make them look at it and make sure that you feel comfortable with this.

It is interesting to note that in other contexts, workers have successfully brought "hostile environment" sexual harassment lawsuits against work organizations that permitted some employees to pin-up nude centerfolds in the workplace. In a 1991 landmark case, Lois Robinson went to court after officials at the Jackonsville Shipyard ignored complaints that pornographic pictures were prominently displayed in the workplace (Petrocelli and Repa 1998). Because their jobs require them to look at nude pin-ups, workers at *Gentleman's Sophisticate* do not define it this way.

Gentleman's Sophisticate will only hire employees who can tolerate exposure to sexual materials that might offend them. This practice may discriminate against women workers if women, in general, are less able to develop this tolerance. Boswell contends that some young interns leave after two days because they can't cope with the sexual materials:

> I've seen interns come in who are just very young. Especially women who are very young and they're here for about two days and they just like, scream and run out of the room because I don't know what they thought, but they obviously weren't thinking. "Oh, gee, I can't do this! Somebody said pussy." I mean,

you know, "Oooh, there was a picture of a breast." You know, "My sister and her powerful group will not approve of me being here." I don't know what it is. But interns sometimes show up, do about two days and then just freak. But they're usually like eighteen to twenty-two and just don't have enough worldliness.

Only those who find ways to cope with the materials stay on; those who can't are quickly weeded out. Importantly, both men and women eventually learn this tolerance; the staff of the editorial department is gender balanced. However, few editors had actually sought out the opportunity to work in the pornography industry. Members of the editorial staff came from backgrounds in journalism, publishing, or business. None of the editors were involved in the sex industry prior to working at the magazine. Moreover, when individuals applied for a job at the parent company (which we have given the pseudonym Publisher's Inc.), some were unaware that they would be working for a men's pornographic magazine. The editors claimed that they accepted a job at *Gentleman's Sophisticate* not because it is pornography, but rather because it is an internationally known publication. Many of the editors talk about a period of adjustment in which they get used to working with the sexually explicit material on a daily basis, and most say that they learn to enjoy the work. This is similar to Salzinger's (2000) study of a maquiladora in Mexico, where she witnessed the process by which women adjusted to the sexual objectification expected of them. *Gentleman's Sophisticate* provides another case of how workers who decide to stay have to find some way to adjust to the norms of their workplace.

Workers at *Gentleman's Sophisticate* often reconcile the tension they experience with sexually explicit material using humor. Humor is one of the main strategies that people use to deal with unsettling or unwanted experiences (Fitzgerald, Swan, and Fischer 1995:120). One person referred to the culture of *Gentleman's Sophisticate* as a "locker room": a place filled with bawdy jokes and sexual bantering. Most of the sexual joking at *Gentleman's Sophisticate* is about the content of the magazine itself. People joke about breast implants, ads for penis enlargements, and the impossibility of certain sexual acts that are described in letters from readers. Editors also joke about the readers who buy the magazine and enjoy it. Boswell claims that most of the editors have contempt for the readers of the magazine, believing that they are all "in federal prisons and trailer camps." In fact, none of the editors claim that they enjoy reading the magazine and looking at the pictures; they consider the overarching view of sexuality portrayed in the magazine to be narrow and outdated.

Although joking is pervasive in the editorial department, it is almost never about personal matters. Tina says joking is "just business and never personal." When Bill is asked if he ever talks about sex at work, he doesn't think to mention sexual joking about the magazine. He says, "No, not at all. I just don't want to talk about sex . . . especially with women, because everything could be misconstrued, especially in these times when people are so sensitive." But when asked if he talks about sex in regard to the magazine, he clarifies that "that" kind of joking happens "all the time":

> Oh yeah, we laugh at a lot of stuff. Some of it is so ridiculous, you know, how many positions can you come up with and have it artful? We laugh at the pictorials. We laugh at the color. We laugh at the choice of girls. Yeah, we do that a lot. Sure. But to me, that's in the abstract. . . . If I met you outside of this environment and I brought a *Gentleman's Sophisticate*

magazine with me . . . and started talking to you about it, that would be like approaching you, hitting on you. For us, it's like an "in" thing. It's like we work here.

Working with the magazine and joking about it is an "in" thing at *Gentleman's Sophisticate* "as long as it is not personal." Talking about sex is fine if it is about the magazine, or if it is "abstract." If it is concrete talk about an individual's sexual behavior or desires, then it is "sensitive" and likely to be "misconstrued." Bill acknowledges that while this "abstract" sexual talk and joking is considered part of the job here, in other contexts, it might be interpreted as an inappropriate "come on" or even as sexual harassment.

On several occasions, the editors shared jokes that were "going around the office that day." During an interview with a male editor, he said, "You'll get good and raunchy jokes and you pass those around. And the popular joke last week was . . . oh yeah, 'Why do women fake their orgasms? [Why?] Because they think we care.'"

Although the editor said that this was a very popular joke with both men and women, the joke only makes sense if told from a male point of view. The joke is "on" women for thinking that men care about their sexual pleasure. Messner (1992) has noted that male locker room jokes are almost always about degrading women. However, at *Gentleman's Sophisticate*, both men and women participate in this type of humor. When the first author arrived for an interview, a woman employee who escorted her to her appointment told her a blow job joke in the hallway, and then "offered" her to a man in the elevator as "his own personal girl." Thus, even though the editorial department at *Gentleman's Sophisticate* is not an all-male domain, the description of the culture in the editorial department as a male locker room is apt given the emphasis on the bawdy depiction and discussion of sex from a male heterosexual point of view, with most of the jokes at women's expense.

But just because the work culture is sexualized does not mean that absolutely anything goes. Boundary lines are still drawn at the organization. Margaret, the managing editor, said:

> I watched in the production room one day and one of the men who works there held open an issue of [a competing pornographic magazine] which happened to have a Black centerfold and said, "Can you imagine what our relationship would be like if you looked like this?" Comments like that are totally inappropriate. It doesn't matter that I work here. It's inappropriate and that's an inappropriate discussion to have. So I think people think they're not crossing the line just because you work here and in reality they really are. That line is still there and should still be there.

Margaret's boundary line between acceptable and harassing sexual behavior is personal sexual innuendo. In this sense, working at *Gentleman's Sophisticate* may really be like the men's locker rooms where there may be lots of fantasy talk and sexual joking, but little actual emotional and personal intimacy (Curry 1991; Lyman 1987).

The racist stereotype embedded in the man's remark is also important in understanding why Margaret used this example to illustrate her boundary line. Both Margaret and the man in the production room are white. His comment insinuates that if she were Black, she would be more sexually available to him, reflecting a popular "controlling image" of Black women (Collins 2000). It is also significant that *Gentleman's Sophisticate* does not regularly publish images of women of color. From a production

standpoint (one that is surely influenced by racist assumptions about sexuality in the larger culture) (West 1993), Black sexuality is defined as unacceptable. In this context, the fact that the centerfold was Black may have marked this "joke" as different from and more offensive than the regular joking about sex that occurs on a daily basis.

According to Lyman (1987) and Curry (1991), joking in all-male settings (sports locker rooms and fraternities) is a form of male bonding. The success of the male bond relies on several things: avoiding talk of personal relationships and other intimate matters, being able to put someone down (often by degrading and objectifying women and gays and lesbians), and being able to "take" a joke without losing one's cool. All-male arenas that are highly sexualized (like locker rooms or fraternities) may foster even more humorous and joking relationships than other contexts because joking is a way of releasing sexual tension, and maybe even denying its existence.

Sexual joking is enjoyed by most editors, unless it crosses the line into the personal. When this happens, editors claim that their organization responds speedily and decisively to protect those who feel victimized. Brian provided one example of this organizational commitment to protecting workers. Part of his job is fielding calls from prospective writers and models. Brian received a phone call from "Ginger Petty" who said she had been doing research on S&M and wanted to submit her work to *Gentleman's Sophisticate*. Over the course of the conversation, Ginger began telling Brian about her own sexual fantasies, and how she would like to be "disciplined" by Brian. Brian thought the incident was "hilarious" and went to tell Margaret, his boss, about it:

> I went over to tell Margaret about the call, laughingly. Just saying, "This really takes the cake!" And she laughed, too,

but she said, "You know, in truth, if it were Nicole [the other woman that was working there at the time], who'd gotten this call, I don't think I'd be laughing right now." She said, "I think I'd be concerned. It would be more than a joke, but 'assault' is the wrong word. Like a harassment type of call." But she asked me, "Do you at all feel offended or whatever?" And I said, "Please! Honestly! I mean, not even close!" But I thought it was very nice that she extended that kind of sensitivity because I could have been.

Margaret is sensitive to the possibility that Ginger Petty's call could be harassment because it seems to cross personal boundaries. It is interesting that this workplace norm allows Margaret to consider the possibility that a man may he harassed by a woman, but Brian does not share Margaret's definition of this particular situation as sexual harassment, although he appreciates his boss's reasoning and her sensitivity.

Margaret attributes Brian's lack of concern over the incident to the fact that he is a man. Brian is also gay, and this may help to explain his decision not to label this incident as sexual harassment. He describes the environment at *Gentleman's Sophisticate* as "liberating" in many ways. He says that he enjoys the freedom of self-expression one is allowed in regards to sexuality. On the one hand, Brian reports that he is out at work and that he enjoys joking with women colleagues and "playing around a little with ideas of gender roles . . . within certain parameters." He also explains that he has learned to slip into what he calls "hyperhetero extreme" talk around his straight friends to make them uncomfortable. He sees himself at the forefront of sexual joking and uses this talk as a way to make his straight friends "squirm." He explains,

I feel like it's a parody. I feel like I'm *really* making fun of *them* and the way they talk and they may not get it that way, but I get a kick out of teasing them and seeing that they really don't feel comfortable with it. . . . Actually, in truth, there's got to be some element of hostility in it too, for me. You know, for the years that I had to listen to this shit. For all the years that I had to swallow and maybe even make believe that it was who I was. Now, I can do it better than you can! I can teach you! And doesn't it make you squirm?

Giuffre and Williams (1994) report a similar incident in their study of sexual harassment in restaurants when a gay waiter explained that the open sexual environment allowed him to make straight coworkers uncomfortable with his sexual banter. He, too, saw this joking as a kind of payback for all the times he and other gay people had been oppressed and excluded by the norms of compulsory heterosexuality. Granted his penchant for engaging in "hyper-hetero-extreme" talk, it is understandable why Brian did not see the Ginger Petty incident as sexual harassment.

Women in other departments said they felt protected from sexual harassment owing to a powerful woman lawyer employed by the firm who they perceived as vigorously pursuing all complaints of harassment. This is consistent with Gruber's (1998) finding that sexual harassment complaints may be less frequent in workplaces with proactive sexual harassment procedures. Women employees at *Gentleman's Sophisticate* said they felt empowered to complain about any individual who crossed the line from "business sex" to "personal sex." This sense of the individual's right to personal autonomy, and protection from individual harassers, is consistent with the overarching values of free choice and individual rights which characterized the organization culture as a whole. Thus, while the norms and values of the locker room might seem to foster sexual harassment, employees in general felt that their workplace was free of sexual harassment, and that anyone who dared cross the line would be quickly reprimanded.

Some editors acknowledged that sexual harassment did sometimes occur at *Gentleman's Sophisticate.* These instances were perceived as the result of a few "Neanderthals" outside the editorial department who didn't understand the difference between joking and harassment.

According to Boswell,

> There's very little sexual harassment that does go on. Probably less than in other companies because again, it's not really an issue. I mean, that's not to say, I don't observe like "Troglodytes speaking coarsely with their women." But the strange thing is that other men will speak up and say, "Hey, knock it off!" or "Gentlemen, stop this!" I mean, for the most part, people cool it. . . . There's a couple of guys that roam around the office that are real sort of pigs, and classic male chauvinists, but because the company is so upwardly mobile, it's just sort of like, "Ahh, he's just a retrograde." There are a couple of people in the organization that are just sort of hardwired into their Italian-Stallion souls and they can be good about it for about a week, but sooner or later, the genetics reassert themselves and you have to slap them again. But in a company of hundreds of people, who cares?

Boswell describes the men who sexually harass women employees as throwbacks to the 1970s, a time when the magazine was at the height of its popularity. They are men who have failed to evolve with the times.

Interestingly, the editors often described the readers of *Gentleman's Sophisticate* in a similar way. They, too, are considered Neanderthals stuck in another era's vision of sexuality. In both instances, the editors attempt to separate themselves from what they perceive as a lower class, unsophisticated view of sexuality and masculinity. This tension between the editors' sexual tastes and preferences, and the expressions of sexual desire represented in the magazine, reflects what Connell (1995) has characterized as a key feature of masculinity. Different forms of masculinity constantly compete for dominance; the hegemonic form of masculinity is always defined in terms of its difference from, and superiority over, alternative forms of masculinity, and all versions of femininity. Thus, the "Neanderthal" readers of *Gentleman's Sophisticate,* and the "Neanderthal" men at the organization who sexually harass women, function as foils for the men editors to define themselves as superior to other men.

By separating business sex from personal sex, the culture of the editorial department supports the idea that sexual harassment is an individual problem and not an organizational issue. Although the editors are subjected to a sexualized work environment, they rarely complain about it or label it sexual harassment. Men and women editors seem to enjoy joking in the locker room environment. Only when sexual bantering crosses over into the personal do some editors feel like they are being sexually harassed. Perhaps for this reason, editors distance themselves from the content of the magazine. Because anyone who enjoys the magazine is a retrograde, lower class "Neanderthal," an employee who took the magazine too seriously and admitted to finding it personally stimulating would likely be looked upon with suspicion by others, perhaps as the sort of "Neanderthal" likely to sexually harass women.

Womyn

The editorial department at *Womyn* employs a staff of 18 women. Included in this number are four unpaid interns. Unlike *Gentleman's Sophisticate*, the editors at *Womyn* are not offered training in sexual harassment policy, nor are they asked to sign any acknowledgment about the sexual content of their magazine. When asked whether the company had a formal sexual harassment policy, the editor-in-chief replied, "We don't have any formal policy here at *Womyn* except we clearly, as feminists, know where we stand on the issue."

Many other members of the editorial staff seemed surprised when asked if they had a formal policy regarding sexual harassment. Most said they weren't sure and then explained that *anybody* who would choose to work at *Womyn* would simply understand that sexually harassing behavior is not tolerated. In other words, the editors saw the feminist norms and values within their workplace culture as protection against sexual harassment.

Working at *Womyn* means knowing where one stands on all sorts of important feminist issues. This feminist sensibility creates an environment where editors believe they are doing more than a "just a job." Brett, a senior editor at *Womyn,* said,

> I think it's hard to work at *Womyn* and look at it as a job in journalism. It's more of a calling. I feel like I live it everyday . . . I don't think my work is just a piece of journalism, I think it's a piece of activism.

The motto, "the personal is political" is very much alive at *Womyn*. People's personal identities are intricately tied to their work identities. This encourages the formation of intimate ties among co-workers. Natasha, a copy editor who was new to the department when she was interviewed, described the sense that when she was being welcomed to the job she was also being welcomed to a "sisterhood":

> I felt this whole school marmish excitement about the way we were speaking to one another. You know, I felt it was like, girls' novels, you know, like eighth grade girls' novels. . . . The image is patent leather shoes and girls who are pledging undying friendship. You know what I mean?

Being an editor at *Womyn* requires a certain amount of personal disclosure, often about sexual matters. Editors at *Womyn* reflect on and share their opinions about topics ranging from date rape to sexual harassment to the nature of sexual pleasure and desire. While it is necessary to consider these topics from an editorial standpoint, sexuality permeates the more informal conversations as well. People talk about their own sex lives and what they do and don't like to do in bed, as well as having serious conversations about their sexual identities and their relationships. Many women at the magazine explain that this sharing creates very close bonds among the workers that extend beyond the walls of the editorial department. This environment of trust leads to an openness about sexuality that some editors described as "dorm room" culture. Stacey describes some aspects of this dorm room:

> It's just like all of us hanging around all the time. We're so touchy. And we're always having parties just together without our partners. And so we're always dancing together and having sleep overs and stuff.

When at work, employees frequently give each other pats on the back, hugs, and the occasional back rub. There is also a great deal of joking about sex. Almost every editor repeated a joke around the office that there are three main topics of conversation: Food, Hair, and Sex. It is quite common for workers to bring snacks and treats to share that are placed for collective consumption at the so-called "trough." Offering food is an effective means of achieving integration into predominately female work groups, as the first author discovered after she donated homemade brownies to the trough (see also, Reskin and Padavic 1994).

When asked for examples of how people joke about sex at *Womyn*, Brett explains that things can get pretty explicit:

> There's always discussion of—literally— what kind of sex people do and what they like. It's very graphic sometimes. It's very technical. . . . And I do think, very much, that that has to do with an all-women staff. I think it's totally comfortable. Both straight and lesbians. It doesn't matter. Everybody talks about everything.

Another member of the staff, Samantha, reinforces the idea that *Womyn* is a very sexualized, but safe environment:

> I think this is a very sexual place in a lot of ways. And there's a lot of sexual energy in here, but it's very positive. And maybe, if it was a place where you felt threatened in some way, that the energy could be a form of harassment, you know what I mean? But it's so non-threatening.

When asked what makes it non-threatening, she replied, "For me, it's probably just the all-women environment."

According to Brett and Samantha, if the same conversations involved men, they would probably consider them sexual harassment. Once again, this indicates how social context matters in the definition of sexual harassment. It also helps to explain why the male/female ratio is an important predictor of the likelihood of experiencing sexual harassment (Gruber 1998). A feminist all-women dorm room culture that encourages personal disclosure about sex shapes the definition of sexual harassment very differently

from the male-dominated locker room culture that promotes impersonal, heterosexual, and often degrading sex talk. While talk of "the personal" is taboo and possibly constitutes harassment in the locker room, it is normative and expected in the dorm room.

Some women may seek out a sex-segregated work environment in hopes of finding this pleasurable, non-threatening atmosphere. In fact, most of the editors described the dorm room environment as very liberating. Vera, a former editor explained, "For the most part, conversations about our emotional and sexual lives are wonderful and liberating and one of the best parts of being at *Womyn*. It is special."

But even in this all-women environment, boundary lines were drawn between acceptable and unacceptable behavior. Here we focus on two examples where power dynamics between workers, especially between editors and interns, led to uncomfortable situations that the editors thought could be defined as sexual harassment.

(1) At *Womyn*, all staff members, including interns, attend and participate in editorial meetings. While internship programs are common in the magazine publishing industry, the high level of participation interns enjoy at *Womyn* seems to be quite unusual. During a staff meeting to generate ideas for a special issue on sexuality, the editor-in-chief asked the interns for their input. She wanted to draw on their experiences going off to college for the first time, dealing with boyfriends and girlfriends, perhaps even handling date rape. When asked whether anyone was ever uncomfortable about the way people talked about sex at work, the assistant to the editor-in-chief said that after the staff meeting about the sex issue, an intern approached her and said:

> "God, can I answer this?" You know, "I feel so embarrassed" or "I wanted to say something, but I was so embarrassed

that everybody's sitting around. You know, can I talk about it?"

The intern did not want to be forced to self-disclose. The request for information in a public forum felt impersonal to her and exploitative, like she was being used, not comforted and supported by her friends.

The interns did not describe these experiences as sexual harassment, however. At *Womyn,* workers give each other the benefit of the doubt that they know what sexual harassment is and they are opposed to it in all its manifestations. Sexual harassment is implicitly defined as something that "other" people do—not feminists. For this reason, some workers at *Womyn* may not feel empowered to complain about a co-worker's or supervisor's behavior, despite its potentially negative impact.

(2) A second incident where people expressed discomfort with sexuality at *Womyn* was linked to the ambiguous hierarchy in the editorial department. The emphasis on sisterhood in the dorm room culture can lead to confusing relationships between members of the organization who hold differing amounts of power. Kara contends that things can get a "bit odd" when people talk or joke about sex at work. When asked for an example of when things "get odd," she said:

> The last batch of interns that we had, one of my interns hit on me—quite strongly. And that was a very uncomfortable situation. But, I think it would have been something that would not have happened at any other office. I had just come to *Womyn* and I wasn't as aware of the demarcation lines. It was horrifying.

Kara explained that after a party at a co-worker's house, a few interns and other *Womyn* staff decided to go dancing. At the end of the night she and one intern were the only ones left and they decided to go to a strip show at a lesbian bar. Kara identifies herself as heterosexual and assumed that the intern she was with was heterosexual as well. Sometime that night the intern made a pass at Kara which she characterized as extremely aggressive and similar to some sexual interactions she had experienced in college "when people were half-drunk." As Kara reflected back on this night, she was clearly upset at herself for taking the intern to a bar. She felt this was completely inappropriate behavior on her part:

> I would have never done that in another workplace. NEVER!! After it happened, I was like, "How could you not see that this was completely inappropriate behavior? You do not take your intern to [a lesbian bar with a strip show]. That is ridiculous!"

There are many important issues that may explain why, at *Womyn,* the lines of demarcation between acceptable and unacceptable sexual expression were unclear to Kara, but one major issue seems to have impacted her definition of this situation as "horrifying": the deemphasis on hierarchy. She says, "Here you have a very strange thing where there is a hierarchy, but we are not supposed to talk about it. We are not supposed to acknowledge it and we are all supposed to be friends."

Oerton (1996) points out that U.S. feminists have been in the forefront of creating flatter, non-hierarchical organizations as part of their effort to transform social inequality. The assumption is that when organizations lack formal hierarchies there will be an absence of gendered and sexualized inequalities. In the case of *Womyn,* a definite hierarchy exists, but its existence is informally denied. Kara implies that the invisible hierarchy at *Womyn* may have encouraged her to think it was acceptable to go out to a bar and socialize with an intern, and for the intern to believe it was acceptable to express sexual interest in Kara. But Kara believes that in a hierarchical situation, sexual relationships should not be permitted because in situations of unequal power, subordinates are vulnerable to abuses of power, including sexual harassment.

In both of these examples, the respondents identified unequal power as the defining feature of sexual harassment. Unpaid interns are seen as especially vulnerable: they fear that the dorm room disclosure of personal sexual information may be exploitative when hierarchical positions come into play, particularly in editorial meetings; or that interns may be easily taken advantage of by those who are more powerful. From the viewpoint of these editors, the key feature of sexual harassment is not that it is sexual, or even personal, but rather, that it involves the exploitation of someone in a less powerful position by someone with organizational power over them.

The dorm room culture at *Womyn* encourages open and frank discussion of sexuality. Editors are expected to discuss their sexual needs and desires. Most staff members say they enjoy the intimacy between coworkers involved in sharing and joking about personal aspects of their lives. Editors at *Womyn* did not consider sexual harassment to be a problem at their organization because there were no men in the department, and perhaps more importantly, because they shared a feminist analysis of sexual harassment as an abuse of power. In this regard, it is interesting that both of the examples of sexual harassment we described were described *not* by the person who was the target of the possible harassment, but by the person occupying the more powerful position who was concerned about the vulnerabilities of those less powerful. The editors at *Womyn* felt safe from sexual harassment because the norms and values of the dorm room culture supported constant vigilance against it, even by those who are in charge.

Discussion

The organizational cultures of the editorial departments at *Gentleman's Sophisticate* and *Womyn* are quite distinct. Imagine that it is your first day of work as an editor at *Gentleman's Sophisticate*. Pictures of naked women are hanging on the walls, and copies of the pornographic magazine lay scattered on coffee tables and on the desks of your colleagues. Your new colleagues stop you in the hallway to tell a dirty joke. Getting "one up" on people by telling especially crude or "politically incorrect" jokes will enhance your status and put you in the "in" crowd. You are told to sign an agreement that says that you understand that exposure to sexually explicit materials will not "count" as sexual harassment in this workplace. If you are shocked or offended by this sexualized atmosphere, you have to let it "roll off your back," or else you'll probably quit or be fired. If you agree to stay on the job, you might begin to define yourself as someone who doesn't let those things bother them. But everyone—including your boss and the legal department—agrees that there is a "line" beyond which the sexual bantering becomes sexual harassment. That line is the personal, and anyone who violates it is likely to be reprimanded.

Now imagine your first day of work at *Womyn*. You learn that "Food, Sex, and Hair" are the popular topics of conversation. Office sex talk requires personal disclosure and soul-searching discussions of the political implications of your intimate sexual relationships. If you don't fully participate in this personal disclosure, you will be marginalized to some degree. You notice that your coworkers share backrubs, go out dancing together, and hold slumber parties. The topic of sexual harassment in this workplace will probably not come up, since everyone here is a feminist who presumably knows where everyone else stands on the issue. The consensus is that sexual harassment is an abuse of organizational power, meaning that the least powerful members of the organization, the interns, are the most vulnerable.

Both workplaces are sexualized, although very differently. Editors at *Womyn* would surely object to normative behaviors at *Gentleman's Sophisticate,* and vice versa. To characterize this difference we have suggested the analogy of the "locker room v. the dorm room." Because locker rooms are implicitly assumed to be male, dorm rooms, female, these gendered metaphors capture both the cultural values of the two workplaces as well as the skewed numerical proportions of men and women who work in high-level management positions in them. We have argued that these different organizational cultures help explain why workers at *Gentleman's Sophisticate* and *Womyn* define sexual harassment differently. While not all individuals at each workplace share the same interpretation of specific interactions, they do seem to share similar understandings of the meaning of sexual harassment and the difference between acceptable and unacceptable sexual behavior.

This finding has important implications for the study of sexual harassment. It challenges the validity of research that uses seemingly objective lists of unwanted sexual behaviors to gauge the prevalence of harassment (Williams 1997). The meaning of sexual harassment varies depending on organizational context. The boundary between acceptable and unacceptable sexual behavior is the result of a complex interplay between the characteristics of individual workers, the structural features of an organization, and the cultural norms in any given workplace. Researchers should consider this context when measuring the prevalence of harassment. This perspective draws on a long tradition of sociologists beginning with Durkheim and later Goffman who suggest that the rituals or performances we engage

in on a daily basis are complicated interactions "which hold society together, but in a stratified way" (Collins 1994:219). Perhaps the definition of sexual harassment as an illegal act has led us to assume that sexual harassment is the exception in the workplace instead of the norm. We suggest that taking a closer look at the workplace norms regarding sexuality that shape interactions and rituals at work will be a more fruitful avenue than focusing on individual behaviors or definitions of sexual harassment taken out of context.

Our research also has important insights for policy makers working to find remedies for sexual harassment. According to legal scholar Vicki Schultz (1998a, 1998b), many sexual harassment policies promote the misguided belief that all forms of sexual expression are harmful to women. In some cases, concern over sexual harassment litigation has led companies to forbid men and women from travelling together on business; in others a "five second rule" has been imposed prohibiting men from looking at women for more than five seconds at a time. These draconian measures, ostensibly imposed to "protect" women, can actually harm them by denying them equal opportunities and respect. Schultz insists that not all sexual behavior is harmful to women. She writes, "sexuality is part of the human experience, and so long as organizations still employ people rather than robots, it will continue to flourish in one form or another. And sexuality is not simply a tool of gender domination; it is also a potential source of empowerment and even pleasure for women on the job" (1998b:14). She urges courts to conduct in-depth investigations of the meaning of sexual expression in a given workplace before determining whether something is sexual harassment.

Our research supports the view that sexual behavior itself is not necessarily harmful to women. Sometimes an offensive nude pin-up is sexual harassment; sometimes it isn't. Sometimes demands for personal disclosure about sexual behavior are sexual harassment; sometimes they aren't. Individuals who experience unwanted sexual behavior take culture into consideration when deciding whether they have experienced sexual harassment; researchers and policy makers should do likewise.

Our research did not uncover rampant sexual harassment at *Womyn* or *Gentleman's Sophisticate,* but it did reveal the type of behaviors that the editors would consider harassment. According to Schultz, this information would be valuable to the courts if one of the editors were to file a complaint of sexual harassment against their employer. She argues that sexually explicit behavior must be examined in the "larger workplace context" to determine if it, along with any objectionable "nonsexual behavior . . . created a discriminatory work environment" (1998a:1795). She would insist that the fact that the workplaces are sexual does not in itself constitute proof that the women employed there were sexually harassed. Schultz writes, "Sex should be treated just like anything else in the workplace: Where it furthers sex discrimination, it should go. Where it doesn't, it's not the business of our civil rights laws" (1998b:15). For a finding of sexual harassment, the complainant would have to link their experience to blocked opportunities or some other form of gender discrimination.

We need more case studies of organizational sexuality in a variety of workplace settings to broaden our understanding of how organizational culture influences workplace definitions of acceptable and unacceptable sexual joking and behavior. In this study, we examined two extreme cases chosen to highlight how culture matters. But what about editors who work for other magazines which are not strongly associated with gender and sexual ideology, such as *Businessweek* and

Time? And how do workers in other industries, like retail or computing, draw boundary lines? By examining organizational sexuality in a number of work contexts, we can begin to understand sexual harassment as part of the larger phenomenon of sexuality at work without falling into the trap of equating all sex at work with harassment. A research agenda attuned to the complex ways that organizational sexuality is put to use in the service of pleasure *and* discrimination will move us closer to the goal of eliminating blocked opportunities for women (and men) without reducing them to helpless victims in need of protection from sex.

REFERENCES

Adkins, Lisa. 1995. *Gendered Work: Sexuality, Family, and the Labour Market.* Buckingham, UK: Open University Press.

Allison, Anne. 1994. *Nightwork: Sexuality. Pleasure, and Corporate Masculinity in a Tokyo Hostess Club.* Chicago: The University of Chicago Press.

Connell, Robert W. 1995. *Masculinities.* Berkeley: University of California Press.

Collins, Patricia Hill. 2000. *Black Feminist Thought: Knowledge, Consciousness, and the Politics of Black Empowerment.* New York: Routledge.

Collins, Randall. 1994. *Four Sociological Traditions.* New York: Oxford University Press.

Curry, Timothy Jon. 1991. "Fraternal bonding in the locker room: A profeminist analysis of talk about competition and women." *Sociology of Sport Journal* 8:119–135.

Fitzgerald, Louise F., Suzanne Swan, and Karla Fischer. 1995. "Why didn't she just report him?: The psychological and legal implications of women's responses to sexual harassment." *Journal of Social Issues* 51, 1:117–138.

Foner, Nancy. 1994. *The Caregiving Dilemma: Work in an American Nursing Home.* Berkeley: University of California Press.

Gherardi, Sylvia. 1995. *Gender, Symbolism and Organizational Cultures.* London: Sage.

Giuffre, Patti A., and Christine L. Williams. 1994. "Boundary lines: Labeling sexual harassment in restaurants. *Gender and Society* 8, 3:378–401.

Goffman, Erving. 1963. *Stigma: Notes on the Management of a Spoiled Identity.* Englewood Cliffs, NJ: Prentice Hall.

Gruber, James E. 1998. "The impact of male work environments and organizational policies on women's experiences of sexual harassment." *Gender and Society* 12, 3:301–320.

Gutek, Barbara A., Aaron Groff Cohen, and Alison M. Konrad. 1990. "Predicting social-sexual behavior at work: A contact hypothesis." *Academy of Management Journal* 33:560–577.

Hearn, Jeff, and Wendy Parkin. 1987. *Sex at Work: The Power and Paradox of Organization Sexuality.* New York: St. Martin's Press.

Hochschild, Arlie Russell. 1983. *The Managed Heart: Commercialization of Human Feeling.* Berkeley: University of California Press.

Hulin, Charles L., Louise F. Fitzgerald, and Fritz Drasgow. 1996. "Organizational influences on sexual harassment." In *Sexual Harassment in the Workplace: Perspectives, Frontiers, and Response Strategies,* Margaret S. Stockdale, ed., 127–150. Thousand Oaks, CA: Sage.

Leidner, Robin. 1993. *Fast Food, Fast Talk: Service Work and the Routinization of Everyday Life.* Berkeley: University of California Press.

Loe, Meika. 1996. "Working for men—at the intersection of power, gender, and sexuality." *Sociological Inquiry* 66:399–421.

Lyman, Peter. 1987. "The fraternal bond as a joking relationship: A case study of the role of sexist jokes in male group bonding." In *Changing Men: New Directions in Research on Men and Masculinity,* Michael Kimmel, ed. Newbury Park, CA: Sage.

Messner, Michael A. 1992. *Power at Play: Sports and the Problem of Masculinity,* Boston: Beacon Press.

Oerton, Sarah. 1996. *Beyond Hierarchy: Gender, Sexuality, and the Social Economy.* London: Taylor and Francis.

Petrocelli, William, and Barbara Kate Repa. 1998. *Sexual Harassment on the Job: What It Is and How to Stop It,* third edition. Berkeley, CA: Nolo Press.

Pierce, Jennifer L. 1995. *Gender Trials: Emotional Lives in Contemporary Law Firms.* Berkeley: University of California Press.

Pryor, John B., Janet L. Giedd, and Karen B. Williams. 1995. "A social psychological model for predicting sexual harassment." *Journal of Social Issues* 51, 1:69–84.

Pryor, John B., Christine M. LaVite, and Lynnette M. Stoller. 1993. "A social psychological analysis of sexual harassment: The person/situation interaction. *Journal of Vocational Behavior* 42:68–83.

Reskin, Barbara, and Irene Padavic. 1994. *Women and Men at Work.* Thousand Oaks, CA: Pine Forge.

Salzinger, Leslie. 2000. "Manufacturing sexual subjects: 'Harassment,' desire and discipline on a Maquiladora shopfloor." *Ethnography* 1:67–92.

Schultz, Vicki. 1998a. "Reconceptualizing sexual harassment." *Yale Law Journal* 107 (April), 6:1683–1805. 1998b. "Sex is the least of it: Let's focus harassment law on work, not sex." *The Nation* (May 25) 266:11–15.

Trice. Harrison M. 1993. *Occupational Subcultures in the Workplace.* Ithaca, NY: ILR Press.

Welsh, Sandy. 1999. "Gender and sexual harassment." *Annual Review of Sociology* 25:169–190.

West, Cornell. 1993. *Race Matters.* New York: Vintage Books.

Williams, Christine L. 1997. "Sexual harassment in organizations: A critique of current research and policy." *Sexuality and Culture* 1:19–43.

Williams, Christine L., Patti Giuffre, and Kirsten Dellinger. 1999. "Sexuality in the workplace: Organizational control, sexual harassment, and the pursuit of pleasure." *Annual Review of Sociology* 25:73–93.

Stories Employers Tell

Employer Perceptions of Race and Skill

Philip Moss and Chris Tilly

Interviewer: Some of the other managers we've talked to have noticed differences between black workers and white workers. Do you agree with that?

Respondent (white male Atlanta-area fast food restaurant owner): Yeah, there's some. Usually whites are a little bit more focused, a little friendlier, and the ones I've had here probably a little bit more dependable. Blacks probably overall make better workers. They're faster, they have more dexterity. They seem to be able to work a little bit longer. They do a more thorough job. White kids are usually more educated. It doesn't mean they make better workers.

Interviewer: I know that you mentioned earlier that Asians were really good workers?

Respondent: Dependability, reliability, responsibility, and all that kind of stuff. Attitudes. They never talk back to you or anything. They have that, and work habits probably stand out more than anything. Not all of them, but the majority of them. All of them are ambitious. Every one I've had has been contemplating going to college, or they are in college, and a lot of them working two and three jobs. They

are determined to make it. A lot of these people over here don't want to do anything.

Respondent (white female supervisor in Michigan Utility): I think that for whatever reason, a higher percentage of minority employees are not as dependable and do not, performance-wise, make it sometimes. I think it gets right back to the family or lack of family, and the support or lack of support, or expectations that single parent or double parents place on the kids. And maybe as the kids see or don't see their own parents working, every day, and leaving at seven-thirty to get to work by eight o'clock, so they know that this is something you do. There's lots of reasons for it, but I think it's culturally based and maybe societal.

In the simplest models of human capital theory, a worker's probability of being employed and his or her wage depend directly on his or her potential productivity. This potential productivity, in turn, is a function of accumulated skill. Racial groups differ in average educational attainment and other skills, so this theory predicts employment and wage differentials as a consequence. But the employer quotations leading off this chapter suggest that it is critically important to examine the employer perceptions that underlie assessments of employee skills. To what extent are assessments of various racial or ethnic groups as "more focused," "friendlier," "faster," or "not as dependable" shaped by stereotypes?

Employer Perceptions of Demographic Groups in the Face-to-Face Survey

In-depth interviews provide an important vantage point for learning about employer perceptions. Multi-City Study interviewers asked managers whether they saw differences in skill or worker quality among whites, blacks, Latinos, and Asians.[1] The questioning focused on differences between black and white workers, particularly in Atlanta and Detroit, where other racial and ethnic groups are relatively small. The SSRC survey focused even more narrowly, contrasting black men with other workers, particularly whites.

Many employers did describe such differences. It is important to note that the *largest* group of respondents consisted of those who answered, "I don't see any differences" or "I don't know" (sometimes citing the fact that their workforce is too segregated to assess different groups). We will return to this "silent majority" later in the chapter. We focus here on the numerous managers who did identify racial skill disparities. We contend that the views employers hold in this regard are partly an accurate perception of the skills that many less educated workers of color bring to the labor market, but also—especially in the case of soft skills—partly stereotype and partly cultural gap. . . .

Employer Views of Black Workers

As tables 1 and 2 document, negative employer views of black workers' skills were frequent, consistent with other studies based on employer interviews. We explored three dimensions of employers' characterizations of black skills: hard skills and the soft skills of interaction and motivation. Managers more often identified shortcomings in interaction skills and, especially, motivation than deficits in hard skills among black workers.

To begin with, consider employers' ratings of black workers' hard skills—reading, writing, math, and so on. Referring to table 1, approximately 20 percent of all respondents had something disparaging to say about the hard skills of black workers or applicants. In Detroit and Atlanta, cities where blacks are the primary minority group, 31 percent and 29 percent of the respondents made such statements. The responses collected at the firm level, presented in table 2, indicate that about 25 to 30 percent of firms across metropolitan locations have a plurality of respondents who believe black hard skills are relatively poor. These percentages are much greater than the proportions of employers who made corresponding statements about Latinos or Asians. Thus, in our survey, *employers have particularly negative assessments of blacks' hard skills.* Negative views of black hard skills are more common in the primary central city than in the suburbs and in other central cities in the metropolitan area. Because relatively more blacks are employed in the primary central city and, therefore, employers there are more familiar with black employees, this finding may be evidence that such gaps are real. Alternatively, however, it may simply be that suburban employees simply do not think about black workers as much.

In some cases, employers made narrow criticisms of blacks' hard skills. For example, at Michigan Utility, the human resource director stated that blacks pass the exam at a much lower rate than whites. More often, managers combined faultfinding about the hard skills *and* soft skills of black applicants or workers. For example, the manager of clerical workers at a Boston hospital stated,

> I think [minorities'] education is maybe on a lesser level. This is not a racial remark, but I can still say that I think that the white secretaries that I have are much more professional. I'm not sure it's fair to say more "intelligent" but

TABLE 1 Percentage of Individual Respondents Reporting Particular Perceptions in Face-to-Face Interviews, by Metro Area

	Atlanta	Boston	Detroit	Los Angeles	Total
Employers who said					
About blacks					
Blacks have lagging hard skills	28.9	9.9	31.1	16.3	20.3
Blacks have lagging interaction skills	20.0	4.0	18.0	18.4	14.6
Blacks have lagging motivation	40.0	15.8	32.8	45.9	33.4
Black women are better than black men	5.6	0.0	8.2	5.1	4.0
Black men are better than black women	0.0	2.0	1.6	1.0	1.1
Blacks are better workers	3.3	——	1.6	2.0	1.7
About Latinos					
Latinos have lagging hard skills	1.1	7.9	——	10.2	5.4
Latinos have lagging interaction skills	——	——	——	4.1	1.1
Latinos have lagging motivation	2.2	7.9	——	9.2	5.4
Latinos are better workers	5.6	14.9	1.6	26.5	13.4
About Asians					
Asians have lagging hard skills	——	2.0	——	4.1	1.7
Asians have lagging interaction skills	——	——	——	2.0	0.6
Asians have lagging motivation	——	——	——	1.0	0.3
Asians are better workers	3.3	8.9	——	14.3	7.4
About immigrants					
Immigrants have a stronger work ethic	5.6	18.8	3.3	20.4	13.1
	N = 90	N = 101	N = 61	N = 98	N = 350

Source: Multi-City In-Depth Employer Survey.

they certainly present themselves that way. They are more higher-caliber.

This manager mixed comments on hard skills (education, intelligence) with evaluations of soft skills (professionalism, self-presentation). In similar fashion, a hospital manager in Los Angeles lamented,

I would have to say that as far as qualifications, the literacy level of the Caucasian is higher. And I'm talking about

TABLE 2   Percentage of Firms Where Respondents Report Particular Perceptions in Face-to-Face Interviews, by Location

	Primary Central City	Other Central Cities	Suburbs	Total
Firms where respondents said				
About blacks				
Blacks have lagging hard skills				
At least one respondent	39.7	32.4	29.0	33.7
Half or more of firm respondents	27.9	29.4	23.2	26.2
Blacks have lagging interaction skills				
At least one respondent	29.4	17.6	29.0	26.7
Half or more of firm respondents	19.1	17.6	18.8	18.6
Blacks have lagging motivation				
At least one respondent	54.4	52.9	46.4	50.6
Half or more of firm respondents	38.2	47.1	37.7	39.5
Black women are better than black men				
At least one respondent	13.2	5.9	2.9	7.6
Half or more of firm respondents	10.3	5.9	2.9	6.4
Black men are better than black women				
At least one respondent	1.5	5.9	1.4	2.3
Half or more of firm respondents	——	5.9	1.4	1.8
Blacks are better workers				
At least one respondent	1.5	5.9	4.3	3.5
Half or more of firm respondents	1.5	2.9	2.9	2.3
About Latinos				
Latinos have lagging hard skills				
At least one respondent	11.8	8.8	8.7	9.9
Half or more of firm respondents	4.4	8.8	4.3	5.2
Latinos have lagging interaction skills				
At least one respondent	2.9	——	1.4	1.7
Half or more of firm respondents	1.5	——	1.4	1.2
Latinos have lagging motivation				
At least one respondent	14.7	8.8	5.8	9.9
Half or more of firm respondents	7.4	8.8	2.9	5.8
Latinos are better workers				
At least one respondent	16.2	26.5	21.7	20.3
Half or more of firm respondents	16.2	20.6	14.5	16.3
About Asians				
Asians have lagging hard skills				
At least one respondent	2.9	2.9	4.3	3.5
Half or more of firm respondents	1.5	2.9	2.9	2.3
Asians have lagging interaction skills				
At least one respondent	1.5	——	1.4	1.2
Half or more of firm respondents	——	——	——	——
Asians have lagging motivation				
At least one respondent	——	——	1.4	0.6
Half or more of firm respondents	——	——	——	——

TABLE 2 *Continued*

	Primary Central City	Other Central Cities	Suburbs	Total
Asians are better workers				
At least one respondent	13.2	17.6	11.6	13.4
Half or more of firm respondents	13.2	17.6	10.1	12.8
About immigrants				
Immigrants have a stronger work ethic				
At least one respondent	14.7	29.4	18.8	19.2
Half or more of firm respondents	11.8	29.4	13.0	15.7
	N = 68	N = 34	N = 69	N = 172

Source: Multi-City In-Depth Employer Survey.
Note: "Other central cities" also include any municipality other than the primary central city that has a black population of 30 percent or more.

verbal communication. I'm talking about written communication. I see that on the reports that I have to read. I can tell where the report came from. With some of the Hispanics, of course, that's because English is the second language. And with African Americans some of it, I feel, is cultural. There's a certain speech quality. That doesn't mean they, certainly, weren't capable, but it's ingrained.

An Atlanta grocery store manager, describing applicants who "tend to be more black," complained, "They come in usually with very little skills and very little training. They really don't have anything to offer, other than just being a body, a person."

In fact, employers' criticisms of blacks' hard skills often shaded over into discussions of soft skills. Recall that employer assessments of "soft skills" may be distant from any objective representation of workers' skills, because of the subjectivity of such assessments and the context sensitivity of worker behavior along these dimensions. Nonetheless, it is instructive to review what employers said about soft skills. We first consider interaction skills, then motivation, and finally examine managers

who made *positive* statements about blacks' soft skills.

Almost 15 percent of respondents complained about blacks' ability to interact well with others in the workplace. The percentage of respondents in Boston who reported negative perceptions of blacks' interaction skills (and of blacks' motivation skills) is substantially less than the proportion in the three other cities. At the firm level, approximately 27 percent of firms had at least one respondent offer such a view, and 19 percent of firms had half or more respondents with this perception of blacks' interaction skills. In the smaller and less representative SSRC sample, 32 percent of businesses had at least one respondent who faulted the interaction skills of black men in particular (not shown). Negative comments on blacks' interaction skills touched on a variety of issues. To start with, numerous managers complained that many African Americans don't know how to apply for a job. The human resource director of a Los Angeles–area department store, for example, complained that few black or Latino men "come in a suit and present that professional image that I need for [commission sales]. They just don't know how to get a job." Quite a few managers, including the Los Angeles hospital manager quoted earlier, also remonstrated African Americans for using a "black" dialect, a problem particularly in jobs involving customer contact. A manager at a retail chain store in Detroit explained that for employers like her, it is important that your language not identify you as black: "I don't want to know when I pick up the phone whether you are black or white."

Respondents' negative comments about blacks' interaction skills went beyond speech patterns. Standard stereotypes about black hostility or oversensitivity abounded, as managers described blacks, and black men in particular, as defensive, combative, or having a difficult "attitude." The content of employers' comments ranged widely. At one extreme, a Latino store manager in a black area of Los Angeles, who hires mostly Latinos, flatly stated, "You know, a lot of people are afraid, they [black men] project a certain image that makes you back off. They're really scary." When asked how much he thought was perception and how much reality, he responded, "I think 80 percent is reality." Other respondents stated that managers see black men as difficult to control. For example, the black female personnel manager of a Detroit retail store commented:

Employers are sometimes intimidated by an uneducated black male. Their appearance really isn't up to par, their language, how they go about an interview. Whereas females, black or white, most people do feel, "I could control this person." A lot of times people are physically intimidated by black men. The majority of our employers are not black. And if you think that person may be a problem, [that] young black men normally are bad, or [that] the ones in this area [are], you say, "I'm not going to hire that person, because I don't want trouble."

A white female personnel official from a Los Angeles area public-sector agency department offered a related perspective, laying part of the blame on white supervisors:

There's kind of a being-cool attitude that comes with walking down the street a certain way and wearing your colors, or challenging those who look at you wrong, and they come to work with an awful lot of that baggage. And they have a very difficult time not looking for prejudice. If a supervisor gives him an instruction, they immediately look to see if it's said different to them because they're black. Or if something goes wrong in the workforce, they have a tendency to blame the race, their being black. And I also think that part of the problem is that the supervisors and managers of these people have their own sets of expectations and their own sets of goals that don't address the diversity of these people, and it's kind of like, "Well, hell, if they're going to come work for me, they're going to damn well do it my way." And my own personal feeling is that a lot of these young black men who are being tough scare some of their supervisors. And so rather than address their behavior problems and deal with the issues, they will back away until they can find a way to get rid of them. We have a tendency to fear what we're not real familiar with.

Other managers agreed that blacks are overly sensitive to discrimination, and/or have expectations that exceed their merits as workers. "It's that old adage, you know, 'The world owes me a living and here I am—give it to me,' type thing," remarked a supervisor of nursing aides in the Los Angeles area. "Even some of them don't want to be told what to do." "With the black workforce for some reason, I've had people say that they weren't being treated fairly," chorused the human resources director of a

Boston-area manufacturer. The head cashier at an Atlanta-area grocery store complained,

> With some of the part-timers you have had a problem where a black associate was asked to clean the bathroom or do some type of cleaning, they basically told us that their grandmother, grandfather, did that when they were a slave and now in this era they shouldn't have to do that anymore.

> And so you kinda gotta watch what you say so that they don't get offended. With a black person you've got to be mainly serious most of the time, you can't crack a joke without making sure you don't say the wrong things. But whereas if I was around the white people or Oriental, we crack jokes and even if they are putting down our race and things like that, it was a joke, nothing more, no harm done, you know, whereas if it was done in the presence of a black person they get easily offended.

Furthermore, some employers deplored blacks' tendency to congregate in cliques and share stories of perceived discrimination—"the grapevine gets going in the wrong direction," as one Atlanta manager put it.

Turning to the issue of motivation, another recurrent soft-skill stereotype depicted blacks as lazy, unmotivated, or undependable. This, too, is a stereotype of African Americans held widely by whites (Hacker 1992; Majors and Mancini Billson 1992; Peffley and Hurwitz 1998; Fiske 1998). Among employers interviewed face to face in the Multi-City Study, one-third of the respondents expressed a negative view of blacks' motivation. Aggregated to the level of the firm, 40 percent had half or more respondents voice disparaging views of the motivation of blacks. About 50 percent of firms had a least one respondent offer this type of sentiment. As with employer views

about hard skills, more primary central city than suburban employers voiced pejorative attitudes about black motivation and work ethic. Again, this differential between the primary central city and suburb might be interpreted as evidence for the accuracy of employer views or for the greater salience of these issues for urban employers. In the SSRC sample, respondents at 40 percent of firms voiced perceptions of black men as unmotivated employees.

As with interaction, comments about black workers' motivation varied widely in substance, but in general were more sharply negative than those about interaction. A Latina female personnel officer of a Los Angeles retail distribution warehouse whose workforce is 72 percent Latino and only 6 percent black stated outright, "Black men are lazy. Who is going to turn over? The uneducated black." The white male owner of a small Detroit-area plastic parts plant (46 percent black, 54 percent white) said that in his experience, black men "just don't care." "Black kids don't want to work" was the opinion of a white male owner of a small auto parts–rebuilding shop in Los Angeles whose workforce is entirely Hispanic women. "Black men are not responsible," added a Latina personnel supervisor for a Los Angeles auto-parts manufacturer located next to a major black neighborhood but with a workforce that is 85 percent Latino and less than 1 percent black. Other typical comments asserted that black workers "tend to work a little slower," "are not as dependable," "have more of an 'I don't care' attitude," "don't really want to work," "are lazy" or are "not as dependable" as immigrant workers because "their job is not as important to them."

Negative views of blacks' interaction skills and motivation were mixed with a smaller number of positive views. About 2 percent of our respondents voiced such positive perceptions, including a slightly higher percentage (3.3 percent) in Atlanta. This is small, indeed, compared with a cumulative total of 46 percent who made negative comments about blacks' hard or soft skills, but it is informative to examine the substance of the positive statements.

Some managers viewed black workers' assertiveness as understandable or even positive. Said the African American director of a Detroit-area social service agency,

> Because of things that we've gone through that maybe people more in the mainstream or majority don't go through, we're just a little more testy, and sometimes people in the majority take that to mean that we don't like them or we're aggressive or real pushy or mean or something.

A white production manager in a Boston-area consulting firm voiced a similar sentiment:

> Those people who have been the underdogs, they are stronger fighters than the people who have had an easy road of it. And perhaps this is where antagonism is created, but it's understandable. If you are an underdog, you're going to fight to do better. And if you're on the other end of the stick, where it's been very easy for you to progress and to achieve and to become successful, you can feel very threatened.

More widespread are employers who see black workers as needing the job more, and therefore more willing to work hard, do menial tasks, and stay at a job longer. Not surprisingly, employers in the suburbs and in other central cities (where the nearby workforce tends to be more affluent) were more likely to hold this belief than their counterparts in the primary central city (see table 2). Managers who lauded blacks as harder workers typically offered lower-paying jobs. At establishments where at least one man-

ager described blacks as better workers, the average starting wage lagged a substantial $1.10 behind the pay level at other firms. The wage gap was 66 cents in cases where half or more of the respondents made such statements. The number of firms yielding praise of blacks as better workers was quite small, making these estimated differences rather imprecise. . . .

The white manager of an Atlanta-area fast food restaurant reported a striking difference between the white and black workers he was able to hire:

> I find the workers in the suburbs to be, if they are white, to be lower-educated. They don't have communication skills. In the store that I am at now and the ones that I worked at in predominantly black neighborhoods, they tend to be higher-educated. They have a better work ethic in general. The middle-class kids that we did have, they didn't want to work as hard because they didn't have the drive. If you are having to pay bills and pay your own tuition, there is a certain incentive that you have to work. If Mom and Dad are paying the bills and when they write the checks in front of you, why do you have to work hard?

A white manufacturing supervisor agreed, reflecting back on his experience hiring at a department store in a previous job:

> Initially the people from the more affluent areas, whether they be white or black, but primarily they were white, from an interviewing and presentation standpoint they were much more polished. So [you would think], "Hey, this is a great person, let me put them on the floor." They can work in the designer area, whatever, and present themselves very well. Whereas the group from the lower-income areas, which were primarily black, may not present themselves

as well at first or may not be as polished or whatever. So you may think, "Well, for this particular position this [upper-income] person presents, better, so we'll go with this person." But the lower-income person may need the job more and may be the more solid employee. If you hire both of them, the lower-income person, the black person or whatever, may stick around longer and be a much more solid citizen than the upper-income person, because [the upper-income person is] always looking for something else to go to.

Some employers thought their black employees were more inclined toward friendly customer service than their white employees. This sentiment was offered by more than one home health agency manager, and also by a Detroit-area dry cleaning manager: "If the truth be told, my black employees are much friendlier on the counter, they make a little bit more of an effort. Yeah, they smile a lot more and they are much more pleasant. They just try harder for the job, I guess."

In short, although substantial minorities of employers criticized blacks' sense of entitlement and lack of commitment, smaller minorities described blacks as willing to settle for less and work hard at the worst jobs. These statements come predominantly from low-wage employers comparing blacks with white, suburban youth. . . .

Employer Explanations of Black Skill Levels

Employers who criticized blacks' skills advanced a number of theories to explain these perceived skill problems. Respondents who noted *hard*-skill differences attributed them above all to educational attainment or school quality. A Boston public agency official griped:

Well, do I see any differences [between workers of different racial or ethnic groups]? Only in the skills level. Again, it goes back to the school system. Whites have abandoned it. It's a minority school system. Those kids who are going through the school system have a different level, a lesser level, of skills than the kids who don't. There's no question about that. . . .

The list of reasons given for lagging soft skills is much longer. The most frequent items on the slate were the influences of family structure, the welfare system, and inner-city life. But we also heard from managers who specifically pointed to class rather than race as the key factor shaping blacks' social skills. And some employers noted the dependency of soft skills on workplace context, implicitly or explicitly raising the question of whether they are skills at all.

Employers frequently portrayed black families as not placing sufficient stress on the value of work and education. The opinion of this manager at County Construction in the Atlanta suburbs is representative:

I think that sometimes they have been raised where a lot is not expected of them, and I think that lends itself to their poor self-confidence and them thinking that they're not capable of it. It's hard to take a person who's lived in an environment where neither of their parents worked and they got along just fine, and then you try and tell them that you've got to work to succeed, and it's something that they just haven't been taught.

The quote above refers to "neither of their parents." More frequent, however, was the view that blacks are likely to have had single mothers, who failed to instill in them a work ethic (or other positive values, such as desire for education) while growing up. Remarks from a manufacturing plant manager exemplify the perceived association between single parenthood and lack of a strong work ethic:

> I think there's a higher percentage chance if you go in the inner city that a black person is going to come from a single-parent home where there has not been any values taught or work ethic, that type thing. But where a black person has come from what I call a quote "normal" home, there is no difference, okay?

The regional vice president of an insurance firm described *hard*-skill consequences of single-parent upbringing as well:

> When you find that a large number of those people [blacks] are unemployed, I think it's because either they don't want to be employed or they're not college-educated. They're high school-educated or less, and they don't have the technical skills required to get a decent job. And that could come from family background or lack of nurturing. Single-parent family could come into that, because education may not be as strong.

In Los Angeles, the comparison goes beyond black and white. This transportation company manager clearly feels that being raised by single mothers is part of the reason blacks are less attractive job candidates than the alternative sources of labor in Los Angeles, Hispanics and Asians:

> One of the key elements of the business code is the word "respect" and the second word is "responsibility." We have found because of family values that, for instance, the Asian worker has a very strong sense of responsibility and respect. We have found a little closer sense of responsibility because of the family value with the Hispanic. We have found less of that being prevalent in the black,

and principally because they don't have the same strong family value. In the economic environment of Los Angeles as a whole, if an Asian applies for a position, you can say in most cases they have come from a family where the mother and father are still living together. In the Hispanic you can say that. In the black you cannot say that.

Many employers also expressed the belief that blacks are more likely than other groups to depend on public welfare, and this contributes to their poor work habits. Most frequently, employers suggested that welfare undermined blacks' upbringing or, in the case of women, their current seriousness about work:

> I have interviewed where I was stunned that their [black women's] expectations were, expecting to be given something for nothing. I believe [it's due to] their environment where there's more of the matriarch, and it's more of the welfare system. More of the black races are on that system where they have children so that they can get more money. And I have interviewed a few of the young ladies who don't see a goal in mind. They don't have any vision of what they could do. It is a day-to-day survival. *(Los Angeles-area hospital manager)*

> They're trying to get the blacks to get their self-esteem back and basically the biggest problem with a lot of people, not just blacks, is the welfare system. Because you've got third- and fourth-generation people on welfare. They can't remember when the last person in that family went to work for a day. *(Boston-area candy factory manager)*

> A welfare mentality to me is people that don't give a damn. After you've been beaten down and beaten down for so long, then they really don't give a damn.

That person feels like, they already don't have a goal in life. They just want a job. They don't care as far as satisfying the customer. They're under no pressure as far as bills go, 'cause the government is taking care of them, so if you ride them too hard they quit. (*personnel director at an Atlanta-area fast food restaurant*)

Our respondents frequently explained blacks' (and, to a lesser degree, Hispanics') labor market problems as a result of growing up in inner-city areas. . . Managers envisioned the inner city as a place where there is a concentration of negative causal factors such as inferior schools, single-parent families, poor role models, and welfare dependence. So we often heard accounts that wove together these various factors. For instance, a custodial supervisor in a Detroit-area public agency said:

> *Respondent:* In some situations perhaps by the environment in which they [blacks] were raised, they are at a disadvantage coming from single-parent families or broken homes or see their parents be on some type of aid.
>
> *Interviewer:* Do you think that's more true among your workers here [in a community immediately adjacent to Detroit] than at Macomb [County, north of Detroit, where the respondent previously employed a white workforce]?
>
> *Respondent:* Yes, I don't know if it's because it's a poorer area and it's put more strain on families and people where they couldn't hold the family together.

Another Detroit-area manager, a senior administrative assistant at the regional headquarters of "ShopKwik," a retail chain, offered a similar analysis: "Well, it's the way that they're brought [up]—I mean, there's gangs out on the streets. There's people hijacking cars and it's the way that, if your mom is not home and you're on welfare, what type of a life can those kids have?"

Single motherhood, reliance on welfare, and inner-city residence are disproportionately present among *low-income* families, not just black families. And quite a few managers, particularly in Detroit, did link blacks' perceived skill problems to class rather than race. As a white manager at a Detroit publishing concern put it, skill disparities are "more a reflection of—the people of that race might fit into this socio-economic structure, and therefore they reflect the values of that socioeconomic structure."

A white supervisor at a Detroit nonprofit stated the case even more strongly:

> See, my thing is the whole, the income level. I wish we would have a day where people would understand how the income level affects work ethics. Because I think they look at it from a racial view. And maybe there are some tie-ins, but I just am bound to confront that race stuff. It's like, have you looked at every other possibility before you went immediately and said it's race?

An African American manager at a government federal agency office in Detroit concurred:

> Black and white, I would think it was more a matter of economics, which would tend to be black and white [laughter]. But I don't think black and white is the issue. I think it's those that come from lower-income levels have lower expectations of themselves and do not necessarily do as well. They don't expect to do as well as those who have lived a middle-class or better life, regardless of the color, have different expectations and then they bring that with them. So with Detroit being primarily black and low-income level in general, then it could appear to be black and white.

The white vice president of operations at an industrial real estate company in the

Los Angeles area agreed in part, but suggested a more complicated story that involves attitudes spawned by poverty and the complementary problem of management prejudice toward blacks:

> I think it could be a combination of their attitude and the way they look at going into a position, and I think you can look at it also on the management's end as prejudice that is still remaining in the minds of a lot of the owners. I think it's a twofold situation. I think there is a history to overcome with the black employee. That they're lazy. I think a lot of times that there are black employees that have that feeling themselves. That they have probably come up out of the poverty without a lot of initiative given behind them. So they go in with the attitude that it is owed to them.

A number of our informants took a quite different line of argument, however. Instead of blaming poor soft skills on blacks' social environments or families, they maintained that such qualities—and particularly motivation—are created within the workplace and labor market. That is, they pointed to the importance of *context*—both current and earlier in someone's work history—in shaping soft skills. As a black human resource official of a Detroit-area insurer expressed it:

> I think business drives the work ethic. If business is lax, then people have casual attitudes about their jobs. You are one thing up to the point of entering the business world, but then you are something else. I'm not the same person I was fifteen years ago. I had to take on certain thoughts and attitudes whether I liked it or not.

Several others agreed that motivation is more a function of management than of the workforce. When asked about racial differences in the work ethic, a white manager of

contracted public-sector workers mused, "I think it's how you motivate each group. Two or three years ago I would have probably said, Well, the black race isn't as motivated as the Oriental or the Hispanic. But I've seen that if you motivate, that you have to motivate each group differently."

A white public-sector human resource official added that work ethic may vary by job:

> If I take security, or I take the basic labor jobs, I'm not so sure that when they were Caucasian-dominated, twenty years ago, that people weren't leaning on a shovel and gold bricking. Many times the classifications we normally associate with being more lazy or finding ways to avoid work are the entry-level, lower-skilled ones. And now those happen to be dominated by blacks and, to a lesser extent, Hispanics.

The black human resource director at an Atlanta-area motel gave a similar account. Asked if there was a racial difference in work quality or work ethic, he responded, "Nah, nah. I think that if they made more, I think they would work a lot better. It's money." And a white Los Angeles hospital executive likewise explained workforce differences by the nature of the jobs held:

> One of my departments is entirely black, and we find their style to be less professional. The radio's going, the workplace is sloppier, there's always food. They have an increasing need to work overtime to get their work done. They have the most boring and tedious jobs, so there's a certain amount of tolerance. That they kind of need to do what makes the day the most enjoyable, to put up with the work and stick around for these boring jobs.

A few respondents also argued that workers can readily be trained to relate well to customers. Even a store manager who commented that "it does take a certain kind of person" to be "fast, fun, and friendly" (the slogan of the Value King chain . . .), added, "but if you work with a person, I think that you could pretty much [get them to] be fast, fun, and friendly."

Although most of these employer comments referred to blacks, we encountered a particularly striking example of the ability of employers to shape worker attitudes in a Latino community. By coincidence, our SSRC sample included two department store distribution warehouses located in the same Latino neighborhood in the Los Angeles area. In one case, personnel officials complained sarcastically about employee laziness, their propensity for theft, the presence of "gang bangers" wearing their gang colors, and even the poor personal hygiene of the workforce. Turnover in this warehouse stands at 25 percent, even after personnel beefed up screening to select for more stable employees. In the second warehouse, however, turnover is 2 percent. Although this warehouse also employs large numbers of present and past gang members, managers have successfully imposed a dress code that bans the wearing of colors. The key to the remarkably low turnover, according to the vice president for human resources, "is simply locating your operation in an area where you don't have an awful lot of competition, and what competition you do have, you meet or exceed all pay and benefits they offer."

Indeed, this warehouse pays its entry-level workers from 50 cents to $2.50 more per hour than its competitor does. The contrast suggests that efficiency wage models, which posit that higher pay will elicit greater effort from workers, help explain worker attitudes (Akerlof and Yellen 1986). A manager at Atlanta-area County Construction described the principles involved. After complaining about laziness, tardiness,

and transportation woes among his entry-level workers, he explained how the business is addressing these problems:

> The biggest strategy is money speaks. We went through a big, major change in our pricing structure here lately, as far as what we start off people. You go to [another business that competes for workers] and you get paid $4.50 an hour. We start entry-level people off at $7.50 an hour. We feel like if we offer you more money, we're offering you good money as far as an entry-level person with no experience, and we expect our money's worth.

As all these examples illustrate, differences in workers' soft skills may be real, yet be effects as well as causes of unequal treatment.

Employer Views of Latinos, Asians, and Immigrants

When asked about "differences between blacks, whites, Latinos, and Asians," most respondents zeroed in on the distinction between blacks and whites. We heard much less about Latinos and Asians, in part because in two of the metropolitan areas under study—Atlanta and Detroit—these groups remain small. When managers did speak to Latinos' and Asians' skills, positive comments outnumbered negative ones—the reverse of the situation for blacks. This is particularly true with regard to soft skills. Since relatively few employers made *any* comment about Latino and Asian skills, it is useful to compute the ratio of positive to negative comments in order to facilitate comparison with employers' views of blacks. For blacks, the ratio of respondents indicating blacks are better workers to those stating that blacks are worse workers (in terms of hard skills or soft skills) was a minuscule .04, meaning that for every respondent with a positive viewpoint there were 25 with negative things to say. For Latinos, positive statements slightly outnumbered negative ones, yielding a ratio of 1.32. For Asians, the ratio was 2.92: nearly three laudatory respondents for each critical one. After reviewing criticisms of Latino and Asian skills, we will turn to analysis of the positive statements.

Start once more by considering hard skills. As table 1 shows, only 5 percent of all respondents criticized Latinos' basic and technical skills. This percentage was considerably higher—over 10 percent—in Los Angeles, where Latinos are the major group of people of color. Asians came in for very little criticism. The responses collected at the *firm* level, presented in table 2, indicate that while a plurality of respondents at 26 percent of firms criticized black hard skills, the percentage judging Latinos this way was a lower 5 percent, and the percentage for Asians lower still.

"I have to say the Hispanics, most of them don't pass the [math] test," commented a Boston-area bank manager. More commonly, however, employers pointed to language problems with Latino, Asian, and other immigrant groups. The personnel director at a Boston-area factory lamented:

I think a lot of the [ethnic groups], especially Hispanic, are not prepared to go into the workforce. Language. Simple math skills, basic reading skills. Some of them have the initiative to go to school and learn the language. Others do not, and it's a big problem. It's a horrendous problem because we're looking at entry-level people, we're looking for people to train on their job. And to train to run a machine, for instance, the drilling machine. We're going to get maybe a high school grad or even less, and we find that it's almost impossible to hire some people, because there's no standards when these people come into the country.

In a Los Angeles nursing home chain, Asians' difficulty with English raised very concrete issues: "Facilities have been written up for language. Like a building I had in [location]. They were cited because the residents couldn't talk to some of the staff members because their English was so poor that they couldn't communicate."

Aside from difficulties with language, no employers disparaged the hard-skill levels of Asian workers. On the contrary, we frequently heard the stereotype of Asians' facility with math and technical tasks. The 4 percent of respondents in Los Angeles and the 2 percent in Boston who criticized Asian hard skills (see table 1) were invariably speaking of problems with English. Of course, in a number of businesses serving immigrant communities, bilingualism, or even speaking the immigrant language, is instead a plus. A manager at a Boston-area public-sector agency noted both sides of this coin: "If you're people from a background where English isn't their first language, yeah, they may have trouble communicating with other people if they're not that good with the English language." But he continued:

Well, I think having some [people for whom English is a second language], it's an advantage, because we do realize that [clients] are from everywhere. And being here, we do look for some people with other languages, again being here in this area there's a lot of Hispanic [clients], so we have a certain pool of Hispanics. If a person gets a call and they don't speak the language, they have a difficulty, we can transfer it to a person who speaks Spanish.

Criticisms of Latino, Asian, or immigrant soft skills were relatively rare. Referring back to table 1, only 1 percent of respondents said anything negative about Latinos' interaction skills; 5 percent faulted

Latinos' motivation. The overall average for Latino motivation is a bit misleading, however, because there are so few Latinos in Detroit and Atlanta. In Los Angeles and Boston the percentages criticizing Latinos' motivation were 9 percent and 7 percent. Fewer than 1 percent of the surveyed managers said negative things about Asians' soft skills.

Detractors of Latinos' soft skills often echoed themes that we heard more often in descriptions of blacks. Some managers complained of Latino pride or prickliness. For instance, the owner of a Boston-area factory commented:

> I had a manager in here and the way he tells them to do things, they thought it was disrespectful, the way he was talking to them. They wanted to see "please" and "thank you" and kind of "kiss my fanny" -type of an attitude. They pretty much thought that the way the authority was delegated by that person, it would have been different if it had been a white person who was going to do the same job.

Motivation issues came up at the same plant, where a manager described Latinos as "more slow-paced because of their background and the countries they came from [that] don't have the hustle and bustle of the United States." Although managers at this plant reported problems with first-generation immigrant Latinos, we more commonly heard praise for the new immigrants' work ethic, coupled with complaints that succeeding generations did not necessarily inherit this attitude. A Los Angeles-based manager of contracted hospital housekeepers identified young, native-born Latina women as the group with the worst ethic, stating that he had encountered high levels of workers' compensation fraud in this population. "There is an issue of respect" with native-born Hispanics, much as with

African Americans, stated a manager at a Los Angeles–area utility.

Outnumbering the negative comments about Latinos and Asians were laudatory statements about their work habits. Closely related were the recurrent paeans to the immigrant work ethic—primarily applying to Latinos, Asians, and Afro-Caribbean migrants in the cities in question. It was not always easy to tell whether employers were praising Latinos or Asians as a group or were praising their immigrant workers (whom these two groups disproportionately represent). When it was not obvious whether a respondent was referring to Latinos or Asians, on the one hand, or immigrants who happened to be Latino or Asian, on the other, we coded *both* a preference for Latino workers or Asian workers *and* an affirmation of a stronger work ethic among immigrants in tables 1 and 2.

As table 1 shows, over 13 percent of all respondents asserted that Latinos are preferred workers (more than six times as many as expressed this view of blacks), and more than 7 percent felt this way about Asian workers. The percentages were much higher in Los Angeles, where there are relatively more Latinos and Asians than in other cities, and higher as well in Boston, where racial diversity is also greater than in Detroit or Atlanta. The firm-level counts in table 2 make the point even more forcefully. Over 16 percent of firms have a plurality of respondents who favor Latino workers, and close to 13 percent of firms have a plurality of respondents who prefer Asians. The chorus who sang the praises of immigrant workers included 13 percent of our respondents, and at almost 16 percent of firms, half or more respondents agreed that immigrants were superior to native workers. Again, this opinion was heard most often in Los Angeles and Boston. When we consider the 13 percent with positive comments as a percentage of those who commented at all on the relative work ethic of immigrants and natives, the results are far more dramatic: 92 percent of those making any comment rated immigrants as more committed. The same was true in the smaller SSRC sample, in which 81 percent of Detroit respondents who ventured an opinion agreed that immigrants have a stronger work ethic than native-born workers, as did 88 percent of Los Angeles respondents. This bodes ill for less skilled African American workers, particularly in Los Angeles, since they increasingly compete with immigrant workers for jobs.

As with blacks, those employers who rate Latinos, Asians, and immigrants as better workers are bestowing a mixed blessing. Since a key issue is willingness to work where natives might turn up their noses, these firms turn out to offer below-average wages. At firms where at least one respondent or at least half of respondents pronounced Latinos better workers, the hourly starting wage averaged 24 and 27 cents less, respectively, than at other firms. Businesses where at least one manager lauded Asians paid 36 cents per hour less than others, and when half of the managers or more jumped on the bandwagon, the gap widened to 93 cents. Praise for the immigrant work ethic, similarly, came with a wage penalty of 39 cents (when at least one manager spoke up) to 96 cents (when half or more did so). One Los Angeles manufacturer made this connection explicit. When asked why most of his workforce was Latino, he explained that as a small business, "We have to have a competitive edge, and our edge is our prices are lower." He added, "All of my guys, practically, start at five dollars an hour," while "some of the competitors that we deal with pay fifteen an hour." This should not surprise us, since immigrants are often comparing their current situation with peasant agriculture, maquiladora-type export assembly jobs, or even low-intensity warfare back home.

Praise for Latino and Asian workers typically focused on motivation, with managers sometimes attributing these groups' high levels of commitment to their recent immigration:

> Spanish people are more willing to work. They are willing to work longer hours. I think the ones that I've known are very dedicated to their jobs. (*Boston-area metal-finishing shop*)

> Your Asian workforce, because it's the newest immigrant in the country, and what I've seen with them is they have a completely different work ethic. You need them for seventy-two hours a day, they'll be there for seventy-two hours a day. (*Boston-area factory*)

If anything, employers were even more positive about Asians than Latinos, as this comment by a Boston-area factory trainer indicates: "[Hispanics] take a lot of pride in what they do, but they also can get very insulted. As a spectrum I see the Asians on the high end of work ethic and working hard and privately and quietly. I probably see Hispanics on the other end because of that pride in their culture."

Some employers compared immigrants favorably to native whites. The remarks of two white Boston-area managers are striking in this regard:

> *Respondent:* [The Latinos] work pretty well. They're trying to support their family.

> *Interviewer:* Would say you have more problems in getting the white people to work?

> *Respondent:* Absolutely. I mean, not that we won't hire them, but we will look twice before we hire just a regular white guy for a floor job. (*factory*)

> The Cape Verdean guys back there [in the kitchen] are my hardest workers. These guys are absolutely fantastic workers. When I was younger in all

restaurants, you always had young, white, American boys washing dishes. Now, you know, I almost try to stay away from them in a way because they're so lazy at times. I get Cape Verdean kids in here and they bust their butt. You know, I get these white kids in here, they're young, sixteen, seventeen, eighteen years old, and they think they're just going to hang out and just be lazy all day. (*restaurant*)

However, in other cases whites are not applying for the jobs in question, so employers compared immigrants favorably to blacks alone. The maintenance supervisor at a Boston-area facility compared *immigrant* blacks to African Americans, and concluded that West Indian immigrants "seem to be a little bit harder workers, will give you a little bit more," whereas "the native black expects a lot more for doing a lot less." The personnel director of an Atlanta-area laundry expressed a strong opinion on the merits of Latino immigrants versus African Americans:

[Hispanics] have a much higher work ethic [than blacks]. Hispanics, while they are employed with you, are very good employees. They're diligent. They do their job. They don't complain as much. [Blacks are] more vociferous than Hispanic people. If we are going to have complaints or we're going to have people not coming into work, it's going to be more predominantly black than it is Hispanic.

In fact, a supervisor at this laundry expressed concern at the prospect that prosperity in Mexico would cut off their labor supply, since blacks don't stay in the jobs and whites don't even apply:

Respondent: The only thing that really bothers us [supervisors] right now is how they say that Mexico is going to start paying more money and all of this kind of stuff. If we didn't

have Mexican people that come in and want jobs like they do now, I believe we'd be in trouble. Because we do not get black people that will come to work and stay here.

Interviewer: Or white people?

Respondent: Oh there's no—you can forget white people, period.

At a Los Angeles garment factory, the manager drew similar conclusions when he compared workers by race and ethnicity: "I think the work ethic for Hispanics is better than it is for blacks," he stated. "Asians are very good workers." Whites, on the other hand, were simply out of the picture for these jobs: "Whites, they wouldn't do the type of job in the back. That's a rarity, especially in Southern California, to see a member of the Caucasian race working in the plants. They just don't have the stamina or the, you know, humility to do that type of job."

In this context, African Americans have fewer opportunities than whites, but higher expectations than immigrants do. A Los Angeles warehouse's operations director quoted black workers as saying, "I'm paraphrasing it: 'You expect me to do that for what? You're not paying me enough for doing what you want me to do'"—and contrasted this with "hard-working" immigrant Latinos.

Customer reservations about dealing with Latino or Asian employees came up far less frequently than for blacks. Nonetheless, customer bias is an issue for these ethnic groups as well, as the examples of an Atlanta supermarket and a Los Angeles car dealership illustrate:

I think in today's world we get more complaints from customers about Hispanics and Orientals than we do blacks. Years ago we used to get complaints when we had "too many blacks" in a particular store. You don't hear that today, but you sure as hell hear about the fact that "You've got nothing but slant-eyes working in this store," or, "All those damn Mexicans are everywhere."

Unfortunately, I've had people come up to me and say, "I want a Caucasian salesperson. I don't want to talk to a Chinese salesperson." I think it's more that than it is the ability of my salesperson.

The Silent Majority: Employers Who Denied Racial Differences

It is important to note that the largest group of respondents consisted of those who did *not* describe differences by race within the workforce. Based on context, some of these answers appear to be sincere, whereas others were almost certainly offered as the socially desirable answer. As one Boston-area public-sector respondent wryly remarked, "we have to be so politically correct these days." Certainly a number of respondents were uncomfortable with the question, as in the case of this clerical supervisor at an Atlanta-area educational institution:

Interviewer: A number of the people that we have talked to in the area have commented on the differences between black and white workers. Could you comment on that?

Respondent: [whispers inaudible words]

Interviewer: But it's confidential.

Respondent: I know, I know. I guess you hear me hedging a little. It just depends on the individuals. But this has been one of our problems. The . . . a lot of it is the . . . and it's not true, it's not true, blanket . . . definitely it's not, but unfortunately in the majority of the cases we have problems that tend to be minority. I am going to close my door in case anyone comes down the hall.

A few managers referred to equal employment opportunity laws in ways that seemed to indicate discomfort at drawing racial distinctions. "That's a loaded ques-

tion," said another Boston-area public-sector manager; "you know, the direction of your question was towards, for lack of a better term, 'protected populations,' and I cannot articulate any particular reason why those populations and/or employees would have any more of a hurdle with regard to their work that I know of."

Moreover, many respondents gave mixed responses, at some points delineating racial differences and at other points denying them. Consider this Atlanta-area restaurateur, who offered a detailed indictment of black job applicants:

When you have white people come in the door [they usually] are more qualified than some of the black people that come in off the street. Because most of the time, black people that come in off the street, they've had sixteen jobs in the last two months just because they're never satisfied with what they have. You never know if they're telling you the truth. Whereas white people, nine out of ten times theirs are pretty much what they write down. A white person will come in dressed in a tie, whereas a black person will come in dressed in, you know, rags. Have four earrings in each ear. In this business you want someone that comes to the table that's not going to intimidate you. You want somebody that's going to look presentable, have good communication skills.

But at the end of this speech, he insisted, "I love my black employees as much as I love my white employees. They do just as much a job, you know." In this case, the respondent is distinguishing between black applicants and the black employees he has actually hired; in other cases, the logic underlying apparently inconsistent statements is far less clear.

Within the majority group who did not describe racial differences, there were four

W.U. — relates to gender neutr.

general categories of responses. First were the respondents who appeared uncomfortable or irritated with the question, or simply wanted to get the topic over with. These interviewees gave the minimal answer, "no," to the question about differences among groups of workers, and to the interviewer probes that often followed a clipped answer of this kind. Such flat denials were frequent, but more numerous was the second class of replies: "it all depends on the individual." For example, the human resource manager from a Boston-area instrument manufacturer stated:

> You might see certain traits or tendencies in individuals, but you can't necessarily say it's based on their race or something like that. So, I don't think it would be fair to make those generalizations. I don't want to sit here and say, "Asians make good workers," and things like that, because it depends more on the individual than the particular racial group.

The manager of a financial services office in Los Angeles gave a similar response:

> I have an Asian lady working for me now. She's a very hard worker. Very dedicated, very dependable. But I've had Asians work with me that were not. The same in the black community and Hispanic. I've had it work both ways. The young lady that worked for me straight out of high school for six years was Hispanic background. Never had office experience in her life. Excellent. And yet I had Hispanics work for me that were lazy, didn't have an interest in the job. So I personally don't think it's too much on the ethnic background as it is the personal individual.

Quite often, this response was phrased not as an answer to the question, but rather as an assertion that color-blind procedures are used at the firm—"we don't consider race, we look at the individual." As the facilities manager at a large Atlanta factory put it: "I'm just color-blind. I know there's a black, white, Asian, Latin, Indian, Korean, whatever the case is. But I just look at them as individual people, simple as that."

In some cases, it appeared that "it depends on the individual" was given as a socially desirable response, since the circumstances of the firm suggested something different. For example, the manager of a contract cleaning firm in Boston offered: "Well, my personal feeling from watching people do this work for twenty years, and when we sold the company before, we had ten thousand cleaners going out every night, okay, so we see a lot of people. And to me, it's not that segment of society, it's the individual."

But earlier, he had indicated that twenty years ago the cleaning crews were almost entirely Portuguese immigrants, and now because the second-generation Portuguese don't want these jobs, the crews are virtually all Latino.

One variant of "it depends on the individual" was a group of employers who dismissed the question of differences between groups of workers by recounting their experience with a successful black (or Hispanic or Asian) employee. Others avoided the question by saying they had no black applicants in recent memory (or, less often, no white applicants), often because of the distance of the firm from the central city or because "blacks just don't apply for these jobs."

Third were the respondents who stated that different groups have different cultures, not necessarily different levels of skill, and that it is management's responsibility to deal with diversity. Here a personnel official at a Boston-area public agency starts out by saying "it's individual," but then goes on to talk about how the office manages diversity: "I really think it's individual rather than looking at the race. In every race, you're gonna find something different. Someone who may not fit. We try to discourage stereotyping in here, too. So we celebrate the different ethnic groups on a regular basis and that's one of the things, we have a committee."

But some respondents who proclaimed the importance of recognizing and respecting diversity voiced what appeared to be very conventional stereotypes at another point in the interview. For example, the Asian human resource director at Anytown College in the Los Angeles area asserted: "Sure, work ethics. I think it has to do with their cultural background. And that's why I think we're talking more about how to deal with diversity, how to value diversity. Because if you don't understand one culture from the other, you tend to have within your workforce problems." Later in the interview, however, he stated, "And you've got your African Americans who think that 'Oh well, they owe it to me, and therefore I can do whatever I want.'"

The final type of "no difference" reply was "there may be some differences out there, but we screen [or train] so effectively that we do not see such differences among our candidates [or employees]." Most public-sector agencies fell into this category. Respondents from these agencies indicated that the need to pass the relevant civil service tests for a job in their organization resulted in slates of candidates, all of whom could do the job.

For example, at a government agency in Massachusetts the personnel manager declared:

> [Differences by race or ethnicity don't] have a whole heck of a lot to do with it. No, a black kid has to be as motivated as a white kid to go up and take these courses on his own. To go up to [a par-

ticular level of] training, to become a [category of specific competence in this training] and that kind of thing. He's got to be as motivated as a white person to be attractive to us. And so by the time we get people, the standard is so high it is foolish for us to do anything less. The black, white, age doesn't, I mean, whatever we've got in that pool, they have to meet that standard.

A Los Angeles public agency manager emphasized training rather than selection:

> People skills? It's pretty across the board, as far as them being able to deal with the public and supervise. I think it's just the constant training at [name of the agency]. We take them when they're seventeen and eighteen, and just keep them here forever, so they're home-grown, and that's it, you know. And maybe that's why we don't see [such differences].

This type of reply was not exclusive to the public sector. After having been asked why the private-sector company for which he worked had developed such a good reputation as a place for African Americans to succeed, this Los Angeles personnel official stated:

> Well, because of the programs we have. That we do take affirmative action seriously. We have great training programs. But it's not just for one ethnicity. Everybody goes through those programs. You really come in and you really do get trained well. And the [company] has continued an atmosphere, environment for people to succeed.

Based on these comments by the "silent majority," we suspect that negative employer views of black workers, and most likely of Latinos and Asians, are more widespread than the numbers in our tables would suggest. Those who cited cultural rather than skill differences, or stated that through screening or training they garner well-performing workers from all racial groups, offered explanations that square their denial of racial differences with the widely known differences in workforce outcomes by race. But most of the silent majority answered the question about racial differences among workers with variants of "no" or "it depends on the individual." These are the answers one would expect of someone giving the socially desirable response to shut off further discussion. While we acknowledge that some managers who told us "it depends on the individual" were most likely stating a sincere, deeply held belief, we suspect that others were not. . . .

Gender Within Race in the Eyes of Employers

Past research leads us to expect that employers will view black women and black men in distinct ways. An extensive literature—not primarily focused on the workplace—explores stereotypes of black men and black women. As we have noted, stereotypes of black men often include laziness, violence, and hostility. Black women are often stereotyped as welfare-dependent, single mothers, and dominating or pushy. Indeed, a common view blames many of the problems of African Americans on widespread single motherhood (Collins 1990; Mullins 1994).

If such stereotypes are prevalent, it should not be surprising to find that many employers refer to them in judging the employability of black men and women. Joleen Kirschenman (1991) found that 39 percent of Chicago-area employers rated inner-city black women as more desirable workers than their male counterparts, whereas only

10 percent expressed a preference for inner-city black men; the remainder did not report seeing any difference between the two groups. Interestingly, employers typically linked both positive and negative perceptions of black women to single motherhood. Positive views of black women tended to emphasize their high level of motivation and commitment, attributed by many employers to their economic role as main supporters of their families. Employers who criticized black women as workers, on the other hand, stressed their unreliability due to their child care obligations. Ivy Kennelly (1999), using a subset of the data analyzed in this chapter (she examined employer interviews from Atlanta, one of the four cities in the larger data set), confirmed Kirschenman's finding of two-sided employer judgments of black women workers keyed to an image of the African American woman as single mother. Unlike Kirschenman, Kennelly found that equal numbers of employers described black women as committed and as unreliable.

Our findings from the four-city sample of face-to-face interviews are generally consistent with Kirschenman's and Kennelly's results. Specifically, we likewise find employer views characterizing black women as single mothers. However, we also find a set of additional employer assessments of the difference between black men and women that are not anchored in single mother, absent father stereotypes: black women as more educated and skilled than black men, black women as better at relating to others, and, conversely, black women as touchier than black men. In addition, we encountered a small number of employers who distinguished between Latino and Latina workers, most often by criticizing the "macho" attitude of the former.

In the interests of truth in advertising, we wish to note that in the in-depth surveys, we learned much more about the distinctions employers drew between black and white workers than about those they drew between black women workers and black men workers. This is due to the structure of the questionnaire itself. Interviewers were instructed to probe first for employer perceptions of racial differences, then gender differences in general, and finally gender differences within race. Because many employers were uncomfortable with these lines of questioning, interviewers had the discretion to cut the series of queries short if they concluded that continuing it would be fruitless and might jeopardize responses to the rest of the survey. As a result, employers spoke directly about differences between black men and women only in a small minority of cases—about one in nine. In coding responses, we did not count employers who simply addressed differences in physical strength ("Women can't lift cases of Coke all day") or commented on workers' gendered preferences for particular jobs.

As table 1 shows, about 4 percent of respondents characterized black women as superior to black men; about 1 percent stated the reverse. When we recalculate these proportions as a percentage of those who expressed an opinion about the *relative skills* of black men and women, they amount to 36 percent who rated black women better than black men and 10 percent who stated the reverse. These rankings are strikingly similar to those found by Kirschenman (1991)—in both cases indicating a strong preponderance of rankings placing black women above black men.

Employers who identified black women as better workers than black men sounded three main themes. The most frequent one, echoing Kirschenman's and Kennelly's findings, pointed to black women's motivation. For instance, the white male manager of a chain restaurant in the Los Angeles area commented: "The black female tends to

work more and harder than the black male. Where the black male tends to slack off, not work. They're the ones who would say, 'Ten-minute break,' or, 'I need a cigarette.' You know, 'I need to get out,' or, 'I need this particular weekend off.'"

A number of employers expressed this superior motivation in terms of being willing to put up with more or settle for less (a pattern also noted by Kennelly). For example, a white male supervisor at a Detroit-area steel plant said, "Sometimes the [black] women are more aggressive," and went on to explain that by "aggressive," he meant able to get beyond "feel[ing] uncomfortable working with white males." He added, "They're accepted because they are aggressive and they are willing to do the job and they don't expect someone else to do their job for them." The human resource director at the same plant, also a white man, commented on the fact that black women "strive" for jobs paying $6 an hour, whereas black men do not. And a white male plant manager in the Atlanta area commented that men, black and white, see the order processor job as "beneath them," whereas women tend to be more content in it. Given comments like this, one might expect that employers who describe black women as better workers than black men might offer lower starting wages—like employers who view blacks as better workers than whites. However, the difference turns out to be negligible (employers who spoke more highly of black women in any way paid, on average, 7 cents an hour more than those who did not; those who specifically lauded black women's superior motivation paid 9 cents an hour less).

Once more echoing Kirschenman and Kennelly, employers argued that black women are more motivated than their male counterparts because they are the main or only sources of support for their families, evoking images of the single mother or matriarch. At Peachtree Foods, an Atlanta-area grocery store, the personnel director stated: "[black] women are the main force in the workplace. And I don't know what's going on with the [black] men—boy, they must be staying at home or something. There are more I know of that the female of the household is the main worker."

The white male owner of a downtown Detroit store agreed: "[black women are better workers] I think because they probably have a child at home that they have to provide for and they have a commitment to it. A woman has a lot more commitment to their family than a man does."

He contrasted black men, who "have a defeated attitude, totally." And a black man who supervises Jack's Junkyard in the Detroit area observed that black women "have learned over a period of time that if you want to have something solid to rely on you'd better rely on yourself and be able to support yourself, because they found out over time you cannot rely on that man to be there to take care of you."

A second theme voiced by employers who expressed a preference for black women over black men was black women's higher education and skill levels. Respondents described black women as having "better communication skills, better work skills in everything," and being "a hell of a lot sharper" and "very impressive" compared to black men, who "tended to be less skilled, less educated." These views match up with the greater presence of black women (relative to black men) in jobs requiring added skilled tasks or credentials. . . .

Finally, a few managers rated black women's interaction skills as better. "I think black women are more aggressive, I mean, more outgoing and more people-oriented as a whole," remarked the human resource director at a Detroit-area manufacturer. Black men, on the other hand, were more often described as hostile and even potentially violent, as we described earlier in this chapter. The manager of the Peachtree Foods store near Atlanta—himself a black man—summed up all three themes by declaring: "I would say that normally the [black and white] females are smarter. I would say that they're probably a little easier to work with. Flexibility, being able to adjust." He contrasted black men within his hiring pool, whom he described as "more trend-binding" and "into the rappers."

Only a very small number of employers rated black men above black women. None referred to hard skills. Instead, they voiced the flip side of the interaction and motivation issues. In terms of interaction, the white male site manager at a home maintenance service complained that women are overly sensitive to perceived discrimination and harassment, and "your real challenge is when you have an ethnic minority person of the female persuasion." At a Detroit food manufacturer whose workforce is 80 percent black, the white male personnel manager said that "guys will say 'Fuck you' and that will be the end of it. Girls will talk behind your back and start these little cliques." As for motivation, while, as noted earlier, a number of employers described women as willing to settle for less, the front desk supervisor at a Boston-area hotel observed that young women, black and white, "seem to have incredible attitude these days." He attributed this attitude problem, which had led him to fire a number of women, to frustration at inability to move up fast enough in the workplace. Finally, while employers invoked the image of black women as single mothers to explain these women's commitment to a job, they also pointed to it as a source of unreliability—due to "baby and boyfriend problems," as one Atlanta manager put it. A white male middle manager at a Boston-area health care facility opined:

You have a lot of single mothers who struggle to survive and that to maintain a full-time, forty-hour position, the kids issues that come up and the disturbances about their work, calling in sick or not being able to make it to work on time and those type of things. Those issues that come in, and I would find more in the black population.

While few employers commented specifically on the disruptive effects of black women's child care responsibilities, many others made such comments about women in general or single mothers in particular. The comparison between Latino men and Latina women came up less frequently in the interviews. When it did, most often the balance tipped toward women, as with blacks. Some employers contrasted "proud" or "macho" Latino men (easily offended and demanding "respect") with more submissive Latina women. At a public agency in Los Angeles, a white female personnel official remarked: "The [Latino] men tend to want to boss the women. And to order them around, even though they're working at the same level. I can't help thinking it has to do with the machismo. Because it has been with the Latin males that we have, that this problem has come up."

And a white male warehouse manager in Los Angeles rated Latino men more willing workers than blacks, but not on a par with Latinas: "I think in general the blacks tend to make sure that you're not pulling the wool over their eyes. A little more the jailhouse lawyer kind of attitude. Hispanic women are extremely hard-working. And Hispanic men kind of like a spectrum of all of those things."

At a Los Angeles accounting firm, however, the white male CEO pointed to the effect of family demands on Latina data entry workers, echoing the "babies and boyfriends" comment about African American women.

"If I've noticed any difference, I'd say I've noticed that the Hispanic women spend more time dealing with personal issues. Their children and their families and stuff like that, and consequently don't get as much production."

In summary, when managers compared men and women *within* the categories of black and Latino, the comparisons primarily redounded to the disadvantage of men. This is consistent with the fact that the presence of most tasks and credential requirements is associated with a greater probability that a woman will be hired within any given racial group (including whites). . . . However, it would be misleading to suggest that women have unambiguous advantages relative to men in our data. In the Employer Survey data, women are still paid less—with a starting wage disadvantage of 10 percent or so, even after controlling for race, ethnicity, human capital, and other factors affecting pay, and a significantly slower rate of wage growth (Hertz, Tilly, and Massagli 2001). In the Multi-City Study Household data, women are four times as likely to report sexual harassment as men, and more than three times as likely to say that they have experienced gender discrimination in promotions or pay raises.

In addition, although relatively few employers commented on child care demands as an employment handicap for women, this issue deserves a closer look. Child care constraints have become more important because mothers of young children increasingly seek paid work: as of 1995, 55 percent of mothers aged fifteen to forty-four were in the Labor market within a year of giving birth (U.S. Department of Commerce 1997). The Multi-City Study Household Survey offers a look at how child care handicaps women's labor force participation. As table 3 shows, child care requirements prevented almost one-third of women from seeking a job (compared to

TABLE 3 Effects of Child Care Constraints on Women's Employment, by Race and Ethnicity

	Total	White	Black	Latina	Asian
In the past twelve months, has a concern about your child care needs caused you to					
Not look or apply for a job	31.6%	33.4%	20.6%	34.2%	26.0%
Turn down a job you were offered	12.5	15.2	8.8	10.5	8.4
Not participate in school or a training program	19.2	24.0	18.0	14.1	13.5
Quit or be fired from your job	11.4	11.4	6.1	12.7	20.6
Hourly wage penalty associated with answering yes to at least one of the above	−10.2	−15.0	−8.7	−9.7	−7.7
	N = 2,238–41	N = 278–395	N = 445–782	N = 328–765	N = 151–287

Source: Multi-City Study of Urban Inequality Household data analyzed by authors; wage penalty data from Browne, Tigges, and Press 2001.
Note: For women with a child under eighteen in Atlanta, Boston, Detroit, and Los Angeles, surveyed from 1992 to 1994. "Quit or be fired" and wage penalty are calculated based on number who worked in last twelve months; others are based on all women with children. Wage penalty data control for education, experience, and a variety of other factors. The low end of each range of sample sizes shows the number of women employed in the last twelve months; sample sizes for the first three variables in the table were all quite close to the high end.

only one man in twelve—not shown), prompted one in eight to turn down a job, and caused one in ten job-holding women to quit or be fired (see Press 2000 for a more detailed analysis of Los Angeles data). Women who reported any kind of child care constraint suffered an hourly wage penalty of 10 percent relative to other women, after controlling for education, experience, and other factors affecting wages (Browne, Tigges, and Press 2001). White, Latina, and Asian women cited child care constraints more often than did black women, but these handcaps are severe for every racial and ethnic group.

REFERENCES

Akerlof, George, and Janet Yellen, J., eds. 1986. *Efficiency Wage Models of the Labor Market.* Cambridge: Cambridge University Press.

Browne, Irene, Leann Tigges, and Julie Press. 2001. "Inequality Through Labor Markets, Firms, and Families: The Intersection of Gender and Race-Ethnicity." In *Urban Inequality: Evidence from Four Cities,* edited by Alice O'Connor, Chris Tilly, and Lawrence Bobo. New York: Russell Sage Foundation.

Collins, Patricia Hill. 1990. *Black Feminist Thought: Knowledge, Consciousness, and the Politics of Empowerment.* New York: Routledge.

Fiske, Susan T. 1998. "Stereotyping, Prejudice, and Discrimination." In *Handbook of Social Psychology,* edited by Daniel T. Gilber, Susan T. Fiske, and Gardner Lindsey. New York: Oxford University Press.

Hacker, Andrew. 1992. *Two Nations: Black and White, Separate, Hostile, and Unequal.* New York: Ballantine.

———. 1999. "'That Single Mother Element': How White Employers Typify Black Women." *Gender and Society,* 13(2): 168–192.

Kirschenman, Joleen. 1991. "Gender Within Race in the Labor Market." Presented at the Urban Poverty and Family Life Conference. Chicago (October 10–12, 1991).

Majors, Richard, and Janet Mancini Billson. 1992. *Cool Pose: The Dilemmas of Black Manhood in America.* New York: Touchstone.

Mullins, Leith. 1994. "Images, Ideology, and Women of Color." In *Women of Color in U.S. Society,* edited by Maxine Baca Zinn and Bonnie Thornton Dill. Philadelphia: Temple University Press.

Peffley, Mark, and Jon Hurwitz. 1998. "Whites' Stereotypes of Blacks: Sources and Political Consequences." In *Perception and Prejudice: Race and Politics in the United States,* edited by Jon Hurwitz and Mark Peffley. New Haven, Conn.: Yale University Press.

Press, Julie E. 2000. "Child Care as Poverty Policy: The Effect of Child Care on Work and Family Poverty." In *Prismatic Metropolis: Inequality in Los Angeles,* edited by Lawrence Bobo, James H. Johnson, Melvin L. Oliver, and Abel Valenzuela. New York: Russell Sage Foundation.

IMMIGRATION, GLOBALIZATION, AND WORKPLACE INEQUALITY

∽ READING 21 ∽

Unionization and Immigrant Incorporation in San Francisco Hotels

Miriam J. Wells

The tremendous surge of immigration into the U.S. over the past several decades raises crucial questions as to the character, determinants, and consequences of immigrant incorporation. Of particular concern is immigrants' engagement in the social relations and institutional structures of work and the effects of this involvement on the strength and character of class-based organizations. In concert with the recent literature examining the role of "mediating institutions" in immigrant incorporation (Bach 1993; Lamphere 1992; Lamphere, Stepick, and Grenier 1994), I contend that the movement of immigrants into U.S. society is neither random nor individual. Rather, it is limited, shaped, and structured—and group boundaries are variously reinforced, reformed, or broken down—by the institutional settings in which immigrants operate. In this [chapter], I aim to lend analytical rigor to our understanding of immigrant incorporation by going beyond the largely descriptive accounts of mediating institutions to systematically distinguish the facets of

work-based institutions that affect working class solidarity, and to identify the conditions under which one facet can prevail.

In this article, I argue that the industries in which immigrants are engaged—in particular their occupational structures, labor processes, and class-based organizations—shape inter-group relations at work, and thus the consequences of immigration for unionization. This study identifies local unions as key determinants of the social relations at work relative to potentially divisive occupational structures and labor processes. It signals the import of union ideology, strategy, and structure, and of understanding exactly when inclusive union initiatives are likely to emerge, and what practices undergird their success. Using the example of the San Francisco hotel industry, it analyzes how an ideologically and operationally inclusive labor union overcame ethnic and immigrant fragmentation and non-conducive occupational structure and labor processes to build a sustained and democratic organization. . . .

This article considers the form and consequences of union intervention. It examines an industry in which workers are fragmented by ethnicity, immigration status, occupational structure, and labor process, but in which a consciously inclusive labor union operating in a supportive political environment—San Francisco–based Local 2 of the Hotel Employees and Restaurant Employees, International

(H.E.R.E.)—has forged a dynamic overarching labor organization. It has done so, moreover, almost twenty years ahead of the U.S. labor movement nationally, using organizing methods informed by an understanding of workforce diversity. In this instance, the presence of immigrants in the workforce has helped the union bridge other workforce cleavages, engendering sweeping changes in the organizing practices and the decision making and contractual structures of the union itself. This study confirms emerging evidence as to the importance of union strategy and structure. It also underscores findings based on the study of national unions as to the conditions that foster union incorporation of lower status groups (Cornfield 1989, 1993). It suggests, however, that distinctive dynamics may be at work in the case of local unions, where social movements in the surrounding community can play pivotal roles in fostering early inclusiveness.

Data for this article are drawn from a research project in progress exploring the relationship between unionization and globalization in the San Francisco hotel industry.[1] A total of 79 interviews, each from one to four hours long, were conducted by the author between October 1996 and March 1999. Repeated interviews with 18 present and former union officers and staff at the local, regional, and national levels covered subjects' life and work histories, the historical periods of union development and change, the character of hotel jobs, and the impacts of immigration on workplace dynamics and union organizing. Interviews were conducted with a total of 36 individuals who work or have worked in the industry, covering individuals' life and work histories, connections with their countries of origin, labor processes and inter-ethnic dynamics at work and in the community, and

perceptions of, and experience with, the union. Two studies of room cleaners completed by union staff and workers were helpful as well. Observations of work and lunchtime dynamics were made while accompanying union staff waiting for interviews.

Information regarding the employers' side of the picture is, as yet, limited, as interviews were conducted with only three hotel managers and three employers' association spokespersons. Repeated interviews with three labor lawyers helped clarify the character of the legal issues surrounding union strategies and immigrant status. Interviews with six representatives of Asian and Latino community and immigrant organizations, and seven local government officials and staff, provided information on patterns of immigration and immigrant settlement, immigrant concerns, and community-union interactions. Demographic data were drawn from union records, the Statistical Year Books of the Immigration and Naturalization Service, and the 5 percent Public Use Microdata Sample data set gathered by the U.S. Bureau of the Census. Local newspapers, International and local union publications, and historical records housed in the San Francisco State University Labor Archives and Research Center, the San Francisco Public Library, and the University of California, Berkeley's Bancroft Library, helped flesh out the picture of the strategy and historical development of the union. Union files on hotel ownership, and reports completed by local government agencies and several firms that do research on the hotel industry, helped develop a picture of the changing structure of the industry.

The analysis proceeds by: 1) showing how immigration has increased the demographic complexity of San Francisco and its hotel industry; 2) clarifying how the occupational structure and labor processes compound and alter the impacts of demographic complexity, elaborating the organizing challenges of the union; 3) showing that it was shifts in the union's organizational structure,

1. This project has been funded by the Cultural Anthropology Program at the National Science Foundation and the University of California, Davis.

ideological orientation, and operating environment that led to its assertive efforts to incorporate immigrants; and 4) analyzing how union initiatives explicitly geared to workers' demographic and economic complexity have overcome sociocultural divisions and non-conducive occupational structure and labor processes to forge a viable labor organization.

The Immigrant Reconstitution of San Francisco and Its Hotel Workforce

Facilitated by the 1965 lifting of the national origins immigration quotas in place for forty years, and by laws in the 1970s and 1980s that eased the admission of refugees and asylees, the composition of San Francisco and its hotel workforce has shifted dramatically. Overall, their minority, immigrant, and non-citizen shares have risen rapidly, while their non-Hispanic, white, and citizen shares have plummeted.[2] Groups with a strong prior base in the city have increased the most. Chief among these are the Chinese, who formed a thriving settlement in San Francisco after the mid-19th century Gold Rush; Filipinos, who began to settle in the early 20th century after

being forced out of California agriculture; and Salvadorans, who have had a substantial residential nucleus in the city's Mission District since the 1930s.

The Changing Demography of San Francisco

San Francisco's immigrant share is remarkable, even for the state that houses the largest portion (34 percent) of the nation's foreign-born residents. Although only 5 percent of San Franciscans were foreign-born in 1970, by 1990, fully 34 percent were foreign-born—about the same proportion as Los Angeles and far greater than the national or state averages (8 and 22 percent respectively). Asian-Pacific Islanders and Hispanics account for the bulk of the influx, constituting 56 and 21 percent of the city's foreign-born residents by 1990.

Overall, the non-Hispanic white portion of the population fell from 87 percent in 1950 to only 47 percent by 1990. Asian-Pacific Islanders quintupled over this period, from about 5 to 29 percent of the population; nearly two-thirds are Chinese and one-fifth Filipino.[3] Hispanics more than tripled, from 3 percent to nearly 13 percent; 38 percent are Central American and 40 percent are Mexican. These immigrant influxes have created a distinctive immigrant population. San Francisco's Asian proportion is unusually large—about three times that of Los Angeles, for example. Its Latino population is unusually, but distinctively diverse: unlike Los Angeles where over 90 percent of Latinos are Mexican, or Miami where they are predominantly Caribbean, San Francisco's Hispanics have no single dominant national origin. Caribbean Hispanics are relatively few in number; Central Americans and Mexicans contribute roughly equal proportions. Blacks make up a relatively small, and declining, share of San Francisco

2. The data regarding the ethnic, racial, and immigrant composition of San Francisco and its hotel workforce were drawn from The U.S. Department of Commerce. Bureau of the Census', *Census of Population and Housing, 1970, 1980, 1990: Public Use Microdata Samples,* 5 percent sample. San Francisco State University's Public Research Institute performed the computations. While there are some discrepancies between the 1970 and the 1980–1990 reports in identifying "Hispanic" or "Spanish-origin" subjects, I agree with Waldinger and Bozorgmehr (1996:471–474) that the discrepancies are not serious enough to preclude analysis over time. "Asian-Pacific Islander" (API) is the aggregate Census term for Asian; "Hispanic" is the term used for Spanish-speaking persons; "White" is the term for non-Hispanic whites. I will use "Latino," the term preferred by Latin American immigrants, interchangeably with "Hispanic."

3. The Census does not specify the number and percent of Asians in San Francisco in 1950. The figure of 4.5 percent is an estimate based on historical accounts and regional Census data.

TABLE 1   Changes in the Ethnicity/Race of Employed Persons in the San Francisco Hotel Industry, 1970–1990

		1970	1980	1990	% Change 1970–1990
White	No.	5,508	4,840	4,215	−23.5
	%	60.0	41.1	34.1	−43.2
Black	No.	1,479	1,420	759	−48.7
	%	16.1	12.1	6.1	−62.1
Asian-Pacific Islander	No.	1,071	3,260	4,409	311.7
	%	11.7	27.7	35.6	204.3
Hispanic	No.	1,122	2,200	2,837	152.9
	%	12.2	18.7	22.9	87.7
Other	No.	0	60	154	n/a
	%	0	0.5	1.2	n/a
Total employed		9,180	11,780	12,374	

Source: U.S. Department of Commerce, Bureau of the Census. 1970, 1980, 1990. *Census of Population and Housing: Public Use Microdata Samples.* Washington. D.C.: U.S.G.P.O.

residents, decreasing from 12 percent in 1970 to 10.7 percent by 1990, as the manufacturing jobs that employed many moved out of the city to the wider Bay Area (Potepan and Barbour 1996).

The Changing Hotel Workforce

San Francisco's recent immigrants are especially concentrated in the service sector, whose immigrant share grew from about 18 percent in 1970 to fully 55 percent by 1990. Within this sector, the hotel industry has been particularly impacted. As Table 1 shows, hotel workers have always been less white and more minority than the city's population as a whole, and this contrast has grown and changed form over the years. Overall, the white and black shares of hotel workers have shrunk, while the Asian and Hispanic shares have exploded (see Table 1).

Immigration is the major cause of this ethnic restructuring. Between 1970 and 1990, the foreign-born share of hotel workers increased from 22 to 48 percent—14 percentage points more than the immigrant share of San Francisco as a whole. As in the city, Asians and

Hispanics are the largest immigrant groups, accounting for 56 and 22 percent of the industry's immigrants, respectively. Currently, immigrants are represented in all groups, although the immigrant shares of Asians (about 93 percent) and Hispanics (84 percent) are most substantial (see Table 2).

As Table 3 demonstrates, hotel workers are now substantially more immigrant and minority than the residents of the city. Moreover, nationality groups in San Francisco that contain a larger proportion of more educated, affluent, and acculturated individuals, such as the Chinese and Japanese, are more highly represented in the city than the industry, while groups with a greater share of recent immigrants and overall lower economic and educational levels, such as Southeast Asians, Filipinos, and Salvadorans, are more highly represented in the industry.

The Changing Demography of Hotel Jobs

Immigrants have moved unevenly into the hotel industry's occupational structure. As Table 4 shows, immigrants increased in all job

TABLE 2 Change in the Hotel Industry in Citizenship Status of Ethnic/Racial Groups, 1970–1990

	1970				1980				1990				% Change, 1970–1990			
	Native	ImmCit	Non-Cit	TotImm	Native	ImmCit	Non-Cit	TotImm	Native	ImmCit	Non-Cit	TotImm	Native	ImmCit	Non-Cit	TotImm
White	83.3	10.2	6.5	16.7	82.6	10.7	6.6	17.3	85.8	6.6	7.6	14.2	3.00	−35.29	16.92	−14.97
Black	100	0	0	0	94.4	4.2	1.4	5.6	89.2	0	10.8	10.8	−10.80	n/a	n/a	n/a
API	61.9	23.8	14.3	38.1	12.9	38	49.1	87.1	7.1	49.1	43.8	92.9	−88.53	106.30	206.29	143.83
Hispanic	40.9	18.2	40.9	59.1	30	20	50	70	16.2	22.4	61.4	83.8	−60.39	23.08	50.12	41.79
Other	0	0	0	0	66.7	0	33.3	33.3	57.8	0	42.2	42.2	n/a	n/a	n/a	n/a

Source: U.S. Department of Commerce, Bureau of the Census. 1970, 1980, 1990. *Census of Population and Housing Public Use Microdata Samples.* Washington. D.C.: U.S.G.P.O.

TABLE 3   Percent of Population in Selected Ethnic/Racial Groups, San Francisco Hotel Industry, City of San Francisco, 1990

	% of Industry Population	% of City Population
White (Non-Hispanic)	34.1	46.9
Black	6.1	10.7
Asian-Pacific Islander	35.6	28.5
Chinese	14.7	17.5
Filipino	13.7	5.4
Japanese	0.3	1.5
Vietnamese	2.1	1.3
Cam/Lao/Thai	0.9	0.5
Asian Indian	0.9	0.3
Korean	1.0	0.9
Indonesian	0.6	0.1
Other Asian-Pacific Islander	1.4	1.0
Hispanic	22.9	13.3
Mexican	6.6	5.2
Puerto Rican	0.5	0.6
Central American	12.7	5.0
Guatemalan	0.5	0.6
Salvadoran	9.0	2.7
Nicaraguan	2.0	1.4
Other Central American	1.2	0.3
South American	2.5	0.8
Other Hispanic	0.6	1.7
Other	1.2	0.6

Source: U.S. Department of Commerce, Bureau of the Census. 1990. *Census of Population and Housing: Public Use Microdata Samples.* Washington. D.C.: U.S.G.P.O.

categories between 1970 and 1990. Food servers, and especially bussers, were more immigrant than other "front-of-the-house" workers (those who have direct contact with guests) in 1970, but had become decidedly so by 1990 (50 and 83 percent respectively). Immigrants have made their greatest impact in the "back of the house": between 1970 and 1990, their share of cooks rose from 43 to 77 percent, food preparers from 67 to 80 percent, and room cleaners from 15 to a striking 85 percent. Because room cleaners comprise about 27 percent of all hotel workers, they currently contribute the largest share (39 percent) of foreign-born workers in the industry. As a result, the largest body of immigrants in the

San Francisco hotel industry are Asian-Pacific-Islander and Hispanic women who clean rooms.[4]

As Table 5 shows, this immigrant influx has increased the ethnic and racial diversity of all job categories. In some jobs, immigrants have almost entirely replaced native-born whites and blacks. Room cleaners are the most striking case in point, shifting from about

---

4. Filipinas and Chinese were the two largest Asian room cleaning groups in 1990, comprising about one-fourth and one-fifth of the job category respectively. Most of the rest were Korean and Southeast Asian. Central American Hispanics were the most numerous, followed by Mexicans (U.S. Dept. 1990).

TABLE 4 Change in the Citizenship Status of Hotel Occupations, 1970–1990

	1970				1980				1990				% Change 1970–1990			
	Native	ImmCit	Non-Cit	Totlmm	Native	ImmCit	Non-cit	Totlmm	Native	ImmCit	Non-cit	Totlmm	Native	ImmCit	Non-Cit	Totlmm
Manager	75	15.6	9.4	25	76.4	9.7	13.9	23.6	62.3	16.3	21.3	37.6	−16.93	73.40	126.60	50.40
Receptionist	100	0	0	0	33.3	33.3	33.3	66.6	76.5	0	23.5	23.5	−23.50	n/a	n/a	n/a
Clerical	100	0	0	0	80	14.3	5.7	20	75.8	10.2	14	24.2	−24.20	n/a	n/a	n/a
Bartender	100	0	0	0	80	10	10	20	54.7	16	29.3	45.3	−45.30	n/a	n/a	n/a
Bellperson	100	0	0	0	66.7	25	8.3	33.3	76.1	10.9	13	23.9	−23.90	n/a	n/a	n/a
Cook	57.1	42.9	0	42.9	21.1	42.1	36.8	78.9	23.3	38.7	38.1	76.8	−59.19	n/a	n/a	n/a
Food Server	53.9	15.4	30.8	46.2	68.9	19.7	11.5	31.2	50	15.4	34.6	50	−7.24	−50.00	12.34	8.23
Food Preparer	33.3	0	66.7	66.7	30.4	21.7	47.8	69.5	19.6	27.9	52.4	80.3	−41.14	−58.17	−21.44	20.39
Busser	71.4	14.3	14.3	28.6	29.2	16.7	54.2	70.9	17.1	37.6	45.3	82.9	−76.05	162.94	216.78	189.86
Room Cleaner	85.3	8.8	5.9	14.7	31.1	31.8	37.1	68.9	14.8	37.4	47.8	85.2	−82.65	533.90	710.17	479.59

Source: U.S. Department of Commerce, Bureau of the Census. 1970, 1980, 1990. *Census of Population, and Housing Public Use Microdata Samples. Washington, D.C.: U.S.G.P.O.*

TABLE 5 Change in the Ethnic/Racial Composition of Hotel Occupations, 1970–1990

	1970					1980					1990				
	White	Black	API	Hispanics	Other	White	Black	API	Hispanics	Other	White	Black	API	Hispanics	Other
Manager	93.8	6.3	0	0	0	75.0	9.7	11.1	4.2	0	67.4	0.8	16.8	10.7	4.3
Receptionist	100.0	0	0	0	0	33.3	0	33.3	33.3	0	76.5	0	0	23.5	0
Clerical Worker	100.0	0	0	0	0	82.9	2.9	2.9	8.6	0	76.1	0	16.6	2.1	5.2
Bartender	100.0	0	0	0	0	50.0	10.0	20.0	20.0	0	54.7	0	28.3	17.0	0
Bellperson	50.0	33.3	16.7	0	0	50.0	0	33.3	16.7	0	68.1	0	31.9	0	0
Cook	14.3	14.3	71.4	0	0	15.8	5.3	73.7	5.3	0	24.0	10.8	48.0	25.3	2.6
Food Server	69.2	0	7.7	23.1	0	70.5	6.6	9.8	13.1	0	37.3	12.1	29.4	22.5	0
Food Preparer	0	33.3	66.7	0	0	8.7	8.7	52.2	30.4	0	0	0	62.4	28.7	0
Busser	42.9	0	28.6	28.6	0	20.8	0	45.8	33.3	0	13.0	6.5	52.8	27.6	0
Room Cleaner	20.6	47.1	11.8	20.6	0	9.1	19.7	41.7	29.6	0	5.8	8.3	51.8	33.6	0.6

Source: U.S. Department of Commerce, Bureau of the Census, 1970, 1980, 1990. *Census of Population and Housing: Public Use Microdata Samples. Washington, D.C.: U.S.G.P.O.*

85 percent native-born (almost half black and a fifth white), to 85 percent immigrant (over half Asian and one-third Hispanic).

Occupational Structure, Labor Process, and Inter-Group Relations

The occupational structures and labor processes of hotel work compound and alter the impacts of increasing demographic complexity, thereby elaborating the organizing challenges of the union. Although the industry's occupational structure fosters workforce fragmentation in some regards, it does not exhibit the coincidence of ethnic and occupational boundaries that so exacerbates inter-group antagonisms and distance in contexts of sharply split labor markets and ethnic niches (Bonacich 1972, 1973; Hechter 1978; Model 1993). Similarly, although some labor processes preserve or intensify inter-group divisions, others erode or soften them. In the case of both potentially divisive influences, the placement of immigrants in the industry helps bridge and mitigate workforce cleavages, creating new groupings of solidarity on which union organizing can build.

The Role of Occupational Structure

The industry's occupational structure introduces important sources of workforce fragmentation through the wide and ranked range of distinct occupations it encompasses, into which sociocultural groupings are differentially channeled. The occupational structure is pyramidal, with a small number of managerial and administrative positions at the top and a large number of service positions at the bottom. Within this pyramid, jobs are clustered by function. Housekeeping is the largest functional cluster; food service and preparation is next largest. "Front-of-the-house" jobs involving regular interaction with guests (e.g., bellman, receptionist, and bartender) are ranked and paid more highly than are "back-of-the-house" jobs (e.g., dishwasher, room cleaner, and janitor). Gender and color contribute to this ranking: white men still hold the most privileged positions; women of color hold the least. Moreover, the qualities required in "front-of-the-house" jobs restrict the involvement of immigrants and minorities and limit their mobility from the back to the front. Most important of these attributes is the ability to speak English; formal training, technical expertise, and middle class self-presentation are others.

Despite varied and sometimes competing occupational concerns, however, and despite the disparate overall privilege of certain workforce segments, the occupational structure lacks the congruence of ethnic and occupational boundaries that can generate serious inter-group friction. As the foregoing census data show, industry-wide, no hotel occupation is comprised solely of one ethnic group, and no group is confined to a single occupation (see Table 5). Rather, all occupations are ethnically mixed, so that those who vary culturally share interests economically. Thus, there is not, at the level of the industry, a labor market split sharply along lines of ethnic status nor an occupation in which such boundaries coincide with occupational designation. Moreover, all ethnic groups encompass natives and immigrants so that ethnic identity bridges the native-immigrant split.

Ethnic job clustering is more marked at the level of the hotel, a pattern that here, as elsewhere, appears to reflect employers' recruitment preferences, immigrant workers' tendencies to use interpersonal networks to locate and gain access to work, and the preferences of certain native (especially black) workers for non-menial positions (Neckerman and Kirschenman 1990; Waldinger 1992, 1997). Thus, hotels catering to an international Asian clientele hire more Asians; "Asian" food and beverage rooms often hire only Chinese and Filipinos; fine "European" dining rooms often employ older white male waiters—and preferably those with European accents; avante-garde cocktail lounges often recruit only young white women as waitresses. Salvadorans and Mexicans have particularly elaborated networks of job acquisition in hotel kitchens, so dishwashers (stewards) may be almost exclusively Latino. In one hotel, room cleaners are only Filipina and Chinese, and some applied for their jobs while still in their homelands. In another, twelve Bosnians join the mix of Latinas, Southeast Asians, and Chinese. Despite this ethnic clustering, however, in all of the hotels observed or of which informants were aware, occupations are mixed in their ethnic and racial composition. Moreover, workers' awareness of ethnic occupational dispersal in other hotels precludes a firm association between ethnicity and economic status overall.

The Role of Labor Processes

Hotel labor processes vary in their tendencies to separate or connect workers, and thus in their impacts on ethnic and occupational divisions. Jobs that involve cooperation and physical proximity—and mobility and authority structures that accord benefits to those who forge linkages outside their own groups—tend to soften inter-group boundaries, generating communication and cohesion among them. By contrast, jobs in which work is dispersed and/or independent, and in which upward mobility channels are limited or absent, tend to leave prior ethnic cleavages intact and may even enhance them. A contrast of housekeeping and food service work helps clarify such labor process distinctions.

The process of cleaning hotel rooms offers little opportunity or encouragement for the formation of bonds among ethnic groups. Housekeeping departments are headed by an executive housekeeper—a management position responsible for the overall management and financial planning of the department. Below this position, the elaboration of the occupational structure depends on the size of the property. In one typical case of a 32-floor hotel, two assistant executive housekeepers manage the day-to-day operation of the department, including scheduling, grievances and problem resolution, discipline, and organizing special projects such as training or the periodic flipping of mattresses. The executive and assistant executive housekeepers may be either male or female and tend to be hired from outside the hotel. Below them are the immigrant operations staff components of the department: linen runners (men, two in this case), who often assign work and do the strenuous work of transporting linens to and from the room cleaners' work sites; housemen (four), who do the heavy cleaning work such as lifting, garbage emptying, and window washing; inspectresses (two), who do spot-checks of the room cleaners' work, oversee the replenishment of supplies, and generally make sure the work process runs smoothly; and room cleaners (here, 48 of them), who clean the rooms after use, in preparation for new occupants.

Although elsewhere room cleaners work in teams, in San Francisco they labor alone. They have no explicit need to interact with, or rely upon, others in completing their daily room quotas. Although they engage fleetingly with linen runners and housemen, these assistants serve a large number of cleaners and their ties with any individual or group tend to be limited. Cleaners assigned to the same floor may see each other in passing, but vigilant supervisors and the demands of the job make it unwise to spend time conversing. Because managers often assign individuals from a single nationality to work on a particular floor, the on-the-job relationships that *are* formed, tend to enhance the cohesiveness of the group. Nor do upward mobility structures in housekeeping foster inter-group ties. The job of inspectress presents the main

Eg.: Little appor. for formation of bonds in house-keeping

avenue for a room cleaner's advancement, since managers often hire inspectresses from the room cleaner ranks to facilitate communication with immigrants. Inspectress positions are few relative to the large number of room cleaners, however, and they require English language proficiency which many cleaners lack. Moreover, the material rewards and advancement possibilities of the position are limited and its stress is substantial, so that many cleaners are not interested in it. In fact, some who have become inspectresses, have moved back to cleaning rooms.

While the promise of upward mobility does not significantly encourage room cleaners to develop inter-occupational links, the power that inspectresses and linen attendants exert over cleaners does motivate some such alliances. Because these low-level managers tend to be relatively long-lived in their positions, they can persecute cleaners they dislike. Linen attendants can discriminate in the assignment of work; inspectresses can scrutinize each finished room for the inevitable streaked mirror corner or patch of dust, or indulge in such humiliating forms of chastisement as wiping off a dusty finger on a negligent room cleaner's cheek. In practice, individuals from particular ethnic groups tend to develop clientelistic ties with same-group managers, so that authority structures reinforce ethnic clustering in housekeeping. In such situations, workers from other groups anticipate unequal treatment, even if no favoritism is actually practiced. When it *is* practiced, ethnic factionalism can become marked. In one such housekeeping department, a Filipino linen attendant is thought to favor Filipina cleaners, causing sustained inter-group friction and rigidifying the boundaries of ethnic groups. In another, Chinese and Latina inspectresses are thought to be easier on their own, again causing cleaners from other groups to ally in their perceived mistreatment. In another case, a heretofore comfortably "Latino"

group was converted into one in which Salvadorans and Mexicans heartily mistrusted each other when a Salvadoran supervisor was employed. Union staff is well aware that it is the structure of authority that engenders divisiveness. In the words of one: "When the going is good, they are all Latinos. But when someone gets special treatment, then it's the Salvadorans against the Mexicans . . . or whoever" (interview, organizer #4, April 14, 1998).

Breaks provide room cleaners with an opportunity for socializing; however, language limitations and the lack of prior acquaintance lead such contacts to replicate prior divisions. Cleaners break for lunch at mid-day and most dine in the employees' cafeteria. At such times—as interviews attest and mid-day visits to cafeterias confirm—they tend to gather in groups of people they already know, or whose manner is comfortable due to shared culture and language. Latina, Korean, Vietnamese, and Chinese room cleaners—their job titles evident from their uniforms and their ethnic identity from their language, appearance (unreliably), and bottles of soy sauce and bowls of salsa and kim chee on their tables—dine at separate tables. In these ways, the labor processes of housekeeping work tend to enhance, or at least leave undisturbed, the divisions of gender, occupation, immigration status, and race/ethnicity. Thus, it is not surprising that union staff and workers report that friendship, trust, and leadership in housekeeping tend to follow ethnic lines. Food service staff, by contrast, have much more opportunity and motivation to interrelate. Food service labor processes vary significantly, depending on the type of dining room involved—be it coffee shop, luncheon grill, fine restaurant, or banquet hall. They vary in some of the tasks performed, in terms of whether servers deal directly with food preparers and bartenders, and in the number and kinds of intermediaries between them. To clarify the contrast with housekeeping for our purposes here, let us confine our discussion to the relations between food servers and their on-the-floor assistants in a typical coffee shop—that is, between waitresses and waiters, and the bussers who set and clear tables, the drink servers who take orders and deliver drinks, and the toast and coffee makers who keep these items flowing during the mealtime rush.

Food servers are relatively well paid and tipped. They are native-born and acculturated immigrant men and women who represent the facility to the public. Theirs is a high-stress job. In addition to the physical demands of lifting and carrying heavy trays, the dizzying pace of the mealtime peaks, and the pressure and organizational skills involved in the rapid filling of complex orders, servers confront the emotional claims, even abuse, of imperious guests who (in the words of one server) "want their chins to be wiped." Supervisors are also a major source of stress as they vie among each other for the best "spread sheet" among hotel dining rooms—the greatest number of customers served, the fewest complaints and employee absentees, the fewest disability claims, and the greatest number of part-time workers without benefits. While meeting such pressures, servers are expected to maintain a demeanor that is, in servers' terms, "as classy as the guests." To maintain their equilibrium and meet the pace and pressures of the job, servers rely on each other. They pick up each others' slack when one falls behind; they protect each other from the supervisor's censure; they exchange outbursts of frustration at the behavior of supervisors and guests; they may even take over a co-worker's difficult customer.

In this process, servers rely heavily on their immediate assistants—especially bussers, many of whom are English-speaking Filipino, Chinese, or Latino immigrants. Here, common language facilitates native-immigrant communication; proximity and the teamwork of carrying out a stressful job engender mutual appreciation and friendship. Just as servers ally with each other against the critical scrutiny of their supervisor, so, too, they ally with their assistants to complete their jobs in a way that makes them all look better. The bonds built by such alliance and cooperation can increase their assistants' incomes and lead to their economic advancement. Upward mobility possibilities for food service assistants are substantial in union hotels because of contract-mandated seniority and workers' right of access to better jobs. Food servers often sponsor English-speaking bussers in their bids to become servers. In non-union hotels, by contrast, union staff and workers observe that mobility out of food service assistance is almost non-existent. Union presence enhances the economic benefit of conscientious assistance in another way as well: while some food servers share their tips with assistants in non-union food service facilities as a matter of personal choice and informal practice, such sharing is actively encouraged in union hotels by the union's norms of member solidarity and mutual respect. As a result, bussers and servers believe that bussers' tip-related income is significantly greater in union shops.

Breaks provide an opportunity to cement such work-based relationships. Meal breaks are staggered in shifts on either side of the customers' mealtimes, and co-working food servers and assistants often take their breaks and dine together. Their tables, at such times, are much more diversely comprised than are those of room cleaners. They include natives as well as immigrants, food servers as well as their assistants, and individuals of diverse class and ethnicity. In sum, the labor processes of food service work tend to bridge the divides of gender, occupation, immigration status, race/ethnicity, and class, engendering natural lines of trust across them.

Finally, the placement of immigrants in the occupational structure tends to moderate—even transform—the potential cleavages of ethnicity, occupation, and labor process. As the foregoing census data demonstrate, the occupational clustering of immigrants is more marked than that of ethnic groups, in that certain occupations, such as cook, dishwasher, busser, and room cleaner are over three-fourths immigrant, and others, such as clerical workers and receptionists are over three-fourths native. This clustered proportion is only approached ethnically by the white share of receptionists and clerical workers (see Tables 4 and 5). Despite this immigrant clustering, however, both natives and immigrants are now represented in all occupations. This mixing has eliminated the strong native/immigrant and white/minority schisms that are anticipated in split labor markets, and were, indeed, present in Local 2 when such occupations as bartender were exclusively native white. As a result, natives and immigrants now share occupational concerns, and the category of "immigrant" constitutes a potential basis of worker identification that can span nationality and occupational divides. As the foregoing discussion of room cleaning and food service demonstrated, the realization of this potential is mediated by labor processes. Let us now turn to the ways that union intervention can, and has, played a role.

The Universalizing Transformation of H.E.R.E. Local 2

The demographic shifts within the hotel workforce, in combination with the mediating influences of occupational structure and labor process, not only elaborated the potential bases for fragmentation within the union's clientele, but created a sharp disjuncture between the increasingly immigrant, minority, and female character of the workforce and the predominantly native-born white male character of union influence

and leadership. This disjuncture and potential for divisiveness alone, however, was insufficient to alter Local 2's orientation toward underrepresented groups. Rather, as has been found in studies of unions nationally (Cornfield 1989, 1993), shifts in the union's organizational structure and ideological orientation, and a crisis in its organizing environment were key to its assertive inclusion of lower-status groups. Local 2 emerged from this embattled period with an established position of legitimacy and power in the industry and an ideology and set of organizational practices that were explicitly inclusive of women, minorities, and immigrants. Its route to this incorporation can be understood through the examination of three temporal periods: 1) the late 1800s until World War II, when hotel unions were formed and became established participants in the industry; 2) 1942 to 1975, when the industry was virtually entirely unionized and strike-free, although locals remained craft-based and operated according to hierarchical, bureaucratic organizational principles; and 3) 1975 to the present, when the craft locals were merged into an industrial union whose operating principles emphasized rank-and-file democracy.[5]

From Formation to Legitimation: The Late 1800s to World War II

San Francisco hotel workers began to unionize in the late 1800s. By the turn of the century, their locals were reported the most dynamic in the country and pro-union sentiment in the city was deemed "so strong that hardly any business man cares to defy it" (Josephson 1956:46). Always more inclusive

---

5. The data for this section have been drawn primarily from interviews with current and former union staff, perusal of local newspapers, and consultation of key historical records as noted at the outset.

than their parent organization, San Francisco locals took the lead within the international in pushing for an industrial, rather than craft, union structure. In 1937, they staged a huge work stoppage that affected about 10,000 workers at the peak of the tourist season, causing losses to hotels estimated at $6,500,000 (Josephson 1956:264–269). This strike established the power of unions in the industry, secured its first continuous collective bargaining agreements, and set the stage for a prolonged and bitter strike initiated in August 1941. It continued into December, when the U.S. entered the War.

Craft Union Hegemony: 1942 to 1975

When the Navy moved forces into San Francisco and housed its personnel in several large hotels, the hotel strike was promptly certified as requiring the emergency mediation of the War Labor Board. The resulting settlement consolidated virtually 100 percent union membership in the industry and ushered in a strike-free period of continuous labor-management contracts that persisted for almost 40 years. It also set up a collective bargaining structure that authorized H.E.R.E.'s Local Joint Executive Board to represent hotel craft locals, and two employer associations to represent hotel owners (Cobble and Merrill 1994; Josephson 1956:293–296; Kennedy 1952).

This craft union structure incorporated considerable internal inequity. Hotel jobs were hierarchically ranked in prestige and rewards, with the most valued and best remunerated positions going primarily to the individuals with the highest social status— native-born white men—and the least desirable positions going to the groups with the lowest social ranking—primarily women of color. Bartenders were at the top of the hierarchy with cooks a close second; room cleaners were at the bottom. As a review of union contracts and interviews with longtime

workers and union staff attest, these rankings were reflected in the attitudes of workers toward each other and in the influence of different groups within the H.E.R.E. Higher ranking crafts and workers were disdainful of those with lower status, friction between skilled and unskilled workers was substantial, and lower status crafts received decidedly poorer treatment in union contracts (see also, Damu 1981; Richmond 1981; Russell 1978). The leadership style of the individual who headed the Local Joint Executive Board from 1947 until 1975—Joseph Belardi (also president of the cook's local)—was authoritarian and personalistic, reflecting the top-down, bureaucratic business unionism prevalent in U.S. labor unions at the time.

Inclusive Industrial Unionism: 1975 to the Present

In the mid-1970s, this structure began to come under fire, due, initially, to changes in the ownership structure of the hotel industry. Beginning in the 1950s, and accelerating thereafter, chains and multinational corporations began to replace locally based hotel owners. In San Francisco, the old aristocracy of grand hoteliers dwindled and names such as I.T.T., T.W.A., Rockefeller, and Mitsubishi appeared on the ownership rosters of luxury hotels. Some of these opened without union contracts and hotel and restaurant union membership faltered. In an effort to stem the national tide of union decline and increase its clout relative to large corporations, H.E.R.E. initiated a nation-wide policy of merging its regional craft locals into inclusive industrial unions. Thus, in 1975 by top-down fiat, H.E.R.E. merged its five prior craft locals in San Francisco (food servers, cooks, bartenders, bellmen and room cleaners, and kitchen help) into a single democratic organization—Local 2.

Joseph Belardi was appointed interim president until elections could be held in

April 1978, bringing his authoritarian leadership style into the new organization. Business agents, who had been elected in the separate craft locals, were now appointed. An elected shop steward system was largely dismantled. Meetings were held rarely and dissenting voices went unrecognized. Belardi stated frequently that professionals, rather than workers, should run labor unions. Increasingly, he employed business agents drawn from hotel management, rather than the rank-and-file (Russell 1978:70—74). This leadership style conflicted with the reconfigured power relationships effected by the merger, which reduced the leverage of smaller, previously privileged crafts, whose members were primarily native-born white males. It also increased the leverage of larger, less privileged occupations, the largest of which was the room cleaners, who were primarily immigrant women of color. This change made the concerns, involvement, and support of previously marginal groups crucial to the success of union leadership and initiatives.

Alongside this change in organizational structure, new strains in organizational ideology entered the union, transmitted from the social movements that were galvanizing the region and state, and finding support from the newly empowered segments of union membership. From the late 1950s on, the San Francisco Bay Area was a dynamic center of political activity for civil rights, free speech, antiwar, environmental, women's, and minority power movements. The United Farm Workers union operated a vigorous boycott organization out of San Francisco. Ethnic communities mobilized around issues of housing, education, health care, and redevelopment (Castells 1983). Out of the ferment, a plethora of left-leaning political organizations sprang up espousing variants of economic and sociocultural democracy. In the late 1960s, individuals imbued with the ideology of these movements began to enter

the hotel industry as a place to implement their principles. By the mid-1970s, virtually every hotel department included workers informed by the principles of rank-and-file democracy and gender, racial, and ethnic equality. Political factions within the union proliferated. Not surprisingly, interim President Belardi's autocratic leadership style was a particular focus of discontent, engendering a range of opposition caucuses in the three-year period preceding the 1978 election. Belardi was soundly defeated in the election by a group of independent leftists and rank-and-file workers, whose slate included the first Asian in top office in the union's history (Damu 1981:69). This election consolidated the legitimacy of the new organizational ideology and brought a new set of players into union leadership.

As the 1975–1980 contract period came to a close, internal pressures peaked to radically reshape the union contract by ending the automatic contract rollovers of the previous 40 years with a strike. To define contract demands, the union initiated a series of "job classification" meetings bringing together workers by job category from across the city to identify shared concerns. These meetings began a process of building solidarity that resulted in a 94 percent pro-strike vote on July 7, 1980. The concerns of Latina and Asian immigrant women dominated the strike's agenda—a focus that union leaders of the period attribute to their ideological belief in rank-and-file democracy, and to the size of the room cleaner group which made their support in meetings and on the picket lines essential. "Respect for the maids" became the strike's rallying cry. Its core demands were an end to racial, ethnic, and gender discrimination in hiring and worker treatment, improved contract enforcement, the empowerment of elected shop stewards, compensatory wage increases for back-of-the-house workers, and room quotas and meals for maids.

Because the union had, as yet, no formal organizing department, member support was elicited by rank-and-file activists operating within certain hotel departments—especially among the room cleaners and food service staff at the St. Francis Hotel. Immigrants proved to be some of the most stalwart strike supporters despite their reputations as timid and unwilling to take a stand. A Chinese American room cleaner was assigned to the union negotiating team and given the floor to express her group's complaints to hotel management. The image of immigrant maids squaring off against corporate hotel managers captured the imagination and support of local newspapers, politicians, students, clergy, community groups, and other unions. The strike's settlement, on August 12, effected dramatic improvements in all demand areas, instituting the highest wages for hotel workers in any city in the nation (Richmond 1981).

The elation of the 1980 victory was soon overshadowed, however, by an accelerating organizing crisis that underscored the importance of securing the allegiance of previously marginal groups. The factional struggles of the late 1970s had caused the loss of some long-standing members, and the advent of several major non-union hotels eroded union density further. In 1984, Local 2 lost a citywide restaurant strike, thereby gutting its previously substantial restaurant membership, a majority of whom were Asian and Latino immigrants. Employers' manipulation of workers' immigrant status was a major contributor to the union's defeat, as employers played factions of Asian and Latino workers off against each other, fanned immigrant fears with the threat and actuality of INS raids, and appealed to the common bonds between ethnic employers and workers in order to undercut union appeals. In that same year, a top-down collective bargaining agreement between the management of the newly opening Ramada Renaissance hotel and several hotel unions was challenged in the courts and found unlawful because a majority of employees did not authorize union representation (Bernhard-Altmann 1961). This ruling disqualified Local 2's major prior means of securing recognition and meant that bottom-up organizing would be required for it to preserve or expand its constituency. In 1985, the restaurant owners' and the large hotel owners' collective bargaining associations disbanded, forcing the union to negotiate separately with each hotel and restaurant owner.

Faced with this organizing crisis and encouraged by its altered ideology and organizational structure, Local 2 responded with a concerted dedication of resources to organizing. The 1980 and 1984 strikes had shown that immigrants and women would have to be won for direct conflicts with employers to succeed. Thus, in preparation for the August 1986 hotel contract negotiations and with help from the International, newly-elected President Sherri Chiesa announced a "back to basics" campaign designed to build member involvement in every unionized hotel. In this campaign, the union developed new methods of reaching members and building commitment explicitly designed to incorporate immigrants. To free up staff for this endeavor and to increase the active involvement of members, it shifted the focus of field representatives away from traditional grievance filing and bureaucratic follow-up toward forms of member servicing that built organization. Rank-and-file workers were trained to take on the initial stages of grievance identification and conflict resolution, so that contracts would continue to be enforced and grievances, heard. A leadership council of rank-and-file leaders was established and met regularly to discuss work-based concerns and organizing strategy. The net for participation in this council was cast widely, including, not only shop stewards, as is conventional in such councils, but as many workers from each hotel department as wanted to take an active role.

This approach generated a strong member showing and good contract results in 1986. It was elaborated, refined, and extended to the city's major non-union hotels in 1989. In January 1996, realizing that an even greater dedication of resources would be necessary to stem the tide of union density erosion, the members voted overwhelmingly to move $200,000 from the union's strike fund to create an organizing fund, and to direct the $2 per member per month strike fund deduction to organizing. Currently, Local 2 assigns about one-third of its staff and financial resources to organizing—an organizing commitment that is one of the largest in the country for a union of its size. This investment has enabled it to maintain collective bargaining agreements with over 80 percent, and contracts with 78 percent, of the city's Class A hotels. These contracts set the standard for the local industry. Their terms are some of the best in the nation.

Immigration and Union Mobilization

Local 2 has had a major impact on intergroup relations at work. Because of its inclusive ideology and commitment to rank-and-file democracy, and also because of its organizational reconfiguration and need to consolidate its membership in the face of an organizing crisis, Local 2 has made an active effort to draw in immigrant workers. Its intervention has not only helped bridge sociocultural and economic cleavages, but effected overarching changes in the mediating institution itself—most importantly, in the organizing practices and in the decision-making and contractual structures of the union.

Organizing Practices and Immigrant Incorporation

Local 2 has evolved organizing practices attuned to the ways that the occupational structure and labor processes shape the relations among workforce groups. These practices involve distinctive ways of making contact acknowledging diversity, and building solidarity.

The 1980 strike not only brought to Local 2's collective attention the strategic importance of immigrant incorporation, it established a base of organizational knowledge as to the scale and manner of their involvement in the industry. One important discovery was that, while ethnicity was a major basis of trust among workers, leadership and interethnic relations were structured differently in different parts of the occupational structure and immigrant status could play a bridging role. This knowledge was utilized as the union developed its formal organizing structure and methods after 1985. Current staff and organizers emphasize the importance of building solidarity from the substratum of ethnicity. As one union officer put it:

Ethnic identity is key to organizing because organizing is about leadership and trust, and these are often structured along ethnic lines. It's all about leadership. You win when you have it and you lose when you don't (interview, officer #3, March 6, 1997).

Or in the words of a seasoned organizer:

Workers involvement is based in ethnicity, so organizing must be too. Organizing is getting people to take initiative, not just go along. If we have just one leader representing a big bunch of people, we don't build the depth of commitment, the sense of responsibility in each member, that we need. But if each member is touched by someone they care about—and that person is often someone from their own group—they have a reason to take risks. We need members to resolve the small problems. We won't survive if we don't reach new people and we can't do that unless existing members pick up the slack. We must have people understand from the start that they are the union, we aren't (interview, organizer #1, March 17, 1997).

Organizers recognize, however, that the kind and extent of ethnic clustering they can expect, and thus the extent to which organizers must treat ethnic groups separately, vary by department and occupation. Organizers assigned to stewarding must speak Spanish, since dishwashers are virtually all Latino and most meetings are held entirely in Spanish. In food service, English is the shared language and organizing approaches are not segmented by ethnicity. In housekeeping, where social relations tend to be confined to the ethnic group, organizers must be fluent in the major languages of the workforce—Spanish, Cantonese, Tagalog, and English. Translators and broken English are used to communicate with native speakers of other languages. Organizers find that there is some interethnic affiliation, even in housekeeping. For example, Chinese and Filipina maids tend to form separate social groupings, while Latinas of diverse nationalities tend to band together because of relatively greater background similarities and more cohesive community contexts.[6] Southeast Asians generally follow suit, although their group is more

loosely-knit and the Vietnamese may split off. Smaller groups affiliate more randomly, according to individual personalities, rather than ethnic background.

Ethnic schisms can be particularly marked and complex in non-union hotels because the discretionary power of managers is not limited by a union contract. In such situations, workers are highly dependent on their personal relationships with line managers. Patron-client ties between the two are often strong and the opportunity for ethnic and immigrant discrimination is great. Some managers try to bolster their status and gain illicit privileges by developing a clientele from a certain ethnic group—a practice that inflames interethnic antagonisms. Other managers play favorites within groups—a practice that fans interpersonal resentments and splinters ethnic groups. Yet others garner personal favors such as free house painting and yard work from undocumented immigrants, or make them pay for the "privilege" of working without overtime or benefits. These practices both anger and chasten immigrants, eliciting union support from some, but dampening the willingness of others to speak out. Not surprisingly, such managers vehemently urge their followers to oppose the union, so that militant pro- and anti-union factions often develop between groups and within the same ethnic group and job category in non-union hotels.

Organizers begin by identifying reputational leaders within each job category and department, a process that, itself, may be ethnically-segmented. One organizer described departmental differences in leadership development:

As an organizer—and the union's hotel field representatives are essentially organizers—you have to be aware of the differences among departments. When I'm dealing with housekeeping, the leaders will almost always be women,

---

6. Not only are the regional, cultural, linguistic, and social class backgrounds of Asian immigrants more diverse, but they tend to live in dispersed neighborhoods where religious, commercial, and social service institutions are segmented by nationality. By contrast, many Latinos co-occupy neighborhoods where contact and shared institutions foster a pan-Latino identity (Otis 1998; Wallace 1986, 1989; Wong 1998).

and you must find one from each (ethnic) group. Ultimately, you try to get the leaders to join forces. But I've never had the experience of having a leader in housekeeping who was from one group, but was so respected by two groups that she could lead both. In food service, though, I never know where my leaders are going to come from. They may be men or women; white, black, Asian, or Latino. In stewarding, you pretty much know your leaders will be Latinos (interview, organizer #3, February 18, 1998).

Another organizer underscored the importance of an ethnically-tailored approach in housekeeping:

In housekeeping, it's best if same leads same . . . both craft and ethnic group. Chinese room cleaners must be found to lead Chinese room cleaners. That's who they are most likely to trust. You can't expect a Chinese leader to move the Filipinas, or a Filipina leader to move the Latinas. This is especially true at the start, though later we may have trust built within a craft that goes beyond the ethnic group. You always have to have leaders within each craft, though, no matter what. People need to know that their leaders share their experience (interview, organizer #4, February 19, 1998).

Leaders from different groups and occupations gather in Local 2's Leadership Council where they hear the concerns of other crafts and groups and discuss strategies and prospects for organizing. Leaders, then, bring this information back to their clienteles with the goal of intensifying their commitment and involvement. Here, immigrant status comes into play. Especially in departments where immigrants are concentrated, but also in those that are predominantly native, organizers encourage the surfacing of pan-immigrant concerns. They identify such concerns as deserving of the attention of the entire organization, thereby bridging the divides of immigration status, ethnicity, and occupation.

The ethnic and immigrant diversity of workers sometimes necessitates creative means of making contact. The backgrounds of certain groups incline them against meetings and stimulate different forms of communication. A case in point is one set of Eastern European waiters who were stalwart union members, but "left their country to get away from meetings." In that instance, organizers met with workers at their regular coffee shop after work, heard their concerns and signed them up. In general, Local 2's organizers find that working through informal networks is a more effective means of expanding immigrant allegiance than is the usual organizational practice of holding formal meetings. They observe that immigrants have more extensive interpersonal networks in the industry than do native-born workers—especially whites and blacks. This interpersonal connectedness has distinct advantages in that it can multiply the consequences of convincing one worker more rapidly than is the case among natives.

Organizing in hotel departments in which immigrant workers are ethnically clustered, and running a union whose members are so organized, also requires meticulous attention to the even-handed treatment of groups. This involves, most fundamentally, respect for all languages—a principle that Local 2 articulated around the 1980 strike as "the equality of languages." Currently, the union's leaflets, contracts, and other written materials are printed in the four main languages of the workforce. Meetings are held in English and translators are present for Cantonese, Spanish, and Tagalog speakers. Translation is provided for smaller groups when co-workers cannot do so.

Organizers must also be careful, during work site visits, not to appear to favor any

Needs to cater to all ethnic (& craft) groups

group. One described this imperative as follows:

> Where groups are important, like in housekeeping, you must show equal respect to each group. It's a political task. If you go to the lunchroom, you start on one side, one day, with the Filipinas. Then, the next day, you start on the other side, with the Latinas—you reverse the order. You always have to practice equality of languages, at least for the major groups. Everything has to be available in at least four languages. Every group has to speak at meetings. Each group has to be heard (interview, organizer #1, March 17, 1998).

The symbolic appeal of the union must also represent all groups. Because the workforce is so diverse, Local 2 cannot base its appeal in the cultural experience of any single group. Leaders contrast its situation with that of H.E.R.E. Local 11 in Los Angeles, where hotel workers are overwhelmingly Latino and predominantly Mexican, so that the union's appeal to a "Mexican immigrant consciousness" is widely representative and effective. By contrast, Local 2 grounds its appeal in the unifying experience of work and gathers immigrant concerns beneath that overarching umbrella. It identifies workplace issues as matters of "respect"—of the equitable and dignified treatment to which all workers are entitled. The special difficulties of immigrants—for example, discrimination in their work assignments and benefits, threats of exposure to the INS, and demands that they perform clientelistic services—are phrased as matters of respect as well. This discourse links immigrants' concerns with those of natives and legitimates them as comparably worthy of union attention and managerial response. While Local 2 employs ethnic symbolism, it does so eclectically to demonstrate the inclusiveness of the organization and the normalcy

Discourse of "respect"

and universality of ethnic identity. Thus, the organization celebrates Chinese New Year as well as Cinco de Mayo. A range of ethnic foods is served on picket lines and chants and songs are translated into, at least, the four major languages. On one fondly-remembered occasion, fortune cookies bearing messages such as "health, happiness, and medical benefits come through a union contract," and "the union makes us strong," were smuggled into a potluck of ethnic foods sponsored by hotel management during a hard-fought organizing campaign.

Finally, the attempt to incorporate immigrant workers has drawn Local 2 into closer involvement with San Francisco's ethnic communities and their concerns. One Chinese American former room cleaner and union officer described the union's conscious reasoning behind this approach during the 1980 strike:

> We felt that immigrant workers could not be defended just by the union: they had to be defended by the communities in which they lived and of which they were part. Asians and Latinos were the most significant groups that had to be represented. Representation required communication in [people's] native languages and involvement in their community organizations (interview, officer #6, February 19, 1998).

Over the years, Local 2 has built ties to San Francisco's Chinese, Vietnamese, Cambodian, Laotian, Salvadoran, Filipino, and Mexican communities. Its contacts include churches, neighborhood associations, organizations that deal with health and affordable housing, various sorts of legal and immigrant defense organizations, as well as several broad community coalitions. Its outreach tends to be sporadic and issue-focused, however: it crescendos during organizing campaigns and subsides between them. Union leaders have taken positions on a range of issues that concern immigrants—from rent control and affordable housing, to U.S. immigration laws and even foreign policies. Such positions can be problematic because the workforce is so diverse. For example, Central American hotel workers include individuals who fled from the Sandinistas, and those who *were* Sandinistas; they include individuals who worked for the government during the civil wars in El Salvador and Guatemala, and those who were their victims. As a result, venturing outside the bounds of workplace concerns is a touchy matter for union leaders, since stances that win the allegiance of some, raise the ire of others.

Union Structures and Immigrant Incorporation

As noted, the 1975 merger formally incorporated immigrants into the organization as equal participants by opening up and democratizing the governance structure and establishing influence on the basis of one-person-one-vote. Beyond this initial externally mandated change, however, Local 2's conscious efforts to incorporate immigrants have stimulated further changes in its decision-making and contractual structures.

The leadership structure of the union was one of the first targets of change. As Local 2 launched its "back to basics" campaign to actively mobilize existing members, it became clear that it would have to challenge the institutional barriers to immigrant participation within the union. One of the most important of such barriers was the stipulation in H.E.R.E. bylaws that only citizens could hold union office. As a result, president-elect Sherri Chiesa brought to the H.E.R.E.'s 1986 annual conference a proposal that this stipulation be eliminated. Immigrants are crucial to hotel unions' success and must be accorded equal treatment, she argued eloquently—not only in San Francisco, but in

other U.S. cities as well. Her proposal encountered heated opposition, but in the end it prevailed. Immigrants have been represented in Local 2's top leadership ever since. Currently, the president is a native-born white man, the vice president is a Salvadoran immigrant man, and the secretary-treasurer is a Vietnamese immigrant woman.

Immigrants have been drawn into the union's organizational structure at lower levels as well. Currently, about 70 percent of its hotel representatives and staff now come from the rank-and-file; about one-fourth are immigrants. Staff readily acknowledge that organizers are not yet "representative enough" (they are still disproportionately native-born white males), and they hope to achieve a more representative mix. Many qualify this aspiration, however, with the observation that the sensitivity of an organizer to workers' concerns is more important than shared background. There are also advantages to being a linguistically-fluent outsider:

> You commonly hear that unions should have multi-ethnic organizing staff, and that's true. But if you are white, it can actually be easier to organize. No one thinks that you will play favorites. Whereas, if you're Latino, the Latinos think you are a countryman and the others think you will be biased toward Latinos. People also respect white organizers because they are clearly from this country; they are citizens and know their way about. Such a person is seen as a "serious person." People look up to you, they respect what you have to say (interview, organizer #6, March 18, 1998).

In October 1994, the union initiated a program in labor-management cooperation that further fostered the incorporation of immigrants. Through a contract signed with a multi-employer bargaining unit comprised of twelve of the largest hotels, it set up labor management teams to solve common problems without resort to the grievance process. These problem-solving teams were based in particular hotel departments and comprised of workers and line managers. They discussed employee training, scheduling, and discipline; they proposed improvements in the kitchen, banquet service, housekeeping, and food and beverage service. Workers and union staff, as well as formal evaluators of the program (Korshak 1995), indicate that it has been highly successful. Not only has it helped resolve important operational problems, but it has enhanced communication among workforce segments. In addition, the program empowers immigrants along with natives as legitimate contributors to the collective project.

Immigrant concerns have altered the terms of union contracts as well, as immigrants have become increasingly active and legitimate participants in the organization's leadership and daily operation. Six such changes are worthy of note. First, an extended leave policy was developed in the 1980–1983 contract, in response to grievances filed by Filipino workers who were denied leave to visit relatives in the Philippines, or who were fired when they failed to return "on time" after such visits.[7] Second, wording was inserted into the 1980–1983 contract specifying that "no employee . . . shall suffer any loss of seniority, compensation, or benefits due to any change in the employee's name or social security number." This provision protects immigrants who gave false names and/or social security numbers at the time of employment, and who either went in to change the information after obtaining legal immigration

status, or who were caught in its inaccuracy through the Social Security Administration's recent practice of verifying the social security numbers of large employers' workers.[8] Third, in the 1986–1989 contract, the union secured an immigrant assistance addendum to the legal benefit plan. This benefit was developed after the 1986 Immigration Reform and Control Act established fines for employers who knowingly employed undocumented workers, initiating a "scramble" among members to legalize their employment status. It has become the most used portion of the union's benefits package.

Fourth, language was inserted into the 1986–1989 contract stating that "in cases where it is appropriate to a particular job and where it is advantageous to the Hotel to have a position staffed by a multilingual employee, the Hotel recognizes this as an asset."[9] This provision was an outgrowth of certain managers' requests that English only be spoken on the job; its positive framing of immigrant "difference" is highly valued by workers. Fifth, as noted above, the labor-management cooperation program initiated in the largest hotels led to the use of the Education Fund—part of the Health and Welfare and Pension benefit package—to hold classes in English as a Second Language. Hotel managers support these classes because they improve the quality of the service they can provide; immigrant workers use them heavily, because language skills are a passport to upward mobility.

---

7. See 1980 Contract, General Rules, Section 14: Leave of Absence. This issue was highly controversial and contested in the contract negotiations, staff report, because it intruded into the realm of work rule restrictions and limited employers' ability to deploy labor as they like.

8. See 1980 Contract, Section 10: Change of Status. Hotel employers obtained a change to this section in the 1983–1986 contract, stating that falsification of such information at the time of employment could be grounds for discipline— even discharge. The union secured a companion change stipulating that the employer would meet with the union to discuss any "job related impact" on employees found to have problems with their residency status.

9. See 1986 Contract, Section 8: No Discrimination.

Finally, in 1994, a Child Care/Elder Care Program was added to the union's Health and Welfare and Pension benefit package. Its child care provision provides for "informal child care," to accommodate the practice common among immigrants of having a relative, rather than a child care professional, take care of children. Its elder care provision responds to the tendency for immigrants to live in extended families and bear responsibility for elders.

Mediating Institutions and Immigrant Incorporation . . .

This study underscores sociologists' claims that labor processes shape social relations at work, and it goes beyond such claims to show that labor processes affect union mobilization and immigrant incorporation as well. It demonstrates that jobs involving cooperation and physical proximity, and those whose mobility and authority structures accord benefits to individuals who forge linkages outside their groups, tend to blur immigrant-native and interethnic boundaries, generating communication and solidarity across them. By contrast, jobs in which work is solitary and independent, upward mobility avenues are limited or absent, and/or authority structures foster unequal ethnic privilege, tend to leave the cleavages of ethnicity and immigration status intact and may even intensify them. These labor process differences form the substratum for union mobilization: they affect the extent and kinds of workforce divisions that organizers encounter, the kinds of approaches that are necessary to bridge them, and the likely success of their solidarity-building efforts. . . .

All in all, the union's role in this process contrasts sharply with the immi-

grant exclusion practiced by many U.S. labor unions—such as the construction unions in Miami, whose exclusion of Cubans contributed to the emergence of a primarily non-union construction sector in which both workers and owners were Cuban immigrants (Grenier, et al. 1992). It also contrasts with the laissez-faire stance toward organizing the unorganized adopted by most established U.S. labor unions during the latter half of the 20th century—a stance that has only recently begun to shift (see Bronfenbrenner, et al. 1998). In the case examined here, far from driving immigrants into a separate labor market, the union has embraced them as legitimate and equal participants in the established one. Moreover, far from leaving them at the passive periphery of the organization, it has drawn them assertively into its leadership and daily decision-making. Because of the extreme diversity of its immigrant workers, Local 2's task has been much more daunting than that of the Clothing Workers' Union which took a comparably inclusive stance toward Latino immigrants in a Los Angeles waterbed factory (Delgado 1993). In the case analyzed here, union intervention has not only enhanced natives' and immigrants' interaction and accommodation, it has given them more to cooperate about. This demonstration signals the importance of further exploring the mix of organizational and contextual influences that shape labor union practices in particular instances.

REFERENCES

Bach, Robert. 1993. *Changing Relations: Newcomers and Established Residents in U.S. Communities.* New York: Ford Foundation.

Bernhard-Altmann. 1961. International Ladies' Garment Workers' Union, AFL-CIO, v. National Labor Relations Board and Bernhard-Altmann, a Texas Corporation. 81 Supreme Court 1603.

Bonacich, Edna. 1972. "A theory of ethnic antagonism: The split labor market." *American Sociological Review* 37, 5:547–559.

1973. "A theory of middleman minorities." *American Sociological Review* 38:583–594.

Bronfenbrenner, Kate, Sheldon Friedman, Richard W. Hurd, Rudolph A. Oswald, and Ronald L. Seeber, eds. 1998. *Organizing to Win: New Research on Union Strategies.* Ithaca and London: ILR/ Cornell University Press.

Castells, Manuel. 1983. *The City and the Grassroots: A Cross-Cultural Theory of Urban Social Movements.* Berkeley: University of California Press.

Cobble, Dorothy Sue and Michael Merrill. 1994. "Collective bargaining in the hospitality industry in the 1980s." In *Contemporary Collective Bargaining in the Private Sector,* Paula Voos, ed., 447–489. Madison, Wisconsin: I.R.R.A.

Cornfield, Daniel B. 1989. *Becoming a Mighty Voice: Conflict and Change in the United Furniture Workers of America.* New York: Russell Sage.

1993. "Integrating U.S. labor leadership: Union democracy and the ascent of ethnic and racial minorities and women into national union offices." *Research in the Sociology of Organizations* 12:51–74.

Damu, Jean. 1981. "Economic repression: The San Francisco hotel workers' strike." *The Black Scholar* 12, 1:68–71.

Delgado, Hector. 1993. *New Immigrants, Old Unions: Organizing Undocumented Workers in Los Angeles.* Philadelphia: Temple University Press.

Grenier, Guillermo, Alex Stepick, Debbie Draznin, Aline LaBorwit, and Steve Morriss. 1992. "On machines and bureaucracy: Controlling ethnic interaction in Miami's apparel and construction industries." In *Structuring Diversity: Ethnographic Perspectives on The New Immigration,* Louise Lamphere, ed., 35–64. Philadelphia: Temple University Press.

Hechter, Michael. 1978. "Group formation and the cultural division of labor." *American Journal of Sociology* 84, 2:293–317.

Horowitz, Morris A. 1960. *The New York Hotel Industry: A Labor Relations Study.* Cambridge, MA: Harvard University Press.

Josephson, Matthew. 1956. *Union House. Union Bar: The History of the Hotel and Restaurant Employees and Bartenders International Union AFL-CIO.* New York: Random House.

Kennedy, Van Dusen. 1952. *Arbitration in the San Francisco Hotel and Restaurant Industries.* Philadelphia: University of Pennsylvania Press.

Korshak, Stuart R. 1995. "Negotiating trust in the San Francisco hotel industry." *California Management Review* 38, 1 (Fall):117–137.

Lamphere, Louise, ed. 1992. *Structuring Diversity: Ethnographic: Perspectives on the New Immigration.* Chicago and London: University of Chicago Press.

Lamphere, Louise, Alex Stepick, and Guillermo Grenier, eds. 1994. *Newcomers in the Workplace: Immigrants and the Restructuring of the U.S. Economy.* Philadelphia: Temple University Press.

Lee, Patricia. 1990. "Sisters at the borders: Asian immigrant women and H.E.R.E. Local 2." In *Building Bridges: The Emerging Grassroots Coalition of Labor and Community.* Jeremy Brecher and Tim Costello, eds. 38–46. New York: Monthly Review Press.

Model, Suzanne. 1993. "The ethnic niche and the structure of opportunity: Immigrants and minorities in New York City." In *The "Underclass" Debate: Views from History,* Michael Katz, ed., 161–193. Princeton: Princeton University Press.

Neckerman, Kathryn M. and Joleen Kirschenman. 1991. "Hiring strategies, racial bias, and inner-city workers." *Social Problems* 38, 4:433–447.

Otis, Eileen M. 1998. "The reach and limits of Asian Pan ethnic identity: A case study of a community-based organization." University of California, Davis, Ph.D. Qualifying Paper, Department of Sociology (May 20).

Reskin, Barbara and Patricia Roos. 1990. *Job Queues, Gender Queues.* Philadelphia: Temple University Press.

Richmond, Al. 1981. "The San Francisco hotel strike." *Socialist Review* 11, 3:87–113.

Russell, James. 1978. "Letter from San Francisco: Rank-and-file union victory." *Radical America* 12, 5:70–74.

Stull, Donald D., Michael J. Broadway, and Ken C. Erickson. 1992. "The price of a good steak: Beef packing and its consequences for Garden City, Kansas." In *Structuring Diversity: Ethnographic Perspectives on The New Immigration,* Louise Lamphere, ed., 1–34. Philadelphia: Temple University Press.

Waldinger, Roger. 1992. "Taking care of the guests: The impact of immigrants on services—an industry case study." *International Journal of Urban and Regional Research* 16, 1:97–113.

Waldinger, Roger. 1997. "Black/immigrant competition re-assessed: New evidence from Los Angeles." *Sociological Perspectives* 40, 3:365–386.

Waldinger, Roger and Mehdi Bozorgmehr. 1996. *Ethnic Los Angeles.* New York: Russell Sage Foundation.

Wallace, Steven P. 1986. "Central American and Mexican immigrant characteristics and eco-

nomic incorporation in California." *International Migration Review* 20, 3:657–671.

Wallace, Steven P. 1989. "The new urban Latinos: Central Americans in a Mexican immigrant environment." *Urban Affairs Quarterly* 25, 2:239–264.

Wong, Bernard. 1998. *Ethnicity and Entrepreneurship: The New Chinese Immigrants in the San Francisco Bay Area.* Boston: Allyn and Bacon.

*[Handwritten notes: Upshot for 21: - The SF HERE Local 2 Union has been extremely successful b/c of its full inclusion & legitimation of immigr. • Immigrant-native & interethnic boundaries can be crossed if work req. cooperation & allows for upward mobility * Including immigrants in activism & leadership can be v. successful]*

READING 22

Behind the Label

The Return of the Sweatshop

Edna Bonacich and Richard P. Appelbaum

The apparel industry is probably the hardest industry the United States Department of Labor has ever faced.

—Gerald M. Hall[1], District Director U.S. Department of Labor

Where does the money from the sale of a $100 dress actually go? (See Figure 1.) The wholesale cost of a $100 dress made in the United States is about $50; half of the $100 sales price goes to the retailer. Of the $50 wholesale cost, 45 percent, or $22.50, is spent by the manufacturer on the fabric. Twenty-five percent, or $12.50, is profit and overhead for the manufacturer. The remaining 30 percent, or $15, goes to the

contractor, and covers both the cost of direct labor and the contractor's other expenses, and profit. Only 6 percent, $6, goes to the person who actually sewed the garment. Furthermore, this individual was more than likely to have been paid by the number of sewing operations performed than by the hour and to have received no benefits of any kind.

Sweatshops have indeed returned to the United States. A phenomenon of the apparel industry considered long past is back, not as a minor aberration, but as a prominent way of doing business. Every once in a while, an especially dramatic story hits the news: an Orange County family is found sewing in their home, where a seven-year-old child works next to his mother. Thai workers in

[Handwritten margin note: thesis]

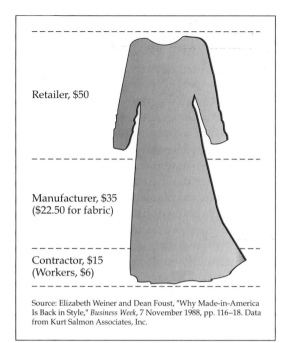

Retailer, $50

Manufacturer, $35
($22.50 for fabric)

Contractor, $15
(Workers, $6)

Source: Elizabeth Weiner and Dean Foust, "Why Made-in-America Is Back in Style," *Business Week*, 7 November 1988, pp. 116–18. Data from Kurt Salmon Associates, Inc.

FIGURE 1 The Distribution of the Proceeds of a $100 Dress

El Monte are found in an apartment complex, held against their will under conditions of semienslavement while earning subminimum wages. Kathie Lee Gifford, celebrity endorser of a Wal-Mart label, discovers that her line is being produced in sweatshops both offshore and in the United States and cries in shame on national television. The United States Department of Labor develops a program to make apparel manufacturers take responsibility for sweatshop violations. The President of the United States establishes the Apparel Industry Partnership to see if a solution can be found to the growth of sweatshops here and abroad. The nation is becoming aware that the scourge of sweatshops has returned.

Sweatshops first emerged in the United States apparel industry in the last decades of the nineteenth century with the development of the mass production of garments in New York City. Immigrant workers, mainly young women, slaved for long hours over their sewing machines in cramped and unsanitary factories, for very low wages. Workers eventually rebelled. In 1909 a major strike by shirtwaist factory workers, sometimes called the uprising of the 20,000, was the first mass strike by women workers in the United States. (Shirtwaists, a style of women's blouse, were the first mass-produced fashion items.) It was followed by strikes in other sectors of the industry. In 1911 the infamous Triangle Shirtwaist factory fire in New York resulted in the deaths of 146 young garment workers, and provoked public outrage. Organized, militant, and supported by an aroused public, the workers founded the garment unions and demanded contracts that would protect them against sweatshop production. New Deal legislation reinforced basic standards of labor for workers and protected their right to join or form independent unions. A combination of government protection and strong apparel unions helped to relegate garment sweatshops to the margins of the industry, until the 1970s, when they began to reappear.

What exactly is a "sweatshop"? A sweatshop is usually defined as a factory or a homework operation that engages in multiple violations of the law, typically the nonpayment of minimum or overtime wages and various violations of health and safety regulations. According to this definition, many of the garment factories in Los Angeles are sweatshops. In a sample survey conducted by the United States Department of Labor in January 1998, 61 percent of the garment firms in Los Angeles were found to be violating wage and hour regulations. Workers were underpaid by an estimated $73 million dollars per year.[2] Health and safety violations were not examined in that study, but in a survey completed in 1997, 96 percent of the firms were found to be in violation, 54 percent with deficiencies that could lead to serious injuries or death.

An emphasis merely on violations of the law fails to capture the full extent of what has been happening. In recent years the garment industry has been moving its production offshore to countries where workers earn much lower wages than are paid in the United States. In offshore production, some manufacturers may follow local laws, but the legal standard is so low that the workers, often including young teenagers, live in poverty, although they are working full time. The same problem arises in the United States. Even if a factory follows the letter of the law in every detail, workers may suffer abuse, job insecurity, and poverty. In 1990, according to the United States census, the average garment worker in Los Angeles made only $7,200, less than three-quarters of the poverty-level income for a family of three in that year. Thus we wish to broaden the definition of sweatshops to include factories that fail to pay a "living wage," meaning a wage that enables a family to support itself at a socially defined, decent standard of living. We include in the concept of a living wage the idea that people should be able to afford decent housing, given the local housing market, and that a family should be covered by health insurance. If wages fail to cover these minima, and if families with working members still fall below the official poverty line, they are, we claim, working in sweatshops.

Why are sweatshops returning to the apparel industry a number of decades after they had more or less disappeared? Why have their numbers grown so rapidly, especially in the last two decades of the twentieth century? And why has Los Angeles, in particular, become a center of garment sweatshops?

Global, Flexible Capitalism

The reemergence of apparel industry sweatshops is part of a much broader phenomenon, namely, the restructuring of global capitalism—a phenomenon we refer to as the new global capitalism. Starting in the 1970s, and accelerating rapidly especially in the 1980s and 1990s, the restructuring included a series of complex changes: a decline in the welfare state in most of the developed industrial countries; a growth in multinational corporations and an increase in global production; entry into manufacturing for export by many countries, among them some of the poorest in the world; a rise in world trade and intensification of competition; deindustrialization in the developed countries; a decrease in job security and an increase in part-time work; a rise in immigration from poorer countries to the richer ones; and renewed pressure on what remains of the welfare state.

These changes are all interconnected, and it is difficult to establish a first cause. Combined, they are associated with an effort by capitalists, supported by national governments, to increase profits and push back the effects of egalitarian movements that emerged in the 1960s and 1970s and that achieved some redistributive policies. The new global capitalism is characterized by an effort to let the free market operate with a minimum of government interference. At the same time, nations are themselves promoting the hegemony of the free market and imposing it as a standard for the entire world.

Among policies that foster the free market are the elimination of trade barriers and the encouragement of international free trade, as exemplified by the North American Free Trade Agreement (NAFTA) and the World Trade Organization (WTO); the insistence by strong states on the rights of their corporations to invest abroad with a minimum of local regulation; and pressure by state-backed, world financial institutions on developing countries that they restructure their political economies so as to foster free markets. Internal policies associated with the disestablishment of the welfare state have included deregulation, the privatization of state functions, and the minimization of state interference in business practices. In the United States, for example, affirmative action, welfare, and other efforts to increase equality through state intervention have come under attack.

The new global capitalism is often touted for its so-called flexibility. The decades of the 1980s and 1990s have been described as post-Fordist; i.e., we have moved beyond huge, mass-production plants making standardized products on the assembly line to a system in which smaller batches of specialized goods are made for an increasingly diverse consumer market. New systems of production, including contracting out the manufacture of specialized goods and services, and the ability to source goods and services wherever they can most efficiently be provided, enhance this flexibility. It is sometimes argued that the new, flexible production allows for more participation by the workers, by enabling them to develop several skills and encouraging them to use their initiative. Instead of repeating the same boring task, as did the workers on the Fordist assembly line, workers in the new factories may engage in more interesting, well-rounded activities. Critics have pointed out that, while some workers may benefit from the new, flexible production arrangements, others face increased job insecurity, more part-time and temporary work, a greater likelihood of working for subcontractors, and less opportunity for unionization. Flexibility for the employer may lead to the expansion of the contingent labor force, which must shift around to find short-term jobs as they arise.

One of the starkest areas of social change in the post–welfare state period has been the attack on organized labor. In the United States, for example, during the postwar period of the late 1940s and continuing until the 1960s, an accommodation was reached between industries and trade unions, whereby both sides accepted that the unions would help to eliminate industrial warfare under a "social contract." The tacit agreement was simple: In exchange for union-demanded wages and benefits, workers would cede control over industrial production to management. The cost of this arrangement would be paid for in the marketplace, through higher prices for goods, rather than in narrower profit margins. This arrangement particularly benefited workers in large, oligopolistic industries, where unions were strong and profits were substantial. The entire economy was seen to benefit from this arrangement because the workers would have enough expendable income to buy the products, thereby stimulating production, creating more jobs, and generating a spiraling prosperity. Even though unions were never popular with business, the major industries, including the apparel industry, came to accept them and accept the fact that they made an important contribution to the well-being of the economy at large.

This view of organized labor has collapsed. Business leaders in the United States now see unions as having pushed the price of American labor too high, thereby limiting the competitiveness of firms that maintain a workforce in this country. Firms in certain industries have increasingly moved offshore to seek out low-wage labor in less developed countries. Business owners and managers also see unions as irrelevant to the new flexible systems of production. Unions grew strong in response to the Fordist production regimes, but with more decentralized systems of production, they are viewed as rigid and impractical. Besides, argue the owners and managers, more engaged and multi-skilled workers no longer need union protection, as they share in a commitment to the firm's goals. Unions interfere with a company's flexibility and therefore hurt everyone, including the firm's employees.

Organized labor has been weakened by various federal policies, among them President Ronald Reagan's dismissal of the air traffic controllers, the appointment of antiunion members to the National Labor Relations

[handwritten top margin: Paradox of new global econ. = capital can move freely but not workers]

[handwritten left margin: How unions have been under-mined (in US)]

[handwritten left margin: ↓ in union membership]

Board, the acceptance of the right of firms to hire permanent replacements for strikers, the passage of NAFTA without adequate protections for workers in any of the three countries involved, and the encouragement of offshore contracting by special tariff provisions. The development of flexible production, with its contracting out and dispersion of production around the globe, has also served to undermine unions because it is much more difficult to organize workers in a decentralized system. As a result, the proportion of the workforce that is unionized has dropped, not only in the United States, but also in other industrial countries: in the United States from a high of 37 percent in 1946 to less than 15 percent of the total workforce in 1995, and only 11 percent of the private sector workforce.[3] These figures are much lower than for the rest of the industrial world.

[handwritten left margin: ? in immigr]

Another significant aspect of the new global economy has been the rise of immigration from the less developed to the industrialized countries. Local economies have been disrupted by the arrival of multinational corporations, and many people see no alternative but to seek a means of survival elsewhere. The involvement of the more developed countries in the economies and governments of the Third World is not a new phenomenon, and it has long been associated with emigration. The countervailing movements of capital and labor in opposite directions have often been noted.

[handwritten left margin: Proletarianization of peasantry]

What is new about the recent phase of global capitalism is the accelerated proletarianization of much of the world's remaining peasantry. Young women, in particular, have been drawn into the labor force to become the main workers in plants that engage in manufacturing for export. In many ways they are the ideal workforce, as they frequently lack the experience and alternatives that would enable them to demand higher

wages and better treatment. The poor working conditions are exacerbated by political regimes, often supported by the United States, that have restricted the workers' ability to organize and demand change.

The increased exploitation of workers in the Third World has a mirror image in the movement of immigrant workers to the more developed countries. Immigrants come not only because of economic dislocations that arise, in part, from the presence of foreign-capital in their homelands, but also because of political struggles that have ensued in connection with the Cold War and its aftermath. A paradox of the new global capitalism is that, although the right of capital to move freely is touted by the supporters of the free market, no such right is afforded labor. Immigration is restricted by state policies. One consequence has been the creation of so-called illegal workers, who are stripped of many basic legal rights. Immigrant workers, especially the undocumented, are more easily exploited than are native workers.

In sum, there has been a shift in the balance of power between capital and labor. Although the working class, including women and people of color, made important gains during the three postwar decades (from the late 1940s through the early 1970s), a backlash began developing in the 1970s and achieved full momentum by the 1980s. This backlash corresponds closely to the "great U-turn" in the United States and other capitalist economies, as a broadly shared postwar rise in living standards came to a halt. Conservative governments in the United States and Europe have implemented policies that favor capital and the free market over labor and other disadvantaged groups. Even political parties that have traditionally supported the working class, such as the Democrats in the United States and the Labour Party in Britain, have shifted to the right.

[handwritten right margin: BHOT]

[handwritten bottom margin: Connects to Wilson]

The reappearance of sweatshops is a feature of the new global, flexible capitalism. The original sweatshops disappeared with the growth of unions and the development of the welfare state. Today, with both of those institutions weakened, markets have been able to drive down wages and reduce working conditions to substandard levels in many labor-intensive industries, such as electronics, toys, shoes, and sports equipment. Indeed, almost every manufacturing industry and some services are pressed to reduce labor costs by minimizing job stability, by contracting out, by using more contingent (part-time and temporary) workers, by reducing benefits, and by attacking unions. But the apparel industry is leading the way.

The Apparel Industry as a Paradigm

The very word *sweatshop* has its roots in the apparel industry. It is ironic that the apparel industry should be a leader in any trend since, as an old industry, it has remained backward in many areas. Significant advances have been made in certain aspects of production, notably computer-assisted design, computer-assisted grading and marking, and computerized cutting, and there have been innovations in sewing machine technology and in the organization of work flow, but the core production process, namely the sewing of garments, is still low-tech. The primary unit of production continues to be a worker, usually a woman, sitting (or standing) at a sewing machine and sewing together pieces of limp cloth.

Garment production is labor intensive, and, unlike many other industries, it does not require much capital to get into the sewing business. Consequently, sewing factories proliferate and the industry is exceedingly competitive—probably more competitive than most. In some ways the apparel industry is the epitome of free market capitalism because the barriers to entry are so low. Less-developed countries take up apparel production as their first manufacturing industry in their efforts to industrialize. In the shift to global production and manufacturing for export, apparel has been in the vanguard. Clothing firms in the United States began to move production offshore to Asia as early as the late 1950s. Today apparel manufacturers in a number of developed countries are opening production facilities and employing workers in almost every country of the world. The result in the United States has been a rise in imports (see Figure 2), which started to grow in the 1960s and 1970s and grew at an explosive rate in the 1980s. In 1962 apparel imports totaled $301 million. They had tripled by the end of the decade, to $1.1 billion; increased another fivefold by 1980, to $5.5 billion; and nearly another fourfold by 1990, to $21.9 billion. By 1997, apparel imports totaled $42 billion; they are projected to exceed $50 billion in 1999. According to estimates by the American Apparel Manufacturers Association, imports accounted for 60 percent of the $101 billion wholesale apparel market.[4] Needless to say, this has greatly increased the level of competition within the industry, creating a pressure to lower wages in the United States garment industry to meet the low wages paid overseas. Global production is certainly expanding in other industries, but apparel is the most globalized industry of all.

The United States is the largest consumer market for apparel in the world. One measure for comparing consumption that does not depend on relative prices is the average per-capita fiber consumption. In 1989–90 (the latest available figures), the average annual world consumption was 17.9 pounds per person. For the United States it was 57.3 pounds. Japan came second with 48.9 pounds per capita. Latin America

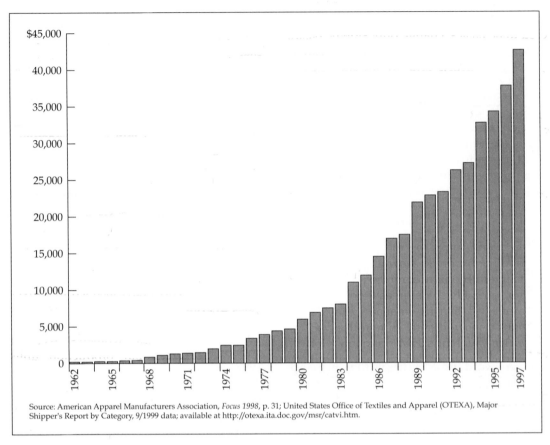

Source: American Apparel Manufacturers Association, *Focus 1998*, p. 31; United States Office of Textiles and Apparel (OTEXA), Major Shipper's Report by Category, 9/1999 data; available at http://otexa.ita.doc.gov/msr/catvi.htm.

FIGURE 2   Apparel Imports to the United States, 1962–1997 ($000,000)

consumed only 12.8 pounds per capita and Africa, 2.9. A primary target for exporting countries, the United States is by far the leading importer of apparel in the world.[5]

The return of sweatshops in the United States apparel industry can be partly, but not entirely, attributed to the dramatic rise in offshore production, and the concomitant increase in cheap imports. Much of the industry is driven by fashion, and sales of fashionable garments are highly volatile. The production of apparel is generally a risky business, which discourages heavy capital investment and limits the availability of capital for firms that want to expand or upgrade. The riskiness is augmented by time. Fashion

can change quickly. Apparel manufacturers want to be sure that any demand is fully met, but must be wary of overproducing garments that may fall out of fashion. The industry needs to be especially sensitive to changes in consumer taste, to respond quickly to these shifts, and to cease production of dying trends in a timely manner.

Needless to say, the industry tries to mold the fickle consumers' tastes as much as possible, by heavy advertising, by producing fashion shows and magazines, and by publicizing the opinions of pundits who predict and help to determine the trends. Indeed, the industry has considerable internal variation in terms of susceptibility to the

♀'s wear vs ♂'s

fashion dynamic. Some garments, considered to be basics, change only slowly. Basics include most underwear and sleepwear, T-shirts, sweatshirts and sweatpants, denim jeans, and men's shirts and pants. The areas of greatest fashion volatility include women's dresses, skirts and tops, women's bathing suits, and the broader area known as women's sportswear (casual clothing). Note that all the traditional basics also can include fashion lines. The Gap made a fortune by turning the basic T-shirt into a personal fashion statement. And denim jeans, when associated with the names of particular designers, have experienced the hot flash of fashion success.

Offshore production usually requires longer waiting times, thereby increasing the risk in making time-sensitive garments. Basics can be planned months in advance without much risk that the garments will go out of fashion. In the United States apparel industry, the production of basics has moved steadily offshore, and highly fashionable apparel is more likely to be made domestically. The distinction is likely to lessen with time as communication and transportation times decrease and as arrangements are made to produce garments in regions closer to their destination market. NAFTA, for example, has led to an enormous growth in Mexico's capacity to produce garments for the United States apparel industry. Because it is much closer to the United States than Asia is, some production has been shifted from Asia to Mexico; and it is possible that the production of more fashion-sensitive garments will also be shifted there. Their proximity also accounts for shifts to the Caribbean and Central America.

The fashion-sensitive sector of the industry is much more concentrated in women's wear than in men's wear, although this may be changing a little. Women in the United States spend twice as much on clothing as do men. The general difference between women's

and men's wear has led to a segregation between the two sectors of the industry. For example, the major industry newspaper is called *Women's Wear Daily*. The two major sectors eventually produced two unions: the International Ladies' Garment Workers' Union (ILGWU), which organized workers in the women's sector, and the Amalgamated Clothing and Textile Workers Union (ACTWU), which organized workers in the textile industry and the men's wear sector. The two unions merged in 1995 into UNITE, the Union of Needletrades, Industrial and Textile Employees, probably less because of a convergence between the two types of garment production than because of the loss of membership that each was suffering.

The differences have also led to a divergence in production systems. Men's wear has generally been produced in larger, mass-production factories, women's wear in smaller, contracted-out production units. Typically, in the production of women's clothing, apparel manufacturers (companies known by the brand names) design and engineer the garments, buy the textiles, and wholesale the completed clothing. The actual production of the garment, the cutting, sewing, laundering, and finishing, is usually done by independent contractors. Most garment contractors are sewing contractors, and they typically receive cut goods that their employees sew. Most garment workers are employed in small, contracting factories, sewing garments for manufacturers, who typically employ several contractors. Contracting out extends at the margins to industrial homework, with a single woman sitting at her home sewing machine, making clothing for a firm that employs her.

The contracting out of apparel production can be seen as an instance of flexible production. It allows apparel manufacturers to deal with fluctuations in fashion and seasons by hiring contractors when they need them and letting them go when they do not.

2 unions

merged

Fashion & prod timing

Contracting out

↓ elasticity

In this respect the apparel industry is at the cutting edge of the new global economy: It has used contracting out for decades and has developed this flexible production system to a fine art. Moreover, the contracting system has been extended to global production. Manufacturers not only employ local contractors, but also often conduct their offshore production through contracting rather than through the ownership of subsidiaries. The lack of fixed assets enables them to move production wherever they can get the best deal in terms of labor cost, taxes and tariffs, environmental regulation, or any other factor that influences the quality and cost of their products.

The virtue of the contracting system for the manufacturers is that they do not need to invest a cent in the factories that actually sew their clothes. Manufacturers engage in arm's-length transactions with their contractors, enabling them to avoid any long-term commitment to a particular contractor or location. The formal commitment lasts only as long as the particular job order. In practice, manufacturers may develop longer-term relationships with a core group of dependable contractors, attempting to ensure that they receive steady work. Nevertheless, the absence of firm ties provides maximum flexibility for manufacturers and the elimination of costly inefficiencies associated with having dependent subsidiaries. Contracting out enables manufacturers to hire only the labor they actually need.

The picture is not quite so rosy from the other side. Contractors, who in the United States and other advanced industrial countries, are often immigrants, must scramble to maintain steady work. And rather than employ a stable workforce, they pass the problems created by flexible production on to their workers. In the United States most garment workers are employed on a piece-work basis, so that they are paid only for the work they actually do. If the work is slow, they do not get paid. In offshore production, workers are more likely to receive an hourly wage rather than piece rate, but they are required to produce an arduous daily quota. Their hours and quotas, like those of piece-rate workers, are determined by the shifting demands of their manufacturers, at the height of the season or if they are producing a hot fashion item, they are required to work long hours. During a lull, they are laid off and go unpaid.

It is out of such a system of contracting out that the sweatshop is born. What provides wonderful flexibility for the manufacturer provides unstable work, impoverishment, and often abusive conditions for the workers.[6] The idea that smaller factories, making specialized goods for an ever-changing market, means that workers are better trained and have more responsibility has not worked out for most garment workers. Instead, they continue to engage in Fordist-style, highly repetitive, boring tasks conducted at high speeds. But because they no longer work in large, centralized production facilities, it is much more difficult for them to join or form unions. In addition, the mobility of the industry makes the task of unionizing formidable because manufacturers can easily shift production away from contractors that show any signs of labor unrest. In sum, flexible production, at least in the apparel industry, has created a much more effective engine for exploiting workers than existed before the new era of global capitalism.

Another feature of the apparel industry that probably portends developments in other industries is the rapidly growing power of retailers in the new global economy, another consequence of the emphasis on increased flexibility. No longer selling to a mass market, retailers now expect to supply consumers with the variety that they want when they want it. Rather than carrying large quantities of inventory in standardized products, the retailers want to be able to order and re-order popular items on short notice. They cherry-pick from designers' and manufacturers' lines, order only the items that they want, and expect them to be delivered rapidly.

The power of retailers in the apparel industry is partly a product of the highly competitive character of the industry, which often gives them the upper hand in dealing with manufacturers. Retailers have also gained power by engaging in their own direct offshore sourcing. Recently, their power has been consolidated by a series of mergers; by 1996 the four largest retailers in the United States accounted for two-thirds of the total value of national apparel retail sales. Consolidation has increased the ability to demand more from manufacturers in terms of price and speed, demands that reverberate all the way down the system to the workers, who bear the brunt of lower wages and faster production.

The idea of fashion and of constantly changing products for specialized markets is spreading far beyond apparel to many other industries. However, the very word "fashion" is deeply associated with the garment industry. It can be seen as the first industry that developed the notion of constantly changing styles. And as we have seen, its highly flexible production system is the most advanced of any industry.

We believe that the way apparel production is organized is a predictor of things to come in many industries and portends the expansion of the sweatshop. One can argue that in the return of the sweatshop we are witnessing a throwback to the earliest phases of the industrial revolution. But it is clear that what is going on is not only "old" but also very new. The apparel industry has managed to combine the latest ideas and technology for the rapid production and distribution of a highly diverse and continually changing product with the oppressive working conditions of the late nineteenth and early twentieth centuries, now coordinated over a global space. Consumers of clothing have never had it so good; the women and men huddled over sewing machines in foreign countries or immigrant enclaves suffer the consequences.

In Figure 3 the chief features of the apparel industry and the forces that are leading to the reemergence of sweatshops are summarized. Briefly, the forces are these. Apparel is a fashion-based, seasonal business and is, therefore, highly risky and competitive (1). It is also a low-tech, labor-intensive industry, particularly at the level of production, with low capital requirements and an ease of entry that encourage competitiveness (2). The unpredictability of the industry leads manufacturers to externalize their risk by contracting out the labor to enhance their flexibility (3). The ease of entry means that apparel production is usually the first industry chosen by countries seeking to industrialize (4). The availability of offshore garment factories with low-wage labor encourages United States apparel manufacturers to move some of their production to those facilities, leading to a rise in garment imports into the United States. Contracting out, both locally and abroad, also contributes to the competitive character of the industry (5 and 6).

The highly competitive nature of the apparel industry enables giant retailers to gain power over the manufacturers, a phenomenon that has increased as retailers have consolidated (7). In turn, the power and consolidation of the retailers adds to the competition between apparel manufacturers, who must jostle for favor with fewer and fewer buyers (8).

The movement of the apparel industry offshore, which is partly encouraged by United States trade and investment policies, combines with interventions by other industries (such as agribusiness) and neoliberal government policies, to create severe economic dislocations among certain segments

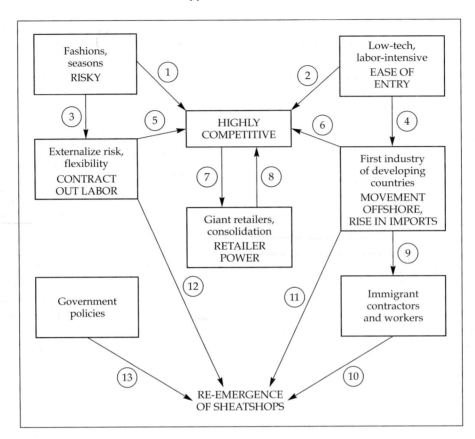

FIGURE 3   The Reemergence of Sweatshops in the United States Apparel Industry

Forces (cont'd) of the population, especially peasants, but also those in some urban occupations. Coupled with the impact of local wars, many with United States involvement, this dislocation results in a rise in immigration to the United States (9). Because of the low capital requirements for garment contracting, those immigrants with small amounts of capital or limited business experience enter the industry as entrepreneurs. Meanwhile, more impoverished immigrants become available to work in garment factories for low wages.

Co-ethnics

The reemergence of sweatshops is a product of the confluence of several forces: the availability of immigrant contractors and workers (10), the competition with low-priced imports (11), and the contracting system (12). These developments have all occurred within a context of government policies that support offshore production, contracting out, weakened organized labor, and a disenfranchised, immigrant working class (13).

The rise in apparel imports has inevitably led to a decline in jobs in the United States garment industry. Peak employment was reached in the early 1970s; since then, employment has more or less steadily decreased. In 1970 the industry employed 1,364,000 people. By 1980 the number had fallen to 1,264,000. In 1990 it was 1,036,000, and in 1997, 813,000. Between 1978 and 1998, in almost every state except California, employment in apparel declined. New York, New Jersey, Pennsylvania, and Massachusetts lost over half their apparel jobs.[7] In California, and mostly in Los Angeles, over 50,000 apparel jobs have been added since 1978.

Garment Production in Los Angeles

To the surprise of many people, Los Angeles is the manufacturing center of the nation, with 663,400 manufacturing jobs in 1997. Los Angeles has 5,900 more manufacturing jobs than the second city, Chicago, and over 200,000 more than Detroit, a distant third.[8] Equally surprising is the fact that the apparel industry is the largest manufacturing employer in Los Angeles County, with 122,500 employees enumerated by the Employment Development Department in April 1998. Thus, almost one out of five manufacturing employees in Los Angeles works in the apparel industry.

Los Angeles has felt the effects of global restructuring. Many high-paying union jobs in the automobile, tire, and aerospace industries have fled the region, while low-wage manufacturing jobs have multiplied. Among these low-wage industries, apparel "has been the lowest paying sector."[9] Nonetheless, Los Angeles is now the apparel manufacturing center of the United States. In Figure 4 apparel employment in the United States and in Los Angeles are compared. Los Angeles paralleled the United States decline during the early 1980s, but then broke away from the national pattern and continued to grow while the apparel industry employment nationwide continued to decline. The discrepancy is even clearer in Figure 5. More people are employed in the apparel industry in Los Angeles

FIGURE 4 Relative Growth in Apparel Employment, 1979–1997, Los Angeles and United States (1979 = 100)

Source: Goetz Wolff, "The Apparel Cluster: A Regional Growth Industry" (pamphlet prepared for the California College Fashion Symposium, Los Angeles, April 1997). Data from United States Bureau of Labor Statistics, Employment and Earnings Unadjusted, State and Area Unadjusted; available: http://stats.bls.gov/cgi-bin/srgate.

Note: Los Angeles accounts for 14 percent of the employment in the apparel industry in the United States.

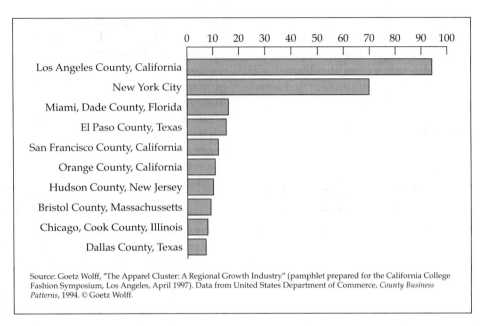

FIGURE 5   United States Counties with Highest Levels of Employment in the Apparel Sector (SIC 23), 1994 (000 Employees)

County than anywhere else in the nation, more than in New York, and far more than in any other center.

Why has Los Angeles become such an important center of garment production? First, the city is a center of design and fashion. The entertainment industry is, through its movies, television, and music, but the most visible manifestation of the city's creation of style. Southern California represents a way of life that is idealized and emulated around the globe. The names Hollywood, California, Disneyland, and even Los Angeles itself conjure up images of fantasy, fun in the sun, the freedom of the western frontier, informality, rebellion, and the end of formal tradition. It is not surprising that Los Angeles attracts people from many different cultures. Los Angeles sells itself along with its products, and its products benefit from all the connotations of the place. The apparel industry finds a natural haven in Los Angeles

in part because of the city's strong connections with fashion and style. The city produces style not only through the entertainment industry but also on its streets: The place creates fashion.

The apparel made in Los Angeles is overwhelmingly women's wear. In 1997 Goetz Wolff, using data from 1994 County Business Patterns, examined the various components of the local apparel industry to compare Los Angeles with the rest of the country. While 25 percent of the United States industry, excluding Los Angeles, was devoted to women's outerwear, 65 percent of the Los Angeles industry was so concentrated. Los Angeles accounts for about 10 percent of all apparel produced in the United States, but almost 25 percent of the women's outerwear. Even in men's wear, Los Angeles tends to specialize in the fashion end, making hip-hop wear, or beach wear, or other garments for which the styles keep changing.

The fact that Los Angeles is also a major center for immigration, especially from Asia, Mexico, and Central America, combines with the industry's focus on fashion to create a location where the most "advanced" forms of flexible production are found. Los Angeles's apparel industry has spawned thousands of contractors who can produce small lots rapidly. In other words, the city's industry is primed for the production of fashion at cheap prices. Immigrants play a vital role in two aspects of the industry. They provide the workforce and the entrepreneurship to run the contracting shops. Many of the immigrant workers are undocumented, which means that they often lack the political wherewithal to resist exploitation. Meanwhile, antiimmigrant movements in California have made immigrants increasingly vulnerable and exacerbated their political disadvantage.

Los Angeles has a long antiunion tradition and has been a harbor for entrepreneurial activity that does not need to worry about union organizing. Many industries are less unionized in Los Angeles than they are in most other major cities in the country, including, importantly, New York and San Francisco. This adds to the attractiveness of Los Angeles as a center of flexible production. Without having to worry about a unionized work force, manufacturers and retailers can arrange production to their own maximal advantage, shifting all the risk to the contractors, and ultimately to the workers. Los Angeles can indeed be described as the "sweatshop capital of the United States."

The Race to the Bottom

The United States is growing more and more unequal, with increasing polarization along race and class lines. In Los Angeles the forces that are shaping inequality in the United States are more sharply focused. The city is characterized by immense wealth, on the one hand, and extreme poverty on the other. A study by a committee of the California legislature found that, between 1989 and 1996, the number of very rich Angelinos, including those with annual incomes over $25 million, doubled, from 165 to 376 individuals, and that, from 1994 to 1996, the numbers of the very poor, those with annual incomes of less that $20,000, grew by 13.5 percent from 2.5 million to 2.9 million people. The authors conclude that there has been a hollowing out of the middle class and that the individuals and families hardest hit by the recession of the early 1990s have been slowest to benefit from the recovery, while the wealthy have benefited strongly.[10] Multimillionaires and even billionaires build mansions in the mountains and canyons and in rich communities such as Beverly Hills and Bel Air, while unemployment soars in the African-American community, and immigrant workers do almost all of the physical labor to eke out a bare survival for themselves and their children. The developments came to a dramatic climax in the so-called riots of April 1992, when all the bitterness of growing inequality in a land of plenty burst out in violent fury.

The apparel industry shows these same extremes. It is an industry in which some people, such as retailers and manufacturers, managers and professionals, bankers and real estate owners, are able to acquire immense wealth. Others, most notably garment workers, are among the poorest, lowest-paid workers in the city. The industry is not only polarized along class lines, it also has a clear racial and ethnic structure and hierarchy. The wealthy at the top are almost all of European extraction. At the bottom, the workers are mainly Latino immigrants, especially from Mexico and Central America, and a minority are Asian immigrants. In the middle are the entrepreneurs who run the contracting shops that employ the workers, and who are mainly immigrants from Asia (and, to a lesser extent, from Mexico and Central America).

Even the phenomenon of Asian middlemen became an issue in the 1992 uprising, as stores owned by Koreans became the target of much of the angry violence. These stores, mainly mom-and-pop operations, came to be seen as the direct oppressors and drainers of African-American and Latino neighborhoods. The situation has parallels in the garment industry. Latino and Asian garment workers come into contact mainly with Asian contractors (among whom Korean immigrants are especially significant) and rarely meet the wealthy whites who are making most of the money generated by their labor.

We must emphasize that the apparel industry is not fundamentally different from other industries in the United States. They all operate on the same principles of private property and competition, and they all demonstrate the same propensity for an increasing accumulation of wealth at the top and growing racial oppression and exploitation at the bottom. Because the apparel industry is one of the worst, it offers a good example of how our society works and how the system produces and reproduces an intensifying polarization by class and race.

NOTES

1. Gerald Hall, the District Director of the Department of Labor (DOL) in Los Angeles, made this statement at a meeting of DOL officials with the Coalition for Garment Workers, a coalition of advocate groups for garment workers, . . . in Los Angeles, 9 July 1998.
2. This figure is arrived at by taking the average back wages owed per factory for ninety days, \$3,631, multiplying it by four to get the back wages owed per year, and then by the estimated 5,000 contractors in Los Angeles. This method of calculating was suggested by Gerald Hall of the DOL, who at a meeting between the DOL and the Coalition for Garment Workers held on July 9, 1998, also reported the amount collected in back wages, per annum.
3. Kate Bronfenbrenner, Sheldon Friedman, Richard W. Hurd, Rudolph A. Oswald, and Ronald L. Seeber, eds., *Organizing to Win: New Research on Union Strategies* (Ithaca, N.Y.: ILR. Press. 1997), 2–3.
4. American Apparel Manufacturers Association, *Focus: An Economic Profile of the Apparel Industry* (Arlington, Va.: AAMA, 1998), 4. The apparel retail market in the United States reached \$180 billion in 1997.
5. Kitty Dickerson, *Textiles and Apparel in the Global Economy,* 2d ed. (New York: Macmillan, 1995), 202–206, 225–26.
6. See Ian M. Taplin, "Flexible Production, Rigid Jobs: Lessons from the Clothing Industry," *Work and Occupations* 22 (November 1995): 412–38; and "Rethinking Flexibility: The Case of the Apparel Industry," *Review of Social Economy* 54 (Summer 1996): 191–220.
7. American Apparel Manufacturers Association, *Focus 1998* (Arlington, Va.), p. 10. In New York City there has recently been a slight rise in apparel employment. The city's apparel and textile manufacturing employment peaked in the mid-1970s at 250,000, but had dropped to 82,500 by 1996. In 1997 it rose to 84,000. "Rebirth of New York's Apparel Industry," *Apparel Industry Magazine,* March 1998, p. 12.
8. Daniel Taub, "L.A. Beats Out Chicago as No. 1 Manufacturing Center," *Los Angeles Business Journal,* 9 March 1998, p. 5. See also Louis Uchitelle, "The New Faces of U.S. Manufacturing: California's Vision of the Future: Thriving, but with Fewer High-Wage Jobs," *New York Times,* 3 July 1994, sec. 3, p. 1; Jack Kyser, *Manufacturing in Los Angeles* (Los Angeles, Calif.: Economic Development Corp., 1997).
9. Taub, "L.A. Beats Out Chicago," p. 5.
10. California Legislature, Assembly Select Committee on the California Middle Class, *The Distribution of Income in California and Los Angeles: A Look at Recent Current Population Survey and State Taxpayer Data* (Sacramento, 1998). The chairman of the committee is Assemblyman Wally Knox.

Upshot: - Increase is sweatshops due largely to new global econ.
•Call for ↑ flexibility shaped by new int'l trade laws &
•Anti-union neolib ideology
- Paradox: System good for manufs, bad for workers
- Apparel industry is worse & LA is center of it in US

∽ **READING** 23 ∽

Maid in L.A.

Pierrette Hondagneu-Sotelo

The title of this chapter was inspired by Mary Romero's 1992 book, *Maid in the U.S.A.*, but I am also taking the pun to heart: most Latina immigrant women who do paid domestic work in Los Angeles had no prior experience working as domestics in their countries of origin. Of the 153 Latina domestic workers that I surveyed at bus stops, in ESL classes, and in parks, fewer than 10 percent reported having worked in other people's homes, or taking in laundry for pay, in their countries of origin. This finding is perhaps not surprising, as we know from immigration research that the poorest of the poor rarely migrate to the United States; they simply cannot afford to do so.

Some of the Latina immigrant women who come to Los Angeles grew up in impoverished squatter settlements, others in comfortable homes with servants. In their countries of origin, these women were housewives raising their own children, or college students, factory workers, store clerks, and secretaries; still others came from rural families of very modest means. Regardless of their diverse backgrounds, their transformation into housecleaners and nanny/housekeepers occurs in Los Angeles. I emphasize this point because images in popular culture and the media more or less

Excerpts from *Domestica: Immigrant Workers Cleaning and Caring the Shadows of Affluence* by Pierrette Hondagneu-Sotelo. Copyright © 2001, The Regents of the University of California. Reprinted by permission of The University of California Press.

identify Latinas with domestic workers—or, more precisely, as "cleaning gals" and "baby-sitters," euphemisms that mask American discomfort with these arrangements. Yet they take on these roles only in the United States, at various points in their own migration and settlement trajectories, in the context of private households, informal social networks, and the larger culture's racialized nativism.

Who are these women who come to the United States in search of jobs, and what are those jobs like? Domestic work is organized in different ways, and in this chapter I describe live-in, live-out, and housecleaning jobs and profile some of the Latina immigrants who do them and how they feel about their work. . . .

Live-in Nanny/Housekeeper Jobs

For Maribel Centeno, newly arrived from Guatemala City in 1989 at age twenty-two and without supportive family and friends with whom to stay, taking a live-in job made a lot of sense. She knew that she wouldn't have to spend money on room and board, and that she could soon begin saving to pay off her debts. Getting a live-in job through an agency was easy. The *señora*, in her rudimentary Spanish, only asked where she was from, and if she had a husband and children. Chuckling, Maribel recalled her initial misunderstanding when the *señora*, using her index finger, had drawn an imaginary

"2" and "3" in the palm of her hand. "I thought to myself, well, she must have two or three bedrooms, so I said, fine. 'No,' she said. 'Really, really big.' She started counting, 'One, two, three, four . . . two-three rooms.' It was twenty-three rooms! I thought, *huy!* On a piece of paper, she wrote '$80 a week,' and she said, 'You, child, and entire house.' So I thought, well, I have to do what I have to do, and I happily said, 'Yes.'"

"I arrived on Monday at dawn," she recalled, "and I went to the job on Wednesday evening." When the *señora* and the child spoke to her, Maribel remembered "just laughing and feeling useless. I couldn't understand anything." On that first evening, the *señora* put on classical music, which Maribel quickly identified. "I said, 'Beethoven.' She said, 'Yeah,' and began asking me in English, 'You like it?' I said 'Yes,' or perhaps I said, '*Sí,*' and she began playing other cassettes, CDs. They had Richard Clayderman and I recognized it, and when I said that, she stopped in her tracks, her jaw fell open, and she just stared at me. She must have been thinking, 'No schooling, no preparation, no English, how does she know this music?'" But the *señora,* perhaps because of the language difficulty, or perhaps because she felt upstaged by her live-in's knowledge of classical music, never did ask. Maribel desperately wanted the *señora* to respect her, to recognize that she was smart, educated, and cultivated in the arts. In spite of her best status-signaling efforts, "They treated me," she said, "the same as any other girl from the countryside." She never got the verbal recognition that she desired from the *señora.*

Maribel summed up her experiences with her first live-in job this way: "The pay was bad. The treatment was, how shall I say? It was cordial, a little, uh, not racist, but with very little consideration, very little respect." She liked caring for the little seven-year-old boy, but keeping after the cleaning of the twenty-three-room house, filled with marble floors and glass tables, proved physically impossible. She eventually quit not because of the polishing and scrubbing, but because being ignored devastated her socially.

Compared to many other Latina immigrants' first live-in jobs, Maribel Centeno's was relatively good. She was not on call during all her waking hours and throughout the night, the parents were engaged with the child, and she was not required to sleep in a child's bedroom or on a cot tucked away in the laundry room. But having a private room filled with amenities did not mean she had privacy or the ability to do simple things one might take for granted. "I had my own room, with my own television, VCR, my private bath, and closet, and a kind of sitting room—but everything in miniature, Thumbelina style," she said. "I had privacy in that respect. But I couldn't do many things. If I wanted to walk around in a T-shirt, or just feel like I was home, I couldn't do that. If I was hungry in the evening, I wouldn't come out to grab a banana because I'd have to walk through the family room, and then everybody's watching and having to smell the banana. I could never feel at home, never. Never, never, never! There's always something invisible that tells you this is not your house, you just work here."

It is the rare California home that offers separate maid's quarters, but that doesn't stop families from hiring live-ins; nor does it stop newly arrived Latina migrant workers from taking jobs they urgently need. When live-ins cannot even retreat to their own rooms, work seeps into their sleep and their dreams. There is no time off from the job, and they say they feel confined, trapped, imprisoned.

"I lose a lot of sleep," said Margarita Gutiérrez, a twenty-four-year-old Mexicana who worked as a live-in nanny/housekeeper. At her job in a modest-sized condominium in Pasadena, she slept in a corner of a three-year-old child's bedroom. Consequently, she found herself on call day and night with the child, who sometimes went several days without seeing her mother because of the latter's schedule at an insurance company. Margarita was obliged to be on her job twenty-four hours a day; and like other live-in nanny/housekeepers I interviewed, she claimed that she could scarcely find time to shower or brush her teeth. "I go to bed fine," she reported, "and then I wake up at two or three in the morning with the girl asking for water, or food." After the child went back to sleep, Margarita would lie awake, thinking about how to leave her job but finding it hard to even walk out into the kitchen. Live-in employees like Margarita literally have no space and no time they can claim as their own.

Working in a larger home or staying in plush, private quarters is no guarantee of privacy or refuge from the job. Forty-four-year-old Elvia Lucero worked as a live-in at a sprawling, canyon-side residence, where she was in charge of looking after twins, two five-year-old girls. On numerous occasions when I visited her there, I saw that she occupied her own bedroom, a beautifully decorated one outfitted with delicate antiques, plush white carpet, and a stenciled border of pink roses painstakingly painted on the wall by the employer. It looked serene and inviting, but it was only three steps away from the twins' room. Every night one of the twins crawled into bed with Elvia. Elvia disliked this, but said she couldn't break the girl of the habit. And the parents' room lay tucked away at the opposite end of the large (more than 3,000 square feet), L-shaped house.

Regardless of the size of the home and the splendor of the accommodations, the boundaries that we might normally take for granted disappear in live-in jobs. They have, as Evelyn Nakano Glenn has noted, "no clear line between work and non-work time," and the line between job space and private space is similarly blurred.[1] Live-in nanny/housekeepers are at once socially isolated and surrounded by other people's territory; during the hours they remain on the employers' premises, their space, like their time, belongs to another. The sensation of being among others while remaining invisible, unknown and apart, of never being able to leave the margins, makes many live-in employees sad, lonely, and depressed. Melancholy sets in and doesn't necessarily lift on the weekends.

Rules and regulations may extend around the clock. Some employers restrict the ability of their live-in employees to receive telephone calls, entertain friends, attend evening ESL classes, or see boyfriends during the workweek. Other employers do not impose these sorts of restrictions, but because their homes are located on remote hillsides, in suburban enclaves, or in gated communities, their live-in nanny/housekeepers are effectively kept away from anything resembling social life or public culture. A Spanish-language radio station, or maybe a *telenovela,* may serve as their only link to the outside world.

Food—the way some employers hoard it, waste it, deny it, or just simply do not even have any of it in their kitchens—is a frequent topic of discussion among Latina live-in nanny/housekeepers. These women are talking not about counting calories but about the social meaning of food on the job. Almost no one works with a written contract, but anyone taking a live-in job that includes "room and board" would assume that adequate meals will be included. But what constitutes an adequate meal? Everyone has a different idea, and using the subject like a secret handshake, Latina domestic workers often greet one another by talking about the problems of managing food and meals on the job. Inevitably, food enters their conversations.

No one feels the indignities of food more deeply than do live-in employees, who may not leave the job for up to six days at a time. For them, the workplace necessarily becomes the place of daily sustenance. In some of the homes where they work, the employers are out all day. When these adults return home, they may only snack, keeping on hand little besides hot dogs, packets of macaroni and cheese, cereal, and peanut butter for the children. Such foods are considered neither nutritious nor appetizing by Latina immigrants, many of whom are accustomed to sitting down to meals prepared with fresh vegetables, rice, beans, and meat. In some employers' homes, the cupboards are literally bare. Gladys Villedas recalled that at one of her live-in jobs, the *señora* had graciously said, " 'Go ahead, help yourself to anything in the kitchen.' But at times," she recalled, "there was nothing, nothing in the refrigerator! There was nothing to eat!" Even in lavish kitchens outfitted with Subzero refrigerators and imported cabinetry, food may be scarce. A celebrity photographer of luxury homes that appear in posh magazines described to a reporter what he sees when he opens the doors of some of Beverly Hills' refrigerators: "Rows of cans of Diet Coke, and maybe a few remains of pizza."[2]

Further down the class ladder, some employers go to great lengths to economize on food bills. Margarita Gutiérrez claimed that at her live-in job, the husband did the weekly grocery shopping, but he bought things in small quantities—say, two potatoes that would be served in half portions, or a quarter of a watermelon to last a household of five all week. He rationed out the bottled water and warned her that milk would make her fat. Lately, she said, he was taking both her and the children to an upscale grocery market where they gave free samples of gourmet cheeses, breads, and dips, urging them all to fill up on the freebies. "I never thought," exclaimed Margarita, formerly a secretary in Mexico City, "that I would come to this country to experience hunger!"

Many women who work as live-ins are keenly aware of how food and meals underline the boundaries between them and the families for whom they work. "I never ate with them," recalled Maribel Centeno of her first live-in job. "First of all, she never said, 'Come and join us,' and secondly, I just avoided being around when they were about to eat." Why did she avoid mealtime? "I didn't feel I was part of that family. I knew they liked me, but only because of the good work I did, and because of the affection I showered on the boy; but apart from that, I was just like the gardener, like the pool man, just one more of their staff." Sitting down to share a meal symbolizes membership in a family, and Latina employees, for the most part, know they are not just like one of the family.

Food scarcity is not endemic to all of the households where these women work. In some homes, ample quantities of fresh fruits, cheeses, and chicken stock the kitchens. Some employer families readily share all of their food, but in other households, certain higher-quality, expensive food items may remain off-limits to the live-in employees, who are instructed to eat hot dogs with the children. One Latina live-in nanny/housekeeper told me that in her employers' substantial pantry, little "DO NOT TOUCH" signs signaled which food items were not available to her; and another said that her employer was always defrosting freezer-burned leftovers for her to eat, some of it dating back nearly a decade.

Other women felt subtle pressure to remain unobtrusive, humble, and self-effacing, so they held back from eating even when they were hungry. They talked a lot about how these unspoken rules apply to fruit. "Look, if they [the employers] buy fruit, they buy three bananas, two apples, two pears. So if I eat one, who took it? It's me," one woman said, "they'll know it's me." Another nanny/housekeeper recalled: "They would bring home fruit, but without them having to say it, you just knew these were not intended for you. You understand this right away, you get it." Or as another put it, *"Las Americanas* have their apples counted out, one for each day of the week." Even fruits growing in the garden are sometimes contested. In Southern California's agriculture-friendly climate, many a residential home boasts fruit trees that hang heavy with oranges, plums, and peaches, and when the Latina women who work in these homes pick the fruit, they sometimes get in trouble.[3] Eventually, many of the women solve the food problem by buying and bringing in their own food; early on Monday mornings, you see them walking with their plastic grocery bags, carting, say, a sack of apples, some chicken, and maybe some prepared food in plastic containers.

The issue of food captures the essence of how Latina live-in domestic workers feel about their jobs. It symbolizes the extent to which the families they work for draw the boundaries of exclusion or inclusion, and it marks the degree to which those families recognize the live-in nanny/housekeepers as human beings who have basic human needs. When they first take their jobs, most live-in nanny/housekeepers do not anticipate spending any of their meager wages on food to eat while on the job, but in the end, most do—and sometimes the food they buy is eaten by members of the family for whom they work.

Although there is a wide range of pay, many Latina domestic workers in live-in jobs earn less than minimum wage for marathon hours: 93 percent of the live-in workers I surveyed in the mid-1990s were earning less than $5 an hour (79 percent of them below minimum wage, which was then $4.25), and they reported working an average of sixty-four hours a week. Some of the most astoundingly low rates were paid for live-in jobs in the households of other working-class Latino immigrants, which

provide some women their first job when they arrive in Los Angeles. Carmen Vasquez, for example, had spent several years working as a live-in for two Mexican families, earning only $50 a week. By comparison, her current salary of $170 a week, which she was earning as a live-in nanny/ housekeeper in the hillside home of an attorney and a teacher, seemed a princely sum.

Many people assume that the rich pay more than do families of modest means, but working as a live-in in an exclusive, wealthy neighborhood, or in a twenty-three-room house, provides no guarantee of a high salary. Early one Monday morning in the fall of 1995, I was standing with a group of live-in nanny/housekeepers on a corner across the street from the Beverly Hills Hotel. As they were waiting to be picked up by their employers, a large Mercedes sedan with two women (a daughter and mother or mother-in-law?) approached, rolled down the windows, and asked if anyone was interested in a $150-a-week live-in job. A few women jotted down the phone number, and no one was shocked by the offer. Gore Vidal once commented that no one is allowed to fail within a two-mile radius of the Beverly Hills Hotel, but it turns out that plenty of women in that vicinity are failing in the salary department. In some of the most affluent Westside areas of Los Angeles—in Malibu, Pacific Palisades, and Bel Air—there are live-in nanny/housekeepers earning $150 a week. And in 1999, the *Los Angeles Times* Sunday classified ads still listed live-in nanny/ housekeeper jobs with pay as low as $100 and $125. Salaries for live-in jobs, however, do go considerably higher. The best-paid live-in employee whom I interviewed was Patricia Paredes, a Mexicana who spoke impeccable English and who had legal status, substantial experience, and references. She told me that she currently earned $450 a week at her live-in job. She had been promised a raise to $550, after a room remodel was finished, when she would assume weekend housecleaning in that same home. With such a relatively high weekly salary she felt compelled to stay in a live-in job during the week, away from her husband and three young daughters who remained on the east side of Los Angeles. The salary level required that sacrifice.

But once they experience it, most women are repelled by live-in jobs. The lack of privacy, the mandated separation from family and friends, the round-the-clock hours, the food issues, the low pay, and especially the constant loneliness prompt most Latina immigrants to seek other job arrangements. Some young, single women who learn to speak English fluently try to move up the ranks into higher-paying live-in jobs. As soon as they can, however, the majority attempt to leave live-in work altogether. Most live-in nanny/housekeepers have been in the United States for five years or less; among the live-in nanny/housekeepers I interviewed, only two (Carmen Vasquez and the relatively high-earning Patricia Paredes) had been in the United States for longer than that. Like African American women earlier in the century, who tired of what the historian Elizabeth Clark-Lewis has called "the soul-destroying hollowness of live-in domestic work,"[4] most Latina immigrants try to find other options.

Until the early 1900s, live-in jobs were the most common form of paid domestic work in the United States, but through the first half of the twentieth century they were gradually supplanted by domestic "day work." Live-in work never completely disappeared, however, and in the last decades of the twentieth century, it revived with vigor, given new life by the needs of American families with working parents and young children—and, as we have seen, by the needs of newly arrived Latina immigrants, many of them unmarried and unattached to families. When these women try to move up from live-in domestic work, they see few job alternatives. Often, the best they can do is switch to another form of paid domestic work, either as a live-out nanny/housekeeper or as a weekly housecleaner. When they do such day work, they are better able to circumscribe their work hours, and they earn more money in less time.

Live-out Nanny/Housekeepers

When I first met twenty-four-year-old Ronalda Saavedra, she was peeling a hard-boiled egg for a dog in the kitchen of a very large home where I was interviewing the employer. At this particular domestic job, the fifth she had held since migrating from El Salvador in 1991, she arrived daily around one in the afternoon and left after the children went to bed. On a typical day, she assisted the housekeeper, a middle-aged woman, with cleaning, laundry, and errands, and at three o'clock she drove off in her own car to pick up the children—a nine-year-old boy, whom she claimed was always angry, and his hyperactive six-year-old brother.

Once the children were put to bed, Ronalda Saavedra drove home to a cozy apartment that she shared with her brother in the San Fernando Valley. When I visited her, I saw that it was a tiny place, about half the size of the kitchen where we had first met; but it was pleasantly outfitted with new bleached oak furniture, and the morning sunshine that streamed in through a large window gave it a cheerful, almost spacious feel. Ronalda kept a well-stocked refrigerator, and during our interview she served me *pan dulce,* coffee, and honeydew melon.

Like many other women, Ronalda had begun her work stint in the United States with a live-in job, but she vastly preferred living out. She slept through the night in peace, attended ESL classes in the morning, ate what she wanted when she wanted it, and talked daily on the phone with her fiancé. All this was possible because live-out jobs are firmly circumscribed. Even when women find it difficult to say no to their employers when they are asked, at the last minute, to stay and work another hour or two, they know they will eventually retreat to their own places. So while the workday tasks and rhythms are similar to those of live-ins, the job demands on live-outs stop when they exit the houses where they work and return to their own homes, usually small and sometimes crowded apartments located in one of Los Angeles' many Latino neighborhoods. For such women with husbands or with children of their own, live-out jobs allow them to actually live with their family members and see them daily.

Live-out nanny/housekeepers also earn more money than live-ins. Most of them work eight or nine hours a day, and of those I surveyed, 60 percent worked five days a week or fewer. Their mean hourly wages were $5.90—not an exorbitant wage by any means, but above the legal minimum, unlike the wages of their peers in live-in jobs. Ronalda earned $350 for her forty-hour workweek, making her hourly wage $8.75. On top of this, her employer gave her an additional $50 to cover gasoline expenses, as Ronalda spent a portion of each afternoon driving on errands, such as going to the dry cleaners, and ferrying the children home from school and then to and from soccer practices, music lessons, and so on. In the suburban landscape of Los Angeles, employers pay an extra premium for nanny/housekeepers who can provide this shuttling service. Only Latina nanny/ housekeepers with experience, strong references, English skills, and an impressive array of certificates and licenses enjoy earnings that reach Ronalda's level.

Today, most Americans who hire a domestic worker to come into their homes on a daily basis do so in order to meet their needs for *both* housecleaning and child care. Most Latina nanny/housekeepers work in households where they are solely responsible for these tasks, and they work hard to fit in the cleaning and laundry (most of them don't cook) while the children are napping or at school. Some of them feel, as one woman said, that they need to be "octopuses," with busy arms extended simultaneously in all directions. A big part of their job requires taking care of the children; and various issues with the children present nanny/housekeepers with their greatest frustrations. Paradoxically, they also experience some of their deepest job satisfaction with these children with whom they spend so much time.

After what may be years of watching, feeding, playing with, and reprimanding the same child from birth to elementary school, day in and day out, some nanny/housekeepers grow very fond of their charges and look back nostalgically, remembering, say, when a child took her first steps or first learned nursery rhymes in Spanish. Ronalda, an articulate, highly animated woman who told stories using a lot of gestures and facial expressions, talked a great deal about the children she had cared for in her various jobs. She imitated the voices of children she had taken care of, describing longingly little girls who were, she said, "*muy* nice" or "*tan* sweet," and recalled the imaginary games they would play. Like many other nanny/housekeepers, she wept freely when she remembered some of the intimate and amusing moments she had spent with children she no longer saw. She also described other children who, she said, were dour, disrespectful, and disobedient.

Many live-out nanny/housekeepers made care work—the work of keeping the children clean, happy, well nourished, and above all safe—a priority over housecleaning duties. This sometimes created conflicts with their employers, who despite saying that their children should come first still expected a spotless house. "The truth is," explained Teresa Portillo, who looked after a child only on the weekends, "when you are taking care of children, you can't neglect anything, absolutely nothing! Because the moment you do, they do whatever little *travesura,* and they scrape their knees, cut themselves or whatever." Nanny/housekeepers fear they will be sent to jail if anything happens to the children.

Feeding the children is a big part of the job. Unlike their live-in peers, when live-out nanny/housekeepers talk about food, they're usually concerned with what the children eat or don't eat. Some of them derive tremendous pleasure and satisfaction from bringing the children special treats prepared at their own homes—maybe homemade flan or *pan con crema,* or simply a mango. Some nanny/housekeepers are also in charge, to their dismay, of feeding and cleaning the children's menagerie of pets. Many feel disgusted when they have to bathe and give eyedrops to old, sick dogs, or clean the cages of iguanas, snakes, lizards, and various rodents. But these tasks are trivial in comparison to the difficulties they encounter with hard-to-manage children. Mostly, though, they complain about permissive, neglectful parents.

Not all nanny/housekeepers bond tightly with their employers' children, but most are critical of what they perceive as their employers' careless parenting—or, more accurately, mothering, for their female employers typically receive the blame. They see mothers who may spend, they say, only a few minutes a day with their babies and toddlers, or who return home from work after the children are asleep. Soraya Sanchez said she could understand mothers who work "out of necessity," but all other mothers, she believed, hired nanny/housekeepers because they just didn't like being with their own kids. "*La Americana* is very selfish,

she only thinks about herself," she said. "They prefer not to be with their children, as they find it's much easier to pay someone to do that." Her critique was shared by many nanny/housekeepers; and those with children of their own, even if they didn't live with them, saw their own mothering as far superior. "I love my kids, they don't. It's just like, excuse the word, 'shitting kids,' " said Patricia Paredes. "What they prefer is to go to the salon, get their nails done, you know, go shopping, things like that. Even if they're home all day, they don't want to spend time with the kids because they're paying somebody to do that for them." For many Latina nanny/housekeepers, seething class resentments find expression in the rhetoric of comparative mothering.

When Latina immigrant women enter the homes of middle-class and upper-middle-class Americans, they encounter ways of raising children very different from those with which they are familiar. As Julia Wrigley's research has shown, the child-rearing values of many Latina and Caribbean nannies differ from those of their employers, but most are eager to do what middle-class parents want—to adopt "time out" discipline measures instead of swatting, or to impose limits on television viewing and Nintendo.[5] Some of them not only adapt but come to genuinely admire and appreciate such methods of child rearing. Yet they, too, criticize the parenting styles they witness close up in the homes where they work.

Some nanny/housekeepers encounter belligerent young children, who yell at them, call them names, and throw violent temper tantrums; and when they do, they blame the parents. They are aghast when parents, after witnessing a child scratch or bite or spit at them, simply shrug their shoulders and ignore such behavior. Parents' reactions to these incidents were a litmus test of sorts. Gladys Villedas, for example, told me that at her job, a five-year-old "grabbed my hair and pulled it really hard. Ay! It hurt so much I started crying! It really hurt my feelings because never in my own country, when I was raising my children, had this happened to me. Why should this happen to me here?" When she complained to her employer, she said the employer had simply consulted a child-rearing manual and explained that it was "a stage." Not all nanny/housekeepers encounter physically abusive children, but when they do, they prefer parents who allow them the authority to impose discipline, or who back them up by firmly instructing their children that it is not okay to kick or slap the nanny. Nanny/housekeepers spoke glowingly about these sorts of employers.

When nanny/housekeepers see parent-child interactions in the homes where they work, they are often put off and puzzled by what they observe. In these moments, the huge cultural gulf between Latina nanny/housekeepers and their employers seems even wider than they had initially imagined. In the home where Maribel Centeno was working as a live-out nanny/housekeeper, she spent the first few hours of her shift doing laundry and housecleaning, but when a thirteen-year-old boy, of whom she was actually very fond, arrived home from school, her real work began. It was his pranks, which were neither malicious nor directed at her, and parental tolerance of these, that drove her crazy. These adolescent pranks usually involved items like water balloons, firecrackers, and baking soda made to look like cocaine. Recently the boy had tacked up on his parents' bedroom door a condom filled with a small amount of milk and a little sign that read, "Mom and Dad, this could have been my life." Maribel thought this was inappropriate behavior; but more bewildering and disturbing than the boy's prank was his mother's reaction—laughter. Another nanny/housekeeper had reacted

with similar astonishment when, after a toddler tore apart a loaf of French bread and threw the pieces, balled like cotton, onto the floor, the father came forward not to reprimand but to record the incident with a camcorder. The regularity with which their employers waste food astounds them, and drug use also raises their eyebrows. Some nanny/housekeepers are instructed to give Ritalin and Prozac to children as young as five or six, and others tell of parents and teens locked in their separate bedrooms, each smoking marijuana.

Nanny/housekeepers blame permissive and neglectful parents, who they feel don't spend enough time with their own children, for the children's unruly behavior and for teen drug use. "The parents, they say 'yes' to everything the child asks," complained one woman. "Naturally," she added, "the children are going to act spoiled." Another nanny/housekeeper analyzed the situation this way: "They [the parents] feel guilty because they don't spend that much time with the kids, and they want to replace that missed time, that love, with toys."

Other nanny/housekeepers prided themselves on taming and teaching the children to act properly. "I really had to battle with these children just to get them to pay attention to me! When I started with them, they had no limits, they didn't pick up their toys, and they couldn't control their tempers. The eldest—oof! He used to kick and hit me, and in public! I was mortified," recalled Ronalda Saavedra. Another woman remarked of children she had looked after, "These kids listened to me. After all, they spent most of the time with me, and not with them [the parents]. They would arrive at night, maybe spend a few moments with the kids, or maybe the kids were already asleep." Elvia Areola highlighted the injustice of rearing children whom one will never see again. Discussing her previous job, she said, "I was the one who taught that boy to talk, to walk, to read, to sit! Everything! She [the child's mother] almost never picked him up! She only picked him up when he was happy." Another nanny/housekeeper concluded, "These parents don't really know their own children. Just playing with them, or taking them to the park, well, that's not raising children. I'm the one who is with them every day."

Nanny/housekeepers must also maneuver around jealous parents, who may come to feel that their children's affections have been displaced. "The kids fall in love with you and they [the parents] wonder, why? Some parents are jealous of what the kids feel toward you," said Ronalda Saavedra, "I'm not going to be lying, 'I'm your mommy,' but in a way, children go to the person who takes care of them, you know? That's just the way it is." For many nanny/housekeepers, it is these ties of affection that make it possible for them to do their job by making it rewarding. Some of them say they can't properly care for the children without feeling a special fondness for them; others say it just happens naturally. "I fall in love with all of these children. How can I not? That's just the way I am," one nanny/housekeeper told me. "I'm with them all day, and when I go home, my husband complains that that's all I talk about, what they did, the funny things they said." The nanny/housekeepers, as much as they felt burdened by disobedient children, sometimes felt that these children were also a gift of sorts, one that parents—again, the mothers—did not fully appreciate. "The babies are so beautiful!" gushed Soraya Sanchez. "How is it that a mother can lose those best years, when their kids are babies. I mean, I remember going down for a nap with these little babies, how we'd cuddle. How is it that a person who has the option of enjoying that would prefer to give that experience to a stranger?" Precisely because of such feelings, many Latina immigrants who have children try to find a job that is compatible with their own family lives. Housecleaning is one of those jobs.

Housecleaners

Like many working mothers, every weekday morning Marisela Ramírez awoke to dress and feed her preschooler, Tomás, and drive him to school (actually, a Head Start program) before she herself ventured out to work, navigating the dizzying array of Los Angeles freeways. Each day she set off in a different direction headed for a different workplace. On Mondays she maneuvered her way to Pasadena, where she cleaned the stately home of an elderly couple; on Tuesdays she alternated between cleaning a home in the Hollywood Hills and a more modest-sized duplex in Glendale; and Wednesdays took her to a split-level condominium in Burbank. You had to keep alert, she said, to remember where to go on which days and how to get there!

By nine o'clock she was usually on the job, and because she zoomed through her work she was able to finish, unless the house was extremely dirty, by one or two in the afternoon. After work, there were still plenty of daylight hours left for Marisela to take Tomás to the park, or at least to take him outside and let him ride down the sidewalk on his kid-sized motorized vehicle before she started dinner. Working as a housecleaner allowed Marisela to be the kind of wife and mother she wanted to be. Her job was something she did, she said, "because I have to"; but unlike her peers who work in live-in jobs, she enjoyed a fairly regular family life of her own, one that included cooking and eating family meals, playing with her son, bathing him, putting him to bed, and then watching *telenovelas* in the evenings with her husband and her sister. On the weekends, family socializing took center stage, with *carne asadas* in the park; informal gatherings with her large Mexican family, which extended throughout Los Angeles; and music from her husband, who worked as a gardener but played guitar in a weekend *ranchera* band.

Some might see Marisela Ramírez as just another low-wage worker doing dirty work, but by her own account—and gauging by her progress from her starting point—she had made remarkable occupational strides. Marisela had begun working as a live-in nanny/housekeeper in Los Angeles when she was only fifteen years old. Ten years later, the move from live-in work to housecleaning had brought her higher hourly wages, a shorter workweek, control over the pace of work, and flexibility in arranging when she worked. Cleaning different houses was also, she said, less boring than working as a nanny/housekeeper, which entailed passing every single day "in just one house, all week long with the same routine, over and over."

For a while she had tried factory work, packaging costume jewelry in a factory warehouse located in the San Fernando Valley, but Marisela saw housecleaning as preferable on just about every count. "In the factory, one has to work very, very fast!" she exclaimed. "And you can't talk to anybody, you can't stop, and you can't rest until it's break time. When you're working in a house, you can take a break at the moment you wish, finish the house when you want, and leave at the hour you decide. And it's better pay. It's harder work, yes," she conceded, "but it's better pay."

"How much were you earning at the factory?" I asked.

"Five dollars an hour; and working in houses now, I make about $11, or even more. Look, in a typical house, I enter at about 9 A.M., and I leave at 1 P.M., and they pay me $60. It's much better [than factory work]." Her income varied, but she could usually count on weekly earnings of about $300. By pooling these together with her husband's

and sister's earnings, she was able to rent a one-bedroom bungalow roofed in red tile, with a lawn and a backyard for Tomás's sandbox and plastic swimming pool. In Mexico, Marisela had only studied as far as fifth grade, but she wanted the best for Tomás. Everyone doted on him, and by age four he was already reading simple words.

Of the housecleaners I surveyed, the majority earned, like Marisela, between $50 and $60 per housecleaning, which usually took about six hours. This suggests an average hourly wage of about $9.50, but I suspect the actual figure is higher. Women like Marisela, who drive their own cars and speak some English, are likely to earn more than the women I surveyed, many of whom ride the buses to work. Marisela was typical of the housecleaners whom I surveyed in having been in the United States for a number of years. Unlike nanny/housekeepers, most of the housecleaners who were mothers themselves had all their children with them in the United States. Housecleaning, as Mary Romero has noted, is a job that is quite compatible with having a family life of one's own.

Breaking into housecleaning is tough, often requiring informal tutelage from friends and relatives. Contrary to the image that all women "naturally" know how to do domestic work, many Latina domestic workers discover that their own housekeeping experiences do not automatically transfer to the homes where they work. As she looked back on her early days in the job, Marisela said, "I didn't know how to clean or anything. My sister taught me." Erlinda Castro, a middle-aged women who had already run her own household and raised five children in Guatemala, had also initially worked in live-in jobs when she first came to Los Angeles. Yet despite this substantial domestic experience, she recalled how mystified she was when she began housecleaning. "Learning how to use the chemicals and the liquids" in the different households was confusing, and, as friends and employers instructed her on what to do, she began writing down in a little notebook the names of the products and what they cleaned. Some women learn the job by informally apprenticing with one another, accompanying a friend or perhaps an aunt on her housecleaning jobs.

Establishing a thriving route of *casas* requires more than learning which cleaning products to use or how to clean quickly and efficiently. It also involves acquiring multiple jobs, which housecleaners typically gain by asking their employers if they have friends, neighbors, or acquaintances who need someone to clean their houses; and because some attrition is inevitable, they must constantly be on the lookout for more *casas*. Not everyone who wants to can fill up her entire week.

To make ends meet when they don't have enough houses to clean, Latina housecleaners in Los Angeles find other ways to earn income. They might prepare food—say, tamales and *crema*—which they sell door-to-door or on the street; or they might sell small amounts of clothing that they buy wholesale in the garment district, or products from Avon, Mary Kay cosmetics, and Princess House kitchenware. They take odd jobs, such as handing out flyers advertising dental clinics or working at a swap meet; or perhaps they find something more stable, such as evening janitorial work in office buildings. Some housecleaners work swing shift in garment factories, while others work three days a week as a nanny/housekeeper and try to fill the remaining days with housecleaning jobs. Some women supplement their husband's income by cleaning only one or two houses a week, but more often they patch together a number of jobs in addition to housecleaning.

Housecleaning represents, as Romero has written, the "modernization" of paid domestic work. Women who clean different houses on different days sell their labor services, she argues, in much the same way that a vendor sells a product to various customers.[6] The housecleaners themselves see their job as far preferable to that of a live-in or live-out nanny/housekeeper. They typically work alone, during times when their employers are out of the home; and because they are paid "by the job" instead of by the hour, they don't have to remain on the job until 6 or 7 P.M., an advantage much appreciated by women who have families of their own. Moreover, because they work for different employers on different days, they are not solely dependent for their livelihood on one boss whom they see every single day. Consequently, their relationships with their employers are less likely to become highly charged and conflictual; and if problems do arise, they can leave one job without jeopardizing their entire weekly earnings. Since child care is not one of their tasks, their responsibilities are more straightforward and there are fewer points of contention with employers. Housecleaning is altogether less risky.

Housecleaners also see working independently and informally as more desirable than working for a commercial cleaning company. "The companies pay $5 an hour," said Erlinda Castro, whose neighbor worked for one, "and the women have to work their eight hours, doing up to ten, twenty houses a day! One does the vacuuming, the other does the bathroom and the kitchen, and like that. It's tremendously hard work, and at $5 an hour? Thank God, I don't have to do that." Two of the women I interviewed, one now a live-out nanny/housekeeper and the other a private housecleaner, had previously worked for cleaning services, and both of them complained bitterly about their speeded-up work pace, low pay, and tyrannical bosses.

Private housecleaners take enormous pride in their work. When they finish their job, they can see the shiny results, and they are proud of their job autonomy, their hours, their pay, and, most important, what they are able to do with their pay for themselves and for their families. Yet housecleaning brings its own special problems. Intensive cleaning eventually brings physical pain, and sometimes injury. "Even my bones are tired," said fifty-three-year-old Lupe Vélez; and even a relatively young woman like Celestina Vigil at age thirty-three was already reporting back problems that she attributed to her work. While most of them have only fleeting contact with their employers, and many said they work for "good people," just about everyone has suffered, they said, "inconsiderate persons" who exhort them to work faster, humiliate them, fail to give raises, add extra cleaning tasks without paying extra, or unjustly accuse them of stealing or of ruining a rug or upholstery. And the plain old hard work and stigma of cleaning always remain, as suggested by the answer I got when I asked a housecleaner what she liked least about her job. "The least?" she said, with a wry smile. "Well, that you have to clean."

Domestic Job Trajectories and Transnational Motherhood

As we have seen, private paid domestic work is organized into sub-occupations, each with different pay scales, tasks, and hours. Although they share many similarities, each job arrangement has its own different problems and rewards. In this section I discuss the movement between the three suboccupations and some of the family characteristics of the women who fill these jobs.

Some researchers have called live-in domestic work "the bridging occupation," because in various periods and places, it allowed rural migrant women to acculturate to the city and learn new ways of living.[7] Unlike Irish immigrant women or the black women who went from the South to the North to work as domestics in the early twentieth century, and unlike many private domestics in Europe and Latin America in the past, most Latina immigrants doing paid domestic work in the United States are *not* new to the city. Yet for many of them in Los Angeles today, especially those who are single and have very limited options for places to work and live, live-in jobs do serve as an initial occupational step. As table 1 shows, new arrivals and women who have lived in the United States five years or less concentrate in live-in jobs (60 percent). In contrast, the majority of housecleaners (83 percent) and live-out nanny/housekeepers (69 percent) have lived in the United States for more than five years. Some begin their live-in jobs literally within forty-eight hours after arriving in Los Angeles, while some housecleaners have lived in the United States for twenty years or more. For newly arrived immigrant

TABLE 1 Type of Domestic Work, Length of Residence in the United States, and Mean Hourly Wages

	Live-Ins (Percent) (n = 30)	Live-Outs (Percent) (n = 64)	Housecleaners (Percent) (n = 59)
Five Years or less in United States	60	31	17
More than five years in United States	40	69	83
Mean hourly wage	$3.80	$5.90	$9.50

women without papers, a live-in job in a private home may feel safer, as private homes in middle- and upper-middle-class neighborhoods are rarely, if ever, threatened by Immigration and Naturalization Service raids.

As the years pass, the women who took live-in jobs learn some English, gain knowledge of other job possibilities, and learn to use their social networks to their occupational advantage. Most of them eventually move out of live-in work. Some return to their countries of origin, and others look to sales, factory work, or janitorial work. But given the low pay of those jobs—in 1999, garment workers in Los Angeles were earning $5.00 an hour, and nonunion janitors with six years of experience were earning $6.30 an hour—many of them transition into some form of domestic day work. As they abandon their live-in positions for live-out nanny/housekeeper and housecleaner jobs, their wages increase. For these women, the initial misery suffered in their live-in jobs makes other domestic work look if not good then at least tolerable—and certainly better than where they started.

For Latina immigrants in Los Angeles today, live-in domestic work does serve as an occupational bridge of sorts, but it often leads only to other types of domestic jobs. These individual trajectories match historical transformations in the occupation. Much as live-in jobs were once the dominant form of paid domestic work, and then gave way to arrangements in which domestics continued to work daily for one employer but lived with their own families, and finally to modernized "job work" or periodic housecleaning, so many Latina immigrants today traverse these three different types of jobs. Some roughly follow the historical order, moving from live-in to live-out nanny/housekeeper jobs, and then to housecleaning, but their modest occupational mobility does not always follow such a linear course.

As Mexican and Central American immigrant women move into live-out and housecleaning jobs, their family lives change. With better pay and fewer hours of work, they become able to live with their own family members. Among those I surveyed, about 45 percent of the women doing day work were married, but only 13 percent of the live-ins were married. Most women who have husbands and children with them in Los Angeles do not wish to take live-in jobs; moreover, their application for a live-in job is likely to be rejected if they reveal that they have a husband, a boyfriend, or children living in Los Angeles. As one job seeker in an employment agency waiting room put it, "You can't have a family, you can't have anyone [if you want a live-in job]." Live-out nanny/housekeepers often face this family restriction too, as employers are wary of hiring someone who may not report for work when her own children come down with the flu.

Their subminimum wages and long hours make it impossible for many live-in workers to bring their children to Los Angeles; other live-ins are young women who do not have children of their own. Once they do have children who are either born in or have immigrated to Los Angeles, most women try to leave live-in work to be with them. Not all the women can do so, and sometimes their finances or jobs force them to send the children "back home" to be reared by grandmothers. Clearly, performing domestic work for pay, especially in a live-in job, is often incompatible with caring for one's own family and home.

The substantial proportion of Latina domestic workers in Los Angeles whose children stay in their countries of origin are in the same position as many Caribbean women working in domestic jobs on the East Coast, and as the Filipinas who predominate in domestic jobs in many cities around the

TABLE 2   Type of Domestic Work, Marital Status, and Location of Children

	Live-Ins (Percent) (n = 30)	Live-Outs (Percent) (n = 64)	Housecleaners (Percent) (n = 59)
Single (includes the widowed, divorced, or separated)	87	55	54
Married	13	45	46
Domestic Workers with Children	*(n = 16)*	*(n = 53)*	*(n = 45)*
All children in United States	18	58	76
At least one child "back home"	82	42	24

globe. This is what I [label] "transnational motherhood" . . . ; in a 1997 article Ernestine Avila and I coined this term as we examined how Latina immigrant domestic workers are transforming their own meanings of motherhood to accommodate these spatial and temporal separations.[8] As table 2 suggests, these arrangements are most common among women with live-in jobs, but live-in domestic workers and single mothers are not the only ones who rely on them.

These transnational arrangements are not altogether new. The United States has a long history of incorporating people of color through coercive systems of labor that do not recognize family rights, including the right to care for one's own family members. As others have pointed out, slavery and contract labor systems were organized to maximize economic productivity, and offered few supports to sustain family life. Today, international labor migration and the job characteristics of paid domestic work, especially live-in work, virtually impose transnational motherhood on many Mexican and Central American women who have children of their own.

At the other end of the spectrum are the housecleaners, who earn higher wages than live-ins (averaging $9.50 an 'hour vs. $3.80) and who work fewer hours per week than live-ins (twenty-three vs. sixty-four). The majority of them (76 percent) have all their children in the United States, and they are the least likely to experience transnational spatial and temporal separations from their children. Greater financial resources and more favorable job terms enhance housecleaners' abilities to bring their children to the United States. As we have seen, weekly housecleaning is dominated by relatively well-established women with more years of experience in the United States, who speak some English, who have a car, and who have job references. Because their own position is more secure, they are also more likely to have their children here. And because they tend to work fewer hours per week, have greater flexibility in scheduling, and earn higher wages than the live-ins, they can live with and care for their children.

With respect to their ability to care for their own children, live-out nanny/housekeepers fall between live-ins and weekly cleaners—predictably, since they are also in an intermediate position in their earnings, rigidity of schedule, and working hours. Live-out domestic workers, according to the survey, earn $5.90 an hour and work an average workweek of thirty-five hours, and 42 percent of those who are mothers reported having at least one of their children in their country of origin.

NOTES

1. Glenn 1986:141.
2. Lacher 1997:E1.
3. One nanny/housekeeper told me that a *señora* had admonished her for picking a bag of fruit, and wanted to charge her for it; another claimed that her employer had said she would rather watch the fruit fall off the branches and rot than see her eat it.
4. Clark-Lewis 1994:123. "After an average of seven years," she notes in her analysis of African American women who had migrated from the South to Washington, D.C., in the early twentieth century, "all of the migrant women grew to dread their live-in situation. They saw their occupation as harming all aspects of their life" (124). . . .
5. Wrigley 1995.
6. Romero 1992.
7. Smith 1973; McBride 1976.
8. Hondagneu-Sotelo and Avila 1997.

REFERENCES

Clark-Lewis, Elizabeth. 1994. *Living In, Living Out: African American Domestics in Washington, D.C., 1910–1940*. Washington, D.C.: Smithsonian Institution Press.
Glenn, Evelyn Nakano. 1986. *Issei, Nisei, Warbride*. Philadelphia: Temple University Press.
Hondagneu-Sotelo, Pierrette, and Ernestine Avila. 1997. "'I'm Here, but I'm There': The Meanings of Latina Transnational Motherhood." *Gender and Society* 11:548–71.
Lacher, Irene. 1997. "An Interior Mind." *Los Angeles Times*, March 16, E1, E3.
McBride, Theresa. 1976. *The Domestic Revolution: The Modernization of Household Service in England and France, 1820–1920*. New York: Holmes and Meier.
Romero, Mary. 1992. *Maid in the U.S.A.* New York: Routledge.
Smith, Margo L. 1973. "Domestic Service as a Channel of Upward Mobility for the Lower-Class Woman: The Lima Case." In *Female and Male in Latin America: Essays*, edited by Ann Pescatello, 192–207. Pittsburgh: University of Pittsburgh Press.
Wrigley, Julia. 1995. *Other People's Children*. New York: Basic Books.

Discussion Questions for Part III

1. Discuss the ways in which global inequality is linked to inequality within the United States.
2. How does jobless poverty differ from other forms of poverty?
3. How is jobless poverty linked to the broader economic and social trends described in previous readings?
4. How have the broader economic and social trends described in previous readings influenced gender and racial inequality in the workplace?
5. Do you expect that gender and racial inequality in the workplace will decline or worsen over the 21st century?
6. In what ways are work organizations "gendered"? Are they "racialized" and "sexualized" as well? Give examples.
7. How do the processes Henson and Rogers describe help maintain the gender segregation of occupations?
8. How do the experiences of men doing "women's work" differ from those of women doing "men's work"? How would you explain these differences?
9. Dellinger and Williams (Reading 19) argue that "employees in a variety of fields encounter unwanted sexual behavior as a routine feature of their jobs but only rarely label this 'sexual harassment.'" How would you explain this?
10. What factors influence the definition of acceptable and unacceptable sexual behavior in a work setting?
11. How do Moss and Tilly (Reading 20) explain the "silent majority" of employers

who claimed that they did not make any racial distinctions among their employees? Do you agree with this explanation? Can employers ever be truly color-blind?

12. What factors might account for employers' having different views of black employees, as compared with Latinos, Asians, or immigrants? What are the sources of employers' views of these different groups of workers?

13. What kinds of jobs are most likely to require soft skills? Is racial or gender discrimination more or less likely to occur in these jobs than in jobs not requiring these skills?

14. How might you expect the racial and ethnic diversity of a firm's workforce to affect its likelihood of unionization and labor solidarity?

15. What advice would you give to unions that are attempting to organize a largely immigrant workforce?

16. Why do Bonacich and Appelbaum refer to the "return" of the sweatshop? Were sweatshops ever really gone from the United States?

17. In what ways is the return of the sweatshop linked to globalization? What other factors help explain the reappearance of sweatshops in American industry?

18. On the basis of these readings, what kinds of social policies or laws would most benefit the rising number of immigrant workers in the United States?

19. What are some of the reasons that Latina immigrants have become so predominant among domestic workers in southern California? What are other examples of ethnic job clusters?

PART IV

Types of Work

▰▰ INDUSTRIAL WORK ▰▰

∽ READING 24 ∽

Thirty Years of Making Out

Michael Burawoy

↳ public sociologist!

Making Out—a Game Workers Play

. . . In this section I propose to treat the activities on the shop floor as a series of games in which operators attempt to achieve levels of production that earn incentive pay, in other words, anything over 100 percent. The precise target that each operator aims at is established on an individual basis, varying with job, machine, experience, and so on. Some are satisfied with 125 percent, while others are in a foul mood unless they achieve 140 percent— the ceiling imposed and recognized by all participants. This game of making out provides a framework for evaluating the productive activities and the social relations that arise out of the organization of work. We can look upon making out, therefore, as comprising a sequence of stages—of encounters between machine operators and the social or nonsocial objects that regulate the conditions of work. The rules of the game are experienced as a set of externally imposed relationships. The art of making out is to manipulate those relationships with the purpose of advancing as quickly as possible from one stage to the next.

def.

Rules

"Art"

At the beginning of the shift, operators assemble outside the time office on the shop floor to collect their production cards and punch in on the "setup" of their first task. If it has already been set up on the previous shift, the operator simply punches in on production. Usually operators know from talking to their counterpart, before the beginning of the shift, which task they are likely to receive. Knowing what is available on the floor for their machine, an operator is sometimes in a position to bargain with the scheduling man, who is responsible for distributing the tasks.

. . . The scheduling man's duties [did not] end with the distribution of work, but . . . he also assumed some responsibility for ensuring that the department turned out the requisite parts on time. Therefore, he is often found stalking the floor, checking up on progress and urging workers to get a move on. Because he has no formal authority over the operators, the scheduling man's only recourse is to his bargaining strength, based on the discretion he can exert in distributing jobs and fixing up an operator's time. Operators who hold strategic jobs, requiring a particular skill, for example, or who are frequently called upon to do "hot jobs" are in a strong bargaining position vis-à-vis the scheduling man. He knows this and is careful not to upset them. . . .

After receiving their first task, operators have to find the blueprint and tooling for the operation. These are usually in the crib, although they may be already out on the floor.

The crib attendant is therefore a strategic person whose cooperation an operator must secure. If the crib attendant chooses to be uncooperative in dispensing towels, blueprints, fixtures, etc., and, particularly, in the grinding of tools, operators can be held up for considerable lengths of time. Occasionally, operators who have managed to gain the confidence of the crib attendant will enter the crib themselves and expedite the process. Since, unlike the scheduling man, the crib attendant has no real interest in whether the operator makes out, his cooperation has to be elicited by other means. For the first five months of my employment my relations with the crib attendant on second shift were very poor, but at Christmas things changed dramatically. Every year the local union distributes a Christmas ham to all its members. I told Harry that I couldn't be bothered picking mine up from the union hall and that he could have it for himself. He was delighted, and after that I received good service in the crib. . . .

While I was able to secure the cooperation of the crib attendant, I was not so fortunate with the truck drivers. When I was being broken in on the miscellaneous job, I was told repeatedly that the first thing I must do was to befriend the truck driver. He or she was responsible for bringing the stock from the aisles, where it was kept in tubs, to the machine. Particularly at the beginning of the shift, when everyone is seeking their assistance, truck drivers can hold you up for a considerable period. While some treated everyone alike, others discriminated among operators, frustrating those without power, assisting those who were powerful. Working on the miscellaneous job meant that I was continually requiring the truck driver's services, and, when Morris was in the seat, he used to delight in frustrating me by making me wait. There was nothing I could do about it unless I was on a hot job; then the foreman or scheduling man might intervene. To complain to the foreman on any other occasion would only have brought me more travail, since Morris could easily retaliate later on. It was better just to sit tight and wait. Like the crib attendants, truckers have no stake in the operator's making out, and they are, at the same time, acutely conscious of their power in the shop. All they want is for you to get off their backs so that they can rest, light up, chat with their friends, or have a cup of coffee—in other words, enjoy the marginal freedoms of the machine operator. As one of the graffiti in the men's toilet put it, "Fuck the company, fuck the union, but most of all fuck the truckers because they fuck us all." Operators who become impatient may, if they know how, hop into an idle truck and move their own stock. But this may have unfortunate consequences, for other operators may ask them to get their stock too. . . .

As they wait for the stock to arrive, each operator sets up his machine, if it is not already set up. This can take anything from a few minutes to two shifts, but normally it takes less than an hour. Since every setup has a standard time for completion, operators try to make out here, too. When a setup is unusually rapid, an operator may even be able to make time so that, when he punches in on production, he has already turned out a few pieces. A setup man is available for assistance. Particularly for the inexperienced, his help is crucial, but, as with the other auxiliary personnel, his cooperation must be sought and possibly bargained for. He, too, has no obvious stake in your making out, though the quicker he is through with you, the freer he is. Once the machine is set up and the stock has arrived, the operator can begin the first piece, and the setup man is no longer required unless the setup turns out to be unsatisfactory.

The quality and concern of setup men vary enormously. For example, on day shift the setup man was not known for his cooperative spirit. When I asked Bill, my day man, who the setup man was on day shift, he replied, "Oh, he died some years ago." This was a reference to the fact that the

All this is emotional labor to an extent

present one was useless as far as he was concerned. On second shift, by contrast, the setup man went about his job with enthusiasm and friendliness. When he was in a position to help, he most certainly did his best, and everyone liked and respected him. Yet even he did not know all the jobs in the shop. Indeed, he knew hardly any of my machines and so was of little use to me. . . .

The assigned task may be to drill a set of holes in a plate, pipe, casting, or whatever; to mill the surface of some elbow; to turn an internal diameter on a lathe; to shave the teeth on a gear; and so on. The first piece completed has to be checked by the inspector against the blueprint. Between inspector and operator there is an irrevocable conflict of interest because the former is concerned with quality while the operator is concerned with quantity. Time spent when an operation just won't come right—when piece after piece fails, according to the inspector, to meet the specifications of the blueprint—represents lost time to the operator. Yet the inspector wants to OK the piece as quickly as possible and doesn't want to be bothered with checking further pieces until the required tolerances are met.

Inspector vs. operator

When a piece is on the margin, some inspectors will let it go, but others will enforce the specifications of the blueprint to the nth degree. In any event, inspectors are in practice, if not in theory, held partly responsible if an operator runs scrap. Though formally accountable only for the first piece that is tagged as OK, an inspector will be bawled out if subsequent pieces fall outside the tolerance limits. Thus, inspectors are to some extent at the mercy of the operators, who, after successfully getting the first piece OK'd, may turn up the speed of their machine and turn out scrap. An operator who does this can always blame the inspector by shifting the tag from the first piece to one that is scrap. Of course, an inspector has ample opportunity to take revenge on an operator who tries to shaft him. Moreover, operators also bear the responsibil-

ity for quality. During my term of employment, charts were distributed and hung up on each machine, defining the frequency with which operators were expected to check their pieces for any given machine at any particular tolerance level. Moreover, in the period immediately prior to the investigation of the plant's quality-assurance organization by an outside certifying body, operators were expected to indicate on the back of the inspection card the number of times they checked their pieces. . . .

When an inspector holds up an operator who is working on an important job but is unable to satisfy the specifications on the blueprint, a foreman may intervene to persuade the inspector to OK the piece. When this conflict cannot be resolved at the lowest level, it is taken to the next rung in the management hierarchy, and the superintendent fights it out with the chief inspector. . . . [P]roduction management generally defeated quality control in such bargaining . . . which reflects an organizational structure in which quality control is directly subordinated to production. Not surprisingly, the function of quality control has become a sensitive issue and the focus of much conflict among the higher levels of Allied's engine division. Quality control is continually trying to fight itself clear of subordination to production management so as to monitor quality on the shop floor. This, of course, would have deleterious effects on levels of production, and so it is opposed by the production management. Particularly sensitive in this regard is control of the engine test department, which in 1975 resided with production management. The production manager naturally claimed that he was capable of assessing quality impartially. Furthermore, he justified this arrangement by shifting the locus of quality problems from the shop floor to the design of the engine, which brought the engineers into the fray. Engineering management, not surprisingly, opposes the trend toward increasing their responsibility for quality. Therefore, the

Conflict hierarchy b/w insp. & open

prod. vs. quality

we all do this (me eg → stuffing envelopes, entering data)

manager of engineering supported greater autonomy for quality control as a reflection of his interest in returning responsibility for quality to the shop floor. . . .

After the first piece has been OK'd, the operator engages in a battle with the clock and the machine. Unless the task is a familiar one—in which case the answer is known, within limits—the question is: Can I make out? It may be necessary to figure some angles, some short cuts, to speed up the machine, make a special tool, etc. In these undertakings there is always an element of risk—for example, the possibility of turning out scrap or of breaking tools. If it becomes apparent that making out is impossible or quite unlikely, operators slacken off and take it easy. Since they are guaranteed their base earnings, there is little point in wearing themselves out unless they can make more than the base earnings—that is, more than 100 percent. That is what Roy refers to as goldbricking. The other form of "output restriction" to which he refers—quota restriction—entails putting a ceiling on how much an operator may turn in—that is, on how much he may record on the production card. In 1945 the ceiling was $10.00 a day or $1.25 an hour, though this did vary somewhat between machines. In 1975 the ceiling was defined as 140 percent for all operations on all machines. It was presumed that turning in more than 140 percent led to "price cuts" (rate increases), and this was indeed the case.

140 %

In 1975 quota restriction was not necessarily a form of restriction of *output,* because operators *regularly* turned *out* more than 140 percent, but turned *in* only 140 percent, keeping the remainder as a "kitty" for those operations on which they could not make out. Indeed, operators would "bust their ass" for entire shifts, when they had a gravy job, so as to build up a kitty for the following day(s). Experienced operators on the more sophisticated machines could easily build up a kitty of a week's work. There was always some

"kitties"

discrepancy, therefore, between what was registered in the books as completed and what was actually completed on the shop floor. Shop management was more concerned with the latter and let the books take care of themselves. Both the 140 percent ceiling and the practice of banking (keeping a kitty) were recognized and accepted by everyone on the shop floor, even if they didn't meet with the approval of higher management.

Management outside the shop also regarded the practice of "chiseling" as illicit, while management within the shop either assisted or connived in it. Chiseling (Roy's expression, which did not have currency on the shop floor in 1975) involves redistributing time from one operation to another so that operators can maximize the period turned in as over 100 percent. Either the time clerk cooperates by punching the cards in and out at the appropriate time or the operators are allowed to punch their own cards. In part, because of the diversity of jobs, some of them very short, I managed to avoid punching any of my cards. At the end of the shift I would sit down with an account of the pieces completed in each job and fiddle around with the eight hours available, so as to maximize my earnings. I would pencil in the calculated times of starting and finishing each operation. No one ever complained, but it is unlikely that such consistent juggling would have been allowed on first shift. . . .

The Organization of a Shop-Floor Culture

So far we have considered the stages through which any operation must go for its completion and the roles of different employees in advancing the operation from stage to stage. In practice the stages themselves are subject to considerable manipulation, and there were occasions when I would complete an operation without ever having been given it by the scheduling man, without having a blueprint,

[handwritten left margin, top: "Whether or not workers are "making out" becomes part of workers' conversation / social interaction."]

or without having it checked by the inspector. It is not necessary to discuss these manipulations further, since by now it must be apparent that relations emanating directly from the organization of work are understood and attain meaning primarily in terms of making out. Even social interaction not occasioned by the structure of work is dominated by and couched in the idiom of making out. When someone comes over to talk, his first question is, "Are you making out?" followed by "What's the rate?" If you are not making out, your conversation is likely to consist of explanations of why you are not: "The rate's impossible," "I had to wait an hour for the inspector to check the first piece," "These mother-fucking drills keep on burning up." When you are sweating it out on the machine, "knocking the pieces out," a passerby may call out "Gravy!"—suggesting that the job is not as difficult as you are making it appear. Or, when you are "goofing off"—visiting other workers or gossiping at the coffee machine—as likely as not someone will yell out, "You've got it made, man!" When faced with an operation that is obviously impossible, some comedian may bawl out, "Best job in the house!" Calling out to a passerby, "You got nothing to do?" will frequently elicit a protest of the nature, "I'm making out. What more do you want?" At lunchtime, operators of similar machines tend to sit together, and each undertakes a postmortem of the first half of the shift. Why they failed to make out, who "screwed them up," what they expect to accomplish in the second half of the shift, can they make up lost time, advice for others who are having some difficulty, and so on—such topics tend to dominate lunchtime conversations. As regards the domination of shop-floor interaction by the culture of making out . . . the idiom, status, tempo, etc., of interaction at work continue to be governed by and to rise out of the relations in production that constitute the rules of making out.

[handwritten left margin, bottom: "all interaction / "social" / is about "making out""]

[handwritten top right: "Everyone eventually buys into game of "making out""]

In summary, we have seen how the shop-floor culture revolves around making out. Each worker sooner or later is sucked into this distinctive set of activities and language, which then proceed to take on a meaning of their own. Like Roy, when I first entered the shop I was somewhat contemptuous of this game of making out, which appeared to advance Allied's profit margins more than the operators' interests. But I experienced the same shift of opinion that Roy reported:

> . . . Attitudes changed from mere indifference to the piecework incentive to a determination not to be forced to respond, when failure to get a price increase on one of the lowest paying operations of his job repertoire convinced him that the company was unfair. Light scorn for the incentive scheme turned to bitterness. Several months later, however, after fellow operator McCann had instructed him in the "angles on making out," the writer was finding values in the piecework system other than economic ones. He struggled to attain quota "for the hell of it," because it was a "little game" and "keeps me from being bored."[1]

Such a pattern of insertion and seduction is common. In my own case, it took me some time to understand the shop language, let alone the intricacies of making out. It was a matter of three or four months before I began to make out by using a number of angles and by transferring time from one operation to another. Once I knew I had a chance to make out, the rewards of participating in a game in which the outcomes were uncertain absorbed my attention, and I found myself spontaneously cooperating with management in the production of greater surplus value. Moreover, it was only in this way that I could establish relationships with others on the shop floor. Until I was able to strut around the floor like an experienced operator, as if I had all the time in the world and could still make out, few but the greenest would condescend to engage me in conversation. Thus, it was in terms of the culture of making out that individuals evaluated one another and themselves. It provided the basis of status hierarchies on the shop floor, and it was reinforced by the fact that the more sophisticated machines requiring greater skill also had the easier rates. Auxiliary personnel developed characters in accordance with their willingness to cooperate in making out: Morris was a lousy guy because he'd always delay in bringing stock; Harry was basically a decent crib attendant (after he took my ham), tried to help the guys, but was overworked; Charley was an OK scheduling man because he'd try to give me the gravy jobs; Bill, my day man, was "all right" because he'd show me the angles on making out, give me some kitty if I needed it, and sometimes cover up for me when I made a mess of things. . . .

What we have observed is the expansion of the area of the "self-organization" of workers as they pursue their daily activities. We have seen how operators, in order to make out at all, subvert rules promulgated from on high, create informal alliances with auxiliary workers, make their own tools, and so on. In order to produce surplus value, workers have had to organize their relations and activities in opposition to management, particularly middle and senior management. . . . For Cornelius Castoriadis, this represents the fundamental contradiction of capitalism:

> In short, it [the deep contradiction] lies in the fact that capitalism . . . is obliged to try and achieve the simultaneous exclusion and participation of people in relation to their activities, in the fact that people are forced to ensure the functioning of the system half of the time *against* the system's own rules and therefore in struggle against it. This fundamental contradiction appears constantly wherever

the process of management meets the process of execution, which is precisely (and par excellence) the social moment of production.[2]

But if the self-organization of workers is necessary for the survival of capitalism, it also questions the foundations of capitalism.

> When the shop-floor collective establishes norms that informally sanction both "slackers" and "speeders," when it constantly constitutes and reconstitutes itself in "informal" groups that respond to both the requirements of the work process and to personal affinities, it can only be viewed as actively opposing to capitalist principles new principles of productive and social organization and a new view of work.[3]

But is making out as radical as Castoriadis claims? Or is it, as Herbert Marcuse would argue, a mode of adaptation that reproduces "the voluntary servitude" of workers to capital? Are these freedoms and needs, generated and partially satisfied in the context of work and harnessed to the production of surplus value, a challenge to "capitalist principles"? Does making out present an anticipation of something new, the potential for human self-organization, or is it wholly contained within the reproduction of capitalist relations?[4] . . .

NOTES

1. Donald Roy, "Work Satisfaction and Social Reward in Quota Achievement," *American Journal of Sociology* 57 (1953): 509–10.
2. Paul Cardan (alias Cornelius Castoriadis), *Redefining Revolution* (London: Solidarity Pamphlet 44, n.d.), p.11.
3. Cornelius Castoriadis, "On the History of the Workers' Movement," *Telos* no. 30 (Winter 1976–77): 35.
4. See, for example, Herbert Marcuse, *One Dimensional Man* (Boston: Beacon Press, 1964), chap. 1; *An Essay on Liberation* (Boston: Beacon Press, 1969); *Eros and Civilization* (Boston: Beacon Press, 1955), chap. 10.

☙ READING 25 ☙

Women on the Line

Tom Juravich

Until recently, the role played by women in the industrial labor force has been severely underestimated. Although the postwar bias emphasized the extent to which women remained in the home, women have played fundamental roles in American industry; as Barbara Wertheimer has written, "We Were There" (Wertheimer, 1977). We tend to forget that it was women who first left the New England farms (leaving the men behind) to work in the new industrial centers of Lawrence, Massachusetts and Manchester, New Hampshire. In addition, entire industries, such as the garment industry, hired primarily female workers.

It is important, however, to characterize the nature of women's participation in the industrial labor force. Despite great shifts in American industry (textiles in New England have been replaced by high-tech, for example), "women's work" has remained essentially the same. For the most part women have occupied the lowest paid, most tedious "handwork" positions. In the textile industry women nimbly replaced spools of thread and tied swift weavers' knots as well as similar handwork. In today's high-tech industry they assemble electrical components and micro chips. As in the garment industry,

women hold the majority of assembly positions (Grossman, 1980).

Thus the women at National [the factory I studied; a pseudonym] are part of a continuing American tradition, one that our conventional view of the industrial workplace has generally downplayed. In what follows we will observe assembly work at National—and see that in addition to low pay and repetition, it is characterized by a considerable degree of chaos.

Women's Work

On the average there were twenty women working on the second floor at National. The number fluctuated greatly while I was there. It plummeted to a low of eight during two different lay-offs, and rose to forty during peak production (for about two months when a four-hour second shift was added). The women were extremely young. A handful were in their forties and fifties, but most were in their early twenties. At least eight were under twenty.

There were ten to fifteen small machines on the floor that were used sporadically for a variety of jobs. Two or three might be running at any given time. But most of the women worked on the three-wire assembly, the major product of the floor. The production of these assemblies was broken down into six separate tasks.

The process began at the SELM, where terminals were placed on various lengths of

Material excerpted from "Women On the Line" from *Chaos on the Shop Floor: A Worker's View of Quality, Productivity, and Management* by Tom Juravich. Copyright © 1985 by Temple University Press. Reprinted by permission of Temple University Press.

wire. It was the operator's job to inspect these leads (wires) as they came off the machine. They were then stacked in cardboard boxes and put in a shelf near the SELM at the back of the floor.

The assembly itself began in the next phase. Between four and eight women took three different colors (and lengths) of wire and inserted them into a small plastic block an inch square and a quarter of an inch deep. This was by far the hardest and most tedious job. Each lead had a square terminal on the end which had to be pushed into a square channel in the plastic block until it locked. It was not an easy task. It took a certain amount of force and some finesse as well. If you held the lead too far back you bent the terminal. If you held the lead too close you banged your fingers.

You could always tell who was new on the job by their bandaged fingers. Without exception, new employees were assigned to "blocking," as this job was called, and without exception their hands bled. If they lasted beyond the first few weeks, which most did not, they developed the calluses necessary to do the job.

Besides being physically difficult, "blocking" demanded speed. The women were expected to block close to two hundred assemblies per hour, although we had no bonus system (where workers can earn extra money by being more productive). If after a training period that rate was not met, the women would be called into the office repeatedly and threatened with dismissal, although to my knowledge that never happened. Usually they quit long before that.

From the blockers the assemblies moved down the line to be sewed. Although I use the phrase "down the line," the assemblies were not moved down a belt or automatic assembly line. They were stacked in boxes which the women shifted from station to station. At any given time the floor was stacked with a variety of boxes containing assemblies at different stages of production. The sewers took assemblies that had been blocked and on specially designed machines sewed around the three wires. Sewing was the most favored job on the line, and it was usually assigned to women who had been at National the longest. The younger women competed hard for these positions.

The assemblies then passed to the singers (singe-ers) and trimmers. The actual stitching of the assemblies was fairly loose, and it was the singer's job to pass a heat gun (which looked like a large hair dryer) over the stitching to shrink the thread around the wires. After singeing, the loose end of the thread was cut off by the trimmers. In many ways the easiest job, trimming, was often held back as a reward or to be done when there was little else to do.

These five steps—making the leads on the SELM, blocking, sewing, singeing, and trimming—produced the assembly. The sixth and final stage was to inspect and pack the finished product. The inspectors checked the length of the wire, the sewing, the blocks (to see that they were not scratched in the blocking process), and a variety of other characteristics. Depending on the work load, one or two women worked as inspectors.

For a while my knowledge of the women's work was only that of an outsider. I had observed them repeating their tasks over and over, but my attention had been focused on the SELMs. Their work seemed straightforward, and although boring, appeared to present little confusion. Yet in the coming months, as I spent more time with the women, I began to understand that their work was quite different. Although these six tasks appeared so simple that one would expect the process to be automatic, it was actually the source of much confusion, conflict, and disagreement. A careful look at the production process reveals why women on the line were beset with their own kind of chaos.

The Craft Knowledge of Deskilled Workers

Much has been written about the deskilling of labor in the twentieth century. Perhaps the best example is Harry Braverman's *Labor and Monopoly Capital* (1974). Throughout the book, as well as in related volumes (see Zimbalist, 1979), we are given numerous examples of how technology has taken away the skill from a job, leaving only routine to the workers.

If there ever were an example of this degradation of labor, it was the kind of work performed by the women at National. There is no way that their work could be seen as exciting, satisfying, or rewarding. It was tolerable at best. Even Carroll recognized this. He once told me, "It takes a special kind of girl [sic] to do this kind of work. The guys could never do it, they don't have the patience. We like the neat ones, the ones who like this close work."

One comes away from Braverman convinced that little skill is necessary to perform most factory jobs. This conviction is very much shared as a conventional wisdom. Yet these "simple" tasks often look quite different from the shop floor.

One of my first jobs working closely with the women involved changing the belts on the sewing machines. The belts were made of leather and stretched or broke over time. Installing a new belt involved cutting a new piece of leather to the proper length and fastening it together with a metal staple. This took about half an hour (until much later when I discovered a special tool which was designed to punch the holes and fasten the staple). The women poked fun at my somewhat clumsy style (the task actually was quite difficult), especially Carol (not to be confused with Carroll), whose machine I started on. She was a large woman in her late thirties with a hot temper but also a good sense of humor.

After replacing the belt, I sat down at her machine and asked her to show me how to sew. I never heard such laughter. The other women thought that a man sewing was the funniest thing they ever saw. It took me five minutes to sew a single assembly, and it came out completely wrong. "You'll never make your rate that way, honey," said Carol. "You think your job is hard," said one of the other sewers. Carroll would also sew while repairing or testing a machine. He was a little better at it than me, but not much. The women used the opportunity to give him all the grief they could. "See if you can keep that up all day," one of the women used to say.

It was clear to me, and to anyone else watching, that a worker could not walk in off the street, sit down at the machine, and make her rate. Yet despite his own experience, this is how Carroll often threatened the women: "Why, I could get somebody right off the street who could do that job faster than you." Perhaps Carroll believed it. The usual explanation is that these jobs require a certain manual dexterity, though no real skill, and some people simply lack the physical coordination. Yet this explanation is not adequate. As I found out, many of our assembly positions required more than deftness.

At one point I was called over to adjust a small press. It applied a spade terminal (like the one on your television antenna) to an already cut and stripped length of wire. The repair amounted essentially to cleaning out the applicator with the air line and some lubricant, but in the process I discovered that Betty, the operator of the machine, had perfected an ingenious technique.

The wire was approximately sixteen inches long, and terminals had to be placed on each end parallel to each other. I had seen other women struggle with this job, placing a terminal on one end, turning the wire around, lining it up and applying the other terminal. Betty, however, had found another way to do it. As I was checking the machine,

I saw her pick up a handful of wires and bounce them in her hand. When I asked what she was doing, she said she was finding the "bend" in the wire. This "bend" she referred to was due to the fact that the wire had originally been coiled on a spool. Although the machine that stripped and cut the wire included a mechanical device called a straightener, it was impossible to remove the bend entirely, and when lined up in a tray, the wires bent one way or the other.

Once Betty had bounced the wires and they lined up the same way (with the ends bending down as she held them), still holding them as a bunch, she put a terminal on one end of all of them. She then turned the bundle around and put terminals on the other end. Because she let the memory of the wire keep the ends turned the same way, the terminals were easily applied in the proper parallel fashion.

I was impressed. This was hardly a deskilled worker performing routine procedures. When I asked her how she learned to do it, she responded casually that she had figured it out doing the job. As I began to see the women's work from the inside, I noticed a host of skills like Betty's that facilitated production. In fact, I was surprised how fundamental this "craft knowledge" was to the day-to-day operation of the mill. By "craft knowledge," most people think of skills possessed by someone like a violin maker. It is knowledge that cannot be rigidly systematized or reduced to procedural rules but is developed through years of experience. I would argue that the women on the line possessed skills very much akin to those of a craftsman.

Even so, I would hardly argue that working in National was anything like making violins. Indeed, as we have seen, the work itself was menial. Yet contrary to Braverman, a job that involves repetitive, boring tasks is not necessarily devoid of skill or craft. As Manwaring and Wood conclude,

the recognition of "working knowledge does not in and of itself refute the deskilling thesis, but it does provide a different vantage point, one in which the central notion is that work is both degrading and constructive, both crippling and enriching" (Manwaring and Wood, 1984: 56).

It is not that craft knowledge at National merely facilitated speedier production. Rather, it was integral to getting the job done at all. Based on research in a paper cone factory, Ken Kusterer (1978) implies this point in his distinction between basic and supplemental (craft) knowledge.

> Basic knowledge includes all the procedures necessary to routinely carry out their work tasks: how to start and stop the machine, clean it in a prescribed manner, "bridge the cones," label the case, etc. Supplemental knowledge includes all the know-how necessary to handle obstacles to this routine work performance that arise from time to time: how to keep the machinery running, overcome "bad paper," diagnose the cause of the defects. (Kusterer, 1978: 45)

Thus, when Carroll told the women that he could replace them with "somebody off the street," what he really meant was, "Provided that all the materials are perfect, the machines are running well, and with constant supervision," then "somebody off the street" would do. But as we have seen, National hardly ever ran under those conditions. The machines were in constant disrepair, the materials were inconsistent, and most of the actual decisions on the floor were made by the women themselves, not by Carroll or June. If the managers had to make every decision themselves, production schedules would never be met.

The high labor turnover at National always threatened production. A new assembler would be trained for a day or two and then left on her own. This worked fine as long as things went smoothly. But a problem could spell disaster. For example, one new blocker was doing fine until she blocked 5,000 assemblies with wire that was too heavy. A more experienced blocker would have detected the overly heavy gauge simply by feeling the wire, and could have avoided the lost time and materials. (In a way Carroll was right about taking workers directly off the street. This blocker had made her rate all right, but her work had to be tossed in the scrap pile.)

Thus, the day-to-day operation of the mill required more than mere routine assembly. Yet the constant need for decision-making had mixed implications for the women on the line.

Chaos on the Line

As Kusterer demonstrates in *Know-How on the job* (1978), all jobs from bank teller to longshoreman demand an insider's knowledge, without which the job cannot be done effectively. This craft knowledge is important to workers in a number of ways. First, it is an important source of pride and dignity. That jobs involve more than menial tasks contributes in fundamental ways to workers' self-esteem. Second, craft knowledge can be an important source of power for workers. Because for the most part it is hidden from management, it can become a tool for workers to assert power in the workplace.

Yet the degree to which this kind of decision-making was constantly needed on the line indicates how confused production really was. The women did not really mind making decisions—it was by far the most interesting part of their day—but making the right decision was not always clear, and the wrong decision often carried strong sanctions.

For example, the leads produced by the SELM were supposed to be measured on an ongoing basis by the operator and once an hour by an inspector. They checked the overall length of the wire, the length of the strip, and how the wire was placed in the terminal. The specifications for these leads were extremely rigid, with the tolerance on each measure plus or minus one-sixty-fourth of an inch. Given the condition of the machines, the quality of the materials, and the experience of the workers, this tolerance was nearly impossible to achieve. In fact, the manual for the machine specified that it would work only to a one-thirty-second of an inch tolerance. In actuality, the machines were running plus or minus one-sixteenth of an inch.

Everyone in the mill, from the operator Alice to the inspectors, was aware of this. They knew that by official specifications most of the leads were beyond tolerance. Yet they also knew that the leads were probably acceptable to the purchaser, and that if they rejected too many items Carroll would be on their backs. Thus everyone was in an ambiguous position that required a constant negotiation of the rules.

From my experience, this goes on in other mills, where official specifications only serve as general guidelines, and where actual specifications are actually much looser. Yet I never witnessed anywhere near the negotiation that occurred daily at National. If the women actually obeyed the specifications, they would do no work. Yet if they accepted (or produced) something beyond an acceptable tolerance, they ran the risk of being held responsible for producing "bad" items.

This uncertainty led to endless "crises" at National. Every two or three weeks, management shut down the production line and called everyone into the cafeteria. Carroll or June would show us some assemblies and ask us what was wrong with them. It was a test. It was amazing how much we could find wrong if we looked hard enough, although what we found was often not what they had in mind. One time the blocks were scratched, another time the tab on the end of the terminals was bent, and once the sewing pulled out. They would chew us out and send us back to the line, usually with some new procedure or inspection to eliminate the problem.

However, if we focused on one detail or aspect of production, the line would immediately slow down. As long as the women stuck close to specifications, the production rate dropped. Interestingly, most of these crises ended the same way. For a week or two the women were very careful, but before long they went back to their old ways. The new inspection or procedure was usually forgotten, and the uncertainty in the production line remained essentially the same. It was amazing to me that despite a series of these crises, the line ran basically the same when I left National as when I arrived.

Much More Than Just a Routine Job

From this in-depth look at the women on the line at National, we have discovered that what they do is much more than just routine work. Not denying that it was boring and repetitive, working at National required constant decision-making and precarious negotiation of what was expected. At first glance, it might be argued that the women at National were "lucky" to have this high level of decision-making, to the extent that it relieved them of the boredom they would otherwise experience. Yet upon further analysis, this constant decision-making cannot be seen as relieving boredom. Decision-making took place in such a confusing and contradictory context that in fundamental ways it added to the pressure.

Workers have a number of ways of dealing with monotony. For some it is dreams of summer vacations or a new car, for others it is the beer at lunch, while others try radios and singing on the job. If you observe a mill carefully, you will notice all kinds of routines that appear pointless at first glance. For example, one of the older women on the floor had a routine she followed religiously. Every day at morning coffee break she went to the corner store and bought a newspaper. She brought it to her table and then went to the bathroom for a paper towel that she spread on her table. She then proceeded to eat half of her sandwich, no more, no less, every working day. There were numerous other examples of women "setting up" their meager possessions—radio, cigarettes, and coffee cup—in similar fashion.

At first you wonder if these routines are the product of working too long in an alienating workplace. Yet over time you see the purpose behind these rituals. Most of what the workers at National did was out of their control. They knew they would produce thousands of assemblies each day, yet had no control over the conditions under which that production occurred. These rituals, then, in important and fundamental ways served to impose some, if only a small amount, of personal impact on the day. The woman who eats just half a sandwich at the same time each day in her own way is imposing some order on the day's events. Although these jobs are clearly "too small for people," it is through this imposition of order that they somehow become "enough."

Jobs become less boring to the extent that workers control their daily activities. For example, if workers' rates were computed by the day instead of by the hour, workers could work harder in the morning when they were fresh, and slower in the afternoon when tired. A break in the work routine, however, when not tied to an increase in control, does not necessarily make a job less boring. For instance, when management stopped production at National because of problems with tolerances, it did not alleviate boredom. Since constant decision-making made the workday more unpredictable, the

Upshot: — Argues against Braverman's hype of deskilled, boring labor.
— Instead, argues that much work req. decisionmaking, creativity
& has actually v/ chaotic.
• This bothered workers, made them feel insecure.

women felt less in control than if their jobs were utterly routine.

Psychologists agree that random punishment is the worst kind because it threatens an individual's sense of control and order. A punishment that follows from a certain behavior or occurs at some fixed interval is much easier to deal with than one that occurs at random times. In a similar fashion, the ongoing decision-making and the confusion that resulted made the work at National difficult to bear.

Especially confusing times (during one of our "crises," for instance) had an obvious effect on the women who worked on the line. Tempers flared, arguments were more common, people took more days off, and some worked as slowly as they could. They complained as well. "I wish they'd make up their damn minds," said one of the blockers to me. "It's bad enough having such boring work, and then there's so much confusion

all the time. One day it'll pass, the next day it won't." As another woman said to me, "All I want to do is to be able to do my job without anyone bothering me, and then go home."

REFERENCES

Braverman, Harry. 1974. *Labor and Monopoly Capital: The Degradation of Work in the Twentieth Century.* New York: Monthly Review Press.

Grossman, Rachael. 1980. "Women's Place in the Integrated Circuit." *Radical America* 14: 29–50.

Kusterer, Ken C. 1978. *Know-How on the Job: The Important Working Knowledge of "Unskilled" Workers.* Boulder, Colo.: Westview Press.

Manwaring, T. and S. Wood. 1984. "The Ghost in the Machine: Tacit Skills in the Labor Process." *Socialist Review,* no. 74 (14), 55–83, 94.

Wertheimer, Barbara Mayer. 1977. *We Were There: The Story of Working Women in America.* New York: Pantheon.

Zimbalist, Andrew, ed. 1979. *Case Studies on the Labor Process.* New York: Monthly Review Press.

∽ READING 26 ∽

Fast Food Nation

The Most Dangerous Job[1]

Eric Schlosser

One night I visit a slaughterhouse somewhere in the High Plains. The slaughterhouse is one of the nation's largest. About five thousand head of cattle enter it every day, single file, and leave in a different form. Someone who has access to the plant, who's upset by its working conditions, offers to give me a tour. The slaughterhouse is an immense building, gray and square, about three stories high, with no windows on the front and no architectural clues to what's

happening inside. My friend gives me a chain-mail apron and gloves, suggesting I try them on. Workers on the line wear about eight pounds of chain mail beneath their white coats, shiny steel armor that covers their

---

hands, wrists, stomach, and back. The chain mail's designed to protect workers from cutting themselves and from being cut by other workers. But knives somehow manage to get past it. My host hands me some Wellingtons, the kind of knee-high rubber boots that English gentlemen wear in the countryside. "Tuck your pants into the boots," he says. "We'll be walking through some blood."

I put on a hardhat and climb a stairway. The sounds get louder, factory sounds, the noise of power tools and machinery, bursts of compressed air. We start at the end of the line, the fabricating room. Workers call it "fab." When we step inside, fab seems familiar: steel catwalks, pipes along the walls, a vast room, a maze of conveyer belts. This could be the Lamb Weston plant in Idaho, except hunks of red meat ride the belts instead of french fries. Some machines assemble cardboard boxes, others vacuum-seal subprimals of beef in clear plastic. The workers look extremely busy, but there's nothing unsettling about this part of the plant. You see meat like this all the time in the back of your local supermarket.

The fab room is cooled to about 40 degrees, and as you head up the line, the feel of the place starts to change. The pieces of meat get bigger. Workers—about half of them women, almost all of them young and Latino—slice meat with long slender knives. They stand at a table that's chest high, grab meat off a conveyer belt, trim away fat, throw meat back on the belt, toss the scraps onto a conveyer belt above them, and then grab more meat, all in a matter of seconds. I'm now struck by how many workers there are, hundreds of them, pressed close together, constantly moving, slicing. You see hardhats, white coats, flashes of steel. Nobody is smiling or chatting, they're too busy, anxiously trying not to fall behind. An old man walks past me, pushing a blue plastic barrel filled with scraps. A few workers carve the meat with Whizzards, small electric knives that have spinning round blades. The Whizzards look like the Norelco razors that Santa rides in

the TV ads. I notice that a few of the women near me are sweating, even though the place is freezing cold.

Sides of beef suspended from an overhead trolley swing toward a group of men. Each worker has a large knife in one hand and a steel hook in the other. They grab the meat with their hooks and attack it fiercely with their knives. As they hack away, using all their strength, grunting, the place suddenly feels different, primordial. The machinery seems beside the point, and what's going on before me has been going on for thousands of years—the meat, the hook, the knife, men straining to cut more meat.

On the kill floor, what I see no longer unfolds in a logical manner. It's one strange image after another. A worker with a power saw slices cattle into halves as though they were two-by-fours, and then the halves swing by me into the cooler. It feels like a slaughterhouse now. Dozens of cattle, stripped of their skins, dangle on chains from their hind legs. My host stops and asks how I feel, if I want to go any further. This is where some people get sick. I feel fine, determined to see the whole process, the world that's been deliberately hidden. The kill floor is hot and humid. It stinks of manure. Cattle have a body temperature of about 101 degrees, and there are a lot of them in the room. Carcasses swing so fast along the rail that you have to keep an eye on them constantly, dodge them, watch your step, or one will slam you and throw you onto the bloody concrete floor. It happens to workers all the time.

I see: a man reach inside cattle and pull out their kidneys with his bare hands, then drop the kidneys down a metal chute, over and over again, as each animal passes by him; a stainless steel rack of tongues; Whizzards peeling meat off decapitated heads, picking them almost as clean as the white skulls painted by Georgia O'Keeffe. We wade through blood that's ankle deep and that pours down drains into huge vats below us. As we approach the start of the line, for the first time I hear the steady *pop, pop, pop* of live animals being stunned.

Now the cattle suspended above me look just like the cattle I've seen on ranches for years, but these ones are upside down swinging on hooks. For a moment, the sight seems unreal; there are so many of them, a herd of them, lifeless. And then I see a few hind legs still kicking, a final reflex action, and the reality comes hard and clear.

For eight and a half hours, a worker called a "sticker" does nothing but stand in a river of blood, being drenched in blood, slitting the neck of a steer every ten seconds or so, severing its carotid artery. He uses a long knife and must hit exactly the right spot to kill the animal humanely. He hits that spot again and again. We walk up a slippery metal stairway and reach a small platform, where the production line begins. A man turns and smiles at me. He wears safety goggles and a hardhat. His face is splattered with gray matter and blood. He is the "knocker," the man who welcomes cattle to the building. Cattle walk down a narrow chute and pause in front of him, blocked by a gate, and then he shoots them in the head with a captive bolt stunner—a compressed-air gun attached to the ceiling by a long hose—which fires a steel bolt that knocks the cattle unconscious. The animals keep strolling up, oblivious to what comes next, and he stands over them and shoots. For eight and a half hours, he just shoots. As I stand there, he misses a few times and shoots the same animal twice. As soon as the steer falls, a worker grabs one of its hind legs, shackles it to a chain, and the chain lifts the huge animal into the air.

I watch the knocker knock cattle for a couple of minutes. The animals are powerful and imposing one moment and then gone in an instant, suspended from a rail, ready for carving. A steer slips from its chain, falls to the ground, and gets its head caught in one end of a conveyer belt. The production line stops as workers struggle to free the steer, stunned but alive, from the machinery. I've seen enough.

I step out of the building into the cool night air and follow the path that leads cattle into the slaughterhouse. They pass me, driven toward the building by workers with long white sticks that seem to glow in the dark. One steer, perhaps sensing instinctively what the other don't, turns and tries to run. But workers drive him back to join the rest. The cattle lazily walk single-file toward the muffled sounds, *pop, pop, pop,* coming from the open door.

The path has hairpin turns that prevent cattle from seeing what's in store and keep them relaxed. As the ramp gently slopes upward, the animals may think they're headed for another truck, another road trip—and they are, in unexpected ways. The ramp widens as it reaches ground level and then leads to a large cattle pen with wooden fences, a corral that belongs in a meadow, not here. As I walk along the fence, a group of cattle approach me, looking me straight in the eye, like dogs hoping for a treat, and follow me out of some mysterious impulse. I stop and try to absorb the whole scene: the cool breeze, the cattle and their gentle lowing, a cloudless sky, steam rising from the plant in the moonlight. And then I notice that the building does have one window, a small square of light on the second floor. It offers a glimpse of what's hidden behind this huge blank facade. Through the little window you can see bright red carcasses on hooks, going round and round.

Sharp Knives

Knocker, Sticker, Shackler, Rumper, First Legger, Knuckle Dropper, Navel Boner, Splitter Top/Bottom Butt, Feed Kill Chain—the names of job assignments at a modern slaughterhouse convey some of the brutality inherent in the work. Meatpacking is now the most dangerous job in the United States. The injury rate in a slaughterhouse is about three times higher than the rate in a typical American factory.[2] Every year more than one-quarter of the meatpacking workers in this country—roughly forty thousand men and women—suffer an injury or a work-related illness that requires medical attention beyond first aid.[3] There is strong evidence that these numbers, compiled by the Bureau of Labor Statistics, understate the number of meatpacking injuries that occur. Thousands of additional injuries and illnesses most likely go unrecorded.

Despite the use of conveyer belts, forklifts, dehiding machines, and a variety of power tools, most of the work in the nation's slaughterhouses is still performed by hand. Poultry plants can be largely mechanized, thanks to the breeding of chickens that are uniform in size. The birds in some Tyson factories are killed, plucked, gutted, beheaded, and sliced into cutlets by robots and machines. But cattle still come in all sizes and shapes, varying in weight by hundreds of pounds. The lack of a standardized steer has hindered the mechanization of beef plants. In one crucial respect meatpacking work has changed little in the past hundred years. At the dawn of the twenty-first century, amid an era of extraordinary technological advance, the most important tool in a modern slaughterhouse is a sharp knife.

Lacerations are the most common injuries suffered by meatpackers, who often stab themselves or stab someone working nearby. Tendinitis and cumulative trauma disorders are also quite common. Meatpacking workers routinely develop back problems, shoulder problems, carpal tunnel syndrome, and "trigger finger" (a syndrome in which a finger becomes frozen in a curled position). Indeed, the rate of these cumulative trauma injuries in the meatpacking industry is far higher than the rate in any other American industry. It is roughly thirty-three times higher than the national average in industry.[4] Many

slaughterhouse workers make a knife cut every two or three seconds, which adds up to about 10,000 cuts during an eight-hour shift. If the knife has become dull, additional pressure is placed on the worker's tendons, joints, and nerves. A dull knife can cause pain to extend from the cutting hand all the way down the spine.

Workers often bring their knives home and spend at least forty minutes a day keeping the edges smooth, sharp, and sanded, with no pits. One IBP worker, a small Guatemalan woman with graying hair, spoke with me in the cramped kitchen of her mobile home. As a pot of beans cooked on the stove, she sat in a wooden chair, gently rocking, telling the story of her life, of her journey north in search of work, the whole time sharpening big knives in her lap as though she were knitting a sweater.

The "IBP revolution" has been directly responsible for many of the hazards that meatpacking workers now face. One of the leading determinants of the injury rate at a slaughterhouse today is the speed of the disassembly line. The faster it runs, the more likely that workers will get hurt. The old meatpacking plants in Chicago slaughtered about 50 cattle an hour. Twenty years ago, new plants in the High Plains slaughtered about 175 cattle an hour. Today some plants slaughter up to 400 cattle an hour—about half a dozen animals every minute, sent down a single production line, carved by workers desperate not to fall behind. While trying to keep up with the flow of meat, workers often neglect to resharpen their knives and thereby place more stress on their bodies. As the pace increases, so does the risk of accidental cuts and stabbings. "I could always tell the line speed," a former Monfort nurse told me, "by the number of people with lacerations coming into my office." People usually cut themselves; nevertheless, everyone on the line tries to stay alert. Meatpackers often work within inches of each other, wielding large knives. A simple mistake can cause a serious injury. A former IBP worker told me about boning knives suddenly flying out of hands and ricocheting off of machinery. "They're very flexible," she said, "and they'll spring on you . . . zwing, and they're gone."

Much like french fry factories, beef slaughterhouses often operate at profit margins as low as a few pennies a pound.[5] The three meatpacking giants—ConAgra, IBP, and Excel—try to increase their earnings by maximizing the volume of production at each plant. Once a slaughterhouse is up and running, fully staffed, the profits it will earn are directly related to the speed of the line. A faster pace means higher profits. Market pressures now exert a perverse influence on the management of beef plants: the same factors that make these slaughterhouses relatively inefficient (the lack of mechanization, the reliance on human labor) encourage companies to make them even more dangerous (by speeding up the pace).

The unrelenting pressure of trying to keep up with the line has encouraged widespread methamphetamine use among meatpackers. Workers taking "crank" feel charged and self-confident, ready for anything. Supervisors have been known to sell crank to their workers or to supply it free in return for certain favors, such as working a second shift. Workers who use methamphetamine may feel energized and invincible, but are actually putting themselves at much greater risk of having an accident. For obvious reasons, a modern slaughterhouse is not a safe place to be high.

In the days when labor unions were strong, workers could complain about excessive line speeds and injury rates without fear of getting fired. Today only one-third of IBP's workers belong to a union.[6] Most of the nonunion workers are recent immigrants; many are illegals; and they are generally employed "at will." That means they can be fired without warning, for just about any reason. Such an arrangement does not encourage them to lodge complaints. Workers who have traveled a great distance for this job, who have families to support, who are earning ten times more an hour in a meatpacking plant than they could possibly earn back home, are wary about speaking out and losing everything. The line speeds and labor costs at IBP's nonunion plants now set the standard for the rest of the industry. Every other company must try to produce beef as quickly and cheaply as IBP does; slowing the pace to protect workers can lead to a competitive disadvantage.

Again and again workers told me that they are under tremendous pressure not to report injuries. The annual bonuses of plant foremen and supervisors are often based in part on the injury rate of their workers. Instead of creating a safer workplace, these bonus schemes encourage slaughterhouse managers to make sure that accidents and injuries go unreported. Missing fingers, broken bones, deep lacerations, and amputated limbs are difficult to conceal from authorities. But the dramatic and catastrophic injuries in a slaughterhouse are greatly outnumbered by less visible, though no less debilitating, ailments: torn muscles, slipped disks, pinched nerves.

If a worker agrees not to report an injury, a supervisor will usually shift him or her to an easier job for a while, providing some time to heal. If the injury seems more serious, a Mexican worker is often given the opportunity to return home for a while, to recuperate there, then come back to his or her slaughterhouse job in the United States. Workers who abide by these unwritten rules are treated respectfully; those who disobey are likely to be punished and made an example. As one former IBP worker explained, "They're trying to deter you, period, from going to the doctor."

From a purely economic point of view, injured workers are a drag on profits. They are less productive. Getting rid of them makes a good deal of financial sense, especially when new workers are readily available and inexpensive to train. Injured workers are often given some of the most unpleasant tasks in the slaughterhouse. Their hourly wages are cut. And through a wide variety of unsubtle means they are encouraged to quit.

Not all supervisors in a slaughterhouse behave like Simon Legree, shouting at workers, cursing them, belittling their injuries, pushing them to move faster. But enough supervisors act that way to warrant the comparison. Production supervisors tend to be men in their late twenties and early thirties. Most are Anglos and don't speak Spanish, although more and more Latinos are being promoted to the job. They earn about $30,000 a year, plus bonuses and benefits. In many rural communities, being a supervisor at a meatpacking plant is one of the best jobs in town. It comes with a fair amount of pressure: a supervisor must meet production goals, keep the number of recorded injuries low, and most importantly, keep the meat flowing down the line without interruption. The job also brings enormous power. Each supervisor is like a little dictator in his or her section of the plant, largely free to boss, fire, berate, or reassign workers. That sort of power can lead to all sorts of abuses, especially when the hourly workers being supervised are women.

Many women told me stories about being fondled and grabbed on the production line, and the behavior of supervisors sets the tone for the other male workers. In February of 1999, a federal jury in Des Moines awarded $2.4 million to a female employee at an IBP slaughterhouse. According to the woman's testimony, coworkers had "screamed obscenities and rubbed their bodies against hers while supervisors laughed."[7] Seven months later, Monfort agreed to settle a lawsuit filed by the U.S. Equal Employment Opportunity Commission on behalf of fourteen female workers in Texas. As part of the settlement, the company paid the women $900,000 and vowed to establish formal procedures for handling sexual harassment complaints.[8] In their lawsuit the women alleged that supervisors at a Monfort plant in Cactus, Texas, pressured them for dates and sex, and that male coworkers groped them, kissed them, and used animal parts in a sexually explicit manner.

The sexual relationships between supervisors and "hourlies" are for the most part consensual. Many female workers optimistically regard sex with their supervisor as a way to gain a secure place in American society, a green card, a husband—or at the very least a transfer to an easier job at the plant. Some supervisors become meatpacking Casanovas, engaging in multiple affairs. Sex, drugs, and slaughterhouses may seem an unlikely combination, but as one former Monfort employee told me: "Inside those walls is a different world that obeys different laws." Late on the second shift, when it's dark outside, assignations take place in locker rooms, staff rooms, and parked cars, even on the catwalk over the kill floor.

The Worst

Some of the most dangerous jobs in meatpacking today are performed by the late-night cleaning crews. A large proportion of these workers are illegal immigrants. They are considered "independent contractors," employed not by the meatpacking firms but by sanitation companies. They earn hourly wages that are about one-third lower than those of regular production employees. And their work is so hard and so horrendous that words seem inadequate to describe it. The men and women who now clean the nation's slaughterhouses may arguably have the worst job in the United States. "It takes a really dedicated person," a former member of a cleaning crew told me, "or a really desperate person to get the job done."

When a sanitation crew arrives at a meatpacking plant, usually around midnight, it faces a mess of monumental proportions. Three to four thousand cattle, each weighing about a thousand pounds, have been slaughtered there that day. The place has to be clean by sunrise. Some of the workers wear water-resistant clothing; most don't. Their principal cleaning tool is a high-pressure hose that shoots a mixture of water and chlorine heated to about 180 degrees. As the water is sprayed, the plant fills with a thick, heavy fog. Visibility drops to as little as five feet. The conveyer belts and machinery are running. Workers stand on the belts, spraying them, riding them like moving sidewalks, as high as fifteen feet off the ground. Workers climb ladders with hoses and spray the catwalks. They get under tables and conveyer belts, climbing right into the bloody muck, cleaning out grease, fat, manure, leftover scraps of meat.

Glasses and safety goggles fog up. The inside of the plant heats up; temperatures soon exceed 100 degrees. "It's hot, and it's foggy, and you can't see anything," a former sanitation worker said. The crew members can't see or hear each other when the machinery's running. They routinely spray each other with burning hot, chemical-laden water. They are sickened by the fumes. Jesus, a soft-spoken employee of DCS Sanitation Management, Inc., the company that IBP uses in many of its plants, told me that every night on the job he gets terrible headaches. "You feel it in your head," he said. "You feel it in your stomach, like you want to throw up." A friend of his vomits whenever they clean the rendering area. Other workers tease the young man as he

retches. Jesus says the stench in rendering is so powerful that it won't wash off; no matter how much soap you use after a shift, the smell comes home with you, seeps from your pores.

One night while Jesus was cleaning, a coworker forgot to turn off a machine, lost two fingers, and went into shock. An ambulance came and took him away, as everyone else continued to clean. He was back at work the following week. "If one hand is no good," the supervisor told him, "use the other." Another sanitation worker lost an arm in a machine. Now he folds towels in the locker room. The scariest job, according to Jesus, is cleaning the vents on the roof of the slaughterhouse. The vents become clogged with grease and dried blood. In the winter, when everything gets icy and the winds pick up, Jesus worries that a sudden gust will blow him off the roof into the darkness.

Although official statistics are not kept, the death rate among slaughterhouse sanitation crews is extraordinarily high. They are the ultimate in disposable workers: illegal, illiterate, impoverished, untrained. The nation's worst job can end in just about the worst way. Sometimes these workers are literally ground up and reduced to nothing.

A brief description of some cleaning-crew accidents over the past decade says more about the work and the danger than any set of statistics. At the Monfort plant in Grand Island, Nebraska, Richard Skala was beheaded by a dehiding machine. Carlos Vincente—an employee of T and G Service Company, a twenty-eight-year-old Guatemalan who'd been in the United States for only a week—was pulled into the cogs of a conveyer belt at an Excel plant in Fort Morgan, Colorado, and torn apart. Lorenzo Marin, Sr., an employee of DCS Sanitation, fell from the top of a skinning machine while cleaning it with a high-pressure hose, struck his head on the concrete floor of an IBP plant in Columbus Junction, Iowa, and died. Another employee of DCS Sanitation,

Salvador Hernandez-Gonzalez, had his head crushed by a pork-loin processing machine at an IBP plant in Madison, Nebraska. The same machine had fatally crushed the head of another worker, Ben Barone, a few years earlier. At a National Beef plant in Liberal, Kansas, Homer Stull climbed into a blood-collection tank to clean it, a filthy tank thirty feet high. Stull was overcome by hydrogen sulfide fumes. Two coworkers climbed into the tank and tried to rescue him. All three men died. Eight years earlier, Henry Wolf had been overcome by hydrogen sulfide fumes while cleaning the very same tank; Gary Sanders had tried to rescue him; both men died; and the Occupational Safety and Health Administration (OSHA) later fined National Beef for its negligence. The fine was $480 for each man's death.[9]

Don't Get Caught

During the same years when the working conditions at America's meatpacking plants became more dangerous—when line speeds increased and illegal immigrants replaced skilled workers—the federal government greatly reduced the enforcement of health and safety laws. OSHA had long been despised by the nation's manufacturers, who considered the agency a source of meddlesome regulations and unnecessary red tape. When Ronald Reagan was elected president in 1980, OSHA was already underfunded and understaffed: its 1,300 inspectors were responsible for the safety of more than 5 million workplaces across the country. A typical American employer could expect an OSHA inspection about once every eighty years. Nevertheless, the Reagan administration was determined to reduce OSHA's authority even further, as part of the push for deregulation. The number of OSHA inspectors was eventually cut by 20 percent, and in 1981 the agency adopted a new policy of

"voluntary compliance." Instead of arriving unannounced at a factory and performing an inspection, OSHA employees were required to look at a company's injury log before setting foot inside the plant. If the records showed an injury rate at the factory lower than the national average for all manufacturers, the OSHA inspector had to turn around and leave at once—without entering the plant, examining its equipment, or talking to any of its workers. These injury logs were kept and maintained by company officials.

For most of the 1980s OSHA's relationship with the meatpacking industry was far from adversarial. While the number of serious injuries rose, the number of OSHA inspections fell.[10] The death of a worker on the job was punished with a fine of just a few hundred dollars. At a gathering of meat company executives in October of 1987, OSHA's safety director, Barry White, promised to change federal safety standards that "appear amazingly stupid to you or overburdening or just not useful." According to an account of the meeting later published in the *Chicago Tribune,* the safety director at OSHA—the federal official most responsible for protecting the lives of meatpacking workers—acknowledged his own lack of qualification for the job. "I know very well that you know more about safety and health in the meat industry than I do," White told the executives. "And you know more about safety and health in the meat industry than any single employee at OSHA."

OSHA's voluntary compliance policy did indeed reduce the number of recorded injuries in meatpacking plants. It did not, however, reduce the number of people getting hurt. It merely encouraged companies, in the words of a subsequent congressional investigation, "to understate injuries, to falsify records, and to cover up accidents." At the IBP beef plant in Dakota City, Nebraska, for example, the company kept two sets of injury logs: one of them recording every injury and illness at the slaughterhouse, the other provided to visiting OSHA inspectors and researchers from the Bureau of Labor Statistics. During a three-month period in 1985, the first log recorded 1,800 injuries and illnesses at the plant. The OSHA log recorded only 160—a discrepancy of more than 1,000 percent.

At congressional hearings on meatpacking in 1987, Robert L. Peterson, the chief executive of IBP, denied under oath that two sets of logs were ever kept and called IBP's safety record "the best of the best." Congressional investigators later got hold of both logs—and found that the injury rate at its Dakota City plant was as much as one-third higher than the average rate in the meatpacking industry. Congressional investigators also discovered that IBP had altered injury records at its beef plant in Emporia, Kansas. Another leading meatpacking company, John Morrell, was caught lying about injuries at its plant in Sioux Falls, South Dakota. The congressional investigation concluded that these companies had failed to report "serious injuries such as fractures, concussions, major cuts, hernias, some requiring hospitalization, surgery, even amputation."

Congressman Tom Lantos, whose subcommittee conducted the meatpacking inquiry, called IBP "one of the most irresponsible and reckless corporations in America."[11] A Labor Department official called the company's behavior "the worst example of underreporting injuries and illnesses to workers ever encountered in OSHA's sixteen-year history." Nevertheless, Robert L. Peterson was never charged with perjury for his misleading testimony before Congress. Investigators argued that it would be difficult to prove "conclusively" that Peterson had "willfully" lied. In 1987 IBP was fined $2.6 million by OSHA for underreporting injuries and later fined an additional $3.1 million for the high rate of cumulative trauma injuries at the Dakota

City plant. After the company introduced a new safety program there, the fines were reduced to $975,000—a sum that might have appeared large at the time, yet represented about one one-hundredth of a percent of IBP's annual revenues.[12]

Three years after the OSHA fines, a worker named Kevin Wilson injured his back at an IBP slaughterhouse in Council Bluffs, Iowa. Wilson went to see Diane Arndt, a nurse at the plant, who sent him to a doctor selected by the company. Wilson's injury was not serious, the doctor said, later assigning him to light duty at the plant. Wilson sought a second opinion; the new doctor said that he had a disk injury that required a period of absence from work. When Wilson stopped reporting for light duty, IBP's corporate security department began to conduct surveillance of his house. Eleven days after Wilson's new doctor told IBP that back surgery might be required, Diane Arndt called the doctor and said that IBP had obtained a videotape of Wilson engaging in strenuous physical activities at home. The doctor felt deceived, met with Wilson, accused him of being a liar, refused to provide him with any more treatment, and told him to get back to work. Convinced that no such videotape existed and that IBP had fabricated the entire story in order to deny him medical-treatment, Kevin Wilson sued the company for slander.

The lawsuit eventually reached the Iowa Supreme Court. In a decision that received little media attention, the Supreme Court upheld a lower court's award of $2 million to Wilson and described some of IBP's unethical practices. The court found that seriously injured workers were required to show up at the IBP plant briefly each day so that the company could avoid reporting "lost workdays" to OSHA. Some workers were compelled to show up for work on the same day as a surgery or the day after an amputation. "IBP's management was aware of, and participated in, this practice," the Iowa Supreme Court noted. IBP nurses regularly entered false information into the plant's computer system, reclassifying injuries so that they didn't have to be reported to OSHA. Injured workers who proved unco-operative were assigned to jobs "watching gauges in the rendering plant, where they were subjected to an atrocious smell while hog remains were boiled down into fertiliz-ers and blood was drained into tanks." Ac-cording to evidence introduced in court, Diane Arndt had a low opinion of the work-ers whose injuries she was supposed to be treating. The IBP nurse called them "idiots" and "jerks," telling doctors that "this guy's a crybaby" and "this guy's full of shit." She later admitted that Wilson's back injury was legitimate. The Iowa Supreme Court con-cluded that the lies she told in this medical case, as well as in others, had been partly motivated by IBP's financial incentive pro-gram, which gave staff members bonuses and prizes when the number of lost work-days was kept low. The program, in the court's opinion, was "somewhat disingenu-ously called 'the safety award system.'"

IBP's attitude toward worker safety was hardly unique in the industry, according to Edward Murphy's testimony before Con-gress in 1992. Murphy had served as the safety director of the Monfort beef plant in Grand Island. After two workers were killed there in 1991, Monfort fired him. Murphy claimed that he had battled the company for years over safety issues and that Monfort had unfairly made him the scapegoat for its own illegal behavior. The company later paid him an undisclosed sum of money to settle a civil lawsuit over wrongful termination.

Murphy told Congress that during his tenure at the Grand Island plant, Monfort maintained two sets of injury logs, routinely lied to OSHA, and shredded documents requested by OSHA. He wanted Congress to know that the safety lapses at the plant were not accidental. They stemmed directly from Monfort's corporate philosophy, which Murphy described in these terms: "The first commandment is that only production counts . . . The employee's duty is to follow orders. Period. As I was repeatedly told, 'Do what I tell you, even if it is illegal . . . Don't get caught.'"

A lawsuit filed in May of 1998 suggests that little has changed since IBP was caught keeping two sets of injury logs more than a decade ago.[13] Michael D. Ferrell, a former vice president at IBP, contends that the real blame for the high injury rate at the com-pany lies not with the workers, supervisors, nurses, safety directors, or plant managers, but with IBP's top executives. Ferrell had ample opportunity to observe their decision-making process. Among other duties, he was in charge of the health and safety pro-grams at IBP.

When Ferrell accepted the job in 1991, af-ter many years as an industrial engineer at other firms, he believed that IBP's desire to improve worker safety was sincere. Accord-ing to his legal complaint, Ferrell later discov-ered that IBP's safety records were routinely falsified and that the company cared more about production than anything else. Ferrell was fired by IBP in 1997, not long after a se-ries of safety problems at a slaughterhouse in Palestine, Texas. The circumstances sur-rounding his firing are at the heart of the lawsuit. On December 4, 1996, an OSHA in-spection of the Palestine plant found a num-ber of serious violations and imposed a fine of $35,125. Less than a week later, a worker named Clarence Dupree lost an arm in a bone-crushing machine. And two days after that, another worker, Willie Morris, was killed by an ammonia gas explosion. Morris's body lay on the floor for hours, just ten feet from the door, as toxic gas filled the building. Nobody at the plant had been trained to use hazardous-materials gas masks or protective suits; the equipment sat in a locked storage room. Ferrell flew to Texas and toured the plant after the accidents. He thought the facility was in terrible shape—with a cooling system that violated OSHA standards, faulty wiring that threatened to cause a mass electrocution, and safety mechanisms that had deliberately been disabled with magnets. He wanted the slaughterhouse to be shut down immediately, and it was. Two months later, Ferrell lost his job.

In his lawsuit seeking payment for wrongful termination, Ferrell contends that he was fired for giving the order to close the Palestine plant. He claims that IBP had never before shut down a slaughterhouse purely for safety reasons and that Robert L. Peterson was enraged by the decision. IBP disputes this version of events, contending that Ferrell had never fit into IBP's corporate culture, that he delegated too much authority, and that he had not, in fact, made the decision to shut down the Palestine plant.[14] According to IBP, the decision to shut it was made after a unanimous vote by its top executives.

IBP's Palestine slaughterhouse reopened in January of 1997. It was shut down again a year later—this time by the USDA. Federal inspectors cited the plant for "inhumane slaughter" and halted production there for one week, an extremely rare penalty imposed for the mistreatment of cattle. In 1999 IBP closed the plant. As of this writing, it sits empty, awaiting a buyer. . . .

Kenny

During my trips to meatpacking towns in the High Plains I met dozens of workers who'd been injured. Each of their stories was different, yet somehow familiar, linked by common elements—the same struggle to receive proper medical care, the same fear of speaking out, the same underlying corporate indifference. We are human beings, more than one person told me, but they treat us like animals. The workers I met wanted their stories to be told. They wanted people to know about what is happening right now. A young woman who'd injured her back and her right hand at the Greeley plant said to me, "I want to get on top of a rooftop and scream my lungs out so that somebody will hear." The voices and faces of these workers are indelibly with me, as is the sight of their hands, the light brown skin criss-crossed with white scars. Although I cannot tell all of their stories, a few need to be mentioned. Like all lives, they can be used as examples or serve as representative types. But ultimately they are unique, individual, impossible to define or replace—the opposite of how this system has treated them.

Raoul was born in Zapoteca, Mexico, and did construction work in Anaheim before moving to Colorado. He speaks no English. After hearing a Monfort ad on a Spanish-language radio station, he applied for a job at the Greeley plant. One day Raoul reached into a processing machine to remove a piece of meat. The machine accidentally went on. Raoul's arm got stuck, and it took workers twenty minutes to get it out. The machine had to be taken apart. An ambulance brought Raoul to the hospital, where a deep gash in his shoulder was sewn shut. A tendon had been severed. After getting stitches and a strong prescription painkiller, he was driven back to the slaughterhouse and put back on the production line. Bandaged, groggy, and in pain, one arm tied in a sling, Raoul spent the rest of the day wiping blood off cardboard boxes with his good hand.

Renaldo was another Monfort worker who spoke no English, an older man with graying hair. He developed carpal tunnel syndrome while cutting meat. The injury got so bad that sharp pain shot from his hand all the way up to his shoulder. At night it hurt so much he could not fall asleep in bed. Instead he would fall asleep sitting in a chair beside the bed where his wife lay. For three years he slept in that chair every night.

Kenny Dobbins was a Monfort employee for almost sixteen years. He was born in Keokuk, Iowa, had a tough childhood and an abusive stepfather, left home at the age of thirteen, went in and out of various schools, never learned to read, did various odd jobs, and wound up at the Monfort slaughterhouse in Grand Island, Nebraska. He started working there in 1979, right after the company bought it from Swift. He was twenty-four. He worked in the shipping department at first, hauling boxes that weighed as much as 120 pounds. Kenny could handle it, though. He was a big man, muscular and six-foot-five, and nothing in his life had ever been easy.

One day Kenny heard someone yell, "Watch out!" then turned around and saw a ninety-pound box falling from an upper level of the shipping department. Kenny caught the box with one arm, but the momentum threw him against a conveyer belt, and the metal rim of the belt pierced his lower back. The company doctor bandaged Kenny's back and said the pain was just a pulled muscle. Kenny never filed for workers' comp, stayed home for a few days, then returned to work. He had a wife and three children to support. For the next few months, he was in terrible pain. "It hurt so fucking bad you wouldn't believe it," he told me. He saw another doctor, got a second opinion. The new doctor said Kenny had a pair of severely herniated disks. Kenny had back surgery, spent a month in the hospital, got sent to a pain clinic when the operation didn't work. His marriage broke up amid the stress and financial difficulty. Fourteen months after the injury, Kenny returned to the slaughterhouse. "GIVE UP AFTER BACK SURGERY? NOT KEN DOBBINS!!" a Monfort newsletter proclaimed. "Ken has

learned how to handle the rigors of working in a packing plant and is trying to help others do the same. Thanks, Ken, and keep up the good work."

Kenny felt a strong loyalty to Monfort. He could not read, possessed few skills other than his strength, and the company had still given him a job. When Monfort decided to reopen its Greeley plant with a nonunion workforce, Kenny volunteered to go there and help. He did not think highly of labor unions. His supervisors told him that unions had been responsible for shutting down meatpacking plants all over the country. When the UFCW tried to organize the Greeley slaughterhouse, Kenny became an active and outspoken member of an anti-union group.

At the Grand Island facility, Kenny had been restricted to light duty after his injury. But his supervisor in Greeley said that old restrictions didn't apply in this new job. Soon Kenny was doing tough, physical labor once again, wielding a knife and grabbing forty- to fifty-pound pieces of beef off a table. When the pain became unbearable, he was transferred to ground beef, then to rendering. According to a former manager at the Greeley plant, Monfort was trying to get rid of Kenny, trying to make his work so unpleasant that he'd quit. Kenny didn't realize it. "He still believes in his heart that people are honest and good," the former manager said about Kenny. "And he's wrong."

As part of the job in rendering, Kenny sometimes had to climb into gigantic blood tanks and gut bins, reach to the bottom of them with his long arms, and unclog the drains. One day he was unexpectedly called to work over the weekend. There had been a problem with *Salmonella* contamination. The plant needed to be disinfected, and some of the maintenance workers had refused to do it. In his street clothes, Kenny began cleaning the place, climbing into tanks and spraying a liquid chlorine mix. Chlorine is a hazardous chemical that can be inhaled or absorbed through the skin, causing a litany of health problems. Workers who spray it need to wear protective gloves, safety goggles, a self-contained respirator, and full coveralls. Kenny's supervisor gave him a paper dust mask to wear, but it quickly dissolved. After eight hours of working with the chlorine in unventilated areas, Kenny went home and fell ill. He was rushed to the hospital and placed in an oxygen tent. His lungs had been burned by the chemicals. His body was covered in blisters. Kenny spent a month in the hospital.

Kenny eventually recovered from the overexposure to chlorine, but it left his chest feeling raw, made him susceptible to colds and sensitive to chemical aromas. He went back to work at the Greeley plant. He had remarried, didn't know what other kind of work to do, still felt loyal to the company. He was assigned to an early morning shift. He had to drive an old truck from one part of the slaughterhouse complex to another. The truck was filled with leftover scraps of meat. The headlights and the wipers didn't work. The windshield was filthy and cracked. One cold, dark morning in the middle of winter, Kenny became disoriented while driving. He stopped the truck, opened the door, got out to see where he was—and was struck by a train. It knocked his glasses off, threw him up in the air, and knocked both of his work boots off. The train was moving slowly, or he would've been killed. Kenny somehow made it back to the plant, barefoot and bleeding from deep gashes in his back and his face. He spent two weeks at the hospital, then went back to work.

One day, Kenny was in rendering and saw a worker about to stick his head into a pre-breaker machine, a device that uses hundreds of small hammers to pulverize gristle and bone into a fine powder. The worker had just turned the machine off, but Kenny knew the hammers inside were still spinning. It takes fifteen minutes for the machine to shut down completely. Kenny yelled, "Stop!" but the worker didn't hear him. And so Kenny ran across the room, grabbed the man by the seat of his pants, and pulled him away from the machine an instant before it would have pulverized him. To honor this act of bravery, Monfort gave Kenny an award for "Outstanding Achievement in CONCERN FOR FELLOW WORKERS." The award was a paper certificate, signed by his supervisor and the plant safety manager.

Kenny later broke his leg stepping into a hole in the slaughterhouse's concrete floor. On another occasion he shattered an ankle, an injury that required surgery and the insertion of five steel pins. Now Kenny had to wear a metal brace on one leg in order to walk, an elaborate, spring-loaded brace that cost $2,000. Standing for long periods caused him great pain. He was given a job recycling old knives at the plant. Despite his many injuries, the job required him to climb up and down three flights of narrow stairs carrying garbage bags filled with knives. In December of 1995 Kenny felt a sharp pain in his chest while lifting some boxes. He thought it was a heart attack. His union steward took him to see the nurse, who said it was just a pulled muscle and sent Kenny home. He was indeed having a massive heart attack. A friend rushed Kenny to a nearby hospital. A stent was inserted in his heart, and the doctors told Kenny that he was lucky to be alive.

While Kenny Dobbins was recuperating, Monfort fired him. Despite the fact that Kenny had been with the company for almost sixteen years, despite the fact that he was first in seniority at the Greeley plant, that he'd cleaned blood tanks with his bare hands, fought the union, done whatever the company had asked him to do, suffered injuries that would've killed weaker men, nobody from Monfort called him with the news. Nobody even bothered to write him. Kenny learned that he'd been fired when his payments to the company health insurance plan kept being returned by the post office. He called Monfort repeatedly to find out what was going on, and a sympathetic clerk in the claims office finally told Kenny that the checks were being returned because he was no longer a Monfort employee. When I asked company spokesmen to comment on the accuracy of Kenny's story, they would neither confirm nor deny any of the details.

Today Kenny is in poor health. His heart is permanently damaged. His immune system seems shot. His back hurts, his ankle hurts, and every so often he coughs up blood. He is unable to work at any job. His wife, Clara—who's half-Latina and half-Cheyenne, and looks like a younger sister of Cher's—was working as a nursing home attendant when Kenny had the heart attack. Amid the stress of his illness, she developed a serious kidney ailment. She is unemployed and recovering from a kidney transplant.

As I sat in the living room of their Greeley home, its walls decorated with paintings of wolves, Denver Broncos memorabilia, and an American flag, Kenny and Clara told me about their financial condition. After almost sixteen years on the job, Kenny did not get any pension from Monfort. The company challenged his workers' comp claim and finally agreed—three years after the initial filing—to pay him a settlement of $35,000. Fifteen percent of that money went to Kenny's lawyer, and the rest is long gone. Some months Kenny has to hock things to get money for Clara's medicine. They have two teenage children and live on Social Security payments. Kenny's health insurance, which costs more than $600 a month, is about to run out. His anger at Monfort, his feelings of betrayal, are of truly biblical proportions.

"They used me to the point where I had no body parts left to give," Kenny said, struggling to maintain his composure. "Then they just tossed me into the trash can." Once strong and powerfully built, he now walks with difficulty, tires easily, and feels useless, as though his life were over. He is forty-six years old.

NOTES

1. This chapter is based largely on interviews that I conducted with dozens of Latino meatpacking workers in Colorado and Nebraska. I also interviewed a former slaughterhouse safety director, a former slaughterhouse nurse, former plant supervisors, and a physician whose medical practice was for years devoted to the treatment of slaughterhouse workers. All of these managerial personnel had left the meatpacking industry by choice; none had been fired; and their reluctance to use their real names in this book stems from the widespread fear of the meatpackers in rural communities where they operate. I am grateful to those who spoke with me and showed me around.

    Deborah E. Berkowitz, the former director of health and safety at the UFCW, was an invaluable source of information about the workings of a modern slaughterhouse and the dangers that workers face there. Her article on meatpacking and meat processing in *The Encyclopaedia of Occupational Health and Safety* (Geneva, Switzerland: International Labour Organization, 1998), cowritten with Michael J. Fagel, is a good introduction to the subject. Curt Brandt, the president of UFCW Local 22 in Fremont, Nebraska, described the various tactics he's seen meatpacking firms use over the years to avoid compensating injured workers. Two Colorado attorneys, Joseph Goldhammer and Dennis E. Valentine, helped me understand the intricacies of their state's workers' comp law and described their work on behalf of injured Monfort employees. Rod Rehm, an attorney based in Lincoln, Nebraska, spent many hours depicting the conditions in his state and arranged for me to meet some of his clients. Rehm is an outspoken advocate for poor Latinos in a state where they have few political allies. Bruce L. Braley, one of the attorneys in *Ferrell v. IBP,* told me a great deal about the company's behavior and sent me stacks of documents pertaining to the case. "Killing Them Softly: Work in Meatpacking Plants and What It Does to Workers," by Donald D. Stull and Michael J. Broadway, in *Any Way You Cut It,* is one of the best published accounts of America's most dangerous job. "Here's the

Beef: Underreporting of Injuries, OSHA's Policy of Exempting Companies from Programmed Inspections Based on Injury Record, and Unsafe Conditions in the Meatpacking Industry," *Forty-Second Report by the Committee on Government Operations* (Washington, D.C.: U.S. Government Printing Office, 1988), shows the extraordinary abuses that can occur when an industry is allowed to regulate itself. After the congressional investigation, Christopher Drew wrote a terrific series of articles on meatpacking, published by the *Chicago Tribune* in October of 1988. The fact that working conditions have changed little since then is remarkably depressing. Gail A. Eisnitz's *Slaughterhouse: The Shocking Story of Greed, Neglect, and Inhumane Treatment Inside the U.S. Meat Industry* (Amherst, N.Y.: Prometheus Books, 1997), suggests that many cattle are needlessly brutalized prior to slaughter. Nothing that these sources reveal would come as a surprise to readers of Upton Sinclair.

2. . . . In 1999, the most recent year for which statistics are available, the injury and illness rate in the nation's meatpacking industry was 26.7 per 100 hundred workers. For the rest of U.S. manufacturing, it was 9.2 per hundred workers. See "Industries with the Highest Nonfatal Total Cases, Incidence Rates for Injuries and Illnesses, Private Industry, 1999," Bureau of Labor Statistics, December 2000; and "Incidence Rates of Nonfatal Occupational Injuries and Illnesses by Selected Industries and Case Types, 1999," Bureau of Labor Statistics, U.S. Department of Labor, December 2000.

3. . . . The meatpacking industry now has about 147,600 workers, and at least 26.7 percent of them suffer workplace injuries and illnesses. See "Industries with the Highest Nonfatal Total Cases." . . .

4. . . . In 1999 the incidence of repeated trauma injuries in private industry was 27.3 per 10,000 workers; in the poultry industry the rate was 337.1; and in the meatpacking industry it was 912.5. See "Industries with the Highest Nonfatal Illness Incidence Rate of Disorders Associated with Repeated Trauma and the Number of Cases in These Industries," Bureau of Labor Statistics, U.S. Department of Labor, December 2000. . . .

5. . . . *beef slaughterhouses often operate at profit margins:* According to Steve Bjerklie, the profit margin for slaughter is about 1 percent, with additional earnings from processing and the sale of byproducts. See Steve Bjerklie, "On the Horns of a Dilemma," in *Any Way You Cut It,* p. 42. . . .

6. . . . Cited in Cohen, "Free Ride with Help from INS."

7. . . . *"screamed obscenities and rubbed their bodies":* A federal judge later reduced the award to $1.75 million. See Lynn Hicks, "IBP Worker Awarded $2.4 Million by Jury," *Des Moines Register,* February 27, 1999; Lynn Hicks, "Worker: Sexism, Racism at IBP," *Des Moines Register,* February 3, 1999; "IBP Told to Pay Attorney's Fees," *Des Moines Register,* December 30, 1999.

8. . . . See "Monfort Beef to Pay $900,000 to Settle Sexual Harassment Suit," *Houston Chronicle,* September 1, 1999.

9. . . . See "Liberal Packing Plant Fined $960," *UPI,* October 19, 1983.

10. . . . See Christopher Drew, "A Chain of Setbacks for Meat Workers," *Chicago Tribune,* October 25, 1988. . . .

11. . . . Quoted in Donald Woutat, "Meatpacker IBP Fined $3.1 Million in Safety Action; Health Problem Disabled More Than 600, OSHA Says," *Los Angeles Times,* May 12, 1988. . . .

12. . . . See Christopher Drew, "IBP Agrees to Injury Plan," *Chicago Tribune,* November 23, 1988; Marianne Lavelle, "When Fines Collapse: Critics Target OSHA's Settlements," *National Law Journal,* December 4, 1989. . . .

13. . . . For Ferrell's side of the case, I have relied upon "Plaintiff's Statement of Specific Disputed Facts and Additional Material Facts," *Michael D. Ferrell v IBP, Inc.,* United States District Court for the Northern District of Iowa, Western Division, May 7, 1999.

14. . . . For IBP's version of events, I have relied upon "Statement of Undisputed Facts in Support of Defendant's Motion for Summary Judgment," *Michael D. Ferrell v IBP, Inc.,* United States District Court for the Northern District of Iowa, Western Division, March 6, 1999.

SERVICE WORK

 READING 27

Over the Counter
McDonald's

Robin Leidner

McDonald's

No one ever walks into a McDonald's and asks, "So, what's good today?" except satirically. The heart of McDonald's success is its uniformity and predictability. Not only is the food supposed to taste the same every day everywhere in the world, but McDonald's promises that every meal will be served quickly, courteously, and with a smile. Delivering on that promise over 20 million times a day in 54 countries is the company's colossal challenge (*McDonald's Annual Report* for 1990: 2). Its strategy for meeting that challenge draws on scientific management's most basic tenets: find the One Best Way to do every task and see that the work is conducted accordingly.

To insure that all McDonald's restaurants serve products of uniform quality, the company uses centralized planning, centrally designed training programs, centrally approved and supervised suppliers, automated machinery and other specially designed equipment, meticulous specifications, and systematic inspections. To provide its customers with a uniformly pleasant "McDonald's experience," the company also tries to mass-produce friendliness, deference, diligence, and good cheer through a variety of socialization and social control techniques. Despite sneers from those who equate uniformity with mediocrity, the success of McDonald's has been spectacular.

McFacts

By far the world's largest fast-food company, McDonald's has over 11,800 stores worldwide (*McDonald's Annual Report* for 1990: 1), and its 1990 international sales surpassed those of its three largest competitors combined (Berg 1991: sec. 3, 6). In the United States, consumer familiarity with McDonald's is virtually universal: the company estimates that 95 percent of U.S. consumers eat at a McDonald's at least once a year (Koepp 1987: 58). McDonald's 1990 profits were $802.3 million, the third highest profits of any retailing company in the world (*Fortune* 1991: 179). At a time when the ability of many U.S. businesses to compete on the world market is in question, McDonald's continues to expand around the globe—most recently to Morocco—everywhere remaking consumer demand in its own image.

As politicians, union leaders, and others concerned with the effects of the shift to a service economy are quick to point out,

---

McDonald's is a major employer. McDonald's restaurants in the United States employ about half a million people (Bertagnoli 1989: 33), including one out of fifteen first-time job seekers (Wildavsky 1989: 30). The company claims that 7 percent of all current U.S. workers have worked for McDonald's at some time (Koepp 1987: 59). Not only has McDonald's directly influenced the lives of millions of workers, but its impact has also been extended by the efforts of many kinds of organizations, especially in the service sector, to imitate the organizational features they see as central to McDonald's success.

For a company committed to standardization, McDonald's inspires strikingly varied reactions, both as an employer and as a cultural icon. On one side, Barbara Garson (1988), for instance, presents work at McDonald's as so systematized, automated, and closely monitored that all opportunity for thought, initiative, and human contact, let alone self-development, has been removed. To other critics, the ubiquity and uniformity of McDonald's epitomize the homogenization of U.S. culture and its imperialist export. At McDonald's, they point out, local culture is invisible and irrelevant, personal interactions are flattened into standardized patterns, and individual preferences are subordinated to efficient production processes. Nutritionists scorn McDonald's menu, environmentalists its packaging.

However, McDonald's has been as widely admired as reviled. To its supporters, McDonald's represents efficiency, order, familiarity, good cheer, and good value. Many business writers hold McDonald's up as an example of excellence in service management (see, e.g., Heskett, Sasser, and Hart 1990; Peters and Austin 1985; Zemke with Schaaf 1989). A pioneer in the standardization and mass-production of food and service, the company is often represented as emblematic of American capitalist know-how. It is a company whose phenomenal growth has resulted from steadfast commitment to its basic promise to customers of fast service, hot food, and clean restaurants.

The relentless standardization and infinite replication that inspire both horror and admiration are the legacy of Ray Kroc, a salesman who got into the hamburger business in 1954, when he was fifty-two years old, and created a worldwide phenomenon.[1] His inspiration was a phenomenally successful hamburger stand owned by the McDonald brothers of San Bernardino, California. He believed that their success could be reproduced consistently through carefully controlled franchises, and his hamburger business succeeded on an unprecedented scale. The basic idea was to serve a very few items of strictly uniform quality at low prices. Over the years, the menu has expanded somewhat and prices have risen, but the emphasis on strict, detailed standardization has never varied.

Kroc set out to achieve the kind of tight control over work routines and product quality that centralized production in factories makes possible, although the fast-food business is necessarily highly decentralized. Not only are the stores geographically dispersed, but approximately 75 percent of McDonald's outlets are owned by individual franchisees rather than by the corporation (*McDonald's Annual Report* for 1989: i). In his autobiography, Kroc describes how he approached the problem of combining standardization with decentralization (Kroc with Anderson 1977: 86):

> Our aim, of course, was to insure repeat business based on the system's reputation rather than on the quality of a single store or operator. This would require a continuing program of educating and assisting operators and a constant review of their performance. It would also require a full-time program of research and development. I knew in my bones that the key to uniformity would be in

our ability to provide techniques of preparation that operators would accept because they were superior to methods they could dream up for themselves.

McDonald's franchise owners retain control over some matters, including pay scales, but the company requires that every store's production methods and products meet McDonald's precise specifications. The company encourages and enforces compliance with its standards in a variety of ways. The franchise agreements detail the obligations of both the owners and the corporation; the corporation requires that all potential owners go through its rigorous store-management training program; the corporation provides training materials for crew people and managers that include step-by-step instructions for every task in the store; raters from the corporation regularly visit franchises to evaluate their quality, service, and cleanliness; and owners must purchase their equipment and food products from suppliers approved by the corporation. For those aspects of store operation not specifically covered by the franchise agreement, the corporation must persuade franchisees that they will maximize their profits by following the recommendations of the corporation. Given McDonald's phenomenal success, this persuasive power is considerable, as Kroc intended.

Luxenberg (1985: 77) writes that "Kroc introduced an extreme regimentation that had never been attempted in a service business." This regimentation is not limited to food-preparation techniques. McDonald's has standardized procedures for bookkeeping, purchasing, dealing with workers and customers, and virtually every other aspect of the business. But it is the assembly-line techniques used to produce and serve identical products in every McDonald's that are most salient for workers and most relevant to customers. These are the procedures

designed to ensure that the food served to customers will be up to McDonald's standards and that customers will not have to wait more than a few minutes for their meal. The most comprehensive guide to corporate specifications for producing and serving "McDonald's quality" food is the "Operations and Training Manual"—McDonald's managers call it "the Bible"—which describes company procedures and standards in painstaking detail. Its 600 pages include, for instance, full-color photographs illustrating the proper placement of ketchup, mustard, and pickle slices on each type of hamburger on the menu. McDonald's stresses that these specifications are not arrived at arbitrarily, but are the accumulated fruits of years of experience and research. Franchise owners are kept up-to-date on corporate specifications by means of regularly issued bulletins.

Enforcement of McDonald's standards has been made easier over the years by the introduction of highly specialized equipment. Every company-owned store in the United States now has an "in-store processor," a computer system that calculates yields and food costs, keeps track of inventory and cash, schedules labor, and breaks down sales by time of day, product, and worker (*McDonald's Annual Report* for 1989: 29). In today's McDonald's, lights and buzzers tell workers exactly when to turn burgers or take fries out of the fat, and technologically advanced cash registers, linked to the computer system, do much of the thinking for window workers. Specially designed ketchup dispensers squirt exactly the right amount of ketchup on each burger in the approved flower pattern. The french-fry scoops let workers fill a bag and set it down in one continuous motion and help them gauge the proper serving size.

The extreme standardization of McDonald's products, and its workers, is closely tied to its marketing. The company advertises on a massive scale—in 1989, McDonald's spent $1.1 billion system-wide on advertising and promotions (*McDonald's Annual Report* for 1989: 32). In fact, McDonald's is the single most advertised brand in the world (*Advertising Age* 1990: 6). The national advertising assures the public that it will find high standards of quality, service, and cleanliness at every McDonald's store. The intent of the strict quality-control standards applied to every aspect of running a McDonald's outlet, from proper cleaning of the bathrooms to making sure the hamburgers are served hot, is to help franchise owners keep the promises made in the company's advertising.

The image of McDonald's outlets promoted in the company's advertising is one of fun, wholesomeness, and family orientation. Kroc was particularly concerned that his stores not become teen-age hangouts, since that would discourage families' patronage. To minimize their attractiveness to teenage loiterers, McDonald's stores do not have jukeboxes, video games, or even telephones. Kroc initially decided not to hire young women to work behind McDonald's counters for the same reason: "They attracted the wrong kind of boys" (Boas and Chain 1976: 19). . . .

One McDonald's Franchise

I was assigned to a McDonald's in the downtown area of a small city near Chicago. It was a new store, only about fifteen months old when I began my fieldwork, but an exemplary one; it had recently won a major McDonald's award. The store was far more elegant than the average McDonald's. Adjacent to an expensive hotel, the restaurant was designed to seem "high-class," not garish or tacky. The interior decor included marble walls, a mahogany dining counter, black Art Deco fixtures, and mauve draperies. Outside were window boxes filled with flowers or greenery, and a relatively small Golden Arches sign, since the city council would not permit a large one.

This McDonald's differed from most in that it had neither a parking lot nor a drive-thru [*sic*] service window. It depended on pedestrian traffic for business, and its clientele included business people, college students, senior citizens, and shoppers. Fewer families came in than is typical for a McDonald's, and more people ordered just coffee or ice cream rather than a full meal; the average check size was accordingly smaller than at most McDonald's stores. At the time of my research in 1986, the store served 1,700 customers on an average day. In the course of a year, those customers collectively spent about one and a half million dollars. (The average McDonald's store brought in $1.34 million in 1985, half of it in drive-thru sales [training center lecture].)

The franchisee who owned the store owned three other McDonald's stores in the Chicago suburbs. The business had made him wealthy, and he proudly showed off a "new toy" to me, a Corvette convertible, complete with telephone. He also had a yacht. He, his wife, and some of their grown children were closely involved in running the store, coming in several times a week, planning improvements, and overseeing the operation. Such involvement is encouraged by the corporation, which wants all of its franchisees to be "owner/operators," not just investors.

This McDonald's store had five salaried managers, all male, three white and two black. The owner's son, another white, also worked as a manager on occasion. In addition, there were as many as five hourly swing managers at a time (all female; three black, one white, one Native American). During my fieldwork, two crew people, a black woman and an Asian man, were promoted to that level of management.

The store's crew fluctuated in size between sixty-five and about one hundred people in the course of six months; the store manager believed that eighty-five was optimal. There were about equal numbers of window workers and grill workers.

Personnel policies at McDonald's franchises, including pay scales, are determined by the franchise owners, not by the corporation. Many press reports have described fast-food franchises raising wages and offering benefits to compete for the declining number of teenage workers, but the crew at this franchise, both grill and window workers, started work at the federal minimum wage, $3.35 in 1986, and they received no benefits such as health insurance, paid holidays, or paid sick days. Merit raises of five or ten cents per hour were granted quarterly, when job performance reviews were made, and crew people promoted to crew trainer or crew chief received raises of five to fifteen cents per hour as well. The pay remained quite low, however. One crew trainer who had worked at the franchise for about a year and a half was earning $3.75.

Most, though not all, male crew members worked on the grill and most female crew members worked on the window. This pattern was usually based on managers' decisions when hiring workers. Some crew people reported having been given a choice about where they would start out, but more than half said that they had been assigned to their first job. A couple of crew people reported that the first women to be cross-trained to work on the grill had to persuade managers that they should be allowed to do so. In my interview sample of window people, 75 percent of the workers were women; according to the store's manager, this proportion accurately approximated the actual gender composition of the job category.

Salaried managers were expected to work forty-six to fifty hours per week. Officially, all of McDonald's crew workers are part-time, but 25 percent of my interview sample of window crew said that they usually worked thirty-five hours or more per week. The number of hours worked by crew people varied greatly, since many of them were students who only wished to work a few hours per week. Those who did want longer hours were expected to compete for them, proving themselves deserving through conscientious job performance. In practice, a core group of about twenty steady workers was sure to get its preferred hours, but cutting back an employee's hours was a standard way the managers showed their displeasure over poor job performance or attitude. The usual strategy for getting rid of poor workers, the store manager told me, was to decrease the hours they were scheduled to work until they got the message.

Through its scheduling practices McDonald's attempted to minimize labor costs without sacrificing speedy service for customers. As in almost all restaurants, McDonald's business normally came in waves rather than in a steady stream, with big rushes at meal times. On the one hand, managers did not want to have to pay crew people for hours they were not needed, since crew labor productivity is one of the main criteria by which managers are judged (Garson 1988: 32). On the other hand, they wanted to be sure to have enough people to keep lines moving quickly when business was brisk. The computerized cash-register system analyzed sales by hour of the day and day of the week, and managers used these figures to schedule work crews.

Since, however, computer projections are never entirely accurate, the schedules at this McDonald's were designed so that workers bore much of the burden of uncertainty. On the work schedule, posted one week in advance, a line for each crew person showed the hours she or he was scheduled to work. A solid line indicated hours the employee could count on working, and a zigzag line marked an additional hour or so. If the store was busy when a worker's guaranteed hours were finished, she or he would be required to work that extra time; if it was not busy, she or he would be asked to leave. In addition, it was quite common at unexpectedly quiet times for managers to tell workers they could leave before their scheduled hours were completed or even to pressure them to leave when they would rather have kept on working. I heard one manager say, "Come on, can't I make a profit today?" when a crew person resisted being sent home fifteen minutes early. Conversely, when the store was busy, managers were reluctant to let workers go when their scheduled hours, including the optional time, were done. When lines of people were waiting to be served, workers—I was one of them—would often have to ask repeatedly to be "punched out" (off the time clock) at the end of their shift.

Workers' preferences for longer or shorter hours varied; some wanted to earn as much as possible, others preferred to have more time for other activities. Whatever their preferences, the scheduling practices made it difficult for workers to plan ahead. Arrangements for transportation, social activities, child care, and so on could be disrupted by unexpected changes in the schedule, and workers could not accurately predict how much money they would earn in a given week. Furthermore, one of the most common complaints among the workers was that they had been scheduled to work at times they had said they were not available. Once on the schedule, they were held responsible for finding a replacement (see Garson 1988: 32–33). Since the McDonald's schedule was made up of such small units of time, however, it was usually relatively easy for workers to arrange hours for their convenience, an advantage McDonald's emphasized in recruitment. For example, workers who played on a high school team could cut down their hours during the sports season, and workers who needed to take a particular day off could usually arrange it if they gave sufficient notice.

The Interview Sample

Thirty-five percent of my sample was of high school age. (It is possible that I undersampled high school students simply because, since they were less likely to work many hours, I had less opportunity to meet them.) Although the majority of my sample (65 percent) were eighteen years old or over, 60 percent of the crew people told me that this was their first job.

The great majority of the crew people in the store were black, although blacks are a minority, albeit a large one, of the city's population. In my interview sample, 80 percent were black (including three Caribbean immigrants), one person was Hispanic-American, one was an Asian immigrant, and the rest were American-born white. A sizable minority of the workers commuted long distances, from the South Side and the West Side of Chicago. A full 25 percent of my sample had one-way commutes that took at least an hour and required at least one change of train, and I knew of several other workers with commutes at least that long. Given that the crew people started work at McDonald's at minimum wage, this pattern strongly suggests that these workers had been unable to find work near their homes or better-paying jobs elsewhere.

About two-thirds of the store's crew people were trained to work at the window. My sample of twenty-six window workers was not completely representative of all of the employees who worked behind the counter during the months I was there. Since my sampling method depended on my meeting the worker in the crew room, I probably oversampled those who worked relatively long or relatively steady hours and missed both those who worked only a few hours per week and those who worked for only a short time before quitting. I oversampled crew trainers and crew chiefs—30 percent of my sample had been promoted to one of these

Handwritten margin note (top): Workers: Thought v. Little & are monitored thru computerized registers

jobs. However, according to the store's manager, my sample was fairly representative of the store's population of customer-service workers in its gender, race, and age distributions. . . .

The Routine

McDonald's had routinized the work of its crews so thoroughly that decision making had practically been eliminated from the jobs. As one window worker told me, "They've tried to break it down so that it's almost idiot-proof." Most of the workers agreed that there was little call for them to use their own judgment on the job, since there were rules about everything. If an unusual problem arose, the workers were supposed to turn it over to a manager.

Many of the noninteractive parts of the window workers' job had been made idiot-proof through automation. The soda machines, for example, automatically dispensed the proper amount of beverage for regular, medium, and large cups. Computerized cash registers performed a variety of functions handled elsewhere by human waitresses, waiters, and cashiers, making some kinds of skill and knowledge unnecessary. As a customer gave an order, the window worker simply pressed the cash register button labeled with the name of the selected product. There was no need to write the orders down, because the buttons lit up to indicate which products had been selected. Nor was there any need to remember prices, because the prices were programmed into the machines. Like most new cash registers, these added the tax automatically and told workers how much change customers were owed, so the window crew did not need to know how to do those calculations. The cash registers also helped regulate some of the crew's interactive work by reminding them to try to increase the size of each sale.

For example, when a customer ordered a Big Mac, large fries, and a regular Coke, the cash register buttons for cookies, hot apple pies, ice cream cones, and ice cream sundaes would light up, prompting the worker to suggest dessert. It took some skill to operate the relatively complicated cash register, as my difficulties during my first work shift made clear, but this organizationally specific skill could soon be acquired on the job.

In addition to doing much of the workers' thinking for them, the computerized cash registers made it possible for managers to monitor the crew members' work and the store's inventory very closely. For example, if the number of Quarter Pounder with Cheese boxes gone did not match the number of Quarter Pounder with Cheese sold or accounted for as waste, managers might suspect that workers were giving away or taking food. Managers could easily tell which workers had brought in the most money during a given interval and who was doing the best job of persuading customers to buy a particular item. The computerized system could also complicate what would otherwise have been simple customer requests, however. For example, when a man who had not realized the benefit of ordering his son's food as a Happy Meal came back to the counter to ask whether his little boy could have one of the plastic beach pails the Happy Meals were served in, I had to ask a manager what to do, since fulfilling the request would produce a discrepancy between the inventory and the receipts. Sometimes the extreme systematization can induce rather than prevent idiocy, as when a window worker says she cannot serve a cup of coffee that is half decaffeinated and half regular because she would not know how to ring up the sale.[2]

The interactive part of window work is routinized through the Six Steps of Window Service and also through rules aimed at standardizing attitudes and demeanors as

Handwritten margin notes (left): Opposite problem of Nork workers; Everything is automated / routinized

Handwritten margin note (right): Workers monitored & limited by computers

[handwritten: Do people do emotion work as customers?]

well as words and actions. The window workers were taught that they represented McDonald's to the public and that their attitudes were therefore an important component of service quality. Crew people could be reprimanded for not smiling, and often were. The window workers were supposed to be cheerful and polite at all times, but they were also told to be themselves while on the job. McDonald's does not want its workers to seem like robots, so part of the emotion work asked of the window crew is that they act naturally. "Being yourself" in this situation meant behaving in a way that did not seem stilted. Although workers had some latitude to go beyond the script, the short, highly schematic routine obviously did not allow much room for genuine self-expression.

[handwritten margin: Emotion work]

Workers were not the only ones constrained by McDonald's routines, of course. The cooperation of service-recipients was crucial to the smooth functioning of the operation. In many kinds of interactive service work . . . constructing the compliance of service-recipients is an important part of the service worker's job. The routines such workers use may be designed to maximize the control each worker has over customers. McDonald's window workers' routines were not intended to give them much leverage over customers' behavior, however. The window workers interacted only with people who had already decided to do business with McDonald's and who therefore did not need to be persuaded to take part in the service interaction. Furthermore, almost all customers were familiar enough with McDonald's routines to know how they were expected to behave. For instance, I never saw a customer who did not know that she or he was supposed to come up to the counter rather than sit down and wait to be served. This customer training was accomplished through advertising, spatial design, customer experience, and the example of other customers, making it unnecessary for

[handwritten margin: Even most customers "know how to behave"]

the window crew to put much effort into getting customers to fit into their work routines.

McDonald's ubiquitous advertising trains consumers at the same time that it tries to attract them to McDonald's. Television commercials demonstrate how the service system is supposed to work and familiarize customers with new products. Additional cues about expected customer behavior are provided by the design of the restaurants. For example, the entrances usually lead to the service counter, not to the dining area, making it unlikely that customers will fail to realize that they should get in line, and the placement of waste cans makes clear that customers are expected to throw out their own trash. Most important, the majority of customers have had years of experience with McDonald's, as well as with other fast-food restaurants that have similar arrangements. The company estimates that the average customer visits a McDonald's twenty times a year (Koepp 1987: 58), and it is not uncommon for a customer to come in several times per week. For many customers, then, ordering at McDonald's is as routine an interaction as it is for the window worker. Indeed, because employee turnover is so high, steady customers may be more familiar with the work routines than the workers serving them are. Customers who are new to McDonald's can take their cue from more experienced customers.

Not surprisingly, then, most customers at the McDonald's I studied knew what was expected of them and tried to play their part well. They sorted themselves into lines and gazed up at the menu boards while waiting to be served. They usually gave their orders in the conventional sequence: burgers or other entrees, french fries or other side orders, drinks, and desserts. Hurried customers with savvy might order an item "only if it's in the bin," that is, ready to be served. Many customers prepared carefully so that they could give their orders promptly when they got to

[handwritten right margin: Advertising, teaches "customers" as does rest. layout]

the counter. This preparation sometimes became apparent when a worker interrupted to ask, "What kind of dressing?" or "Cream and sugar?", flustering customers who could not deliver their orders as planned.

McDonald's routines, like those of other interactive service businesses, depend on the predictability of customers, but these businesses must not grind to a halt if customers are not completely cooperative. Some types of deviations from standard customer behavior are so common that they become routine themselves, and these can be handled through subroutines (Stinchcombe 1990: 39). McDonald's routines work most efficiently when all customers accept their products exactly as they are usually prepared; indeed, the whole business is based on this premise. Since, however, some people give special instructions for customized products, such as "no onions," the routine allows for these exceptions. At the franchise I studied, workers could key the special requests into their cash registers, which automatically printed out "grill slips" with the instructions for the grill workers to follow. Under this system, the customer making the special order had to wait for it to be prepared, but the smooth flow of service for other customers was not interrupted. Another type of routine difficulty was customer dissatisfaction with food quality. Whenever a customer had a complaint about the food—cold fries, dried-out burger—window workers were authorized to supply a new product immediately without consulting a supervisor.

These two kinds of difficulties—special orders and complaints about food—were the only irregularities window workers were authorized to handle. The subroutines increased the flexibility of the service system, but they did not increase the workers' discretion, since procedures were in place for dealing with both situations. All other kinds of demands fell outside the window crew's purview. If they were faced with a

dispute about money, an extraordinary request, or a furious customer, workers were instructed to call a manager; the crew had no authority to handle such problems.

Given the almost complete regimentation of tasks and preemption of decision making, does McDonald's need the flexibility and thoughtfulness of human workers? As the declining supply of teenagers and legislated increases in the minimum wage drive up labor costs, it is not surprising that McDonald's is experimenting with electronic replacements. So far, the only robot in use handles behind-the-scenes work rather than customer interactions. ARCH (Automated Restaurant Crew Helper) works in a Minnesota McDonald's where it does all the frying and lets workers know when to prepare sandwich buns, when supplies are running low, and when fries are no longer fresh enough to sell. Other McDonald's stores (along with Arby's and Burger King units) are experimenting with a touch-screen computer system that lets customers order their meals themselves, further curtailing the role of the window worker. Although it requires increased customer socialization and cooperation, early reports are that the system cuts service time by thirty seconds and increases sales per window worker 10–20 percent (Chaudhry 1989: F61).

Getting Workers to Work

The extreme routinization does not mean that McDonald's work is undemanding. I found that the company asked a lot of its workers, and the stresses of the job could be considerable. Especially when the store was busy, window work was extraordinarily hectic. From the grill area came the sounds of buzzers buzzing and people shouting instructions. Workers dashed from side to side behind the counter to pick up the various products they needed. Just getting around was extremely difficult.

— Again, problematizes idea of 'unskilled'

Why McD's employees work so hard for min. wage

Many difficulties & chaotic moments

There might be six window workers, a manager or two overseeing the flow of food from the grill and backing up window workers, and another worker in charge of french fries, all trying to maneuver in a very small area, all hurrying, often carrying drinks, ice cream cones, stacks of burgers. Workers with pails of soapy water would frequently come to mop up the greasy floor, leaving it slippery and treacherous even for workers in the regulation nonskid shoes. Traffic jams formed around the soda machines and the salad cases. In the course of a shift various supplies would run out, and there would be no lids for the large cups, no clean trays, no Italian dressing, no ice, until someone found a moment to replenish the stock. Food products were frequently not ready when needed, frustrating window workers' efforts to gather their orders speedily—the supply of Big Macs in the food bin could be wiped out at any moment by a worker with an order for four of them, forcing several other workers to explain to their customers that they would have to wait for their food. The customers, of course, could be a major source of stress themselves. All in all, McDonald's work may be regarded as unskilled, but it was by no means easy to do well. Window workers had to be able to keep many things in mind at once, to keep calm under fire, and to exhibit considerable physical and emotional stamina.

Even when the store was not crowded, workers were expected to keep busy, in accordance with the McDonald's slogan "If there's time to lean, there's time to clean." I was struck by how hard-working most of the crew people were:

> Matthew moves very fast, sweeps up whenever he has a spare moment. In fact, all of the crew people work like beavers— backing each other up, cleaning, etc.

Considering workers' low wages and limited stake in the success of the enterprise, why did they work so hard? Their intensity of effort was produced by several kinds of pressures. First, it seemed to me that most workers did conceive of the work as a team effort and were loath to be seen by their peers as making extra work for other people by not doing their share. Even workers who had what managers would define as a "bad attitude"—resentment about low wages, disrespectful treatment, or any other issue— might work hard in order to keep the respect of their peers.

Naturally, managers played a major role in keeping crew people hard at work. At this store, managers were virtually always present behind the counter and in the grill area. During busy periods several managers would be there at once, working side by side with the crew as well as issuing instructions. Any slacking off by a worker was thus very likely to be noticed. Managers insisted on constant effort; they clearly did not want to pay workers for a moment of nonproductive time. For instance, I heard a manager reprimand a grill worker for looking at the work schedule: "Are you off work? No? You look at the schedule on your time, not on my time." A handwritten sign was posted recommending that window workers come in fifteen minutes early to count out the money in their cash-register drawers on their own time so that, if the amount was wrong, they would not later be held responsible for a shortage. Crew trainers and crew chiefs were encouraged to let managers know about any workers who were shirking or causing problems.

The presence of customers on the scene was another major factor in intensifying workers' efforts. When long lines of people were waiting to be served, few workers had to be told to work as swiftly as possible. The sea of expectant faces provided a great deal of pressure to keep moving. Window workers in particular were anxious to avoid antagonizing customers, who were likely to take

Pressures (neg.)

Why hard workers
(cont'd)

out any dissatisfactions on them. The surest way to keep people happy was to keep the lines moving quickly. The arrangement of the workplace, which made window workers clearly visible to the waiting customers as they went about their duties, and customers clearly visible to workers, was important in keeping crew people hard at work. This pressure could have an effect even if customers did not complain. For example, on the day I was to be trained to work window during breakfast, I spent quite a while standing behind the counter, in uniform, waiting to be given instructions and put to work. I was acutely aware that customers were likely to wonder why I did not take their orders, and I tried to adopt an air of attentive expectancy rather than one of casual loitering, in the hope that the customers would assume there was a good reason for my idleness.

These sorts of pressures were not the only reasons crew people worked hard and enthusiastically, however. Managers also tried to motivate them to strenuous efforts through positive means. The managers' constant presence meant that good work would not go unnoticed. McDonald's Corporation stresses the importance of acknowledging workers' efforts, and several workers mentioned that they appreciated such recognition. Indeed, I was surprised at how much it cheered me when a manager complimented me on my "good eye contact" with customers. Various incentive systems were in place as well, to make workers feel that it was in their individual interest to work hard. Free McDonald's meals (instead of the usual half-priced ones) and free record albums were some of the rewards available to good workers. Contests for the highest sales totals or most special raspberry milk shakes sold in a given hour encouraged window workers to compete in speed and pushiness. The possibility of promotion to crew trainer, crew chief, or swing

⟵ Pressures (positive)

manager also motivated some workers to work as hard as possible.

Group incentives seemed to be especially effective in motivating the crew. As part of a national advertising effort stressing service, all of the stores in McDonald's Chicago region competed to improve their speed. The owner of the store where I worked promised that if one of his stores came out near the top in this competition, the entire crew would be treated to a day at a large amusement park and the crew trainers would be invited for a day's outing on his yacht. The crew trainers and many other workers were very excited about this possibility and were willing to try to achieve unprecedented standards of speed. (They did not win the prize, but the crew of one of the owner's other stores did.) Some workers, though, especially the more disaffected ones, had no desire for either promotions or the low-cost rewards available and spoke derisively of them.

Managers also tried to make workers identify with the interests of the store, even when it clearly resulted in harder work for the same pay. At a monthly meeting for crew trainers, a manager acknowledged that workers were always asking why the store would not pay someone for an extra fifteen minutes to sweep up or do other such tasks not directly related to production, instead of making workers squeeze these tasks in around their main duties. He explained the importance to management of keeping labor costs down:

"Say we use four extra hours a day—we keep extra people to [wash] the brown trays" or some other tasks. He reels off some calculations—"that's 120 hours a month, times—let's pay them the minimum wage—times twelve months. So that's 1,440 hours times $3.35, equals $4,825." There are oohs and ahs from the trainers—this sounds like a lot of money to them. I don't think it sounds like that much out of $1.5 million (which he had just said the store brought in annually). The manager went on, "So how do we get extra labor? By watching how we schedule. A $200 hour [an hour with $200 in sales], for instance, will go smoother with four window people, but three good people could do it. We save money, and then we can use it on other things, like training, for instance."

The crew trainers were willing to agree that it was only reasonable for the store to extract as much labor from them as possible, though resentments about overwork certainly did not disappear. The manager was also successful enough in getting the crew trainers to identify with management that they were willing to give the names of crew people who were uncooperative. . . .

For the most part, it seemed that sticking to corporate directives on proper management produced good results, while, predictably, more authoritarian and arbitrary interactions with staff produced resentment. The apparently respectful, even-handed, psychologistic management style that McDonald's encourages helped make the repetitive, fast-paced, low-autonomy, low-paid jobs tolerable to workers. Workers learned to accept even rules that were quite disadvantageous to them when they perceived those rules to be fairly administered by people who regarded them as human beings. The official McDonald's stance was likely to anger workers, however, when, faced with customers who did not treat the crew as human beings, managers felt it was more important to satisfy the paying public than to defend the workers' dignity. . . .

Overview

. . . Most McDonald's work is organized as low-paying, low-status, part-time jobs that give workers little autonomy. Almost every decision about how to do crew people's tasks has been made in advance by the corporation, and many of the decisions have been built into the stores' technology. Why use human workers at all, if not to take advantage of the human capacity to respond to circumstances flexibly? McDonald's does want to provide at least a simulacrum of the human attributes of warmth, friendliness, and recognition. For that reason, not only workers' movements but also their words, demeanor, and attitudes are subject to managerial control.

Although predictability is McDonald's hallmark, not all factors can be controlled by management. One of the most serious irregularities that store management must deal with is fluctuation in the flow of customers, both expected and unexpected. Since personnel costs are the most manipulable variable affecting a store's profitability, managers want to match labor power to consumer demand as exactly as possible. They do so by paying all crew people by the hour, giving them highly irregular hours based on expected sales—sometimes including split shifts—and sending workers home early or keeping them late as conditions require. In other words, the costs of uneven demand are shifted to workers whenever possible. Since most McDonald's crew people cannot count on working a particular number of hours at precisely scheduled times, it is hard for them to make plans based on how much money they will earn or exactly what times they will be free. Workers are pressured to be flexible in order to maximize the organization's own flexibility in staffing levels. In contrast, of course, flexibility in the work process itself is minimized.

Routinization has not made the crew people's work easy. Their jobs, although highly structured and repetitive, are often demanding and stressful. Under these working conditions, the organization's limited commitment to workers, as reflected in job security, wages, and benefits, makes the task of maintaining worker motivation and discipline even more challenging. A variety of factors, many orchestrated by the corporation, keeps McDonald's crew people hard at work despite the limited rewards. Socialization into McDonald's norms, extremely close supervision (both human and electronic), individual and group incentives, peer pressure, and pressure from customers all play their part in getting workers to do things the McDonald's way. . . .

NOTES

1. Information about McDonald's history comes primarily from Boas and Chain 1976; Kroc with Anderson 1977; Love 1986; Luxenberg 1985; and McDonald's training materials. Reiter's (1991) description of Burger King reveals numerous parallels in the operation of the two companies, although Burger King, unlike McDonald's, is a subsidiary of a multinational conglomerate.

2. Thanks to Charles Bosk for this story.

REFERENCES

Advertising Age. 1990. "Adman of the Decade: McDonald's Fred Turner: Making All the Right Moves." (January 1): 6.

Bertagnoli, Lisa. 1989. "McDonald's: Company of the Quarter Century." *Restaurants and Institutions* (July 10): 32–60.

Boas, Max and Steve Chain. 1976. *Big Mac: The Unauthorized Story of McDonald's.* New York: New American Library.

Chaudhry, Rajan. 1989. "Burger Giants Singed by Battle." *Nation's Restaurant News* (August 7): F36.

Fortune. 1991. "Fortune Global Service 500: The 50 Largest Retailing Companies." (August 26): 179.

Garson, Barbara. 1988. *The Electronic Sweatshop: How Computers Are Transforming the Office of the Future into the factory of the Past.* New York: Simon and Schuster.

Heskett, James L., W. Earl Sasser, Jr., and Christopher W. L. Hart. 1990. *Service Breakthroughs: Changing the Rules of the Game.* New York: Free Press.

Koepp, Stephen. 1987. "Big Mac Strikes Back." *Time* (April 13): 58–60.

Kroc, Ray, with Robert Anderson. 1977. *Grinding It Out: The Making of McDonald's.* Chicago: Contemporary Books.

Love, John F. 1986. *McDonald's: Behind the Arches.* New York: Bantam Books.

Luxenberg, Stan. 1985. *Roadside Empires: How the Chains Franchised America.* New York: Viking.

McDonald's Annual Report. Various years. Oak Brook, Ill.

Peters, Tom and Nancy Austin. 1985. *A Passion for Excellence: The Leadership Difference.* New York: Random House.

Reiter, Ester. 1991. *Making Fast Food: From the Frying Pan into the Fryer.* Montreal: McGill-Queen's University Press.

Stinchcombe, Arthur L. 1990. *Information and Organizations.* Berkeley: University of California Press.

Wildavsky, Ben. 1989. "McJobs: Inside America's Largest Youth Training Program." *Policy Review* 49: 30–37.

Zemke, Ron, with Dick Schaaf. 1989. *The Service Edge: 101 Companies That Profit from Customer Care.* New York: NAL Books.

Upshot: - McD's has perfected the routinized, uniform sales of fast food.
   - This study looks @ practices, routines, behaviors in 1 Chicago-area McD's.
- 1st: Explores McD's sci. mgmt philosophy & world's love-hate rxn to McD's.
   • Biggest result: Everything is standardized, routinized, & automated → little thought req. of workers
- Work is unskilled but still stressful, chaotic, & demanding
- Workers work hard b/c of various neg & pos pressures
⊛ Emotional labor req.!!

⁓ READING 28 ⁓

Lives on the Line

Low-Wage Work in the Teleservice Economy

Ruth Buchanan

Cindy is twenty-three years old and works full time at a call center in New Brunswick, Canada, taking reservations for hotel chains in Canada and the United States.[1] She has worked there for two and a half years, at a wage of $7.50 an hour (Canadian). At the time of the interview, she earned almost $8 an hour. Cindy began working part time while she was going to school, but when she graduated from college with a degree in marine biology, she could find no jobs in her field. So she stayed on full time with the call center, describing the job as "just a way to make money." The center is open twenty-four hours a day and her shifts can begin as early as 7 A.M. and end as late as two o'clock the following morning. Every day she deals with several hundred telephone calls automatically relayed to her headset from a queue. She must handle each call quickly in order to meet her 150-second-per-call target, and to keep other callers waiting as briefly as possible. Yet she also must be sure not to deviate from a carefully written global script. In addition to working quickly and cleanly within her script, Cindy must be a convincing saleswoman for the hotels in her chain, as her

"conversion" rate—the proportion of calls that result in reservations—is closely monitored. Indeed, the computer keeps track of every minute of her working day, including any time that she is not available to take calls (which is not allowed to exceed a half hour, in addition to scheduled breaks). Despite the low wage and highly regulated working conditions, Cindy has few complaints and no immediate plans to leave her job. Rather, her attitude is one of pragmatic acceptance. "It's not bad. I wish I had something degree-related. That's what I tell everyone. But it's not going to happen right now."

A constitutive tension between the privilege of being employed and the marginal nature of that employment underpins Cindy's call-center experience. This tension is not unique to call-center work, but is a central dynamic of the expanding market for low-wage labor in Canada in the 1990s. Labor markets in Canada and the United States have in recent decades become increasingly segmented, divided between a shrinking core of highly skilled, well-paid jobs and an expanding periphery of low-wage jobs. A growing gap in job creation between the few good jobs and a lot of bad jobs has become increasingly apparent in the fast-growing service sector of the economy (Economic Council of Canada 1990). In Canada, recent trends in labor markets also have led to an increase in nonstandard employment (most of which also tends to be lower waged), which includes temporary, part-time, and casual jobs.

[handwritten margin note top: ♀ & young adults overrep. in new srvc. jobs ⊗]

In comparison to many low-wage workers, Cindy is seemingly fortunate to hold a full-time job that provides her with some benefits. Yet in other ways, her circumstances are similar to those of many other low-wage workers. Women and young people such as Cindy are overrepresented in low-wage jobs, particularly in the expanding service sector. Fast-food restaurant service, insurance sales, debt collection, and retail sales all are work that has become increasingly routinized, scripted, and monitored by firms anxious to maximize productivity and reduce labor costs (Leidner 1993). In many of these jobs, employees are not only expected to competently perform assigned tasks, but they also must look and sound as though they are enjoying themselves at the same time. Through the scripting of employees' interactions with the public, firms attempt to control unpredictability (and ensure consistency) in the interpersonal encounters at the heart of a service economy.

In addition to being positioned in the expanding periphery of polarized labor markets, low-wage service work is marginal in several other ways. Service employees exist at the furthest edges of a firm's organization, geographically remote from the head office and distanced from opportunities for internal advancement. Moreover, service employees often function as a buffer between the dictates of the firm and the demands of the customer; they must absorb the frictions and stresses of this position as intermediary. Their interpersonal skills are tested on a daily basis, yet this hidden emotional labor remains largely uncompensated and unacknowledged. When employees burn out owing to the stress and difficulty of the work, employers have no trouble refilling the positions, often with people just as apparently overqualified as Cindy. While most low-wage workers, such as Cindy, consider themselves fortunate just to have a job, as a

[handwritten margin note left, vertical: Marginalization of l-wage srvc.]

society we need to examine more closely the personal and social costs associated with widespread low-wage employment. In terms of mounting everyday stresses, underutilized talent, and forgone opportunities, the low-wage labor market may be pricier than we imagine. . . .

[handwritten margin note right: ⊗ RQ/ main rsch. puzzle]

Working the Phones: The High-Tech, Low-Wage Ghetto

Technological developments and corporate restructuring have transformed the ways in which services are provided, consumers are researched, and products marketed. The integration of communications and software technologies means that telephone and Internet interactions between producers and consumers frequently supplement and even replace the face-to-face service encounter in the bank, post office, courier company, airline, hotel chain, or department store. Increasingly, Canadians and Americans are called at home and asked (politely) whether they would like to switch long-distance carriers, purchase insurance, sign up for a new credit card, participate in a consumer information survey, or donate money to deserving children in a remote part of the world.

As companies turn to the telephone as a cheap and efficient means to service customers and market products, working the phones is an increasingly dominant feature of the low-wage labor market in Canada and the U.S. Although the vast networks of people, products, and services accessible via the Internet attract much media attention to the so-called information highway, much less public scrutiny is given to the most widespread applications of telecommunications and software technologies in call centers. Even less attention is devoted to the scores of faceless and placeless people who animate these scripts of the postindustrial economy.[2]

[handwritten margin note right: Imp. of research]

360   *Ruth Buchanan*

Nonetheless, attracting this type of work has become a preoccupation of local economic development agencies in a number of sites in Canada, including Winnipeg and New Brunswick, where interviews were conducted for this study. Local governments use the promise of available pools of well-educated, bilingual, unemployed individuals as bait to attract call-center investment (and tax dollars) to their localities. In areas where wage rates are generally low and unemployment is high, call centers might seem to be ideal vehicles for job creation. Yet policy makers know very little about the composition of this workforce and its longer-term implications for improving the skills and career opportunities of workers. In an effort to address some of these questions, this chapter investigates in detail the backgrounds and circumstances of people who do telephone work; it is drawn from a study of call centers in Canada that surveyed firms and interviewed workers in Winnipeg, Toronto, and three cities in New Brunswick.[3] The primary goal of the study was to better understand the impacts of globalization-driven restructuring within Canada on those who are positioned at its social and geographic margins. The study was designed to find out who performed this type of work, the economic, social, and educational circumstances that led them to it, and how it fit into their plans and aspirations. Was call-center work seen as a career in itself, a steppingstone to something better and more lasting, or simply a last-ditch way to pay the bills?

The people with whom I spoke often found themselves doing telephone work as a last resort. Many of them, such as Cindy, had some postsecondary education and aspired to more challenging work. Most occupied positions with little or no opportunity for advancement. Their experiences are reflective of the narrowing range of employment options in Canada . . . , especially for women and youth, who make up the bulk of the call-center labor force. As a type of work that is easy to get but has little opportunity for advancement, and that draws on a labor force with few other employment options, call-center work can be described as a type of high-tech, low-wage ghetto.

Within the call-center industry, however, is a considerable amount of diversity. Not all workers are just marking time and eager to move on. Some are paid considerably more than $8 per hour, enjoy job security and benefits, and do not find the work overly stressful. A few felt they were able to learn and develop their skills on the job. For some, call-center work represents a step up from a previous job. Acknowledging these differences, the larger study aspires to provide some insights into the ways in which labor markets for telephone work are differently constituted in a range of locations and workplaces, and how these differences affect the opportunities of frontline telephone workers. While this diversity is evident in the following accounts, exploring fully geographic and sectoral variations within the call-center industry in Canada is beyond the scope of this chapter. Rather, this chapter presents a number of accounts of telephone work from the perspective of those performing it, in a range of locations and workplaces. The focus is on the substantial commonalities, rather than the differences, among these narratives.

Two interrelated processes—globalization and restructuring—provide the backdrop to the emergence of call-center work in Canada. Globalization here can be defined as the qualitative expansion of flows of money, goods, people, and ideas across international borders (Giddens 1990; Twining 2000). In recent years, these accelerated processes of integration and exchange have had a profound impact on the way in which corporations and governments do business. Increasing flows of international investment have led firms to reorganize their operations across provincial and national borders, seeking the most attractive environments in which to operate. Factors that influence firms' location decisions include the cost and quality of the local labor force and the regulatory environment. As firms have become more mobile, governments at a subnational level have become even more actively involved in courting those firms, and the jobs and investment they bring with them (Kassab and Luloff 1993; Milne 1995). Local economic development strategies include the active marketing of a locality, its workforce and regulatory environment, as well as the provision of financial incentives and the development of increasingly targeted training and job-creation policies. Often, restructuring strategies adopted by firms and facilitated by local governments in response to globalization converge on an issue at the heart of this . . . chapter: the location and recruitment of a low-wage workforce.

Globalization

The prairie city of Winnipeg or the even smaller urban centers of St. John, Fredericton, and Moncton in the tiny province of New Brunswick (home to only three quarters of a million people) might seem unlikely places to look for evidence of an increasingly globalized economic order. Yet the rapid emergence of call centers in these unlikely locations is an excellent illustration of the complex realignments of institutional, physical, and human geography taking place in the globalized economy. Call centers bring together a number of familiar globalization themes: the expanding significance of the service economy, diffusion of new technologies, restructuring of firms through downsizing and relocation, and heightened competition for investment and jobs among provincial and local governments. Call centers bridge the old divide between core and periphery in new ways,

linking marginal workers and locations with global networks of capital while at the same time reinscribing hierarchies of place and identity. Field studies, such as the research reported in this chapter, attempt to locate this reorganized low-wage work within the context of these larger shifts. . . .

This empirical study of call-center work is one such attempt. It examines the interrelationship between global flows of investment and technology and local governments and labor markets. Call centers are made possible by telematics—the combination of telecommunications and software technologies that can coordinate, through the predictive dialing of outbound or switching of inbound calls, the simultaneous connection of a telephone call and the display of account information to a service representative. Although this technology is not particularly new, its dissemination to such places as New Brunswick facilitates the corporate reorganizations that are bringing the call centers there as well. Back officing—the corporate restructuring strategy that brings jobs to places such as Moncton and Winnipeg—creates a particularly footloose type of investment. Most firms rent their premises and bring in computers and other equipment purchased elsewhere. Telephones ordinarily are supplied by the local phone company, and the provincial government provides significant "training" grants to offset whatever remaining costs might be associated with the relocation. . . .

Restructuring . . .

The rapid emergence of the call-center industry is commonly attributed to developments in telematics over the last several decades. Had firms not perceived any advantages to reorganizing their operations to utilize these technologies, however, the transformation would not have taken place. Providing services or marketing products over the phone today presents a number of opportunities for firms to reorganize work. First, workers who perform these tasks are centralized in less costly work locations, away from the head office. Relocating these workers away from the rest of the firm also in some cases facilitates the segregation of internal labor markets—that is, limiting the opportunities of teleworkers to obtain more desirable positions within the firm. Finally, the implementation of information systems that enable the tracking of a courier package by a teleworker for a customer, for example, also presents the opportunity for management to track the performance of the teleworker with similar precision. With telematics, it becomes possible to monitor every minute of the employee's working day and implement productivity quotas so that poor performers are weeded out. Many companies base their evaluation of employees on these quantitative indicators, despite the possible distortions or subversions they might reproduce or encourage. In addition, most of the teleworkers with whom we spoke had their calls monitored randomly, so that, as in Bentham's Panopticon, the employee effectively internalized the experience of being under constant surveillance with only a limited amount of actual observation. Lower-skilled jobs such as telemarketing, teleservice, data entry, and rate or credit checking now can be segregated from the rest of a firm's operations and relocated to a suburban or offshore location where labor, rents, and other costs are generally lower. Preferred locations for call centers therefore are usually in towns or areas where other opportunities are limited—places such as Moncton, Winnipeg, Halifax, or Hamilton. In addition to taking advantage of preexisting geographic divisions in the labor market to reap immediate productivity gains, call centers also take advantage of localized gender and racial labor market hierarchies. Indeed, the call center has become a prime example

of the growing category of feminized labor on the periphery: a majority of women perform the work, and those men who do it are often young, gay, or otherwise marginalized.

The approach to back officing reflected in the call-center phenomenon has been described as the "dark side" of flexible production (Harrison 1994). Opportunities for advancement and skills acquisition in these positions usually are limited, so that one would expect employees to invest little in their jobs and continue to seek employment elsewhere. In labor markets where opportunities are plentiful, this job seeking leads to an unattractive (that is, for firms) combination of high turnover and low productivity. By relocating to labor markets where few other options exist, such as New Brunswick or Winnipeg, the returns for firms can be significant. Yet the gains produced by relocating work are fixed; firms seeking further advantage are forced either to increase the productivity of their workforce by other means, or relocate production farther offshore in search of even cheaper labor (Appelbaum 1993). From the perspective of the employees, this can mean being presented with ongoing demands for more work with negligible wage increases (sweated labor) in a context where unsatisfactory performance can mean the loss of the company to another location.

The extent to which labor markets are locally constructed and the ways that companies are able to exploit these local differences became apparent during research for this project, which involved conducting interviews in Winnipeg, Toronto, and three smaller cities in New Brunswick (Fredericton, St. John, and Moncton). For example, interviewees in New Brunswick suggested that wages and working conditions in call centers there compared unfavorably with those in other parts of the country. An employee with one firm that had another call center in London, Ontario, said, "People sort of know that the rules are quite different in London—they

[handwritten margin note: Contrasts in local labor mkts.]
[handwritten margin note: Training]

don't know in a big way, but they don't work overnight shifts. They, you know, I think they've got more clout in London."[4] A similar observation was made by a service representative from Ontario, who recently transferred to a newly opened St. John call center.[5] Based on information he had gained from many years of experience with the company and his recent access to work logs at other locations, this worker concluded that the company had established higher productivity quotas at the New Brunswick location. He further speculated that the longer-term goal would be to phase out more costly centers in other locations, on the basis of the convenient argument that they were not performing as well.

The contrast between local labor markets also was reinforced by interviews conducted with call-center employees in Toronto, who generally represented their jobs as marginal, temporary stop-gaps until something better came along. Teleworkers in Toronto often had worked at many different call centers; if one place did not work out, finding work at another was easy enough. One eighteen-year-old interviewed had worked at nine telemarketing or survey research firms in the two years that she had been doing part-time phone work.[6]

In New Brunswick, while jobs tend to occupy the same marginalized place in firms' organizational structures, most employees interviewed did not intend for their call-center position to be temporary. For most, it was their first job, and no one had worked at more than two different call centers. Several of the younger employees interviewed in New Brunswick reported that they had picked teleservice as their chosen career. The seriousness with which New Brunswick call-center employees approach their jobs is bolstered by the fact that most of those who work at the centers have had at least some postsecondary education, including some with two-year degrees from newly minted community college courses in teleservice. Some had even paid

$1,400 for a thirty-five-week course offered by a private firm that boasts of placing 90 percent of its graduates directly into local teleservice jobs. Yet when the idea of community college training programs for call-center work was raised in interviews with teleworkers in Winnipeg, several laughed spontaneously, and one described it as "a joke."[7] While some teleworkers interviewed in Winnipeg were attending a university, no one with a completed degree was still working the phones.

Local governments were actively involved in assisting companies to recruit employees, particularly in smaller centers. In New Brunswick, in addition to the community college programs, local industry job fairs functioned as gathering points for those interested in getting involved in telework. Firms rarely advertised positions. Rather, openings were communicated by word of mouth, or additional employees were hired through temporary employment agencies. The temporary agencies drew on the lists of those "available for telework" generated at the job fairs, where people were invited to fill out a form listing their qualifications and contact information. The forms were entered into a database that was used as a means of hiring new employees, but also as a marketing tool for the business development association to use in its efforts to attract more call centers to the locality. The local job fair played an important role in the social construction of call-center work, as it was an opportunity for firms and economic development agencies to represent telework as steady, professional, and desirable employment.

[handwritten margin note: workers recruited thru local efforts like job fairs]

Lives on the Line: Telephone Workers in Canada . . .

This section looks more closely at three aspects of [my] interviews that reveal the links between call-center employment and low-wage work more generally: the circumstances

3 poi

that push people into telephone work; the personal impact of such routinized and monitored work; and the potential for telephone workers to realize a life after telework.

Telephone Work as a "Last Resort"

Most telework requires little more than basic keyboarding skills and the ability to talk on the phone. Many interviewees explained that they had turned to the work after other avenues had failed because it was not difficult to get hired. As one woman in Winnipeg put it, "There's a lot of companies. . . . You can go through the newspaper any day and within an hour have a job phoning people, as a telemarketer, either selling furnace cleanings or carpet cleanings. . . . A lot of them are starting at $5.45—minimum wage, and people are taking the jobs because, you know, they need to work so they're taking the jobs." Jane started working in teleservice after her retail employer went bankrupt and she had been unemployed for several months. She described it as "a last resort." She had dropped off over a hundred resumes, but at that time in Winnipeg (just after Christmas), "It was next to impossible to get a job. . . . [I was out of work] I think four months, and then somebody suggested Survey Research because they'll hire anybody and everybody, so I thought, well, I've tried everywhere else, so I'll try that, and lo and behold, I became a Survey Research worker."

"Need" for even min. wage jobs

At first she was pleased with the work, because the wage was a bit above the minimum (though approximately what she had made at her previous retail sales job), but it soon "lost its appeal."[8] For others, telework offers a way out of a difficult situation, or a step up the employment ladder. Anthony, for example, now in his midtwenties, started doing telework part time for extra cash in a survey research firm when he was sixteen, while also working at McDonald's. When he graduated from high school, he took on full-time hours at the survey research firm so that he could get out of a difficult living situation at home. Looking back, Anthony understood that not going to the university limited his longer-term options, but he defended his choice as the right one.

> I just didn't think [going to the university] was viable considering that my home situation was a mess. If I'd gone to school and kept working at Survey Research part time, I wouldn't have been able to afford to move out on my own. The idea was that I was going to stay at my dad's place, despite these family problems, and go to school. To me, that was just absurd. Not that it would totally hinder me, but it would have an effect. . . . It made more sense to me to branch out on my own and get an apartment, work full time and just take it from there.[9]

Angela, who had been working night shifts as a baker at a donut shop for many years for minimum wage, had been fired from her last position without cause. Rather than attempting to bring a complaint against her employer, she shortly found a telemarketing position through a friend. Angela said she was happy about the change as telework paid more, she worked daytime shifts, and the work environment was an improvement over her baking jobs. She also enjoyed working with her mostly female coworkers at the call center better than the male cohort with whom she had worked previously.[10] In Winnipeg, a relatively large number of gay youth worked in a couple of large outbound centers. Telework offered some of these youth an opportunity both to live on their own and connect with the downtown gay community through their new coworkers. Outbound call centers, particularly in Winnipeg, tended both to rely on a high proportion of part-time employees and on young people.[11] Many youth reported that

various reasons for taking jobs

[handwritten: workers express ambivalence about nature of work/their happiness doing it]

telework was a way to pay some bills while going to the university. Many kinds of phone work—survey research and telemarketing in particular—have short flexible shifts that are easily worked around school or other obligations. That these jobs usually are part time is an advantage rather than a shortcoming for students who need extra cash. Some firms encourage hiring student employees, particularly when a firm's work fluctuations fit well with the academic calendar.

Although the work can be very useful for those youth who want or need part-time shifts, others have found themselves trapped in call-center work at the beginning of their working lives, with few alternatives later on. Moreover, when one has no other economic assistance, to try to support oneself and go to school on call-center wages can be daunting. One twenty-year-old, Jane, told us that after several years of telework and living on her own, she thought she had "missed the boat" on getting an education.

> I know it's a job that I got because I couldn't get another job or because it's a real slack job, and it didn't encourage me to go any further as a young person, like I didn't go to school, which I should have done because I thought I could do this as a job.[12]

[handwritten margin: Missed out on other oppors...?]

Later in the interview, Jane talked about how the part-time evening shifts fit in well with the "party" lifestyle that she and many of her teleworking friends found easy to slip into.

> You know, I had the whole day to sleep, and it was only five hours out of my life every day, and I made super good money, and I think I lost a lot of time doing that, and I can guarantee that this is the same way that a lot of the people at Survey Research think because I'm friends with a lot of those people, and I

would go and party with a lot of those people. Like it's the same thing, and once you get in that cycle it's not helping anybody. I think it set me back a lot because I didn't have a goal, and what's my life? I could make money and I could do good and I could save and I could buy a house and I could do all these great things, but I wasn't becoming a better person. I wasn't getting any professional training in anything.

Jane's regrets about missed opportunities might be easy to dismiss as the product of individual lack of initiative. Yet others in very different circumstances frequently echoed the sense of ambivalence that is at the heart of Jane's comments. An older teleworker, also in Winnipeg, said,

> I've always felt exploited doing that kind of work, but yet, in another sense, it is work, and it's very flexible work, and it's there if you want it, and if you don't want it, then give it to somebody else. You don't have to be forced to take it.[13]

That most people choose telework with some awareness of its limits is true, but they often do so under circumstances of considerable social and financial constraint. The lack of real alternatives also can keep many in telephone work much longer than they had anticipated or would have hoped.

[handwritten: Constrained oppor.]

Unskilled Labor?

Lisa is a twenty-two-year-old woman from Cape Breton Island, an economically depressed region in the province of Nova Scotia. Unemployment levels there, since the decline of the coal mining industry two decades ago, have been steady at about 20 percent. Eighteen months prior to our interview, unemployed, Lisa made the eight-hour trip to Fredericton, New Brunswick, in a last-ditch effort to find work. Within a few weeks, someone at her church told her that a large corporation, which had recently consolidated its national call-center operations in the city, was hiring. She applied for the job, was hired immediately, and within a couple of weeks was working the phones as a customer service representative. She considers herself very fortunate, since her workplace is unionized and offers good wages (up to $15 per hour), benefits, and job security well beyond that found in most similar workplaces in the province.

Nonetheless, Lisa was close to quitting her job because of what she described as the "constant negative" that made up her working day. In a year and a half of taking dozens of calls a day, she said, only three people said something positive about the service. People were regularly abusive to her on the phone. Most of the time she did not have the authority to provide real assistance to customers. Handling irate callers often left her "pretty frustrated" and a "ball of tension." While difficult callers seemed to be the primary source of her work stress, the workplace itself did not seem set up to help. Lisa described the working environment as "very Big-Brotherish. You needed an identification card to get into the locked office. Once inside, the workday was highly regulated. One had to account for every minute."

At Lisa's workplace, once a person logged onto the computer, a record was made of the entire day. Like most other call centers, performance was evaluated in part through monitoring telephone calls. Lisa had received some negative reviews from her supervisors, and not much encouragement. While she made an effort to put a positive spin on her experience at the call center ("I'm tougher now; I don't get intimidated easily"), Lisa felt that it was only a matter of time before she would have to move on. "I don't think of myself as a quitter, but I want a future in my job."

When I returned six months later to speak with her again, Lisa was still working at the same teleservice position. She was also still trying to leave. For Lisa, "the money's a trap" that so far had kept her in a highly stressful, dead-end job. She was certain that her stress levels, after two years on the job, had begun to affect her life outside work. "I don't talk the same, I say things backwards, I can't think of words, I can't think clearly . . . that's not me." The company refused a request for unpaid leave, which she had hoped would give her some time to look for another job, without the insecurity of quitting. She now felt that her only alternative was to take stress leave, even though she thought it would reflect badly on her as a person. "I feel like a loser because I'm only twenty-two and I already have to take stress leave. . . . I feel less of a person, I feel like I can't handle life or something." Lisa said she was a person who believed in looking on the bright side. Yet despite the job security and comfortable pay she admittedly enjoyed at the call center, for her to be optimistic about the two years she had spent there was difficult. "I wish there was more positive to say about it, but it hasn't changed at all."

Lisa's narrative highlights the demanding nature of the emotional and interpersonal labor required by even inbound call-center work. The requirements go beyond the simple, unflaggable projection of a friendly telephone persona to the necessity of being able to "read" callers, anticipate their needs and expectations, and develop the ability to defuse (or at least "handle") difficult, angry, or unreasonable customers ("irates"). Some service representatives appear to be dramatically more effective at dealing with irates than others. People doing this work also appear to vary significantly in the extent to which negative calls affect them. Those workers who could establish a degree of emotional distance between themselves and callers appeared to be the least likely to experience overwhelming stress. Lisa, who describes herself as a "sensitive person," is an example of someone who, over time, found the work of dealing with irate callers to be increasingly draining, even as she reportedly improved at handling them.

While telephone jobs initially are attractive because they're flexible, easily obtained, and generally pay better than the minimum-wage alternatives, many workers such as Lisa quickly find that these jobs are far more demanding and stressful than they had anticipated. One of the reasons for this reaction is that telephone work, like much interactive service work that includes expectations about the performance of emotional labor, seems to have a much more direct impact on the employee's sense of self. Some (particularly young people) reported that they experience this aspect of the job as empowering, because they learned not to let anything get to them or can handle themselves better in difficult situations. Many others, however, such as Lisa, find the work to be full of dilemmas and confrontations that demean and undermine their sense of self.

Emotional Labor and the Gendering of Telephone Work

Dealing with difficult callers is one issue in which gendered differences in telephone service work experience seemed to emerge in individual interviews. Yet these personal differences must be seen in the context of how the work is socially constructed and understood. While the gender breakdown varies somewhat across work sites and sectors of the industry (men being much better represented in telemarketing, finance, and technology-related firms), this study revealed that women make up a substantial majority of the call-center workforce in each of the sites within Canada. This is not surprising, given existing research on the feminization of low-wage labor markets in Canada and elsewhere (Armstrong and Armstrong 1994; Duffy and Pupo 1992; Jensen 1989, 1996). Although some suggest that transformations brought about by information technologies might serve to break down perceived boundaries between men and women's white-collar work, this has not happened in call-center work (Webster 1993; Belt, Richardson and Webster 1999). Rather, existing gendered hierarchies have become reinscribed in new positions and restructured work sites (McDowell 1991, 1997).

One of the mechanisms through which this process of reinscription has taken place in telephone sales, and service work in particular, is through the performative aspects of the job. Employees must enact scripts that reflect social expectations and assumptions, many of which have a significantly gendered nature. Studies of flight attendants and waitresses illustrate ways in which the social understandings about "good service" require workers to "do gender" by showing deference through accepting treatment as a subordinate, smiling, and flirting (Hall 1993; Hochschild 1983). Arlie Hochschild, in her influential study of flight attendants, described this performative, gendered, and largely invisible work as *emotional labor*. (Reading 8) Emotional labor brings into focus one of the least visible ways in which women's social roles in their private lives are extrapolated into workplace expectations, so that they become required but not compensable. Just as women have been socialized into managing the emotional dimensions of their personal relationships, it is expected that they will voluntarily perform these functions in the workplace as well.

Work in the call centers, whether teleservice or telemarketing, is gendered in this way. The only difference is the narrow bandwidth of the method of communication. Call-center workers must have the ability to immediately communicate a friendly, helpful, and professional demeanor in a few spoken words. The work involved in projecting friendliness over the phone appears to be quite similar to that described in studies of waitresses and flight attendants, where a key component of the job is the ability to continue to smile regardless of how you feel or how others treat you. One call-center employee said that workers were told to smile while they were speaking to customers on the phone because it would make them sound friendlier. She said that she believed that it did work, and if she were having trouble with a particular caller, she would silently ask herself whether she was smiling. Not only must workers be able to sound friendly on the phone, they also must continue to be friendly when unhappy or upset customers complain and criticize, enacting the script of the deferential servant over the phone. Moreover, as in waitressing, call-center work apparently involves a component of scripted flirtation. Several young women, each of whom was a top performer in a telemarketing position, admitted that they were most successful in selling to men and that they used a different tone of voice for men and women. The pitch for men was higher, more singsong, and definitely more flirtatious; the pitch for women was lower, firm, and businesslike. One of these women had been told by her boss that she ought to pursue a career in "phone sex" because of the "seductive" quality of her voice. She quit telemarketing shortly thereafter.[14]

The gendered quality of telephone work is also reflective of wider trends in low-wage work. Not surprisingly, in Toronto, youth and recent immigrants also found themselves disproportionately represented in these feminized jobs. A significant amount of gender segregation appears within telephone work, with men concentrated in higher-paying technical or financial-oriented positions and women being disproportionately represented in frontline customer service and sales positions. All of these divisions reveal the extent to which low-wage labor markets are socially produced: they are the effects of institutions and practices that divide, sort, and channel people's opportunities by race, gender, class, and age. The social processes by which labor is feminized—far from becoming less relevant in contemporary labor markets—are seamlessly woven into corporate decision making through the economic calculus of labor costs and productive benefits. Yet this calculus hardly conceals its underlying gendered assumptions: what it means to "give good service" and the difference between valuable *skills* and natural *attributes* that enables employers to describe these jobs as unskilled.

Hidden Talents: The Misrecognized Skills of Call-Center Workers

Despite the large number of call-center employees who reported that they found their jobs both stressful and monotonous, many of the younger employees responded positively to questioning about what they had learned from their call-center experience. One twenty-year-old woman reported that, after a year and a half of teleservice, the way she "deals with people" dramatically improved for the better. . . . In particular, she said that she could "no longer be intimidated, easily or at all," and that she was "tougher." After describing the pettiness of some of the customer complaints, she added that little things didn't bug her anymore. She had learned to expect to be treated with courtesy by customer service agents with whom she dealt. A twenty-one-year-old man reported that he enjoyed learning how to establish a professional, yet human, connection with the people with whom he spoke during the day.[15] He was a bilingual francophone from Moncton, and had learned to "tone down" his Acadian accent in a professional context. Irate calls were his favorites, he said, because he had become very effective at calming people down.

Call-center work thus calls for a number of interpersonal competencies that in other contexts (such as international diplomacy or business negotiation) indeed might be considered skills. Although firms and employees clearly are aware of a range of skills required for the delivery of high-quality customer service, the work continues to be referred to and understood by all as low-skilled labor. Since call-center work requires the development and use of interpersonal skills—including work I've described as emotional labor—both workers and employers understand it in terms of personal development rather than job skills. This assumption reveals another process by which work is gendered—the distinction between skill and talent (Jensen 1989). While work typically performed by men is identified as requiring certain kinds of skills, what women do is more often described as the utilization of their so-called natural talents. "Many of the skills which women demonstrate in their work— patience, consideration, friendliness, supportiveness, et cetera—are too often regarded as personal attributes" (Poynton 1993, 167). Moreover, the perception of women's competencies in the workplace is further eroded by equating certain functions they perform with female roles in the private sphere—the secretary as "office wife" being the prime example (Webster 1993, 1996).

This gendered misidentification of skill in call centers also means that firms are more inclined to undervalue quality service in favor of efficiency in the organization of call-center work. While some firms now attribute more value to quality customer service in terms of how they organize work and evaluate their employees, this has not translated directly into higher wages for workers, although it may have a significant effect on job satisfaction and working conditions. Other firms exacerbate job stress by binding employees between the competing demands of satisfying the customer and minimizing talk time, and penalizing employees who take extra time with a difficult customer or to help a colleague.

Another implication of failing to recognize skills developed in the call-center workplace is the failure to promote call-center employees to other positions within the firm. Anthony, introduced earlier as someone who had started telephone research part-time at age sixteen, found himself without further options for advancement at age twenty-five. Eight years later, he remains with the company, now a full-time supervisor, but still only making about a dollar per hour more than the frontline callers. Anthony had applied for a number of other positions within the firm without success.[16]

> I got the impression that it was basically because I had long hair and didn't conform to any kind of appearance standards that are somewhat backhandedly enforced in the sense that they hire their own. Their own are the people who wear starched shirts and blue jeans. That's about as casual as they'll get. They'll wear their shirt and tie and they'll be wearing blue jeans too and sneakers. I've pretty much been told—not told directly—indirectly that because I don't have any university aspirations in terms of market research courses and because I don't have any university period because I decided to work full-time for the company that I'm not qualified for a variety of positions which they've given to other people who have less qualifications than me and some who haven't even gone to university.

The first step in having call-center employees' skills more effectively utilized and compensated is to name and recognize them as such. An example where work-related skills of call-center employees were made visible to an employer occurred in Toronto in a recent successful union drive at a telemarketing center. One key organizer explained how she and her colleagues were able to succeed in signing up the requisite number of employees in their workplace, despite serious opposition from their employer:

> We are telemarketers, right? We were using telemarketing techniques to sign people up! What better people. It got to the point where there were so many people we were signing up that we had almost like a script. . . . We used good selling techniques, so we would explain the situation to people, tell them how urgent it was, make them feel as if they were involved in something special, that's another technique. Tell them this is the first telemarketing center in Canada to have an organizing drive . . . you could just sort of figure out who you were dealing with and find their Achilles' Heel and use it.[17]

Unfortunately, the opportunities for most call-center employees to better utilize their capacities is limited by the structure of the industry and the dominant forms of workplace organization. Although most express a desire to move on to other, more rewarding work, their ability to realize these aspirations is likely to be similarly constrained.

Everyday Stresses and Survival Strategies

Individuals who did telephone work for any length of time developed myriad strategies for managing job stress or at least ameliorating its impact on their well-being and sense of self. These strategies were highly individual; for many, they simply amounted to certain ways of thinking about the work or representing it to others, while others manifested more concrete forms of subversion or resistance in how they performed the work and dealt with employers. While leaving was an option for some, most telephone workers

opted for safer and more private techniques for everyday survival. Some developed a critical and evocative appreciation of the organization and mechanics of the workplace, describing the work in terms of "performance," or more vividly, as prostitution. Rosa, the call-center employee turned union organizer quoted earlier, described her relationship to workplace technology in terms of the *standing reserve*, that is, in Heidegger's (1977) words, "things that are not even regarded as objects, because their only important quality has become their readiness for use."[18] As Rosa put it, "you are standing waiting until that call comes in to use you to make money. And you are simply another part of that machine."

In addition to hidden expectations for the performance of emotional labor, firms often create more explicit conflicts for employees. For example, in outbound call-center work, supervisors commonly pressure employees to meet steep quotas. In telefundraising, this may include expectations about how much money to request from potential donors. Asking for large amounts from people whose income may be limited, such as senior citizens, did not sit well with many employees. Some simply set their own expectations and settled for fewer bonuses. Others found that their unwillingness to engage in high-pressure sales tactics jeopardized their jobs.

When asked for comparisons between telemarketing and other types of work performed, employees often ranked phone work below waitering or retail sales. The difference seemed to lie in the greater scope for authenticity in the interpersonal relations of in-person service jobs. The scripted and monitored nature of telephone work led employees to feel that they were unable to "be themselves" at work. This usually was reinforced by the organization of work space and how call centers were managed. Employees generally had very little room for autonomy or individuality. Dress codes were common, despite the fact that employees were not seen by customers. While the extent and nature of supervisory discipline of behavior varied, several people commented that they were disciplined for laughing or talking between calls. Some workplaces allowed workers to read, knit, or draw if work was slow, while at other companies, only firm-related work was permitted. A very few were allowed to personalize their work spaces. One survey research worker commented, "It's almost like the army. It's very regimented. You punch in with a time clock. You come in and sit down, and the numbers are all computerized. As soon as you finish a call, the minute you hang up, another call comes up. It's just this constant, all day, repetitious, . . . constant sort of beating on a drum, but day after day."[19]

The effort to maintain a notion of one's self as a "good employee" or even as a "good person," however, often led people to persist in unsatisfactory workplace conditions. Lisa persisted in a job with which she was struggling because she knew she had no better options, but also because she "wasn't a quitter." Another woman, who was consistently the highest performer at her insurance sales center, put up with significantly lower pay than she knew she was entitled to as an insurance agent, because for her, "money wasn't the issue," it was doing the work well that mattered.[20] Although this perspective was most pronounced in New Brunswick, many call-center workers were anxious to be seen and to see themselves as good workers and reasonable people. The extent to which this impulse might work to the employer's benefit was observed by another woman working part-time shifts at a financial services firm that routinely sent workers home halfway through their shift if work was slow, even though many commute significant distances:

> But I guess I think companies owe—I think people are going more than

halfway. The employees are good people, you know, they don't want the sun and the earth. There are just some things that would be fairer. They wouldn't say that, I don't think. So, I have been sitting on the fence watching, but people are pretty happy—I think the potential is there to abuse the situation.[21]

Among some workers, reluctance to complain may stem as much from fear of reprisal as from a general attitude of acceptance. Most call centers are not unionized and make no secret of their hostility toward the idea of unionization. Although many might agree that unionization could improve conditions, one employee observed, "They're so afraid of that word because immediately they think they are going to lose their job if they talk union at all."[22] Fear and skepticism concerning the benefits of unionization appeared to be strongest in New Brunswick, where a recent history of polarized labor relations has left a negative impression on the province's young people. Unfortunately, fears regarding job security and the Panopticon-like nature of the workplace leaves most call center workers isolated in both their critical analysis and symbolic acts of resistance.

Call-Center Careers?

Call centers tend to have a high rate of employee turnover. One of the driving forces behind locating centers in more remote areas is to obtain a more secure and stable workforce. This has been successful to some extent in the New Brunswick example, where new centers report lower rates of turnover than existing centers in other locations. Yet only one of the interview subjects had worked full-time at a call center for longer than three years, and that was in a supervisory capacity. Most people do not seem able to do telephone work indefinitely, even if they start out thinking they can. The story of Lois, a former telemarketer, is an extreme but illuminating case in point.

Lois is fifty years old and had worked at a number of other jobs, including restaurant manager and real estate agent.[23] For a little over a year, Lois worked thirty hours a week at an outbound center for $7.50 per hour with no benefits, but with the possibility of earning a few hundred extra dollars in bonuses for high performance. Her employer was an American-owned telemarketing company that obtained most of its contracts from large retail firms. For Lois, this meant two years of selling insurance to credit card customers of one of those firms. Although she had taken the initiative to become licensed as an insurance agent, the company refused to pay her at an agent's rate ($11 per hour) despite the fact that she would then be able to "verify" all of her own calls.

Lois was one of her company's top performers and a loyal employee. The first time I spoke with her, she had been hand-picked by her manager for the interview. She was a model employee. Lois had few complaints about the management, wages, or working conditions. She claimed that working hard at a job she is good at is more important to her than the money. This is why she continued to work at the telemarketing firm, with no plans to quit or look elsewhere, even though she admitted she was not being adequately compensated for the insurance-agent work she was doing.

The second time I spoke with Lois, she was no longer working with the telemarketing firm. She had started a small home business selling candles and associated ornaments and was making approximately twice the income of her call-center job, with far less effort. Her doctor had advised against continuing at the call center after she collapsed at work from high blood pressure and was taken to the hospital on a stretcher.

I had no lunch. They didn't allow us any lunch that day. It was too busy. See, they were just seeing dollar signs. Sales, sales, sales like crazy. . . . And the next thing I knew, I just went to Cathy and I said, "Cathy, I can't. . . . I gotta go outside, I gotta go outside." Oh, I didn't want to go, but I had to, I couldn't handle it. . . . So anyway I went out there and leaned against the next building— just to get some fresh air. I had to get some fresh air. So then I got that I could hardly stand up, so I came back inside and sat down on the stairs. And that was it. I just passed right out. And then I couldn't talk. . . . I was that close to a stroke. . . . my doctor told me not to go back. He said, "You just can't." He said, "If you want to kill yourself, you go back."[24]

Lois's experience is uncommon, although many of the people who work in call centers report that they soon begin to find the work stressful. Even in "good" centers, with pleasant surroundings, well-designed work stations, and adequate rest breaks, the combination of monotony and the emotional strain of dealing with high numbers of irate callers can lead to burnout within a few years for many competent and willing workers.

Within the last decade in Canada, new approaches to labor market policy, emerging local economic development strategies, and the reorganization of firms have functioned to produce new markets for low-wage workers, particularly in sites such as New Brunswick and Manitoba. A market-oriented approach to labor policy would evaluate these developments as unequivocal successes; firms have found workers, and workers have found jobs. Yet this chapter has sought to establish another foundation on which to evaluate the social utility of these low-wage labor markets, using the accounts of workers themselves. Evaluating work from the perspective of those who do it reveals a number of troubling issues particular to low-wage service work at the end of the century.

Much of the frontline service work performed by low-wage workers, including teleworkers, is both highly routinized and monitored. Employees are given little or no autonomy, and yet firms hire them to act as a lubricant, smoothing out the rough spots between the corporate need for profitability and the public's demand for service. Telemarketing employees face even more friction as they invade people's homes for the purpose of selling their companies' products on commission. The emotional and interpersonal demands of these positions are large, yet the employees themselves are considered unskilled. They operate at the geographic and organizational margins of the corporate hierarchy and have only limited opportunities to gain transferable job skills or move to a better position within the firm. Job security is limited, benefits often are nonexistent, and the hours are either shifts, highly variable, part-time, or all three. The routinization of the work means predictability for employers but stress, monotony, and eventual burnout for employees. Further, wage and scheduling flexibility for employers translates into uncertainty and insecurity for low-wage employees, making it difficult for individuals to keep friends, find day care, pay their rent, or go to school.

A troubling backdrop to routinization and flexibility, which have become central features of the low-wage employment landscape, is the fact that policy makers seem not to have grasped its inherent contradictions. The highly demanding nature of "unskilled" work and severe personal and financial constraints imposed by "flexible" employment simply are not parts of the dominant policy discourse. Although call centers, for example, have become highly visible on the policy horizon as the targets of local economic development strategies, the only independent studies commissioned have been comparative cost estimates designed to encourage firms to make relocation decisions.

When this project was undertaken, no information was publicly available on the gender and age composition of the call-center workforce. The difficult situations that lead many young people, most often women, into telework is not considered, nor are the workplace environments that lead so many to quit or lose their jobs within a year or two. Very few of those interviewed maintained they could imagine themselves doing such work full-time for more than a couple of years. Some suggested that the companies depend on the high turnover to keep their phones supplied with eager and productive newcomers. Strategies for dealing with the problem of high turnover (where policy makers acknowledge it) fail to identify the sources of the problems in the workplaces themselves. Rather, they focus on facilitating employers' recruitment among particular groups, notably high school students, or on developing community college training programs, which function more as recruitment avenues for firms than as training centers.

This chapter has argued that the problems of the low-wage worker have been exacerbated by the responses of both governments and firms to the perceived dictates of globalization. In response to dominant understandings of the globalization script, restructuring firms and retrenching governments have operated in concert to produce the flexible, yet predictable, frontline worker who is the mainstay of the new service economy. Although we have few tools at our disposal for appreciating the social costs of this convergence of purpose, the accounts herein at least have revealed some of the ways in which opportunities are lost, skills are misrecognized, and aspirations are crushed in these workplaces. In bringing together first-person accounts of low-wage work with dominant understandings of the globalization script, this chapter illuminates the inherent contradictions embedded within current approaches and challenges scholars and policy makers to continue the effort to produce alternative scripts in which both the perspectives and personhood of low-wage workers are recognized.

NOTES

1. Cindy is a pseudonym for a call-center worker interviewed by the author in December 1997, St. John, New Brunswick (hereafter all names given for interviewees are pseudonyms).

2. The term *teleworker* is used to identify collectively those whose work is performed primarily over the telephone, whether answering questions or providing services to callers who have requested them over a 1–800 number (inbound), or using the phone to make sales, perform surveys, or raise money for charities (outbound). Along with Heather Menzies, I make a distinction between *telework* and *telecommuting,* using the latter to refer to those who work outside a central office at their own discretion (see Menzies 1997).

3. This chapter draws on approximately sixty interviews with telephone workers in Moncton, St. John, Fredericton, Toronto, and Winnipeg conducted between June 1996 and July 1998. The interviews were conducted with Sarah Koch-Schulte as part of a larger study, funded in part by Status of Women Canada (see Buchanan and Koch-Schulte 2000b).

4. Call-center employee, interview with author, July 1996, Fredericton, New Brunswick.

5. Tony, interview with author, 12 June 1997, - St. John, New Brunswick.

6. Lisa, interview with author, 6 July 1998, Toronto.

7. Anthony, interview with author, 9 June 1998, Winnipeg.

8. Jane, interview with author, 11 June 1998, Winnipeg.

9. Anthony, interview with author, 9 June 1998, Winnipeg.

10. Angela, interview with author, 12 June 1998, Winnipeg.

11. A survey mailed to personnel managers at all forty call centers in Winnipeg revealed that 45 percent of the employees worked under nonstandard (that is, temporary or part-time) employment contracts; across all study sites the average figure was 38 percent nonstandard employment. Across all study sites

and all employment categories, the percentage of youth workers was significant, ranging from a low of 37 percent of full-time workers in Winnipeg to a high of 70 percent of temporary workers in Toronto (Buchanan and Koch-Schulte 2000).

12. Jane, interview with author, 11 June 1998, Winnipeg.

13. Ellen, interview with author, 12 June 1998, Winnipeg.

14. Maia, interview with author, 9 July 1998, Toronto.

15. Jacques, interview with author, 12 June 1997, St. John, N.B.

16. Anthony, interview with author, 9 June 1998, Winnipeg.

17. Rosa, interview with author, 18 November 1996, Toronto.

18. Heidegger 1977.

19. Ellen, interview with author, 18 December 1997, Moncton.

20. Lois, interview with author, November 1996, St. John, New Brunswick. . . .

21. Jill, interview with author, 14 July 1996, St. John, New Brunswick.

22. Moura, interview with author, 13 June 1996, St. John, New Brunswick.

23. Lois, interview with author, 4 November 1996, St. John, New Brunswick.

24. Lois, follow-up interview with author, December 1997, St. John, New Brunswick.

REFERENCES

Appelbaum, Eileen. 1993. "New Technology and Work Organisation: The Role of Gender Relations." In *Pink Collar Blues: Work, Gender and Technology,* edited by Belinda Probert and Bruce Wilson. Melbourne: Melbourne University Press.

Armstrong, Pat, and Hugh Armstrong. 1994. *The Double Ghetto: Canadian Women and Their Segregated Work.* 3d ed. Toronto: McLelland and Stewart.

Bakker, Isabella, ed. 1996. *Rethinking Restructuring: Gender and Change in Canada.* Toronto and Buffalo: University of Toronto Press.

———, ed. 1994. *The Strategic Silence: Gender and Economic Policy.* London, UK, and Atlantic Highlands, N.J.: Zed Books/North-South Institute.

Belt, Vicki, Ranald Richardson, and Juliet Webster. 1999. "Smiling Down the Phone: Women's Work in Telephone Call Centers." Presented at the RGS-IBG Annual Conference, University of Leicester. Unpublished paper (on file with author).

Bourdieu, Pierre, and Loic J. D. Wacquant. 1992. *An Invitation to Reflexive Sociology.* Chicago: University of Chicago Press.

Boyer, Robert, and Daniel Drache, eds. 1996. *States Against Markets: The Limits of Globalization.* London and New York: Routledge.

Buchanan, Ruth. 1995a. "Border Crossings: NAFTA, Regulatory Restructuring and the Politics of Place." *Indiana Journal of Global Legal Studies* 2: 371.

———. 1995b. "The Flexible Woman: Gendered Implications of Post-Fordist Narratives." University of Toronto Feminism and Law Working Paper Ser. 95–96(3).

———. 2000. "1-800 New Brunswick: Economic Development Strategies, Firm Restructuring and the Local Production of 'Global' Services." In *Globalizing Institutions: Case Studies in Regulation and Innovation,* edited by Jane Jenson and Boaventura de Sousa Santos. Aldershot, U.K.: Ashgate.

Buchanan, Ruth, and Sarah Koch-Schulte. 2000. *Gender on the Line: Technology, Restructuring, and the Reorganization of Work in the Call Center Industry.* Ottawa: Status of Women Canada Policy Research.

Casey, Catherine. 1995. *Work, Self and Society: After Industrialism.* London and New York: Routledge.

Curtis, James E., Edward G. Grabb, and L. Neil Guppy, eds. 1998. *Social Inequality in Canada: Patterns, Problems, and Policies.* Scarborough, Ontario: Prentice Hall.

Day, Shelagh, and Gwen Brodsky. 1998. *Women and the Equality Deficit: The Impact of Restructuring Canada's Social Programs.* Status of Women Canada Policy Research.

Duffy, Ann, and Noreen Pupo. 1992. *Part-Time Paradox: Connecting Gender, Work and Family.* Toronto: McClelland and Stewart.

Economic Council of Canada. 1990. *Good Jobs, Bad Jobs: Employment in the Service Industry.* Ottawa: Ministry of Supply and Services.

Evans, Patricia. 1993. "From Workfare to the Social Contract: Implications for Canada of Recent U.S. Welfare Reforms." *Canadian Public Policy-Analyse de Politiques* 19(1): 54–67.

Evans, Patricia, and Gerda Wekerle. 1997. *Women and the Canadian Welfare State: Challenges and Change.* Toronto and Buffalo: University of Toronto Press.

Freeman, Carla. 2000. *High Tech and High Heels in the Global Economy: Women, Work and Pink-Collar Identities in the Caribbean.* Durham, N.C.: Duke University Press.

Giddens, Anthony. 1990. *The Consequences of Modernity.* Stanford, Calif.: Stanford University Press.

Hall, Elaine. 1993. "Smiling, Deferring and Flirting: Doing Gender by Giving 'Good Service.'" *Work and Occupations* 20: 452–71.

Hanson, Susan, and Geraldine Pratt. 1995. *Gender, Work and Space.* London and New York: Routledge.

Harrison, Bennett. 1994. *Lean and Mean: The Changing Landscape of Corporate Power in the Age of Flexibility.* New York: Basic Books.

Heidegger, Martin. 1977. *The Question Concerning Technology and Other Essays.* New York: Harper and Row.

Hirst, Paul, and John Zeitlin. 1992. "Flexible Specialization Versus Post-Fordism: Theory, Evidence and Policy Implications." In *Pathways to Industrialization and Regional Development,* edited by Michael Storper and Alan John Scott. London and New York: Routledge.

Hochschild, Arlie Russell. 1983. *The Managed Heart: Commercialization of Human Feeling.* Berkeley: University of California Press.

Jensen, Jane. 1989. "The Talents of Women, the Skills of Men: Flexible Specialization and Women." In *The Transformation of Work? Skill, Flexibility and the Labour Process,* edited by Stephen Wood. London and Boston: Unwin Hyman.

———. 1996. "Part-Time Employment and Women: Range of Strategies." In *Rethinking Restructuring: Gender and Change in Canada,* edited by Isabella Bakker. Toronto and Buffalo: University of Toronto Press.

Johnson, Andrew F., Stephen McBride, and Patrick J. Smith, eds. 1994. *Continuities and Discontinuities: The Political Economy of Social Welfare and Labor Market Policy in Canada.* Toronto and Buffalo: University of Toronto Press.

Kassab, Cathy, and A. E. Luloff. 1993. "The New Buffalo Hunt: Chasing the Service Sector." *Journal of the Community Development Society* 24: 175–95.

Lamphere, Louis, Helena Ragone, and Patricia Zavella, eds. 1997. *Situated Lives: Gender and Culture in Everyday Life.* New York: Routledge.

Leidner, Robin. 1993. *Fast Food, Fast Talk: Service Work and the Routinization of Everyday Life.* Berkeley: University of California Press.

Lowe, Grahame S. 1999. "Labor Markets, Inequality, and the Future of Work." In *Social Inequality in Canada: Patterns, Problems, and Policies,* edited by James E. Curtis, Edward G. Grabb, and L. Neil Guppy. Scarborough, Ontario: Prentice Hall.

Massey, Doreen. 1994. *Space, Place and Gender.* Minneapolis: University of Minnesota Press.

McDowell, Linda. 1991. "Life Without Father and Ford: The New Gender Order of Post-Fordism." *Transactions: Institute of British Geographers* 16: 400–19.

———. 1997. *Capital Culture: Gender at Work in the City.* Oxford and Malden, Mass: Blackwell.

Menzies, Heather. 1997. "Telework, Shadow Work: The Privatization of Work in the New Digital Economy." *Studies in Political Economy* 53: 103–23.

Milne, William. 1995. "Regional Development Policies: Time for New Solutions." *Policy Options* 16: 31–35.

Peck, Jamie. 1996. *Work-Place: The Social Regulation of Labor Markets.* New York: Guilford Press.

Piore, Michael, and Charles Sabel. 1984. *The Second Industrial Divide: Possibilities for Prosperity.* New York: Basic Books.

Pollert, Anna. 1988. "Dismantling Flexibility." *Capital and Class* 34: 42.

Poynton, Cate. 1993. "Naming Women's Workplace Skills: Linguistics and Power." In *Pink Collar Blues: Work, Gender and Technology,* edited by Belinda Probert and Bruce Wilson. Melbourne: Melbourne University Press.

Sabel, Charles. 1995. "Bootstrapping Reform: Rebuilding Firms, the Welfare State and Unions." *Politics and Society* 23: 5.

———. 1991. "Moebius Strip Organizations and Open Labor Markets: Some Consequences of the Reintegration of Conception and Execution in a Volatile Economy." In *Social Theory for a Changing Society,* edited by Pierre Bourdieu and James Coleman. Boulder, Colo.: Westview Press.

Sassen, Saskia. 1996. *Losing Control? Sovereignty in an Age of Globalization.* New York: Columbia University Press.

———. 1995. "When the State Encounters a New Space Economy: The Case of Information Industries." *American Journal of International Law and Policy* 10: 769.

Streeck, Wolfgang. 1996. "Public Power Beyond the Nation-State." In *States Against Markets: The Limits of Globalization,* edited by Robert Boyer and Daniel Drache. London and New York: Routledge.

Twining, William. 2000. *Globalization and Legal Theory.* London: Butterworths.

Webster, Juliet. 1993. "From the Word Processor to the Micro: Gender Issues in the Development of Information Technology in the Office." In *Gendered by Design? Information Technology and Office Systems,* edited by Eileen Green, Jenny Owen, and Den Pain. London and Washington, D.C.: Taylor and Francis.

———. 1996. *Shaping Women's Work: Gender, Employment and Information Technology.* London and New York: Longman.

Wharton, Amy. 1993. "The Affective Consequences of Service Work." *Work and Occupations* 20: 205–32.

Wilson, Patricia. 1996. "Future Directions in Local Economic Development." In *Local Economic Development in Europe and the Americas,* edited by Christopher Demaziere and Patricia Wilson. London: Mansell.

Upshot: - Explores low-wage workers in call centers in 3 Canadian towns.

- Frames these call centers as signs of a changing labor market, due to & responding to globalization & corp. restructuring. → Call centers separate srvc. from HQs & take adv. of captive pop. of desperate workers

- Workers rarely see this as a 'career' & burn out soon
* Workers must engage in emotional labor using interpersonal skills

- Most workers are ♀, minorities/immigrants, gay or otherwise marginalized.

- Have to frequently de-stress & often don't feel "like themselves"

∽ **READING 29** ∽

The House Rules

Autonomy and Interests Among Service Workers
in the Contemporary Casino Industry

Jeffrey J. Sallaz

Dealers come on shift knowing that it is they who must face the hard intent of
players to win and coolly stand in its way, consistently blocking skill, luck, and
cheating, or lose the precarious reputation they have with management.

—Erving Goffman, Aspiring Croupier, 1967

Hell, if a player's tipping who cares if he's winning? It ain't my money I'm
giving away!

—Maria, Blackjack Dealer, 1998

It is 9 p.m. on a busy Friday night at "Jack-pot," a large corporate casino in Nevada.[1] I am a "break-in" blackjack dealer about to begin my first shift, squirming nervously in my "black and whites" (worker slang for their hot and uncomfortable tuxedo attire). Management has assigned Joanne—at 33 one of the oldest and most experienced of Jackpot's young, primarily female and immigrant dealers—to watch over me. She stands at my side as I deal two cards to each of the three middle-aged, middle-class men at the table. The casino's interior, with its opulent decor, dim lighting, and free cocktails, is designed to provide these players a fantasy realm of conspicuous consumption in which everyday worries and concerns do not hold.

For me, however, the casino represents a critical if extreme research site for the sociology of service work. Not only are Nevada's casinos notorious for their despotic labor control strategies (Frey, 1986; R. Smith, Preston, & Humphries, 1974), but the industry over the past decade has expanded throughout the United States and become highly competitive (Eadington, 1999; Marfels, 1999). Such developments, scholars of service work predict (Hochschild, 1983, p. 8; Leidner, 1999, p. 84; MacDonald & Sirianni, 1996, p. 9), should have increased the relevance of customer service to the individual casino and, thus, intensified managerial attempts to control workers' "interactive labor" (Leidner, 1993).

A mere 10 minutes into my first night of fieldwork, however, a surprise comes. All three players are winning but not offering me any tips. I smile and make conversation anyway, as house procedure dictates. Joanne, though, whispers to me, "Listen kid, your attitude sucks. When they're winning but not toking [tipping], you ain't supposed to be

"The House Rules: Autonomy and Interests Among Service Workers in the Contemporary Casino Industry" by Jeffrey J. Sallaz from *Work and Occupations*, Vol. 29, No. 4, November, 2002: pp. 218–238. Copyright © 2002 Sage Publications. Reprinted by permission of Sage Publications, Inc.

nice. Dummy up and deal. Get them outta here." I would soon discover that although dealers are required to simultaneously deal quickly, protect against cheating, and produce in customers a happy, carefree, emotional state, they regularly violate these "house rules" to increase their tip incomes. Why do dealers refuse to identify with casino management? And considering the considerable resources the firm mobilizes to ensure compliance with its tripartite goals of *speed, security,* and *service*—intense work routinization, video surveillance, emotional labor requirements—how are workers able to break its shop-floor rules? Although the emergent sociology of service work has highlighted novel dilemmas of autonomy and interests for management, it too narrowly focuses on the service labor process and, thus, cannot fully account for the genesis and functions of the casino's system of labor control.

Theory: Situating the Service Labor Process

The proportion of U.S. workers employed in service industries has grown steadily throughout [the 20th] century (from 30% in 1900, to 50% in 1950, to 75% today). Sociologists and scholars of the workplace, however, did not begin to theorize how this transition affected our traditional, manufacturing-based understandings of labor relations until the past few decades. Specifically, they have argued that the immediate presence of clients at the point of production complicates managerial strategies for organizing the labor process and monitoring/disciplining workers. These dilemmas have been described as being of two main types: those of worker autonomy and interests.

Regarding *autonomy,* researchers have pointed out the possibilities of increased worker surveillance and control offered by the presence of clients. Management may, for instance, surreptitiously monitor and

evaluate service providers using electronic surveillance (Garson, 1988; MacDonald & Sirianni, 1996), "secret shoppers" (Benson, 1986), or customers themselves (Fuller & Smith, 1991). In general, though, service labor may offer workers greater autonomy than does manufacturing labor because they perform not just physical tasks but "emotional" or "interactive" labor as well (Hochschild, 1983; Leidner, 1993; Sutton, 1991). The product being "sold" by a service firm, that is, is often intangible, such as an experience or a feeling. And insofar as despotic control strategies produce standardized, "inauthentic" emotional expressions, they become inappropriate for organizing work (Frenkel, Korczynski, Shire, & Tam, 1999, p. 203; Gutek, 1995; Hochschild, 1983; Van Maanen & Kunda, 1989). Workers must therefore be granted a much wider degree of autonomy to customize their service offerings (Gottfried, 1991; Rafaeli & Sutton, 1987; V. Smith, 1996). In addition, the alignment of *interests* cannot be conceptualized as a simple dichotomy in which managers and workers clash against one another (Leidner, 1999; Troyer, Mueller, & Osinsky, 2000). Rather, the interests and resources of clients themselves must be considered, especially the extent to which two of these groups may form an alliance against the third. And whereas such alliances will continually shift within any one workplace, one pattern will dominate (Leidner, 1993).

I began ethnographic fieldwork in the casino equipped with two conceptual "tools": the notions of "emotional labor" and "three-way interest alliance." And whereas they worked well initially—management did ask us to smile, laugh, and provide players an overall gaming "experience," though dealers often aligned themselves with clients versus the House—I soon found them limited in two important ways. First, I began researching the history of casino dealing in Nevada and found that the current emotional labor demands and interest alliance on the gambling tables were of recent origin. As the structure of the casino industry had changed throughout the century, so had managerial strategies for organizing casino dealing. Yet the service work literature offers few tools for understanding how industrial and organizational change affect the fine details of the actual labor process. As Heimer and Stevens (1997) stated, these studies have neglected or ignored how "the content of [service and professional] work is altered by external demands placed on the organization in which it is embedded . . . organizational environments matter" (pp. 135–136). Second, whereas my fieldwork revealed why it was "rational" for workers to break the casino's rules regarding service, I was initially unable to understand why management allowed this to happen (especially in a heavily monitored workplace such as the casino). Did workers' infractions in fact serve some function for the firm beyond the immediate horizon of the labor process? "Do [workers'] 'games' or coping practices in the service sector . . . display contradictory impulses?" (McCammon & Griffin, 2000, p. 284). . . .

Method and Data

Considering that legal gambling has throughout the majority of U.S. history been confined to a single, sparsely populated state, a surprisingly large amount of primary and secondary source materials exist on the work experiences of Nevada's casino dealers throughout the 20th Century. My historical analysis in this article is thus based on a series of oral histories of early Nevada casino workers collected by historians at the University of Nevada, several ethnographies of casino dealing, management publications, employee handbooks, and my own interviews with veteran casino workers.

The ethnographic portion of the article, in turn, is based on a 4-month stint as a casino dealer. In late spring, I moved to Nevada and, as must all aspiring croupiers today, enrolled in a state-licensed vocational school offering standardized courses in dealing. Completion of such a program constitutes a prerequisite for applying to dealing jobs. In June (a peak in the hiring season), I applied to the Jackpot Corporation as a blackjack dealer. I specifically chose Jackpot as a potential research site because of its current structural position in the U.S. casino industry. The prevailing image of the contemporary casino is still that of the glamorous, Disney-esque, megacasino on the Las Vegas Strip catering to a high-rolling, often international clientele. As the gambling industry has spread across the United States over the past decade, however (38 of the 50 U.S. states now allow casinos), the typical casino has become smaller, less glitzy, and more geared toward a "locals market" (Bear, Stearns and Co., 2001; Eadington, 1999). Jackpot casino— located "off the strip" and catering to a competitive market of budget-conscious tourists and locals—is thus an ideal representative of the "new generation" of American casinos.

Through considerable good fortune I was hired by Jackpot as a swing-shift (9 p.m. to 5 a.m.) blackjack dealer. . . . Though technically classified as part-time, I like all dealers regularly worked 10 to 12 hours per night and 50-plus hours per week. During my tenure as a croupier, I kept my status as researcher hidden from both management and co-workers. When asked about myself on job applications or by other workers in the casino, I would reply that I was between jobs or looking for a new line of work. Although aware of the ethical issues associated with covert ethnographic research, I decided before entering the field that such dissembling was not only safe for my subjects—my presence would pose no danger for my coworkers, whereas I would take all necessary steps to ensure anonymity—but necessary for two reasons. First, because of the illicit workplace behavior I might observe, I was worried that other dealers would not trust their secrets to one associated with management and/or academia. And second, I wanted to ensure that I received no special treatment from corporate or floor management. Indeed, throughout my fieldwork, I could discern no major differences in how I was treated by management or my coworkers. In fact, the process of gaining entrée and winning the trust of fellow dealers was easier than expected because of the worker solidarity induced by the industry's shared tip structure, in which individual dealers' tips are pooled together and split evenly among all workers. Because the most experienced dealer's income was dependent on the tip-making ability of the greenest of dealers, new workers are quickly "taken under the wing" of veteran dealers and taught explicitly the work group's multiple tip-making tactics. . . .

A House Divided: Corporate Versus Floor Management Schemas for Organizing Work

Although Jackpot targets budget-conscious locals and working-class tourists, like all casinos it must be prepared to handle high-roller action as well. Corporate management has thus officially organized dealing work—from initial "auditions" to the ubiquitous black globes above each table—to maximize speed, security, and service. Upon applying to Jackpot, I was first required to attend an eight-person group interview at which personnel specialists evaluated our interaction skills through conversation exercises and role-playing games. The next day, three of us were invited back for an audition on the casino floor itself. We took turns dealing at a dead table for Rick, a young corporate manager who informed us that

> We're looking for "people people." Those who can carry on a conversation. We can

always teach technical skill, but we need good personalities. As a matter of fact, we had a gentleman recently who didn't even know how to deal, but was so outgoing and fun that we had to hire him. And we did and we trained him and now he's the best dealer in the house.

The initial decision to hire is thus based as much on the applicant's personality as her or his technical skill. Before starting work, though, the new dealer must pass both a drug test and a police background check of her or his criminal record. In sum, management uses the results of various prehire tests (friendly demeanor, no drug use, clean police record) as indicators of certain desirable traits (amiability, honesty, sobriety) to select workers they feel will readily perform service- and security-related directives.

The physical organization of the casino floor functions to maximize security by "creat[ing] conditions of regularity and visibility" (Skolnik, 1978, p. 71). Groups of 8 to 16 gaming tables are numbered and placed facing outward in oval-shaped patterns called *pits*. One or two supervisors monitor each pit.[2] The oval design lets them constantly keep multiple tables in their field of vision, while a black ceiling globe housing a video camera is mounted above each table and relays to a central control room staffed by surveillance specialists. Even dealers' uniforms are designed to maximize security rather than comfort or aesthetics; long-sleeved shirts with tight cuffs ensure they do not slide chips up their sleeves, while aprons prevent them from accessing their pockets while on the tables. This sophisticated network of surveillance is intended to function as a panopticon, insofar as management can potentially monitor workers at all times, whereas the individual dealer should have no knowledge of if or when she or he is under observation (Foucault, 1979).

The organization of the labor process it-self is constrained by both the basic rules of blackjack and the structure of the tipping system. A blackjack table is a semicircle of green felt with betting circles for seven players. Once all bets are placed, the dealer gives each player, including herself or himself, two cards. The idea of the game

> is for the player and dealer to get as close to a card count of 21 as possible, without "breaking" (going over that number). The most straightforward way to reach 21 is by drawing an ace (which counts for either 11 or 1) and a 10-card. The two-card 21 is called "blackjack" [and is paid 3 to 2; a regular winner is paid 1 to 1]. (Skolnik, 1978, pp. 56–57)

After the initial cards are dealt, each player decides whether to "hit" (take another card) or "stand." If a hit breaks the player, the dealer takes his or her cards and bet immediately. After all players have played their hands, the dealer exposes both her or his cards and plays out the hand. At this point,

> the critical items are . . . dealers must draw on 16 and stand pat on 17, and ties are a standoff . . . the player is not playing against the other players but only against the dealer; and the dealer is totally lacking in discretion. (Skolnik, 1978, p. 57)

The standard method of tipping one's dealer is to offer a "toke bet." Here, the player places a smaller side bet "for the dealer" next to his or her bet before the hand begins. If the player loses, both bets are collected and go into the tray (to the house). If the player wins, the dealer pays both bets and collects for herself or himself both the original toke bet and its winnings. These tip earnings are then deposited in a common "toke box" and evenly distributed among all dealers at the end of the shift. Two important characteristics of this tipping system must be emphasized. First, the dealer is

tipped only when the player wins; otherwise, both bets go the house. Second, the shared tip system encourages dealer cooperation to collectively maximize the tip income for all.

Although the basic rules of blackjack are simple enough and seemingly would allow dealers considerable latitude to perform their tasks, this is far from the case. The *noninteractive components* of dealing (how dealers handle cards, chips, etc.) have been routinized to maximize speed and security. "Procedure" consists of a series of brief actions that, taken together, constitute a "hand" and are repeated over and over. They are as follows:

1. holding the deck,
2. dealing two cards to each player (the "pitch") and the dealer,
3. hitting each player's hand,
4. exposing and playing the dealer's hand,
5. collecting losing bets,
6. paying winning bets, and
7. shuffling the deck.

There is one precise way to perform each of these tasks, specified to such a degree of detail that the placement of every finger at every moment is predetermined.

The house also regulates seven aspects of the *interactive component* of dealing—how croupiers converse with customers and each other. First, to maximize speed, dealers must teach novice players the procedures of play so they do not unnecessarily hold up the game. This education, though, must involve only rules of play, not game strategy. Computer simulations have determined the "proper" blackjack strategy that maximizes the player's win percentage. It allows the player to win nearly half (49%) of the time. The average player, though, plays around the 35% to 45% level (Vogel, 1994). Dealers of course know the basics of the proper strategy but are prohibited from advising players on how to play their hands to maximize security (i.e., the house advantage on individual hands and thus the overall house edge). Third, dealers must constantly monitor their tables for possible cheating and report any unusual player behavior to the floor supervisor. Fourth, all official game-related communication between dealer and players must be signaled visibly so both supervisors and cameras can monitor the action from afar. And fifth, on the casino floor, dealers cannot "carry on unnecessary conversations with other employees"; this is to prevent interemployee cheating schemes (Jackpot employee manual).

The remaining two areas of interactive regulation serve to ensure customer service. The Jackpot employee manual instructs dealers to create a fun table atmosphere in which each player feels like a guest: "Greet each player with a friendly 'hello,'" "introduce yourself to each player," "show a general interest in your players," and "say 'thank you' when players leave your game." Certain behaviors are prohibited: "Never display any body language that could be interpreted as negative or unfriendly" and "never ignore a player." The final directive prevents dealers from "hustling tokes," that is, aggressively pressuring players to tip, and thus creating an "unfun" table atmosphere:

- Never imply that a player should tip.
- Never say "let's make some money."
- No differential treatment of players who tip. (Jackpot employee manual)

Were the above policies to be enforced completely—a technically possible task—dealers would undoubtedly perform simultaneously speed, security, and service. Actual practices on the casino floor, however, diverge from the official organization of the labor process. As my fieldwork proceeded, I discovered a difference on the shop floor for dealers between the roles of pit bosses and those of corporate management. From the point of view of dealers, corporate management demands they provide speed, security, and service for all clients. Yet Jackpot's pit bosses, although officially salaried representatives of the corporation, were all former dealers and acted as middlemen between dealers and corporate management. Through observations of and informal conversations with pit bosses, I found that they are evaluated according to their pit's nightly "win" (overall profit), a function of both volume of play and the house's win percentage on a given evening. Floor managers thus perform strategically within their own game by (a) maximizing speed for low-rollers by letting the tipping system regulate the labor process, even though this entails sacrificed security and service provision; and (b) maximizing security and service for high-rollers by imposing despotic control, even though speed is here sacrificed.

The Daily Grind: Autonomy for Low-Rollers

Low-rollers (those who play $3 to $20 hands) constituted around 90% of Jackpot's clientele. During many shifts, in fact, a dealer would only encounter low-rollers. And although corporate management directs dealers to provide service to and ensure security for all players, pit bosses care only about maximizing speed for low-rollers. They thus here withdrew control, allowing the logic of the tipping system to regulate the labor process. For just as pit bosses seek to maximize the overall volume of low-rollers' small-stake wagers, dealers understand that more hands dealt means more tipping opportunities and therefore spontaneously maximize their speed. Players would often complain about the pace at which we dealt or even ask us to slow down. Invariably a dealer would respond, "Sorry, but we have to deal this way" or "Can't help it. The hand is quicker than the eye." Consent was thus secured as well over the intense routinization of dealing work. At no point during my fieldwork did I hear workers complain about the severe standardization of their every move, for on the shop floor itself, dealing according to procedure was understood as—and as far as I could tell *was*—the fastest way to deal and thus to make tips.

Yet the flip side of the maximum-speed performance generated by the tipping system is sacrificed security and service provision. The toke bet system, that is, creates incentives both to assist players who are tipping and to treat nontippers rudely to force them off. And the autonomy to do so is granted by floor supervisors in three ways. First, surveillance is withdrawn when low-rollers are playing. Pit bosses pay close attention primarily to high-stakes games, whereas video surveillance too neglects "grind play." As a new dealer, I soon discovered this fact of life on the casino floor: The vast majority of our work is not monitored.

> Tonight I accidentally paid a woman on her $5 bet when we both have 18 [ties in blackjack are a standoff]. Even worse, I paid and collected her $1 tip bet too. At first I panicked. What if the cameras saw that? Will they fire me? But then I rationalized it, telling myself that this place is so packed tonight, while the players at my table were playing such small bets. What are the odds that one or two guys in surveillance, monitoring all the action on all the tables, saw one little mispay? And sure enough the night ended without anyone in management having noticed.

Second, pit bosses encourage dealers to break official norms of service to maintain a fast pace of play on their tables by disciplining slow—usually drunk—low-rollers. Whereas official procedure requires workers to treat all players as guests, floor management would here deflate player status and grant dealers the right to treat them with coldness:

> Two middle-aged men are among the six players at my table. They are drinking Budweisers as fast as the waitress can bring them, and the guy on my far right is so drunk he keeps passing out at the table and spilling his beer. He somehow manages to keep putting up bets, though, so I must deal to him. But he is too drunk to read his cards or make the proper signals, so I must repeatedly ask, "Would you like to hit sir?" and then interpret his garbled response. The other players are getting annoyed, and Larry the pit boss is now standing permanently at my side. Larry nags him. "One hand on the cards." "Keep your beer behind your bet." "Sir, look up, it's your turn." Eventually the two drunk guys get the hint and stumble off. Larry says to me, "If they're slowing you down like that, you gotta get on their case, bug 'em, get 'em outta there."

Floor supervisors direct dealers to force off slow players by withholding service. Dealers comply and, in return, are able to withhold service from, and even openly antagonize, low-rolling nontippers.

Third, pit bosses ask dealers to operate outside of procedure regarding security to improve the house edge in key situations (for instance, when dealing to suspected cheaters or a low-roller in the midst of a lucky winning streak). They here emphasize that dealers are not, as official rules proclaim, passive mediators between players and the house but can influence game outcomes:

> Melissa, another new dealer, and I are sitting in the cafeteria waiting to clock out. Chuck, a pit boss, walks over and says, "You two are new, so there's something I want to tell you. When you're dealing, pay attention to how many 10s are out of your deck. If they ain't coming out [remember, the player's odds are improved in proportion to the number of 10-valued cards left in the deck], break your deck

[shuffle sooner than procedure dictates] and we have the advantage again. Just something to think about."

Although requests such as these were honored when players were not tipping or workers were being directly monitored (i.e., when high-rollers were playing), dealers would use these same techniques in the opposite way when dealing to a tipping low-roller:

> Melissa and I nod intently while Chuck is speaking and say, "Sure, sure." When he leaves, though, we both bust out laughing. "Whatever," says Melissa. "If he's tipping I ain't gonna push him off," I say. "Yeah. As long as no one's behind me [i.e., I'm not being watched] I'm gonna help the man out."

In sum, when low-rollers are on the table, pit bosses withdraw surveillance and allow workers to break routinized procedure and refuse to identify with the house. Workers in turn experience such autonomy as a highly complicated and serious game on the tables—one that, unlike the "official" games, involves three parties: players, the house, and dealers.

"A Game of Making Tokes"

Once I began work and collected my bearings, I learned that not only the act of dealing itself but practically all aspects of worker culture—break-room conversations, after-work gripe sessions, hints granted to break-ins by veterans—revolve around "making tokes." Jackpot dealers earn about $20 each night in salary, $60 to $100 in tips. To maximize their tip incomes, they deploy a variety of tip-making tactics.

Classifying Players

Jackpot dealers categorize players into two broad types: tippers and nontippers ("georges" and "stiffs," respectively). When a new player sits down, however, the dealer does not know whether he or she is a tipper and so immediately embarks upon a process of information gathering. A new player, for instance, can announce he is a tipper:

> Win me a couple hands, buddy, and I'll be a generous fellow.
>
> All right, pal, let's make *us both* some money!

In addition, an unspoken protocol of tipping exists on the tables. After a series of wins (approximately three to five) or a single big win (such as a blackjack), table norms dictate a tip. A blackjack, though, offered a special test of tipping status, because as part of such a win, players often receive a 50-cent piece ($3 bet = $4.50 payoff, $5 bet = $7.50 payoff, etc.). This coin, paid out after a large win and, literally, "small change" (both in terms of monetary denomination and its size relative to the larger plastic gaming chips), represented a perfect opportunity for even a moderate tipper to get on a dealer's good side. Too small for use as a cocktail waitress tip or slot machine token, it could easily be bet as a potential $1 tip for the dealer. A player who pocketed the 50-cent piece or, far worse, used it as part of his or her next bet (referred to invidiously by dealers as "putting the silver on top") immediately betrayed his or her status as a nontipper.

Often, though, a new player will be "cold," losing game after game. Because even the most generous george does not tip during a losing streak, dealers can use jokes or stories to discern a player's true colors; that is, they can slyly "hustle" an initial tip:

> While riding home from work with Claudia, a Chinese woman in her 40s, we talk about how to get players to start toking. She tells me that she doesn't wear her wedding ring at work because it gets dirty from handling money all

night. "Once while I was dealing," she says, "a man asked me if I was married. 'Yes, yes,' I said. 'Well where's your ring?' 'Oh we can't afford one right now, but we are saving up to buy one.' 'Did you hear that?' he says to the table. 'C'mon, let's put some tips up for her.'" We both laugh.

Educating Novices

The only customers who can escape—albeit briefly—an initial tipper/nontipper classification are true novices: players, usually tourists, who simply are not aware of the basic tipping procedure. When dealing with such a player, one must first draw attention to the tipping structure:

> I tell Kim, a fellow dealer, that it seems like a lot of players are nice but don't know how to tip. She says, "Well wait until you have one player at the table who does tip. When they do, make a big deal of it in front of the other players: 'Thank *you*, sir!'" [in exaggerated tone, tapping the tip conspicuously].

Having made players aware of the toke system, dealers must make clear that tips are not mere gratuities or gifts but rather a fee for a service rendered. They will, for instance, whisper advice to players to emphasize that such hints are not only not a part of their job duties but against the rules as well. And when an initial tip is offered, a dealer's demeanor changes dramatically from indifference to active engagement with the action on the table.

Communicating Information to Other Dealers

Information on player tipping behavior is not only collected but shared among workers as well. I discovered that during relief changes, dealers utilize a complex, though unformalized, code communicating customer tipping behavior—a veritable dealer semiotics. When relief arrives, a dealer must finish the current hand and inform the table that she or he is leaving. Through this act of saying goodbye to the players, though, the exiting dealer communicates to the incoming dealer vital information about tipping status—who is tipping, how much, how frequently. For example, a dealer in good spirits who thanks the table at large is a sure sign that multiple tippers are playing. And if the dealer singles out one player with a smile and "good luck to you, sir" upon leaving the table, then this player is obviously the only tipper. I did not become fully aware of the range of this code, though, until about a month into my fieldwork. While working relief one night, a veteran dealer offered me information concerning the miserly tipping behavior on his table:

> I am relieving Juan [a veteran Filipino dealer] tonight. As I am finishing a relief shift, three new players—two men and a woman—come to the table with about $100 each and begin playing $5 hands. After their first hand, Juan comes back and I move on. When I return in an hour to relieve Juan again, the three players are now all laughing and have about $200 each in front of them [signifying that they have been winning]. And yet there are no tips behind Juan's tray. As Juan turns to leave he says nothing to the players but gives me an exasperated look and says, "Good luck, Jeff." I've never had an exiting dealer wish *me* good luck, I think. It is not until I have already dealt out my first hand that I catch on. He wants these stiffs to lose!

Helping Tippers Win

Workers' tactics for dealing with and to players they have labeled tippers fall into two broad categories: helping them win ("improving their luck") and providing extra emotional labor ("treating them right"). When executed successfully, they both enable (in terms of the first tactic) and encourage (in terms of the second) players to continue tipping. Blackjack dealers can help players win in two ways. First, they can offer advice on basic blackjack strategy. Splits are key opportunities to offer assistance.

> Sam [an African American male in his 20s] and I are talking after work about helping out players who are tipping. Sam says, "if they try to split 10s, I'll say, 'Are you *sure* you want to do that?'"

More generally, dealers can advise players whether to hit their hand.

> I tell Sam that I do this too, "Like when I can see that a person has 14 and my up-card is a 6 and they start to swipe [signal a hit], I'll go,'Now be careful here' and then wait for them to give the hit signal again."

To offer assistance, the dealer must deploy a minitactic to see the player's cards. The dealer can crane her or his neck to catch a glimpse of the player's hand; she or he can, with varying degrees of subtlety, ask the player for this information; or the player himself or herself can verbally or visually convey it:

> It is late in the night and I am dealing to Troy, an outgoing salesman from Los Angeles. He is a tipper and puts me up frequently, referring to "*us* winning." But I soon realize that he is not the smartest of players and so help him out as best I can. He begins turning his cards face up on the table when he receives them—so I will be able to see his hand—and giving me ambiguous hit signals. I respond by doing everything I can to assist him, practically playing the hands for him. "We're good there," I say. "That 13's gonna need some help." Eventually the pit boss notices,

strolls over and tells Troy to stop exposing his cards, casting me a dirty look as well. While this reprimand would have scared me early in my fieldwork, I now merely tone down my assistance. The exchange of tips—dollar chips for helpful hints—continues, albeit more covertly.

The second way that dealers can help tippers is to pay attention to the cards that have been played from the deck and time their shuffle to increase the player's odds of winning. Whereas official procedure dictates that the deck be shuffled only when exactly two thirds of the way through, if after the first hand the deck is disadvantageous to players (i.e., a disproportionately high number of 10s have been played), a dealer can shuffle early. Conversely, she or he can shuffle later than procedure dictates when the deck is favorable to players. If, however, despite all attempts to the contrary, a dealer is "hot" and unable to lose, she or he can still go to great lengths to emphasize that she or he is, in fact, on the player's side and as much a victim of bad luck as they:

> After work tonight I take $50 of my tip money and go to play blackjack at a neighboring casino with a coworker. We immediately make our status as tippers known, and the dealer, a young Asian man, responds by cracking jokes and laughing with us. He keeps turning up blackjacks and 20s however, so our tip bets go into the chip tray [to the House]. I see that he is continually breaking the deck early, but to no avail. With each winning hand, he looks increasingly distraught and says apologetically, *"I'm trying! I'm trying!"*

Emotional Labor for Tippers

The second type of tactic is the provision of extra emotional labor for the tipper, the most basic unit of which is the smile:

I am talking before work with Teresa, a rather shy dealer from Mexico. "To make tips," she tells me, "you have to please the customer." "Well, how do you do that?" I ask. "You smile at them."

In addition, dealers "read" players and offer appropriate emotional displays depending on their age, gender, general disposition, and so on. In general, female, young, and grind players were offered informal, relaxed, and "fun" forms of service. Experienced dealers would constantly offer me advice on procuring tips from such players. "Flirt!" many told me. "Bullshit with them." "Laugh at their jokes," Claudia once said, "even if they're totally dumb." Dealers can also make jokes and provide general entertainment on the tables. I for instance developed a working repertoire of funny comments for use during the games:

> I begin my shift at a $5 blackjack table. The players tip occasionally but are really sedate. I am in top form, though, and provide a humorous running commentary to the game. After calling for insurance and checking my hand when my up-card is an ace, I give the players a sorrowful expression so they will think I have a blackjack. When they all go, "Awww!" I say quickly, "Oh, calm down, I'm just pulling your legs." This gets lots of laughs. And after the game is briefly interrupted by a tray fill, I say to the players, "And now back to the regularly scheduled blackjack game." Soon the table is in an uproar and they are offering toke bets practically every hand. In fact, when my shift ends, the woman at third base hands me a $5 chip and tells me with a big, genuine smile, "You were fun!"

Dealers also personalize their interactions with tippers more than with nontippers. They ask and address them by their first names, inquire about where they are from and what they do, and so on. They refer to the tipper's play as a joint enterprise: "We almost got that one," "Where's that 5 when we need it?" And they appear to be more emotionally invested in game outcomes than they actually are by smiling or laughing when players win and frowning when they lose.

Older players and men playing alone, in contrast, are more serious about their game play and expect reserved, deferential, and status-enhancing emotional labor. Maria, a Hispanic blackjack dealer in her 20s, explains one of her tactics for these players:

> "You know how these old guys are. They like to be taken care of. So you pay attention to what he's drinking and when the cocktail waitress comes around, if I see he needs another drink, I'll go ahead and order his drink for him." This impresses him, she thinks, and encourages more tips.

More generally, the dealer calls these players by their last names. During the game, she or he "takes care of them" by watching and learning their basic game strategy to then assist them with it. And the dealer makes their play seem central to table outcomes. For instance, if there is only one such tipper at a table full of players, the dealer, on busting, can say to him or her, "Good play, sir. That'll get everyone paid," regardless of whether his or her play had been the deciding factor in breaking the dealer. At a table packed full of players, all of whom are following the game closely, the difference in a dealer's treatment of a tipper vis-à-vis others is both conspicuous to all and a sure source of additional toke bets.

Forcing Off Nontippers

When dealing to stiffs, however, dealers conspire to force them off the table as quickly as possible to make room for players who tip.

Dealers are landlords, I was told, and nontippers tenants who do not pay the rent:

> You know how some players be sitting there for three or four hours at a time but never put down a bet for you? You go to break, come back and they're *still there.* No offense. Sit down and play a few hands, but don't be taking up that seat all night long if you ain't gonna pay some rent. (Hugo, a 23-year-old Hispanic man)

Dealers attempt to force out these players by making them lose. They can, for example, simply follow procedure by withholding assistance they would normally grant even the most modest tipper. They merely say nothing when the player splits 10s or does not split 8s. And they respond to requests for advice by saying, "That's a tough call" or "I don't know . . . are you feeling lucky?"

Dealers can also bend the house rules slightly by altering their shuffle (i.e., dealing sooner or later than procedure dictates) to change a bad run of the cards (here, one that is going well for the player). Joanne, my first-night "trainer," introduced me to this technique of "shuffling your shuffle":

> It is late in the evening and the players at my table are winning big, but not tipping. Joanne tells me to change my shuffle, "Take a third from the top or shuffle an extra time. It doesn't matter. Just do something different." I'm not quite sure why she is saying this, but I assume it is because I am doing something wrong. On the next break, though, she explains, "They were winning but they weren't tipping. You got to change the flow of the cards, try to break them up a bit."

And once dealers do find a good run of cards (here, one that is going poorly for the player), they simply concentrate on dealing extremely rapidly, knowing that after all, the odds are in their (and the house's) favor. In the words of Kim, a veteran dealer, "Just find a sweet spot in the deck and wipe' em out."

At the far extreme, dealers may directly, and with the pit bosses' implicit approval, manipulate game outcomes. The following anecdote, involving the game roulette, vividly illustrates this arrangement:

> It is a slow night so they send me to help the dealer at a roulette table in the back of the casino. Cathy, a middle-aged White woman, is dealing. A group of three players has just joined the two already at the table. As the game is about to begin, she whispers to me, "Watch this. Time to make some money." As she spins the ball, she announces to the table, "28 black, put your money on 28 black." Three players do and, sure enough, the ball comes to rest on 28 black. (I am in awe.) As she is paying out the winners, I softly ask her how she did it. "Honey, I'm a big fish in a little pond here at Jackpot. Twenty years at the Mint." As she finishes paying out, not a single player tips her or offers her a tip bet for the next spin. "Not one goddamn cent," she hisses to me, "My checks are starting to bounce from all the smiles and thank-yous I've been depositing." As she gets ready to spin the ball again, she says, "Now watch this. Let's put it where they ain't." Sure enough on the next spin the 4 hits, one of the few numbers nobody is on. Several players leave the table. I ask her if she's scared of getting caught. "No," she replies, "there's no way the cameras are watching this one little table in the back. And Mark (the pit boss) wouldn't say anything 'cause last Saturday night I was on his roulette table and it was packed full of big bettors. I set it down on the only empty number and you should've seen the smile he flashed me."

TABLE 1   House-Dealer Interest Alignment by House Goal and Type of Player

	Speed	Security	Service
Tipper	Maximize (in house's interest)	**Help player win (against house's interest)**	Provide (in house's interest)
Nontipper	Maximize (in house's interest)	Make player lose (in house's interest)	**Withhold (against house's interest)**

Note: Cells in boldface indicate "hot spots" when high-rollers are on the table.

Here, Cathy exercised her autonomy to make tokes by manipulating the game to allow players to win their bets. When the players "failed the test" (did not tip), she knew they were nontippers and proceeded to force them off. Conscious too of the lack of surveillance at "this one little table in the back," she acknowledges her obligation to the pit boss to work the same technique to the house's advantage in a high-action situation, regardless of the players' tipping status.

Antagonizing Stiffs

Dealers also force off nontippers by withholding emotional labor. On one particularly bad tip night in early August, eight of us dealers gathered at a large table in the cafeteria during break to complain about our tables:

> Helen brings up a Jackpot regular notorious for engaging dealers in endless conversations yet not tipping. "Just talk, talk, talk and no tip. I don't want to talk, mother. I am tired. Put up a dollar here and there and I will talk, but no money and I am tired." Phil launches into a diatribe against the most despised of players: those who look rich and are on a winning streak but don't tip. "I love to take those people's money. To dummy up and deal. I hate 'em."

Two of my coworkers went even further, explaining how they openly antagonize nontippers:

> "Sometimes I'll piss them off on purpose, 'Oh, you lost again sir, too bad.'" [All laugh.] "Yeah! Or just smile a little when they lose. That usually gets to them."

So this is the cost to the house, at the level of the labor process, of making workers dependent on customers' tips. The toke bet system creates a pattern of alliances between dealers, players, and the house in which it is rational for workers to break official rules (see Table 1). The autonomy to do so, however, is granted and regulated by pit bosses as one part of a larger regime, the dual nature of which comes into full focus when we consider their strategies for handling potential "hot spots" (indicated in boldface in Table 1) when high-rollers are on the table.

To Protect and to Serve: Despotic Control for High-Rollers

About 10% of Jackpot's players were high-rollers (clients who regularly play at least $25 hands), for whom floor managers seek to maximize security and provide personalized service. For such clients, pit bosses would impose despotic control (tight supervision, harsh penalties) over workers to ensure maximum security and proper service provision. For dealers, the passage from autonomy to despotism is audibly marked by the procedure for announcing the arrival of a high-roller. On seeing a player put down a "high-action" bet such as a brown $100 chip, a dealer must yell, "Brown plays" and wait for a pit boss to come to the table before dealing the hand. Though this slows the action down considerably, the immediate presence of a supervisor not only ensures that dealers do not treat a (nontipping) high-roller rudely, it also allows the pit boss to perform customer service by personally thanking the player for his or her patronage or offering a complementary dinner. To further ensure that dealers do not assist a (tipping) high-roller, both floor supervisors and video surveillance carefully monitor high-action play:

> The moment someone slaps down a $100 bet, you can *feel* the cameras zooming in. (Joanne)

Punishments, too, are intensified; the only two dealers fired during my time at Jackpot were accused of assisting high-rollers.

. . . About 10% of Jackpot's clientele are high-rollers. For them, management imposes despotism to ensure adequate security and service at the expense of speed, whereas for low-rollers, a tipping system guides the labor process. And on average, approximately 40% of Jackpot's low-rollers were tippers. Thus, for every 90 low-rollers, 36 will be tippers and 54 nontippers. Speed is of course maximized for both. Yet tippers receive good service/poor security, whereas nontippers get bad service/maximum security. Overall, 90% of players receive adequate speed, 64% adequate security, and 46% adequate service. So although the onset of competition has led Jackpot to promote service as a method of product differentiation, the casino's system of labor control generates it for less than half of all players.

Having specified why worker autonomy and noncompliance are rational for both floor managers and dealers, one may ask, insofar as this labor regime neither fully unites workers' interests with manage-

ment's (Table 1) nor maximizes customer service, . . . why does it persist? Although my data do not allow claims concerning the extent to which corporate management was conscious of shop-floor practices, I can specify why this system is rational, or at least functional, for the firm as a whole. First, allowing a tipping system to regulate the labor process constituted a loss of labor control, insofar as the ability to distribute a primary workplace reward—monetary payment—is transferred to customers, whose interests are of course never fully aligned with the firm's. By doing so, however, the casino lowered labor costs: Under U.S. labor law, tipped employees can be paid one half the federal minimum wage with no benefits and laid off in response to seasonal fluctuations in demand (Harrison, 1994; Wessels, 1997).

Second, whereas the breadth of service was compromised—not all, and in fact less than half, of players received service—the depth of service was maximized. The tipping system, that is, by establishing a micro-economy in which dealers must continually produce the appropriate "emotional capital" to exchange for "financial capital," served as a highly effective mechanism of product customization:

> Kim, a young Vietnamese dealer of 2 years, understands immediately that the two businessmen who have just sat down at her table expect friendly smiles and entertaining small talk. She provides both and they fulfill their end of the bargain: the two men tip frequently and well. Soon, though, they both lose several large hands and become irritable. Now her smiles are inappropriate. "Why are you so happy? Do you like to see us lose like this?" She becomes quiet and serious, dealing quickly and without expression as the two men play their hands intensely. Soon they have won

their original money back and more. The cocktails take effect and they now are loud and boisterous. Kim laughs along with them, occasionally cracking jokes herself. The cycle repeats several times, as it does every night.

In addition, the distribution of tippers among all players was not random. Locals, regulars, and high-rollers tended to be "wise" to the tipping system, whereas tourists and low-rollers were more apt to either not understand or refuse to participate in it. And insofar as the former groups constitute the contemporary casino's most desired target markets (Cabot, 1996), the tipping system ensured the provision of service to the firm's most highly prized clients.

Conclusion . . .

Blackjack dealing is an admittedly extreme occupation. Its practitioners work in an environment of potentially total surveillance, intense routinization of their labor, and no union protection. Precisely because of these factors, however, dealing offers a unique opportunity to refine the understanding of the labor process for tipped service workers. For if new service demands have *here* led to a hegemonic labor regime, then one should expect to find similar arrangements in less strictly regulated workplaces. In fact, since 1965, the number of U.S. employees who work for tips has tripled from approximately 1.9 million to 5.6 million (Jacobs, 2001; U.S. Department of Labor, 1965). Scholars of service work, however, have glossed over tipping, treating it as just one mechanism among many for inducing service provision from workers. This omission stems from a lack of attention to a second pressure generated by increased competition in service industries; while emotional

labor demands arise, so do pressures to cut costs. And although the efficacy of new managerial strategies for inducing service from workers is well documented, one must not forget that their costs (in terms of training, supervision, etc.) are high. Tipping, insofar as it simultaneously lowers labor costs and spontaneously generates customized service provision, thus represents an attractive system for organizing work, albeit one with costs to the firm. . . .

. . . In conclusion, as the U.S. service economy continues to expand and become increasingly competitive, we would expect management, when possible, to allow tipping systems to regulate the labor process as a means of both lowering labor costs and inducing workers to perform service with a smile. The noncompliance that results will in turn be regulated in accordance with the financial or otherwise status of the "player," thus constituting a hegemonic regime of service provision.

NOTES

1. Jackpot is a pseudonym, as are all proper names in this article.
2. Of the 11 supervisors who worked the swing, there were 5 White men, 1 White woman, 3 minority men (2 Asian, 1 Hispanic), and 2 minority women (both Asian).

REFERENCES

Bear, Stearns and Co. (2000). *Native American gaming in California: Nevada's biggest risk?* New York: Smith Barney.

Bear, Stearns and Co. (2001). *Global gaming almanac: 2001 edition.* New York: Smith Barney.

Benson, S. (1986). *Counter cultures.* Chicago: University of Illinois Press.

Binion, L. B. (1973). *Some recollections of a Texas and Las Vegas gaming operator.* Reno: University of Nevada Oral History Program.

Braverman, H. (1974). *Labor and monopoly capital.* New York: Monthly Review Press.

Cabot, A. N. (1996). *Casino gaming: Policy, economics and regulation.* Las Vegas: University of Nevada, Las Vegas, International Gaming Institute.

Demos, P. (1991, June). *How to build extraordinary customer service.* Paper presented at World Gaming Conference and Expo, Las Vegas, NV.

DiBenedetto, B. (1996). Bells and whistles: Service is people, but these days smiles are never enough. *Casino Executive Magazine, 2*(10), 66.

Eadington, W. R. (1984). The casino gaming industry: A study of political economy. *Annals of the American Academy of Political and Social Science, 474,* 23–35.

Eadington, W. R. (1990). *Indian gaming and the law.* Reno: University of Nevada Press.

Eadington, W. R. (1998), Casino management in the 1990's: Concepts and challenges. In K. J. Meyer-Arendt & R. Hartmann (Ed.), *Casino gambling in America: Origins, trends, and impacts* (pp. 16–36). New York: Cognizant Communication.

Eadington, W. R. (1999). The economics of casino gambling. *Journal of Economic Perspectives, 13*(3), 173–192.

Enarson, E. (1993). Emotion workers on the production line: The feminizing of casino card dealing. *NWSA Journal, 5*(2), 218–232.

Findlay, J. M. (1986). *People of chance.* New York: Oxford University Press.

Foucault, M. (1979). *Discipline and punish: The birth of the prison.* New York: Vintage Books.

Frenkel, S. J., Korczynski, M., Shire, K. A., & Tam, M. (1999). *On the front line: Organization of work in the information economy.* Ithaca, NY: Cornell University Press.

Frey, J. (1986). Labor issues in the gaming industry. *Nevada Public Affairs Review, 2,* 32–38.

Fuller, L., and Smith, V. (1991). Consumers' reports: Management by customers in a changing economy. *Work, Employment and Society, 5,* 1–16.

Garson, B. (1988). *The electronic sweatshop.* New York: Simon & Schuster.

Goffman, E. (1959). *The presentation of self in everyday life.* New York: Anchor Books.

Goffman, E. (1967). Where the action is. In *Interaction ritual: Essays on face-to-face behavior* (pp. 149–270). Garden City, NY: Anchor Books.

Gottdiener, M., Collins, C. C., and Dickens, D. R. (1999). *Las Vegas: The social production of an all American city.* Malden, MA: Blackwell.

Gottfried, H. (1991). Mechanisms of control in the temporary help industry. *Sociological Forum, 6*(4), 699–713.

Graves, R. L. (1978). *Take no as a starter: The Life of Richard L. Graves.* Reno: University of Nevada Oral History Program.

Greenlees, E. M. (1988). *Casino accounting and financial management.* Las Vegas: University of Nevada Press.

Gutek, B. A. (1995). *The dynamics of service: Reflections on the changing nature of customer/provider interactions.* San Francisco: Jossey-Bass.

Harrah, W. F. (1978). *My recollections of the hotel-casino industry and as an auto collecting enthusiast.* Reno: University of Nevada Oral History Program.

Harrison, B. (1994). *Lean and mean: The changing landscape of corporate power in the age of flexibility.* New York: Basic Books.

Hashimoto, K., Kline, S. F., & Fenich, G. G. (1996). *Casino management for the 90's.* Dubuque, IA: Kendall/Hunt.

Heimer, C. A., & Stevens, M. L. (1997). Caring for the organization: Social workers as frontline risk managers in neonatal intensive care units. *Work and Occupations, 24,* 133–163.

Hochschild, A. R. (1983). *The managed heart: Commercialization of human feeling.* Berkeley: University of California Press.

Horowitz, B. (1975). *Situational aspects of public interaction: The "21" game, personal impressions.* Unpublished master's thesis, University of Nevada, Reno.

International Gaming and Wagering Business. (1999). *The Month in Stocks, 20*(8).

Jacobs, E. E. (Ed.) (2001). *Handbook of U.S. labor statistics.* Lanham, MD: Bernan Press.

Leidner, R. (1993). *Fast food, fast talk.* Berkeley: University of California Press.

Leidner, R. (1999). Emotional labor in service work. *Annals of the American Academy of Political and Social Science, 561,* 81–95.

MacDonald, C. L., & Sirianni, C. (1996). *Working in the service society.* Philadelphia: Temple University Press.

Macomber, D. M. (1984). Management policy and practices in modern casino operations. *Annals of the American Academy of Political and Social Science, 474,* 80–90.

Marfels, C. (1995). Casino gaming. In W. Adams & J. R. Brock (Eds.), *The structure of American industry* (pp. 223–245). Englewood Cliffs, NJ: Prentice Hall.

Marfels, C. (1999). Concentration, competition and competitiveness in the casino gaming industry. In W. R. Eadington & J. A. Cornelius (Eds.), *Gaming: Economic and management issues* (pp. 29–44). Reno, NV: Institute for the Study of Gambling and Commercial Gaming.

McCammon, H. J., & Griffin, L. J. (2000). Workers and their customers and clients. *Work and Occupations, 27,* 278–293.

Mello, A. (1997). Vegas teetering on brink of odds war. *Casino Executive Magazine, 6,* 14.

Nelson, W. (1978). *Gaming from the old days to computers.* Reno: University of Nevada Oral History Program.

Nevada Gaming Control Board. (1970, 1979, 1988, 2000). *Nevada gaming abstract.* Carson City, NV: Author.

Noble, D. F. (1984). *Forces of production: A social history of industrial automation.* New York: Oxford University Press.

Petricciani, S. (1982). *The evolution of gaming in Nevada: The twenties to the eighties.* Reno: University of Nevada Oral History Program.

Rafaeli, A., & Sutton, R. I. (1987). Expression of emotion as part of the work role. *Academy of Management Review, 12*(1), 23–37.

Ray, C. (1991). *Black politics and gaming in Las Vegas: 1920's to 1980's.* Reno: University of Nevada Oral History Program.

Reid, E., & Demaris, O. (1963). *The green felt jungle.* New York: Trident Press.

Ring, R. A. (1972). *Recollections of life in California, Nevada gaming, and Reno and Lake Tahoe business and civic affairs.* Reno: University of Nevada Oral History Program.

Saiger, M. (1985). *An interview with Morton Saiger* (R. T. King, Interviewer). Reno: University of Nevada Oral History Program.

Sanders, R., & Knight. R. (1997). Raw deal? Grasping the art of the deal can pay off for a casino's entire culture. *Casino Executive Magazine, 2*(6), 27.

Skolnick, J. (1978). *House of cards.* Boston: Little, Brown.

Smith, R., Preston, F., & Humphries, H. (1974). Alienation from work: A study of casino card dealers. In W. R. Eadington (Ed.), *Gambling and society* (pp. 102–139). Springfield, IL: Charles C Thomas.

Smith, V. (1996). Employee involvement, involved employees: Participative work arrangements in a white-collar service occupation. *Social Problems, 43*(2), 166–179.

Solkey, L. (1980). *Dummy up and deal.* Las Vegas: GBC Press.

Sutton, R. I. (1991). Maintaining norms about expressed emotions: The case of bill collectors. *Administrative Science Quarterly, 36,* 245–268.

Thompson, W. N., & Comeau, M. (1992a). *Casino customer service.* New York: Gaming and Wagering Business.

Thompson, W. N., & Comeau, M. (1992b). Lagniappe: The key to customer service in a buyer's market. In W. R. Eadington & J. A. Cornelius (Eds.), *Gambling and commercial gaming: Essays in business, economics, philosophy and science* (pp. 13–39). Reno: University of Nevada Press.

Troyer, L., Mueller, C. W., & Osinsky, P. I. (2000). Who's the boss? A role-theoretic analysis of customer work. *Work and Occupations, 27,* 406–427.

U.S. Department of Labor. (1965). *Occupational outlook handbook.* Washington, DC: Bureau of Labor Statistics.

Van Maanen, J., & Kunda, G. (1989). "Real feelings": Emotional expression and organizational culture. *Research in Organizational Behavior, 11,* 43–103.

Vinson, B. (1986). *Las Vegas: Behind the tables!* Grand Rapids, MI: Gollehon Press.

Vogel, H. L. (1994). *Entertainment industry economics: A guide for financial analysis.* New York: Cambridge University Press.

Wessels, W. J. (1997). Minimum wages and tipped servers. *Economic Inquiry, 35,* 334–349.

PROFESSIONAL AND MANAGERIAL WORK

∽ READING 30 ∽

Rambo Litigators

Emotional Labor in a Male-Dominated Job

Jennifer L. Pierce

Late in the afternoon, I was sitting with Ben and Stan. . . . They were complaining about being litigators, or as they put it, how "litigation turns people into bastards—you don't have any real choices." Stan said that if you don't fit in, you have to get out because you won't be successful. And Ben added, "To be a really good litigator, you have to be a jerk. Sure you can get by being a nice guy, but you'll never be really good or really successful."

—FIELD NOTES"

The comments made by these two young lawyers suggest that the legal profession often requires behavior that is offensive not only to other people, but to oneself: "To be a really good litigator, you have to be a jerk." In popular culture and everyday life, jokes and stories abound that characterize lawyers as aggressive, manipulative, unreliable, and unethical. This image is expressed in the joke about why the lawyer who falls overboard in shark-infested waters is not eaten alive—it's professional courtesy. Our popular wisdom is that lawyers are ruthless con artists who are more concerned with making money than they are with fairness (Post 1987; *National Law Journal* 1986). Few consider, as these two young men do, that the requirements of the profession itself support and reinforce this behavior. . . .

Gamesmanship and the Adversarial Model

Popular wisdom and lawyer folklore portray lawyering as a game, and the ability to play as gamesmanship (Fox 1978; Spence 1988). As one of the trial attorneys I interviewed said,

The logic of gamesmanship is very interesting to me. I like how you make someone appear to be a liar. You know, you take them down the merry path and before they know it, they've said something pretty stupid. The challenge is getting them to say it without violating the letter of the law.

Lawyering is based on gamesmanship—legal strategy, skill, and expertise. But trial lawyers are much more than chess players; their strategies are not simply cerebral, rational, and calculating moves, but highly emotional, dramatic, flamboyant, shocking presentations that evoke sympathy, distrust, or outrage. In litigation practice, gamesmanship involves the utilization of legal strategy through a presentation of an emotional self that is designed specifically to influence the feelings and judgment of a particular legal audience—the judge, the jury, the witness, or opposing counsel. Furthermore, in my definition, the choices litigators make about selecting a particular strategy are not simply individual; they are institutionally constrained by the structure of the legal profession, by formal and informal professional norms, such as the American Bar Association's Model Code of Professional Responsibility (1982), and by training in trial advocacy, through programs such as those sponsored by the National Institute of Trial Advocacy.

The rules governing gamesmanship derive from the adversarial model that underlies the basic structure of our legal system. This is a method of adjudication in which two advocates (the attorneys) present their sides of the case to an impartial third party (the judge and the jury), who listens to evidence and argument and declares one party the winner (Luban 1988; Menkel-Meadow 1985). As Menkel-Meadow (1985) observes, the basic assumptions that underlie this set of arrangements are "advocacy, persuasion, hierarchy, competition and binary results (win/ lose)." She writes: "The conduct of litigation is relatively similar . . . to a sporting event—there are rules, a referee, an object to the game, and a winner is declared after play is over" (1985: 51).

Within this system, the attorney's main objective is to persuade the impartial third party that his client's interests should pre-

vail (American Bar Association 1982: 34). However, clients do not always have airtight, defensible cases. How then does the "zealous advocate" protect his client's interests and achieve the desired result? When persuasion by appeal to reason breaks down, an appeal to emotions becomes paramount (Cheatham 1955: 282–83). As legal scholar John Buchan writes, "the root of the talent is simply the power to persuade" (1939: 211–13). And in "Basic Rules of Pleading," Jerome Michael writes:

> The decision of an issue of fact in a case of closely balanced probabilities therefore, must, in the nature of things, be an emotional rather than a rational act; and the rules regulating that stage of a trial which we call the stage of persuasion, the stage when lawyers sum up to the jury. . . . The point is beautifully made by an old Tennessee case in which the plaintiff's counsel, when summing up to the jury began to weep. . . . The lawyer for the defendant objected and asked the trial judge to stop him from weeping. Weeping is not a form of argument. . . . Well, the Supreme Court of Tennessee said: "It is not only counsel's privilege to weep for his client; it is his duty to weep for his client." (1950: 175)

By appealing to emotions, the lawyer becomes a con man. He acts as if he has a defensible case; he puffs himself up; he bolsters his case. Thus, the successful advocate must not only be smart, but, as the famous turn-of-the-century trial lawyer Francis Wellman observed, he must also be a good actor (1986 [1903]: 13). In *The Art of Cross-Examination,* first published in 1903 and reprinted to the present, Wellman describes how carefully the litigator must present himself to the judge and jury:

> The most cautious cross-examiner will often elicit a damaging answer. Now is the

time for the greatest self-control. If you show by your face how the answer hurt, you may lose by that one point alone. How often one sees a cross-examiner fairly staggered by such an answer. He pauses, blushes, [but seldom regains] control of the witness. With the really experienced trial lawyer, such answers, instead of appearing to surprise or disconcert him, will seem to come as a matter of course, and will fall perfectly flat. He will proceed with the next question as if nothing happened, or else perhaps give the witness an incredulous smile, as if to say, "Who do you suppose would believe that for a minute." (1986 [1903]: 13–14)

More recently, teacher and lawyer David Berg (1987) advises lawyers to think of themselves as actors and the jury as an audience:

> Decorum can make a difference, too. . . . Stride to the podium and exude confidence, even if there is a chance that the high school dropout on the stand is going to make you look like an idiot. Take command of the courtroom. Once you begin, do not grope for questions, shuffle through papers, or take breaks to confer with cocounsel. Let the jury know that you are prepared, that you do not need anyone's advice, and that you care about the case . . . because if you don't care, the jurors won't care. (1987: 28)

Wellman and Berg make a similar point: in the courtroom drama, attorneys are the leading actors. Appearance and demeanor are of utmost importance. The lawyer's manner, his tone of voice, and his facial expressions are all means to persuade the jury that his client is right. Outrageous behavior, as long as it remains within the letter of the law, is acceptable. Not only are trial lawyers

expected to act, but they are expected to act with a specific purpose in mind: to favorably influence feelings of the judge and jurors.

This emphasis on acting is also evident in the courses taught by the National Institute for Trial Advocacy, where neophyte litigators learn the basics of presenting a case for trial. NITA's emphasis is on "learning by doing" (Kilpatrick quoted in Rice 1989). Attorneys do not simply read about cases but practice presenting them in a simulated courtroom with a judge, a jury, and witnesses. In this case, doing means acting. As one of the teachers/lawyers said on the first day of class, "Being a good trial lawyer means being a good actor. . . . Trial attorneys love to perform." Acting, in sociological terms, constitutes emotional labor, that is, inducing or suppressing feelings in order to produce the outward countenance that influences the emotions of others. The instructors discuss style, delivery, presentation of self, attitude, and professionalism. Participants, in turn, compare notes about the best way to "handle" judges, jurors, witnesses, clients, and opposing counsel. The efforts of these two groups constitute the teaching and observance of "feeling rules," or professional norms that govern appropriate lawyerly conduct in the courtroom. . . .

Intimidation

> Litigation is war. The lawyer is a gladiator and the object is to wipe out the other side.
>
> —CLEVELAND LAWYER QUOTED IN THE *NEW YORK TIMES*, AUGUST 5, 1988

The most common form of emotional labor associated with lawyers is intimidation. In popular culture, the tough, hard-hitting, and aggressive trial lawyer is portrayed in television shows such as *L.A. Law* and *Perry Mason* and in movies such as *The Firm, A Few Good Men,* and *Presumed Innocent.* The news media's focus on famous trial attorneys such as Arthur Liman, the prosecutor of Oliver North in the Iran-Contra trial, also reinforces this image. Law professor Wayne Brazil (1978) refers to this style of lawyering as the "professional combatant." Others have termed it the "Rambo litigator" (a reference to the highly stylized, super-masculine role Sylvester Stallone plays in his action movies), "legal terrorists," and "barbarians of the bar" (Margolick 1988; Sayler 1988; Miner 1988). Trial attorneys themselves call litigators from large law firms "hired guns" (Spangler 1986). And books on trial preparation, such as McElhaney's *Trial Notebook* (1987), endorse the litigator-as-gladiator metaphor by portraying the attorney on the book's dust jacket as a knight in a suit of armor ready to do battle (McElhaney 1987).

The recurring figure in these images is not only intimidating but strongly masculine. In the old West, hired guns were sharpshooters; men who were hired to kill other men. The strong, silent movie character Rambo is emblematic of a highly stylized, supermasculinity. The knight in shining armor preparing to do battle on the front cover of McElhaney's *Trial Notebook* is male, not female. Finally, most of the actors who play tough, hard-hitting lawyers in the television shows and movies mentioned above are men. Thus, intimidation is not simply a form of emotional labor associated with trial lawyers, it is a masculinized form of labor.

Intimidation is tied to cultural conceptions of masculinity in yet another way. In a review of the literature on occupations, Connell (1987) observes that the cult of masculinity in working-class jobs centers on physical prowess and sexual contempt for men in managerial or office positions (1987: 180). Like the men on the shop floor in Michael Burawoy's (1979) study who brag about how much they can lift or produce, lawyers in this study boast about "destroying witnesses," "playing hard-ball," and "taking no prisoners" and about the size and amount of their "win." In a middle-class job such as the legal profession, however, intimidation depends not on physical ability but on mental quickness and a highly developed set of social skills. Thus, masculinizing practices such as aggression and humiliation take on an emotional and intellectual tone in this occupation. . . .

In the sections on cross-examination at NITA, teachers trained lawyers to "act mean." The demonstration by the teachers on cross-examination best exemplified this point. Two male instructors reenacted an aggressive cross-examination in a burglary case. The prosecutor relentlessly hammered away until the witness couldn't remember any specific details about the burglar's appearance. At the end of his demonstration, the audience clapped vigorously. Three male students who had been asked to comment responded unanimously and enthusiastically that the prosecutor's approach had been excellent. One student commentator said, "He kept complete control of the witness." Another remarked, "He blasted the witness's testimony." And the third added, "He destroyed the witness's credibility." The fact that a destructive cross-examination served as the demonstration for the entire class underscores the desirability of aggressive behavior as a model for appropriate lawyer-like conduct in this situation. Furthermore, the students' praise for the attorney's tactics collectively reinforce the norm for such behavior.

Teachers emphasized the importance of using aggression to motivate oneself as well.

Before a presentation on cross-examination, Tom, one of the students, stood in the hallway with one of the instructors trying to "psyche himself up to get mad." He repeated over and over to himself, "I hate it when witnesses lie to me. It makes me so mad!" The teacher coached him to concentrate on that thought until Tom could actually evoke the feeling of anger. He said later in an interview, "I really felt mad at the witness when I walked into the courtroom." In the actual cross-examination, each time the witness made an inconsistent statement, Tom became more and more angry: "First, you told us you could see the burglar, now you say your vision was obstructed! So, which is it, Mr. Jones?" The more irate he became, the more he intimidated and confused the witness, who at last completely backed down and said, "I don't know" in response to every question. The teacher characterized Tom's performance as "the best in the class" because it was "the most forceful" and "the most intimidating." Students remarked that he deserved to "win the case."

NITA's teachers also utilized mistakes to train students in the rigors of cross-examination. For example, when Laura cross-examined [a] witness . . . , a teacher commented on her performance:

> Too many words. You're asking the witness for information. Don't do that in cross-examination. You tell them what the information is. You want to be destructive in cross-examination. When the other side objects to an answer, you were too nice. Don't be so nice! Next time, ask to talk to the judge, tell him, "This is crucial to my case." You also asked for information when you didn't know the answer. Bad news. You lost control of the witness.

By being nice and losing control of the witness, Laura violated two norms underlying the classic confrontational cross-examination. A destructive cross-examination is meant to impeach the witness's credibility, thereby demonstrating to the jury the weakness in opposing counsel's case. In situations that call for such an aggressive cross-examination, being nice implies that the lawyer likes the witness and agrees with her testimony. By not being aggressive, Laura created the wrong impression for the jury. Second, Laura lost control of the witness. Rather than guiding the witness through the cross with leading questions that were damaging to opposing counsel's case, she allowed the witness to make his own points. As we will see in the next section . . . , being nice can also be used as a strategy for controlling a witness; however, such a strategy is not effective in a destructive cross-examination.

Laura's violation of these norms also serves to highlight the implicitly masculine practices utilized in cross-examination. The repeated phrase, "keeping complete control of the witness," clearly signals the importance of dominating other women and men. Further, the language used to describe obtaining submission—"blasting the witness," "destroying his credibility," pushing him to "back down"—is quite violent. In addition, the successful control of the witness often takes on the character of a sexual conquest. One brutal phrase used repeatedly in this way is "raping the witness." Within this discursive field, men who "control," "destroy," or "rape" the witness are seen as "manly," while those who lose control are feminized as "sissies" and "wimps," or in Laura's case as "too nice."

The combative aspect of emotional labor carries over from the courtroom to other lawyering tasks, such as depositions, negotiations, communications with opposing counsel, and discovery. Attorneys "shred" witnesses not only in the courtroom but in depositions as well. When I worked at the private firm, Daniel, one of the partners, employed what he called his "cat and mouse game" with one of the key witnesses, Jim, in a deposition I attended. During the deposition, Daniel aggressively cross-examined Jim. "When did you do this?" "You were lying, weren't you?" Jim lost his temper in response to Daniel's hostile form of interrogation— "You hassle me, man! You make me mad!" Daniel smiled and said, "I'm only trying to get to the truth of the situation." Then he became aggressive again and said, "You lied to the IRS about how much profit you made, didn't you, Jim!" Jim lost his temper again and started calling Daniel a liar. A heated interchange between Daniel and opposing counsel followed, in which opposing counsel objected to Daniel's "badgering the witness." The attorneys decided to take a brief recess.

When the deposition resumed, Daniel began by pointing his index finger at John, the other attorney, and accusing him of withholding crucial documents. Opposing counsel stood up and started yelling in a high-pitched voice—"Don't you ever point your finger at me! Don't you ever do that to me! This deposition is over. . . . I'm leaving." With that he stood up and began to cram papers into his briefcase in preparation to leave. Daniel immediately backed down, apologized, and said, "Sit down John, I promise, I won't point my finger again." He went on to smooth the situation over and proceeded to tell John in a very calm and controlled voice what his objections were. John made some protesting noises, but he didn't leave. The deposition continued.

In this instance, the deposition, rather than the courtroom, became the "stage" and Daniel took the leading role. His cross-examination was confrontational, and his behavior with the witness and opposing counsel was meant to intimidate. After the deposition Daniel boasted to me and several associates about how mad he had made the witness and how he had "destroyed his cred-

ibility." He then proceeded to reenact the final confrontation by imitating John standing up and yelling at him in a falsetto voice. In the discussion that followed, Daniel and his associates gave the effects of his behavior on the "audience" utmost consideration. Hadn't Daniel done a good job forcing the witness to lose control? Hadn't he controlled the situation well? Didn't he make opposing counsel look like a "simpering fool"?

The reenactment and ensuing discussion reveal several underlying purposes of the deposition. First, they suggest that for the attorney the deposition was not only a fact-finding mission but a show designed to influence a particular audience—the witness. Daniel effectively flustered and intimidated the witness. Second, Daniel's imitation of John with a falsetto voice "as if" he were a woman serves as a sort of "degradation ceremony" (Garfinkel 1956). By reenacting the drama, he ridicules the man on the other side before an audience of peers, further denigrating him by inviting collective criticism and laughter from colleagues. Third, the discussion of the strategy builds up and elevates Daniel's status as an attorney for his aggressive, yet rational control of the witness and the situation. Thus, the discussion creates an opportunity for collectively reinforcing Daniel's intimidation strategy. . . .

Masculine images of violence and warfare—destroying, blasting, shredding, slaying, burying—are used repeatedly to characterize the attorney's relationship to legal audiences. They are also used to describe discovery tactics and filing briefs. Discovery tactics such as enormous document requests are referred to as "dropping bombs" or "sending missiles" to the other side. And at the private firm, when a lawyer filed fourteen pretrial motions the week before trial, over three hundred pages of written material, he referred to it as "dumping an avalanche" on the other side.

Strategic Friendliness

Mr. Choate's appeal to the jury began long before final argument. . . . His manner to the jury was that of a friend, a friend solicitous to help them through their tedious investigation; never an expert combatant, intent on victory, and looking upon them as only instruments for its attainment. (Wellman 1986 [1903]: 16–17)

The lesson implicit in Wellman's anecdote about famous nineteenth-century lawyer Rufus Choate's trial tactics is that friendliness is another important strategy the litigator must learn and use to be successful in the courtroom. Like aggression, the strategic use of friendliness is a feature of gamesmanship, and hence, a component of emotional labor. As Richard, one of the attorney/teachers at NITA, stated, "Lawyers have to be able to vary their styles; they have to be able to have multiple speeds, personalities, and style." In his view, intimidation did not always work, and he proposed an alternative strategy, what he called "the toe-in-the-sand, aw-shucks routine." Rather than adopting an intimidating stance toward the witness, he advocated "playing dumb and innocent": "Say to the witness, 'Gee, I don't know what you mean. Can you explain it again?' until you catch the witness in a mistake or an inconsistent statement." Other litigators such as Leonard Ring (1987) call this the "low-key approach." Ring describes how opposing counsel delicately handled the cross-examination of a child witness:

The lawyer for the defendant . . . stood to cross-examine. Did he attack the details of her story to show inconsistencies? Did he set her up for impeachment by attempting to reveal mistakes, uncertainties and confusion? I sat there praying that he would. But no, he did none of the things a competent defense lawyer is supposed to do. He was old enough to

be the girl's grandfather [and] the image came through. He asked her very softly and politely: "Honey, could you tell us again what you saw?" She told it exactly as she had on my direct. I felt relieved. He still wasn't satisfied. "Honey, would you mind telling us again what you saw?" She did again exactly as she had before. He still wasn't satisfied. "Would you do it once more?" She did. She repeated, again, the same story—the same way, in the same words. By that time I got the message. The child had been rehearsed by her mother the same way she had been taught "Mary Had a Little Lamb." I won the case, but it was a very small verdict. (1987: 35–36)

Ring concludes that a low-key approach is necessary in some situations and advises against adhering rigidly to the prototypical combative style.

Similarly, Scott Turow (1987), the lawyer and novelist, advises trying a variety of approaches when cross-examining the star witness. He cautions against adopting a "guerrilla warfare mentality" in cross-examination and suggests that the attorney may want to create another impression with the jury:

Behaving courteously can keep you from getting hurt and, in the process, smooth the path for a win. [In one case I worked on] the cross examination was conducted with a politesse appropriate to a drawing room. I smiled to show that I was not mean-spirited. The chief executive officer smiled to show that he was not beaten. The commissioners smiled to show their gratitude that everybody was being so nice. And my client won big. (1987: 40–42)

Being nice, polite, welcoming, playing dumb, or behaving courteously are all ways that a trial lawyer can manipulate the witness in order to create a particular impression for the jury. I term this form of gamesmanship strategic friendliness. Rather than bully or scare the witness into submission, this tactic employs friendliness, politeness and tact. Yet it is simply another form of emotional manipulation of another person for a strategic end—winning one's case. For instance, the attorney in Ring's account is gentle and considerate of the child witness for two strategic reasons. First, by making the child feel comfortable, he brings to light the fact that her testimony has been rehearsed. Second, by playing the polite, gentle grandfatherly role, he has made a favorable impression on the jury. In this way he improves his chances for winning. As, in fact, he did. Although he didn't win the case, the verdict for the other side was "small."

Although strategic friendliness may appear to be a softer approach than intimidation, it carries with it a strongly manipulative element. Consider the reasoning behind this particular approach. Ring's attorney is nice to the child witness not because he's altruistically concerned for her welfare, but to achieve the desired result, as simply a means to an end. This end is best summed up by litigator Mark Dombroff: "So long as you don't violate the law, including the rules of procedure and evidence or do violence to the canons of ethics, winning is the only thing that matters" (1989: 13).

This emphasis on winning is tied to traditional conceptions of masculinity and competition. Sociologist Mike Messner (1989) argues that achievement in sporting competitions such as football, baseball, and basketball serve as a measure of men's self-worth and their masculinity. This can also be carried over into the workplace. For example, as I have suggested, by redefining production on the shop floor as a "game," Burawoy's factory workers maintain their sense of control over the labor process, and hence, their

identity as men. In her research on men in sales, Leidner (1991) finds that defining the jobs as competition becomes a means for construing the work as masculine:

> The element of competition, the battle of wills implicit in their interactions with customers, seemed to be a major factor which allowed agents to interpret their work as manly. Virtually every step of the interaction was understood as a challenge to be met—getting in the door, making the prospect relax and warm up, being allowed to start the presentation. . . making the sale, and perhaps even increasing the size of the sale. (1991: 168)

For litigators, keeping score of wins in the courtroom and the dollar amount of damages or settlement awards allows them to interpret their work as manly. At Bonhomie Corporation and at Lyman, Lyman and Portia, the first question lawyers often asked others after a trial or settlement conference was "Who won the case?" or "How big were the damages?" Note that both Ring and Turow also conclude their pieces with descriptions of their win—"I won the case, but the verdict was small" and "I won big." Trial attorneys who did not "win big" were described as "having no balls," or as being "geeks" or "wimps." The fact that losing is associated with being less than a man suggests that the constant focus on competition and winning is an arena for proving one's masculinity.

One important area that calls for strategic friendliness and focuses on winning is jury selection or voir dire. The main purpose of voir dire is to obtain personal information about prospective jurors in order to determine whether they will be "favorably disposed to you, your client, and your case, and will ultimately return a favorable verdict" (Mauet 1980: 31). Once an attorney has made that assessment, biased jurors can be eliminated through challenges for cause and peremptory challenges. In an article on jury selection, attorney Peter Perlman maintains that the best way to uncover the prejudices of the jury "is to conduct voir dire in an atmosphere which makes prospective jurors comfortable about disclosing their true feelings" (1988: 5). He provides a checklist of strategies for lawyers to utilize which enable jurors to feel more comfortable. Some of these include:

> Given the initial intimidation which jurors feel, try to make them feel as comfortable as possible; approach them in a natural, unpretentious and clear manner.
>
> Since jurors don't relate to "litigants" or "litigation," humanize the client and the dispute.
>
> Demonstrate the sincere desire to learn of the jurors' feelings.
>
> The lawyer's presentation to the jury should be positive and radiate sincerity. (1988: 5–9)

Perlman's account reveals that the underlying goal of jury selection is to encourage the jury to open up so that the lawyer can eliminate the jurors he doesn't want and develop a positive rapport with the ones who appear favorable to his case.

This goal is supported not only by other writings on jury selection (Blinder 1978; Cartwright 1977; Mauet 1980; Ring 1983; Wagner 1981) but also through the training offered by NITA. As one teacher, a judge, said after the class demonstration on jury selection, "Sell your personality to the jury. Try to get liked by the jury. You're not working for a fair jury, but one favorable to your side." This fact is also recognized by a judge in Clifford Irving's best-selling novel *Trial*: "Assuming his case has some merit, if a lawyer gets a jury to like him and then trust him more than the son of a bitch who's arguing against him, he's home free" (1990: 64).

At NITA, teachers emphasized this point on the individual level. In their sessions on voir dire, students had to select a jury for a case which involved an employee who fell down the steps at work and severely injured herself. (Jurors for the case were classmates, including me.) Mike, one of the students, began his presentation by explaining that he was representing the woman's employer. He then went on to tell the jury a little bit about himself: "I grew up in a small town in Indiana." Then he began to ask each of the jurors where they were from, whether they knew the witness or the experts, whether they played sports, had back problems, suffered any physical injuries, and had ever had physical therapy. The instructor gave him the following comments:

> The personal comments about yourself seem forced. Good folksy approach, but you went overboard with it. You threw stuff out and let the jury nibble and you got a lot of information. But the main problem is that you didn't find out how people feel about the case or about their relatives and friends.

Another set of comments:

> Nice folksy approach, but a bit overdone. Listen to what jurors say, don't draw conclusions. Don't get so close to them, it makes them feel uncomfortable. Use body language to give people a good feeling about you. Good personality, but don't cross certain lines. Never ask someone about their ancestry. It's too loaded a question to ask. Good sense of humor, but don't call one of your prospective jurors a "money man." And don't tell the jury jokes! You don't win them over that way.

The sporting element to voir dire becomes "winning over the jury." This theme also became evident in discussions student lawyers had before and after jury selection. They discussed at length how best "to handle the jurors," "how to get personal information out of them," "how to please them," "how to make them like you," and "how to seduce them to your side." The element of sexual seduction is apparent in the often used phrase "getting in bed with the jury." The direct reference to sexual seduction and conquest suggests, as did the intimidation strategy used in cross-examination, that "winning over the jury" is also a way to prove one's masculinity. Moreover, the desired result in both strategic friendliness and intimidation is similar: obtaining the juror's submission, and winning.

Strategic friendliness is also utilized in the cross-examination of sympathetic witnesses. In one of NITA's hypothetical cases, a woman dies of an illness related to her employment. Her husband sues his deceased wife's employer for her medical bills, lost wages, and "lost companionship." One of the damaging facts in the case, which could hurt his claim for "lost companionship," was the fact that he had a girlfriend long before his wife died. In typical combative, adversarial style, some of the student lawyers tried to bring this fact out in cross-examination to discredit his claims about his relationship with his wife. The teacher told one lawyer who presented such an aggressive cross-examination:

> It's too risky to go after him. Don't be so confrontational. And don't ask the judge to reprimand him for not answering the question. This witness is too sensitive. Go easy on him.

The same teacher gave the following comments to another student who had "come on too strong":

> Too stern. Hasn't this guy been through enough already! Handle him with kid gloves. And, don't cut him off. It generates sympathy for him from the jury when you do that. It's difficult to control a sympathetic witness. It's best to use another witness's testimony to impeach him.

And to yet another student:

> Slow down! This is a dramatic witness. Don't lead so much. He's a sympathetic witness—the widower—let him do the talking. Otherwise you look like an insensitive jerk to the jury.

. . . Strategic friendliness carries over from the courtroom to depositions. Before deposing a particularly sensitive or sympathetic witness, Joe, one of the attorneys in the private firm, asked me whether "there is anything personal to start the interview with—a sort of warm-up question to start things off on a personal note?" I had previously interviewed the woman over the phone, so I knew something about her background. I told him that she was a young mother who had recently had a very difficult delivery of her first child. I added that she was worried about the baby's health because he had been born prematurely. At the beginning of the deposition later that afternoon, Joe said in a concerned voice that he understood the witness had recently had a baby and was concerned about its health. She appeared slightly embarrassed by the question, but with a slow smile and lots of encouragement from him, she began to tell him all about the baby and its health problems. By the time Joe began the formal part of the deposition, the witness had warmed up and gave her complete cooperation. Later, the attorney bragged to me and one of the associates that he had the witness "eating out of his hand."

After recording these events in my field notes, I wrote the following impressions:

> On the surface, it looks like social etiquette to ask the witness these questions because it puts her at ease. It lets her know he takes her seriously. But the

"personal touch" is completely artificial. He doesn't care about the witness as a person. Or, I should say, only insofar as she's useful to him. Moreover, he doesn't even bother to ask the witness these questions himself the first time around. He asks me to do it. I'm to find the "personal hook" that he can use to manipulate her to his own ends.

Thus an innocuous personal remark becomes another way to create the desired impression with a witness and thereby manipulate him or her. Perhaps what is most ironic about strategic friendliness is that it requires a peculiar combination of sensitivity to other people and, at the same time, ruthlessness. The lawyer wants to appear kind and understanding, but that is merely a cover for the ulterior motive—winning. Although the outward presentation of self for this form of emotional labor differs from intimidation, the underlying goal is the same: the emotional manipulation of the witness for a favorable result.

Attorneys also employed strategic friendliness when dealing with clients. As I mentioned in the previous section, intimidation is rarely used with clients, particularly at the private firm, who are typically treated with a politesse, courtesy, and reassurance. The sensitivity to the client's needs and interests does not reflect genuine concern, however, but rather serves as a means to an end—obtaining and maintaining the client's current and future business. The importance of clients to lawyers can be gauged by one of the criteria for determining partnership at private law firms: the ability to attract and maintain a client base (Nelson 1988; Smigel 1969). In this light, clients become another important legal audience for whom the lawyer performs and obtaining a client's business is construed as another form of "winning."

Articles in legal newspapers such as the *National Law Journal* address the importance of lawyers' efforts to attract new clients (O'Neil 1989; Foster and Raider 1988). These articles underscore the importance not only of obtaining business but of appealing to clients through "communication," "cultural sensitivity," and "creating good first impressions." Thus, "finding" new clients is not simply an instrumental role as Nelson (1988) suggests, it also carries with it an emotional dimension.

"Wooing clients" to the firm, or "making rain," as lawyers call it, is a common practice at the private firm. Partners were rewarded in annual bonuses for their ability to bring in new business. In informal conversations, partners often discussed the competition between firms for the clients' business. For example, when one of the partners procured a case from a large San Francisco bank that typically did business with another large firm in the city, he described it as a "coup." Attorneys boasted not only about bringing clients into the firm but about how much revenue "their client" brought into the firm's coffers. The constant focus on capturing clients, "making rain," and making big money betrays male lawyers' need to prove themselves through accomplishments and achievements. Further, those who lost big clients were considered "weak," "impotent," and no longer "in with the good old boys." In this way, winning clients' business is also associated with manly behavior. . . .

REFERENCES

American Bar Association. 1982. *Model Code of Professional Responsibility and Code of Judicial Conduct.* Chicago, Ill.: National Center for Professional Responsibility and the American Bar Association.

Berg, David. 1987. "Cross-Examination." *Litigation: Journal of the Section of Litigation, American Bar Association* 14, no. 1 (Fall):25–30.

Blinder, Martin. 1978. "Picking Juries." *Trial Diplomacy* 1, no. 1 (Spring):8–13.

Brazil, Wayne. 1978. "The Attorney as Victim: Toward More Candor About the Psychological

Price Tag of Litigation Practice." *The Journal of the Legal Profession* 3:107–17.

Buchan, John. 1939. "The Judicial Temperament." In his *Homilies and Recreations.* 3d ed. London: Hodder and Stoughton.

Burawoy, Michael. 1979. *Manufacturing Consent: Changes in the Labor Process Under Monopoly Capitalism.* Chicago: University of Chicago Press.

Cartwright, John. 1977. "Jury Selection." *Trial* 28:13.

Cheatham, Elliott. 1955. *Cases and Materials on the Legal Profession.* 2d ed. Brooklyn: Foundation Press.

Connell, Robert. 1987. *Gender and Power: Society, the Person and Sexual Politics.* Stanford, Calif.: Stanford University Press.

Dombroff, Mark. "Winning Is Everything!" *National Law Journal,* 25 September 1989:13.

Foster, Dean and Ellen Raider. "Bringing Cultural Sensitivity to the Bargaining Table." *San Francisco Banner,* 17 October 1988:14.

Fox, Priscilla. 1978. "Good-bye to Game Playing." *Juris Doctor* (January):37–42.

Garfinkel, Harold. 1956. "Conditions of Successful Degradation Ceremonies." *American Journal of Sociology* 61, no. 11 (March):420–24.

Irving, Clifford. 1990. *Trial.* New York: Dell.

Leidner, Robin. 1991. "Serving Hamburgers and Selling Insurance: Gender, Work, and Identity in Interactive Service Jobs." *Gender & Society* 5, no. 2:154–77.

Luban, David. 1988. *Lawyers and Justice: An Ethical Study.* Princeton, N.J.: Princeton University Press.

Margolick, David. "At the Bar: Rambos Invade the Courtroom." *New York Times,* 5 August 1988:B5.

Mauet, Thomas. 1980. *Fundamentals of Trial Techniques.* Boston: Little Brown.

McElhaney, James. 1987. *McElhaney's Trial Notebook.* 2d ed. Chicago: Section of Litigation, American Bar Association.

Menkel-Meadow, Carrie. 1985. "Portia in a Different Voice: Speculations on a Women's Lawyering Process." *Berkeley Women's Law Review* 1, no. 1 (Fall):39–63.

Messner, Michael. 1989. "Masculinities and Athletic Careers." *Gender & Society* 3, no. 1 (March): 71–88.

Michael, Jerome. 1950. "The Basic Rules of Pleading." *The Record: New York City Bar Association* 5:175–99.

Miner, Roger. "Lawyers Owe One Another." *National Law Journal,* 19 December 1988:13–14.

National Law Journal. "What America Really Thinks About Lawyers." October 1986:1.

Nelson, Robert. 1988. *Partners with Power: The Social Transformation of the Large Law Firm.* Berkeley and Los Angeles: University of California Press.

O'Neil, Suzanne. "Associates Can Attract Clients, Too." *National Law Journal,* 16 January 1989:17.

Perlman, Peter. 1988. "Jury Selection." *The Docket: Newsletter of the National Institute for Trial Advocacy* (Spring):1.

Post, Robert. 1987. "On the Popular Image of the Lawyer: Reflections in a Dark Glass." *California Law Review* 75, no. 1 (January):379–89.

Rice, Susan. "Two Organizations Provide Training, In-House or Out." *San Francisco Banner,* 24 May 1989:6.

Ring, Leonard. 1987. "Cross-examining the Sympathetic Witness." *Litigation: Journal of the Section of Litigation, American Bar Association* 14, no. 1 (Fall):35–39.

Sayler, R. "Rambo Litigation: Why Hardball Tactics Don't Work." *American Bar Association Journal,* 1 March 1988:79.

Smigel, Erwin. 1969. *The Wall Street Lawyer: Professional or Organizational Man?* 2d ed. New York: Free Press.

Spangler, Eve. 1986. *Lawyers for Hire: Salaried Professionals at Work.* New Haven, Conn.: Yale University Press.

Spence, Gary. 1989. *With Justice for None.* New York: Times Books.

Turow, Scott. "Crossing the Star." 1987. *Litigation: Journal of the Section of Litigation, American Bar Association* 14, no. 1 (Fall):40–42.

Wagner, Ward. 1981. *The Art of Advocacy: Jury Selection.* New York: Matthew Bender.

Wellman, Francis. 1986 [1903]. *The Art of Cross-Examination: With the Cross-Examinations of Important Witnesses in Some Celebrated Cases.* 4th ed. New York: Collier.

⸙ READING 31 ⸙

The Social Structure of Managerial Work

Robert Jackall

I

The hierarchical authority structure that is the linchpin of bureaucracy dominates the way managers think about their world and about themselves. Managers do not see or experience authority in any abstract way; instead, authority is embodied in their personal relationships with their immediate bosses and in their perceptions of similar links between other managers up and down the hierarchy. When managers describe their work to an outsider, they almost always first say: "I work for [Bill James]" or "I report to [Harry Mills]" or "I'm in [Joe Bell's] group," and only then proceed to describe their actual work functions. Such a personalized statement of authority relationships seems to contradict classical notions of how bureaucracies function but it exactly reflects the way authority is structured, exercised, and experienced in corporate hierarchies.

American businesses typically both centralize and decentralize authority. Power is concentrated at the top in the person of the chief executive officer (CEO) and is simultaneously decentralized; that is, responsibility for decisions and profits is pushed as far down the organizational line as possible. For example, Alchemy Inc. is one of several operating companies of Covenant

Corporation. When I began my research, Alchemy employed 11,000 people; Covenant had over 50,000 employees and now has over 100,000. Like the other operating companies, Alchemy has its own president, executive vice-presidents, vice-presidents, other executive officers, business area managers, staff divisions, and more than eighty manufacturing plants scattered throughout the country and indeed the world producing a wide range of specialty and commodity chemicals. Each operating company is, at least theoretically, an autonomous, self-sufficient organization, though they are all monitored and coordinated by a central corporate staff, and each president reports directly to the corporate CEO. Weft Corporation has its corporate headquarters and manufacturing facilities in the South; its marketing and sales offices, along with some key executive personnel, are in New York City. Weft employs 20,000 people, concentrated in the firm's three textile divisions that have always been and remain its core business. The Apparel Division produces seven million yards a week of raw, unfinished cloth in several greige (colloquially gray) mills, mostly for sale to garment manufacturers; the Consumer Division produces some cloth of its own in several greige mills and also finishes—that is, bleaches, dyes, prints, and sews—twelve million yards of raw cloth a month into purchasable items like sheets, pillowcases, and tablecloths for department stores and chain stores; and the Retail Division operates an import-export business, specializing in the quick turnaround of the fast-moving cloths desired by Seventh Avenue designers. Each division has a president who reports to one of several executive vice-presidents, who in turn report to the corporate CEO. The divisional structure is typically less elaborate in its hierarchical ladder than the framework of independent operating companies; it is also somewhat more dependent on corporate staff for essential services. However, the basic principle of simultaneous centralization and decentralization prevails and both Covenant and Weft consider their companies or divisions, as the case may be, "profit centers." Even Images Inc., while much smaller than the industrial concerns and organized like most service businesses according to shifting groupings of client accounts supervised by senior vice-presidents, uses the notion of profit centers.

The key interlocking mechanism of this structure is its reporting system. Each manager gathers up the profit targets or other objectives of his or her subordinates and, with these, formulates his commitments to his boss; this boss takes these commitments and those of his other subordinates, and in turn makes a commitment to his boss. At the top of the line, the president of each company or division, or, at Images Inc., the senior vice-president for a group of accounts, makes his commitment to the CEO. This may be done directly, or sometimes, as at Weft Corporation, through a corporate executive vice-president. In any event, the commitments made to top management depend on the pyramid of stated objectives given to superiors up the line. At each level of the structure, there is typically "topside" pressure to achieve higher goals and, of course, the CEO frames and paces the whole process by applying pressure for attainment of his own objectives. Meanwhile, bosses and subordinates down the line engage in a series of intricate negotiations—managers often call these "conspiracies"—to keep their commitments respectable but achievable.

This "management-by-objective" system, as it is usually called, creates a chain of commitments from the CEO down to the lowliest product manager or account executive. In practice, it also shapes a patrimonial authority arrangement that is crucial to defining both the immediate experiences and the long-run career chances of individual managers, In this world, a subordinate owes fealty principally to his immediate boss. This means that a subordinate must not overcommit his boss, lest his boss "get on the hook" for promises that cannot be kept. He must keep his boss from making mistakes, particularly public ones; he must keep his boss informed, lest his boss get "blindsided." If one has a mistake-prone boss, there is, of course, always the temptation to let him make a fool of himself, but the wise subordinate knows that this carries two dangers—he himself may get done in by his boss's errors, and, perhaps more important, other managers will view with the gravest suspicion a subordinate who withholds crucial information from his boss even if they think the boss is a nincompoop. A subordinate must also not circumvent his boss nor ever give the appearance of doing so. He must never contradict his boss's judgment in public. To violate the last admonition is thought to constitute a kind of death wish in business, and one who does so should practice what one executive calls "flexibility drills," an exercise "where you put your head between your legs and kiss your ass goodbye." On a social level, even though an easy, breezy, first-name informality is the prevalent style of American business, a concession perhaps to our democratic heritage and egalitarian rhetoric, the subordinate must extend to the boss a certain ritual deference. For instance, he must follow the boss's lead in conversation, must not speak out of turn at meetings, must laugh at his boss's jokes while not making jokes of his own that upstage his boss, must not rib the boss for his foibles. The shrewd subordinate learns to efface himself, so that his boss's face might shine more clearly.

In short, the subordinate must symbolically reinforce at every turn his own subordination and his willing acceptance of the obligations of fealty. In return, he can hope for those perquisites that are in his boss's gift—the better, more attractive secretaries, or the nudging of a movable panel to enlarge his office, and perhaps a couch to fill the added space, one of the real distinctions in corporate bureaucracies. He can hope to be elevated when and if the boss is elevated, though other important criteria intervene here. He can also expect protection for mistakes made, up to a point. However, that point is never exactly defined and depends on the complicated politics of each situation. The general rule is that bosses are expected to protect those in their bailiwicks. Not to do so, or to be unable to do so, is taken as a sign of untrustworthiness or weakness. If, however, subordinates make mistakes that are thought to be dumb, or especially if they violate fealty obligations—for example, going around their boss—then abandonment of them to the vagaries of organizational forces is quite acceptable.

Overlaying and intertwined with this formal monocratic system of authority, with its patrimonial resonance, are patron-client relationships. Patrons are usually powerful figures in the higher echelons of management. The patron might be a manager's direct boss, or his boss's boss, or someone several levels higher in the chain of command. In either case, the manager is still bound by the immediate, formal authority and fealty patterns of his position but he also acquires new, though more ambiguous, fealty relationships with his highest ranking patron. Patrons play a crucial role in advancement, a point that I shall discuss later.

It is characteristic of this authority system that details are pushed down and credit is pulled up. Superiors do not like to give detailed instructions to subordinates. The official reason for this is to maximize subordinates' autonomy. The underlying reason is, first, to get rid of tedious details. Most hierarchically organized occupations follow this pattern; one of the privileges of authority is the divestment of humdrum intricacies. This also insulates higher bosses from the peculiar pressures that accompany managerial work at the middle levels and below: the lack of economy over one's time because of continual interruption from one's subordinates, telephone calls from customers and clients, and necessary meetings with colleagues; the piecemeal fragmentation of issues both because of the discontinuity of events and because of the way subordinates filter news; and the difficulty of minding the store while sorting out sometimes unpleasant personnel issues. Perhaps more important, pushing details down protects the privilege of authority to declare that a mistake has been made. A high-level executive in Alchemy Inc. explains:

> If I tell someone what to do—like do A, B, or C—the inference and implication is that he will succeed in accomplishing the objective. Now, if he doesn't succeed, that means that I have invested part of myself in his work and I lose any right I have to chew his ass out if he doesn't succeed. If I tell you what to do, I can't bawl you out if things don't work. And this is why a lot of bosses don't give explicit directions. They just give a statement of objectives, and then they can criticize subordinates who fail to make their goals.

Moreover, pushing down details relieves superiors of the burden of too much knowledge, particularly guilty knowledge. A superior will say to a subordinate, for instance: "Give me your best thinking on the problem with [X]." When the subordinate makes his report, he is often told: "I think you can do better than that," until the subordinate has worked out all the details of the boss's predetermined solution, without the boss being specifically aware of "all the eggs that have to be broken." It is also not at all uncommon for very bald and extremely general edicts to emerge from on high. For example, "Sell the plant in [St. Louis]; let me know when you've struck a deal," or "We need to get higher prices for [fabric X]; see what you can work out," or "Tom, I want you to go down there and meet with those guys and make a deal and I don't want you to come back until you've got one." This pushing down of details has important consequences.

First, because they are unfamiliar with— indeed deliberately distance themselves from—entangling details, corporate higher echelons tend to expect successful results without messy complications. This is central to top executives' well-known aversion to bad news and to the resulting tendency to kill the messenger who bears the news.

Second, the pushing down of details creates great pressure on middle managers not only to transmit good news but, precisely because they know the details, to act to protect their corporations, their bosses, and themselves in the process. They become the "point men" of a given strategy and the potential "fall guys" when things go wrong. From an organizational standpoint, overly conscientious managers are particularly useful at the middle levels of the structure. Upwardly mobile men and women, especially those from working-class origins who find themselves in higher status milieux, seem to have the requisite level of anxiety, and perhaps tightly controlled anger and hostility, that fuels an obsession with detail. Of course, such conscientiousness is not necessarily, and is certainly not systematically, rewarded; the real organizational premiums are placed on other, more flexible, behavior.

Credit flows up in this structure and is usually appropriated by the highest ranking officer involved in a successful decision or resolution of a problem. There is, for instance, a tremendous competition for ideas in the corporate world; authority provides a license to steal ideas, even in front of those who originated them. Chairmen routinely appropriate the useful suggestions made by members of their committees or task forces; research directors build their reputations for scientific wizardry on the bricks laid down by junior researchers and directors of departments. Presidents of whole divisions as well are always on the lookout for "fresh ideas" and "creative approaches" that they can claim as their own in order to put themselves "out in front" of their peers. A subordinate whose ideas are appropriated is expected to be a good sport about the matter; not to balk at so being used is one attribute of the good team player. The person who appropriates credit redistributes it as he chooses, bound essentially and only by a sensitivity to public perceptions of his fairness. One gives credit, therefore, not necessarily where it is due, although one always invokes this old saw, but where prudence dictates. Customarily, people who had nothing to do with the success of a project can be allocated credit for their exemplary efforts. At the middle levels, therefore, credit for a particular idea or success is always a type of refracted social honor; one cannot claim credit even if it is earned. Credit has to be given, and acceptance of the gift implicitly involves a reaffirmation and strengthening of fealty. A superior may share some credit with subordinates in order to deepen fealty relationships and induce greater efforts on his behalf. Of course, a different system obtains in the allocation of blame.

Because of the interlocking character of the commitment system, a CEO carries enormous influence in his corporation. If, for a moment, one thinks of the presidents of operating companies or divisions as barons, then the CEO of the corporation is the king. His word is law; even the CEO's wishes and whims are taken as commands by close subordinates on the corporate staff, who turn them into policies and directives. A typical example occurred in Weft Corporation a few years ago when the CEO, new at the time, expressed mild concern about the rising operating costs of the company's fleet of rented cars. The following day, a stringent system for monitoring mileage replaced the previous casual practice. Managers have a myriad of aphorisms that refer to how the power of CEOs, magnified through the zealous efforts of subordinates, affects them. These range from the trite "When he sneezes, we all catch colds" to the more colorful "When he says 'Go to the bathroom,' we all get the shits."

Great efforts are made to please the CEO. For example, when the CEO of Covenant Corporation visits a plant, the most significant order of business for local management is a fresh paint job, even when, as in several cases, the cost of paint alone exceeds $100,000. If a paint job has already been scheduled at a plant, it is deferred along with all other cosmetic maintenance until just before the CEO arrives; keeping up appearances without recognition for one's efforts is pointless. I am told that similar anecdotes from other corporations have been in circulation since 1910, which suggests a certain historical continuity of behavior toward top bosses.

The second order of business for the plant management is to produce a book fully describing the plant and its operations, replete with photographs and illustrations, for presentation to the CEO; such a book costs about $10,000 for the single copy. By any standards of budgetary stringency, such expenditures are irrational. But by the social standards of the corporation, they make perfect sense. It is far more important to please

the king today than to worry about the future economic state of one's fief, since, if one does not please the king, there may not be a fief to worry about or indeed vassals to do the worrying.

By the same token, all of this leads to an intense interest in everything the CEO does and says. In all the companies that I studied, the most common topic of conversation among managers up and down the line is speculation about their respective CEO's plans, intentions, strategies, actions, style, public image, and ideological leanings of the moment. Even the metaphorical temper of a CEO's language finds its way down the hierarchy to the lower reaches of an organization. In the early stages of my fieldwork at Covenant Corporation, for example, I was puzzled by the inordinately widespread usage of nautical terminology, especially in a corporation located in a landlocked site. As it happens, the CEO is devoted to sailboats and prefers that his aides call him "Skipper." Moreover, in every corporation that I studied, stories and rumors circulate constantly about the social world of the CEO and his immediate subordinates—who, for instance, seems to have the CEO's ear at the moment; whose style seems to have gained approbation; who, in short, seems to be in the CEO's grace and who seems to have fallen out of favor. In the smaller and more intimate setting of Images Inc., the circulation of favor takes an interesting, if unusual, tack. There, the CEO is known for attaching younger people to himself as confidants. He solicits their advice, tells them secrets, gets their assessments of developments further down in the hierarchy, gleans the rumors and gossip making the rounds about himself. For the younger people selected for such attention, this is a rare, if fleeting, opportunity to have a place in the sun and to share the illusion if not the substance of power. In time, of course, the CEO tires of or becomes disappointed with particular individuals and turns his attention to others. "Being discarded," however, is not an obstacle to regaining favor. In larger organizations, impermeable structural barriers between top circles and junior people prevent this kind of intimate interchange and circulation of authoritative regard. Within a CEO's circle, however, the same currying and granting of favor prevails, always amidst conjectures from below about who has edged close to the throne.

But such speculation about the CEO and his leanings of the moment is more than idle gossip, and the courtlike atmosphere that I am describing more than stylized diversion. Because he stands at the apex of the corporation's bureaucratic and patrimonial structures and locks the intricate system of commitments between bosses and subordinates into place, it is the CEO who ultimately decides whether those commitments have been satisfactorily met. The CEO becomes the actual and the symbolic keystone of the hierarchy that constitutes the defining point of the managerial experience. Moreover, the CEO and his trusted associates determine the fate of whole business areas of a corporation.

Within the general ambiance established by a CEO, presidents of individual operating companies or of divisions carry similar, though correspondingly reduced, influence within their own baronies. Adroit and well-placed subordinates can, for instance, borrow a president's prestige and power to exert great leverage. Even chance encounters or the occasional meeting or lunch with the president can, if advertised casually and subtly, cause notice and the respect among other managers that comes from uncertainty. Knowledge of more clearly established relationships, of course, always sways behavior. A middle manager in one company, widely known to be a very close personal friend of the president, flagged her copious memoranda to other managers with large green paperclips, ensuring prompt attention to her requests. More generally, each major division of the core textile group in Weft Corporation is widely thought to reflect the personality of its leader—one hard-driving, intense, and openly competitive; one cool, precise, urbane, and proper; and one gregarious, talkative, and self-promotional. Actually, market exigencies play a large role in shaping each division's tone and tempo. Still, the popular conception of the dominance of presidential personalities not only points to the crucial issue of style in business, a topic to be explored in depth later, but it underlines the general tendency to personalize authority in corporate bureaucracies.

Managers draw elaborate cognitive maps to guide them through the thickets of their organizations. Because they see and experience authority in such personal terms, the singular feature of these maps is their biographical emphasis. Managers carry around in their heads thumbnail sketches of the occupational history of virtually every other manager of their own rank or higher in their particular organization. These maps begin with a knowledge of others' occupational expertise and specific work experience, but focus especially on previous and present reporting relationships, patronage relationships, and alliances. Cognitive maps incorporate memories of social slights, of public embarrassments, of battles won and lost, and of people's behavior under pressure. They include as well general estimates of the abilities and career trajectories of their colleagues. I should mention that these latter estimates are not necessarily accurate or fair; they are, in fact, often based on the flimsiest of evidence. For instance, a general manager at Alchemy Inc. describes the ephemeral nature of such opinions:

> It's a feeling about the guy's perceived ability to run a business—like he's not a good people man, or he's not a good

numbers man. This is not a quantitative thing. It's a gut feeling that a guy can't be put in one spot, but he might be put in another spot. These kinds of informal opinions about others are the lifeblood of an organization's advancement system. Oh, for the record, we've got the formal evaluations; but the real opinions—the ones that really count in determining people's fates—are those which are traded back and forth in meetings, private conferences, chance encounters, and so on.

Managers trade estimates of others' chances within their circles and often color them to suit their own purposes. This is one reason why it is crucial for the aspiring young manager to project the right image to the right people who can influence others' sketches of him. Whatever the accuracy of these vocabularies of description, managers' penchant for biographical detail and personal histories contrasts sharply with their disinclination for details in general or for other kinds of history. Details, as I have mentioned, get pushed down the ladder; and a concern with history, even of the short-run, let alone long-term, structural shifts in one's own organization, constrains the forward orientation and cheerful optimism highly valued in most corporations. Biographical detail, however, constitutes crucial knowledge because managers know that, in the rough-and-tumble politics of the corporate world, individual fates are made and broken not necessarily by one's accomplishments but by other people. . . .

II

. . . Here I want to highlight a few basic structures and experiences of managerial work, those that seem to form its essential framework. First of all, at the psychological level, managers have an acute sense of organizational contingency. Because of the interlocking ties between people, they know that a shake-up at or near the top of a hierarchy can trigger a widespread upheaval, bringing in its wake startling reversals of fortune, good and bad, throughout the structure. Managers' cryptic aphorism, "Well, you never know . . . ," repeated often and regularly, captures the sense of uncertainty created by the constant potential for social reversal. Managers know too, and take for granted, that the personnel changes brought about by upheavals are to a great extent arbitrary and depend more than anything else on one's social relationships with key individuals and with groups of managers. Periods of organizational quiescence and stability still managers' wariness in this regard, but the foreboding sense of contingency never entirely disappears. Managers' awareness of the complex levels of conflict in their world, built into the very structure of bureaucratic organizations, constantly reminds them that things can very quickly fall apart.

The political struggles at Covenant Corporation, for instance, suggest some immediately observable levels of conflict and tension.

First, occupational groups emerging from the segmented structure of bureaucratic work, each with different expertise and emphasis, constantly vie with one another for ascendancy of their ideas, of their products or services, and of themselves. It is, for instance, an axiom of corporate life that the greatest satisfaction of production people is to see products go out the door; of salesmen, to make a deal regardless of price; of marketers, to control salesmen and squeeze profits out of their deals; and of financial specialists, to make sure that everybody meets budget. Despite the larger interdependence of such work, the necessarily fragmented functions performed day-to-day by managers in one area often put them at cross purposes with managers in another.

Nor do competitiveness and conflict result only from the broad segmentation of functions. Sustained work in a product or service area not only shapes crucial social affiliations but also symbolic identifications, say, with particular products or technical services, that mark managers in their corporate arenas. Such symbolic markings make it imperative for managers to push their particular products or services as part of their overall self-promotion. This fuels the constant scramble for authoritative enthusiasm for one product or service rather than another and the subsequent allocation or re-allocation of organizational resources.

Second, line and staff managers, each group with different responsibilities, different pressures, and different bailiwicks to protect, fight over organizational resources and over the rules that govern work. The very definition of staff depends entirely on one's vantage point in the organization. As one manager points out: "From the perspective of the guy who actually pushes the button to make the machine go, everyone else is staff." However, the working definition that managers use is that anyone whose decisions directly affect profit and loss is in the line; all others in an advisory capacity of some sort are staff. As a general rule, line managers' attitudes toward staff vary directly with the independence granted staff by higher management. The more freedom staff have to intervene in the line, as with the environmental staff at Alchemy or Covenant's corporate staff, the more they are feared and resented by line management. For line managers, independent staff represent either the intrusion of an unwelcome "rules and procedures mentality" into situations where line managers feel that they have to be alert to the exigencies of the market or, alternatively, as power threats to vested interests backed by some authority. In the "decentralized" organizations prevalent today in the corporate world, however, most staff are entirely dependent on the line and must market their technical, legal, or organizational skills to line managers exactly as an outside firm must do. The continual necessity for staff to sell their technical expertise helps keep them in check since line managers, pleading budgetary stringency or any number of other acceptable rationales, can thwart or ignore proffered assistance. Staff's dependent position often produces jealous respect for line management tinged with the resentment that talented people relegated to do "pine time" (sit on the bench) feel for those in the center of action. For instance, an environmental manager at Weft Corporation comments on his marginal status and on how he sees it depriving him of the recognition he feels his work deserves:

> I also want recognition. And usually the only way you get that is having a boss near you who sees what you do. It rubs me raw in fact. . . . For instance, you know they run these news releases when some corporate guy gets promoted and all? Well, when I do something, nothing ever gets said. When I publish papers, or get promoted, and so on, you never see any public announcement. Oh, they like me to publish papers and I guess someone reads them, but that's all that's ever said or done. . . . I can get recognition in a variety of arenas, like professional associations, but if they're going to recognize the plant manager, why not me? If we walked off, would the plants operate? They couldn't. We're *essential*.

This kind of ambivalent resentment sometimes becomes vindictiveness when a top boss uses staff as a hammer.

Staff can also become effective pitchmen; line managers' anxious search for rational solutions to largely irrational problems, in fact, encourages staff continually to invent and disseminate new tactics and schemes.

Alternatively, social upheavals that produce rapid shifts in public opinion—such as occurred in the personnel or environmental areas in the aftermath of the 1960s—may encourage proliferation of staff. In either circumstance, staff tend to increase in an organization until an ideological cycle of "organizational leanness" comes around and staff, at least those of lower rank, get decimated.

Third, powerful managers in Alchemy Inc., each controlling considerable resources and the organizational fates of many men and women, battle fiercely with one another to position themselves, their products, and their allies favorably in the eyes of their president and of the CEO. At the same time, high-ranking executives "go to the mat" with one another striving for the CEO's approval and a coveted shot at the top. Bureaucratic hierarchies, simply by offering ascertainable rewards for certain behavior, fuel the ambition of those men and women ready to subject themselves to the discipline of external exigencies and of their organization's institutional logic, the socially constructed, shared understanding of how their world works. However, since rewards are always scarce, bureaucracies necessarily pit people against each other and inevitably thwart the ambitions of some. The rules of such combat vary from organization to organization and depend largely on what top management countenances either openly or tacitly.

Nor are formal positions and perquisites the only objects of personal struggle between managers. Even more important on a day-to-day basis is the ongoing competition between talented and aggressive people to see whose will prevails, who can get things done their way. The two areas are, of course, related since one's chances in an organization depend largely on one's "credibility," that is, on the widespread belief that one can act effectively. One must therefore prevail regularly, though not always, in small things

to have any hope of positioning oneself for big issues. The hidden agenda of seemingly petty disputes may be a struggle over long-term organizational fates.

At the same time, all of these struggles take place within the peculiar tempo and framework each CEO establishes for an organization. Under an ideology of thorough decentralization—the gift of authority with responsibility—the CEO at Covenant actually centralizes his power enormously because fear of derailing personal ambitions prevents managers below him from acting without his approval. A top official at Alchemy comments:

> What we have now, despite rhetoric to the contrary, is a very centralized system. It's [the CEO] who sets the style, tone, tempo of all the companies. He says: "Manage for cash," and we manage for cash. The original idea . . . was to set up free-standing companies with a minimum of corporate staff. But . . . we're moving toward a system that is really beyond what we used to have, let alone modeled on a small corporate staff and autonomous divisions. What we used to have was separate divisions reporting to a corporate staff. I think we're moving away from that idea too. I think what's coming is a bunch of separate businesses reporting to the corporation. It's a kind of portfolio management. This accords perfectly with [the CEO's] temperament. He's a financial type guy who is oriented to the bottom line numbers. He doesn't want or need intermediaries between him and his businesses.

In effect, the CEO of Covenant, who seems to enjoy constant turmoil, pits himself and his ego against the whole corporation even while he holds it in vassalage. Other CEOs establish different frameworks and different tempos, depending on self-image and temperament. The only firm rule seems to be that articulated by a middle-level Covenant manager: "Every big organization is set up for the benefit of those who control it; the boss gets what he wants."

Except during times of upheaval, the ongoing conflicts that I have described are usually hidden behind the comfortable and benign social ambiance that most American corporations fashion for their white-collar personnel. Plush carpets, potted trees, burnished oak wall paneling, fine reproductions and sometimes originals of great art, mahogany desks, polished glass tables and ornaments, rich leather upholstery, perfectly coiffured, attractive and poised receptionists, and private, subsidized cafeterias are only a few of the pleasant features that grace the corporate headquarters of any major company. In addition, the corporations that I studied provide their employees with an amazing range and variety of services, information, and social contacts. Covenant Corporation, for instance, through its daily newsletter and a variety of other internal media, offers information about domestic and international vacation packages; free travelers' checks; discounted tickets for the ballet, tennis matches, or art exhibits; home remedies for the common cold, traveling clinics for diagnosing high blood pressure, and advice on how to save one's sight; simple tests for gauging automotive driving habits; tips on home vegetable gardening; advice on baby-sitters; descriptions of business courses at a local college; warning articles on open fireplaces and home security; and directions for income tax filing. The newsletter also offers an internal market for the sale, rental, or exchange of a myriad of items ranging from a Jamaican villa, to a set of barbells, to back issues of *Fantasy* magazine. Covenant offers as well intracompany trapshooting contests, round-robin tennis and golf tournaments, running clinics, and executive fitness programs. Weft Corporation's bulletin is even more elaborate, with

photographic features on the "Great Faces" of Weft employees; regular reports on the company's 25- and 50-year clubs; personal notes on all retirees from the company; stories about the company's sponsorship of art exhibits; human-interest stories about employees and their families—from a child struggling against liver cancer to the heroics of a Weft employee in foiling a plane hijacker; and, of course, a steady drumbeat of corporate ideology about the necessity for textile import quotas and the desirability of "buying American."

My point here is that corporations are not presented nor are they seen simply as places to work for a living. Rather, the men and women in them come to fashion an entire social ambiance that overlays the antagonisms created by company politics; this makes the nuances of corporate conflict difficult to discern. A few managers, in fact, mistake the first-name informality, the social congeniality, and the plush exterior appointments for the entire reality of their collective life and are surprised when hard structural jolts turn their world upside down. Even battle-scarred veterans evince, at times, an ambivalent half-belief in the litany of rhetorics of unity and cohesive legitimating appeals. The latter are sometimes accompanied by gala events to underline the appeal. For instance, not long after the "big purge" at Covenant Corporation when 600 people were fired, the CEO spent $1 million for a "Family Day" to "bring everyone together." The massive party was attended by over 14,000 people and featured clowns, sports idols, and booths complete with bean bag and ring tosses, foot and bus races, computer games, dice rolls, and, perhaps appropriately, mazes. In his letter to his "Fellow Employees" following the event, the CEO said:

> I think Family Day made a very strong statement about the [Covenant] "family"

of employees at [Corporate Headquarters]. And that is that we can accomplish whatever we set out to do if we work together; if we share the effort, we will share the rewards. The "New World of [Covenant]" has no boundaries only frontiers, and each and everyone can play a role, for we need what *you* have to contribute.

The very necessity for active involvement in such rituals often prompts semi-credulity. But wise and ambitious managers resist the lulling platitudes of unity, though they invoke them with fervor, and look for the inevitable clash of interests beneath the bouncy, cheerful surface of corporate life. They understand implicitly that the suppression of open conflict simply puts a premium on the mastery of the socially accepted modes of waging combat.

The continuous uncertainty and ambiguity of managerial hierarchies, exacerbated over time by masked conflict, causes managers to turn toward each other for cues for behavior. They try to learn from each other and to master the shared assumptions, the complex rules, the normative codes, the underlying institutional logic that governs their world. They thus try to control the construction of their everyday reality. Normally, of course, one learns to master the managerial code in the course of repeated, long-term social interaction with other managers, particularly in the course of shaping the multiple and complex alliances essential to organizational survival and success.

Alliances are ties of quasiprimal loyalty shaped especially by common work, by common experiences with the same problems, the same friends, or the same enemies, and by favors traded over time. Although alliances are rooted in fealty and patronage relationships, they are not limited by such relationships since fealty shifts with changing work assignments or with organizational upheavals.

Making an alliance may mean, for instance, joining or, more exactly, being included in one or several of the many networks of managerial associates that crisscross an organization. Conceptually, networks are usually thought of as open-ended webs of association with a low degree of formal organization and no distinct criteria of membership. One becomes known, for instance, as a trusted friend of a friend; thought of as a person to whom one can safely refer a thorny problem; considered a "sensible" or "reasonable" or, especially, a "flexible" person, not a "renegade" or a "loose cannon rolling around the lawn"; known to be a discreet person attuned to the nuances of corporate etiquette, one who can keep one's mouth shut or who can look away and pretend to notice nothing; or considered a person with sharp ideas that break deadlocks but who does not object to the ideas being appropriated by superiors.

Alliances are also fashioned in social coteries. These are more clublike groups of friends that, in Weft Corporation, forge ties at the cocktail hour over the back fence on Racquet Drive, the road next to the company's tennis courts where all important and socially ambitious executives live; or in Friday night poker sessions that provide a bluff and hearty setting where managers can display their own and unobtrusively observe others' mastery of public faces, a clue to many managerial virtues. In other companies, coteries consist of "tennis pals" who share an easy camaraderie over salad and yogurt lunches following hard squash games or two-mile jogs at noon. They are also made up of posthours cronies who, in midtown watering holes, weld private understandings with ironic bantering, broad satire, or macabre humor, the closest some managers ever get to open discussion of their work with their fellows; or gatherings of the smart social set where business circles intersect with cliques from intellectual and artistic worlds and where glittering, poised, and precisely vacuous social conversation can mark one as a social lion. In one company, a group of "buddies" intertwine their private lives with their organizational fates in the most complete way by, for example, persuading an ambitious younger colleague to provide a woodsy cabin retreat and local girls for a collegial evening's entertainment while on a business trip. At the managerial and professional levels, the road between work and life is usually open because it is difficult to refuse to use one's influence, patronage, or power on behalf of another regular member of one's social coterie. It therefore becomes important to choose one's social colleagues with some care and, of course, know how to drop them should they fall out of organizational favor.

Alliances are also made wholly on the basis of specific self-interests. The paradigmatic case here is that of the power clique of established, well-placed managers who put aside differences and join forces for a "higher cause," namely, their own advancement or protection. Normally, though not always, as Brown's case at Covenant shows, one must be "plugged into" important networks and an active participant in key coteries in order to have achieved an organizational position where one's influence is actively counted. But the authority and power of a position matter in and of themselves. Once one has gained power, one can use one's influence in the organization to shape social ties. Such alliances often cut across rival networks and coteries and can, in fact, temporarily unite them. Managers in a power clique map out desired organizational tacks and trade off the resources in their control. They assess the strengths and weaknesses of their opponents; they plan coups and rehearse the appropriate rationales to legitimate them. And, on the other hand, they erect requisite barriers to squelch attempted usurpations of their power.

Cliques also introduce managers to new, somewhat more exclusive networks and coteries. Especially at the top of a pyramid, these social ties extend over the boundaries of one's own corporation and mesh one's work and life with those of top managers in other organizations.

I shall refer to all the social contexts that breed alliances, fealty relationships, networks, coteries, or cliques, as circles of affiliation, or simply managerial circles. Now, the notion of "circles," as it has been used in sociological literature as well as colloquially, has some drawbacks for accurately delineating the important features of the web of managerial interaction. Specifically, a circle suggests a quasiclosed social group made up of members of relatively equal status without defined leadership and without formal criteria for membership or inclusion. In a bureaucratic hierarchy, nuances of status are, of course, extremely important. Moreover, since business cannot be conducted without formal authorization by appropriate authorities, one's formal rank always matters even though there is ample scope for more informal charismatic leadership. Finally, the most crucial feature of managerial circles of affiliation is precisely their establishment of informal criteria for admission, criteria that are, it is true, ambiguously defined and subject to constant, often arbitrary, revision. Nonetheless, they are criteria that managers must master. At bottom, all of the social contexts of the managerial world seek to discover if one "can feel comfortable" with another manager, if he is someone who "can be trusted," if he is "our kind of guy," or, in short, if he is "one of the gang." The notion of gang, in fact, insofar as it suggests the importance of leadership, hierarchy, and probationary mechanisms in a bounded but somewhat amorphous group, may more accurately describe relationships in the corporation than the more genteel, and therefore preferable, word "circle," In any event, just as managers must continually please their boss, their boss's boss, their patrons, their president, and their CEO, so must they prove themselves again and again to each other. Work becomes an endless round of what might be called probationary crucibles. Together with the uncertainty and sense of contingency that mark managerial work, this constant state of probation produces a profound anxiety in managers, perhaps the key experience of managerial work. It also breeds, selects, or elicits certain traits in ambitious managers that are crucial to getting ahead.

⨾ READING 32 ⨾

Blacks on the Bubble

The Vulnerability of Black Executives in White Corporations

Sharon M. Collins

Since at least the 1960s, a significant number of blacks appear to be entering the middle class via mainstream avenues to economic success and well-being (Freeman 1976; Farley 1984). Yet, the position of economically disadvantaged blacks has deteriorated during the same time period (Jaynes and Williams 1989). Stark contrasts between blacks in the middle class and the ghetto have raised important questions among researchers about what influences economic opportunities for black Americans. Researchers ask whether a new system of stratification in the labor market is evolving to respond more to attributes associated with class (such as education and family background) than to racial attributes. Most studies look at overall trends or concentrate on the black underclass to address this issue. In contrast, this article explores the relationship between race and economic opportunity by examining the careers of blacks in white corporate management.

Seventy-six of the highest level black executives employed in major Chicago-based white corporations were interviewed to analyze the characteristics of managerial jobs. I distinguished two type of jobs: racialized jobs and mainstream jobs. Racialized jobs are jobs in white-owned companies that were created or reoriented during the 1960s and 1970s to carry out pro-black governmental policies and mediate black-related issues. Affirmative action and community relations jobs are examples. Mainstream jobs are line and support jobs that lack racial implications in a company. Since racialized jobs in white companies evolved to address black-related political issues more than profitability, I explore the impact of racialized versus mainstream jobs on these managers' current status in white companies. For example, the decline of black protest and federal government support for race-based social policy during the 1980s may undermine the rational for racialized positions. Moreover, since racialized jobs implement political requirements and mainstream jobs do not, I examine the implications of filling these jobs for attaining mainstream corporate assignments.

Perspectives on Race and Economic Attainment

In both theoretical and practical viewpoints, scholars increasingly view socioeconomic attributes associated with class, that is, family background and educational attainment, as more influential than racial discrimination in mediating black economic opportunities.

Some scholars maintain that discrimination remains an obstacle to blacks' full economic participation regardless of human capital and related advantages (see Jones 1986; Lazear 1979; Zweigenhalft 1987; Zweigenhalft and Domhoff 1991). However, others argue convincingly that blacks' economic chances more likely are mediated by "nonracial" factors (Featherman and Hauser 1976; Hout 1984; Smith and Welch 1983, 1986). Researchers advance the perspective that black job opportunities are not anchored to racial discrimination per se (Wilson 1978, 1987). The idea that racial barriers are eroding presumes that as blacks in the middle class attain quality educations and ascend occupational ladders they are assimilating into the economic mainstream. It is a view in which culture and macroeconomic factors increasingly restrict opportunities available to disadvantaged blacks (see Becker 1981, ch. 11; Harrington 1984; Murray 1984; Wilson 1978, 1987). Simultaneously, these factors—in the form of valued human capital and the expansion of skilled and high-paying jobs in service industries—benefit better educated blacks in the middle class. Put another way, the same macroeconomic trends that elaborated the underclass (e.g., shifts in technology and the increased numbers of white-collar jobs generated by service industries) created new and better opportunities for blacks to become middle class. Growth market factors combined with improvements in the supply of black labor to erode long-standing racial barriers to blacks with skills.

In this perspective, the structure of occupations has become increasingly color-blind. Black social dysfunction fed by welfare dependence, family background, and limited job skills explains race-related job inequality and low status. Conversely, the increased acquisition of marketable work skills and quality education explain blacks' better ability to gain middle-class lifestyles and successfully compete with whites.

Nonracial explanations for blacks' economic status not only shape theoretical issues; they also justify strategies for practical solutions to current economic problems. In particular, they rationalize dismantling race-specific programs, although visions for future federal strategies vary among potential advisors. For instance, researchers have argued that many of the contemporary problems of blacks are unresponsive to race-based governmental interventions. Moreover, many argue that black leadership and misguided government actions actually have fostered black problems (Wilson 1978, 1981, 1987; Loury 1985; Murray 1984; Sowell 1983; and Williams 1982).

Race-specific programs and policies are under attack and their future is in question. However, a consensus seems to be building that color-blind labor markets, not race-conscious policies, will protect and sustain black gains in jobs once closed to them.

The Problem of Race and Economic Attainment

Theoretical and practical perspectives on racial inequality in the contemporary economy hinge on the ability of some blacks to make occupational advancements. However, characteristics associated with the jobs blacks hold—which might shed more light on the role of race and public policy—remain out of focus. Only two sets of researchers (i.e., Brown and Erie 1981; Collins 1983, 1989) incorporate the possibility that a by-product of race-conscious policies and programs was a new employment structure in which highly educated blacks could be of value. In addition, existing research fails to look closely at the ways in which blacks earn income because such research is not easily accessible. I based my study of black executives on the idea that the lack of these data may obfuscate ways in which race-specific programs expanded economic opportunities for blacks. A related idea is that blacks might partially depend on these programs to secure their economic opportunities. I suggest that better jobs for blacks may not just be a factor of education or, even, the effect of affirmative action. Better jobs may depend also on substantive changes in the organization of jobs, changes growing out of employers' need to appease black constituents and obey government regulations. This article explores the notion that political pressures on white employment and social institutions produced a new source of economic opportunities for middle-class blacks. Demands for black-oriented programs and employment policies altered the organization of jobs and institutions to distribute more services and financial resources to blacks. That is, during the 1960s and 1970s administrative functions and race-specific programs essentially were created, expanded, or reinterpreted to respond to black needs. In this perspective, the expansion of programs that targeted blacks increased the number of professional and administrative jobs available to middle-class blacks. More significant is that opportunities for good jobs in white-dominated settings emerged in a race-oriented delivery system. Blacks, therefore,

remained "functionally segregated" in the labor market. By this, I mean that black professionals in white institutions were ghettoized to the extent that they filled roles tied to black-related demand factors versus the demand of total, or predominantly white, constituencies. . . .

Methodology

Between May 1986 and January 1987, I specifically sought to identify and interview 76 of the 87 highest-ranking black executives working in Chicago-based Fortune 500 companies.[1] I set this goal since when researchers, public policymakers, and the general public talk about black breakthroughs, these are some of the people they are talking about. In focusing on this group, I studied people at a level where conformity to corporate cultures and personal networks are key factors in individual mobility. So, too, is skill a key factor for success. Therefore, I conceive these people to be at a level of attainment where the influence of race appears to be absent or to not matter anymore. These executives exemplify black middle-class beneficiaries of the civil rights movement and seem clearly to have broken racial barriers.[2]

To locate these managers, I used *Chicago Reporter* (1983, 1986) "Annual Corporate Survey" lists citing the 52 largest white-owned industrials, utilities, retail companies, transportation companies, and banks in Chicago. I then asked knowledgeable informants familiar with the white corporate community in Chicago to identify black officers in these firms. These same informants also identified employees of the targeted companies who might be able to provide names of higher-level black officers. I asked these new "in-house" informants to identify blacks at the selected levels of management. Finally, I asked black executives who participated in the study to identify other top blacks in the selected Chicago firms.

I sought out black executives at the highest levels in companies and information from informants and articles in the press suggests I found them. Knowledgeable sources, such as executive headhunters, confirmed that I defined and located nearly the entire population of senior-level black executives employed in Chicago. However, it is difficult to specify the exact number of blacks who met the study criteria. Nevertheless, publications such as *Dollars and Sense* (e.g., 1985) highlight the nation's top-ranking black executives and the people I interviewed routinely appear in these accounts.

The executives hold some of the more desirable and prestigious positions in Chicago corporations. About two-thirds (56 of 76) had the title of director or above, including two chief officers, 30 vice-presidents, and 24 unit directors. (The total includes three people with the title of "manager" whose rank within the organization was equivalent to vice-president or director.) In addition to being the top people in Chicago, participants in this study were among the highest-ranking black executives in the country. Five of them were the only blacks in the nation to have achieved their level in a company. Almost half (32 of 76) were the highest-ranking blacks in a company's nationwide management structure.

Using vitae respondents sent to me prior to the interview, I conducted semi-structured interviews in which respondents were asked to describe, in detail, each job they had held over the course of their careers. I differentiated the "racialized" and "mainstream" tasks for each job held by a manager. I considered jobs racialized when the description of a job showed a substantive or a symbolic connection to black communities, to black issues, or to civil rights agencies at any level of government.[3]

While obviously there are a variety of jobs in management, I propose that it is not just color-blind skill and economic shifts that support the position of these managers in corporations. I believe these managers also benefit from filling jobs created by race-specific programs that grew out of civil rights demands and the ensuing legislation. Therefore, the first question asks whether their relationship to the economy became functionally segregated over the course of their careers. That is, did the managers I interviewed fill corporate slots that are distinguishable along racial lines?[4]

Placement in Race-Based Jobs

Figure 1 shows that one-third of the people I interviewed (25 of 76 managers) never performed a racialized job. Their corporate careers were completely in the mainstream. Conversely, two-thirds experienced some functional segregation in a company by having had one or more racialized jobs.

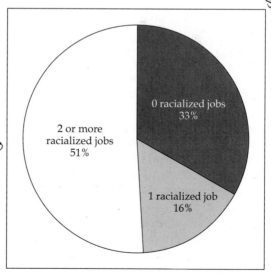

FIGURE 1 Percent of 76 Managers Who Had Racialized Jobs

[handwritten top margin: W.U. → Begs question: If Wilson's hyp. is juxtaposed w/ this one, would ties to m.c. blacks do much for ghetto blacks?]

Managers in the mainstream of a company have careers made up of jobs interfacing with total constituencies. They do not act in an intermediary role presiding between white corporations and black consumer, manpower, or political issues. The career of a vice-president and regional sales manager for a Fortune 500 company in the manufacturing and retail food industry provides an illustration. This manager was hired as a market researcher for a Fortune 15 east coast oil company in 1961 where his job involved marketing only to the total (predominantly white) consumer market not to "special" (predominantly black) markets. In 1968, this manager accepted a position as a salesman with his current employer and, again, reported he was never assigned a black territory, although sales territories in his current company were segmented by race. He said:

[handwritten left margin: "main stream" jobs]

> Those kinds of things even happen now, so that . . . in New York . . . especially in Harlem, the Bronx, Brooklyn, you would basically have black sales reps or Hispanic. At that time [in 1968] . . . it happened a lot [but] I happened not to get caught in that because I lived in New Jersey and they want your territory to be closer to home . . . there were no blacks.

[handwritten left margin: egs–]

The manager moved up through the sales hierarchy from salesman to sales manager, from zone manager to district manager, from area manager, to division manager, finally to his present job in the company as an officer in the firm. He was not assigned to black territories as a salesman nor as a sales manager, neither was he responsible for a predominantly black sales force nor for strategic marketing to the black community when he managed geographical areas.

A heavily recruited vice-president of investor relations with an MBA from the University of Chicago is a similar example of upward mobility within the mainstream job

[handwritten left margin: 2)]

structure of companies. In 1968, this manager entered the white private sector and worked her way up in banking until, in 1984, she was recruited by a major food manufacturer in Chicago to become an assistant vice-president and director. After a brief tenure, she again was recruited, this time by her current employer, and became a full vice-president and officer. At no point did her jobs with these three firms link her to blacks or to issues relating to blacks. She was not used by firms to give financial advice primarily to black organizations, nor was she the interface between company and black consumers or investors. Neither did she work on any federally funded loan programs administered in the private sector targeting minority constituencies, such as Small Business Administration (SBA) programs. Although firms she worked for had affirmative action, manpower, and community affairs programs she was never approached to manage, nor did she ever administer, programs of this kind.

Black executives with mainstream careers are the successful products of moral and legislative commitments made to incorporate blacks into the higher-paying occupations in white-dominated institutions. However, Figure 1 also shows that most managers (55 of 76) had racialized jobs. Twelve of 76 managers had held one job created by companies to respond to black protest and governmental requirements. Over half the managers (39 of 76) had held two or more jobs produced by social policy mandates and protest.

[handwritten right margin: BUT most are racial ized]

The account of a vice-president and director of urban affairs is one example. This manager moved up in the white banking sector through a series of newly-created community relations and corporate affairs jobs. Throughout, this man was a company ombudsman whose task was to "promote the visibility and good name" of the bank in the black community in Chicago.

Similarly, the career of a senior vice-president of sales for a Fortune 500 printing and publishing company was interspersed with black community relations jobs that "develop[ed] a good corporate citizenship image among blacks and . . . work[ed] with . . . local [black] agencies."

A senior vice-president and zone manager who works for a major firm in the fast-food industry and who is, nationally, one of highest-ranking black executives in the white corporate sector, also spent part of his tenure in an "urban affairs" job. He said:

> After the civil disorders, the riots . . . there was a tremendous movement . . . to have black ownership in [black] communities around the country. Basically [my] job was to work with the licensee department and coming up with minority candidates around the country to become licensees.

Racialized functions showed up in the range of jobs held by respondents. People employed in operations took on racialized functions managing predominantly black workforces and mediating black-white relationships in racially volatile employment settings. Public relations executives took on racialized functions in which they interacted predominantly with black community organizations for white corporations. Sales executives became involved in helping white corporations orient product advertisements specifically to black markets and developing socially sensitive corporate programs to project positive images to black consumers. Personnel managers helped companies in the recruitment and training of blacks and in tasks otherwise designed to ease the entry and promotion of blacks within white-dominated institutions.

Racialized jobs show up in most of these successful managerial careers and a question naturally arises: what caused employment opportunities to be skewed this way?

One explanation would be that jobs tied to blacks are part of the ordinary make-up of corporate operations. They do not indicate racial divisions. For instance, it would be difficult for black managers employed in personnel in major metropolitan areas not to be in jobs tied to concentrations of blacks. Blacks make up a large proportion of blue-collar workers. However, having blacks in racialized jobs implies more than this routine involvement. Racialized jobs have political goals that evolved because of pressures on companies to ameliorate black problems and administer government regulations. I suggest that careers took this course because black activism and governmental regulations provoked an administrative crisis in businesses' operating environments. Corporations solved their problem with blacks by funneling race-specific policy through these managers.

The career of a black director of testing for an educational test and supply company shows this. In 1965, this manager was promoted from an entry-level customer-representative job to become manager of community relations. During this period, his company was in jeopardy of losing a lucrative market in a New Orleans public school district. The year 1965 was in the middle of an era when blacks were demanding more representation and community control, and a change of school district management put blacks in key buying positions. The manager stated flatly that he was promoted because "the company was abruptly shut out [and] they needed somebody black to represent [it]" to this sales constituency. A new political mandate emerged in his company to pacify blacks in a militant consumer population. The movement of this manager into community relations was a response to political demands.

Similar dynamics can be identified in his promotion to personnel manager in the same company. He explained that, at the

[handwritten note at top: Upshot: Good jobs for Blacks emerged & expanded b/c of political pressures on corps. by gov't.]

time, the company was one-third black and most were "secretaries and [office] administrative types." Top white management explicitly stated the purpose behind this second promotion. Because blacks were ghettoized within the low-paying jobs in the company he explained:

> I was told that there was a lot of dissatisfaction in the ranks [and] there was a definite need for someone [black] to be visible in personnel. [My job was] to make blacks in the company feel they were being related to . . . to present a positive image to the staff [and] to show them they could make it.

An executive for a major steel company provides a second illustration of black-related crises faced by white-dominated environments. This man shifted from construction project manager to a public affairs job in 1974 when a major construction project came under attack by the Chicago Defender, a black newspaper. He said, " [The company] wanted me to get them out of trouble . . . big trouble. [Blacks] were threatening to picket . . . the minority community . . . was threatening the project." The black media—as well as the black community which surrounded the construction site—criticized the company's lack of black suppliers and contractors. This manager's job in public affairs was created to develop a minority procurement program to put this public protest to rest.

Figure 2 shows the total number of people who were ever employed in major fields (i.e., in personnel, public relations, sales, production, and technical fields). Figure 2 also shows the proportion of blacks who filled at least one job, while in a field, which targeted black consumers, black labor, or black constituencies. Figure 2 shows that managers had racialized jobs in each area. The largest number of people had at least one racialized job in public

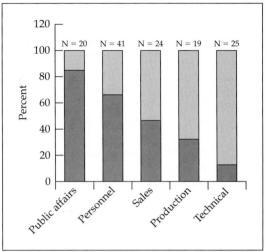

FIGURE 2 Managers in Racialized Functions, by Field

relations and personnel areas. The large presence of managers in racialized personnel and public relations jobs is consistent with the idea that good jobs for blacks emerged or expanded because of political pressures on corporations. The federal government and black communities demanded accommodations which increased the need for companies to have blacks visible in these key departments. In public relations, for instance, corporate giving programs needed broadened initiatives because of increasing pressures from black communities and from changing urban environments. Even more distinctively, personnel departments underwent dramatic transitions to address hiring priorities established by the government.

Political pressures on corporations were great which created a demand for blacks in these areas. Forty-five of the 56 managers who had racialized jobs specifically had personnel and public relations jobs managing affirmative action and urban affairs programs. Twenty-two of these 45 managers

(49 percent) were working in mainstream areas and were approached by company management to take these jobs. Twelve of these 22 approached managers (55 percent) were personally solicited for these jobs by senior-level management. Senior vice-presidents and chief executive officers asked them to take these jobs. Nine of these 22 managers (41 percent) turned these jobs down and were approached a second time by top management. Eleven of the 22 approached managers (50 percent) were given salary increases, more prestigious job titles, and promises of future rewards. One respondent commented somewhat ironically:

> It was during the early 1970s, and there weren't very many people around that could do anything for minorities. . . . I mean, they were really, all the companies were really scrambling. . . . All you saw was minorities functioning in that . . . and it doesn't take much brain power to figure out that that's where most of us were going to end up.

Both economic and political demands of consumer constituencies can produce employment opportunities. Employment opportunities tied to economic mandates occur in response to consumer preferences and buying patterns, and demands that stem from the marketplace create these opportunities. Employment opportunities resulting from political mandates are tied to protest and pressure; they are outgrowths of social policy and governmental intervention. The data I use above highlight the segment of black opportunities that are protest related and result from political influences on labor-market demand. Such labor-market demand benefited blacks to the extent that it created and expanded black opportunities in higher-paying and previously-closed positions, such as managerial jobs. On the other hand, if this demand responds to the disruptiveness and the pervasiveness of black protest, then as political pressures abate, this demand will decline. Therefore, do racialized jobs become expendable?

Status of Current Jobs

This section of the article asks: is this system of opportunity within white corporate environments vulnerable to changing political conditions? I explore the possibility that the attack on race-based programs and the reduction of black community pressures contribute to a race-based vulnerability in these managers' corporate careers.

In the 1980s, the federal government's 20-year commitment to policies and practices that assisted blacks to compete economically experienced a dramatic reversal. Throughout the decade, a clear message was sent of White House opposition to race-based policies and protections, particularly the policy of affirmative action (Hudson and Broadnax 1982). Similarly, a decade of U.S. Supreme Court appointments and decisions also signaled a retreat from the endorsement of the principle of race-based remedies to overcome historic discrimination (Wilson et al. 1991). (Although the court did twice endorse affirmative action policies during the decade the majority of decisions clearly indicated that the use of preferential hiring policies was now on soft ground.)

The attack on race-specific programs reduced the role of the federal government as a strong advocate of black employment. If federal policies assisted in the creation of jobs for middle-class blacks, then a retreat from racial policies may undermine blacks' gains in the labor market. For instance, a race-neutral federal stance would cause employers to retreat from past affirmative action (i.e., numerical) commitments. Of interest in this article, however, is whether there are substantive characteristics that make black jobs particular targets to be let go in companies. The hypothesis here is that because of the race-specific focus of these jobs, this administrative structure will fluctuate along with political conditions.

Managers were asked if their jobs had changed in title, scope of responsibilities, budget, or functions since 1980. I asked, for example if any of their responsibilities had been increased, reassigned to other managers, or dissolved. I also asked about departmental changes, that is, if budgets and staff had increased or decreased. Racialized jobs in corporations were the most recent employment for over one-third (30 of the 76) of the managers I interviewed. Figure 3 compares the reports of 45 mainstream managers with these 30 managers in racialized jobs. One chief executive officer was excluded from this summary since CEOs might be fired by a corporate board but the job itself would not be increased, downsized, or eliminated.

This figure conforms to what my hypothesis would predict. Black executives in racialized jobs (50 percent versus 11 percent) reported the company had eliminated, reduced, or redistributed some of their

functions to managers in other areas of a company much more than did black executives in mainstream jobs.

An example is a vice-president of urban affairs who began his career in the financial industry in the early 1970s in affirmative action. Due to the intensity of racial pressures in Chicago, his job evolved into a community liaison position that primarily focused on placating blacks. He summarizes his job this way:

> I kept my hands on the pulse of the [black] community—I sold the bank's story out to the community. I conducted the social audit, finding out where the bank was deficient, where they could come up to speed.

In the next quote, this manager makes explicit the different futures of the two tracks of functions in public relations, mainstream and racialized (i.e., black). The mainstream functions are responsible for maintaining traditional, that is, white, civic contributions. The black function, for which this manager was responsible, was essentially an appeasement role. In the late 1970s, the rationale for appeasement was undermined by an atmosphere in which pressure from blacks was absent, and the black community affairs function was cut back. He said:

> They kept talking, they had this term "the long hot summer" and up to about 1976 [or] 1977, they were talking about the long hot summer [but] nothing happened. [So] they just cut the money. I mean, their traditional lines of support . . . for the [Chicago] symphony, and the [Chicago] Art Institute and those kinds of things, they were still maintaining a level. But no [money for] community groups, grass-roots types. There was just a withdrawal.

It can also be seen in Figure 3, however, that mainstream as well as racialized jobs

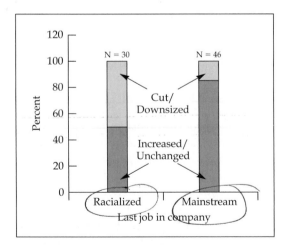

FIGURE 3 Changes in Mainstream and Racialized Jobs Since 1980

[Handwritten at top: Upshot: Racialized jobs have been esp. expendable w/ lack of pol. pressure → Will this Transf?]

experienced vulnerability. Therefore, job vulnerability cannot be viewed merely as a product of racial inequality in the job structure. Stories of white-collar workers, including middle managers and financial-industry employees, illustrate that job fragility is also a feature of macroeconomic changes such as greatly diminished growth in service-sector jobs (Forbes 1991; Hertz 1990). Indeed, in the post-1980 era of corporate mergers and economic restructuring, news reports indicate that both white and black managers have been victims of job loss in major corporations (*New York Times* 1987; *U.S. News & World Report* 1987). Job insecurity confronts individuals who are in high-status occupations, not blacks per se. However, are there substantive differences within this strata of jobs that make black fragility in management a somewhat different phenomenon?

[Handwritten in left margin: overall loss of jobs tho]

The next series of quotes illustrate how politically useful jobs in white companies become economically expendable, particularly in a context of corporate buyouts and economic reorganization. A director of community affairs and public affairs managed the black component of public relations for a major retail firm in Chicago. Since 1972, this respondent was charged with "keeping [up] the image" of the company in the black community and represented the company at conventions, on community boards, and on the committees of black community organizations. Between 1981 and 1982, the company began streamlining the workforce to maximize profits and, in a way similar to the case just recounted, when pressure waned the company image among black consumers became less important. During this period, the respondent reported, his job in community affairs "just wasn't important to them—they just didn't want to spend money on that any more." The manager reported, "they wanted to cut the job, they just didn't want to cut me" and the black component of community affairs was dismantled completely. Throughout,

managers in racialized jobs told similar stories. For instance, I spoke with a 20-year manager of corporate contributions and community relations for a steel company who was "looking for opportunities elsewhere." He reported that the programs he ran were funded by company reserves set aside during the 1960s and 1970s following black riots in Chicago. These reserves were once large but project funding diminished as company profits diminished in the comparatively calm racial atmosphere of the 1980s. He said, "[The department] will have a totally different look. . . . [It] will honor the commitments we made for this year and phase out. That includes me and part of my staff."

Even managers who have not experienced immediate reductions say that racialized functions are easy targets because of the political climate and corporate reorganization. An example is a manager who designed a minority purchasing program for his company. This program identifies minority businessmen and helps them compete to supply goods and services to the company via contracts that ordinarily went to larger white firms. This manager was considering retirement, and he indicated that although his program budget had increased over the years, the company would probably cut his job when he resigns. The company began streamlining in 1984, reducing purchasing requirements and its base of minority and majority suppliers. He said:

[Handwritten in right margin: jobs phased out]

> They haven't tried to cut back my program, my budget grows every year. But they're trying to eliminate the supplier base. . . . They reduced it by half between last year and this and they want to reduce it again by half next year. [Do you think the company will fill your job once you leave?] No. When I leave I'm not even grooming anybody to take my job. As far as I know, I don't think the company is [grooming someone] either.

The job was created in a highly specialized area to assist black and other minority businessmen gain company contracts. The mainstream, less specialized, counterpart is in the area of purchasing. The mainstream purchasing functions, although vulnerable, will remain. But the respondent's part of the purchasing function—which is oriented toward blacks—apparently will be allowed to dissolve.

The apparent explanation is that racialized jobs were created when economic expansion and race-specific employment demands converged. In the 1980s, these trends reversed. Political pressure placed on employers by government and black publics weakened, at the same time as competition for market share intensified. Racial functions, therefore, have greatly reduced value.

Job Security

The hypothesis indicated that these jobs would vary according to conditions. It therefore suggests that a race-based structure of job opportunities actually works both ways. Where pressure declines jobs become unstable, but where pressure is stable so are these jobs. Race would make blacks in these jobs vulnerable, but these jobs can also protect blacks from job loss.

Not all managers who have racialized responsibilities expressed concern about their future in a company. Half of the managers (15 of 30) reported that their jobs had been downgraded or cut and half reported that their jobs had not (see Figure 3). Does variability in the reports of these managers undermine my thesis that fragility is a component in racialized careers? It does not if managers' reports of greater relative job security coincide with areas where remnants of political pressure remain on employers.

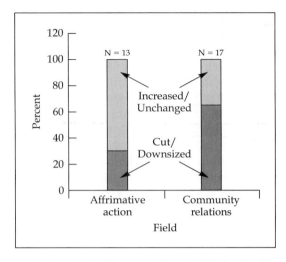

FIGURE 4 Job Changes Since 1980, by Field

Figure 4 summarizes reports of job changes that have occurred among the 30 respondents in race-relations areas. The jobs of these managers are sorted into two fields, affirmative action and community relations. I classified managers with equal employment opportunity, personnel, and staff-training functions as affirmative action, and managers with urban affairs, corporate contributions, marketing, and public relations functions as community relations. People who filled affirmative action jobs reported fewer cuts than those filling community affairs jobs. About one-third of the managers (four of 13) in affirmative action reported job cuts compared to two-thirds of the managers (11 of 17) in community relations.

Although the numbers are admittedly small, black jobs in community relations especially have been cut. These data support linking political pressures to job vulnerability since variability in political pressure can be located here. Affirmative action jobs are produced from a less volatile source of political pressure than community relations jobs since they are tied to government requirements. Thus, it is reasonable to presume that affirmative action jobs are less vulnerable because of

Comm. relations jobs less stable than affirm. acn. jobs

the regulatory environment. For instance, two affirmative action managers who reported that their responsibilities had increased also reported that their current employers were under consent decrees. Obviously, the rationale that created these jobs still remains, even if attenuated. Even if a company wished to cut affirmative action slots, it would still have visits from compliance officers and government regulations to contend with.

Black community-relations jobs, on the other hand, were created in response to community pressures and a need for visibility among black constituencies. A recent model for this phenomenon is a major consumer goods company in Chicago. This company was negotiating with a grass-roots group of black activists who targeted the company because of its poor performance in minority hiring. As a result, a mainstream company job in corporate giving was transformed into a community affairs job and a new (black) community affairs manager was hired. Given this context, it seems reasonable to argue that as pressures from the government abate (as have pressures from the black community), affirmative action jobs will also become increasingly expendable in companies.

Overall, this pattern is one in which relatively stable positions are grounded in the residuals of political pressure. Therefore, these managers' reports concerning job stability do not undermine the thesis of political dependency. They appear to be the exception but they are part of the rule. Political conditions erode these managers' jobs and, conversely, protect them. Job security is anchored to the governmental and black community pressures that remain in place today. Moreover, this pattern supports the idea that job security is contingent on racial factors. Under conditions in which racial pressures abate, the vulnerability of these positions would increasingly emerge and these jobs would be eliminated.

Attempts at Job Enhancement

Having shown that the racialized structure of jobs is distinctive, the next question is whether taking these jobs marginalizes blacks in companies. During post-1980 cutbacks, some managers made attempts to break out of racialized slots and into the mainstream of a company. Did the degree to which they succeeded hinge, at least in part, on their previous work experience? That is, is racialized human capital a factor perceived to limit managers' value in mainstream corporate functions? People whose careers incorporate some, but not a majority, of racialized jobs are coded as having "mixed" careers. People who had a majority of racialized jobs are coded as having "segregated" careers. Although illustrative rather than conclusive, the following comparisons of segregated and mixed careers suggest that career segregation makes black managers dependent on racial politics because they lack requisite experience in core corporate areas.

The experience of a past community relations manager for a major electronics corporation highlights that the skills that once were in demand now are a contributing factor to these managers' economic vulnerability. This man reported that his company's commitment to urban affairs began to decrease and, observing the handwriting on the wall" as he put it, he made multiple attempts to get out of urban affairs. He reported:

> I was just not able to make that break. I talked to [people] in various divisions that I was interested in, and I got the lip service that they would keep [me] in mind if something opened up. As it happened, that just did not develop. I can never remember being approached by anyone. Nothing [happened]—that I can really hang [onto] as an offer. People would ask, "have you ever run a profit and loss operation?"

Finally, he described himself as taking "hat in hand" and approaching senior management in 1982 to request duties he knew to be available in a general administrative area. He said:

> Frankly, this was an attempt to seize an opportunity. This time I went and I asked for a [new assignment]. We had some retirement within the company and some reorganization. I saw an opportunity to help myself. The urban affairs was shrinking. A number of jobs we created [in urban affairs] were completely eliminated. It just happened that the opportunity [to pick up administrative services] was there. It had a significant dollar budget and profit and loss opportunity. . . . It was concrete and useful. So I asked for it.

He was only temporarily successful in his attempt to exchange urban affairs for a more stable assignment in administrative services. One year later, he was invited to resign from the company because of poor performance.

An urban affairs manager who tried to move to warehouse distribution in a retail company was similarly constrained. This manager constructed a successful career, but the trade-off for rising in a company in race-oriented jobs was that he became cut off from mainstream areas. He failed in his shift from what he termed the "money-using" to the "money-producing" part of the business:

> I was too old to do what you had to do to compete. . . . I was competing with 21- and 22-year-olds to get into the system. They couldn't charge [my salary] to a store and have me doing the same thing the others [were] doing [for much less money]. You need the ground-level experience. When I should have gotten it, I was busy running an affirmative action department.

I explored with him possibilities for placement in other areas of the company. I asked why he didn't expand his job into mainstream public relations, an area he was (apparently) more qualified to pursue. He responded:

> I thought about it very seriously. I wondered where I was going with the system. It came up quite often. I talked about it when I first accepted this job. And at the end, they told me, "We don't know. We'll have to get back to you." They never did.

That his superiors never got back to him may result from the fact that the organization needed him precisely where he was placed. Or, it may result from senior management's perception that he lacked the necessary skills to compete with younger mainstream managers who had moved up through that field. In either event, these people identified two routes to buffer their position in a company. One was to move laterally into an entirely different corporate area associated with mainstream planning, production, or administration. The second was to move laterally to the mainstream component of the racialized area. These quotes illustrate that people who specialize in affirmative action and community relations are stymied in both routes. In exchange for establishing an expertise in racialized functions, these managers' value is reduced in other areas. Because of limited skills and career "track records," people who were concentrated in racialized roles lacked the human capital to compete in mainstream company areas. The same skills that made them valuable later constrained them.

A director of affirmative action in his mid-40s talked about this dead end when he said, "Nobody ever told me . . . that if you stay in [this] job you'd be in [this] job forever. You don't move to vice-president of personnel from manager of EEO."

People with mixed careers, in contrast, had more flexibility. They could enlarge their roles within core areas in the company. For example, a director of community affairs and area personnel manager with a major Chicago retailer had a 19-year career which alternated between personnel and labor relations, and urban affairs and affirmative action. In 1985, he was appointed as the replacement for an exiting black vice-president of community affairs. His new position in community affairs was a downgraded version of the old job; his title was director of community affairs. In 1986, the community affairs staff and budget once again were reduced. In the next quote, he explains how he aggressively was able to enlarge his role, which had become a meaningless position:

> I went into my boss and told him I could do it with one hand tied behind my back. I had a director title for something that took one day a week to do. I told him that he had to give me some more responsibilities in personnel. So that's how I got that. [The commitment to affirmative action had] gotten so bad, the firm moved its headquarters from O'Hare to Salt Lake City. I guess that's one way of getting the monkey off your back.

The fact that company headquarters moved out of Chicago, which has a highly politicized urban black environment, to a much less confrontational and predominantly white environment, may indeed be partially the reason for reducing the budget for community affairs. To protect his future in the company, this manager asked for, and received, more responsibilities in mainstream personnel. Had he not had critical experience in personnel functions, it is likely that continuing cutbacks in community affairs eventually would have placed him in the ranks of vulnerable managers.

Summary and Conclusions

In this article I have illustrated that mobility within the black middle class since 1960 may be tied to a racial division of labor that emerged as a result of civil rights initiatives. I used interviews with highly successful and apparently fully assimilated black executives in white corporations. I then showed that many of these executives are utilized in a racialized niche of managerial jobs that are linked to black needs. Blacks who occupy this job structure experience double jeopardy—the threat of downward mobility comes from changes both in the structure of the economy and in the public policy agenda. Twenty years ago, affirmative action and community relations jobs represented a new source of corporate management jobs for blacks. Ironically, however, these avenues of upward mobility also infused a race-based fragility into black managerial gains 20 years later. Corporate affirmative action, community relations, and other "black" jobs are administrative outgrowths of specific political conditions. The decline of protest and governmental support for race-based social policy during the 1980s undermined the rationale for racialized positions.

My data on black managers both support and differ from current views of growth in the black middle class. They support the idea that race-specific programs and higher educational attainment enabled blacks to climb occupational and income hierarchies historically closed to them. But they do not support the assumption that mobility within the middle class is a sign that blacks are assimilating into a color-blind labor market. Rather, the data suggest that governmental solutions to racial inequality have been resisted and not incorporated into the workplace. Interviews are from blacks who have "made it" by most standards, yet they illustrate that careers in management have race-regulated ceilings and systems of mobility. Broad occupational titles and income alone do not necessarily tell the story. Indeed, they may overstate the case for black advancement. . . .

Employers should recommit to a proactive recruitment strategy and have in place a sufficient organizational structure to implement it. For instance, companies need to reward officers and managers for the recruitment and development of a diverse workforce. Moreover, affirmative action and human resources development as it relates to minorities should not be dismantled. These functions should not be viewed as marginal activities. Instead, recruitment and development should be viewed as a job that, if done well, will increase company profitability at every level. Similarly, community relations departments are also in jeopardy because they are seen as peripheral in white companies. But community enhancement, in the form of training programs, corporate donations, and minority business partnerships, should also be seen as having an important purpose. Pro-active involvement in urban communities is a way of developing a work force the company may draw from in the future.

Acknowledgments

This research was supported by a grant from the National Science Foundation. The author especially thanks William Domhoff, Joe Feagin, Arnold Feldman, Cedric Herring, Anthony Orum, R. Stephen Warner, and William J. Wilson for their advice on this manuscript.

NOTES

1. One person declined to be interviewed; ten people did not interview because of logistical reasons or they did not meet my criteria.

2. I considered blacks to be "top executives" if: (1) they were employed in a banking institution and had a title of comptroller, trust officer, vice-president (excluding "assistant" vice-president), president, or chief officer; or (2) they were employed in a nonfinancial institution with a title of department manager, director, vice-president, or chief officer.

3. For example, one manager was hired by the chief executive officer of a major retailer in 1968 specifically to eradicate discriminatory employment practices used in the personnel department to exclude blacks from higher-paying positions in the company. I coded this job "racialized" since it was designed to improve black opportunities in the company at a time when the federal government increasingly was requiring it. Jobs that were described in a way that revealed neither explicit nor implicit connections to blacks were labeled "mainstream." When a managers' description left me undecided about the nature of a job or when it was not feasible to examine careers on a job-by-job basis, I asked respondents a broad question to identify jobs that were racialized. Specifically, I asked, "During the 1960s and the early 1970s, social programs such as EEO, manpower training, and community affairs were hot items in some corporations. Did you ever have a job in any of these areas?"

4. The role of gender in this context is not discussed; only eight of 76 were women.

REFERENCES

"Annual Corporate Survey." 1983. *Chicago Reporter.* (December): 2–6.

———. 1986. *Chicago Reporter.* (January): 7–10.

Becker, Gary. 1981. *A Treatise on the Family.* Cambridge: Harvard University Press.

Brown, M. K. and S. P. Erie. 1981. "Blacks and the Legacy of the Great Society: The Economic and Political Impact of Federal Social Policy." *Public Policy* 29: 299–330.

Chicago Reporter. 1965. *Dark Ghetto: Dilemmas of Social Power.* New York: Harper & Row.

Collins, Sharon M. 1983. "The Making of the Black Middle Class." *Social Problems* 30: 369–382.

———. 1989. "The Marginalization of Black Executives." *Social Problems* 36: 317–331.

Dollars and Sense. 1965. "Annual Careers/Black History" issue. (February/March).

Farley, Reynolds. 1984. *Blacks and Whites: Narrowing the Gap?* Cambridge: Harvard University Press.

Featherman, David L. and Rober M. Hauser 1976. "Prestige or Socioeconomic Scales in the Study of Occupational Achievement." *Sociological Methods and Research* 4: 403–422.

Freeman, Richard. 1976. *The Black Elite.* New York: McGraw-Hill.

Farrington, Michael. 1984. *The New American Poverty.* New York: Holt, Rinehart & Winston.

Heckman, James J. and Brook S. Payner. 1989. "Determining the Impact of Federal Antidiscrimination Policy on the Economic Status of Blacks: A Study of South Carolina." *The American Economic Review* 79: 138–177.

Hertz, Diane. 1990. "Worker Displacement in a Period of Rapid Job Expansion: 1983–87." *Monthly Labor Review* (May): 21–33.

Hout, Michael. 1984. "Occupational Mobility of Black Men." *American Sociological Review* 49: 308–322.

Jaynes, Gerald David and Robin M. Williams, Jr. 1989. *A Common Destiny: Blacks and American Society.* Washington, DC: National Academy Press.

Jones, Edward W. 1986. "Black Managers: The Dream Deferred." *Harvard Business Review* 86: 85–93.

Lazear, Edward. 1979. "The Narrowing of Black-White Wage Differentials Is Illusory." *American Economic Review* 69: 553–564.

Leonard, Jonathan S. 1984. "The Impact of Affirmative Action on Employment." *Journal of Labor Economics* 2: 439–464.

Loury, Glenn C. 1985. "The Moral Quandary of the Black Community." *The Public Interest* 79: 9–22.

Murray, Charles. 1984. *Losing Ground: American Social Policy, 1950–1980.* New York: Basic Books.

New York Times. 1987. "The Ax Falls on Equal Opportunity." January 4, Section 4: 1–7.

Smith, James P. and Finis R. Welch. 1983. "Longer Trends in Black/White Economic Status and Recent Effects of Affirmative Action." Paper prepared at the Social Science Research Council Conference at the National Opinion Research Center, Chicago.

———. 1986. *Closing the Gap: Forty Years of Economic Progress for Blacks.* Santa Monica, CA: Rand Corporation.

Sowell, Thomas. 1983. *The Economics and Politics of Race.* Transcript of "The Firing Line" television program, taped in New York City in November 1983 and telecast later by PBS.

U.S. News & World Report 1987. "You're Fired," pp. 50–54.

Williams, Walter. 1982. "Rethinking the Black Agenda." Pp. 16–18 in *Proceedings from The Black Alternatives Conference.* Distributed by The New Coalition for Economic and Social Change, San Diego, CA.

Wilson, Cynthia A., James H. Lewis and Cedric Herring. 1991. *The 1991 Civil Rights Act: Restoring Our Basic Protections.* Chicago: Chicago Urban League and Chicago Lawyers' Committee for Civil Rights Under Law.

Wilson, William J. 1978. *The Declining Significance of Race.* Chicago: University of Chicago Press.

———. 1981. "The Black Community in the 1980s: Questions of Race, Class, and Public Policy." *Annals of the American Academy of Political and Social Sciences* 454(March): 26–41.

———. 1987. *The Truly Disadvantaged: The Inner City, the Underclass, and Public Policy.* Chicago: University of Chicago Press.

Zweigenhaft, Richard L. 1987. "Women and Minorities of the Corporation: Will They Make It to the Top?" Pp. 37–62 in *Power Elites and Organizations,* edited by G. William Domhoff and Thomas R. Dye. Beverly Hills, CA: Sage Publications.

Zweigenhaft, Richard L. and G. William Domhoff. 1991. *Blacks in the White Establishment? A Study of Race and Class in America.* New Haven, CT: Yale University Press.

MARGINAL, CONTINGENT, AND
LOW-WAGE JOBS

⊙ READING 33 ⊙

Are We Not Temps?

Jackie Krasas Rogers

Here's how Ludy Martinez responded when the temporary agency she worked for refused to raise her rate:

Well, that's the only thing you have as a temp, the only advantage you had was to be connected to ten different temp agencies so that when one didn't treat you right, you'd go to another. Or you'd play them against each other. Being able to compare the different pay scales. And I in fact had a couple of agencies. One place I temped at had temps from, like, five different agencies there, and I can't remember if I was there longer than the others, but certain other temp agencies tried to woo me away from the one that I was at. And I couldn't remember if I had an ethical question about that. Just say, "How does this agency treat you?" Well then screw that. You know, and the rule was supposed to be you couldn't work at that company unless you had a separation period for, like, six months where you stopped temping and all that. And that was the time when I just threw that rule out the door because I said you have not earned that right from me, you

know. And I was never called on the carpet for that either. But I just decided this is all a temp has. If one agency treats you badly, you have a right to accept a job even if you met these people because you were placed originally. I mean, that was the first time I felt really mercenary about it. And they didn't care because the turnover at their agency was so [bad]. I never got reprimanded for it. (Ludy Martinez, thirty-six-year-old Filipina)

The Missing Subject

Studies of work seem to fall into two categories with regard to workers' subjectivity. One perspective portrays workers as having very little will of their own, as mindless drones with no ideas or opinions. They seem to be completely controlled by their circumstances. Workers appear oversocialized, their behavior easily predictable according to their role in the labor process. At times, it seems an almost fruitless inquiry to locate any knowledge that is not predetermined and scripted by the organization of work.

The second perspective, derived largely from the human relations school, focuses simply on job satisfaction and its effects on productivity. These studies seem lost in a completely subjectivist orientation that fails to recognize very real constraints on human behavior.

Over time, more sophisticated analyses have emerged wherein identity and subjectivity are explored, even if they are under-theorized with regard to the organization of work. Attending to workers' subjectivities helps us to understand how some workers may experience the very same work conditions as oppressive while other workers do not. For example, workers do not uniformly experience work routinization as oppressive (Leidner 1993).

Leidner (1993) also identifies a contradiction in workers being socialized to be themselves. She reveals one insurance agent's practice of reminding himself to act authentically by keeping visible in his car a note stating "Be Kevin." Implicit in the analysis is the notion that work routines are imposed on a worker's true self. One might also want to investigate the problem of workers maintaining a secure identity, and the results of their efforts. Actions do not take place outside power relations, and the pursuit of a stable identity may itself be a means through which power relations are reproduced. The very notion of authenticity can help to reproduce power relations in routinized service work. Some service workers experience routinization as helpful because it protects important aspects of their identity. Thus the imperative to protect one's identity shapes workers' feelings and actions such that it diminishes resistance to managerial prerogatives.

This chapter explores temporary clerical workers' subjectivities and their role in challenging or reproducing power relations. Important questions remain about how temporary workers feel about their employment relationship. Several researchers, myself included, have demonstrated the exploitative structures of temporary employment, but do temporary workers actually *feel* exploited? How do temporary workers characterize their acts of resistance? Do temporary workers embrace the temporary industry's efforts to shape their understandings of the employment relationship?

More complicated are issues of identity. Given a work situation where social relationships are constantly in flux, what are temporary workers' struggles with identity? In trying to maintain a stable identity, temporary workers may help to reproduce the very power relations that constrain them. In other words, temporaries' subjectivities may contribute to the "outflanking" of their resistance.

From existing studies we can already see a preoccupation of temporary workers with their identity. For instance, some temporaries tell a "cover story" to alleviate the stigma of temporary employment: Temporary workers are actors waiting to be discovered, entrepreneurs in the making, and just passing through on their way to the top. Others proudly and self-consciously reject the hierarchical values from which the stigma derives; climbing the corporate ladder just gives them vertigo, so they take a first-floor job.

Whatever the case, these examples show temporary clerical workers trying to maintain a stable identity. Just how these attempts are intertwined with organizational power/knowledge relations and what their consequences are warrants investigation.

I Temp, Therefore I Am Not

If the temporary workers I interviewed had one experience in common, it was the experience of being a "nonperson." One symptom of non personhood in temporary clerical employment concerned naming practices. Many temporaries reported being referred to not by their name, but simply as "the temp." "Give it to the temp," "Oh, she's the temp," "Where's the temp?" I found this naming practice to be quite common. When I arrived at one assignment in particular, I found a letter with instructions left by the "permanent" secretary. The letter was addressed, "Dear temp." Many times, I was introduced to co-workers with the simple phrase "This is our temp."

These naming practices occur both for practical reasons, and because of temporary clerical workers' low status. Often they are not in a workplace long enough to have others learn their names, so they and others like them become "the temp." Co-workers' tendency to replace an individual's name with "temp" may also reflect asymmetrical naming practices with regard to social status. Subordinates must properly name their bosses (proper title, the correct name, no first names); however, bosses need not reciprocate and seldom show the same consideration or respect.

What struck me in my observations as well as from the interviews was the extent to which the people around temporary workers did not find this practice troublesome, while at the same time most temporary workers seemed bothered by it. Being labeled "the temp" denied some temporary workers important aspects of their identity (Rogers 1995).

> And it didn't really matter if you were good at your job as a temp; you were still identified as a temp; you were going to be treated in that way. (Ludy Martinez, thirty-six-year-old Filipina)

> Sometimes you get in a situation where no matter what you do it's not good enough because of the fact you're a temp. Sometimes being just totally alienated because you're a temp. They're like, "Oh that's the temp." And the reputation of some temporaries have followed temps on down the road. So sometimes you have to override that stereotype. One strike already against you. But then you override the stereotype. (Larry Landers, thirty-eight-year-old African American)

As illustrated by Larry, most temporaries reported wanting to show that they were "better" than the temp label they were given. Because one's work is still a principle means of identity formation and maintenance in U.S. society, temporary workers not surprisingly appear to be overly preoccupied with, or fetishize, their identity. Certainly, the structure of temporary employment with its transitoriness and its construction of the temporary as a nonperson helps to place further emphasis on identity issues. Imagine starting a new job every day or every week: "The unpredictability and variability of social relations inevitably renders identity precarious or uncertain" (Sturdy 1992, 140). The following quote represents the feelings of many of the temporaries I interviewed.

> You have to know that you don't mind arriving in different clothes, meeting all different kinds of people. It's not safe. It's not comfortable a lot of times. If you're doing different things with different people in different environments. A lot of change. A lot of change. And that's difficult for a lot of people. (Doug Larson, thirty-nine-year-old white man)

Many temporary workers experience the unpredictability as problematic, not only for important practical reasons (scheduling, budgeting), but because constant flux presents a challenge to maintaining a stable identity.

However, we cannot simply predict temporary workers' subjectivity from the structure of temporary employment. Individuals' differential attempts at maintaining a stable identity can reproduce or challenge unequal relations in temporary employment. Some will identify with temporary agencies and corporate clients even as they experience the negative aspects of temporary employment. Others can draw on their experiences to unveil exploitative, if interdependent, relationships. Neither of these cases is without its contradictions.

Identity fetishism, an excessive preoccupation with identity, often results in temporary workers' attempting to gain a sense of competence through a variety of means. While earlier we saw how this results in work intensification, here the focus is on how it accomplished the individualization of temporaries as subjects, the result of which is often the reproduction of power relations.

Part of each "cover story" told by temporaries is the notion that they are not "just a temp." Rather, they are an artist, a teacher, a student, an actor, an upwardly mobile yet unrecognized talent, a professional who has been laid off. Temporary workers who invoke these cover stories are not lying; rather, they are rejecting the label of temp and its associated stigma. The larger implication of these identity struggles is the individualization of temporaries. Temporaries do not feel or act as part of the group "temporaries" but feel attached to the groups they identify in their cover story. Changing the conditions of temporary employment is much less a priority for many temporaries than is getting out of temporary employment.

Still other temporaries asserted their individuality by emphasizing their upbringing as a differentiating factor between "real temporaries" and themselves.

I was raised that way, sort of compulsive. Even though you're a temp, you don't blow it off. You know and usually, especially if I were working for people I respected I didn't want to do a shoddy job just because I know how important it is. And I have a good friend who is doing a temp stint right now for somebody in the entertainment business that's just a total whack-off. And she's an out-of-work producer right now, and she's just absolutely compulsive about doing a good job, and she's carrying the ball and he's a nitwit. You run into the same

types. Just some of us were raised to believe in no matter what you're doing even if it's just for a few bucks, you just don't do a shoddy job. (Ellen Lanford, thirty-eight-year-old white woman)

These descriptions, although couched in highly individualistic terms, are imbued with class and racial understandings of what constitutes a good employee—that is, *not* a temp. Temporary employment relations value middle-class femininity and whiteness (Rogers and Henson 1997), but they do so in a way that grants those who can "do" white, middle-class femininity a reprieve from being classified as a temp. Successful "performance" of white, middle-class femininity does not result in one being praised for being a good temporary worker; rather, one is rewarded for *not* being just a temp. The pejorative label "temp" is reserved for those who, for whatever reason, do not "fit in" to the dominant corporate culture. As Ludy explains,

I would see other temps coming in that also didn't have a clue and were usually also the ones who were not used to temping or sort of undereducated in a lot of ways. They did not have a clue either of how to behave and read signals or, um, what to do to even just look busy. And a lot of them would just sit there and say, "Well, nobody's given me anything to do." And they didn't know to ask for more work. And those were the ones that would sit there with *People* magazine and say, "Can I leave early?" because there's nothing to do [laughs]. But, yeah, there were probably a few that I realized proper screening would eliminate. You know sometimes they weren't educated enough, not really brought up to understand that they were working in the white corporate world and didn't really know how to blend in. You know you don't speak

Black English on the phone; you know [you don't] chew gum; you know you don't interrupt. (Ludy Martinez, thirty-six-year-old Filipina)

Thus, socially constructed differences in class and race accomplish the further individualization of temporary workers. Those who can successfully identify as not temporary receive the added bonus of having confirmed for them their class or racial privilege. Although of Filipino descent, Ludy emphasizes her education and class standing in opposition to another "minority" group to whom she attributes a lack of education and communication skills.

Many temporary workers, the men in particular, felt stigmatized because temporary work was not seen as a "real job," which implies stable, full-time employment. The notion that "real men have real jobs" is explained by Harold Koenig:

Like they're thinkin', "Gee, what's the deal?" Shouldn't you be, I don't know, doing something else?" They never say that, but that's just me projecting that. More so now the older I get. I mean, it's like sort of fine if you're just out of school. They kind of expect you're doing this until you get a regular job. It's like I get the feeling now that they're thinking, "Why? Why? I'm suspicious of you." (Harold Koenig, twenty-nine-year-old white man)

Harold and other men reported feelings that could be characterized as masculinity struggles. For those like Harold (white, with an upper-middle-class background), the masculinity struggles seemed most intense. Working in a "feminized" occupation (secretarial and temporary employment) seemed to threaten aspects of their masculine identity. Male temporaries felt that they were perceived by others as somehow defective and lacking in character because they were not in a position of power and were not on the fast track to one. Particularly troublesome was the sporadic nature of the work. As with part-time work, temporary work is seen as viable for women, whose work still is often constructed as secondary to men's. Similarly, women's location in contingent work arrangements is often "explained" by reference to their home and family duties regardless of whether they actually have these duties. Thus, there seems to be no legitimate reason for a man to be employed temporarily, especially in secretarial work, so the identity of male workers is questioned from the outset.

Most acutely felt by the heterosexual men among the workers I spoke with was the fear of being labeled "homosexual," as their logic dictated that a man in a feminine occupation was of questionable sexual orientation. Both straight and gay men conflated sexuality and gender in their discussions of men in temporary employment. While most straight men felt the association of gay men with temporary work was problematic and stigmatizing, at least one gay man, Michael Glenn, had a different perception. By far the exception, Michael Glenn positively constructs temporary work as feminized to include gay men, whom he sees as feminized as well. Despite other problems he had with temporary employment, Michael was not troubled by this aspect of temporary work. But just as Ludy was able to confirm her class privilege at the expense of other temporaries, straight men who deride temporary employment as something beneath them, as women's work (or gay men's work), are able to confirm both their gender and sexual privilege over women and gay men at the same time that they reduce the likelihood of identification with them. While Michael Glenn's characterization of the gendered nature of temporary employment is not derisive, it *is* individualizing in

[handwritten margin note: Lock of unity fails to challenge dom. pwr. structure]

that it does not "challenge the dominant/subordinate statuses of male/female" (Rogers and Henson 1997, 223). Heterosexual men still are conceived of as problematic in temporary employment, while women's and gay men's temporary employment is naturalized rather than considered in conjunction with the low pay, low status, and lack of power of temporary workers. Thus the problems associated with temporary employment are deemed problems only as they relate to *individual* workers, and in this case individual male workers. Solutions therefore are aimed at individuals escaping temporary employment rather than transforming power relations within temporary employment.

[handwritten margin note: too indiv. focused]

So stigmatizing is temporary employment that many temporaries go so far as to hide their temporary employment experience from potential permanent employers by rewriting their résumés, as did Larry Landers:

> I don't list a lot of temporary experience. I don't like to list a lot of my temp [work]. I maybe list skills-wise. But a lot of jobs don't like temp experience, because it shows instability. And you always want to project stability. Don't show them that you've been jumping from here to here to here. Don't want to show that. They frown on that. (Larry Landers, thirty-eight-year-old African American)

In their recognition of employers' dislike of the supposed instability of temporaries, these people once again deny their membership in the ranks of temporary workers. They again constitute themselves as individuals free from the stigmatizing label of temporary employment. The need to do so derives not only from identity fetishism but real material requirements for obtaining a secure position that might otherwise be denied were they to reveal their stint of temporary work.

Despite the fact that many of the temporaries I interviewed had been at it for more than a year, and that many of them have recurring periods of temporary employment, no one actually identified himself or herself as a temporary worker. By its very definition, *temporary* is a condition that cannot be part of a solidified or stable identity. Collective identification, much less collective resistance, seems difficult at best when dealing with highly individualized subjects, a topic I investigate further at the end of this chapter.

Freedom

. . . The temporary industry and client companies try to influence temporaries' perceptions to their favor. Temporary employment is cast as an exchange relationship entered into by equal parties—the temporary and the client company are said to be "free" to "try out" each other. In fact, the temporary industry proclaims that temporary workers' freedom to leave a job is one of the greatest benefits of temporary employment. Appeals to freedom resonate with basic cultural values of agency in the United States, wherein individuals are seen as "free" to succeed or fail.

> Temping is not bad. But when you take a permanent job you're locked in. You're locked into this personality, that personality. If they don't like you, you always have to have a backup plan. Like for me, if one agency doesn't work, I call all the agencies. If one doesn't work, another one will. (Larry Landers, thirty-eight-year-old African American)

> You get to see the whole dynamics of the company, and if you really want to work there or not. Because they treat

you completely different. When you're a temp, you get all the shitty work. Excuse me. But you can always tell them, "Thank you very much, but I won't be back tomorrow." You get to see how everyone works, and you get to decide if you really want to work there or not. So temping allows me to, you know, kind of test the waters. (Doug Larson, thirty-nine-year-old white man)

I think temping is the best. Because you just say, "No more; I'm out." You know, you don't have to put up with anything. No commitment. That's the best part about temping. (Shari Jensen, thirty-three-year-old African American)

Yet few temporaries ever question this "fact." First, individuals in the United States are not legally prohibited from leaving a job when they wish. Why should this differ for temporary workers? More important, the freedom appeal is devoid of any recognition of power relations that might constrain temporaries' opportunities to use this freedom. In fact, few temporaries report ever taking advantage of their new-found ability to leave, as this quote from Shari Jensen exemplifies:

But now I ran out of unemployment; I have no choice, you know. That's why you go back to temping. But I like the no commitment, you know. I hated being a secretary. Because I don't like being told what to do. That's why I guess I like temping, because I don't have to put up with it. I can just pick up and go any-time. *But I'm not like that. I cannot do it. If I say yes, I cannot break it.* But you can al-ways give them a week or something. That's good. And you know it's short-term, so you feel good. You don't have to put up with it for a long time. (Shari Jensen, thirty-three-year-old African American; my italics)

Although the temporary workers I in-terviewed seldom took advantage of their loose employment affiliation, the possibility that they could do so was important to their understanding and appraisal of temporary employment. Despite the fact that many faced serious, material constraints on their ability to leave a temporary assignment, they did not feel locked into a situation that, if permanent, would feel oppressive to them. Temporary work provides an escape from some types of work pressure. Seeing temporary employment as an escape from the pressures of "permanent" work helps mute conflict because the negative aspects of temporary work are framed as a necessary trade-off to other types of work pressure.

In reality, temporary workers are asked to commit to the duration of each assign-ment, somewhat reducing their freedom to leave a job willy-nilly. In fact, one agency I visited went as far as to have their tempo-rary workers sign the following contract:

I, _____, understand that if I am ever employed by [Amanu-ensis Temporary Agency], it will be on a temporary, not permanent, basis. I therefore am never guaranteed continu-ous full or part time employment and my temporary association can be dis-continued at any time with no notice or explanation necessary.

I understand that if I am employed by [Amanuens[is] Temporary Agency], I am committed to complete the agreed upon assignment term. If, for any reason, I am unable to complete the as-signment, I will give [Amanuensis Tem-porary Agency], two (2) weeks written notice.

I also understand that if I do not report to work when scheduled, or fail to call to report off work before scheduled, my af-filiation with [Amanuensis Temporary Agency] will be terminated immediately.

Those temporaries who exercise their freedom to leave are generally labeled as "flakes" by clients, agencies, and other temporaries. Just as there are pressures for "regular" workers to remain in a job, temporary workers experience pressures to remain in an assignment. Leaving an assignment prior to its completion is not looked upon kindly by temporary agencies and may result in work deprivation for the temporary. Nevertheless, it was important to many temporary workers I spoke with to characterize these pressures differently from the pressures associated with permanent employment.

> On the one hand, I would like to have a permanent job. I would like to have the benefits. I'd like to have the security. I'd like to have a decent wage. But on the other hand, being a temp offers me the freedom to leave a job when I want. But you can also only be so finicky when you have to work. So, um, I would say frankly there's much more disadvantages to working temporary than there are working permanent, other than [the] freedom to not being tied down. I mean, to not have a complete commitment. That's the good thing, but not for everybody. For me it's good, but at the same time nobody has a commitment to you. They could let you go tomorrow and not tell you. So you have absolutely no security and no guarantees and no insurance and no benefits. (Albert Baxter, thirty-one-year-old white man)

Albert Baxter recognizes the limitations on his ability to leave a job, along with several other disadvantages of temporary employment. This does not, however, diminish the importance for him of being able to leave (at least in theory) an assignment to pursue other interests. In fact, he is reluctant to take on a permanent job:

> If a permanent job came to me—[and] right now I'm not looking very hard for one, not at all really—then I'd have to consider it. And consider, like, a career. I mean, my planned career is just writing, period. I'm not gonna settle for anything else. And people say, "Here's this wonderful opportunity to become an insurance broker." And I say, "No I don't think so." (Albert Baxter, thirty-one-year-old white man)

It is important to remark that Albert Baxter is not representative of temporary workers because, unlike most, he would not prefer "permanent" employment (Polivka 1996). Among the workers who did not desire a permanent job, however, Albert's reasons were not uncommon. Albert does represent a small minority of people who do not want a traditional employment arrangement. This population of workers, while it does exist, is vastly overemphasized by the temporary industry. The "freedom" sought by a few is manipulated to appear as a desire of many and benefit to all, despite mounting evidence to the contrary.

Exploitation

Some temporaries come to adopt the views of management by identifying with the cost-cutting imperatives of business and today's labor market. Yet if we re-examine the words of these temporaries, we find at least some ambivalence toward the temporary industry line. Apparently, efforts at discursive control are far from complete.

> You get in, like I said before. And I think that is the only reason people are doing it. And employers are reducing their overhead by hiring a lot more temps. It's working out for both, *but I think you'll see some type of revolt against temping in the next ten years. People won't be able to afford*

to do it. They want more than that. Right now it's a stopgap measure for the people not working and for the companies strapped financially. (Doug Larson, thirty-nine-year-old white man; my italics)

Considering comments like this, we need to question whether efforts at discursive control are successful at all. Temporaries often reject industry discourses even as they invoke them, and they create a counterdiscourse out of lived experiences. One of the temporary workers I interviewed, Linda Mejia, told me that her extensive experience with a number of agencies helped her to know how they work, and what she could actually get from them if she pushed hard enough. But this knowledge does not come easily. In fact, this knowledge may be hidden intentionally from temporary workers. Agencies are well-served by making their actions (such as construction of pay rates and methods of work allocation) invisible. Temporary workers with less experience (as temporaries) feel mystified when confronted with the barriers to knowledge constructed by the temporary industry (for instance, prohibition of discussing pay rates, lack of reasons for assignment termination, client evaluation of the temporary's performance, and agency markups).

Ironically, increasing the extent and duration of temporary employment may help to reveal the exploitative nature of the temporary employment relationship, which relies on transitoriness both to control workers and to obfuscate that control. Thus, one of the contradictions of temporary work is that while it is a stream of "unfair" experiences designed to keep the worker in the dark, the longer the stream becomes, the more likely the worker is to develop a critical understanding of the organization of temporary work. Recall Doug Larson's account in

which he feels taken advantage of because he is working for seven dollars an hour. These feelings gave rise to a budding sense of unfairness.

Doug believed that after his initial stint, he would be granted a pay increase, which never materialized. While he does not cast temporary employment as "exploitation" per se, he does question its fairness. Although Doug was unable to clearly articulate just what it was that bothered him about temporary employment, it seems obvious that he was upset about the failure of existing work structures to accommodate workers' needs for flexibility without workers bearing all the costs. And while Doug continually emphasized the need for the freedom inherent in temporary employment to pursue his acting career, he unfortunately did not find his ideal solution in temporary employment.

In addition to Lucy Martinez's other temporary employment experiences, she temped for a friend in San Francisco. Because of Lucy's vast experience, her friend asked her to help size up the competition for temporary workers:

I remember sitting down doing a little project for my friend Donna and comparing what a word processor was getting at different agencies because I'd been with so many of them. And I had to tell her, "You're on the low end." You know, this same job is posted over at this lady's agency and it's $11 an hour, and you're $9.50. That's ridiculous. And I remember going to certain agencies that I was registered with and, um, balking at going to certain places temping saying I've worked for another agency, and they paid me at least ten bucks and you're offering me eight. That's ridiculous. And they were, like, "Oh, you have an attitude." But I felt like I at least had to say that because they were saying,

[handwritten: Is this all a type of emotional labor?]

"Well, we pay whatever the market will bear." Well, what do you know about the *market?* (Ludy Martinez, thirty-six-year-old Filipina)

Ludy learned that pay scales are not as scientifically constructed as agencies claim them to be. In fact, Ludy questions the legitimacy of the very idea of market determination of wages. As she recounted this story to me, she laughed and emphasized the word *market* with disdain, as if to dispute its very meaning. Later, Ludy told me, "Temporaries definitely can be treated like a commodity. And even when they're treating you well, you know that they're treating you well as like a good business practice as opposed to actually having respect for you or caring about getting you a job." (Ludy Martinez, thirty-six-year-old Filipina)

[handwritten margin note: Empli start to question system after doing offender]

Although Albert Baxter described feeling exploited and actually used the word *exploited,* he carefully qualified his expression of these feelings in terms of his "freedom" to choose:

I know that I definitely do feel exploited. I don't like it, but it's also a position I've chosen to put myself in. And I can see that I can leave it. Whereas some other people cannot if they don't have the skills and ability. (Albert Baxter, thirty-one-year-old white man)

Once again, the construction of temporary employment as freedom from something else potentially obscures what might otherwise be understood as exploitative.

Don Birch, an "elite" temporary with the Yale degree who thought he had successfully negotiated a dollar-an-hour increase for an assignment. When he received his paycheck, the increase was nowhere to be found. He told me that before this incident he realized that relations between temporaries and agencies were "inherently unequal"; however, this experience prompted him to characterize the temporary industry in the following way:

It's fraught with problems and exploitation, and it's inherently an unequal, anti-labor exercise in which, you know, you don't get any benefits and you're exploited. You're just literally exploited. And it's a total step backwards. It's . . . very destructive for families and for people who are trying to plan and look longer term. (Don Birch, twenty-four-year-old white man)

While most temporary workers did not describe their feelings as pointedly as Don, many characterized the structure of the economic relationship between temporaries and their agencies as "a rip off." Cindy Carson was upset when she learned that temporaries doing the same work earned a higher hourly wage than she:

[handwritten margin note: Temps recognized their exploitation]

I got really angry with them recently. I mean, I'm not making that much money there, but then again the clerical positions don't make that much. But this is the first time that I've been doing temp work in my life that I feel like I'm getting ripped off. I never felt that way before. I felt like I was making an adequate wage. So I asked for a raise. . . . I thought I put it in a very diplomatic fashion. I said to this one woman who was always there handing out the checks, "Oh, can you find me a higher-paying assignment?" I thought that would be a way to say it. . . . And the next assignment they sent me on was two days, and I got fifty cents an hour more, which I was really happy about at the time, you know. Then . . . this office manager gets on the phone and says, "We have an assignment today; it pays seven dollars an hour. Do you want it?" She was really snippy with me, and I knew that this other lady had probably said to her that

I wanted a raise. And I said, "OK, fine, I'll go there." And it was only supposed to be for a few weeks. So then I was there for three and a half months, and I just got really, really angry. I became more and more angry. (Cindy Carson, thirty-eight-year-old white woman)

Cindy's "raise" was short-lived, and her feelings of exploitation grew. When I asked her if there was anything she would change about temporary employment, she discussed the pay structure at length, citing profit margin and capriciousness as problems with the current system.

I would change the pay structure because I think it should be set. Like, I think they shouldn't be getting any more than like 25 percent of what you're making. Something like that maximum. And then the second thing would be some sort of system where if you're really having a problem that you can feel comfortable saying, "Well, they're saying this to me, and I'm really stressed out." . . . [There should be a system] where you won't lose the job. But, I mean, my main concern is the money, because I think it shouldn't be a barter system. Like, they're paying some people more to do the same job. . . . I'm really angry about that. I think it should be if you're superior then, OK, give you fifty cents an hour more or a dollar an hour more. But there shouldn't be this huge range. . . . They bill the company; that's another thing. That office manager told me how much they were charging for me. . . . It was really giving me the creeps. They were charging them $10.99, and I was getting $7. And I was *really* angry. Because I think they have a set fee. . . . We charge $10 for people to come empty trash cans, we charge $10.99 for filing, we charge $12 for phones. And then what they do is they

kind of play with the temps and give them what they think will pay. When they ask you to write down the lowest you'll take, that's all you get. (Cindy Carson, thirty-eight-year-old white woman)

Cindy's and the others' accounts of the exploitative nature of the temporary employment relationship exemplify the process through which any apparent consensus is broken: "When the self-defeating or self-denying nature of the practice is experienced most acutely, conflict occurs" (Sturdy 1992, 141). Discursive controls fail most dramatically when actual experiences sharply diverge from attempts to shape consciousness.

Knowing the Score

How, then, can we explain the lack of action in light of the awareness of exploitation articulated by so many of the temporary workers interviewed? Simply put, knowledge can be a double-edge sword. In the scenarios depicted in this chapter, knowledge enabled temporary workers to perceive and articulate exploitative employment relations. Knowledge, however, can result in a type of organizational "outflanking" of temporary workers, which prevents them from resisting. Specifically, knowing the high cost of resistance often prevents temporary workers from taking any action. For example, knowledge of the financial arrangement between agencies and clients makes temporary workers aware of the pecking order that places the client well above the worker. Clients, not workers, pay the temporary agency, and therefore, the loss of a client and any anticipated repeat business poses more of a threat to the success of the agency than the loss of a single, expendable temporary worker. This is particularly true in an area where competition among temporary agencies is high at the same time that unemployment is high. Thus, knowledge as well as ignorance can temper resistance.

Contrary to popular theories that find temporaries acting impulsively and irrationally, temporary workers often weigh all the potential consequences of resistance. With the knowledge that temporary agencies have no obligation to their workers, Cindy Carson struggled with her decision to publicly express anger to her agency supervisor. Cindy was sure she would lose her job after she "stomped out of the office," but she did not. While she chose to express her anger in this case, Cindy remarks that in every other similar situation, she did nothing because of the knowledge of the tenuous nature of her position:

> But I got so desperate the past couple years that I just put up with it. It was awful, but I used to be very desperate. But when you're not desperate, I think you do the right thing. But when you're desperate you can't always. (Cindy Carson, thirty-eight-year-old white woman)

Cindy no longer characterizes herself as desperate, because she is only partially dependent on temporary employment for her income. She has had a relatively steady stint of part-time employment in the evenings, which she is able to supplement with temporary employment to provide an adequate, if not substantial, income.

One of the most savvy temporaries I interviewed, Ludy, expressed how a veiled threat from an agency prevented her from complaining about any problems in her assignments. Eventually, Ludy even refrained from mentioning clients' requests to alter her time cards, a practice that is clearly against agencies' policies. She understood that the small loss the agencies would experience from the alteration of her time card was insignificant when compared to the permanent loss of that client.

Thus, knowledge of the structure of interests in temporary clerical employment, while theoretically empowering, can also limit resistance when that knowledge also highlights the marginal status of individual workers in the temporary employment triad. Despite agencies' avowals that temporaries are valuable assets, clients and agencies are clearly the dominant parties in the transaction. Temporaries may be valuable assets, but they are aware that they often are replaceable valuable assets.

Similarly, knowledge of the individualization of temporary workers leads many temporary workers to conclude that resistance is futile.

> Obviously I wouldn't get involved in trying to change it. I mean, I'm getting out of this now. There are some things that would be nice to change, but I don't even know any other temps. I guess laws could be changed, but people are in and out of this business. (Jean Masters, thirty-four-year-old African American)
>
> Who is looking out for the temp's interest? The agency isn't looking out for the worker's interest. The business isn't looking out for the worker's interest. So I should start a temp union! I wouldn't want to organize that. Jimmy Hoffa of the temps. No, no, no. No one stays in one place. You all have your own thing going. No way. (Doug Larson, thirty-nine-year-old white man)

. . . . With few means of conducting collective resistance, temporary workers inevitably emphasize leaving temporary employment over improving it. Many personal acts of resistance, including sabotage, do take place, but only a few attempts at collectively improving material conditions of employment ever surface. Most of temporaries' efforts at resistance are in the discursive realm, debunking temporary industry myths, shaking off stereotypes, and reaffirming one's identity often at the expense of other temporaries. In short, there is much evidence here to support the assertion that "resistance against perceivedly overwhelming odds tends to be through existential and symbolic gestures" (Clegg 1994, 294). Thus temporary workers' preoccupation with rejecting the stigma of temporary employment does not come from some inherent personal need, but rather is a byproduct of the highly asymmetrical power relations characteristic of temporary clerical employment. At the same time, this preoccupation can reproduce the very relations that prompted the preoccupation to begin with. Consequently, the knowledge of one's odds of success limits much resistance to the symbolic realm, where identity fetishism acts to individualize subjects.

Although many, but not necessarily all, temporary clerical workers feel exploited in their employment relationship, only a low incidence of collective resistance is evident. Temporary employment produces individuals who, in trying to secure a stable identity in opposition to the stigmatized "temp" identity, may help perpetuate the status quo. Their knowledge of the power imbalance in temporary employment outflanks their resistance before it begins. Gender, race, and class shoot through and surround individualized resistance when privileged positions are confirmed as a means of solidifying one's identity against and at the expense of the "other." How then, might temporary workers better their situation collectively?

These data show the challenges that potential organizers face with regard to the subjectivity of temporary workers. The data also demonstrate, however, the power of experience in revealing the asymmetries in temporary employment. Although most clerical temporaries seem too overwhelmed by their circumstances to take action themselves, if presented with realistic possibilities of successful labor organizing, they might be open to union membership. Few temporaries might lead, but many might follow.

Perhaps the struggle needs to be waged simultaneously on the symbolic and material fronts. To constitute temporary workers collectively instead of as individuals, organizers might reclaim the fluid identity of the "temp" and give it the dignity it lacks, providing temporary workers with the legitimacy to demand social justice. Reclaiming the fluid identity of "temp" may enable temporary workers to . . . recognize their common plight despite their differences, real or constructed.

∞ **READING** 34 ∞

American Untouchables

Homeless Scavengers in San Francisco's Underground Economy

Teresa Gowan

An early morning at Bryant Salvage, a Vietnamese recycling business, finds a variety of San Francisco's scavengers converging to sell their findings. Vehicle after vehicle enters the yard to be weighed on the huge floor scale before dumping its load in the back; ancient pickup trucks with wooden walls, carefully loaded laundry carts, canary Cadillacs stuffed to overflow with computer paper, the shopping carts of homeless men, a 1950s ambulance carrying newspaper, and even the occasional gleaming new truck. The homeless men unload their towers of bottles and cardboard while young Latino van recyclers shout jokes across them. Middle-aged Vietnamese women in jeans and padded jackets buzz around on forklifts or push around great tubs full of bottles and cans, stopping occasionally to help elderly people with their laundry carts. The van recyclers repeatedly honk their horns at the homeless guys to get out of the way. The homeless recyclers, silently methodical in their work, rarely respond.

Equivalent scenes can be found in Jakarta, San Salvador, or Calcutta. The collection and sale of other people's trash is a common means of survival for very poor people all over the world. At the moment

Abridgment of "American Untouchables: Homeless Scavengers in San Francisco's Underground Economy," by Teresa Gowan, presented at the Regular Session on the Informal Economy, ASA 1995. Reprinted by permission of the author.

full-time scavenging is most prevalent in poorer countries, where a huge variety of people collect, sort out and clean rags, paper, cardboard, metals, and glass, often living on the dumps where they work. They either sell these materials for recycling, or directly recycle them into new products themselves. The United States and Western Europe have had their own share of trash pickers. The wharf rats and the tinkers, the rag and bone men, the mudlarks and the ragpickers, all lived off working the garbage of industrialization until the early twentieth century. However, in these countries welfare capitalism eventually absorbed most poor people into the waged working class, leaving only the formal municipal garbage workers and an insignificant scrap economy supplied by eccentric junk lovers, schoolchildren, and the occasional part-time cardboard or can recycler.

Trash is back. Over the last ten years the US recycling industry has mushroomed on both the formal and informal levels, taking the form of a double tiered system which relies heavily on informal labor for sorting and collection, while reprocessing is dominated by large capital enterprises. Informal labor in recycling falls into two distinct groups: the general population who sort their own household recycling for free (sometimes required by law), and those who collect and sort in order to sell. This paper is concerned with the second group. . . .

Informal Recycling in the Broader Political Economy

Homeless men are the most immediately visible group of San Francisco's recyclers, as they work in the daytime and collect from unsorted public and private trash. Making only a few dollars a load, many recyclers work more than 12 hours a day, sometimes taking in two or even three loads of 100–200 pounds each. However, the greatest volume of informal recycling is brought in by the van recyclers. Latinos and Asian Americans, many of them first generation and undocumented immigrants, use vans to collect large quantities of cardboard and bottles. Known by their competitors in the city's official recycling company as the "mosquito fleet," the van recyclers work at night and in the early morning, preempting the weekly runs of the curbside recycling program trucks or collecting the boxes and bottles put out by bars and restaurants every night. Small numbers of African American and white car-drivers specialize in computer paper and newsprint. Yet another significant group are elderly people who gather unobtrusively from public trash using plastic bags which they usually consolidate into laundry carts when they go to the recycling companies.

The increases in volume reported by the recycling business is repeated in the accounts of homeless recyclers. Clarence, who has recycled in the southern part of the So-Ma district since 1991, says that there are now 25–30 men working a patch that used to only support five of them. Sam reckoned that there were five times more recyclers in the 24th Street area than when he began five years ago.

The Loss of Formal Work

The increase of informal recycling has occurred in the context of the radical transformations of the country's political economy since the 1970s. These changes include a sharp decrease in industrial jobs, especially union ones, a scaling down of formalized relationships between the state and economic enterprises, and a general decentralization of economic activity.

California suffered the effects of restructuring later than the older manufacturing regions of the United States. The state was insulated from the manufacturing collapse of the early 1980s by its disproportionate share of defense contracts, its large share of booming computer and bio-tech companies, and a real-estate frenzy financed by the spectacular but ephemeral successes of the LA-based junk-bond market. The inability of these industries to really sustain the bulk of California's working class is now revealed. Working class Californians are suffering from a prolonged and severe recession, losing 1.5 million jobs in 1990–2, including 1/4 of all manufacturing jobs. Construction, always the best bet for unskilled male labor, has practically stopped—the rate of housing starts is the lowest since the Second World War. Within San Francisco the very disjunction between the collapse of heavy industry and the still booming informational industries has added to the problems of blue collar workers by bringing in large numbers of younger people with high disposable incomes who are willing and able to pay increasingly fantastic rents and house prices.

The experience of the recyclers I've interviewed suggests that the rise of recycling is at least in part a direct product of this job crisis. The new full-time scavengers started recycling as a last resort, after failing to find better paid work. Victoriano, a Mexican van recycler, described how he and several other van recyclers moved to California with the idea of getting construction work, but have had to settle for recycling instead. Anita, an elderly recycler, started the work when her daughter's data entry job was cut back to 20 hours a week.

For the homeless recyclers the process of moving into recycling was more drawn out and complex, given that they only noticed this line of work after they had already become homeless. The story tends to be that the multiple economic and emotional strains of long-term unemployment propelled these men on to the street. While they didn't even consider cart recycling before, once they were homeless recycling became "making the best of it," a partial solution to both extreme financial hardship and the indignities of their condition. The stories of Bill, Jordan, and Victor are typical in this regard. Bill previously worked for PG&E as a mechanic for 17 years, but was laid off in cutbacks in the fall of 1988. Jordan had a relatively well-paid union job as a forklift operator in Oakland before his company closed down. According to both of these men, unemployment transformed a controllable alcohol habit into a major problem, their families left them, and they became homeless. Victor, a skilled carpenter who moved here from New Mexico in 1994, spent six months unsuccessfully looking for construction work before ending up sleeping under the 101 freeway and recycling.

The Contraction of Welfare Benefits

The devastating effect of the job losses on the current Californian recession are intensified by their coincidence with severe welfare cuts on both the local and federal levels. While laid-off workers in Northern and Western Europe are still at least partially protected by social democratic safety nets, Americans left unemployed by the vast job losses of the last few years have had only minimal help from the welfare system, once their unemployment eligibility has run out.

Conditions have always been harsh for Americans living on benefits. However, the political and economic restructuring of the last 20 years has included a substantial reduction of the standard of living for the disabled, the unemployed, and their dependents. The US welfare system's historical principle of "less eligibility" requires that welfare benefits pay less than work, with the argument that people will only work when they can make more by working than by claiming benefits. Union-busting, capital flight, and the subsequent mushrooming of temporary work and subcontracting combined to drive the going wage for the working poor below the existing level of welfare benefits.[1] . . .

Welfare contraction has not been coupled with looser work rules for those still receiving benefits. As a result, the benefit cuts force recipients into participation in the underground economy. Elderly people without family support or private pension schemes, single adults on disability, women with children on AFDC, and above all single able-bodied adults on welfare ("General Assistance" in California), simply cannot get by without supplementing their income through other means. Mary, a woman with bad arthritis who brings in about 70 lbs. of recycling every morning, started recycling after her SSI entitlement was reduced. . . . Most homeless recyclers are only eligible for GA, which comes to $345 a month, barely enough to cover a month's rent in a welfare hotel. The welfare system therefore simultaneously requires claimants to work and forces this work underground by surveilling and penalizing any work for money in the formal economy.

The "Capital Strategy" Analysis

For working class people caught between unemployment and welfare contraction, recycling has become an important subsistence strategy, attracting increasing numbers of homeless men, recent Filipino, Chinese and Latino immigrants, Southeast Asian refugees on welfare, and poor elderly people.

Through which wide-angle lens should we view this booming underground economy in trash? The dominant practice in the informal economy literature has been to see the growing underground economy as just one more element of the systemic offensive of capital against organized labor and government regulation. In this model, the formal and informal economies are not in competition but instead form interlocking systems which combine to maximize the profits of large capital. Castells and Portes clearly articulate this perspective when they describe the informal economy as "a new form of control characterized by the disenfranchisement of a large sector of the working class, often with the acquiescence of the state."[2] . . .

Castells and Portes' conception of informal economic activity as a capital strategy effectively explains the case of the recycling industry, where informal "production" is clearly dependent on a close relationship with large capital. The recycling collected in the informal sector eventually ends up in the hands of large corporations, as reprocessing technology is too expensive for small capital. Informal recyclers, therefore, function as essential intermediaries between consumers and capital, with thousands of informal recyclers in the Bay Area feeding perhaps a hundred small recycling companies, which in turn feed a smaller number of large buyers who export fiber, metal, and glass all over the world. In this globalized industry bottles, cans, and cardboard collected on neighborhood streets are more likely to end up in Asia or Australia than in local recycled products.[3]

Control by large capital is apparent on the local level. San Francisco's garbage giant, Norcal, dominates both the legal and the informal economies in trash. Norcal holds the city contract for both garbage collection and curbside recycling. The company also owns the two largest recycling companies in the city, both of which overwhelmingly buy from the professional scavengers of the informal economy.

It is unlikely that Norcal's official collection company would find it profitable to take over the frequent and comprehensive collection performed by informal recyclers across the city. Their weekly curbside program is too infrequent for small restaurants and bars with limited storage space, whereas the informal recyclers have a nightly circuit. In addition, the homeless and elderly recyclers get much of their material from unsorted trash which would end up as garbage. Through its recycling companies, Norcal still ends up with most of the recycling collected by the informals. "What do you say," laughs Samuel Stewart II of the city recycling department, "yes, we still make money from it!" In practice the informals provide a recycling labor force which is cheaper than the union workers of Norcal's curbside program, and greatly increases the company's volume of recycling.

The "capital strategy" implementation of San Francisco's recycling industry is therefore persuasive on the purely economic level. Rather than competing with formal industry, the informal recyclers serve as a cheap collection service for a few large companies, primarily Norcal's vertically integrated conglomerate. These companies would not have been able to rely on the efforts of the informal recyclers without so many other businesses shrinking their formal operations, creating a "fourth world" of workers permanently pushed off the bottom of the formal labor market and only partially supported by the state. Recycling is therefore both typical of capital restructuring and dependent on it at the same time.

There are, however, serious problems with the "capital strategy" model. The argument tends towards functionalism, jumping too quickly from what capital needs to what capital gets. I now turn to my participant observation with homeless recyclers, in hopes of showing that such an assumption strips away the living center of social life, thereby obscuring the processes by which informal economic arrangements are sustained and reproduced from day to day.[4]

Meanings of Recycling for Homeless Men

Even for men on the street, recycling is a choice, although it is a choice made within severe constraints. Homeless people are doing all sorts of things to get by: panhandling, washing car windows or shop windows, drug dealing, selling the Street Sheet paper, doing the service agency shuffle, performing music or poetry, stealing, selling clothes or books, and turning tricks.

All these occupations vary to some extent along the lines of race and gender. The typical recycler is a man in his 30s or 40s, most often African American, but with large minorities of whites and Latinos. The racial breakdown of recyclers is therefore not noticeably dissimilar from that of the general homeless population, although there are perhaps a few more white men. Gender, on the other hand, is extremely skewed. Out of hundreds of homeless recyclers on the San Francisco scene I have encountered only four women, all classically "butch," with a muscular and taciturn self-presentation. The two I know have long histories of doing male-dominated jobs. One of them used to be a traffic cop, the other a van driver. Recycling is almost exclusively a man's job. In general there are still many more men than women on the street.[5] However, the extreme scarcity of female recyclers is better explained by the gendered nature of the work. There are, after all, several homeless women who walk around with their husbands and boyfriends as they work; however, they studiously ignore the process of recycling,

rarely even touching the cart, let alone actually doing any dumpster diving. While recycling can be made to fit certain masculinities, it repulses women with mainstream conceptions of femininity. One woman selling clothes on the street described recycling as a filthy job which "no woman should have to do. I'd rather stand in line all day."

If anything is clear from my field work it is that even for these most socially excluded and degraded informal workers, their work couldn't be further from the analytically empty space of hand to mouth "survival." Despite the low pay, many of the homeless recyclers really get into their work with enthusiasm. They do not express the sullen resentment of people acting only out of economic compulsion—a self-presentation which is overwhelmingly in evidence in social welfare establishments. The work is inherently hard. Clarence, a very strong but not particularly obsessive recycler, works 7 or 8 hours daily, dragging two carts tied together for about nine miles and collecting 250 pounds of recycling for his average $20 receipt. Bill the Mechanic has put in at least 16 hours on the days I've spent with him, barely ever stopping for a break. His daily income of under $30 works out at about $1.80 per hour of intense physical labor. Yet recyclers often push themselves beyond reasonable goals, working obsessively fast and energetically. Keeping their carts on the road for speed they steam along, leaning hard into their loads and darting searching glances from side to side. Several recyclers I know work for 12 or more hours a day, and it's not unusual to find lonely carts full of recycling whose owners have passed out from dehydration and exhaustion.

The recyclers are also eager to display their great efforts to other people. Sam, a middle-aged white man who died by the side of his recycling cart earlier this year, was always concerned with asserting the validity of his work to others. The first time I ever met him he pointedly told me a story of an argument with a "resident" the night before. "Hey, keep the noise down, I've got to *work* in the morning," the man had shouted out of a window. "What do you think I'm doing," Sam had shouted in return. "They just don't think, you know," he said in retrospect. "They think we do this for fun or something. I work hard, I clear up the neighborhood. Don't beg, don't steal, don't deal drugs. You'd think people could be civil to me." Although Sam was unusual in his willingness to fight back at housed people, the same eagerness to impress the serious nature of their work on others is standard among the recyclers. Their physical movements themselves have elements of mime. Like the superhard stare of the gang-banger or cop, the obsessively workaholic self-presentation of many recyclers suggests how much they have to prove by *how* they do their work. We are already a long way from the simple economic self-preservation implied by the capital strategy model.

Why should the homeless recyclers be so emotionally involved in a job which is physically exhausting, low paid, and most of all, significantly stigmatized by much of the general population as not only disgusting but akin to stealing? To get at this question we need to take the experience of homelessness seriously, not only as an indication of extreme economic hardship, but as an extraordinary dehumanizing and frightening location on the American social map.

The Dominant Constructions of Homelessness

The recyclers are fighting a formidable and ancient set of discourses which set up homeless people as powerful symbols of deviance and decay. These can be simplified into two dominant strands which I call the exclusion discourse and the social welfare discourse.

The exclusion discourse sets up homelessness as a representation of fundamental and threatening outsiderness. Here homelessness is characterized by madness, the rejection of rules, and general failure or refusal to control the physical and emotional manifestations of the animal self. The disproportionately large number of African-Americans who are homeless adds in three centuries worth of white race-think which places people with dark skin somewhere on the border between culture and nature, human and animal. Through this lens people who are not homeless intuitively attribute disgusting and irrational impulses to homeless people. In the case of recyclers, the symbolic connection of homelessness and trash is often so powerful that others don't require any rational explanation for their dumpster diving activities at all. One of the bartenders I interviewed seemed surprised at the idea of homeless recyclers selling the bottles they collect every night from his bar. "Oh yes, I suppose they do sell them—I've never really thought about it," he said.

The exclusion discourse has recently taken on a new intensity. As long as homeless people were relatively rare, they could safely symbolize intemperance, dirt, and savagery without being considered a real threat. But with the huge growth in homelessness since the early 1980s, the meaning of homeless people in public space is in the process of reinterpretation. No longer isolated *representations* of disorder, the exclusion discourse represents the "new homelessness" as a full-scale *invasion* by disruption, madness, dirt, criminality, and free-roaming idleness. Exclusive practices against homeless people have become more hostile and the use of institutional force has intensified. Local politicians, police departments, and chambers of commerce have responded to the appearance of large numbers of extremely poor people who have nowhere to disappear to by redefining public space as private space with selective access for people who don't look poor. In the same commercial strips where "consumers" are encouraged to "browse" and "linger," homeless people are moved on, cited, and arrested. In the last year, San Francisco police have issued 15,000 tickets under the "Matrix" program for "encampment," "aggressive panhandling," "urinating in public" or "obstructing freedom of movement."

The exclusion discourse attacks homeless people as a threat to the shared values of the wider society. In contrast, the degrading practices of the welfare agencies set them up as incompetent victims. Welfare and health agencies move to analyze and tame the people outside by curing the poor of their problems and reincorporating them into housed society. In this kinder discourse, the problem of homelessness is now a pitiful state entered involuntarily, and the solution is a technical question of how to best help the vulnerable poor rehabilitate themselves. Homelessness represents not a free space but a pathetic and mundane condition. The dangerous, even visionary madness and hedonistic abandon portrayed in the exclusion discourse are contained and tamed by the social welfare discourse's mechanistic categories of involuntary mental illness, social disconnection, and substance abuse.

The American social welfare discourse is profoundly individualistic. Inability to prosper is an individual failure, stemming from personal deficiencies. For example, any analysis of a homeless person's economic activity focuses on how they consume resources, rather than how they produce value. Although agencies may recognize that a single person especially cannot live on GA alone, money-earning activity is uniformly classified as deviance rather than subsistence. By setting up "the problem of poverty" in this way the social welfare discourse draws a curtain over the self-sustaining (and self-defining) parts of poor people's lives.

Fighting Hostile Images of "the Homeless"

What both the exclusion discourse and the social welfare discourse have in common is their assertion that the state of homelessness is but an external representation of a profound internal difference from the rest of society. The response of the homeless recyclers is to argue through their work that they are neither strange nor evil nor incompetent, but just decent working men down on their luck. Rejecting both the criminality and insanity attributed to them by the exclusion discourse and the feminizing picture of pathetic incompetence and vulnerability created by the social welfare discourse, recyclers aggressively assert their normality, hard work, competence, and self-sufficiency.

Recyclers often complain of the indignities of social welfare institutions. Although few go so far as to quit the welfare system completely, recyclers turn their back on their status as welfare clients and embrace an identity based on their work. Differentiating themselves strongly from "stiffs" and "winos," recyclers are not heavy users of soup kitchens or shelters, only moving inside if they get sick or the weather hits freezing. Many would agree with Jordan: "I hate the shelters, don't like being around all the bums. It's depressing. You can't keep any self-respect."

For those who have spent long years in prison, dealing with the welfare system takes on an added significance. After doing eight years inside in the 1980s, James, a white man in his early forties, has turned his back on what he calls the "poverty system" completely. "When you've been in the joint, shit, you've done your time and you don't want to do any more. I'm a citizen . . . (sigh). Dealin' with the welfare and the hotels, it's like another sentence, it really is. I have to go through that any more? No. It's about time for life, real life." I asked him if recycling was real life. He laughed. "Well, that's a question. Mm. Yes, yes it is . . . it's *more* of a life anyway. You do your own thing, you know." After looking life in the eye from both locations James has decided that he prefers recycling and sleeping rough to living in the hotels and spending long hours in service agency lines. In defiance of the wider society's stigmatization of homelessness he insists that the recycling life allows him to be a man worthy of respect.

Rejecting the social welfare construction of the homeless man as a pathetic dependent, recyclers use their work to demonstrate that they are both self-sufficient and competent. Some emphasize physical strength and effort, others formal knowledge and resourcefulness. Those with technical education will often apply it to their work. Dobie is an African American recycler who works the prosperous Richmond neighborhood. He has customized a big cart, adding wheels with real tires and inner tubes. He demands respect for his work, striding along in the middle of the road, holding up traffic with imperious hand signals. Like Bill the Mechanic, Dobie applies technical concepts to the haulage aspects of recycling. Bill explains the best angle to hold your cart in relation to the road using math formulas. Dobie blinds with science in his discussions of the mechanics of weight distribution and cart design.

The recyclers are equally concerned with struggling against the exclusion discourse's representations of homelessness as criminality, madness, and disorder. Recyclers uniformly pride themselves on living as much within the law as is possible for a homeless person. Many people say explicitly that recycling is a way for them to do an honest day's work, without having to hustle or cheat. At the extreme is a person like Clarence, an African American man in his late thirties who had a desk job in the army for several years. Clarence sends in every receipt he gets to General Assistance, and will not touch the dumpsters rented out by the

Norcal recycling company. Sam, who usually dropped by every couple of days, avoided me for weeks out of embarrassment over a small loan he was unable to repay.

A major priority for most recyclers is to build regular, exclusive relationships with suppliers in businesses and apartment buildings. Apart from the obvious benefits of stabilizing income, such connections are important points of pride, ways to convince themselves and others that people who are not homeless rely on their services and trust them to keep to a routine. These relationships are often referred to in formal business language: "I try not to default on my schedule," says Dobie. "I've got several long-standing accounts in the Castro area," says Jordan.

Relationships with suppliers make recyclers feel that they can claim to be part of "the community," rather than outside. To be seen to get on with one another is equally important. The exclusion discourse pictures homeless people as living outside rules and social restraint, acting on impulse. Two bartenders who refused to let homeless recyclers take their bottles both explained their decisions by their wish to avoid fights. "See, that would cause fights. We can't have them fighting outside the bar, it's bad for business," said one man. Neither of them had seen a fight between recyclers—but this is how they expected homeless people to behave.

Knowing that others are likely to see them in this way, recyclers strongly reject suggestions that they compete with each other for resources. Rather than fighting over scraps, recyclers treat each other as solidaristic blue collar workers. "There's no shortage, we don't need to be competing" is the accepted wisdom. It's not unusual to hear men who are only superficial acquaintances comparing their night's work after they have sold their load, telling each other where they found the best stuff. "Well, a man wouldn't just take that information and go and clean up ahead of me," Sam explained. "I mean, well, he would be embarrassed." Even Clarence, who has big plans for expanding into van recycling, and thinks of himself as an "entrepreneurial dude," puts group solidarity before financial gain. A couple of years ago he was working the area around where he lives too intensively and some of the older men asked him to cool off a bit. "Come on, Clarence, a man needs a smoke now and then." "And that was cool," says Clarence. "I don't want to be getting in anyone else's way. There's plenty out there for everyone."

Another way that the recyclers reject the antisocial characteristics attributed to them by the exclusion discourse is by forging a strict separation between work and leisure. They are acutely aware that the "unemployed" man becomes marked out from "decent" working class men when the crucial masculine work/leisure distinction blurs into the more ambiguous state of "hanging out." The recyclers' stigmatization as homeless people and their lack of privacy for leisure time combine to create a presumption of guilt—any moment of rest is liable to be interpreted by others as indication that they are a "bum." Many respond to this problem by hiding away alone in secluded space when they are not working. Others create clear spatial and temporal breaks between "work" and "leisure" by alternating vigorous work with a scheduled "breakfast break" or "lunch-hour" where they abandon their carts to socialize, eat, or drink in parks or street corners. One group of younger and more sociable African Americans in the So-Ma area regularly get together to barbecue and drink on a Friday or Saturday night. "We're single men, you know. We like to party."

Who Is Attracted to Recycling?

Men move towards recycling not just because it provides a way to demonstrate certain qualities, but also because it is the informal job they are best *able* to do. The majority of the homeless recyclers in my sample have a substantial history of stable blue-collar employment and only hit skid row life in their 30s or later. This kind of life-history tends to produce a man who is either uncomfortable or inexperienced with using his "personality" for direct economic gain. Socialized as a routinized blue collar worker, the typical recycler finds it difficult to change himself into a hustler, even an uncriminalized hustler such as a car washer or "street sheet" vendor. Victor describes himself as "an old-fashioned guy. I'm not real sociable. This (recycling) suits me because, in general I mean, no one bothers you much, you can get your pay without having to bullshit about it." Victor's self-contained, taciturn masculinity was sustainable, perhaps even essential in the lower-middle-class, Latino community where he spent most of his previous life. Now that he is homeless his refusal to take on a more communicative, more subordinate role has become a luxury he can afford by doing recycling.

Recycling therefore gives people an opportunity of making a living which is culturally and often spatially removed from the usual walkways of ghetto life. While this chance to make an honest buck outside of the ghetto economy is most clearly welcomed by men who feel profoundly "away from home" on skid row, recycling also appeals to cons and hustlers looking for a change. Spike spent two years stealing from cars with his best buddy Valentino, but now they are using recycling to keep straight:

> I've changed, don't want to get in trouble any more. I got one felony, I don't intend to get the other two. But I don't want to do that shit anyway. This is better. I like recycling. It's real interesting what you find out there when you put your mind to it. And you're not doin', anyone any harm.

Those recyclers who work the most strenuously tend to be men who previously held long-lasting and decently paid semi-skilled or skilled jobs in the formal economy. Many of them are white, but by no means exclusively. These mostly older men are more intense about their work, and rarely sociable with other recyclers. Clarence, who is a charitable sort of guy, says, "It's not that they're alienated or anything . . . they're just doin' their route, no time to chat." I disagree. My impression is that those men who have achieved some part of the American dream but then lost it find their homeless state a continual source of pain and shame. As a result they can't get much comfort from others in the same position. Only by totally immersing themselves in their recycling work can they feel that they are still men in the way they learned to think of manhood in their formative years.

The almost obsessive effort that these recyclers put into their work becomes understandable when you realize that every heave of the cart is a blow against the ever-present image of the welfare bum. This helps to explain why Bill the Mechanic, who has fallen from the prosperity of a suburban ranch house and two cars, works every waking hour; why his brother Sam worked himself to death on the job at 48.

Using Recycling to Redefine Homelessness

No matter how hard recyclers like Bill and Sam work, they cannot escape other people's perception of them as just another faceless private in the homeless army. In truth, far from proving difference from "the homeless" as constructed in mainstream discourses, doing recycling is a clear mark of the condition of homelessness, at least for work age men. These men have only got into recycling since they became homeless. In many years under the poverty line Valentino

and Spike had never considered recycling, yet they instantly gravitated towards recyclers as a natural peer group within the homeless population, making their first rounds only one day after they had to move onto the street. I knew Valentino before he became homeless, and he called me a couple of days after he moved outside. "We've been sleeping in this alley down by Folsom, doin' just fine," he said. "We met some nice guys down here. Showed us the tricks of recycling." Only one of the sample had done recycling before becoming homeless, and he was using a truck to collect valuable scrap metals like copper and brass.

Recyclers respond to the close connection between homelessness and recycling in two ways. Some still try to escape a homeless identity by trying to look as un-homeless as possible in their personal appearance, and by working all the time and not socializing with other homeless people. Neither Danny nor Jordan ever use the term "homeless" at all. Still in shock, Jordan looks only to the past or the future. "I'm just waiting for something to come up," he says. "I've got a (truck-driving) license, you know. . . . A man with a *license* shouldn't be in this position."

Others accept that they will be seen as homeless and consciously use their work to assert a "positive" homeless identity which contradicts the exclusion and social welfare discourses. In order to do this they often end up drawing new lines of exclusion: "Us recycling guys, well we're different from other homeless you know. We don't just bum around and do drugs."

Some of the recyclers have a more militant homeless identification. James is extremely angry about the collective abuse of the homeless by the SFPD, intensified under the current "Matrix program." Using a standard American individualist conception of citizenship he argues that recyclers provide for themselves economically and they harm no one. He therefore deserves the same presumption of innocence, the same common respect, and the same civil liberties as any other citizen.

While these approaches are radically different in their political implications, at the level of everyday self-presentation they work out much the same. All of these people work hard to present an image of competence and industry to the rest of the population, an image which contradicts the dominant meanings of homelessness.

In this way the recyclers make of their work a cultural project to transform the stigma of dumpster-diving into a public demonstration of normality and self-sufficiency. They thereby challenge the symbolic fault lines which separate homeless people from everyone else, making the implicit (and often explicit) argument that the problem of homelessness is not created by the differences and deficiencies of homeless people themselves, but is both part and product of the wider society.

> It makes me so mad when people are disrespectful. I mean, can't they see? It could have happened to them, to anybody almost, you know. I mean, you can't protect yourself against bad luck. I'm not a bad man. Can't they see?

Luther's question, "Can't they see?", is both metaphorical and literal. As he sees it, those who see *him* hard at work recycling should be able to figure out that he is an ordinary, decent man, rather than some shadowy representation of what they themselves are not.

Abstract Versus Situated Labor

The capital strategy perspective emphasizes macro-structural limitations rather than the practices people develop within them. At its most extreme, it reduces the efforts of informal workers to pre-social survival by adaptation. But while objective constraints are indeed massive for the homeless recyclers, this desperately poor and socially degraded group refuse to compete aggressively or treat each other instrumentally, insisting instead on respect and solidarity as the basis of their relationships. Rather than scrabbling for survival as faceless victims of structural forces, the recyclers use their work to enact the principles they believe in: self-sufficiency, community, work ethic, "dependable" behavior.

Although they are experiencing extreme poverty and often despair, homeless recyclers don't experience their work lives as new grooves "distributed" by capital to take advantage of their desperation. Within the harsh constraints imposed by homelessness, they have taken up this particular work because it suits their needs, skills, and sense of self better than the other ways they could make money. Other people on the street have very different orientations; Valentino described his friends among the street crack dealers as "*not* impressed" by his recycling. He thought it highly unlikely that any of them would try recycling, seeing as they had always been "different" from him. Most typically, recyclers welcome the opportunity to earn cash from "good honest labor" without either hustling or enacting dependency. Choosing the hard labor of recycling over the various forms of "hustling" performed by other homeless men, the recyclers tend to share a specific previous life experience— that of the male blue collar worker in a routinized workplace in the formal economy.

The move into recycling reflects not only a particular past but a particular reaction to being homeless. Without the status crisis of homelessness these proud native men would not even consider recycling, let alone invest it with such symbolic significance. However, once they become homeless, recycling becomes thinkable. And once they become recyclers, that experience becomes part of what they are and what they can and cannot do, shaping their future possibilities and limitations, likes and dislikes. Labor is part of a life, past, present, and future.

To say that recyclers make a social world out of picking up garbage, and that they have adopted this particular form of work available to homeless people because it "suits" them does not necessarily challenge the capital strategy analysis. It does, however, fill it out substantially. When we do ethnography, we are forced to replace the automatons of macro-social theory with real people. In this case, qualitative fieldwork shows us the concrete ways that a group of informal workers come to "consent" to their economic activity, even making of it a centerpiece of their lives. While the capital strategy analysis may outline the origins of informal recycling, only a closer look at the social world of the recyclers explains how it is sustained and reproduced by the people who do it. . . .

In the meantime, as the recyclers say, the recycling companies are a haven, the only environment where their homelessness does not become the basis for separate and unequal treatment. The recycling staff are generally curt but fair, the rationalized economic transaction is free from the usual compulsory humiliation rituals. "No hustle, no bullshit," as Carlos puts it. Given their stigmatized social position, recyclers are choosing to concentrate their efforts on using their work to redefine themselves as people with full humanity rather than victims. In this way they not only pull themselves back into the flows of capital, but also create self-respect in a hostile world.

NOTES

1. Blau, Joel. *The Visible Poor: Homelessness in the United States.* New York: Oxford University Press, 1992, p. 49.
2. Castells, Manual and Alejandro Portes. "World Underneath: The Origins, Dynamics, and Effects of the Informal Economy." In *The Informal Economy,* p. 27.
3. *San Francisco Business Times,* September 16, 1994.
4. Since September 1994 I have used a combination of participant observation and informal interviewing to study homeless recyclers working in San Francisco. I have got to know 21 of the recyclers well, by working with them and talking as we go. I have also had occasional conversations with about 30 other men. I have also interviewed 14 bartenders about the relationship between bars and the recyclers that collect from them, four Latino van recyclers, a recycling consultant to Alameda County, an official in the San Francisco City Recycling Department, and a manager at one of the smaller recycling companies.

   I made contact with the homeless recyclers by approaching them in the street or in the recycling company yards. I focused on two yards, the largest and best-known in the city, and a smaller Vietnamese-run business. Eight of the recyclers, five white and three Latinos, are based in the Mission, a large racially and ethnically mixed neighborhood of mostly low-income people. From the Mission they travel out to the more prosperous Noe Valley and Castro neighborhoods. Another eight, six of them African American live in the main "skid row" areas of the city—the So-Ma and Tenderloin neighborhoods—from which they have access to the hundreds of bars and restaurants surrounding the downtown area. The other members of the group each recycle in different neighborhoods of the city; the wealthy Pacific Heights and Richmond areas; the heavily touristed North Beach; the mixture of high fashion and ghetto in Hayes Valley; and the predominantly African American neighborhoods of Hunters Point and Bayview.
5. Samples taken in eight American cities in the mid-eighties ranged from 78% to 97% male composition (see Snow, David A. and Leon Anderson, *Down on Their Luck: A Study of Homeless Street People* (1993), Berkeley: University of California Press). Many homeless women may be invisible to such tracking samples, as they are approached in male-dominated places like soup lines and public parks. Yet there are good structural reasons that there should be considerably more men than women on the street, not least the differences between AFDC and GA.

∽ **READING 35** ∽

Toward a 24 Hour Economy

The U.S. Experience and Implications for the Family

Harriet B. Presser

As we begin the twenty-first century, we are witnessing an important yet often overlooked trend: the movement toward a twenty-four-hour, seven-days-a-week economy. Increasingly, there is a demand for people to work evenings, nights, and weekends. Labor force scholars have long studied *how many* hours and days people are employed, but they have typically neglected to consider *which* hours or days they work—and why this matters. . . .

Basic Parameters

Before presenting some basic parameters, I would like to briefly review the definitions of nonstandard work schedules I am using.

First, let us consider the definitions of *work shifts*, which categorize hours of employment in a broad way. The specific definitions of each shift are as follows:

Fixed day: at least half the hours worked most days last week fell between 8 A.M. and 4 P.M.

Fixed evening: at least half the hours worked most days last week fell between 4 P.M. and midnight.

Fixed night: at least half the hours worked most days last week fell between midnight and 8 A.M.

Rotating: schedules that change periodically from days to evenings or nights.

When I refer to standard hours of employment, I mean fixed days; nonstandard shifts refer to nondaytime employment: fixed evenings, nights, and rotating shifts. These are conservative definitions, producing minimal estimates of the percentage working nonstandard hours, since at least half of one's hours of employment need to be before 8 A.M. or after 4 P.M., or rotating. Also, I would like to make clear that when I speak of nonstandard work shifts, I am not referring to flexitime, in which employees can set the time they begin and end work within a few hours of the core schedule for personal reasons. Nonstandard work shifts, in contrast, are set by employers to meet their needs, not those of their employees.

By working nonstandard *days*, I am referring to weekends: Saturday and/or Sunday.

Nonstandard work *schedules*, accordingly, refer to nonstandard hours and/or nonstandard days.

With these clarifications in mind, let us look at some basic facts. The source of these data is the May 1991 *Current Population Survey* (known as the CPS)—a survey of about 55,000 households in the United States. This is our best and most recent source of nationally representative data on the wok schedules of employed Americans. I have limited the sample to those employed aged eighteen and over. Here are some of the basic parameters on the prevalence of nonstandard hours and days in 1991, as reported in my earlier research (Presser 1995):

- One in five employed Americans works evenings, nights, or rotating schedules.
- One in four employed Americans works Saturday and/or Sunday.
- Only 31.5 percent of employed Americans work during the daytime, 5 days a week, Monday through Friday, 35–40 hours a week: the "standard" work schedule.
- When dropping the restriction of 35–40 hours above, the percentage with such a work schedule is 55.1, a bare majority.
- Women are as likely as men to work late or rotating schedules and on weekends, although men are more likely to work nights vs. evenings and Sundays vs. Saturdays.
- Unmarried people are more likely to work nonstandard schedules than married people.
- The presence of children, for both married and unmarried parents, increases their likelihood of working nonstandard schedules.

Research that I have done specifically on "dual earners" (Presser 1988, 1989a)—that is, for married couples with both spouses employed—reveals that one in four are "split-shift" couples: one spouse works during the daytime and the other evenings, nights, or on a rotating schedule (hours changing from days to evenings to nights, or the reverse). And for dual-earner couples *with preschool-aged children*, the ratio is one in three. Moreover, for *young* dual-earner couples with young children—that is, those with at least one spouse aged nineteen to twenty-seven, who typically are recently married and the most economically vulnerable—

the ratio increases further to one in two; that is, one-half of young dual-earner American couples with preschool-aged children are split-shift couples. (This latter figure is based on the 1984 National Longitudinal Survey of Youth, the NLSY; the other data are based on the 1991 CPS.)

I shall come back to these figures when I talk about possible consequences for the presumably "intact" family.

It is not just the married who experience a high prevalence of nonstandard work schedules; indeed, single people are more likely to have nonstandard work schedules than married people, and single mothers with young children more so than their married counterparts. Further, the more children, the more likely the nonstandard schedule. But the phenomenon is widely experienced by all subgroups within American society—both married and unmarried; those with and without children; blacks, whites, and Hispanics; the better and less educated, etc.—even though there are differences in prevalence among these subgroups.

What is driving the growing demand for employment during the evening, night, and weekends, and why do Americans accommodate to this growing demand? Is it due mostly to an increasing lack of daytime job opportunities, or to people's preference for working odd hours to accommodate their personal or family needs?

Demand

My thesis concerning demand is that the growth of the service economy, linked to the increasing employment of women and the aging of the population, is intensifying the demand for nonstandard work schedules. As more and more women are employed during the *daytime*, the demand for nondaytime and weekend services increases, because women are less available to shop during the daytime and on weekdays.

Increasingly, family members are eating out and purchasing other homemaking services that previously would have been performed by full-time housewives. Moreover, the rise in families' real income due to the growth of dual-earner couples has heightened the demand for recreation and entertainment during evenings, nights, and weekends. Further, the aging of the population has increased the demand for medical services over a twenty-four-hour day, seven days a week.

[margin handwriting: Why — new sources of demand for 24-hour services]

Technological changes are also moving us to a global economy. The ability to be "on call" at all hours of the day and night to others around the world generates a need to do so. For example, the rise of multinational corporations, along with the use of computers, faxes, etc., increases the demand that branch offices operate at the same time that corporate headquarters are open. Similarly, international financial markets are expanding their hours of operation.

The future trend in the United States will undoubtedly be toward greater diversity in work schedules, particularly among employed women. Table 1 demonstrates this. This table lists the ten occupations that are projected to grow the most between 1992 and 2005 (on the basis of moderate projections), as well as the distributions of work schedules and the percent female for these occupations as of May 1991. We see that in most of these occupations, unusually high percentages work nonstandard hours and/or days. Future growth in nonstandard hours and days of employment should be especially evident among women because seven of these ten growth occupations are disproportionately female and account for 18.5 percent of the overall projected growth in employment in this period. Thus I would expect further increases not only in the employment of women, but more of them—including mothers with young children—will be working nonstandard hours and days. Moreover, the feedback between women's daytime and nondaytime employment is sure to continue, along with

the aging of the population and the resulting demand for continuous twenty-four-hour medical care.

Supply

Turning to the supply side, why do Americans agree to work nonstandard hours? The limited data we have suggest it is more because it is a job requirement than for family or personal reasons—or, as the U.S. Bureau of Labor Statistics puts it, for "involuntary" rather than "voluntary reasons." Even though women are much more likely than men to report family reasons, for both men and women, most report involuntary reasons— even women with preschool-aged children. This can be seen in Table 2, which reports the main reasons given by those who work nonstandard shifts.

[margin handwriting: Not v. voluntary to work non-std. hours.]

It is particularly notable that less than 5 percent of employed Americans who work evenings, nights, or rotating schedules indicate they do so for better pay (a voluntary personal reason). The pay differentials in the United States, when they exist, are generally not substantial.

An approach I have taken to indirectly assess gender differences in the importance of family characteristics for working nonstandard schedules is a multivariate analysis of the 1991 CPS data (Presser 1995). This analysis controlled for job and background characteristics. It showed that being married reduces women's but not men's likelihood of employment during nonstandard hours. Moreover, the presence of children affects women's but not men's hours of employment. Interestingly, having preschool-aged children *increases* the likelihood of women working nonstandard hours but having school-aged *decreases* the likelihood women will work such hours. Insofar as school substitutes for child care, this difference suggests that the full-time child care demands of preschoolers are an important inducement

TABLE 1 Occupations in 1992 with the Largest Projected U.S. Job Growth (Moderate Estimates) for 2005, the Percentage in These Occupations Who Work Nonstandard Schedules in May 1991, and the Percentage Female in These Occupations in May 1991

	Employment (in 1000s)		% Work Nonstandard Schedules: May 1991			% Female May 1991
Job Growth Rank/Occupation	1992 (Actual)	2005 (Projected)	% Nonday or Rotating Hours	% Weekend Variable Days	% Nondays + Weekends or Variable Days	
1. Salespersons	3,660	4,446	24.7	73.6	75.2	55.5
2. Registered nurses	1,835	2,601	40.1	63.2	67.4	96.7
3. Cashiers	2,747	3,417	43.4	74.9	80.2	80.2
4. General office clerks	2,688	3,342	7.4	14.0	17.5	80.5
5. Truck drivers, light and heavy	2,391	3,039	16.2	36.8	42.8	3.6
6. Waiters and waitresses	1,756	2,394	58.6	83.0	90.0	84.1
7. Nursing aids, orderlies, and attendants	1,308	1,903	40.7	68.9	75.9	89.0
8. Janitors and cleaners, including maids and housekeeping cleaners	2,862	3,410	29.6	38.0	56.2	41.2
9. Food counter, fountain, and related workers	1,223	1,748	48.5	76.2	86.5	71.7
10. Computer scientists and systems analysts	455	956	3.6	11.8	14.4	33.6

Source: Presser (1995) and *Statistical Abstract of the United States.*

Healthcare? (caregivers)

TABLE 2 Percentage of Distribution of Main Reason Reported for Working Nondays (Including Rotators), by Gender and Age of Youngest Child: May 1994

Main Reason	Total	Male				Female			
		Total Male	No Child	Child <5	Child 5–13	Total Female	No Child <5	Child <5	Child 5–13
Voluntary reasons	36.1	29.5	30.8	24.4	29.0	44.7	40.7	56.7	46.7
Better pay	4.9	4.8	4.3	4.9	7.2	4.9	5.6	2.8	5.1
Better child care arrangements	5.1	1.5	.1	5.3	4.2	9.9	0.8	32.4	19.9
Better arrangements for care of other family members	3.5	1.7	1.0	3.1	3.9	5.8	2.6	12.7	11.0
Allows time for school	9.9	8.6	11.5	2.3	.6	11.6	16.0	3.2	3.3
Other voluntary	12.7	12.9	13.9	8.8	13.1	12.5	15.7	5.6	7.4
Involuntary reasons	58.7	65.4	63.9	71.1	66.8	49.8	54.6	36.3	46.5
Requirement of the job	52.4	58.9	57.2	64.8	60.7	43.7	48.3	31.2	40.4
Could not get any other job	4.9	5.0	5.4	4.1	4.1	4.8	5.1	4.5	3.8
Other involuntary	1.4	1.5	1.3	2.0	2.0	1.3	1.2	0.6	2.3
No response/don't know	5.2	5.1	5.3	4.6	4.2	5.5	4.7	7.0	6.8
Total %	100.0	100.0	100.0	100.0	100.0	100.0	100.0	100.0	100.0
No. of cases (N)	(7930)	(4372)	(3045)	(757)	(570)	(3558)	(2333)	(713)	(512)

Note: Percentages are weighted; *N* are unweighted. Percentages for underlined reasons indicate the sum for all responses in that group.
Source: Presser (1995).

for some women to work nonstandard hours—even though they may not be a primary reason for most.

This analysis also showed that nonstandard work schedules are pervasive throughout the occupational hierarchy, but men and women employed in service occupations, particularly in personal services, and in service industries such as eating and drinking places, are most likely to work these schedules, net of family and background factors.

Consequences

So much for what we know about the causes or determinants—which is not that much. What about the consequences? Here, too, our knowledge is limited.

We know that, biologically, working nights and rotating schedules alters one's circadian rhythms, often leading to sleep disturbances, gastrointestinal disorders and chronic malaise. Such negative health and psychological consequences are extensively documented (see, for example, U.S. Congress 1991), although there are problems in the design of many of these studies (small samples, lack of control groups, etc.).

Putting aside these important considerations of health and psychological consequences, I wish to address here the implications of nonstandard work schedules for family life, including marital formation and dissolution, the timing and number of children, and child rearing. I say "implications," as we have very little empirical data on this topic.

Clearly, working nonstandard schedules typically puts one's availability for family interaction and leisure out of sync with others. I have argued that the "at-home" structure of family life is changing dramatically in the United States because of the growth of the twenty-four-hour economy (Presser 1989a); for example, among presumably "intact" families, dinner time—in my view, the most cohesive daily activity for families—has many absent fathers and mothers as a consequence of shift work.[1] A national U.S. study showed that working late or rotating hours was associated with greater difficulty in scheduling family activities and more time spent on housework; also, working weekends or variable days was linked with less time in family roles and with higher levels of work/family conflict and family adjustment (Staines and Pleck 1983). Another national U.S. study (White and Keith 1990) found a modest negative effect of shift work on marital quality and significantly increased the likelihood of divorce over a three-year period. (This is the only longitudinal analysis of work schedules that I am aware of, although I am in the process of conducting such an analysis with the first and second waves of the U.S. National Survey of Families and Households.)

[margin note:] studies of fx

Earlier work I have done on the relationship between work schedules and child care showed that, among dual-earner American couples who work different shifts and have preschool-aged children, virtually all fathers who are at home when mothers are employed care for their children during this time (Presser 1988). Thus, although couples may not have chosen different work hours because of child care, their work schedule behavior facilitates the sharing of child care when both are employed. Similarly, many single as well as married employed mothers in the United States rely on grandmothers who are also employed to share child care with them, and this is possible because they work different hours (Presser 1989b). Thus, what may be stressful for the marriage or for intergenerational relations may be good for children: more fathering or grandparenting rather than substitute care. I have also shown that nonstandard work schedules among dual earners cause an increase in men's share of household tasks (Presser 1994), although one may question whether this is the best route to gender equality in this regard.

As for the issue of work schedules and fertility behavior, there have been no studies to date on this, in the United States or elsewhere. Yet one might expect that nonstandard work schedules decrease the frequency of sexual behavior, postpone the timing of births, and decrease overall family size desires.

Conclusions and Implications

To conclude, there is clear evidence that nonstandard work schedules are pervasive in the United States, they are most evident in service occupations and industries, and although employed men and women are equally engaged in such schedules, future growth will be disproportionately female. Whereas family considerations are not the predominant reason for working nonstandard schedules, the consequences of such employment may be profound in both negative and positive ways. On the negative side, such employment radically alters the at-home structure of family life, perhaps increasing marital instability; on the positive side—at least from the child's perspective— it increases men's and grandmother's participation in child care; and from women's perspective, it increases men's participation in household tasks. *to a point*

Clearly, there are other potential consequences that merit investigation that have not been studied. I find this an especially interesting research area because it addresses the linkage between changes in the economy and changes in the family—that is, how macro changes alter the nature of the family at the micro level. I believe research in this area tends to be neglected because there is no clear policy directive. We have not yet been able to adequately cope with *day* care problems: who wants to deal with night care problems? And if split shifts among couples are shown to increase the risk of divorce, should we discourage such employment—and could we, when this is where much of the job growth lies?

To conclude, it is clear to me that the twenty-four-hour, seven-days-a-week economy is increasingly becoming a reality, and we need to pay more attention to what this means for the quality of family life and the health and well-being of individual family members.

NOTE

1. Based on my preliminary analysis of the data from the 1986–1987 National Study of Families and Households, for all married couples—regardless of employment status—only 71.0 percent of mothers and 51.0 percent of fathers ate dinner with their children all seven days of the prior week, and both parents were present all seven days for only 40.8 percent. More interesting is the fact that 10.2 percent of the mothers and 24.2 percent of fathers did not eat dinner with their children at least five days in the prior week (although rarely were both missing more than two days).

REFERENCES

Presser, Harriet B. 1988. "Shift Work and Child Care Among Young Dual-Earner American Parents." *Journal of Marriage and the Family* 50:133–48.
———. 1989a. "Can We Make Time for Children?: The Economy, Work Schedules, and Child Care." *Demography* 26:523–43.
———. 1989b. "Some Economic Complexities of Child Care Provided by Grandmothers." *Journal of Marriage and the Family* 51:581–91.
———. 1994. "Employment Schedules Among Dual-Earner Spouses and the Division of Household Labor by Gender." *American Sociological Review* 59 (June): 348–64.
———. 1995. "Job, Family, and Gender: Determinants of Nonstandard Work Schedules Among Employed Americans: 1991." *Demography* 32: 577–98.
Staines, Graham L. and Joseph H. Pleck. 1983. *The Impact of Work Schedules on the Family*. Ann Arbor: Institute for Social Research, The University of Michigan.
U.S. Congress. 1991. *Biological Rhythms: Implications for the Worker*, OTA-BA-463. Washington, DC: Office of Technological Assessment.
White, Lynn and Bruce Keith. 1990. "The Effect of Shift Work on the Quality and Stability of Marital Relations." *Journal of Marriage and the Family* 52:453–62.

[Handwritten top margin: Upshot: The 1996 TANF (& Personal Resp. Act) have not been as successful & productive as many portray]

[Handwritten: — Logic of system is flawed: rigid bureaucracy to instill independence & ambition...?]

READING 36

Flat Broke with Children

Enforcing the Work Ethic

Sharon Hays

[Handwritten left margin: —(most) ¢ not on welfare due to lacking work ethic!]

[Handwritten left margin: — Participation & reporting regs are confusing]

[Handwritten left margin: — System degrades people & family]

[Handwritten right margin: messages to "be a good worker"]

The first thing you see on entering the Arbordale welfare office is a large red banner, 12 feet long, 2 feet high, reading, "HOW MANY MONTHS DO YOU HAVE LEFT?" Underneath that banner is a listing of jobs available in the area—receptionist, night clerk, fast-food server, cashier, waitress, data entry personnel, beautician, forklift operator. In most cases, the hours, benefits, and pay rates are not listed. The message is unmistakable: you must find a job, find it soon (before your months run out), and accept whatever wages or hours you can get.

Contrary to the hopes of many politicians, the promotion of family values seemed less than a minor distraction when compared to the massive amount of time the welfare offices of Arbordale and Sunbelt City dedicated to the pursuit of welfare reform's work requirements. Among the piles of paper that clients received in their visits to those offices, I uncovered none that proclaimed, "Marriage is the foundation of a successful society." There were no dating services offered, no family planning programs touted. And there was nothing in the Agreement of Personal Responsibility each applicant was required to sign that implied that marriage was an alternative route to self-sufficiency.

[Handwritten left margin: welfare to work]

There were, however, materials stressing time limits, describing employers' expectations of employees, providing job search tips, leading clients to the job hot line for public employees, and informing clients where to acquire clothes for work, where to seek help in writing a resume, and how to decide on the proper childcare provider. One pamphlet, "Taking Charge of Your Future," was designed to teach welfare mothers how to behave at a job interview: "Shake hands firmly. Don't criticize a former employer. Use good eye contact. Smile. Show enthusiasm. Sell yourself." Another handout outlined the principle that "Work Is Better Than Welfare," reminding clients that they have a responsibility to work and offering platitudes that included "All jobs are good jobs," "As long as people are on welfare, they will be poor," and "Work is the first priority. Any earnings are good."

Welfare recipients, of course, are not merely being encouraged to work. In Arbordale and Sunbelt City, they were reminded repeatedly that work requirements are backed up by strictly enforced time limits—two years at the state level, five years overall—and they were continuously admonished to "save their months." Welfare caseworkers and supervisors, for their part, were painfully aware of the time limits, and they were also aware that the work requirements are enforced through federal "participation rates" requiring states to place increasing percentages of their welfare clientele in jobs. Should a state fail in this task, its federal financial allotment will be decreased. If a caseworker failed in her piece

[Handwritten right margin: 1996 & after TANF work regs.]

[Handwritten bottom margin: Federal rules → Dictate state's funding → Caseworkers aware of limits (& wanting security & own jobs)]

[Handwritten annotations at top: Theses: 1) A number of problems w/ logic of welfare to work 2) Program's rigid bureaucratic nature robs people of their dignity. 3) Key problems: -Assumptions of laziness -Lack of concern for mothers]

of this task, she could lose her job. For welfare mothers, this translated into constant and intense pressure to find work. The symbolic device of the "ticking clock" measuring one's time on welfare was used incessantly by Arbordale and Sunbelt caseworkers and quickly found its way into the vocabulary of the welfare mothers I met.

Just as most of the public and the popular media have assumed all along, welfare reform's Work Plan thus takes center stage in the welfare office. According to the logic of this plan, if the welfare office can train mothers to value work and self-sufficiency, the need for welfare receipt will be eliminated, and former recipients will become respectable, "mainstream" American workers. In this model, the ideal of independence— long associated with values of citizenship, self-governance, and full social membership in Western culture—is thereby transformed into a simple demand for paid work.

There are a number of problems with that logic, as this chapter will demonstrate. A foundational problem is the false assumption that most welfare recipients were previously lacking the motivation to work. Another problem, apparent to anyone who has ever tried to survive on a minimum wage job, is that the low-wage work typically available to welfare recipients offers neither financial independence nor the independence associated with the higher ideals of American citizenship. These difficulties, I soon discovered, are made worse by the procedural enactment of reform. Immersed in a bureaucratic machine, the rigid rules and demanding regulations of reform not only diminish the dignity of the people being served, they also degrade the values that the Personal Responsibility Act purports to champion.

Added to all this is a final key failure of the Work Plan of welfare reform. This model seems to forget that the target group for welfare reform is mothers with children. In our culture, children are assumed to be "dependent" on their parents. To the extent that

we expect welfare mothers to continue to care for their children, those mothers cannot be "independent" in an unfettered sense, and what the law is asking of them is far more than "self" sufficiency.

Nonetheless, as many scholars of American culture have pointed out, the work ethic is a central value in this society. Although the care of one's children is certainly work and surely represents a contribution to the larger good, given that many mothers in American society today are called upon to juggle both paid employment and the care of their families, it is worth examining just what happens when the welfare system sets out to enforce its vision of independent, working motherhood.

Valuing Work

The work requirements of welfare reform are based on the argument that past welfare policy provided a financial incentive to eschew work and thus contributed to a steady decline in the work ethic among the poor. The system of reform is therefore intended to instill the commitment to work that welfare recipients are presumed to lack. The trouble is, as I've noted, that the assumption underlying this logic is wrong.

The majority of welfare mothers already *have* a work ethic. There is a tremendous amount of research available to show that long before welfare reform, most welfare recipients wanted to work and most had worked, at least part of the time. Half of all mothers entering the welfare office in the early 1990s came off the rolls in less than two years. At least one-third worked on or off the books while they were on welfare. Eighty-three percent had some work experience, 65 percent had been recently employed, and two-thirds would leave welfare with jobs. At one time or another, many did find themselves out of work, desperately poor, and back at the welfare office again—about 40 percent

[Handwritten margin annotations: "Logic of Work Plan", "Thesis", "Thesis 2", "Pressure recipients to work (intensely)", "Tied to Chap. 2", "Argues there is a (strong) work ethic among mothers/welfare recipients", "(stats)", "(starts)"]

[handwritten margin note: Underlines importance of personal stories & lack of right effectiveness of]

who left the rolls would later become repeat customers. But nearly all welfare recipients would ultimately spend three times as many of their adult years off the welfare rolls as on.[1]

In considering these facts, it is important to realize that most of the people who apply for benefits at the welfare office are, of course, a different portion of the population from your average yuppie, and the work opportunities available to them differ correspondingly. Nearly half are without high school diplomas (47 percent); just 19 percent have had some college. The work experience of many is in low-skilled, dead-end jobs. And the mainly single women who face the requirements of reform have, on average, two children to worry about when they consider the costs and benefits of the types of jobs that are open to them.[2]

[handwritten margin note: demog. of recips. ↓ underprivileged]

The reasons that this group of Americans cycles between welfare and work, and the reasons that some have difficulty ever finding suitable jobs, are therefore multiple, though ultimately neither mysterious nor unfamiliar. Problems with childcare, problems with the physical or mental health of themselves or their children, obligations to extended family members, unexpected financial difficulties, low wages, overly demanding employers, job layoffs, changing work schedules, the indignities of bottom-end employment, and a commitment to properly responding to the needs of their children can all lead hardworking, "independent" women to seek out the help of the welfare office, as will become increasingly clear.

As a start, consider Carolyn. A oncemarried, black Sunbelt City welfare mother with a high school diploma, her story contained a number of the patterns I saw in the lives of welfare recipients. She had worked for most of her adult life, and she had also spent nearly all her life hovering somewhere close to the poverty line. She had been employed as a waitress, a clerk at the District Attorney's office, a telephone operator, a

[handwritten margin note: Case — Carolyn]

nurse's aide, a receptionist at the power company, a childcare worker, and a discount-store cashier. She initially went on welfare when she had her first and only child with a man she planned to marry. Carolyn cried when she told me the story of how that man began to physically abuse her and ultimately raped her during her pregnancy: "When I first met him, he was a really good man," she said. "But then he started taking drugs. It was terrible. I was afraid all the time." Shortly after the rape, she escaped that situation and moved in with her sister, but lost her job. By the time she gave birth, she was suffering from a nervous breakdown. ("He had drove me insane: that's what they said, in the letter from the psychiatrist.") It was following her hospitalization for that breakdown, ten years before I met her, that she first went on welfare with her then two-month-old baby girl.

By the time her daughter was two years old, Carolyn went back to work. Three years after that she took on the full-time care of her three nieces (aged 3, 9, and 12) when their mother was imprisoned for selling drugs and Carolyn learned that those children were otherwise bound for the foster care system. At that point, she took a second job to care for those four kids, and tried hard to avoid returning to welfare. But after a few years her carefully organized (though always precarious and stressful) work/family balance was thrown into disarray. Her brother and sister-in-law who had been helping with childcare and transportation moved out of town. This left Carolyn trying to manage with the public bus system, paid caregivers, and after-school programs for her daily round of transportation to two jobs, the childcare provider, the older kids' schools, and back home again—along with all the added expenses that went with this new strategy.

Then came the final straw. Carolyn was laid off one of her jobs. By this time, she was

[Handwritten at top: Upshot: People (♀) NOT in welfare office due to a lacking work ethic!]

deeply in debt and ill: the stress of her situation had contributed to serious heart problems, and her doctor was urging her to "take it easy." All these difficulties—transportation, relationships, low wages, precarious jobs, ill health, and the care of children—came together and landed her in the welfare office where I met her. It was clear to me that, at that point in her life, Carolyn was hoping for a little rest and recuperation. But the terms of the newly reformed welfare office, as you'll soon see, required just the opposite.

[Handwritten margin note: complexity]

Although the poor mothers I met in Arbordale and Sunbelt City all came from different circumstances, many of them shared at least some of the troubles from which Carolyn had suffered. The primary point is that, in the vast majority of cases, when women end up on welfare it is not because they have lost (or never found) the work ethic. It is only because a moral commitment to work is, by itself, not always sufficient for the practical achievement of financial and familial stability.

Constructing the Work Ethic

The model used to train low-income mothers like Carolyn in the work requirements of the Personal Responsibility Act is a model of behaviorism. This model—made famous by the training of Pavlov's dogs—posits that a system of rewards for proper behavior and punishments for improper behavior can teach people to behave in the desired way. Under reform, the central punishments used to prod clients into the labor market are time limits, work "participation" rules, and the system of sanctions. The central rewards designed for that purpose are "supportive services" and "income disregards."

[Handwritten margin note: Personal Resp. Act → behaviorism]

Welfare reform's system of supportive services allows caseworkers to subsidize the costs of childcare, provide bus token and gasoline vouchers, pay for clothing and supplies for work, and, under certain conditions, cover expenses like rent and utility payments. Arbordale and Sunbelt caseworkers could also use supportive services, in special cases, to help welfare mothers repair their cars, buy prescription eyeglasses, pay the deposit on a new apartment, or partially cover the costs of reconstructive dental surgery. In accordance with the rules of reform, all this support is time-limited and must be work-related. And with the exception of childcare subsidies, all this support is provided at the discretion of welfare caseworkers.

[Handwritten margin note: ↑discretion for welfare case-workers.]

In addition to these potentially quite helpful subsidies, paid work is made more attractive to welfare clients through the system of income disregards. Once a welfare mother gets a job, a portion of her wages will be "disregarded"—that is, she can continue to receive all or part of her welfare check along with her paycheck until her income reaches the poverty line (or until her time limit is reached). Given just how far below the poverty line many welfare mothers and their children have lived in the past, this is a big boost for a number of them, providing more income than they have ever experienced.

[Handwritten margin note: system of income disregard]

As helpful as these services are, they pale in comparison to the system of strictly enforced rules—all backed up by the threat of punishment. The first set of rules is the "work participation" requirements designed to keep welfare mothers busy pursuing employment from the moment they set foot in the welfare office. The second set is the "reporting" rules, designed to assure that clients maintain contact with the welfare office at all times so that their work and their welfare eligibility can be constantly monitored. The precise sequencing and specifics of these requirements vary somewhat from state to state, but the system's outlines are established by the edicts of the Personal Responsibility Act.

[Handwritten margin notes: RULES; 1st set]

The demanding and often humiliating characteristics of these rules are best understood through the eyes of the recipient. After you have been through your two-hour appointment to establish your eligibility for benefits, after you have signed your Agreement of Personal Responsibility and vowed to commit yourself to self-sufficiency, you are required to meet with an employment caseworker, You will then be given a literacy test, your work history will be documented, and your employment-related skills assessed.

Your initial participation requirement is to make 40 job contacts in 30 days. This is known as your "job search." There are workers at the welfare office that check on these job contacts, so you cannot simply go downtown and fill out an application at every establishment you pass. You are instructed to meet only with employers who actually have jobs. If it should be discovered that you were offered a job that you did not take, you will be punished (as I will explain in a moment).

During this time, you must also attend a series of "job readiness" or "life skills" classes. The courses I attended in Arbordale and Sunbelt City were three- to five-day workshops that included reiterations of the rules of welfare reform, motivational speeches on the sense of pride engendered by paid work, and therapeutic sessions on how to manage stress and how to determine whether your relationships with family and friends are furthering or thwarting the goal of self-sufficiency. These courses also included sessions on how to dress for an interview, defer to your employer, get along with your co-workers, manage childcare, budget your time, balance your checkbook, speak proper English rather than street slang, and, of course, discover the job or career that is right for you.

If you have not found a job at the end of your 30-day search, you must enter a training program that your caseworker chooses for you or with you. Both Arbordale and Sunbelt City, like many states, chose training programs in accordance with a "work first" policy emphasizing expedient entry into the labor market rather than long-term, career-oriented training. Even though many of the caseworkers I met recognized that low-wage jobs were inadequate to cover the costs of raising children, state policymakers deemed the work first model the most realistic strategy given the time limits and federal work participation demands. Nearly all the training programs offered in Arbordale and Sunbelt City are therefore geared to low-wage service sector and clerical jobs (and nearly all are in fields traditionally defined as "women's work"). These include training sessions for office skills, nursing assistants, introductory computer use, food service employment, cook's helpers, certification for childcare work, and preparation for the high school equivalency exam. In Sunbelt City there is even a workshop for aspiring "guest room attendants"—otherwise known as hotel maids. Local employers (phone companies, factories, hotel chains, insurance companies) also sometimes offer workshops to train welfare recipients for positions that need to be filled; at the completion of training, employers pick the best trainees for paying jobs, leaving the rest to fend for themselves.

If you are not in training or a job within a specified period, or if you or your caseworker decide you are not yet ready for a paying job, you will be assigned a Community Work Experience (workfare) position. In this case you will be required to do unskilled work for a state, county, city, or other non-profit agency—sweeping streets, answering phones, sorting papers, serving food at a school cafeteria, or working as a childcare provider, groundskeeper, bus driver, or custodian. All of these jobs are without pay, and all are pitched as work experience. In

Arbordale and Sunbelt City, once you are signed up for a workfare placement, you must follow through for the contracted period (usually three to six months), even if you should be offered a paying job elsewhere.

At the same time you are following these participation rules, you must also manage your reporting responsibilities. You must, for instance, meet with your welfare employment worker every 30 days to discuss your progress toward self-sufficiency. You must inform the caseworker immediately if you fail to attend a day or an hour of your training program or workfare placement. You must notify your caseworker immediately if you change your childcare provider, open a bank account, take out a life insurance policy, change your address, buy a used car, or let a friend stay in your home.

If you should get a job, you must, of course, quickly contact your welfare worker. At this point you have the option of closing your welfare case or continuing to take advantage of the programs of supportive services and income disregards. If you choose the latter path, your clock will keep ticking and you will remain under the watchful eye of the welfare office and remain obligated to notify welfare caseworkers of any change in your circumstances. These reporting requirements will now also include, for instance, a ten-cent raise, a shifting work schedule, or a day you miss work to take your child to a doctor's appointment.

If you should quit your job, participation rules require you to prove "good cause." Not liking your work, having problems with childcare, experiencing other family problems, having a sick child, your own illness, arguments with supervisors, having your apartment building burn down—none of these counts as good cause. If you are fired from a job, you must prove that it occurred through no fault of your own. Otherwise, this is treated as equivalent to quitting a job without good cause.

If you should fail in any of these tasks, you will receive a "sanction."

The system of sanctions is key. Sanctions are the central form of punishing welfare mothers for their failure to comply with welfare rules—their failure, in other words, to behave appropriately. To be sanctioned means that all or part of your welfare benefits are cut. In most states, sanctions operate on a graduated system, becoming increasingly punitive for repeated violations. In Arbordale, for instance, the first sanction costs you one month of welfare benefits, the second sanction means three months without welfare, the third lasts for six months. In Sunbelt City, you lose an increasing percentage of your welfare check for an ever-longer period of time, and with your third sanction you become *permanently* ineligible for welfare benefits. This system, I discovered, operates quite effectively to keep nearly all welfare recipients in line, since most of them learn to fear that they might be punished in this way.

Being sanctioned is the harshest status of all. You receive little or no welfare money, yet your "clock" is ticking and you are using up your lifetime allotment of welfare benefits. Nationwide, at any given time, it is estimated that about one-quarter of welfare clients are under sanction for their failure to comply with welfare regulations—more than double the number of recipients who suffered such punishment prior to welfare reform. Failure to make job contacts, attend a scheduled meeting with a welfare caseworker, go to all your job readiness classes, arrive at your workfare placement on time, or cooperate with child support enforcement, or quitting a job without good cause or getting fired from a job because of some mistake—all these are sanctionable offenses. Sanction rates were so high in Sunbelt that one caseworker worked full time on nothing but the sanctioned cases. In both offices, there were separate workshops just for sanctioned clients. I attended a number of these "sanction workshops," so I became quite familiar with the responses they elicited.

[margin note: Rxns, to Sanctioning]

Most of the sanctioned welfare mothers I encountered were surprised and angered by being sanctioned. As many as half, I would estimate, didn't fully understand the reason for the sanction when it occurred. Even though these mothers received "official" notification of the requirements in advance and received written notice of the sanction when it occurred, the system of participation and reporting requirements they face is extraordinarily complex. Welfare caseworkers contend with these rules day in and day out, and most still have a hard time remembering them all. I was therefore not surprised that a good number of welfare clients were uncertain as to which rule they had broken.

Most clients, I learned, would just "sit out" their sanction, treating it as yet another welfare regulation with which they must comply. Some sanctioned welfare mothers simply drifted away and disappeared (given that they were receiving no support, they presumably left to seek out alternative sources of income elsewhere). A few thought they might "beat" the system by temporarily removing themselves from the welfare rolls. This last strategy was ineffectual however: their clocks kept ticking, they were ineligible to reapply until their sanctioned period was over, and if they did reapply, they would have to start over from the beginning—certification, the wait for the first check, then the job search, life skills classes, training, employment, or unpaid work-experience placement.

[margin note: Upshot — Confusing, demanding & insulting]

Overall, the rules designed to enforce work emerge as a relatively confusing mix of commands, backed up by some welcome gifts, and many, many, less welcome requirements. In pondering this system of rules, rewards, and punishments, the observer might consider to what extent it adds up to a model of the values of "mainstream" America.

The welfare clients I met heard two pieces of this message loud and clear: they knew they were expected to find jobs, and they knew they were expected to obey the rules. Many of them also heard, more faintly perhaps, the enthusiasm that was often conveyed by the caseworkers who enforced those rules, an enthusiasm for genuinely improving the lives of welfare families. Yet, just as the behaviorist model of welfare mixes rewards with punishments, that enthusiasm was also mirrored by another implicit message, one that emerged from the constant pressure, echoed persistently in the background, and was assimilated by most of the welfare mothers I encountered: "You are not wanted here. Americans are tired of helping you out, and we will not let you rest, not even for an instant, until you find a way to get off welfare."

[margin note: msg most recips gleaned]

The message of the importance of paid work is a very powerful message indeed.

Bureaucracy and Autonomy: A Sidebar

Given the decline of the welfare rolls in the years following reform, it is clear that the work requirements and time limits and sanctions of the Personal Responsibility Act have played a role in convincing poor mothers to get off the welfare rolls, faster, than they did in the past. Also impacting this process is the organization of the welfare system that has structured the enforcement of those work requirements and time limits and sanctions.

The welfare office is, first and foremost, a bureaucracy. It is a world of rigid rules and formal procedures. It is a world where every new welfare client can be represented as a series of numbers: a case number, a number of children, a number of fathers of those children, a number of dollars in cash income, a number of months on welfare, a number of required forms, oaths, and verifications. It is also a world where every welfare client has come to symbolize a potential case of fraud and a potential "error" in the calculation of appropriate benefits.* It is no surprise, therefore, that the congressional Work Plan was simply translated into a complex system of bureaucratic rules and regulations. When this bureaucratic system is used to promote an ethic of independence, however, a number of contradictions emerge.

Most Americans have some experience with rigid bureaucracies, if only the Department of Motor Vehicles, the Internal Revenue Service, a credit agency, or an insurance company. Such bureaucracies are efficient precisely because they are cold and impersonal. Operating like human assembly lines, they apply uniform rules, follow regularized procedures, and ignore the particular circumstances of each case as far as possible. Bureaucracies also serve as a powerful form of social control. Every rigid, unforgiving rule signals yet another demand with which the client must comply. The messiness of human existence is precluded, and no excuses are allowed.

Welfare mothers thus learn the message of reform in a context that most people experience as dehumanizing and degrading. This arrangement also means that they first hear the messages of "personal responsibility" and "self-sufficiency" in a context where they are required to be deferential and compliant, obediently following the rules

laid down by others. Of course, given the sheer number of welfare clients and welfare rules, the welfare bureaucracy could be construed as a necessary evil. But it seems to me that if human dignity is an issue, one can ask the question of whether all the rules of welfare are absolutely essential. And if the achievement of national values is an important goal, one can also consider just what happens to the cultural ideals of proud workers and independent, self-determining citizens when those values are immersed in a bureaucratic system of social control.

The most striking example of this bureaucratic system is the initial eligibility interview. A glimpse of this one- to three-hour interrogation is crucial to understanding how poor mothers experience welfare. By the time the potential client reaches this point, she has already filled out a 14-page form asking about every aspect of her familial and financial situation. Much of the "intake" interview simply repeats those questions. Among the many intake interviews I sat through, this one, conducted by a highly competent and thoughtful caseworker named Gail, went quite smoothly, in part because Gail was so experienced and in part because the client was so well-prepared, polite, and compliant. Like all eligibility interviews, it began with a jumbled mix of inquiries:

You're applying for yourself and who else? Your children's names? Their social security numbers? Are you working? Are you going to school? Where? Are there any medical reasons why you are not able to work at this point? Do you receive any money for your children of any kind—child support, disability benefits? What is your address?

And have you ever gone under any other last name? Is this your maiden name? Does your mother receive welfare? Where were you born? Is anyone you're applying for pregnant, blind,

---

*Caseworkers, localities, and states are all judged for their "error" rates, the mistakes made in determining eligibility and benefit amounts. The federal government rewards states that have few errors and punishes those that have many. Prior to welfare reform, when "work participation" rates became a key method for judging effectiveness, error rates were central. They now sit alongside "participation" as one of the two things that everyone in the welfare office has to worry about.

disabled, needed at home to take care of someone who is disabled?

Is your child in day care? Have you come up with an agreement or signed an agreement for the cost? Do you have a contract? Do you have any children that do not live with you that you have to pay child support for?

useful info @ interview?

Some of these questions seemed reasonable enough, but by the time this portion of the interview was over (about a half hour later) the client and I were having a hard time determining the point of all these inquiries. Still, it wasn't difficult to surmise that the client's primary job was to offer simple answers and passively comply.

The next set of questions involved the all-important issue of "resources"—that is, the prospective recipient's current and potential sources of income. Many of these questions have been added over time as politicians and the public have become more and more worried about welfare cheats (with Cadillacs and rental properties on the side):

Do you have any cash right now, like in your purse, at home? Do you have a

*I later asked Gail if she'd encountered any welfare clients with rental properties, boats, or campers, or if she'd come across any who fished or farmed for profit. She responded in the negative. Of the welfare mothers I met, a good number were without checking accounts, almost all had spent any savings they had before coming to the welfare office, and none were holding stocks or bonds. Although it is true that many welfare clients supplement their (inadequate) welfare checks with aid from relatives and boyfriends and with minor side jobs (like "doing hair"), and although it is true that a tiny proportion of welfare clients engage in serious fraud, Gail was well aware that this line of questioning was probably not the most effective way to uncover fraud. "But," she said, "I just do my job. This is what the state wants me to do."

checking account, or a savings account? Where? Do you have your recent statements? Do you have anything like stocks or bonds, U.S. savings bonds, retirement plans? Any houses or land? Or is your name on someone else's property, like your parents have a joint deed with you or anything like that?

assets → financial?

Do you own any cars or trucks, motorcycles, campers, boats, motor homes? Do you have any kind of health insurance at all? Any life insurance policies? In the last two years have you traded, sold, or given away any of these resources that we talked about or listed on the application? Any lawsuits you might be receiving a settlement on?

physical or legal?

Do you receive any kind of commissions, bonuses, tips? Do you receive any money from doing baby-sitting or day care? Do you receive any income from farming, fishing, raking leaves, mowing lawns, any kind of odd jobs like that? Do you have any kind of contract income, like our school bus drivers, they get a contract and they pay x amount of dollars, anything like that? Are you self-employed in any way? Do you have a private business on the side, do you do hair or nails or that sort of thing? Okay, any other kind of self-employment where you have stuff that you sell, at the flea market or anything?

extra income? (informal)?

You've indicated no other money coming into the household. Is that correct? And, anyone outside of your household, like parents, aunts, uncles, anyone like that paying your rent? Now, do you have any scholarships or grants to pay for school? Are you expecting any changes coming up in your income?

grants, etc.?

Gail knew that many of these questions were intrusive, and she also found some of them completely unnecessary.* But she pressed on. At this point in the interview, she began reviewing the checklist of required "verifications," one of the more tedious and time-consuming portions of the intake process. In order to receive benefits, the client must produce, for instance, children's social security cards, birth certificates, and immunization records; rent receipts or a lease from the landlord; a verification of the number of people living in the household; statements from banks and insurance companies; childcare contracts; utility receipts; and school enrollment records. Most Americans would have a hard time coming up with everything on this list. If a welfare client should fail to do so, she will be deemed ineligible for benefits.

paper-work nec. to enroll

And this is just the beginning. The intake was less than one-quarter of the way through. There would be many more questions, more forms, additional explanations, and preliminary calculations.

Some people might argue that welfare recipients deserve to be made humble, to pay homage. The conservative critics of welfare have implied as much. But none of the welfare caseworkers I met saw it this way. They empathized with clients' discomfort, and they were sorry that the system had become so bureaucratic. In fact, the massive number of rules faced by contemporary recipients are primarily the result of decades of welfare "reforms"—no intentional humiliation, just too many fingers in the pot for too long, and too little attention to how complex it has all become. This latest round of welfare reform has increased the rules and requirements by about one-third, coming with hundreds of specific regulations and nearly doubling the size of state procedural manuals. Very few of the rules that were there before were changed, and all that came after 1996 were simply *added,* as they had been so many times before. All this has created an impossible bureaucratic morass.

Is this humiliation right?

Just a result of "too many reforms"

For caseworkers as well as clients, one of the central consequences of welfare's bureaucratic maze is that it often becomes difficult to remember the larger social and moral purposes of those endless rules and regulations. Once again, the welfare eligibility interview provides a useful illustration of the nature of this problem. By the time we got to the long-winded explanation of welfare reform, we were nearly an hour into the intake, about halfway through. Our caseworker, Gail, was speaking quickly now, partly because she knew this speech by heart, and partly because she knew how tiring this process can be. (My only job had been to listen quietly, and I was already feeling dull-witted.)

The program TANF stands for Temporary Assistance to Needy Families. It was called AFDC before, welfare checks, lots of names for it. Now it's Temporary Assistance for Needy Families, and that's because of changes with welfare reform.

TANF Specifics

With federal welfare reform, over the course of your lifetime, you can receive assistance for a total of 60 months. And what happens is that you have a big clock that ticks. Each time you receive a TANF check, one month of that clock is used up. Let's say this time you need assistance for six months, you finish your classes, and you're doing fine. Three years from now your child will be six, you lose your job for some reason, you receive assistance for another three months. That will be a total of nine months. Each time you get a check, your clock is ticking. And when you hit that magic number of 60 you can no longer receive TANF assistance for your lifetime.

Federal

Okay, that's the federal requirements. In this state we have our own system of welfare reform, and what we have is another big clock that ticks. This clock says

& then State-by-state specifics

[handwritten top margin: Upshot: B/w federal & (various) state regs., TANF is a confusing bureaucratic mess! → AND a system of social control]

that you can receive TANF assistance for a total of 24 months. And when you hit that magic number of 24 months, there's then a two-year period where you cannot receive TANF checks at all.

Gail then went on to explain the job search, the unpaid workfare placements, the income disregards, the supportive services of childcare and transportation, and the fact that finding a job is the best way to avoid the "hassles" of welfare. Finally, without pausing to take a breath, she concluded this first round of introductions to welfare reform with the following:

[handwritten margin: Is this why they don't want to clean it up?]

The enhanced disregards, the transportation services and the day care you will get. So we're not gonna just put you out there working. You'll have the supportive services. At the end of those 24 months, you continue with your day care, you continue with the medical assistance, you continue with the transportation, though it might be a little bit more limited, and the supportive services are even more limited than before.

At the end of this one year transitional, you then have that two years off of assistance completely. That's two years on, with us doing all we can do to get you a job or keep you employed. Okay? So this is all under the regular monthly check. Okay?

The client looked at me quizzically. Our heads were spinning. Federal requirements? State requirements? Supportive services? Transitional services? Ticking clocks? Enhanced disregards? The magic number? What did you say?

[handwritten margin: Confusing]

Clearly, in this context, it is difficult to decipher the central point of welfare reform. Every step of the way, for both clients and caseworkers, the higher goals they strive for are repeatedly muddied and obscured by the unrelenting stream of complex rules and requirements. Although welfare mothers ultimately read welfare reform as the insistence that they find paid work, what they experience initially and most acutely is this system of social control.

This returns us to the cumulative impact of the welfare bureaucracy—the contradiction between demanding individual autonomy and exercising social control. The symbolic logic of the Work Plan implies that reform will overcome welfare dependence by training clients in "personal responsibility," yet the routines and procedures of the welfare office systematically require of recipients obedience, deference, and passive compliance. How can welfare caseworkers convince their clients that they recognize them as independent, assertive, self-seekers while simultaneously demanding their unquestioning deference to an impossible system of rules? How will clients understand their paid employment as a positive individual choice when it is presented as one of many absolute demands, backed up by multiple threats of punishment? As many scholars have pointed out, the operations of bureaucracies are simply not conducive to instilling a sense of individual self-determination.

[handwritten margin: key → breakdown of logic]

Even though welfare's combination of bureaucratic control, behaviorist methods, and demands for autonomy is a very odd one, it could be interpreted in a different, less contradictory light—though not one that supports most politicians' rhetoric about the goals of welfare reform. If we really want to include welfare mothers as active citizens, full-fledged participants in society, and the social equals of both men and the middle class, it doesn't make sense to use bureaucratic mechanisms to mentor and inspire them. If, on the other hand, what we are actually preparing them for is to serve our fast food, clean our toilets, answer our phones, ring up our receipts, and change our bed pans, the bureaucratic operations of *[handwritten top margin: ⊗ System (bur.) degrades workers, offers no real training]*

[handwritten: brilliant!]

welfare could be construed as a very effective route. Deference and obedience are, after all, important qualities for many low-wage workers. And the message that getting a job, any job, is better than staying on welfare is certainly congruent with this interpretation. Similarly, the "work first" model used by Arbordale and Sunbelt City, as expedient and realistic as it may be for some welfare clients, precludes the possibility of the kind of education and training that could offer lasting financial stability and self-determination rather than inadequate, unskilled, low-paid labor.

[handwritten margin: ⊗ Upshot]

Thus, the trouble with bureaucratic welfare is not just that its procedures are demeaning and degrading, picturing welfare recipients as childlike and manipulative and burying the goals of reform in a bureaucratic swamp. There is also a real danger that the more valuable versions of the principles of independence and citizenship have been debased by this process, transformed into a demand for a new form of wage slavery, where the lives of welfare mothers and their children are treated as worth far less than those of the American middle class.

Complications on the Road to "Self-Sufficiency"

The bureaucratic rigidity, the interrogation, the time limits, the sanctions, the unpaid workfare placements of the Personal Responsibility Act certainly do not offer an unequivocally positive image of the values of the nation. Still, this system has contributed to a dramatic drop in the number of welfare recipients nationwide. Further, as the proponents of welfare reform so regularly emphasize, it is also true that 60 percent of former welfare clients had at least temporary jobs by 2002. These two facts—the decline of the rolls and the employment of former welfare mothers— are the central basis for the positive national

assessments of welfare reform. These two facts, however, hide a much more disturbing reality. By 2002, a full 40 percent of former welfare recipients remained unemployed. Of the 60 percent who were working, half were without sufficient wages to raise their families out of poverty.[3] At the same time, many of the mothers who had left welfare with jobs had lost them and were returning to the welfare office once again. From where I stood, it seemed that the glass was at least half empty.

[handwritten margin: SCARY stats, ⊗ tho!]

In the welfare offices of Arbordale and Sunbelt City, caseworkers and I witnessed these realities in a direct and immediate way. It wasn't easy to keep track of the proportions from that vantage point, but we could tell that some families were doing well and a larger portion were not so lucky. Of course, the triumphs mattered. Everyone in the welfare office was happy about all those families who were significantly better off as a result of the training and material support offered by reform. But in considering the long-range prospects for the majority of poor families, the view from the welfare office left me and most of the people who worked there with a much less optimistic outlook than those who have unequivocally embraced reform. In fact, it was apparent to us that many of the former welfare recipients categorized by national statistical renderings as "successful" looked little different from those who were marked as failures. A few introductory examples will help to clarify the nature of some of the problems involved.

Andrea, who had found a job and left the rolls, would be labeled as one of the "success" stories of the Personal Responsibility Act. When I met her in 1999 she was making $5.75 an hour, working a 35-hour-week at a Sunbelt City convenience store. Twenty-eight years old, with two children, she paid $475 a month for housing and utilities and $200 for food. This left her with about $50 to pay for clothing, transportation, medical bills, childcare, laundry, school

[handwritten margin: Case: Andrea (success)]

*[handwritten bottom margin: ⊗ 2 reasons for + assessment of TANF:
• ↓ in welfare rolls & • ↑ employment of welfare mothers]*

costs, furniture and appliances, and cleaning supplies for a family of three. She couldn't make it. Her kids didn't have proper shoes. Her oldest daughter wanted a new outfit for the school year. Her phone had been turned off the month before. She wasn't sure if she'd be able to pay the current month's rent. She worried about what would happen when winter came. She stayed on the "transitional benefits" offered by the welfare office that provided her with continued help with the costs of childcare and transportation, even though she knew this strategy was not only time-limited but would also ultimately prolong her period of ineligibility for welfare.

If Andrea did not have children, her $5.75 would still be inadequate, but its consequences would be altogether different. The depth of her worries about rent and utility bills and shoes and winter coats and even the availability of a telephone had everything to do with her concern for those children. What would happen to her children if she was laid off her job? What was going to happen when she got too far behind in her bills? What if one of the kids got sick? What kind of career ladder was available to her, as a convenience-store clerk, that might guard her against future hardship? When last I saw Andrea, she had used up 16 months of her lifetime welfare benefits and was deeply in debt. Her youngest child was then two years old.

Clara would be considered a "failure" by the standards of the Personal Responsibility Act. She found herself in the Arbordale welfare office after the delicatessen where she worked for five years was closed down. Thirty years old, with a three-year-old daughter and a nine-year-old son, her caseworker sent her to a job at McDonald's. I first met her two weeks later when she came into the welfare office to tell her caseworker that she just couldn't manage the required speed of fast-food service: "I know how to make sandwiches," she anxiously explained, "but this work is just too fast. My boss keeps telling me to 'pick up the pace.' But I can't do it!"

"Just hang in there," her caseworker replied, "and we'll see if we can't find you something better soon."

Clara was sobbing by then, and talking about how the stress of the job was taking a toll on her two kids as well, "I have to get them up at five in the morning, and they don't want to go. I yell at them. They don't deserve it. *Please* don't make me go back."

Her caseworker could only repeat the suggestion to "hang on" (even though she later told me how much she wished there was some other option). Five days later Clara quit her job. Her caseworker empathized, but rules are rules, and since Clara had quit without "good cause," she was sanctioned, leaving her and the kids without any income for a month. By the time I saw Clara again she was back on benefits and looking for a new job (40 contacts in 30 days). She was broke and exhausted, and owed money to all her family members and friends. She had used up six months of her lifetime welfare benefits.

Kendra, one of the first clients I interviewed, would be categorized among the "successes" of reform in that she was no longer on the welfare rolls. But hers is a story that continues to break my heart. Nearly everyone in the Arbordale welfare office knew and loved Kendra. She was very sweet, and shy, and deeply earnest. At the time I met her in 1998, she was 26, with two daughters aged six and eight. After a long history of working part-time, on and off, in unskilled jobs, she had finally landed a secure and meaningful job, she thought, working at the homeless shelter run by the Salvation Army. It was the night shift, but she was happy about it, since it made her feel especially good to be helping out the homeless. Given her own experiences, she thought she had a special empathy for their hardship. Additionally, the graveyard shift worked

[Handwritten margin notes: "?", "If you get people used to these, how can you take them away?", "Case: Clara (failure)", "Case: Kendra (success)"]

well, she said, because it allowed her to have time with her two daughters during the day. She had worked out childcare with a neighbor who worked the day shift. She was not making enough money to get by without the extra help from the welfare office and public housing, but she was planning on asking for a small raise, thinking that she could work her way up, or maybe take a second job. She was also studying for the high-school equivalency test. She was hopeful, cheerful, and she was proud of herself. She felt particularly grateful to her welfare caseworkers and to her foster parents, who had been kind enough to raise her and her two brothers from a young age. She wanted these people to be proud of her as well, and she felt that she was on her way for the first time in her life, largely thanks, she told me, to all the supplemental services and caseworker support she experienced as a result of welfare reform. We talked about strategies for how she might make ends meet without the help of the welfare office.

Two months later, all Kendra's dreams came to a crashing halt. Her brothers got into an argument, and one brother shot and killed the other. One was dead, the other was on his way to prison. She fell apart emotionally, missed too many days at work, and lost her job. She left the welfare rolls and moved out of public housing. Although Arbordale caseworkers made a special effort to track her down (a rare undertaking and one that was certainly not a part of their job descriptions), no one could find her. All of us worried about what would become of Kendra and her daughters. . . .

Assessing the Work Plan

Watching the ongoing political celebrations of the decline of the welfare rolls in the years following reform, I had to wonder if I was missing something. There were certainly some successes involved, but the applause of the proponents of reform seemed both premature and neglectful of much of the ground-level hardship faced by poor families. It was also apparent to me that those proponents were ignoring a number of additional complicating factors.

First, there was the question of how much of the declining welfare rolls of the late 1990s could be credited to reform and how much of it to the then-booming economy. Scholars continue to debate this question. Historically speaking, the relative number of welfare recipients has always been connected to fluctuations in the economy, and this connection seems to be confirmed by the rapid decline of welfare receipt in the late 1990s and the slowdown of that decline when the economy began to stall in 2001. But it also makes sense that the new law and the new procedures of welfare offices have had an impact. The best historical comparison in this case is the major policy changes of the late 1960s that clearly affected the size of the welfare rolls in the 1970s and 1980s. Still, conclusive figures on the comparative importance of the law and the economy are hard to come by, and vary widely. Taking into account the range of existing literature on this question, and recognizing that many welfare mothers left the welfare rolls with jobs long before the passage of reform, one could optimistically credit the Personal Responsibility Act with half the welfare employment exits that occurred from 1996 to 2002.[4]

On the positive side, as I've suggested, there is little doubt that the system of training, supportive services, and income supplements provided by reform has heightened the employability of some welfare mothers—offering just the kind of temporary economic support and training needed to create a financially stable work and family life. For the majority, however, these programs are not a sufficient basis for lasting stability.

[Margin annotations: Remaining question 1) How much of "success" due to reform or 90s boom?]

The 40 percent of former welfare clients who were without work in 2002 had *no discernible source of income*. And, as noted, of the 60 percent of former welfare recipients who were employed, only half had found jobs paying above-poverty wages. Even more disheartening, national studies estimate that about two-thirds of those who do find work will, for one reason or another, lose those jobs over the course of a year. Hence, the 40 percent who are without jobs or welfare include not just those who never found work, but also all those who once had jobs and lost them. This 60/40 split of employed versus unemployed former welfare recipients has remained fairly steady from 1998 to 2002. This means that every time someone in the nonworking 40-percent category finds a job, some family in the working 60-percent category loses their job. And remember, of the jobs that these parents are competing for, only half pay enough to support their families above the poverty line.

Thus, what we are actually seeing when we look at the decline of the welfare rolls is millions of mothers desperately striving to work their way out of poverty and continuously moving in and out of low-wage jobs. Some of these women and children are managing to rise above the poverty level, at least for a time, but most are not. Some keep their jobs for longer than others, some have better jobs than others, some have found little work at all. Very few—optimistically 10 to 20 percent—have achieved relatively permanent, above-poverty stability. Of those who go long periods without work or welfare, given that they are no longer in the "system," there is currently no reliable data on their fate, though there is every reason to believe that most are in situations of dire poverty.

All these consequences of welfare reform were measured during a period of tremendous economic prosperity. And all the celebrations of the declining welfare rolls ignore not just the hardships of unemployed and underemployed former welfare recipients, they also ignore the millions who are still on welfare, still trying to cope with the rules of reform, and still trying to comply with Americans' stated demand that they leave the rolls as fast as they can.

It is also important to recognize that the hardships and chronic instability we are talking about have not only impacted the 12 million temporarily poor and persistently poor families who were on welfare in 1996. This law has also impacted all the millions of newly poor, returning poor, and temporarily poor who have ended up on welfare since then—and tens of millions more will be affected by this law over time. Although there is some good news in this, overall, it is surely not a rosy picture of happily employed, independent women who are effortlessly juggling their work and family lives.

In the end, the results of the Work Plan of reform tell us a story not just about the hardship of present and former welfare recipients but also about the nature of the American labor market—and about deeper problems in achieving the American dream. Recognizing the realities of low-wage work, one could argue that the underlying logic of the Personal Responsibility Act is either punitive or delusional. On the punitive side, the work rules of reform might be interpreted as implicitly aimed at creating a vast population of disciplined and obedient workers who are hungry enough (and worried about their children enough) to take any temporary, part-time, minimum-wage job that comes their way, no matter what the costs to themselves or their family. More positively (but nearsightedly), one could interpret the Work Plan as following from the assumption that there is an unlimited number of career ladders available for every American to climb. The time-limited nature of welfare reform's childcare,

Handwritten note at top: Personal Respon. Act model = mythological 'bootstrap' mentality

transportation, and income supports, for instance, suggests a middle-class (and increasingly mythological) model of working one's way to the top. From the file room to the front office, from flipping burgers to managing one's own franchise, from cleaning toilets to running the county maintenance division, from sorting mail to programming computers—everyone, this model implies, has the chance to achieve financial success. But given the nature of most of the low-wage jobs available in the United States today, the supportive benefits required to enable recipients to make ends meet are very unlikely to be covered by the wage increases that most clients will receive by the time they become ineligible for further welfare help. And given rising income inequalities and the widening division between low-wage service workers and the educated, technologically savvy professional class, it is very unlikely that the majority of welfare mothers will have a chance to climb permanently out of poverty—at least for as long as they have children to care for.

Whether intended or not, it may ultimately be true that the Work Plan of welfare reform is more effective as a form of punishment than it is as a positive strategy for independence. Of course, the Work Plan *is* somewhat effective at pressing mothers into jobs. The Work Plan *can,* as national statistics testify, contribute to a significant decline in the absolute number of people on welfare. And this plan *has* provided some welfare families with valuable supportive benefits and new hope. Yet given the realities of low-wage work and single parenting, the Work Plan will not elevate the majority of welfare families above the poverty line. In the long run, many will need to go back on welfare or will need to be dependent on the help of men, extended family members, friends, charitable community services, or illegal activities. Whether the latter forms of dependence are, by some measure, superior

to "welfare dependency" is a matter of one's goals, and a question I will explore further.

Many policymakers were well aware of existing research from the start, and they knew that the odds of raising welfare recipients out of poverty were not good. But arguably, the symbolic message that paid work *should* lead to independence was, from the beginning, more important than the practical issue of poverty itself. What we have achieved with the decline of the welfare rolls is, in fact, the *appearance* of independence. This has surely helped to maintain faith in our system, but it is nonetheless insufficient if we are truly committed to the values of familial stability and inclusive citizenship.

In the meantime, the work rules of reform have suggested to the nation that we have no responsibility to address the inadequacy of low-wage work. And the individualistic logic of these rules has also ignored the fact that something more than "personal" responsibility is at stake here. Children, these rules imply, can be managed by simply putting them aside in childcare centers. In fact, if work requirements were the only feature of welfare legislation it might appear that mothers in American society have been completely "freed" from the responsibility of parenting. We need to ask ourselves what has happened in this process to the cultural ideals of independence and commitment to others.

―――――

In the face of the Work Plan's moral and practical inadequacies, we might be tempted to change our angle of vision, and perhaps set our sights on some alternative plan. One might, for instance, begin to hope that welfare mothers will simply find themselves a good man—to help them with the bills and to help them care for their children. As it turns out, prior research suggests that finding a good man and marrying him is, indeed, a very good way to get off and stay off welfare. So what do family values look like when they are instituted at the level of the welfare office? Is the Family Plan the answer?

NOTES

1. Bane and Ellwood (1994), Edin and Lein (1997), Sidel (1996A), Harris (1996, 1997). See also Dodson (1998), Horowitz (1995), Seccombe (1999), Zucchino (1997).
2. U.S. Department of Health and Human Services (1999B).
3. Moffit (2002).
4. See Bell (2001) for an in-depth analysis of the (very complicated) debate over economy versus policy; see also National Campaign for Jobs and Income Support (2001A), Blank (1997). . . .

REFERENCES

Bane, Mary Jo and David T. Ellwood. 1994. *Welfare Realities: From Rhetoric to Reform.* Cambridge, MA: Harvard University Press.

Bell, Stephen H. 2001. *Why Are Welfare Caseloads Falling?* Assessing the New Federalism 01–02. Washington, DC: Urban Institute.

Blank, Rebecca M. 1997. *It Takes a Nation: A New Agenda for Fighting Poverty.* New edition. Princeton, NJ: Princeton University Press.

Dodson, Lisa. 1998. *Don't Call Us Out of Name: The Untold Lives of Women and Girls in Poor America.* Boston: Beacon Press.

Edin, Kathryn and Laura Lein. 1997. *Making Ends Meet: How Single Mothers Survive Welfare and Low-Wage Work.* New York: Russell Sage Foundation.

Harris, Kathleen Mullan. 1996. "Life After Welfare: Women, Work, and Repeat Dependency." *American Sociological Review* 61 (June): 407–426.

Harris, Kathleen Mullan. 1997. *Teen Mothers and the Revolving Welfare Door.* Philadelphia: Temple University Press.

Horowitz, Ruth. 1995. *Teen Mothers: Citizens or Dependents?* Chicago: University of Chicago Press.

Moffitt, Robert A. 2002. *From Welfare to Work. What the Evidence Shows.* Welfare Reform and Beyond: Policy Brief #13. Washington, DC: Brookings Institution.

National Campaign for Jobs and Income Support. 2001A. *A Recession Like No Other: New Analysis Finds Safety Net in Tatters as Economic Slump Deepens.* Washington, DC: National Campaign for Jobs and Income Support.

Seccombe, Karen. 1999. "So You Think I Drive a Cadillac?" *Welfare Recipients' Perspectives on the System and Its Reform.* Boston: Allyn and Bacon.

Sidel, Ruth. 1996A [1998]. *Keeping Women and Children Last: America's War on the Poor.* Revised edition. New York: Penguin Books.

U.S. Department of Health and Human Services 1999B. *Temporary Assistance for Needy Families Program: Second Annual Report to Congress.* Washington, DC: U.S. Government Printing Office.

Zucchino, David. 1997. *Myth of the Welfare Queen.* New York: Touchstone.

Discussion Questions for Part IV

1. How do workers cope with boring, highly routinized jobs?
2. Why are employers so rarely prosecuted for having unsafe working conditions?
3. Compare the emotional labor required of casino workers with that of workers in other jobs, such as fast food and teleservice.
4. What are some strategies workers use to increase their tips? How do these strategies differ for different kinds of workers?
5. Many of the authors in this part discuss the interests of workers vis-à-vis employers. Under what conditions do workers' and employers' interests coincide? Under what conditions do these interests diverge?
6. In what professions are workers required to perform emotional labor? Compare

the emotional labor performed by teachers or doctors to that performed by the litigators in Pierce's study.

7. In what ways (if any) do you think Jackall's conclusions would be different had he studied African-American managers' experiences? Female managers' experiences?

8. Based on these readings, what career advice would you give an African-American college graduate interested in management?

9. Do you agree with Rogers that temporary workers are stigmatized for not being "real workers"? Are there any other types of workers who experience a similar stigma?

10. What are the advantages and disadvantages of working as a temp?

11. Discuss the links among work, moral worth, and identity in American society. How do the readings in this part illustrate these connections?

12. What are the social and personal costs of the move to a 24/7 economy? What are the social and personal benefits of this shift?

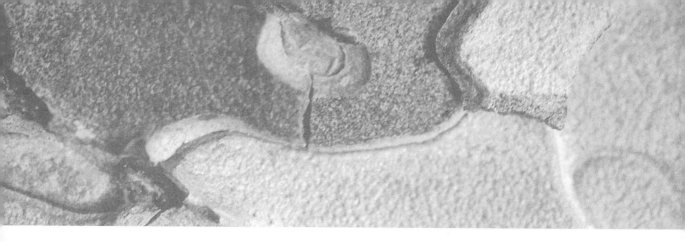

PART V

Work and Family

CARE WORK: PAID AND UNPAID

∽ READING 37 ∾

Love and Gold

Arlie Russell Hochschild

Whether they know it or not, Clinton and Princela Bautista, two children growing up in a small town in the Philippines apart from their two migrant parents, are the recipients of an international pledge. It says that a child "should grow up in a family environment, in an atmosphere of happiness, love, and understanding," and "not be separated from his or her parents against their will . . ." Part of Article 9 of the United Nations Declaration on the Rights of the Child (1959), these words stand now as a fairy-tale ideal, the promise of a shield between children and the costs of globalization.

At the moment this shield is not protecting the Bautista family from those human costs. In the basement bedroom of her employer's home in Washington, D.C., Rowena Bautista keeps four pictures on her dresser: two of her own children, back in Camiling, a Philippine farming village, and two of children she has cared for as a nanny in the United States. The pictures of her own children, Clinton and Princela, are from five years ago. As she recently told *Wall Street Journal* reporter Robert Frank, the recent photos "remind me how much I've missed."[1]

She has missed the last two Christmases, and on her last visit home, her son Clinton, now eight, refused to touch his mother. "Why," he asked, "did you come back?"

The daughter of a teacher and an engineer, Rowena Bautista worked three years toward an engineering degree before she quit and went abroad for work and adventure. A few years later, during her travels, she fell in love with a Ghanaian construction worker, had two children with him, and returned to the Philippines with them. Unable to find a job in the Philippines, the father of her children went to Korea in search of work and, over time, he faded from his children's lives.

Rowena again traveled north, joining the growing ranks of Third World mothers who work abroad for long periods of time because they cannot make ends meet at home. She left her children with her mother, hired a nanny to help out at home, and flew to Washington, D.C., where she took a job as a nanny for the same pay that a small-town doctor would make in the Philippines. Of the 792,000 legal household workers in the United States, 40 percent were born abroad, like Rowena. Of Filipino migrants, 70 percent, like Rowena, are women.

Rowena calls Noa, the American child she tends, "my baby." One of Noa's first words was "Ena," short for Rowena. And Noa has started babbling in Tagalog, the language Rowena spoke in the Philippines. Rowena lifts Noa from her crib mornings at 7:00 A.M., takes her to the library, pushes her on the swing at the playground, and curls up with her for naps. As Rowena explained to Frank, "I give Noa what I can't give to my children." In turn, the American child gives Rowena what she doesn't get at home. As Rowena puts it, "She makes me feel like a mother."

Rowena's own children live in a four-bedroom house with her parents and twelve other family members—eight of them children, some of whom also have mothers who work abroad. The central figure in the children's lives—the person they call "Mama"—is Grandma, Rowena's mother. But Grandma works surprisingly long hours as a teacher—from 7:00 A.M. to 9:00 P.M. As Rowena tells her story to Frank, she says little about her father, the children's grandfather (men are discouraged from participating actively in child rearing in the Philippines). And Rowena's father is not much involved with his grandchildren. So, she has hired Anna de la Cruz, who arrives daily at 8:00 A.M. to cook, clean, and care for the children. Meanwhile, Anna de la Cruz leaves her teenage son in the care of her eighty-year-old mother-in-law.

Rowena's life reflects an important and growing global trend: the importation of care and love from poor countries to rich ones. For some time now, promising and highly trained professionals have been moving from ill-equipped hospitals, impoverished schools, antiquated banks, and other beleaguered workplaces of the Third World to better opportunities and higher pay in the First World. As rich nations become richer and poor nations become poorer, this one-way flow of talent and training continuously widens the gap between the two. But in addition to this brain drain, there is now a parallel but more hidden and wrenching trend, as women who normally care for the young, the old, and the sick in their own poor countries move to care for the young, the old, and the sick in rich countries, whether as maids and nannies or as daycare and nursing-home aides. It's a care drain.

The movement of care workers from south to north is not altogether new. What is unprecedented, however, is the scope and speed of women's migration to these jobs. Many factors contribute to the growing feminization of migration. One is the growing split between the global rich and poor. In 1949 Harry S. Truman declared in his inaugural speech that the Southern Hemisphere—encompassing the postcolonial nations of Africa, Asia, and Latin America—was underdeveloped, and that it was the role of the north to help the south "catch up." But in the years since then, the gap between north and south has only widened. In 1960, for example, the nations of the north were twenty times richer than those of the south. By 1980, that gap had more than doubled, and the north was forty-six times richer than the south. In fact, according to a United Nations Development Program study, sixty countries are *worse off* in 1999 than they were in 1980.[2] Multinational corporations are the "muscle and brains" behind the new global system with its growing inequality, as William Greider points out, and the 500 largest such corporations (168 in Europe, 157 in the United States, and 119 in Japan) have in the last twenty years increased their sales sevenfold.[3]

As a result of this polarization, the middle class of the Third World now earns less than the poor of the First World. Before the domestic workers Rhacel Parreñas interviewed in the 1990s migrated from the Philippines to the United States and Italy, they had averaged $176 a month, often as teachers, nurses, and administrative and clerical workers. But by doing less skilled—though no less difficult—work as nannies, maids, and care-service workers, they can earn $200 a month in Singapore, $410 a month in Hong Kong, $700 a month in Italy, or $1,400 a month in Los Angeles. To take one example, as a fifth-grade dropout in Colombo, Sri Lanka, a woman could earn $30 a month plus room and board as a housemaid, or she could earn $30 a month as a salesgirl in a shop, without food or lodging.

But as a nanny in Athens she could earn $500 a month, plus room and board.

The remittances these women send home provide food and shelter for their families and often a nest egg with which to start a small business. Of the $750 Rowena Bautista earns each month in the United States, she mails $400 home for her children's food, clothes, and schooling, and $50 to Anna de la Cruz, who shares some of that with her mother-in-law and her children. As Rowena's story demonstrates, one way to respond to the gap between rich and poor countries is to close it privately—by moving to a better paying job.

Even as the gap between the globe's rich and poor grows wider, the globe itself—its capital, cultural images, consumer tastes, and peoples—becomes more integrated. Thanks to the spread of Western, and especially American, movies and television programs, the people of the poor south now know a great deal about the rich north. But what they learn about the north is what people *have,* in what often seems like a material striptease.

Certainly, rising inequality and the lure of northern prosperity have contributed to what Stephen Castles and Mark Miller call a "globalization of migration."[4] For men and women alike, migration has become a private solution to a public problem. Since 1945 and especially since the mid-1980s, a small but growing proportion of the world's population is migrating. They come from and go to more different countries. Migration is by no means an inexorable process, but as Castles and Miller observe, "migrations are growing in volume in all major regions at the present time."[5] The International Organization for Migration estimates that 120 million people moved from one country to another, legally or illegally, in 1994. Of this group, about 2 percent of the world's population, 15 to 23 million are refugees and asylum seekers. Of the rest, some move to join family members who have previously migrated. But most move to find work.

As a number of studies show, most migration takes place through personal contact with networks of migrants composed of relatives and friends and relatives and friends of relatives and friends. One migrant inducts another. Whole networks and neighborhoods leave to work abroad, bringing back stories, money, know-how, and contacts. Just as men form networks along which information about jobs are passed, so one domestic worker in New York, Dubai, or Paris passes on information to female relatives or friends about how to arrange papers, travel, find a job, and settle.

Today, half of all the world's migrants are women. In Sri Lanka, one out of every ten citizens—a majority of them women—works abroad. That figure excludes returnees who have worked abroad in the past. As Castles and Miller explain:

> Women play an increasing role in all regions and all types of migration. In the past, most labor migrations and many refugee movements were male dominated, and women were often dealt with under the category of family reunion. Since the 1960s, women have played a major role in labor migration. Today women workers form the majority in movements as diverse as those of Cape Verdians to Italy, Filipinos to the Middle East and Thais to Japan.[6]

Of these female workers, a great many migrate to fill domestic jobs. Demand for domestic servants has risen both in developed countries, where it had nearly vanished, and in fast-growing economies such as Hong Kong and Singapore, where, write Miller and Castles, "immigrant servants—from the Philippines, Indonesia, Thailand, Korea and Sri Lanka—allow women in the richer economies to take up new employment opportunities."[7]

Vastly more middle-class women in the First World do paid work now than in the past. They work longer hours for more months a year and more years. So they need help caring for the family.[8] In the United States in 1950, 15 percent of mothers of children aged six and under did paid work while 65 percent of such women do today. Seventy-two percent of all American women now work. Among them are the grandmothers and sisters who thirty years ago might have stayed home to care for the children of relatives. Just as Third World grandmothers may be doing paid care work abroad in the Third World, so more grandmothers are working in the First World too—another reason First World families are looking outside the family for good care.

Women who want to succeed in a professional or managerial job in the First World thus face strong pressures at work. Most careers are still based on a well-known (male) pattern: doing professional work, competing with fellow professionals, getting credit for work, building a reputation, doing it while you are young, hoarding scarce time, and minimizing family work by finding someone else to do it. In the past, the professional was a man; the "someone else" was his wife. The wife oversaw the family, itself a flexible, preindustrial institution concerned with human experiences the workplace excluded: birth, child rearing, sickness, death. Today, a growing "care industry" has stepped into the traditional wife's role, creating a very real demand for migrant women.

But if First World middle-class women are building careers that are molded according to the old male model, by putting in long hours at demanding jobs, their nannies and other domestic workers suffer a greatly exaggerated version of the same thing. Two women working for pay is not a bad idea. But two working mothers giving their all to work is a good idea gone haywire. In the end, both First and Third World women are small players in a larger economic game whose rules they have not written.

———

The trends outlined above—global polarization, increasing contact, and the establishment of transcontinental female networks—have caused more women to migrate. They have also changed women's motives for migrating. Fewer women move for "family reunification" and more move in search of work. And when they find work, it is often within the growing "care sector," which, according to the economist Nancy Folbre, currently encompasses 20 percent of all American jobs.[9]

A good number of the women who migrate to fill these positions seem to be single mothers. After all, about a fifth of the world's households are headed by women: 24 percent in the industrial world, 19 percent in Africa, 18 percent in Latin America and the Caribbean, and 13 percent in Asia and the Pacific. Some such women are on their own because their husbands have left them or because they have escaped abusive marriages. In addition to these single mothers, there is also a shadow group of "almost" single mothers, only nominally married to men who are alcoholics, gamblers, or just too worn down by the hardships of life to make a go of it. For example, one Filipina nanny now working in California was married to a man whose small business collapsed as a result of overseas competition. He could find no well-paid job abroad that he found acceptable, so he urged his wife to "go and earn good money" as a lap dancer in a café in Japan. With that money, he hoped to restart his business. Appalled by his proposal, she separated from him to become a nanny in the United States.

Many if not most women migrants have children. The average age of women migrants into the United States is twenty-nine, and most come from countries, such as the Philippines and Sri Lanka, where female identity centers on motherhood, and where the birth rate is high. Often migrants, especially the undocumented ones, cannot bring their children with them. Most mothers try to leave their children in the care of grandmothers, aunts, and fathers, in roughly that order. An orphanage is a last resort. A number of nannies working in rich countries hire nannies to care for their own children back home either as solo caretakers or as aides to the female relatives left in charge back home. Carmen Ronquillo, for example, migrated from the Philippines to Rome to work as a maid for an architect and single mother of two. She left behind her husband, two teenagers—and a maid.[10]

Whatever arrangements these mothers make for their children, however, most feel the separation acutely, expressing guilt and remorse to the researchers who interview them. Says one migrant mother who left her two-month-old baby in the care of a relative, "The first two years I felt like I was going crazy. You have to believe me when I say that it was like I was having intense psychological problems. I would catch myself gazing at nothing, thinking about my child."[11] Recounted another migrant nanny through tears, "When I saw my children again, I thought, 'Oh children do grow up even without their mother.' I left my youngest when she was only five years old. She was already nine when I saw her again, but she still wanted me to carry her."[12]

Many more migrant female workers than migrant male workers stay in their adopted countries—in fact, most do. In staying, these mothers remain separated from their children, a choice freighted, for many, with a terrible sadness. Some migrant nannies, isolated in their employers' homes and faced with what is often depressing work, find solace in lavishing their affluent charges with the love and care they wish they could provide their own children. In an interview with Rhacel Parreñas, Vicky Diaz, a college-educated schoolteacher who left behind five children in the Philippines, said, "the only thing you can do is to give all your love to the child [in your care]. In my absence from my children, the most I could do with my situation was to give all my love to that child."[13] Without intending it, she has taken part in a global heart transplant.

As much as these mothers suffer, their children suffer more. And there are a lot of them. An estimated 30 percent of Filipino children—some eight million—live in households where at least one parent has gone overseas. These children have counterparts in Africa, India, Sri Lanka, Latin America, and the former Soviet Union. How are these children doing? Not very well, according to a survey Manila's Scalabrini Migration Center conducted with more than seven hundred children in 1996. Compared to their classmates, the children of migrant workers more frequently fell ill; they were more likely to express anger, confusion, and apathy; and they performed particularly poorly in school. Other studies of this population show a rise in delinquency and child suicide.[14] When such children were asked whether they would also migrate when they grew up, leaving their own children in the care of others, they all said no.

Faced with these facts, one senses some sort of injustice at work, linking the emotional deprivation of these children with the surfeit of affection their First World counterparts enjoy. In her study of native-born women of color who do domestic work, Sau-Ling Wong argues that the time and energy these workers devote to the children of their employers is diverted from their own children.[15] But time and energy are not all that's involved; so, too, is love. In this sense, we can speak about love as an unfairly distributed resource—extracted from one place and enjoyed somewhere else.

Is love really a "resource" to which a child has a right? Certainly the United

Nations Declaration on the Rights of the Child asserts all children's right to an "atmosphere of happiness, love, and understanding." Yet in some ways, this claim is hard to make. The more we love and are loved, the more deeply we can love. Love is not fixed in the same way that most material resources are fixed. Put another way, if love is a resource, it's a *renewable* resource; it creates more of itself. And yet Rowena Bautista can't be in two places at once. Her day has only so many hours. It may also be true that the more love she gives to Noa, the less she gives to her own three children back in the Philippines. Noa in the First World gets more love, and Clinton and Princela in the Third World get less. In this sense, love does appear scarce and limited, like a mineral extracted from the earth.

Perhaps, then, feelings *are* distributable resources, but they behave somewhat differently from either scarce or renewable material resources. According to Freud, we don't "withdraw" and "invest" feeling but rather *displace* or redirect it. The process is an unconscious one, whereby we don't actually give up a feeling of, say, love or hate, so much as we find a new object for it—in the case of sexual feeling, a more appropriate object than the original one, whom Freud presumed to be our opposite-sex parent. While Freud applied the idea of displacement mainly to relationships within the nuclear family, it seems only a small stretch to apply it to relationships like Rowena's to Noa. As Rowena told Frank, the *Wall Street Journal* reporter, "I give Noa what I can't give my children."

Understandably, First World parents welcome and even invite nannies to redirect their love in this manner. The way some employers describe it, a nanny's love of her employer's child is a natural product of her more loving Third World culture, with its warm family ties, strong community life, and long tradition of patient maternal love

of children. In hiring a nanny, many such employers implicitly hope to import a poor country's "native culture," thereby replenishing their own rich country's depleted culture of care. They import the benefits of Third World "family values." Says the director of a co-op nursery in the San Francisco Bay Area, "This may be odd to say, but the teacher's aides we hire from Mexico and Guatemala know how to love a child better than the middle-class white parents. They are more relaxed, patient, and joyful. They enjoy the kids more. These professional parents are pressured for time and anxious to develop their kids' talents. I tell the parents that they can really learn how to love from the Latinas and the Filipinas."

When asked why Anglo mothers should relate to children so differently than do Filipina teacher's aides, the nursery director speculated, "The Filipinas are brought up in a more relaxed, loving environment. They aren't as rich as we are, but they aren't so pressured for time, so materialistic, so anxious. They have a more loving, family-oriented culture." One mother, an American lawyer, expressed a similar view:

> Carmen just enjoys my son. She doesn't worry whether . . . he's learning his letters, or whether he'll get into a good preschool. She just enjoys him. And actually, with anxious busy parents like us, that's really what Thomas needs. I love my son more than anyone in this world. But at this stage Carmen is better for him.

Filipina nannies I have interviewed in California paint a very different picture of the love they share with their First World charges. Theirs is not an import of happy peasant mothering but a love that partly develops on American shores, informed by an American ideology of mother-child bonding and fostered by intense loneliness and longing for their own children. If love is a precious resource, it is not one simply extracted from the Third World and implanted in the First; rather, it owes its very existence to a peculiar cultural alchemy that occurs in the land to which it is imported.

———————

For María Gutierrez, who cares for the eight-month-old baby of two hard-working professionals (a lawyer and a doctor, born in the Philippines but now living in San Jose, California), loneliness and long work hours feed a love for her employers' child. "I love Ana more than my own two children. Yes, more! It's strange, I know. But I have time to be with her. I'm paid. I am lonely here. I work ten hours a day, with one day off. I don't know any neighbors on the block. And so this child gives me what I need."

Not only that, but she is able to provide her employer's child with a different sort of attention and nurturance than she could deliver to her own children. "I'm more patient," she explains, "more relaxed. I put the child first. My kids, I treated them the way my mother treated me."

I asked her how her mother had treated her and she replied:

> "My mother grew up in a farming family. It was a hard life. My mother wasn't warm to me. She didn't touch me or say 'I love you.' She didn't think she should do that. Before I was born she had lost four babies—two in miscarriage and two died as babies. I think she was afraid to love me as a baby because she thought I might die too. Then she put me to work as a 'little mother' caring for my four younger brothers and sisters. I didn't have time to play."

Fortunately, an older woman who lived next door took an affectionate interest in María, often feeding her and even taking her in overnight when she was sick. María felt closer to this woman's relatives than she did to her biological aunts and cousins. She had been, in some measure, informally adopted—

a practice she describes as common in the Philippine countryside and even in some towns during the 1960s and 1970s.

In a sense, María experienced a premodern childhood, marked by high infant mortality, child labor, and an absence of sentimentality, set within a culture of strong family commitment and community support. Reminiscent of fifteenth-century France, as Philippe Ariès describes it in *Centuries of Childhood,* this was a childhood before the romanticization of the child and before the modern middle-class ideology of intensive mothering.[16] Sentiment wasn't the point; commitment was.

María's commitment to her own children, aged twelve and thirteen when she left to work abroad, bears the mark of that upbringing. Through all of their anger and tears, María sends remittances and calls, come hell or high water. The commitment is there. The sentiment, she has to work at. When she calls home now, María says, "I tell my daughter 'I love you.' At first it sounded fake. But after a while it became natural. And now she says it back. It's strange, but I think I learned that it was okay to say that from being in the United States."

María's story points to a paradox. On the one hand, the First World extracts love from the Third World. But what is being extracted is partly produced or "assembled" here: the leisure, the money, the ideology of the child, the intense loneliness and yearning for one's own children. In María's case, a premodern childhood in the Philippines, a postmodern ideology of mothering and childhood in the United States, and the loneliness of migration blend to produce the love she gives to her employers' child. That love is also a product of the nanny's freedom from the time pressure and school anxiety parents feel in a culture that lacks a social safety net—one where both parent and child have to "make it" at work because no state policy, community, or marital tie is reliable enough to sustain them. In that sense, the love María gives as a nanny does not suffer from the disabling effects of the American version of late capitalism.

If all this is true—if, in fact, the nanny's love is something at least partially produced by the conditions under which it is given—is María's love of a First World child really being extracted from her own Third World children? Yes, because her daily presence has been removed, and with it the daily expression of her love. It is, of course, the nanny herself who is doing the extracting. Still, if her children suffer the loss of her affection, she suffers with them. This, indeed, is globalization's pound of flesh.

Curiously, the suffering of migrant women and their children is rarely visible to the First World beneficiaries of nanny love. Noa's mother focuses on her daughter's relationship with Rowena. Ana's mother focuses on her daughter's relationship with María. Rowena loves Noa, María loves Ana. That's all there is to it. The nanny's love is a thing in itself. It is unique, private—fetishized. Marx talked about the fetishization of things, not feelings. When we make a fetish of an object—an SUV, for example—we see that object as independent of its context. We disregard, he would argue, the men who harvested the rubber latex, the assembly-line workers who bolted on the tires, and so on. Just as we mentally isolate our idea of an object from the human scene within which it was made, so, too, we unwittingly separate the love between nanny and child from the global capitalist order of love to which it very much belongs.

———

The notion of extracting resources from the Third World in order to enrich the First World is hardly new. It harks back to imperialism in its most literal form: the nineteenth-century extraction of gold, ivory, and rubber from the Third World. That openly coercive, male-centered imperialism, which persists today, was always paralleled by a quieter imperialism in which women were more central. Today, as love and care become the "new gold," the female part of the story has grown in prominence. In both cases, through the death or displacement of their parents, Third World children pay the price.

Imperialism in its classic form involved the north's plunder of physical resources from the south. Its main protagonists were virtually all men: explorers, kings, missionaries, soldiers, and the local men who were forced at gunpoint to harvest wild rubber latex and the like. European states lent their legitimacy to these endeavors, and an ideology emerged to support them: "the white man's burden" in Britain and *la mission civilisatrice* in France, both of which emphasized the benefits of colonization for the colonized.

The brutality of that era's imperialism is not to be minimized, even as we compare the extraction of material resources from the Third World of that time to the extraction of emotional resources today. Today's north does not extract love from the south by force: there are no colonial officers in tan helmets, no invading armies, no ships bearing arms sailing off to the colonies. Instead, we see a benign scene of Third World women pushing baby carriages, elder care workers patiently walking, arms linked, with elderly clients on streets or sitting beside them in First World parks.

Today, coercion operates differently. While the sex trade and some domestic service is brutally enforced, in the main the new emotional imperialism does not issue from the barrel of a gun. Women choose to migrate for domestic work. But they choose it because economic pressures all but coerce them to. That yawning gap between rich and poor countries is itself a form of coercion, pushing Third World mothers to seek work in the First for lack of options closer to home. But given the prevailing free market ideology, migration is viewed as a "personal choice." Its consequences are seen as "personal problems." In this sense, migration creates not a white man's burden but, through a series of invisible links, a dark child's burden.

———————

Some children of migrant mothers in the Philippines, Sri Lanka, Mexico, and elsewhere may be well cared for by loving kin in their communities. We need more data if we are to find out how such children are really doing. But if we discover that they aren't doing very well, how are we to respond? I can think of three possible approaches. First, we might say that all women everywhere should stay home and take care of their own families. The problem with Rowena is not migration but neglect of her traditional role. A second approach might be to deny that a problem exists: the care drain is an inevitable outcome of globalization, which is itself good for the world. A supply of labor has met a demand—what's the problem? If the first approach condemns global migration, the second celebrates it. Neither acknowledges its human costs.

According to a third approach—the one I take—loving, paid child care with reasonable hours is a very good thing. And globalization brings with it new opportunities, such as a nanny's access to good pay. But it also introduces painful new emotional realities for Third World children. We need to embrace the needs of Third World societies, including their children. We need to develop a global sense of ethics to match emerging global economic realities. If we go out to buy a pair of Nike shoes, we want to know how low the wage and how long the hours were for the Third World worker who made them. Likewise, if Rowena is taking care of a two-year-old six thousand miles from her home, we should want to know what is happening to her own children.

If we take this third approach, what should we or others in the Third World do?

One obvious course would be to develop the Philippine and other Third World economies to such a degree that their citizens can earn as much money inside their countries as outside them. Then the Rowenas of the world could support their children in jobs they'd find at home. While such an obvious solution would seem ideal—if not easily achieved—Douglas Massey, a specialist in migration, points to some unexpected problems, at least in the short run. In Massey's view, it is not underdevelopment that sends migrants like Rowena off to the First World but development itself. The higher the percentage of women working in local manufacturing, he finds, the greater the chance that any one woman will leave on a first, undocumented trip abroad. Perhaps these women's horizons broaden. Perhaps they meet others who have gone abroad. Perhaps they come to want better jobs and more goods. Whatever the original motive, the more people in one's community migrate, the more likely one is to migrate too.

If development creates migration, and if we favor some form of development, we need to find more humane responses to the migration such development is likely to cause. For those women who migrate in order to flee abusive husbands, one part of the answer would be to create solutions to that problem closer to home—domestic-violence shelters in these women's home countries, for instance. Another might be to find ways to make it easier for migrating nannies to bring their children with them. Or as a last resort, employers could be required to finance a nanny's regular visits home.

A more basic solution, of course, is to raise the value of caring work itself, so that whoever does it gets more rewards for it. Care, in this case, would no longer be such a "pass-on" job. And now here's the rub: the value of the labor of raising a child—always low relative to the value of other kinds of labor—has, under the impact of globalization, sunk lower still. Children matter to their parents immeasurably, of course, but the labor of raising them does not earn much credit in the eyes of the world. When middle-class housewives raised children as an unpaid, full-time role, the work was dignified by its aura of middle-classness. That was the one upside to the otherwise confining cult of middle-class, nineteenth- and early-twentieth-century American womanhood. But when the unpaid work of raising a child became the paid work of child-care workers, its low market value revealed the abidingly low value of caring work generally—and further lowered it.

The low value placed on caring work results neither from an absence of a need for it nor from the simplicity or ease of doing it. Rather, the declining value of child care results from a cultural politics of inequality. It can be compared with the declining value of basic food crops relative to manufactured goods on the international market. Though clearly more necessary to life, crops such as wheat and rice fetch low and declining prices, while manufactured goods are more highly valued. Just as the market price of primary produce keeps the Third World low in the community of nations, so the low market value of care keeps the status of the women who do it—and, ultimately, all women—low.

One excellent way to raise the value of care is to involve fathers in it. If men shared the care of family members worldwide, care would spread laterally instead of being passed down a social class ladder. In Norway, for example, all employed men are eligible for a year's paternity leave at 90 percent pay. Some 80 percent of Norwegian men now take over a month of parental leave. In this way, Norway is a model to the world. For indeed it is men who have for the most part stepped aside from caring work, and it is with them that the "care drain" truly begins.

In all developed societies, women work at paid jobs. According to the International Labor Organization, half of the world's women between ages fifteen and sixty-four do paid work. Between 1960 and 1980, sixty-nine out of eighty-eight countries surveyed showed a growing proportion of women in paid work. Since 1950, the rate of increase has skyrocketed in the United States, while remaining high in Scandinavia and the United Kingdom and moderate in France and Germany. If we want developed societies with women doctors, political leaders, teachers, bus drivers, and computer programmers, we will need qualified people to give loving care to their children. And there is no reason why every society should not enjoy such loving paid child care. It may even be true that Rowena Bautista or María Guttierez are the people to provide it, so long as their own children either come with them or otherwise receive all the care they need. In the end, Article 9 of the United Nations Declaration on the Rights of the Child—which the United States has not yet signed—states an important goal for both Clinton and Princela Bautista and for feminism. It says we need to value care as our most precious resource, and to notice where it comes from and ends up. For, these days, the personal is global.

NOTES

1. Information about Rowena Bautista is drawn from Robert Frank, "High-Paying Nanny Positions Puncture Fabric of Family Life in Developing Nations," *Wall Street Journal,* December 18, 2001. All interviews not otherwise attributed were conducted by the author. . . .

2. *New York Times,* September 1, 2001, A8.

3. William Greider, *One World, Ready or Not: The Manic Logic of Global Capitalism* (New York: Simon and Schuster, 1997), p. 21.

4. Castles and Miller, 1998, p. 8. See also Hania Zlotnik, "Trends of International Migration Since 1965: What Existing Data Reveal," *International Migration,* vol. 37, no. 1 (1999), pp. 22–61.

5. Castles and Miller, 1998, p. 5.

6. Castles and Miller, 1998, p. 9. Also see the Technical Symposium on International Migration and Development, the United Nations General Assembly, Special Session on the International Conference on Population and Development, The Hague, The Netherlands, June 29–July 2, 1998, Executive Summary, p. 2. See also *Migrant News*, no. 2 (November 1998), p. 2.

7. Castles and Miller, 1998, p. xi.

8. Arlie Russell Hochschild, *The Time Bind: When Work Becomes Home and Home Becomes Work* (New York: Avon, 1997) pp. xxi, 268.

9. Nancy Folbre, *The Invisible Heart: Economics and Family Values* (New York: The New Press, 2001), p. 55.

10. Rhacel Parreñas, "The Global Servants: (Im)Migrant Filipina Domestic Workers in Rome and Los Angeles," Ph.D. dissertation, Department of Ethnic Studies, University of California, Berkeley, 1999, p. 60.

11. Parreñas, 1999, pp. 123, 154.

12. Parreñas, 1999, p. 154.

13. Parreñas, 1999, p. 123.

14. Frank, 2001.

15. Sau-Ling Wong, "Diverted Mothering: Representations of Caregivers of Color in the Age of 'Multiculturalism,'" in *Mothering: Ideology, Experience and Agency*, ed. Evelyn Nakano Glenn, Grace Chang, and Linda Rennie Forcey (London: Routledge, 1994), pp. 67–91.

16. Philippe Ariès, *Centuries of Childhood: A Social History of Family Life* (New York: Vintage, 1962); Sharon Hays, *The Cultural Contradictions of Motherhood* (New Haven: Yale University Press, 1996).

✑ READING 38 ✑

Capitalism and the Erosion of Care

Paula England and Nancy Folbre

When everything is for sale, the person who volunteers time, who helps a stranger, who agrees to work for a modest wage out of commitment to the public good, who desists from littering even when no one is looking, who forgoes an opportunity to free-ride, begins to feel like a sucker.

—ROBERT KUTTNER, *EVERYTHING FOR SALE*[1]

Robert Kuttner's warning can be rephrased in terms that highlight its resonance with the interface between capitalism and family values. When

"Capitalism and the Erosion of Care" by Paula England and Nancy Folbre from *Unconventional Wisdom: Alternative Perspectives on the New Economy,* edited by Jeff Madrick. Copyright © 2000. Reprinted with permission from The New Century Foundation, Inc., New York.

everything is for sale, the woman who devotes herself to her children, who agrees to work for a nonprofit that cannot afford to pay market wages, who takes care of sick and elderly relatives that no one else will tend to, or who passes up an opportunity to get something for nothing, begins to feel like a sucker. A growing feminist literature on caring labor emphasizes a cruel paradox. On one hand, capitalist development tends to destabilize forms of patriarchal power that once gave women little choice but to specialize in caring for others. This is to be welcomed. On the other hand, it creates competitive pressures that tend to penalize women, men, and institutions that seek to provide genuine care for other people.[2]

In this chapter, we argue that feminist theory offers important insights into the evolution of care services in the economy as a whole. Although we apply some of the conventional tools of both neoclassical and Marxian economics, we draw more heavily from ecological economics, arguing that personal forms of care for others create "externalities" or unanticipated spillover benefits from individual transactions. We argue that increased competition in the provision of services tends to intensify efforts to offload care costs (to make someone else pay), to reduce care services, and to obscure negative effects on the quality of care. These processes, similar to those that lead to pollution and deterioration of the natural environment, erode the supply of care. Ironically, patriarchal control over women has traditionally provided a partially effective— though extremely unfair—buffer of protection for some members of U.S. society, especially children. We need to build a better and more equitable buffer to protect our families and communities from the corrosive effects of the self-interested opportunism that market forces sometimes reward. . . .

I. The Economics of Caring Labor

Neither a stand-alone competitive market nor a centrally planned society (nor any simple combination of the two) can guarantee an adequate quantity or quality of caring labor. The feminist analysis of caring labor insists that something is missing from both neoclassical and Marxian economic theory. Care is more than an input

into the development of human capital. It is also an *output,* something we generally would like to have more of for its own sake. The experiences of being a parent, a neighbor, a friend, or a lover, for example, offer direct rewards. For many people, they are ends in themselves.

Worrying about care reminds us that economic growth is simply a means to these ends. As Nobel laureate Amartya Sen points out, our social goal should be to maximize the development of human capabilities— measured by such indicators as life expectancy, literacy, and other skills—rather than trying to maximize collective consumption or even collective happiness.[3] Care is necessary to develop human capabilities, but is also an important capability in and of itself.

Care cannot be planned from the top down, or simply assigned. It flows from social norms and individual preferences. It is also a skill that must be developed and exercised, one that relies heavily on what some psychologists call "emotional intelligence."[4] But we must keep in mind that despite the intrinsic reward, care is also susceptible to economic incentives. In the long run, care that goes unrewarded is likely to diminish over time.

Can we rely on the forces of supply and demand to provide care? Perhaps to some extent. After all, if the demand for caring services goes up, people who provide them should be able to charge more. One obvious problem, however, is that truly caring individuals are less directly motivated by pecuniary concerns, and often reluctant to bargain by threatening to withhold their services. A "rational" economic person, observing the result, might conclude that it is best to avoid situations in which one might begin to care too much.

A more subtle problem emerges from a consideration of the distinctive nature of care services. The price of these services (whether paid as a wage or as a share of family income) is not a good measure of their value, because care creates the positive externalities already mentioned. Many people share in the benefits when children are brought up to be responsible, skilled, and loving adults who treat each other with courtesy and respect. There is a long list of beneficiaries. Employers profit from access to competent, disciplined, and cooperative workers. The elderly benefit from the Social Security taxes paid by the younger generation. Fellow citizens gain from having law-abiding rather than predatory neighbors.

A central economic problem, however, is that these broad gains cannot be fully captured by those who create them. Parents can't demand a fee from employers who hire their adult children and benefit from their productive efforts. Nor can they send a bill to their children's spouses and friends for the value of parental services consumed. Individual transactions cannot compensate them for the value they provide.

When child care workers or elementary school teachers genuinely care for their students, they foster an eagerness to learn and willingness to cooperate that later teachers and employers benefit from. When nurses do a good job, patients' families and employers benefit. Anyone who treats another person in a kind and helpful way creates a small benefit that is likely to be passed along. A growing body of research on social capital shows that an atmosphere of trust and care contributes not only to the development of human capital but also to economic efficiency.

Like other externalities, however, those created by care create an incentive to *free-ride*—that is, to let others pay the costs. Thus, in the absence of collective coordination, or what we might call good "rules of the game," less than optimal amounts of care will be provided because care providers are not fully compensated for their services. Quite the contrary, they often tend to be crowded out by services that can be sold at full value to buyers able to pay for them directly—such as legal or banking services. To explore this dilemma, we need to look more carefully at how care is defined, how it has been affected by the weakening of patriarchal power in this country, and why it is so difficult to provide within unregulated markets.

Defining Care

Care is a word with many complex interrelated meanings, most of which revolve around the basic notion of concern for other people, especially dependents such as children, students, the sick, and the elderly. Many economists might interpret it as a form of altruism, but we argue that it also includes important elements of trust and social obligation. Care may flow from affection, but it often requires work—a very different kind of work from that which economists typically focus on. It is work that requires personal attention, services that are normally provided on a face-to-face or first-name basis, often for people who cannot clearly express their own needs. In our view, the motive underlying this work often affects its quality. Emily Abel and Margaret Nelson put it this way: "Care givers are expected to provide love as well as labor, 'caring for,' while 'caring about.'"[5]

Some writing on care treats it as an activity that is not only intrinsically rewarding, but also morally transcendent. But many feminist economists shun overly sweet descriptions of caring labor, rejecting the implication that it is necessarily more enjoyable or fulfilling than other types of work. Indeed, much attention focuses on the contradictory dimensions of care as an activity that is frustrating as well as rewarding. Workers are forced to engage in such "emotional" labor, required to be polite, encouraging, and cheerful, whether they feel that way or not.[6]

Scholars on the left have traditionally emphasized the importance of unalienated labor, the virtues of producing for direct use rather than for sale in the market. But as the history of slavery, feudalism, and patriarchy shows, work can be exploitative whether it is part of a market economy or not. Did we ever live in a golden age in which personal, family-based relationships fostered egalitarian communities? This is the implication of much communitarian writing, which blames the growth of the modern, impersonal marketplace for many of our social woes. Feminist scholars question this implication for the obvious reason that personal relations have often been patriarchal relations, seemingly designed to assign most of the economic burdens of care to women so as to allow men more freedom to compete or pursue other wants.

The line between caring and "un-caring" labor simply does not coincide with the line between the family and the market. Indeed, feminist scholarship emphasizes the remarkable similarity between women's responsibilities for care in the home and their responsibilities for care in paid jobs such as teaching and nursing. By emphasizing this similarity, the concept of caring labor focuses attention on the gendered character of social norms that shape the division of labor in both the family and the market. Women are expected, even required, to provide more care than men. This expectation is rooted deeply within the history of patriarchal society in the United States and elsewhere.

Capitalism and the Weakening of Patriarchal Control over Women

Where does care come from? Economists have traditionally avoided this question by confining their attention to the behavior of self-interested adults in the marketplace, and leaving dependents entirely out of the picture. Even neoclassical theory, which is premised on the individual pursuit of self-interest, has treated altruism within the family as a "natural" and therefore relatively uninteresting phenomenon, at least for economic purposes. According to neoclassical economists, women specialize in the provision of care for others either because they have a comparative advantage (they are more "efficient" at it than men) or because they get more pleasure out of it than men do—enough pleasure to compensate them directly for the time, money, and energy required.

But if this particular form of specialization is completely natural and automatic, it is difficult to explain why so many social institutions have historically imposed much greater restrictions on women than on men. As a large body of feminist scholarship shows, women have traditionally had little choice but to specialize in the care of dependents. Explicit restrictions on their access to education and to work outside the home have both reduced their bargaining power and lowered the opportunity cost of time devoted to care. Because they didn't have other opportunities, they weren't giving up as much in order to provide care. Even in relatively egalitarian societies like our own, social norms put greater pressure on women than on men to take care of others, especially family members.

Feminist theory emphasizes the coercive dimensions of social norms of masculinity and femininity. A set of social rules that assigns women greater responsibility than men for the welfare of others can be understood as a system of "discriminatory obligation."[7] It can also be interpreted as a form of "socially imposed altruism" in which women are socialized to act in more caring ways than men, especially toward children.[8] Precisely because these responsibilities were imposed from above, they have been weakened as women's opportunities outside the home have increased, enhancing their bargaining power. Many women are now asking why moms should be expected to give up more than dads.

It is difficult to name a precept more central to the neoclassical vision than its confidence in individual pursuit of self-interest. This confidence has historically been lodged in the presumption, as we have noted, that women would tend to family responsibilities, providing necessary levels of altruism and care. Needless to say, this presumption has been shaken by the destabilization of the patriarchal family and the dramatic movement of wives and mothers into paid employment in the United States. Once it becomes apparent that the family is susceptible to economic reorganization and change, it can no longer be so easily excluded from the larger picture, and it becomes apparent that the larger economy has never been entirely based on the individual pursuit of self-interest. Market economies have always depended on strict rules for the nonmarket provision of care, especially for dependents.

Both personal experience and formal game theory models show that it is generally easier for an individual to avoid responsibilities for the care of others than it is to persuade someone else to assume those responsibilities. Providing care for another is risky, since you cannot be sure it will be reciprocated (hence Kuttner's point about good people being made to feel like suckers). The competitive marketplace is a bit akin to a footrace in which anyone carrying a child or another dependent is at a disadvantage. They do not get their just economic rewards and get left further and further behind. Unless the rules of the race are redefined so that everyone is required to carry a certain share of the burden of obligation, individual competitors have every

incentive to offload and outsource their care responsibilities.

Incentives For Care

Many feminist economists will agree that it is better to pay for care services in the market than to extract it coercively from women in the home. That is no reason to ignore the problems built into market provision. As pointed out earlier, care provides externalities that will never be fully rewarded through individual transactions. Furthermore, the nature of care makes it difficult to assure the quality of the services being provided.

One difficulty with creating appropriate incentives for caregiving is that it is difficult to monitor. Economists have long recognized that some forms of work cannot be efficiently based on purely extrinsic rewards for this very reason. Workers who seek to minimize effort per unit of pay can often conceal their level of effort. It is relatively expensive to monitor workers who provide caring labor, because their "product" cannot be weighed or counted. A nanny who seems perfectly loving and nurturing with infants or toddlers when her employers are present may completely ignore them as soon as the parents leave. Some day-care centers now provide videocams accessible from the Web that allow parents to view what is going on from moment to moment. On the other hand, constant scrutiny of someone else's care can take almost as much time as directly providing that care.

Economists studying jobs in the manufacturing sector observe that employers may offer their workers a higher-than-market-clearing wage in part to foster a sense of reciprocity that encourages effort, or simply to increase the cost of losing their job if they are caught shirking. Workers are particularly likely to command such an "efficiency wage" (high enough to elicit greater effort) when employers can easily discern the effects of effort on product quality. But in care work the difficulty of monitoring worker effort is compounded by the fact that outputs are diffuse, difficult to measure, and enjoyed by parties other than those actually paying the costs.

Gathering good information about caregiving is not an easy task. Expert psychologists, much less parents, are uncertain about the effects of caregivers' characteristics on children's development. Social scientists find it extraordinarily difficult to measure the kinds of neighborhood effects that lead to "collective efficacy."[9] So-called third-party problems further complicate matters. We can't necessarily trust children's assessments of whether their teachers are doing a good job or not.

In general, personal and emotional forms of labor have a subtle character that is far more difficult to assess than most other dimensions of work performance. Who is the best teacher? The best parent? It is often very hard to say. The teacher who improves children's test scores the most may not be the one who makes them feel confident and self-motivated. The parent with the hottest temper may, ironically, also be the one who has the strongest emotional connection with the child. Obviously, skill matters. But motivation also matters—we tend to trust caregivers who convey a sense that they genuinely care for their students, patients, or clients.

Workers who provide care must love their work, we tell ourselves (especially if they are cheap, convenient, and polite to those paying the bill). Otherwise, why would they do it for such low pay? As advocates of pay equity have pointed out for years, many nurses are paid less than tree-trimmers, and parking lot attendants earn more than day-care workers. These differences cannot be explained by the characteristics of the people in these jobs. A small but significant pay penalty is discernible for workers in caring occupations, holding education, experience, and other important factors equal.[10] Some people indeed enter caring jobs because they are intrinsically motivated. However, many others enter them simply because no other options are open to them. Furthermore, the conditions of work, which include low pay and little job security, do little to foster genuine commitment. As a result, even our best caregivers often burn out.

Women who specialize in caring for young children, spouses, or elders at home are vulnerable to similar problems. Because pay is strongly affected by job experience, women who leave employment to care for family members suffer wage penalties for years after they reenter the job market.[11] Statistical analysis shows that mothers who work part-time while their children are young also pay a penalty since part-time experience has a lower return than full-time experience.[12] Being employed fewer years also affects mothers' pensions and Social Security benefits. These effects are particularly consequential when caregivers lack the financial assistance of a partner specializing in market work. Children and others dependent on the caregiver suffer as well.

We should expect and demand as much care from men as from women. But no amount of moralistic finger-wagging is going to persuade individuals to make choices that put them at a competitive disadvantage in a race for ever-greater financial benefits. We don't know what level of care can be sustained in an economy that rewards the individual pursuit of self-interest far more generously than the provision of care for others.

2. The Care Sector

Most service-oriented companies are less immediately affected by the growing international mobility of capital than manufacturing firms are. In the future, we may ship off our children, sick, and elderly to low-wage countries to be cared for—or simply import more low-wage immigrants to care for them here. In the meantime, increased competitive pressure in the production of tangible goods has the indirect effect of intensifying efforts to cut the costs of maintaining and producing our labor force. These efforts impinge directly on the provision of care.

Yet we lack a clear picture of what we could call the "care sector" of the economy. As we know, the nonmarket work of women, a primary source of caring labor, has been explicitly excluded from most economic analysis. The tripartite distinction among agriculture, industry, and services emerged as a classification of types of products without reference to their personal or emotional content. "Services" have always been distinguished simply by their lack of a material output that could be counted or weighed.

Still, we can patch existing bits of data on time-use and the composition of the labor force together in ways that help explain why caring labor is likely to become an increasingly important economic concern. William Baumol predicted long ago that we would suffer a "cost disease" of the service sector, with increases in relative costs resulting from less adaptability to technological change.[13] His predictions have not been completely borne out. In recent years many services, including banking, retail, and entertainment, have been transformed by waves of innovation. But in an important respect, his prediction was spot on. Productivity growth has been and is likely to continue to be slowest in care services requiring personal and emotional contact. These services have simply been redistributed and in some ways concentrated as other dimensions of work have been transformed.

The Decline of Household Production

The two most conspicuous trends shaping the historical organization of care in our economy have been fertility decline and women's entrance into paid employment, both under way for more than 150 years. The first of these trends has reduced our overall demand for caring labor by reducing the number of children relative to the working-age population — an effect increasingly countervailed by the growing proportion of the elderly. The second of these trends has reduced the supply of caring labor outside the market by raising its opportunity cost: Women now have access to better-paying jobs than they used to—as a result, the cost of not working for pay has increased. On the other hand, caring occupations such as teaching, nursing, and home health care have increased dramatically as a percentage of the paid labor force in recent years.

The harder one thinks about these trends, the more arbitrary and misleading our conventional picture of economic development begins to seem. We look back on a history of economic growth that we have carefully constructed by "cooking the books." We divided the economy into two parts—the family (considered, like environmental assets, a part of nature) and the market. Household labor was simply not included in the Gross Domestic Product. When women reallocated their work from an arena in which it wasn't measured to the market economy, where it showed up in dollar terms, we registered significant economic growth. But what happened to the underlying quantity and quality of care services? We don't really know.

Economists have just begun reconstructing quantitative estimates that reveal the magnitude of mismeasurement over time. If we assume that women devoted about as much productive effort to combined paid and unpaid work as men did to paid work—an assumption justified by historical research and early census surveys—we can reconstruct estimates of the total labor force of the United States that include housewives with other paid workers providing domestic and personal services. Thus revised, this category accounts for a larger share of the workforce than any other for much of our history. In 1930, for instance, if we combine housewives and mothers without paid employment with other workers providing paid domestic and personal services, we find that they comprised 41 percent of all workers, compared to the 24 percent of all workers providing other types of services and 20 percent in manufacturing, mechanical, and mining jobs.[14] The development of new cooking and cleaning technologies made household work much more efficient— possibly affecting the productivity growth of the economy as a whole more than even railroad and automotive technologies.

The simplest (and also the crudest) way of estimating the value of women's unpaid domestic and personal services is to multiply the number of full-time equivalent workers in these jobs times women's average wages in paid employment in this sector. It is widely conceded that this number represents an underestimate for two reasons. Women traditionally faced discrimination in paid employment that lowered their market wages. Furthermore, if women choose not to work for a wage, it is often because the true value of their home work is higher than the pay being offered, so even a nondiscriminatory wage understates their productivity. Acknowledging this caveat, studies of Australia, Canada, and the United States show that nonmarket activities valued solely on the basis of labor inputs account for a very significant proportion—between 40 percent and 60 percent — of the total value of all output.[15] Total Economic Product (including the value of nonmarket work)

grows at a very different rhythm and rate over time than Gross Domestic Product. One summary of these findings suggests that, when declines in the stock of natural resources and environmental health are taken into account along with declines in nonmarket work, we have made no economic progress in the United States since 1970—even though Gross Domestic Product per capita has almost doubled.[16]

Even less appreciated is another measurement problem, rooted in the tendency to ignore the qualitative dimensions of caring labor. Much of what housewives did—and do—involves complex multitasking that defies assignment to any one sector of the economy. Serving a salad, for instance, could entail harvesting greens from a kitchen garden while teaching children the names of the plants (agriculture plus education), preparing a dressing while keeping an eye on an infant (manufacturing plus child care), setting the table and welcoming family members to the table (restaurant plus personal services). The modern parent may collect raw materials from the salad bar at the supermarket rather than the garden (hunting and gathering rather than agriculture) but the point remains the same. And within this mix of activities, those with personal and emotional significance—such as choosing something a family member especially likes, or preparing it in a special way—are often far more important than the market value of the meal itself.

Modern time-use surveys often emphasize the distinction between a primary activity and a secondary activity that may be performed simultaneously but is considered of a lower priority, not the "main activity." Examples include listening to the radio while cooking or keeping an eye on a child while doing the laundry. Secondary time-use is particularly relevant to the analysis of child care, which is often combined with other activities. Estimates suggest that somewhere between one-half and three-quarters of all time spent in child care may be accompanied by another activity.[17] These forms of joint production greatly complicate valuation of nonmarket activities.

The entire exercise of imputing market values is based on the notion that there is easy substitutability between home-produced goods and services and market substitutes. This is almost certainly the case for most material goods, and it may even be the case for many services. It matters little to most people, for instance, who vacuums their floors or cleans their toilets. But purchased services are only partial substitutes for personal services in which the identity of the care-provider and the continuity of the care relationship matter. Purchased care can be a good substitute for the custodial and educational component of child care, and for some portion—but not all—of the emotional component. Even parents who rely on paid care during the work day spend significant amounts of time with their children, and the quality of this time is extremely important.

As families purchase more services, they probably reallocate their nonmarket time and effort away from material production toward the personal and emotional dimensions of care. In an analysis of historical time-use data, for instance, Keith Bryant and Kathleen Zick show that parents may actually have increased the amount of time they spend in primary and secondary child care time *per child,* implying that paid child care may largely have displaced secondary or "on-call" time when most of parental attention was actually elsewhere—cooking dinner, for instance, while kids played in the yard next door.[18] Thus, the overall quantity of family care time has declined—but its quality has probably increased. Increased freedom to explore work opportunities outside the home means that the time that women spend on home care is more freely—and perhaps more joyously—given than before.

Whether improvements in quality of nonmarket work have been sufficient to compensate for declines in quantity we cannot say. But the greater the role that personal and emotional care play in nonmarket work, the greater the downward bias in market-based estimates of its value. There are some things you cannot buy perfect substitutes for. Nowadays the personal and emotional content of home life is becoming more and more concentrated in a relatively small number of activities—such as sharing meals or telling bedtime stories. Past a certain point—which we have yet to carefully define or negotiate—family time cannot be reduced without adverse consequences for all family members.

The Growth of the Service Sector

The growth of service jobs is a much-remarked-upon feature of modern economic development, associated with the expansion of women's labor force participation. Services vary considerably along the dimension of personal contact. Some involve working purely with information, and some involve working purely with people, with many permutations in between.

Women tend to move into jobs that resemble their traditional responsibilities for family care, a factor that contributes to occupational segregation. By one recent estimate, 53 percent of workers in the United States would need to change jobs to equalize the occupational distribution by gender.[19] That women are for the most part segregated in lower-paying jobs than men accounts for as much as 40 percent of the gender gap in earnings.[20]

The exact distribution of workers in jobs that involve care is difficult to specify. Hochschild estimates that about one-third of American workers have jobs that demand emotional labor.[21] But not all emotional labor is caring labor—some simply requires relatively shallow affective performance. Such performance may be stressful for workers but does not have serious consequences for consumers. It matters less—and is more difficult to ascertain—if an airline attendant is faking cheerfulness than if a nurse is faking concern for patients.

The two high-skilled occupations that most distinctly require care are nursing and teaching, two subcategories within the Professional, Technical, and Related category that are poorly paid, considering the amount of education they require. In the United States in 1991, almost half of all women in professional and technical work were either nurses or teachers. Throughout the world professional women are overrepresented in these two occupations.[22] Among occupations with lower education requirements there are two within the category of Service Workers that clearly embody care—child care workers and elderly care workers. The percentage of the labor force in these occupations tends to increase in the course of economic development, and working conditions within them are a particular cause of concern in the OECD countries.

But caring responsibilities are not limited to the most explicitly caring occupations. Ethnographic studies of work show that secretaries are expected to protect their bosses from stress and construct a supportive and reassuring environment. Waitresses are encouraged to be kind as well as personable. Airline attendants are expected to be heroic in crises as well as cheerful in serving beverages. Paralegals are expected to mother the lawyers engaged in tough-guy litigation. Conventional categories cannot be used to tally up the exact percentage of jobs that fit the profile of caring labor.

Furthermore, the forms of personal contact involved in jobs are strongly affected by technological innovation and industrial organization. Both urbanization and increased geographic mobility probably reduce the likelihood that employers form personal relationships with workers or workers with consumers. But in the market as well as in the family the reduction of opportunities for personal interaction may heighten the importance of those opportunities that remain. Relationships among workers may acquire increased significance. Services requiring relatively long-term relationships, such as those provided by psychotherapists and personal athletic trainers, become conspicuously sought-after luxuries.

The nature of caring work is often defined by professional standards or by cultural norms that esteem and reward intrinsic values of care. Just because work is paid for doesn't mean that it is not also motivated by genuine concern. As competitive pressures intensify, however, employers may be forced to reduce expenditures on the least profitable forms of care. The particular features of care discussed here, particularly the difficulty of monitoring and measuring its effects, mean that the negative effects of cost-cutting may not be immediately apparent.

3. Cutting Care Costs

Karl Polanyi argued long ago that economic development tended to "disembed" companies from the communities in which they operate.[23] Over the last twenty years it has become increasingly apparent that the intensification of global competition imposes harsh penalties on companies that are not strict profit-maximizers. Privatization of services previously provided by the public sector has a similar effect. Especially when defined in ways that include emotional well-being, quality of care is far more difficult to measure than out-of-pocket cost.

A process that can be termed "the commodification of care" is under way in virtually all countries. Clearly, this process has some good features, beyond the obvious possibilities for increases in efficiency. But we need to pay closer attention to the ways in which emphasis on "fee for service" affects quality. As Clare Ungerson puts it, "the social, political, and economic contexts in which payments for care operate and the way in which payments for care are themselves organized are just as likely to transform relationships as the existence of payments themselves."[24]

The National Income and Products Accounts are not designed to study these issues, and their strict separation between private industry and government makes it difficult to measure expenditures on care services as a whole. However, a good approximation of the value of private market services can be derived by adding expenditures on Personal Services, Health, Education, Social, Other and Miscellaneous, and Private Households. These have increased from about 4.3 percent of Gross Domestic Product in 1959 to about 10.6 percent in 1997.[25] Clearly, care services represent a growing sector of the market economy.

Good illustrations of the negative impact of competitive pressure on quality emerge from even a brief consideration of health care, child care, and elder care. Expenditures in these areas have risen significantly over the past thirty years, while institutional restructuring has created new openings for profit-oriented providers. There can be little doubt that the introduction of profit-based competition helps reduce the escalation of costs. What is at issue is whether it also reduces the quality of services in ways that consumers may be slow to recognize and even slower to act upon.

Health Care

The reorganization of the health care industry in the United States has significantly reduced the escalation of health costs. But the overall quality of care is threatened. Health maintenance organizations (HMOs) charge their members a fixed amount, creating obvious pecuniary incentives for them to cut costs and to discourage unhealthy applicants. Most of their cost savings come from lower rates of hospitalization. In recent years, many HMOs have eliminated coverage for senior citizens on Medicare. A recent study published in the *Journal of the American Medical Association* found that several measures of the quality of care are significantly lower in for-profit than in nonprofit HMOs.[26]

Hospitals have dramatically reduced the length of stays by sending patients home more quickly than ever before, offloading care costs onto family members and friends. Measures of cost-effectiveness do not take these hidden costs into account. Nor have the health effects been closely scrutinized. Forced cutbacks in hospital stays created so much bad publicity that Congress passed legislation in 1996 prohibiting so-called drive-by deliveries, and requiring insurance companies to reimburse at least two days of hospital care for a normal childbirth. A recent article in *Forbes* magazine noted that hospitals are increasingly reusing medical devices that were designed to be disposable—and advised their readership not to sign surgical consent forms without specifying a ban on "unapproved re-use."[27] Even congressional Republicans voted recently in favor of a patients' bill of rights (in an effort to forestall stronger regulation by Democrats).

These well-publicized issues, however, are less troubling than the less visible deterioration in the emotional dimensions of care. As a recent *New York Times* article put it, critics say "hit and run nursing has replaced Florence Nightingale."[28] Bedside nurses have been replaced by unlicenced "care technicians." A survey of over 7,500 nurses released in 1996 reported that 73 percent felt that they had less time to comfort and educate patients.[29] At the same time, reimbursements to home health care workers have been cut back. Deborah Stone, who has extensively interviewed home health care workers, reports, "The more I talked with people, the more I saw how financial tightening and the ratcheting up of managerial scrutiny are changing the moral world of caregiving, along with the quantity and quality of care."[30] These are not changes for the better.

Child Care

Paid child care can serve as a very good complement for parental time. Although there is some controversy over the amount of time very young children should spend away from their parents, there is no evidence that paid child care per se has negative effects. The *quality* of both custodial and parental time is paramount. But experts and parents differ widely in their assessments of quality of paid care (children themselves are seldom consulted!). The time and effort required to monitor quality is quite costly, especially for parents constrained by a tight budget. A recent comprehensive survey argues that the physical and emotional environment in many child care centers remains relatively poor, partly because of poor regulation in many states.[31] Pay levels for child care workers are seldom much above minimum wage, and high turnover rates in the child care industry, averaging about 40 percent per year, preclude the development of long-term relationships between caregivers and young children.

Voluntary accreditation by the National Association for the Education of Young Children tends to improve quality. A recent California study, for instance, rated 61 percent of accredited centers as good in 1997, compared to only 26 percent of those seeking accreditation the previous year. Nationwide, however, only 5,000 out of the nation's 97,000 child care centers were accredited.[32] Furthermore, many children in paid child care are in small, informal family settings, where quality is even more variable than it is in centers. In the rush to expand child care slots to accommodate the exigencies of welfare reform, some states have provided child care vouchers that can be used virtually anywhere and may actually have a negative effect on quality.

The links among regulation, industrial organization, and quality of care are just beginning to be explored. In general, for-profit child care centers do not seem to emphasize "curbside appeal" at the expense of more difficult-to-monitor aspects of quality. However, for-profit child care centers that are part of national chains do seem to follow this strategy. What looks attractive to the parent is not necessarily what is best for the child—shiny new toys matter less than skill and commitment levels of the workers providing care.

Elder Care

Quality issues are still more salient, even shocking, in elder care. Nursing homes now employ more U.S. workers than the auto and steel industries combined. Almost 95 percent of these homes are privately run, though most are subsidized with public dollars. Turnover rates among workers are high, amounting to almost 100 percent within the first three months. According to *Consumer Reports,* about 40 percent of nursing homes repeatedly fail to pass the most basic health and safety inspections.[33] In 1999, the General Accounting Office reported that government inspections of nursing homes across the country each year show that more than one-fourth cause actual harm to their residents.[34]

Given their poor track record at meeting even basic needs, it is chilling to consider how poorly nursing homes meet the emotional needs of the elderly. Susan Eaton describes the things companies "can't bill for, but that make all the difference if you're living in a nursing home: time to listen to somebody's story, time to hold their hand, time to comfort somebody who is feeling troubled. And you can't exactly put that on your bill; imagine finding 'holding hands' on the bill. You have to have a 'treatment,' you have to have some formal procedure."[35] What we really need is some radical treatment for our larger problems of care.

4. Conclusion

Our diagnosis begins with the observation that traditional patriarchal laws and norms in the United States provided a partially effective device for assuring a supply of caring labor. They made it very difficult for women to do anything but care for family members, a form of coercive specialization that lowered women's bargaining power and guaranteed that the costs of care would remain relatively low—at least for men. With the weakening of patriarchal control over women in this country, the price of care has gone up. The impulse to make somebody else pay for care, or to cheapen it by lowering its quality, has shaped the emergence of new market-provided services. Intensified competition and privatization are worsening these trends, with traumatic results for individuals who are too poor, too weak, or too sick to effectively demand the care they require.

The solution to this problem is not to send women back home. Strict forms of patriarchal control are unacceptable—as well as unfair. Nor is the solution to find cheap market substitutes that inevitably lower the quality of care. There are alternatives between the devil and the deep blue sea. We need to forge a new social contract that shares responsibilities for care between men and women. We also need to support and protect caring work in a number of ways—by reducing the pressures of paid employment on family life, by setting strict quality standards for the provision of market care, and by fostering the development of new levels of skill and commitment among paid care workers. This will require rethinking the organization of work in both the private and the public sectors.

The supply of caring labor to the market economy resembles the supply of unpriced natural resources such as air and water. None of these resources appear to have much value until their quality deteriorates to the point that they threaten to become scarce. By that time, however, it may be too late to replenish them.

Efficiency in the use of easily measurable inputs is achieved by displacing costs into an arena in which they are not so easily monitored, sweeping the dirt under the rug. Sooner or later, however, negative externalities such as pollution become apparent—and costly.

The environmental metaphor is compelling. By the time we realized that an invisible ozone layer was protecting us from ultraviolet rays our chemical emissions had already put a hole in it that is impossible to repair. By the time we fully realize what is happening to our social environment, it too may be hard to patch back together. The Humpty-Dumpty of children's storybooks is a fragile, egg-shaped creature. When he falls off a wall, all the king's horses and all the king's men try—but fail—to put Humpty together again.

NOTES

1. Robert Kuttner, *Everything for Sale: The Virtues and Limits of Markets* (New York: Knopf, 1997).
2. Paula England and Nancy Folbre, "The Cost of Caring," *Annals of the American Academy of Political and Social Science* 561 (January 1999): 39–51; Nancy Folbre and Thomas Weisskopf,

"Did Father Know Best? Families, Markets, and the Supply of Caring Labor," in Avner Ben-Ner and Louis Putterman, eds., *Economics, Values, and Organization* (Cambridge: Cambridge University Press, 1998); Nancy Folbre, "Care and the Global Economy," in "Globalization with a Human Face," *Human Development Report,* vol. 1 (New York: United Nations, 1999), pp. 57–84.

3. Amartya K. Sen, "Capability and Well-Being," in Martha Nussbaum and Amartya Sen, eds., *The Quality of Life* (Oxford: Clarendon Press, 1993), pp. 30–53; Amartya K. Sen, "Human Capital and Human Capability," in *World Development* 25, no. 12 (December 1997): 1959–61.

4. Paula England and Nancy Folbre, "Reconceptualizing Human Capital," in Werner Raub and Jeroen Weesie, eds., *The Management of Durable Relations* (Amsterdam: Thela Thesis Publishers, 1999); Daniel Goleman, *Emotional Intelligence* (New York: Bantam, 1995).

5. Emily K. Abel and Margaret K. Nelson, "Circles of Care: An Introductory Essay," in Emily K. Abel and Margaret K. Nelson, eds., *Circles of Care: Work and Identity in Women's Lives* (New York: State University of New York Press, 1990), p. 4.

6. Arlie Hochschild, *The Managed Heart: Commercialization of Human Feeling* (Berkeley: University of California Press, 1983).

7. Deborah Ward, "The Kin Care Trap: The Unpaid Labor of Long Term Care," *Socialist Review* 23, no. 2 (1993): 103.

8. Folbre and Weisskopf, "Did Father Know Best?"

9. Robert J. Sampson, Stephen W. Raudenbush, and Felton Earls, "Neighborhoods and Violent Crime: A Multilevel Study of Collective Efficacy," *Science* 16 (January 1997).

10. Paula England and Nancy Folbre, "The Cost of Caring," *Annals of the American Academy of Political and Social Science,* 561 (January 1999): 39–51.

11. Jane Waldfogel, "The Effect of Children on Women's Wages," *American Sociological Review* 62, no. 2 (1997): 209–17.

12. Paula England, Karen Christopher, and Lori L. Reid, "How Do Intersections of Race/Ethnicity and Gender Affect Pay Among Young Cohorts of African Americans, European Americans, and Latino/as?" in Irene Browne, ed., *Race, Gender, and Economic Inequality:* *African American and Latina Women in the Labor Market* (New York: Russell Sage Foundation, 1999).

13. William Baumol, "Macroeconomics of Unbalanced Growth: The Anatomy of Urban Crisis," *American Economic Review* 57, no. 3 (1967): 415–26.

14. Barnet Wagman and Nancy Folbre, "Household Services and Economic Growth in the U.S., 1870–1930," *Feminist Economics* 2, no. 1 (Spring 1996): 50.

15. Robert Eisner, *The Total Incomes System of Accounts* (Chicago: University of Chicago Press, 1989); Duncan Ironmonger, "Counting Outputs, Capital Inputs, and Caring Labor: Estimating Gross Household Product," *Feminist Economics* 2, no. 3 (Fall 1996): 3.

16. Herman E. Daly, *Beyond Growth: The Economics of Sustainable Development* (Boston: Beacon Press, 1996). For quantitative estimates, see the Redefining Progress Web site at http://www.rprogress.org.

17. John Robinson and Geoffry Godbey, *Time for Life: The Surprising Ways Americans Use Their Time* (University Park: Pennsylvania State University Press, 1997), p. 107; W. Keith Bryant and Cathleen D. Zick, "Are We Investing Less in the Next Generation? Historical Trends in Time Spent Caring for Children," *Journal of Family and Economic Issues* 17, no. 3 (1996): 385–92; Michael Bittman and Jocelyn Pixley, *The Double Life of the Family: Myth, Hope, and Experience* (Sydney: Allen and Unwin, 1997), p. 94.

18. W. Keith Bryant and Cathleen D. Zick, "An Examination of Parent-Child Shared Time," *Journal of Marriage and the Family* 58 (1996): 227–37.

19. Francine D. Blau, "Trends in the Well-being of American Women, 1970–1995," *Journal of Economic Literature* 36, no. 1 (March 1998): 112–65.

20. Trond Petersen and Laurie A. Morgan, "Separate and Unequal: Occupation-Establishment Sex Segregation and the Gender Wage Gap," *American Journal of Sociology* 101, no. 2 (September 1995): 329–65.

21. Hochschild, *The Managed Heart.*

22. Richard Anker, *Gender and Jobs: Sex Segregation of Occupations in the World* (Geneva: International Labour Office, 1998), p. 163.

23. Karl Polanyi, *The Great Transformation* (Boston: Beacon Press, 1957).

24. Clare Ungerson, "Social Politics and the Commodification of Care," *Social Politics* (Fall 1997): 377.

25. Figure for 1959 from Robert E. Yuskavage, "Improved Estimates of Gross Product by Industry, 1959–94," *Survey of Current Business* (August 1996): Table 11. Figure for 1997 from Bureau of Economic Analysis National Accounts Data, "Gross Domestic Product by Industry in Current Dollars as a Percentage of Gross Domestic Product, 1992–1997," http://www.bea.doc.gov/bea/dn2/gposhr.htm.

26. Sheryl Gay Stolberg, "Report Says Profit-Making Health Plans Damage Care," *New York Times,* July 14, 1999.

27. Neil Weinberg, "Blood Money," *Forbes,* March 22, 1999, p. 123.

28. Peter T. Kilborn, "Nurses Put on Fast Forward in Rush for Cost Efficiency," *New York Times,* April 9, 1998, p. A1.

29. Suzanne Gordon, *Life Support: Three Nurses on the Front Lines* (New York: Little, Brown, 1998), p. 255.

30. Deborah Stone, "Care and Trembling," *American Prospect* 10, no. 43 (March–April 1999): 62.

31. Suzanne Helburn, ed., *Cost, Quality, and Child Outcomes in Child Care Centers,* technical report (Denver: University of Colorado Press, 1995).

32. Marcy Whitebook, *NAEYC Accreditation and Assessment* (Washington, D.C.: National Center for the Early Childhood Work Force, 1997).

33. Susan C. Eaton, "Beyond 'Unloving Care': Promoting Innovation in Elder Care Through Public Policy," Radcliffe Public Policy Institute, Changing Work in America Series, Cambridge, Mass., 1996.

34. Editorial, *New York Times,* April 26, 1999.

35. Eaton, "Beyond 'Unloving Care,'" p. 7.

⌒ **READING 39** ⌒

Maid to Order

The Politics of Other Women's Work

Barbara Ehrenreich

In line with growing class polarization, the classic posture of submission is making a stealthy comeback. "We scrub your floors the old-fashioned way," boasts the brochure from Merry Maids, the largest of the residential-cleaning services that have sprung up in the last two decades, "on our

hands and knees." This is not a posture that independent "cleaning ladies" willingly assume—preferring, like most people who clean their own homes, the sponge mop wielded from a standing position. In her comprehensive 1999 guide to homemaking, *Home Comforts,* Cheryl Mendelson warns: "Never ask hired housecleaners to clean your floors on their hands and knees; the request is likely to be regarded as degrading." But in a society in which 40 percent of the wealth is owned by 1 percent of households while the bottom 20 percent reports negative assets, the degradation of others is readily purchased. Kneepads entered American political discourse as a tool of the sexually subservient, but employees of Merry Maids, The Maids International, and other corporate cleaning services spend hours every day on these kinky devices, wiping up the drippings of the affluent.

I spent three weeks in September 1999 as an employee of The Maids International in Portland, Maine, cleaning, along with my fellow team members, approximately sixty houses containing a total of about 250 scrubbable floors—bathrooms, kitchens, and entryways requiring the hands-and-knees treatment. It's a different world down there below knee level, one that few adults voluntarily enter. Here you find elaborate dust structures held together by a scaffolding of dog hair; dried bits of pasta glued to the floor by their sauce; the congealed remains of gravies, jellies, contraceptive creams, vomit, and urine. Sometimes, too, you encounter some fragment of a human being: a child's legs, stamping by in disgust because the maids are still present when he gets home from school; more commonly, the Joan & David–clad feet and electrolyzed calves of the female homeowner. Look up and you may find this person staring at you, arms folded, in anticipation of an overlooked stain. In rare instances she may try to help in some vague, symbolic way, by moving the cockatoo's cage, for example, or apologizing for the leaves shed by a miniature indoor tree. Mostly, though, she will not see you at all and may even sit down with her mail at a table in the very room you are cleaning, where she would remain completely unaware of your existence unless you were to crawl under that table and start gnawing away at her ankles.

———

Housework, as you may recall from the feminist theories of the Sixties and Seventies, was supposed to be the great equalizer of women. Whatever else women did—jobs, school, child care—we also did housework, and if there were some women who hired others to do it for them, they seemed too privileged and rare to include in the theoretical calculus. All women were workers, and the home was their workplace—unpaid and unsupervised, to be sure, but a workplace no less than the offices and factories men repaired to every morning. If men thought of the home as a site of leisure and recreation— a "haven in a heartless world"—this was to ignore the invisible female proletariat that kept it cozy and humming. We were on the march now, or so we imagined, united against a society that devalued our labor even as it waxed mawkish over "the family" and "the home." Shoulder to shoulder and arm in arm, women were finally getting up off the floor. . . .

A couple of decades later, however, the average household still falls far short of that goal. True, women do less housework than they did before the feminist revolution and the rise of the two-income family: down from an average of 30 hours per week in 1965 to 17.5 hours in 1995, according to a July 1999 study by the University of Maryland. Some of that decline reflects a relaxation of standards rather than a redistribution of chores; women still do two-thirds of whatever housework—including bill paying, pet care, tidying, and lawn care—gets done. The inequity is sharpest for the most despised of household chores, cleaning: in the thirty years between 1965 and 1995, men increased the time they spent scrubbing, vacuuming, and sweeping by 240 percent—all the way up to 1.7 hours per week—while women decreased their cleaning time by only 7 percent, to 6.7 hours per week. The averages conceal a variety of arrangements, of course, from minutely negotiated sharing to the most clichéd division of labor, as described by one woman to the *Washington Post*: "I take care of the inside, he takes care of the outside." But perhaps the most disturbing finding is that almost the entire increase in male participation took place between the 1970s and the mid-1980s. Fifteen years after the apparent cessation of hostilities, it is probably not too soon to announce the score: in the "chore wars" of the Seventies and Eighties, women gained a little ground, but overall, and after a few strategic concessions, men won.

Enter then, the cleaning lady as *dea ex machina,* restoring tranquillity as well as order to the home. Marriage counselors recommend her as an alternative to squabbling, as do many within the cleaning industry itself. A Chicago cleaning woman quotes one of her clients as saying that if she gives up the service, "my husband and I will be divorced in six months." When the trend toward hiring out was just beginning to take off, in 1988, the owner of a Merry Maids franchise in Arlington, Massachusetts, told the *Christian Science Monitor,* "I kid some women. I say, 'We even save marriages. In this new eighties period you expect more from the male partner, but very often you don't get the cooperation you would like to have. The alternative is to pay somebody to come in. . . .'" Another Merry Maids franchise owner has learned to capitalize more directly on housework-related spats; he closes between 30 and 35 percent of his sales by making follow-up calls Saturday mornings, which is "prime time for arguing over the fact that the house is a mess." The micro-defeat of feminism in the household opened a new door for women, only this time it was the servants' entrance.

In 1999, somewhere between 14 and 18 percent of households employed an outsider to do the cleaning, and the numbers have been rising dramatically. Mediamark Research reports a 53 percent increase, between 1995 and 1999, in the number of households using a hired cleaner or service once a month or more, and Maritz Marketing finds that 30 percent of the people who

hired help in 1999 did so for the first time that year. Among my middle-class, professional women friends and acquaintances, including some who made important contributions to the early feminist analysis of housework, the employment of a maid is now nearly universal. This sudden emergence of a servant class is consistent with what some economists have called the "Brazilianization" of the American economy: We are dividing along the lines of traditional Latin American societies—into a tiny over-class and a huge underclass, with the latter available to perform intimate household services for the former. Or, to put it another way, the home, or at least the affluent home, is finally becoming what radical feminists in the Seventies only imagined it was—a true "workplace" for women and a tiny, though increasingly visible, part of the capitalist economy. And the question is: As the home becomes a workplace for someone else, is it still a place where you would want to live?

———

Strangely, or perhaps not so strangely at all, no one talks about the "politics of housework" anymore. The demand for "wages for housework" has sunk to the status of a curio, along with the consciousness-raising groups in which women once rallied support in their struggles with messy men. In the academy, according to the feminist sociologists I interviewed, housework has lost much of its former cachet—in part, I suspect, because fewer sociologists actually do it. Most Americans, over 80 percent, still clean their homes, but the minority who do not include a sizable fraction of the nation's opinion-makers and culture-producers—professors, writers, editors, politicians, talking heads, and celebrities of all sorts. In their homes, the politics of housework is becoming a politics not only of gender but of race and class—and these are subjects that the opinion-making elite, if not most Americans, generally prefer to avoid.

Even the number of paid houseworkers is hard to pin down. The Census Bureau reports that there were 549,000 domestic workers in 1998, up 9 percent since 1996, but this may be a considerable underestimate, since so much of the servant economy is still underground. In 1995, two years after Zoe Baird lost her chance to be attorney general for paying her undocumented nanny off the books, the *Los Angeles Times* reported that fewer than 10 percent of those Americans who paid a housecleaner reported those payments to the IRS. Sociologist Mary Romero, one of the few academics who retain an active interest in housework and the women who do it for pay, offers an example of how severe the undercounting can be: the 1980 Census found only 1,063 "private household workers" in El Paso, Texas, though the city estimated their numbers at 13,400 and local bus drivers estimated that half of the 28,300 daily bus trips were taken by maids going to and from work. The honesty of employers has increased since the Baird scandal, but most experts believe that household workers remain, in large part, uncounted and invisible to the larger economy.

One thing you can say with certainty about the population of household workers is that they are disproportionately women of color: "lower" kinds of people for a "lower" kind of work. Of the "private household cleaners and servants" it managed to locate in 1998, the Bureau of Labor Statistics reports that 36.8 percent were Hispanic, 15.8 percent black, and 2.7 percent "other." Certainly the association between housecleaning and minority status is well established in the psyches of the white employing class. When my daughter, Rosa, was introduced to the wealthy father of a Harvard classmate, he ventured that she must have been named for a favorite maid. And Audre Lorde can perhaps be forgiven for her intemperate accusation at the feminist confer-

ence . . . when we consider an experience she had in 1967: "I wheel my two-year-old daughter in a shopping cart through a supermarket . . . and a little white girl riding past in her mother's cart calls out excitedly, 'Oh look, Mommy, a baby maid.'" But the composition of the household workforce is hardly fixed and has changed with the life chances of the different ethnic groups. In the late nineteenth century, Irish and German immigrants served the northern upper and middle classes, then left for the factories as soon as they could. Black women replaced them, accounting for 60 percent of all domestics in the 1940s, and dominated the field until other occupations began to open up to them. Similarly, West Coast maids were disproportionately Japanese American until that group, too, found more congenial options. Today, the color of the hand that pushes the sponge varies from region to region: Chicanas in the Southwest, Caribbeans in New York, native Hawaiians in Hawaii, whites, many of recent rural extraction, in Maine.

The great majority—though again, no one knows exact numbers—of paid housekeepers are freelancers, or "independents," who find their clients through agencies or networks of already employed friends and relatives. To my acquaintances in the employing class, the freelance housekeeper seems to be a fairly privileged and prosperous type of worker, a veritable aristocrat of labor—sometimes paid $15 an hour or more and usually said to be viewed as a friend or even treated as "one of the family." But the shifting ethnic composition of the workforce tells another story: this is a kind of work that many have been trapped in—by racism, imperfect English skills, immigration status, or lack of education—but few have happily chosen. Interviews with independent maids collected by Romero and by sociologist Judith Rollins, who herself worked as a maid in the Boston area in the early Eighties, confirm that the work is undesirable to those who perform it. Even when the pay is deemed acceptable, the hours may be long and unpredictable; there are usually no health benefits, no job security, and, if the employer has failed to pay Social Security taxes (in some cases because the maid herself prefers to be paid off the books), no retirement benefits. And the pay is often far from acceptable. The BLS found full-time "private household cleaners and servants" earning a median annual income of $12,220 in 1998, which is $1,092 below the poverty level for a family of three. Recall that in 1993 Zoe Baird paid her undocumented household workers about $5 an hour out of her earnings of $507,000 a year.

At the most lurid extreme there is slavery. A few cases of forced labor pop up in the press every year, most recently—in some nightmare version of globalization—of undocumented women held in servitude by high-ranking staff members of the United Nations, the World Bank, and the International Monetary Fund. Consider the suit brought by Elizabeth Senghor, a Senegalese woman who alleged that she was forced to work fourteen-hour days for her employers in Manhattan, without any regular pay, and was given no accommodations beyond a pull-out bed in her employers' living room. Hers is not a particularly startling instance of domestic slavery; no beatings or sexual assaults were charged, and Ms. Senghor was apparently fed. What gives this case a certain rueful poignancy is that her employer, former U.N. employee Marie Angelique Savane, is one of Senegal's leading women's rights advocates and had told *The Christian Science Monitor* in 1986 about her efforts to get the Senegalese to "realize that being a woman can mean other things than simply having children, taking care of the house."

Mostly, though, independent maids—and sometimes the women who employ them—complain about the peculiar intimacy of the employer-employee relationship.

Domestic service is an occupation that predates the refreshing impersonality of capitalism by several thousand years, conditions of work being still largely defined by the idiosyncrasies of the employers. Some of them seek friendship and even what their maids describe as "therapy," though they are usually quick to redraw the lines once the maid is perceived as overstepping. Others demand deference bordering on servility, while a growing fraction of the nouveau riche is simply out of control. In August 1999, the *New York Times* reported on the growing problem of dinner parties being disrupted by hostesses screaming at their help. To the verbal abuse add published reports of sexual and physical assaults—a young teenage boy, for example, kicking a live-in nanny for refusing to make sandwiches for him and his friends after school.

But for better or worse, capitalist rationality is finally making some headway into this weird preindustrial backwater. Corporate cleaning services now control 25 to 30 percent of the $1.4 billion housecleaning business, and perhaps their greatest innovation has been to abolish the mistress-maid relationship, with all its quirks and dependencies. The customer hires the service, not the maid, who has been replaced anyway by a team of two to four uniformed people, only one of whom—the team leader—is usually authorized to speak to the customer about the work at hand. The maids' wages, their Social Security taxes, their green cards, backaches, and child-care problems—all these are the sole concern of the company, meaning the local franchise owner. If there are complaints on either side, they are addressed to the franchise owner; the customer and the actual workers need never interact. Since the franchise owner is usually a middle-class white person, cleaning services are the ideal solution for anyone still sensitive enough to find the traditional employer-maid relationship morally vexing.

In a 1997 article about Merry Maids, *Franchise Times* reported concisely that the "category is booming, [the] niche is hot, too, as Americans look to outsource work even at home." Not all cleaning services do well, and there is a high rate of failure among informal, mom-and-pop services. The "boom" is concentrated among the national and international chains—outfits like Merry Maids, Molly Maids, Mini Maids, Maid Brigade, and The Maids International—all named, curiously enough, to highlight the more antique aspects of the industry, though the "maid" may occasionally be male. Merry Maids claimed to be growing at 15 to 20 percent a year in 1996, and spokesmen for both Molly Maids and The Maids International told me that their firms' sales are growing by 25 percent a year; local franchisers are equally bullish. Dan Libby, my boss at The Maids, confided to me that he could double his business overnight if only he could find enough reliable employees. To this end, The Maids offers a week's paid vacation, health insurance after ninety days, and a free breakfast every morning consisting—at least where I worked—of coffee, doughnuts, bagels, and bananas. Some franchises have dealt with the tight labor market by participating in welfare-to-work projects that not only funnel employees to them but often subsidize their paychecks with public money, at least for the first few months of work (which doesn't mean the newly minted maid earns more, only that the company has to pay her less). The Merry Maids franchise in the city where I worked is conveniently located a block away from the city's welfare office.

Among the women I worked with at The Maids, only one said she had previously worked as an independent, and she professed to be pleased with her new status as a cleaning-service employee. She no longer needed a car to get her from house to house and could take a day off—unpaid of course—to stay home with a sick child without risking the loss of a customer. I myself could see the advantage of not having to deal directly with the customers, who were sometimes at home while we worked and eager to make use of their supervisory skills: criticisms of our methods, and demands that we perform unscheduled tasks, could simply be referred to the franchise owner.

But there are inevitable losses for the workers as any industry moves from the entrepreneurial to the industrial phase, probably most strikingly, in this case, in the matter of pay. At Merry Maids, I was promised $200 for a forty-hour week, the manager hastening to add that "you can't calculate it in dollars per hour" since the forty hours include all the time spent traveling from house to house—up to five houses a day—which is unpaid. The Maids International, with its straightforward starting rate of $6.63 an hour, seemed preferable, though this rate was conditional on perfect attendance. Miss one day and your wage dropped to $6 an hour for two weeks, a rule that weighed particularly heavily on those who had young children. In addition, I soon learned that management had ways of shaving off nearly an hour's worth of wages a day. We were told to arrive at 7:30 in the morning, but our billable hours began only after we had been teamed up, given our list of houses for the day, and packed off in the company car at about 8:00 A.M. At the end of the day, we were no longer paid from the moment we left the car, though as much as fifteen minutes of work—refilling cleaning-fluid bottles, etc.—remained to be done. So for a standard nine-hour day, the actual pay amounted to about $6.10 an hour, unless you were still being punished for an absence, in which case it came out to $5.50 an hour.

Nor are cleaning-service employees likely to receive any of the perks or tips familiar to independents—free lunches and coffee, cast-off clothing, or a Christmas gift of cash. When I asked, only one of my coworkers could recall ever receiving a tip, and that was a voucher for a free meal at a downtown restaurant owned by a customer. The customers of cleaning services are probably no stingier than the employers of independents; they just don't know their cleaning people and probably wouldn't even recognize them on the street. Plus, customers probably assume that the fee they pay the service—$25 per person-hour in the case of The Maids franchise I worked for— goes largely to the workers who do the actual cleaning.

But the most interesting feature of the cleaning-service chains, at least from an abstract, historical perspective, is that they are finally transforming the home into a fully capitalist-style workplace, and in ways that the old wages-for-housework advocates could never have imagined. A house is an innately difficult workplace to control, especially a house with ten or more rooms, like so many of those we cleaned; workers may remain out of one another's sight for as much as an hour at a time. For independents, the ungovernable nature of the home-as-workplace means a certain amount of autonomy. They can take breaks (though this is probably ill-advised if the homeowner is on the premises); they can ease the monotony by listening to the radio or TV while they work. But cleaning services lay down rules meant to enforce a factorylike— or even conventlike—discipline on their far-flung employees. At The Maids, there were no breaks except for a daily ten-minute stop at a convenience store for coffee or "lunch"—meaning something like a slice of pizza. Otherwise, the time spent driving between houses was considered our "break" and the only chance to eat, drink, or (although this was also officially forbidden) smoke a cigarette. When the houses were spaced well apart, I could eat my sandwich in one sitting; otherwise, it would have to be divided into as many as three separate, hasty snacks.

Within a customer's house, nothing was to touch our lips at all, not even water—a rule that, on hot days, I sometimes broke by drinking from a bathroom faucet. TVs and radios were off-limits, and we were never, ever, to curse out loud, even in an ostensibly deserted house. There might be a homeowner secreted in some locked room, we were told, ear pressed to the door, or, more likely, a tape recorder or video camera running. At the time, I dismissed this as a scare story, but I have since come across ads for devices like the Tech-7 "incredible coin-sized camera" designed to "get a visual record of your babysitter's actions" and "watch employees to prevent theft." It was the threat or rumor of hidden recording devices that provided the final capitalist-industrial touch— supervision.

What makes the work most factorylike, though, is the intense Taylorization imposed by the companies. An independent, or a person cleaning his or her own home, chooses where she will start and, within each room, probably tackles the most egregious dirt first. Or she may plan her work more or less ergonomically, first doing whatever can be done from a standing position and then squatting or crouching to reach the lower levels. But with the special "systems" devised by the cleaning services and imparted to employees via training videos, there are no such decisions to make. In The Maids' "healthy touch" system, which is similar to what I saw of the Merry Maids' system on the training tape I was shown during my interview, all cleaning is divided into four task areas—dusting, vacuuming, kitchens, and bathrooms—which are in turn divided among the team members. For each task area other than vacuuming, there is a bucket containing rags and the appropriate cleaning fluids, so the biggest decision an employee has to make is which fluid and scrubbing instrument to deploy on which kind of surface; almost everything else has been choreographed in advance. When vacuuming, you begin with the master bedroom; when dusting, with the first room off of the kitchen; then you move through the rooms going left to right. When entering each room, you proceed from left to right and top to bottom, and the same with each surface—top to bottom, left to right. Deviations are subject to rebuke, as I discovered when a team leader caught me moving my arm from right to left, then left to right, while wiping Windex over a French door.

It's not easy for anyone with extensive cleaning experience—and I include myself in this category—to accept this loss of autonomy. But I came to love the system: First, because if you hadn't always been traveling rigorously from left to right it would have been easy to lose your way in some of the larger houses and omit or redo a room. Second, some of the houses were already clean when we started, at least by any normal standards, thanks probably to a housekeeper who kept things up between our visits; but the absence of visible dirt did not mean there was less work to do, for no surface could ever be neglected, so it was important to have "the system" to remind you of where you had been and what you had already "cleaned." No doubt the biggest advantage of the system, though, is that it helps you achieve the speed demanded by the company, which allots only so many minutes per house. After a week or two on the job, I found myself moving robotlike from surface to surface, grateful to have been relieved of the thinking process.

The irony, which I was often exhausted enough to derive a certain malicious satisfaction from, is that "the system" is not very sanitary. When I saw the training videos on "Kitchens" and "Bathrooms," I was at first baffled, and it took me several minutes to realize why: There is no water, or almost no

water, involved. I had been taught to clean by my mother, a compulsive housekeeper who employed water so hot you needed rubber gloves to get into it and in such Niagaralike quantities that most microbes were probably crushed by the force of it before the soap suds had a chance to rupture their cell walls. But germs are never mentioned in the videos provided by The Maids. Our antagonists existed entirely in the visible world—soap scum, dust, counter crud, dog hair, stains, and smears—and were attacked by damp rag or, in hard-core cases, by a scouring pad. We scrubbed only to remove impurities that might be detectable to a customer by hand or by eye; otherwise, our only job was to wipe. Nothing was ever said, in the videos or in person, about the possibility of transporting bacteria, by rag or by hand, from bathroom to kitchen or even from one house to the next. Instead, it is the "cosmetic touches" that the videos emphasize and to which my trainer continually directed my eye. Fluff out all throw pillows and arrange them symmetrically. Brighten up stainless steel sinks with baby oil. Leave all spice jars, shampoos, etc., with their labels facing outward. Comb out the fringes of Persian carpets with a pick. Use the vacuum to create a special, fernlike pattern in the carpets. The loose ends of toilet paper and paper towel rolls have to be given a special fold. Finally, the house is sprayed with the service's signature air freshener—a cloying floral scent in our case, "baby fresh" in the case of the Mini Maids.

When I described the "methods" employed to housecleaning expert Cheryl Mendelson, she was incredulous. A rag moistened with disinfectant will not get a countertop clean, she told me, because most disinfectants are inactivated by contact with organic matter—i.e., dirt—so their effectiveness declines with each swipe of the rag. What you need is a detergent and hot water, followed by a rinse. As for floors, she judged the amount of water we used—one half of a small bucket—to be grossly inadequate, and, in fact, the water I wiped around on floors was often an unsavory gray. I also ran The Maids' cleaning methods by Don Aslett, author of numerous books on cleaning techniques and self-styled "number one cleaner in America." He was hesitant to criticize The Maids directly, perhaps because he is, or told me he is, a frequent speaker at conventions of cleaning-service franchise holders, but he did tell me how he would clean a countertop: first, spray it thoroughly with an all-purpose cleaner, then let it sit for three to four minutes of "kill time," and finally wipe it dry with a clean cloth. Merely wiping the surface with a damp cloth, he said, just spreads the dirt around. But the point at The Maids, apparently, is not to clean so much as it is to create the appearance of having been cleaned, not to sanitize but to create a kind of stage setting for family life. And the stage setting Americans seem to prefer is sterile only in the metaphorical sense, like a motel room or the fake interiors in which soap operas and sitcoms take place.

But even ritual work takes its toll on those assigned to perform it. Turnover is dizzyingly high in the cleaning-service industry, and not only because of the usual challenges that confront the working poor—child-care problems, unreliable transportation, evictions, and prior health problems. As my long-winded interviewer at Merry Maids warned me, and my coworkers at The Maids confirmed, this is a physically punishing occupation, something to tide you over for a few months, not year after year. The hands-and-knees posture damages knees, with or without pads; vacuuming strains the back; constant wiping and scrubbing invite repetitive stress injuries even in the very young. In my three weeks as a maid, I suffered nothing more than a persistent muscle spasm in the right forearm, but the damage would have been far worse if I'd had to go home every day to my own housework and children, as most of my coworkers did, instead of returning to my motel and indulging in a daily after-work regimen of ice packs and stretches. Chores that seem effortless at home, even almost recreational when undertaken at will for twenty minutes or so at a time, quickly turn nasty when performed hour after hour, with few or no breaks and under relentless time pressure.

So far, the independent, entrepreneurial housecleaner is holding her own, but there are reasons to think that corporate cleaning services will eventually dominate the industry. New users often prefer the impersonal, standardized service offered by the chains, and, in a fast-growing industry, new users make up a sizable chunk of the total clientele. Government regulation also favors the corporate chains, whose spokesmen speak gratefully of the "Zoe Baird effect," referring to customers' worries about being caught paying an independent off the books. But the future of housecleaning may depend on the entry of even bigger players into the industry. Merry Maids, the largest of the chains, has the advantage of being a unit within the $6.4 billion Service-Master conglomerate, which includes such related businesses as TruGreen-ChemLawn, Terminix, Rescue Rooter, and Furniture Medic. Swisher International, best known as an industrial toilet-cleaning service, operates Swisher Maids in Georgia and North Carolina, and Sears may be feeling its way into the business. If large multinational firms establish a foothold in the industry, mobile professionals will be able to find the same branded and standardized product wherever they relocate. For the actual workers, the change will, in all likelihood, mean a more standardized and speeded-up approach to the work—less freedom of motion and fewer chances to pause.

———

The trend toward outsourcing the work of the home seems, at the moment, unstoppable. Two hundred years ago women often manufactured soap, candles, cloth, and clothing in their own homes, and the complaints of some women at the turn of the twentieth century that they had been "robbed by the removal of creative work" from the home sound pointlessly reactionary today. Not only have the skilled crafts, like sewing and cooking from scratch, left the home but many of the "white collar" tasks are on their way out, too. For a fee, new firms such as the San Francisco–based Les Concierges and Cross It Off Your List in Manhattan will pick up dry cleaning, babysit pets, buy groceries, deliver dinner, even do the Christmas shopping. With other firms and individuals offering to buy your clothes, organize your financial files, straighten out your closets, and wait around in your home for the plumber to show up, why would anyone want to hold on to the toilet cleaning?

Absent a major souring of the economy, there is every reason to think that Americans will become increasingly reliant on paid housekeepers and that this reliance will extend ever further down into the middle class. For one thing, the "time bind" on working parents shows no sign of loosening; people are willing to work longer hours at the office to pay for the people—house cleaners and baby-sitters—who are filling in for them at home. Children, once a handy source of household help, are now off at soccer practice or SAT prep classes; grandmother has relocated to a warmer climate or taken up a second career. Furthermore, despite the fact that people spend less time at home than ever, the square footage of new homes swelled by 33 percent between 1975 and 1998, to include "family rooms," home entertainment rooms, home offices, bedrooms, and often bathrooms for each family member. By the third quarter of 1999, 17 percent of new homes were larger than 3,000 square feet, which is usually considered the size threshold for household help,

or the point at which a house becomes unmanageable to the people who live in it.

One more trend impels people to hire outside help, according to cleaning experts such as Aslett and Mendelson: fewer Americans know how to clean or even to "straighten up." I hear this from professional women defending their decision to hire a maid: "I'm just not very good at it myself" or "I wouldn't really know where to begin." Since most of us learn to clean from our parents (usually our mothers), any diminution of cleaning skills is transmitted from one generation to another, like a gene that can, in the appropriate environment, turn out to be disabling or lethal. Upper-middle-class children raised in the servant economy of the Nineties are bound to grow up as domestically incompetent as their parents and no less dependent on people to clean up after them. Mendelson sees this as a metaphysical loss, a "matter of no longer being physically centered in your environment." Having cleaned the rooms of many overly privileged teenagers in my stint with The Maids, I think the problem is a little more urgent than that. The American overclass is raising a generation of young people who will, without constant assistance, suffocate in their own detritus.

If there are moral losses, too, as Americans increasingly rely on paid household help, no one has been tactless enough to raise them. Almost everything we buy, after all, is the product of some other person's suffering and miserably underpaid labor. I clean my own house (though—full disclosure—I recently hired someone else to ready it for a short-term tenant), but I can hardly claim purity in any other area of consumption. I buy my jeans at The Gap, which is reputed to subcontract to sweatshops. I tend to favor decorative objects no doubt ripped off, by their purveyors, from scantily paid Third World craftspersons. Like everyone else, I eat salad greens just picked by migrant farm workers, some of them possibly children. And so on. We can try to minimize the pain that goes into feeding, clothing, and otherwise provisioning ourselves—by observing boycotts, checking for a union label, etc.—but there is no way to avoid it altogether without living in the wilderness on berries. Why should housework, among all the goods and services we consume, arouse any special angst?

And it does, as I have found in conversations with liberal-minded employers of maids, perhaps because we all sense that there are ways in which housework is different from other products and services. First, in its inevitable proximity to the activities that compose "private" life. The home that becomes a workplace for other people remains a home, even when that workplace has been minutely regulated by the corporate cleaning chains. Someone who has no qualms about purchasing rugs woven by child slaves in India or coffee picked by impoverished peasants in Guatemala might still hesitate to tell dinner guests that, surprisingly enough, his or her lovely home doubles as a sweatshop during the day. You can eschew the chain cleaning services of course, hire an independent cleaner at a generous hourly wage, and even encourage, at least in spirit, the unionization of the housecleaning industry. But this does not change the fact that someone is working in your home at a job she would almost certainly never have chosen for herself—if she'd had a college education, for example, or a little better luck along the way—and the place where she works, however enthusiastically or resentfully, is the same as the place where you sleep.

It is also the place where your children are raised, and what they learn pretty quickly is that some people are less worthy than others. Even better wages and working conditions won't erase the hierarchy between an employer and his or her domestic help, because the help is usually there only because the employer has "something better" to do with her time, as one report on the growth of cleaning services puts it, not noticing the obvious implication that the cleaning person herself has nothing better to do with her time. In a merely middle-class home, the message may be reinforced by a warning to the children that that's what they'll end up doing if they don't try harder in school. Housework, as radical feminists once proposed, defines a human relationship and, when unequally divided among social groups, reinforces preexisting inequalities. Dirt, in other words, tends to attach to the people who remove it—"garbagemen" and "cleaning ladies." Or, as cleaning entrepreneur Don Aslett told me with some bitterness—and this is a successful man, chairman of the board of an industrial cleaning service and frequent television guest—"The whole mentality out there is that if you clean, you're a scumball."

One of the "better" things employers of maids often want to do with their time is, of course, spend it with their children. But an underlying problem with post-nineteenth-century child-raising, as Deirdre English and I argued in our book *For Her Own Good* years ago, is precisely that it is unmoored in any kind of purposeful pursuit. Once "parenting" meant instructing the children in necessary chores; today it's more likely to center on one-sided conversations beginning with "So how was school today?" No one wants to put the kids to work again weeding and stitching; but in the void that is the modern home, relationships with children are often strained. A little "low-quality time" spent washing dishes or folding clothes together can provide a comfortable space for confidences—and give a child the dignity of knowing that he or she is a participant in, and not just the product of, the work of the home.

There is another lesson the servant economy teaches its beneficiaries and, most troublingly, the children among them. To be cleaned up after is to achieve a certain magical weightlessness and immateriality. Almost everyone complains about violent video games, but paid housecleaning has the same consequence-abolishing effect: you blast the villain into a mist of blood droplets and move right along; you drop the socks knowing they will eventually levitate, laundered and folded, back to their normal dwelling place. The result is a kind of virtual existence, in which the trail of litter that follows you seems to evaporate all by itself. Spill syrup on the floor and the cleaning person will scrub it off when she comes on Wednesday. Leave *The Wall Street Journal* scattered around your airplane seat and the flight attendants will deal with it after you've deplaned. Spray toxins into the atmosphere from your factory's smokestacks and they will be filtered out eventually by the lungs of the breathing public. A servant economy breeds callousness and solipsism in the served, and it does so all the more effectively when the service is performed close up and routinely in the place where they live and reproduce.

Individual situations vary, of course, in ways that elude blanket judgment. Some people—the elderly and disabled, parents of new babies, asthmatics who require an allergen-free environment—may well need help performing what nursing-home staff call the "ADLs," or activities of daily living,

and no shame should be attached to their dependency. In a more generous social order, housekeeping services would be subsidized for those who have health-related reasons to need them—a measure that would generate a surfeit of new jobs for the low-skilled people who now clean the homes of the affluent. And in a less gender-divided social order, husbands and boyfriends would more readily do their share of the chores.

However we resolve the issue in our individual homes, the moral challenge is, put simply, to make work visible again: not only the scrubbing and vacuuming, but all the hoeing, stacking, hammering, drilling, bending, and lifting that goes into creating and maintaining a livable habitat. In an ever more economically unequal culture, where so many of the affluent devote their lives to such ghostly pursuits as stock-trading, image-making, and opinion-polling, real work—in the old-fashioned sense of labor that engages hand as well as eye, that tires the body and directly alters the physical world—tends to vanish from sight. The feminists of my generation tried to bring some of it into the light of day, but, like busy professional women fleeing the house in the morning, they left the project unfinished, the debate broken off in midsentence, the noble intentions unfulfilled. Sooner or later, someone else will have to finish the job.

▨▨▨ **BALANCING WORK AND FAMILY LIFE** ▨▨▨

∞ **READING 40** ∞

The Time Bind

Men

Arlie Russell Hochschild

"I've just talked to two men who took paternity leave."

—ARLIE HOCHSCHILD

"Oh? Who's the other one?"

—AMY TRUETT

*Connect
to Sweden*

Sam Hyatt was a gifted engineer, seven years with the company, and the father of a three-month-old baby boy. In 1990 he was one of two men in the company who requested and received formal parental leave. Amerco, like many companies nationwide, offers six weeks of paid leave to the mother. Beyond that, it allows twenty weeks of unpaid leave that can be split in any fashion between husband and wife. Sam and Latesha Hyatt decided that Latesha should take eighteen weeks and Sam two.

After the birth of a child, many men at Amerco arranged informally with their bosses to take a few unpaid days off using accumulated sick leave because the forms for parental leave were said to be "a hassle." To his astonishment and dismay, Sam discovered that he was the first man in the company to apply formally for paternity leave. I asked Sam, a

Excerpts from *The Time Bind: When Work Becomes Home and Home Becomes Work* by Arlie Russell Hochschild. Copyright © 1997 by Arlie Russell Hochschild. Reprinted by permission of Henry Holt and Company, LLC.

gentle thirty-three-year-old African American man with an easy laugh, to tell me how he ended up being a trailblazer at Amerco.

"I come from a family of six children in Cleveland," he replied. "My mother was a single parent and worked several jobs to support us. I'm the third oldest and I had some responsibilities for my younger brother and sisters. We went through tough times, not just financially but emotionally." He described how he took college preparatory courses in a public school, was accepted by California Polytechnic Institute, and graduated in three years with a degree in mechanical engineering. While in college, he learned of an Amerco summer scholarship/intern program. The company offered him an internship and, pleased with his summer work, offered him a job upon his graduation. Along the way, he met and married Latesha, a chemical engineer who also worked for Amerco.

Amerco was a predominantly white company as was the town of Spotted Deer and its surrounding valley communities. But in pursuit of its mission to increase diversity, Amerco began in the late 1980s actively recruiting gifted minority students at technical colleges and universities, hiring them as summer interns, and, if all went well, offering them jobs when they graduated.

This pathway to Amerco placed Sam Hyatt in a curious mix of circumstances. The company was eager to draw the best from every racial and ethnic talent pool and was busy trying to make minority newcomers feel welcome. So, for example, Amerco made sure that one local radio station played music likely to appeal to many African Americans. The company also hired the only local barber skilled in black hairstyles. Yet it was also true that blacks, Chicanos, and Asians together still made up a very small percentage of Amerco's workforce. And the community lacked the sort of racial mix that might have reduced Sam's occasional sense that people expected him to represent the "black position" on whatever came up.

In fact, what the working-class whites who lived in the surrounding countryside knew about African Americans they seemed to have learned mainly from television shows about violent crime. When Sam first came to Spotted Deer, he got lost driving on a mountain road and stopped at a bar-restaurant to ask for change to make a call. The steely-eyed faces that greeted him made him think of some sheriff's posse in a small Mississippi town in the 1950s. He froze and backed out. That only had to happen once to impress him with a sense of his vulnerability as a black man in this white valley.

Still, at Amerco and at home, life was good. With a flourishing career, a loving wife, and a new house Sam happily prepared for the birth of their first child. Latesha planned to take four and a half months of maternity leave, and Sam's first official act as a father-to-be was to ask the company for time off.

Two months before Latesha was due, I approached my supervisor, somewhat unsure about how he would respond. Amerco had just published a paternity-leave policy in 1988. When I got my hands on it, I didn't realize that I was the first to use it. I'm not sure if I'm still the only one. I filled out the form and took it to my supervisor. We get along really well. I'm not uptight with him generally, but for some reason I was this time. He sensed my nervousness and said, "Don't worry about it, this is great." In a matter of days or a week, it was signed by my manager. The form acted as an agreement that I could take leave without pay for two weeks.

Sam was doing well at work. His supervisor's professional development report noted that he "continuously met and usually exceeded his customers' requirements, and that he was doing a superior job as a department supervisor after a very short time in the position." When his wife was just about to have the baby, Sam noted,

> I was working on a big project to design, fabricate, and test equipment, and it was time to install it—a difficult time to be away from work. But my father had missed my birth and then my boyhood, and maybe that's why I wanted to be there for my own child from the beginning.

After eight hours at the hospital, Sam greeted a squalling, eight-pound baby boy, wrapped him in a blue blanket, and laid him in his bassinet. As he nursed his wife back to health, he cared for the house and spent hours attuning himself to this new small being, whom they named Adam.

When, two weeks later, he returned to his nine-hour days, he encountered a wide variety of reactions:

> To the women at the office, I was a great hero. Sam *cooks!* Sam does *laundry!* Sam

takes *paternity leave!* But most of the guys I'm not close to ignored it. They all knew, but they acted as if they weren't supposed to know. They were thinking, "Where were you? On vacation?" My close friends teased me, "It must have been fun, what did you do? Did you change diapers? Come on, it must have been a *great* time. You sat around and watched TV." They thought I was using this time as an excuse to get away.

They saw Sam's paternity leave as time when he was not working, but relaxing, goofing off. They didn't link paternity leave to paternity.

Sam faced a choice. He could let the playful jabs about "catching up on the soaps" go and accept the obvious implications: that because women give birth to babies, babies are a women's thing; that men have no role at or around birth, so paternity leave is unnecessary or silly. Or he could respond. But he would have to be careful, he felt. He couldn't be too "politically correct" because, for many of his colleagues, the issue of paternity leave was fraught with unacknowledged tension. Many of them were feeling pressure from working wives who had sacrificed time from their own budding careers and yearned for appreciation as well as some parallel gesture of commitment, no matter how small.

Sam stood his ground but parried the jabs lightly:

I let them know what I really did. And I told them what it meant to me. They responded, "Well, it's not for me, but great, if that's what you want," that type of thing. I tried to convey the idea that this is a great opportunity for men. If I had it to do all over again, I told them, I'd take *more* time off.

A few younger men who perhaps dreamed of taking paternity leave themselves someday applauded Sam, as did a few older men who imagined that they might have taken one, had they been given the chance.

At home, Sam's leave, however brief, established a pattern:

I comb Adam's hair every morning and dress him. I hear guys say, "I'm going home to babysit." Or they say, "I have to play Mr. Mom," as if there's no such thing as Daddy or Father. I don't say anything, but I despise these statements. I correct them when they say, "Do you have to babysit?" When they ask me, "What are you doing?" I say, "I'm going home to be a dad." Or, "I'm going home to be with my family." I don't honestly know if they sense the difference between "babysitter" and "dad."

After four and a half months, when Latesha returned to her regular schedule, they both began waking up at 5:30 A.M. to spend more time with Adam. At 7:30 A.M., they dropped Adam at his sitter's. "We rarely get a chance to see him at lunch," Sam continued. "We just can't manage the time. We pick him up at 5:30 P.M. and go home." After a year, Latesha decided to take part time, cutting her working day back to six hours. As Sam explained,

We've named Latesha as the primary caregiver. Still, my role is not to help, it's to act. All the time we're talking about who does what. We're still working it out. Latesha would like an equal partnership. But I wouldn't be comfortable being the one going part time. First, because of my work, and second, because she's more organized than I am.

As it was, Sam had begun to feel that he was pressing the limits of acceptability at Amerco. Because he rarely took work home and rarely worked weekends, he felt his superiors were watching him with an eagle eye. As he put it,

> My use of time doesn't come close to that of my superiors. I don't know if I'm going to change or if, eventually, they are. I love the work. I just don't like the workaholism. Higher-level managers all tell you that family is "number one." Every moment they get, they talk about how their child just won the fifty-yard dash and show you pictures. It's number one to them, but you look at how they live and you have to wonder. To me, family life really is number one.

Still, Sam often found it hard to get out the office door anywhere near 5 P.M.:

> Often, I have a four to five o'clock meeting. Then I have to clean off my desk, return a few calls. If it's my turn to pick up Adam, I may call the babysitter and ask if she can hold out another twenty minutes or so. To leave at five o'clock, I need a good excuse. Adam's not a good excuse.

Sam and Latesha were still resisting the press of work, but without many allies. Their home life was not anchored to a circle of kin who called, visited, meddled, and supported. Both had moved far from their hometowns. Latesha missed her mother and sisters in particular. Even though she found most people at Amerco friendly and outgoing, a semiconscious vigilance against unwanted looks or remarks proved a strain for her, and so she found their time alone together a particular relief. She was as unwilling to give up their family time as Sam was to give up his idea of being a "real dad."

Upon learning that there were only two men in the company who had formally applied for paternity leave, a white manager asked me who the other one was. When I mentioned Sam Hyatt, he mused, "Maybe he got to take it because he's black." That made me wonder: Did the men who ribbed Sam for "catching up on the soaps" think that an exception had been made for him? Were they not asking for their paternity leaves because they were *white* and so had little chance of getting them? It was hard to know how Sam could win.

Certainly, if a boss wanted to resist setting a paternity-leave precedent in his division, he could always behave disagreeably when prospective fathers requested leaves. One worker found himself locked in a fierce struggle with his boss over his request for a single week of paternity leave.

"Call it vacation," his boss suggested.

"I'd like it in addition to vacation," the worker said. "Can you deduct it from my pay?"

"Take it for free, then," his boss replied, irritated.

"I'm not asking for something free," came the response.

"Well, I can't give you paternity leave. It's too much paperwork. Why don't you just take it unofficially?" The following summer, the worker discovered to his dismay that his boss had deducted his paternity leave from his vacation time. When that boss left for another job, the worker had to struggle with his new boss to restore his lost week of vacation time. Such were the isolated trials of male time-pioneers.

Had this worker and Sam Hyatt become fathers in Sweden, however, they would have been among the half of Swedish fathers who take six weeks *paid* paternity leave. In middle-class Swedish families, it would have been very much the thing to do, and even in working-class circles they would have encountered few objections. But at Amerco, the few pioneers of paternity leave were largely invisible and knew little of one another.

Sam Hyatt had, for instance, never heard of John West, who, like him, was consciously attempting to atone for an absent father (as well as an absent mother) by being there for his child. John was a shy, thin, thirty-two-year-old man with blond hair, who initially seemed more eager to tell the story of his wife's family than his own. "My wife's father was a workaholic veterinarian who put in ten- to sixteen-hour days. She didn't want me to be like her father." It was his wife's strong desire for him to take paternity leave that led him to request it.

As for his own story, he quickly filled in the details of his family's slow-motion collapse in Southern California—a childhood without Christmases, Thanksgivings, or any other symbols of family time or connection. By age sixteen, he found himself in a "no-parent" family:

> My brother and I were left unsupervised for days at a time when we were in elementary school, really for ten years of our lives. It made us less trusting but more self-reliant. My brother cooked and I cleaned. Both of us still do that in our marriages today.

While John at first saw himself as merely his wife's proxy on the issue of paternity leave ("This was *really* important to her!"), his own eagerness for it soon showed through as well:

> As soon as Tamara was pregnant, I approached my supervisor. So I gave him six to seven months' notice. My supervisor is new at Amerco and he said, "Oh? Okay." I brought him the book, pointed to the page, and he said, "We'll see as time gets closer if it really fits into our work schedule." I hounded him and I got two weeks.

I asked John how it was being home on paternity leave.

> I cleaned and cooked and did all that good stuff while Tamara recuperated from her delivery. I tried to keep her in bed as much as possible, and I took care of the baby. It worked out really well.

His male coworkers were surprised to learn of the paternity-leave program and quick to evaluate it in financial terms:

> At first, they envied me a bit until I pointed out that it was unpaid. So then the envy went away, and they said, "Oh gosh, I'd never do that, I'd go broke." Well, *I* don't think they'd go broke.

For John, far more than money was at stake:

> In my family, there's nothing left. My mom lives in an apartment. My dad lives in a condo. I have no idea where all the toys and clothes and mementos I had when I was growing up are. I can't find the crib I was born in.

> When we go to visit my in-laws, I realize what a close family is. Tamara goes home to see her room with all her furniture and pictures just as it was. She can pass on to our daughter the toys she herself played with as a baby. Christy is wearing dresses Tamara used to wear. I can't tell you how much I enjoy that.

John also gave some tentative thought to trying to cut back his work hours:

> Tamara goes back to full time in January. I brought it up: "Hey, maybe I could go part time." We could split days so that I'm home when she's not, and she's home when I'm not.

> In the Research and Development Division where I work, there are some young couples who are breaking the ice with part time. So I think if I was ever to ask to work twenty to thirty hours a week, it might be possible.

But in the end John could not bring himself to ask for fewer hours, a decision he rationalized in this way:

> I'm a closet workaholic. There are times my wife has to jolt me back into family life. The last hour at work I get nervous

that I've stayed at work too long. Going home in the car, I worry she'll be in a bad mood. My family comes first, but sometimes I ask myself, do I really *need* to be home? Or is this a passing thing? If I don't get home for an hour, is Tamara going to die? No, probably not. But if I don't meet this deadline at work, maybe the consequence will be severe.

When Tamara was home on maternity leave, John happily left it to her to be the watchdog of family time. She then declared that 6:30 P.M. would be their official dinnertime.

> Tamara keeps telling me that if I really work hard for eight hours, I can get everything done. I can come home and forget about work. So I try to gear myself to that. But sometimes I also want to linger and talk to colleagues and not dash right home.

John nevertheless wanted Tamara to keep him on what he called "the straight and narrow." He liked the idea of being called home by a waiting wife.

Interestingly enough, when Tamara returned to work after her maternity leave, John found himself taking on the same role, helping Tamara to limit her work time:

> My wife is very conscientious about work. She says, "I have to make this deadline," and, "Oh my God, I'm never going to make it, I'm so far behind." I ask her, "What happens if you postpone your deadline? Is there a problem with that?" She thinks it's dangerous not to meet her deadlines. But work isn't school. Nobody's grading you. Even project schedules aren't written in stone. You can talk to all the people who establish your deadline and see if you can get it moved.

Though both John and Tamara talked seriously of their need for more time at home—and each actually made moves to

recapture small amounts of work time for their family life, for their child—their efforts to rein in each other's schedule told a somewhat different story. Whatever they believed their deepest time-desires to be, both of them were voting with their feet. For each of them, the pull of work was stronger than the pull of home, and only the constant application of self-control (or the control the other could apply) could right the balance. As for so many other two-job couples like them, there was no one in the company, at home, or in the neighborhood capable of weighing in on the side of the family.

John's workplace response to his situation at home was a curious one. He began putting a certain amount of effort into helping colleagues get up the nerve to ask for flextime schedules. He recounted one such story:

> My coworker Betty told me her daughter was doing badly in school, but she couldn't get home from work early to help her. Betty told me, "I'm working so hard; there's no way I can go half time." So we talked about her coming in early, leaving at three o'clock, and taking a computer home. She said, "What if my boss says no?" I said, "So what?" "He's going to think badly of me," she said. I answered, "For two days. Then he's going to forget it." Eventually, Betty went to her supervisor and cut a deal. She leaves at three o'clock and works two hours at home on the computer.

John also went out of his way to encourage men to get on the paternity-leave bandwagon:

> I was talking to a guy on the company softball team I play on. His wife is expecting, and the guy was saying, "Oh, I could never ask for paternity leave. My boss wouldn't let me." I said, "How do you know? Did you ask him?" "No, no, but he just wouldn't let me." So I told

him, "Asking is the hardest part. *Ask him!*"

John became an informal chronicler of people's efforts to get shorter hours. He told this story of a woman who wanted to come back part time after she'd had a child:

> Her boss hated the idea but didn't think he had the right to hate it. So he sabotaged it by killing her with kindness. He eliminated all her responsibilities and arranged for her to still get paid. She was devastated. She was a very hard-driving person who wanted to do the work, not just get paid. In the end, her boss left the company, and now she's back full time.

By acting like a self-taught prison "lawyer" whom other inmates consult, John seemed almost to have convinced himself that he had actually altered his own schedule. But, in truth, he was an armchair revolutionary, part of an invisible army of working fathers who dream up hypothetical selves who share the second shift, play with their kids, and seldom postpone family time; while they themselves work like mad.

The Men Who Didn't Ask

Five years after the birth of his son, Jimmy Wayland felt he had completely missed the boat. A handsome, dark-haired consultant specializing in overseas sales, Jimmy had not even thought of paternity leave when his child was born. In fact, he had felt that his wife wanted the entire experience of a new infant for herself, and yet, to his puzzlement, she seemed to resent being left alone. "I had no idea what was stewing in her mind," Jimmy remarked. Both his mother and his mother-in-law pampered and fretted over the baby. Jimmy felt excluded and responded by immersing himself in his work.

As Jimmy described his domestic story,

My wife was in a hurry for us to reach what she felt was success. She's a good person, she just wanted to move more quickly than I did. She saw me as too "laid back." She was always dreaming about the next house, the next job, the next stage of life. My philosophy was to enjoy the one we had. She'd come home from work and start cleaning. If I had a sandwich in my hand, she'd be cleaning up the mayonnaise before I'd finished. Maybe she was just nervous, but she expressed it by trying to make everything "perfect," the kitchen, the house, me.

With the pressure of a small baby and both of our jobs, my wife felt she was doing it all. And she felt it was too much to handle. I didn't have a clue she was as mad as she was. It was actually the day she was supposed to go part time that she left me and the baby.

She'd been so good all her life. At home, she was good. At community college, she had a 4.0 average. Then, when she got unhappy with me, she ran off with a rambling man and left me and Joshua when he was a year and a half. We had a big custody battle. Everyone sided with me and I won.

For a long time, Jimmy, who was thirty-two when I first met him, had felt his personal life was "in a shambles" while his work life flourished. But after the custody battle, he miraculously reestablished a friendship with his wife and in time gave her back half the custody he had legally won. Soon, they were "discussing everything" and splitting holiday care of their son. Each took care of Joshua when the other had to travel.

Jimmy's parents would pick up Joshua from the sitter if Jimmy had to work late or go back into work after dinner, and this helped. But even with the new, more collaborative arrangement, Jimmy felt there was a problem. "Joshua works an eight-to-five job just like I do," Jimmy remarked, "which is tough because he loves being home with me. Life has been hard enough for him, so I feel like he needs all the time I can give."

Jimmy elaborated,

> Joshua is never going to know what a summer is like without having to get up and be shuffled off somewhere. He's never going to experience free time with me around. So I spoil him. I give him some leeway at home. If he doesn't want to eat supper right away, I don't force him, and sometimes he goes to bed later at night than he should. Maybe he's stalling for time, but he says the most hilarious things at nine-thirty at night. We have our best conversations then.

At work, Jimmy described himself as "not a sixty-hour man":

> Here in the plant, we have a macho thing about hours. Guys say, "I'm an eighty-hour man!" as if describing their hairy chests. I personally work about forty-four to forty-eight hours. My boss is a nice guy. I can't tell you that my boss or my boss's boss refuses me permission to take time off. I almost wish they *would*. Then I'd *really* give them a piece of my mind.

Jimmy thought he spent too much time at Amerco not doing "real work," and this meant that he needed to add time at the end of the workday to get it all done:

> Work begins at 7 A.M. since we start getting calls from overseas then. Between nine and nine-thirty, three people might grab me to talk about a sale. Then I have a meeting from ten-thirty to eleven, and probably between eleven-thirty and twelve noon someone will ask me to go out to lunch. I go around in a caffeine high from one meeting to another to another. Meetings are a whirlwind job within the job. It's like a tornado.

> I really like my coworkers, but I now spend so much time saying, "No, I can't" take on more work or do more favors that those relations are getting strained. There are so many things to do on a given day. I'm gone for a couple of hours, and I have twenty electronic messages on my computer when I get back. People are working weekends; you can see by the dates. They send things Friday at 10 P.M., Saturday mornings at 9 A.M., Sundays at 9 P.M. Of the twenty messages on my machine, I have to do something about twelve of them. My head spins. At the end of the day, finally, I'll think out a memo. That's my real work, and that edges out an early pick-up for Joshua.

In his heart of hearts, Jimmy wanted to rise up the Amerco ladder. But he also wanted Amerco to understand, if not honor, men like himself who were caught between the demands of work and home. As he explained,

> You have the high-risers grabbing all they can. Then you have the discontent of the lower-downs. Then you have confused people in the middle like me. A day doesn't go by where I don't talk about overload. It's an underground conversation here. You don't want to say it too loud. We're in this whirlwind; we work ourselves to death. Then when we die: What purpose did we serve? Is it worth it? But we're afraid to get off the roller coaster for fear we won't be able to get back on.

What made it hard on working parents like himself, Jimmy mused, was the absence of an "honorable middle rank." He continued,

> Amerco isn't doing a good enough job matching people's opportunities for money or job titles to their family values.

What if you don't want to go for the top, but you don't want to level out? We need to be assured that it's okay if we make that middle choice. We need to be told, "You may lose out on some money or a promotion down the road, but we still value you." A lot of us feel we can grow and should be rewarded—without becoming top managers. I don't worry about seeming like a loser, a goof-off, deadwood. I worry about not seeming like a serious player. We need to change the definition of serious player. A serious player now means someone who has aspirations to go as high as he can, someone who puts in an incredible amount of time, often at the expense of the family. Amerco needs to recognize serious players with serious families.

Three years later, when I visited Jimmy again, he seemed to be turning into the very man his ex-wife had wanted him to be—a rushed, rising executive who had left the "honorable middle" behind. Just as in 1990 he had thought managers in general "couldn't have a life," now he was a manager without much of a life. He had, he claimed, simply moved the "ambition bar" one notch upward. He had also found a steady girlfriend who had quit work to be a "wonderful stepmom" to Joshua. The result was that he and Joshua did fewer things together. "Joshua can play with his little sports figures on the floor for hours, then go outside and shoot baskets by himself," Jimmy commented wistfully. "Now, I have to invite myself to do things with him."

If, in 1990, Jimmy had agonized more openly about his situation than most of the other middle-level male professionals I interviewed, others found themselves, however silently, trapped in the same dilemma. These men ranged from middle managers to technicians, data entry workers to administrative support personnel. Those in the "middle," like Jimmy, often secretly dreamed of a more moderate work pace and way of life. Men in such jobs tended to be neither fully absorbed into a cult of professional workaholism nor pressed by desperate economic need. They worked hard. They wanted to be, as Jimmy put it, serious players. But half of Amerco's male middle managers had working wives; two-thirds had children under thirteen. In the absence of help from housekeepers or kin, they faced the need and often a fair amount of pressure to pitch in at home. So, many of them seemed inclined to resist very long hours.

Such men in the middle might seem poised to resist the process by which the worlds of home and work were being reversed; but they felt torn between the pressure to do more at home and a company-supported image of the serious player as a long-hours man. Even the smallest actual exchange of work time for home time became a monumental decision in their minds. Sam Hyatt took two weeks off for his child's birth, then tried to hold the line on extra hours, but when he was promoted and sent to another state, even that minimal level of resistance to the pull of work crumbled. John West and Jimmy Wayland both talked a good line about the need for more time at home, but neither of them could bring themselves to "walk the talk," and both ended up as long-hours men.

The sociologist William Goode has observed that upper-middle-class fathers advocated a greater role for men at home, though the pressures of career often prevented them from living out what they claimed to believe. Working-class men, on the other hand, often actually did more at home than they thought they should. Today, a confused group of men may be emerging between the other two, men who feel even more strongly than the upper-middle-class fathers that they *should* be doing more, and are even less able to live up to their ideals.

As Amerco's surveys showed, Amerco women were far more interested than Amerco men in expanding time at home, more informed about Amerco's family-friendly policies, and more likely to say they valued these policies. More surprising was the gap between men at the top and men in the middle. Larger percentages of men in the middle with children in childcare, for instance, supported paternity leave than did men above them in the corporate hierarchy. In one 1990 Amerco survey, 13 percent of top male employees thought childcare leave for new fathers was a policy of "great value," while 26 percent of men one level down and 43 percent of administrative and technical men did. (Hourly workers were not surveyed.) Among women, 43 percent of top employees supported childcare leave for new fathers, while 38 percent of workers one level down and only 27 percent of administrative and technical workers agreed.

I can think of two possible explanations for these differences. Men in lower management were younger than men in upper management and perhaps more sympathetic to the idea of participating at home. In the administrative ranks, men were also more likely to work among women. In fact, over half of all administrative workers were women, which meant that these men talked with women every day. Maybe as a result they came to see the world a bit more from a woman's point of view. But no matter why they wanted more time for family life, the vast majority of them still weren't pressing for it. The reasons they gave for their inaction did not have to do mainly with money

or job security, nor did they generally lack information about policies such as paternity leave or job sharing, nor were they avoiding the evil eye. Many of them simply could not imagine bucking Amerco and the kind of recognition it promised in return for a full-scale dedication of their time to the company. Both Amerco's official managed culture and the informal male culture of the workplace proved so overwhelmingly powerful that there seemed to be a silent pact to acquiesce to long hours. Did men submit to these hours because they "had" to, because the other guys were doing it, because they liked being at work, or because the pull of family life was too weak?

Jimmy Wayland spoke for many when he said, "I don't define my success as career success, but I'm living as if I do." In the end, for these men—and for increasing numbers of women as well—work was winning out. What had transpired both at Amerco and in society at large was a subtle but complete recasting of the notion of the "family man." Traditionally, "family man" meant a good provider, one who demonstrated his love of wife and children by toiling hard at the office or factory. In the modern workplace, however, "family man" has taken on negative overtones, designating a worker who isn't a serious player. The term now tacitly but powerfully calls into question a worker's masculinity. It was precisely to avoid being classified as a "family man" that the majority of men at Amerco, including Jimmy Wayland and John West, stayed clear of the policies that one might have expected a "family man" to embrace.

⊱ READING 41 ⊰

Motherhood on the Night Shift

Anita Ilta Garey

"My grandmother worked in a cannery for forty years, and I never knew it! She was just my grandmother. We'd go to her house and she'd bake cookies and—she was just *there*. I never knew she worked. I never knew she was a cannery worker." In the seminar in which my students interviewed their mothers and grandmothers about their work histories, they were now exchanging "discoveries." Many students were amazed to find that their mothers had been employed while their children were school-age. One student asked herself aloud: "How could I not know she worked?" How indeed?

In the aggregate, women's labor-force participation can be "invisible" in a number of ways. Feminist scholars, through their research and writing in the 1970s and 1980s, reclaimed what had been a hidden history of women's employment and economic production. Women's economic role had been omitted from most historical accounts, and feminist historians put women back in (Kessler-Harris 1982). The invisibility of mothers' labor-force participation has also resulted from the way in which survey and census data have been collected. Women engaged in agricultural labor, for example, are disproportionately undercounted in the censuses of most countries (Dixon 1982). Christine Bose found that, despite changes

over time in the technical definitions of "employment," women's employment has been consistently undercounted in U.S. censuses. Bose argues that although changes in the way employment is counted have corrected a great deal of the undercount of women's employment that occurred in censuses before 1940, much of women's employment in the informal or irregular economy is still not counted (for example, in-home child care, piece work, domestic service, or giving piano lessons). Her larger point is that "census definitions, enumeration, and verification methods can be molded to conform to, and thus support, gender- or race-related ideologies" (Bose 1987:109). In other words, employment can be counted so that certain types of employment and employment of certain types of people remain invisible.

The students who were surprised to learn that their mothers and grandmothers had been employed were pointing to a different kind of invisibility. Rather than the aggregate invisibility of histories and censuses, they had touched upon the ways an individual woman's employment can be rendered invisible. Patricia Zavella's interviews with Chicana cannery workers revealed that although these women had worked in the cannery for many years, some of their husbands would deny the fact that their wives were employed by discounting seasonal work or by describing as temporary and short term a work history that had become ongoing and long term (Zavella 1987). The refusal to recognize their wives' employment status is connected to an ideology that sees women's labor-force participation as secondary, nonessential, and a potential threat to men's identification with being the family provider (Potuchek 1997). Mothers themselves often downplay their employment, and together wives' and husbands' presentations of self perpetuate the ideology of the male breadwinner (Hochschild and Machung 1989; Potuchek 1997; Zavella 1987). For example, many women emphasize maternal visibility in relation to their children by restricting their hours of employment to the hours their children are in school or to the hours their children are asleep. This strategy can render less visible the fact of a woman's employment. It is this kind of invisibility that my students discovered when they took the time to ask their mothers and grandmothers about their labor force participation.

Night-shift work takes place when no one is looking, when the house is quiet and everyone is asleep. Mothers who choose the night shift talk about their reasons for doing so in remarkably similar terms. None of them refers to herself as a night person; all of them talk about their fatigue and their need for more sleep; and all of them describe how working the night shift allows them to be the kind of mothers they want to be. The night shift enables these women to implement a strategy of being a mother that most closely resembles nonemployed "at-home mothers."*

Mothers who work the night shift (11:00 P.M. to 7:30 A.M.) link their strategies of

---

*The common phrase "at-home mothers" infers that mothers who are employed are not in their homes, when clearly employed mothers are at home some of the time and nonemployed mothers are not at home all the time. It serves the same purpose as the phrase "full-time mothers," which is to signify that employed mothers are not "fully" fulfilling their roles as mothers. I use quotation marks to indicate that I am using these phrases to refer to the cultural conceptions embedded within them, conception with which both employed and nonemployed mothers must contend.

being a mother to which hours they are at work—or, more accurately, *to which hours they are at home.* They leave for work after their children are in bed for the night and usually arrive back home after their children have left for school or day care. During the night, children have been with fathers or other relatives, and it is predominantly the fathers who get the children off to school in the morning. One thing that mothers who work the night shift thus avoid is the morning rush at home. Mothers who work day shifts at the hospital, which begin at 7:30 A.M., either have to leave before their children are awake, or they have to get both themselves and their children up and out the door at a very early hour. The morning is not only rushed and tense, but the mother's work schedule and her child's needs and wants are brought into head-on collisions on a daily basis. Some of the night-shift workers reported getting home before their children left for school, and these mothers emphasized the fact that they could then make sure that their children looked "cared for" before they left for school. But they were not the ones who actually got the children ready, and they did not need to hurry their children because of their own schedules, but only in terms of the children's school schedules. Night-shift nurses tiptoe out after the children are asleep and thus avoid the conflicts of a frantic morning exit.

Night-shift workers are home at the other end of their children's school day, when their school-age children return at around 2:00 or 3:00 in the afternoon. Day-shift hospital workers, on the other hand, leave work at around 4:00 or 4:30 in the afternoon and head into rush-hour traffic for the commute home. They rush to pick up children at child care, or they return to waiting children and dinner preparation as soon as they walk in the door. The importance of this after-school and evening time to mothers who choose the night shift becomes evident when we compare them to workers on the evening shift. If mothers work the evening shift (3:30 to 11:00 P.M.), they are home in the mornings to get their children up and off to school, and they are there during the day to be with their preschool-age children, but they are not there in the afternoons and evenings to help with homework, have dinner with the family, or put the children to bed.

In general, mothers with school-age children do not find the evening shift conducive to their strategies of being a mother, and the mothers I talked to who worked the evening shift fell into two categories: they worked part time and had children who were not yet in school, or they worked full time and had children who were grown and out of school. Thus being at home when children returned from school was not an issue for the women in these two groups.

Mothers who work the night shift use shift work to present themselves as mothers in ways that resemble the voluntary part-time workers' strategies of being employed mothers. Although most of the full-time night shift nurses said they would prefer to work part time, they did not have the economic resources that would enable them to take part-time employment. All of the night shift nurses I interviewed worked full time. Most of them were married, but their husbands were not employed in the professions and had less education and lower positions in the occupational hierarchy than the husbands of the voluntary part-time nurses. In addition to needed income, wives' full-time employment at the hospital often provided the medical insurance coverage and other benefits that the family needed.

There are direct economic reasons for nurses to choose the night shift. For example, the hospital gives a pay differential to nurses for working nights, and so nurses on the night shift earn more per hour than they would on the day shift. But my interviews reveal that financial factors are only one part of a matrix of reasons for choosing the night shift and not the sole determining factor. Several nurses reported turning down opportunities for promotion and higher pay because the promotions would have entailed increasing their hours or being responsible as a supervisor even during their hours at home. Nurses explained their choice of shift in terms of their relationship to the profession, their children's needs, their definition of successful mothering, and their husbands' schedules, as well as their family's financial needs.

Another economic benefit of the night shift is that child-care costs are reduced because other family members are home at night to look after children. Night-shift nurses may not have the economic resources to work part time, but they are able to draw on family support resources for nighttime child care. The use of shift work by couples with young children is clearly a way of solving the child-care problems of availability, quality, and expense, and many dual-earner couples deal with the issue of child care by working different shifts and sharing the care of their children (Hertz and Ferguson 1996). Dual-earner couples with children under fourteen years are more likely to work non-day shifts than are dual-earner couples with children older than fourteen (Presser 1987:108). In one-third of dual-earner couples with children under six years of age, at least one parent works a non-day shift, and there is a strong correlation between non-day shifts and high rates of child care performed by family members, including fathers (Presser 1988, 1989).

But child care by family members was not primarily motivated by economic considerations. When it is the woman who works a night shift, the solution resolves more than the provision of child care. Concerns about leaving children with nonfamily child-care providers, coupled with concerns about their identities as primary caregiver mothers, were strong forces motivating these women's child-care arrangements.

When their wives are working, the husbands of the married night-shift nurses are the primary caretakers of their children. For the most part, it was fathers who got their children up and ready for school. Fathers' contributions to the care of their children remain important even when we remember that most of this care occurs between 10:00 P.M. and 8:00 in the morning. It does not occur during the hours when children are doing their homework, going to after-school or weekend activities, having their dinner, taking their baths, being read to, or getting tucked in for the night. The nighttime care of children does not occur when children have appointments with doctors and dentists, during parent-teacher conferences, during friends' birthday parties, or when the stores are open so that one can buy school supplies, clothes, Halloween costumes, sports equipment, dancing shoes, and the present for the friend who is having the birthday party. When fathers care for children while their wives are working night shifts, most of the care occurs while the children, and the fathers, are sleeping.

These men are not necessarily trying to escape parenting work. It is true that men are often resistant to sharing the second shift (Hochschild and Machung 1989), but some women are also reluctant to surrender symbolically key activities, especially those connected to their identities as mothers. In his study of dual-earner couples, Scott Coltrane notes that "the routine care of home and children are seen to provide opportunities for women to express and reaffirm their gendered relation to men and to the world" (Coltrane 1989:473). In addition, Coltrane found that fathers who perform activities normatively assigned to mothers often face negative reactions from male coworkers. Men may refuse to take on these responsibilities for the same reasons that many women are reluctant to relinquish them: because the performance of these activities is symbolically linked to constructions of gender. The night shift enables mothers of school-age children to maximize "family time"—it does not take up after-school time or evening family time, and it gives mothers the most waking time with their children. Working the night shift is the way that some women attempt to reconcile the structural conflicts and the conflicting vocabularies of motive attached to motherhood and employment.

Night-Shift Nurses at Sierra Hospital

Most of the hospital workers who work nights are nurses. My interviews with night-shift workers included registered nurses and nurses' aides, in addition to involuntary part-time janitorial workers. At night, the physicians, physical therapists, social workers, secretaries, receptionists, administrators, and food service workers have all gone home. Several of the night-shift nurses remarked that this was one of the things they liked about working at night.

At Sierra Hospital, the night-shift nurses work eight-hour shifts, which begin at 11:00 P.M. and end at 7:30 in the morning. Many of these nurses live outside the city where the hospital is located and have commutes of up to an hour each way. Most of them reported getting home between 8:30 and 9:00 in the morning. Although they are entitled to a half-hour break during the night, heavy patient loads and exceptionally busy nights often mean that these breaks are not taken in an effort to keep up or catch up with the work that needs to be done. One night shift nurse put it this way:

> Doing a midnight shift on my area, *rarely* do we get half an hour break— *rarely*. You've got to move real fast. Why should I move real fast constantly? You know, even if you take the half an hour break, I'd be so far behind.

Skipping their break also helps them to leave work on time or reduces the amount of time that they must stay after their shift ends. Before a nurse can leave her shift, she must update each patient's chart. Often nurses cannot finish their charting until the next shift arrives to take over the direct patient care. Nurses reported having to extend their workdays by thirty to forty-five minutes in order to finish their charting. Although nurses are technically entitled to overtime if they work after their shift, overtime is frowned upon by a budget-conscious administration, and the message conveyed to nurses is that "good nurses" finish their charting during their shift. Therefore, nurses who don't get their charting finished before their shift ends do so on their own time rather than risk being judged inefficient.

Being a worker is important to the night-shift nurses. However, while part-time nurses were sometimes frustrated by the extra effort it took to stay connected at the workplace when they came in only a few days a week, many of the night-shift nurses preferred the way that the night shift separated them from the daily activities of the ward. One nurse noted that working the night shift was "a family-like business" and different from the day shift, when "the bosses and everybody are there." Night-shift nurses were more removed from the professional aspects of their positions than were either part-time or full-time, day-shift nurses, and they interacted far less with other health professionals such as physicians, physical therapists, and social workers. This had its disadvantages, and several nurses remarked that they were not likely to be promoted or to have opportunities for specialization while they remained on the night shift.

Of the thirty-seven mothers I interviewed, seven were currently working full time on the night shift. All but one of these women had children under the age of twelve years, and the person who didn't have young children had worked the night shift since her children, now grown, were young. In addition, many of the older nurses who were working full-time day shifts when I interviewed them had worked the night shift when their children, now teenagers or adults, were young. Mothers who no longer worked the night shift reported either that they couldn't handle the fatigue of working nights or that they had changed their shifts when their children were older or when there were changes in their circumstances, such as the availability of family child care.

While there are patterns and conclusions to be drawn, there is both overlap and diversity within the group of night shift workers. Short sketches of six of these women illustrate their commonalities and differences as well as the contexts in which each weaves a life.

Shirley Roberts

Shirley Roberts is a sixty-year-old, African-American practical nurse who has worked the night shift for twenty-six years. She is married, has five adult children and eight grandchildren, and lives in a older, working-class neighborhood with well-built and well-maintained Spanish-style homes and well-tended gardens. After her youngest child was born, Shirley went to night school for a year to get her practical nursing training, and her husband stayed with the children while she was in school. Shirley noted that after being home with five children for more than twelve years, evening classes had provided a break for her: "It was an outing for me also, to get away from the house." When her youngest child was six years old and in school, Shirley started to work at the hospital.

> So my husband would be home with them at night and I would be home in the daytime. They would be in school until like 3:00, so that gave me a chance to sleep in the daytime, get up and cook dinner, then, you know, help them with

their homework. And then that's what I been doing ever since.

Shirley does not live far from the hospital, and she does not have to do charting as the registered nurses do, so she is able to get home soon after her shift ends. When her children were growing up, she made sure that she got home before they left for school.

I always got home before they went to school, and I would see that they had their breakfast—their daddy would start it sometimes—and comb their hair, make sure they're okay when they're underage and all.

Shirley told me that her husband, who is a skilled laborer with a civil service position, worked the evening shift when the children were growing up. He would come home at night just as she was leaving for work. Between work schedules and sleeping, Shirley and her husband didn't see each other very much. Shirley explained:

But you have to be able to understand that. . . . You have to have a nice husband who understands that and helps you with the children. You can't do that alone, it's too hard. I mean mothers are doing it, but it's really hard. You need someone to help you. Fortunately, my husband was nice. . . . I didn't have no trouble with the children either.

Shirley never had to rely on nonfamily child care. She was home with the children while they were young, and when she went to work nights, her husband was with them. If the children were ill, Shirley would take vacation days or take the sick child to her mother's house. In the summer the boys would go to summer camp, and the girls would split the summers between both sets of grandparents. At Christmas, Shirley would take vacation time, which she told me was "a big family time for them." Now that

her children are grown and she is near retirement, Shirley continues to prefer the night shift because, she explains, the workload is lighter than on the day shift, when patients have to be fed, bathed, and moved. At sixty, Shirley finds that the night shift continues to work for her.

Janice Ramos

Janice Ramos is a thirty-year-old, Filipina registered nurse. She immigrated to the United States with her parents when she was a teenager. Janice is married and has two children, an eight-year-old child and a fourteen-month-old baby. Her husband, also a Filipino immigrant, works as a technician. The family lives in a large, custom-built, two-story house in a small town about a forty-five-minute drive from the city where Janice and her husband work.

Janice was very articulate, but there was a flatness in her voice, a lack of intonation and a strain that conveyed long-term fatigue. Janice is a planner: their children were planned, their house was planned, her continuing education and career goals were planned. "We plan our life situation," she told me. But Janice has had to face the unplanned and unexpected. Janice's ultimate goal is to become a nurse practitioner. That plan, however, was postponed when Janice's second child was born with health problems. The baby was in the hospital for five months and was still plagued by respiratory illnesses. This experience affected Janice's plans to continue her education and her and her husband's plans about future children (they decided not to have any more).

Doris Chavez

Doris Chavez is a thirty-four-year-old, Mexican-American registered nurse. Her parents both had eighth-grade educations, and she was the first in her family to attend college, where she earned her B.S.N. degree. She is proud of her parents, whom she described as having come from very poor families and as working hard and doing well. Doris and her husband, an electrician, have two children, ages seven years and four years.

I interviewed Doris at the hospital just after her shift ended at 7:30 in the morning. Doris's home is an hour's drive from the hospital and, although she makes this commute four days a week, she feels more sympathy for her husband, whose commute is almost twice as long. Doris and her husband could not afford to buy a house in either of the urban areas where they work, and commuting is the price they pay for buying a house in a more affordable outlying area. Doris added that where they live is "calmer" than the urban area where she works, and that she liked that for her family.

Doris had a lively manner and a quick sense of humor. While she did not hesitate to say that being a "working mother" is "hard" and that "it's not easy to do," Doris thinks of herself as fortunate. Often, after describing a problem or a difficult situation, she concluded, "But we do okay," or "But it works out."

Angela Cordova

Angela Cordova is a forty-three-year-old, Filipina registered nurse who immigrated to the United States when she was sixteen years old. Both of her parents and all four of her siblings have also immigrated. Her mother lives "mainly" with her, but "goes around" to the houses of her other children, being cared for by them and helping them to care for their own children. "In my family," Angela said, "we help one another." When she returned to work when her second child was six weeks old, it was her mother who cared for the baby: "She's the best—the mother of the mother."

Angela is married and has two school-age children, ages nine years and six years. Her husband, also a Filipino immigrant, has a college degree but has been unable to find a job commensurate with his education and now works for a package delivery company. The Cordova family lives in a large, six-bedroom house in a suburb that is a forty-five-minute drive from the city in which Angela and her husband work. When I arrived at her door, Angela opened it and told me that she had just woken up and that her house was not clean. I sat on the sofa while she darted around picking things up and cleaning off the dining room table, where we would sit to conduct the interview.

Angela was friendly and eager to help me with my research project. She was also very tired, and several times during the interview, when I thought she was too tired, I would start to wind it up, at which point she would launch off on another topic with renewed enthusiasm.

Julia Ginzburg

Julia Ginzburg is a forty-three-year-old, Jewish-American registered nurse. Julia's upper-middle-class parents had higher ambitions for her than nursing, but Julia worked in poorly paid social service jobs after college, became pregnant with her first child, and married a man with no education or skills. A nursing degree for Julia was seen as an answer to the problem of how to support her family while her husband obtained his GED and went to college. Julia, her husband, and her first child lived with Julia's parents, who paid for her nursing education, while she went to nursing school. After Julia began her career as a nurse, she and her husband moved into their own rented apartment and had another baby.

At the time I interviewed her, Julia had been working as a nurse for three years, and her children were nine years old and one year old. While still considering themselves a married couple, Julia and her husband have recently separated and live apart. Julia is the primary and often the only breadwinner in the family. Julia's husband takes care of the children during the nights she works at the hospital, and he is there many evenings on her days off, but the bulk of the child care and daily maintenance is left to Julia. Unlike Janice, Doris, or Angela, she is renting the house they live in, and she said of herself, "I'm old, I'm forty-three, and I've got—I've got—nothing—to fall back on."

My overriding impression of Julia was of weariness and disappointment; unlike Janice, Doris, and Angela, hers was not a story of upward mobility, future aspirations, and hope. Julia grew up in an upper-middle-class family; her mother stayed home to raise the children and support her husband's career, and a college education for Julia and her sisters was assumed. Julia's background and the idealism and optimism of the period in which she came of age promised expanding opportunities, but that sense of possibility and promise is no longer a part of Julia's perspective on life.

Patricia Anderson

Patricia Anderson is a fifty-three-year-old, African-American registered nurse. She has worked as a nurse for twenty years, is divorced, and has three adult children and a twelve-year-old daughter. Patricia and her daughter live in a two-bedroom rented apartment in a new apartment complex in a middle-class section of the city. Although most of the full-time nurses at Sierra Hospital work four shifts a week, Patricia works five shifts a week because, she told me, her daughter's dance lessons and other activities are expensive, and she needs the money.

Patricia likes being a nurse and she likes interacting with patients, but she does not like working in the hospital because of the administration, the paperwork, and the speed-up on the ward. If she got married

again, which she would like to do, she said she would change her schedule from full time to part time. When I asked if she would quit working altogether if she could, she replied that she wouldn't take that risk and would stay working two days a week to keep her hand in "in case anything goes wrong."

Nationally, African-American nurses comprised only 4.2 percent of registered nurses in 1996 (Malone and Marullo 1997), and the number of African-American registered nurses at Sierra Hospital is larger than the national average but still a small minority. In an occupation in which 90 percent of the total population is white, Patricia had experienced a number of incidents that she characterized as "subtle racism." Patricia explained, for example, that whenever she was in a new situation, white people would assume she was not a nurse. Applying for her first nursing job twenty years earlier, she was told that applicants for the janitorial positions should apply at the office down the hall. After working as a nurse for a number of years, she interviewed for a different nursing position and discovered halfway through the interview that the personnel director assumed she was applying for a position as a nurses' aide. At Sierra Hospital, nurses and nurses' aides can be sent from their regular wards and loaned to another ward if needed; this is called floating. Patricia remarked that different assumptions were made when white women and black women "floated": "If a white person floats to another floor, they assume she's an R.N. If I float, they assume I'm a nurses' aide."

Most of the African-American nurses I interviewed mentioned both institutional and personal racism in the hospital. Different hospitals and different units within the same hospital had varying reputations regarding whether they were better or worse places for black nurses to work. "Each floor has a personality," Patricia told me, "like states—Louisiana is a man's state; Illinois is a white man's state; and California is strictly for kids." Sierra Hospital was considered a better place than many of the other hospitals in the immediate area, but some wards were considered definitely better than others.

A Mother's Place: "Being" at Home

The house as a symbol of family life is a recurring theme in the stories my interviewees told. Regardless of shift or occupational category, most of the women I talked to emphasized the importance of owning their own homes in the context of their feelings and plans about children. But there was another way in which the house as symbol was particularly salient for the night-shift workers. A house, to be a home, is where a mother is.

One of the most powerful images in modern theater is the door shutting as Nora Helmer leaves her husband and children in Ibsen's *A Doll's House* (1958 [1879]:68). This image juxtaposes the physical boundary of the house with its symbolic importance in the definition of family. Houses, the spaces within which homes are made, are important symbols in the construction of meanings about family. Ibsen represents Nora's desertion of her family with the sound of a closing door, by which the audience knows that she has crossed the threshold and is outside the physical space of the house. When the woman is removed from the house, definitions of home and family are called into question and must be reconstructed to account for or to conceal the fact of their missing central element.

The emotional content of home is mirrored in cliches such as "Home is where the heart is" and "Home is the place where they have to take you in." Another well-known saying is "A woman's place is in the home," the corollary of which may be "A home is where the woman is"—especially where a mother is. Night-shift "working mothers,"

in common with nonemployed mothers, are able to be home during the day.

Being at home during the day is related to cultural ideas of what a mother *does* and what a mother *is*, to both *doing* and *being*. To be at home during the day is to emulate nonemployed mothers, often referred to as full-time mothers. The term "full-time mothers" incorporates the idea that to be employed lessens the fullness or completeness of one's mothering. It is in response to this perspective that the night-shift workers are constructing a "working mother" who is a "full-time mother" because she does what "full-time" (nonemployed) mothers do. Even if her husband and children are not at home, the woman *of* the house is the woman *in* the house.

Janice Ramos, Doris Chavez, and Julia Ginzburg each have one child in elementary school and a child under five years old in some form of day care. Despite differences in ethnicity, age, and seniority at the hospital, their stated reasons for working the night shift are remarkably similar.

Janice had been at Sierra Hospital for less than a year but had worked in several hospitals before that, and I asked her if she had worked the night shift in her previous positions. Janice responded:

> I was always working nights. 'Cause it's easier to work nights with my young children. I like to be home with them, even [if] I'm sleeping, I like to be, you know, around.

Doris, who had worked at Sierra Hospital for ten years, immediately mentioned both owning a house and being home during the day when I said, "Tell me about working and having children." Doris replied:

> It's hard, real hard. I want my kids to go to college; we bought a house. I want them to have a house. The things that I feel are important and so that's why I do it. And that's one of the reasons I work

night shift. I feel more comfortable being at home in the daytime while
they're—well, they go to day care. So
my husband takes them to day care and
then I get home in the morning and
sleep. And I know that I'm home by the
phone in case something happens to
them. The school's right down the street
so during school time it's nice—he
walks home.

Julia, who had been at Sierra Hospital for almost three years, gave a similar response to
my question about her reasons for working
the night shift.

> For me, it allows—I mean, if—I'm avail-
> able. There's always a parent at home. If
> there's anything that comes up; if the kid
> is sick, it's no big deal, I'm here. Like now,
> when—during the summer—when my
> son is finished with his program at noon
> he comes home. I'm here. He can handle
> himself around the house. My small one
> I have in child care, but the big one comes
> home and can go and play with friends,
> he can go to the library himself, but—
> I'm here. . . . I'm asleep! But I'm here. If
> something comes up, I'm available.

"I'm here," "I'm home," "I'm around," "I'm
available": these are striking refrains in two
ways. First, they are coupled with the statement "I'm asleep." Second, for a large part
of the time when these women are home,
their children are not. Notice that both Doris
and Julia use the word "comfortable" to describe their reasons for wanting to be home
in the daytime. But being at home during the
day, even if they are asleep and their children are at school or in child care, fits with
their definition of motherhood. It not only
enables them to respond instrumentally to
daytime child-related needs and emergen-
cies and to be home when children return
from school, but it places them in the symbolically appropriate place for mothers: in

the home. A look at how each organizes her
daily schedule illustrates this.

Janice gets home from the hospital at
about 8:30 in the morning. Her husband, who
has to be at work by 9:00 A.M., has already
gotten their older child off to school, taken
the baby to the neighbor who does child care
for them, and left for work. Janice returns to
an empty house and immediately goes to
sleep. At 1:30 in the afternoon, she wakes up,
gets the baby from the neighbor's house, and
meets her son at the bus stop. She spends the
next few hours feeding the children, playing
with the baby, and helping her son with his
homework. When her husband returns from
work between 4:30 and 5:00 P.M., she goes
back to bed and sleeps until about 9:00 P.M., at
which time she gets up to leave the house at
10:00 P.M. for another night shift.

Shirley Roberts reported a similar method
of getting enough sleep by going to bed as
soon as she got home from work in the
morning, sleeping until the children got
home at 3:00 P.M., and then going back to bed
after dinner and sleeping for another two or
three hours. These routines are exceptions to
the pattern reported by most of the other
night-shift nurses, who don't go back to bed
in the afternoon or evening for additional
hours of sleep. Janice's intended routine
gives her more sleep than the other nurses I
interviewed. However, my interview with
Janice indicated that things were often not
routine in her household and that she averages far less sleep than claimed in her report
of a typical day.

Except for her two days off each week,
Janice spends about three of the thirteen-
and-a-half hours she is home during the day
with her children. The rest of the time the
children are at school or child care, or they
are home and Janice is sleeping. For Janice,
working nights cannot be a way of spending
more time with her children, since day-shift
workers would have about as many child contact hours as Janice does. Nor does working

nights give Janice more time with her husband, who takes over the care of the children as soon as he returns from work so that Janice can sleep. But, as Janice says, what working nights does do is to allow her to "be home with them"—to "be around."

Long commutes contribute to mothers' concerns about being at home during the day, near their children's schools and child-care locations. While the concern with being far from home does exist for commuters, many women cited the same reasons for working nights even when they had lived near the hospital in which they worked. Julia Ginzburg and Patricia Anderson, both of whom live within five miles of the hospital, talked about being home during the day in the same terms as did those with long commutes: they wanted to be around, to be available, to be home.

Doris Chavez lives over an hour from the hospital and usually does not get home until 9:00 in the morning. Her husband, who has a two-hour commute to work, gets the children up at 5:00 A.M., leaves the house by 5:30 to drop them at the child-care center, five minutes from their house, and then continues on his way to work. Their oldest child will be at the child-care center until 8:00 A.M., when he is bused to his elementary school, which is also near their home. Unlike Janice, Doris does not immediately go to sleep when she gets home; she does some housework, thinks about dinner preparations, unwinds a bit. She said she usually sleeps between 10:00 A.M. and 3:00 P.M., but when I asked her if that meant that she usually gets five hours of sleep, she told me that she averages about four hours of sleep on the days she works. She wakes at about 3:00 P.M. to welcome her son home from school and goes to pick up her youngest child from the child-care center. Doris spends the rest of the afternoon preparing dinner, helping with homework, and caring for the children. When her husband comes home from work,

they all have dinner together. Doris reported that evenings are spent playing games, reading with the children, or facilitating the oldest child's participation in sports or Cub Scouts. Doris tries to have the children in bed by 8:00 P.M., a challenge in the summer during daylight savings time, so that she can take a half-hour nap on the sofa in the living room before getting ready for work. She leaves the house at 9:30 at night to drive back to the hospital for another night shift.

Doris and Janice differ in the number of hours they are home and awake while their children are home and awake. Doris reported spending about twice as much contact time with her children as Janice, but for both of them what is salient is *which hours* they are home. As Doris said, "I know that I'm home by the phone in case something happens to them." Doris told me that the "overlap" period from 5:30 A.M. until 9:00 every morning, during which neither she nor her husband are at home, is a concern to her, and adds:

> But I'm usually home by nine, and I have been called before [by the school] and they know I'm sleeping. I get that straight with the teacher [laughs] right off the bat. You know, "I work nights, I'm home."

Doris lets her children's teachers know, and she emphasized the importance that they know, that she is a mother at home during the day. The work of making her presence at home visible to her children's teachers illuminates the symbolic nature of Doris's behavior. She is gesturing to herself, to her children, and to relevant others that she is an at-home mother.

Julia Ginzburg's separation from her husband and her position as the primary earner in her family make her life very different from both Janice's and Doris's, but her schedule is similar to the others. When I interviewed Julia, she was trying to implement and maintain a healthier sleep schedule than had been the case for the previous three years. She had been sleep deprived for so long that she reported that she was beginning to have physical and emotional problems. Before she took a break and got some rest, it would often take Julia two hours to leave the hospital after her shift, because she was so tired it would take her that long to finish her charting.* On her new schedule, Julia gets home between 8:30 and 9:00 A.M., after her husband has taken the children to school and child care. She sleeps until about 3:00 P.M., when her nine-year-old son comes home from school, at which time she leaves to pick the baby up from child care. In the summer, her older child gets home at noon from a summer program but takes care of himself while she sleeps.

Julia did not report as structured a family life as Doris did, but Julia is just as concerned about preserving certain symbols that represent a particular construction of motherhood, particularly one in which a mother is home during the day. Although Julia is asleep when her son returns from school, the fact that she is in the house is important to her, not only in terms of being physically present in case of an emergency, but also in symbolic terms. Julia explained:

> If I were working in the daytime, I wouldn't be comfortable with him coming home to an empty house. I don't want him to be—*I don't feel like he's a latchkey kid.* I'm here. I'm asleep! But I'm here.

Patricia Anderson expressed a similar sentiment when I asked her if it was her choice to work nights:

> I'd rather because—since I'm divorced and [my twelve-year-old daughter] is

into a whole lot of different things [dance and sports activities]—to make sure that no one ever has an excuse for saying [in a singsong voice], "Well, my mommy wasn't home and I hit the streets"—just like that.

In Doris's, Julia's, and Patricia's narratives, there is an emphasis not only on the importance of being at home during the day, but also on the importance of being *seen* as mothers who are at home. Doris emphasizes that her children's teachers know that she is home during the day and available to be called; Julia stresses that her son is not a "latchkey kid"; and Patricia says that she works nights in part so that no one can say, retrospectively, that she neglected her daughter because she was away at work during the day. All three are emphasizing maternal visibility. There are two concerns being conveyed in their explanations: one is with the immediate safety of the child, and the second is with potential problems that might be said to be caused by the mother's behavior.

Being there in the afternoon to welcome children home from school and in the evening to supervise dinner, homework, baths, and bedtime is extremely important to these women. The night shift, unlike day or evening shifts, allows them to be present during both of these crucial times. Angela Cordova used a parable to explain her reasons for working the night shift:

> It's better for a mother to stay home in the evening. Because the children will be more calm. See, I grew up in the country, and I could see the chickens and the chicks, like when the sun is setting. The chicks is "cheep cheep cheep" and then the mother hen will sit down and all goes underneath.

For Angela, being at home in the evening is part of a natural order that is pan-species but sex-specific.

---

*Other nurses I interviewed confirmed Julia's exhaustion and the time it took her to finish charting and leave the hospital in the morning.

A woman's presence at home in the evening has a symbolic, emotional, and instrumental importance. If mothers are at home during the afternoons and evenings, they can supervise older children during those hours when children are most likely to act independently or in association with their peers. The theme of supervision was particularly salient with Shirley, Angela, and Patricia, the night-shift workers with the oldest children. Angela told me with great amusement:

> I have only two [children] and I told my husband, "We have to watch them like a hawk" [laughs]—"a friendly hawk, though," I say. [Laughs.]

Shirley also mentioned the parental supervision of children as a reason for working the night shift:

> Working at night was good for my family. It kept them together. You keep your children out of trouble. . . . I don't think children should be left alone. I think that's where you find the problems. I think children should be supervised at all times.

When I asked Patricia if she ever considered changing shifts as her daughter got older, she replied:

> You know, see, every time I want to change [shifts] I see a [television] show or something about teenagers and so I think [about the] things they could do, and I know how I was. I was the goody goody two shoes *only* because my parents were exceptionally strict.

What these mothers are saying is not just that children need supervision, but that *mothers* need to be the ones who are supervising at particular times or in particular circumstances. The supervision that only mothers can do is directly linked to concepts of being—being mothers and being at home. Men (fathers) are often seen by the women I interviewed as unable to provide this all-encompassing kind of supervision and are sometimes seen as either needing supervision themselves or being incapable of adequately supervising their children. Yolanda Lincoln, an African-American ward secretary who worked full time on the day shift, remembered the problems she had when she once tried working an evening shift.

> It was hard for the kids because I didn't get to spend as much time in the evening with them. And even my husband, you know, he said today he would never work evening again while the kids are little. It's family time, and especially as a mother and with children in school, just to oversee that they are doing their homework and things like that. My husband is capable, but sometimes he can be lax, you know? Because a lot of times of time [when] I worked evenings . . . a lot of times I would come home and homework wouldn't be done and he would say, "Oh, she didn't tell me she had homework." So I knew then I could never work evenings.

Like caring for younger children, being at home to supervise older children is gendered. It is considered a mother's responsibility not only to teach young children right from wrong, but also, by her presence, to keep older children from doing wrong. Angela told me that when her nephew got into trouble and was sent to Juvenile Hall, she looked to the structure of her brother and sister-in-law's home for an explanation of "what went wrong." Angela's sister-in-law works an evening shift, from 3:30 P.M. to 11:00 P.M., and Angela blames her sister-in-law for being absent during those crucial hours. She admits that when her sister-in-law goes to work, her brother goes out to see his friends and leaves the children with Angela's mother. Angela's sister-in-law feels that her husband should stay home and help with the children, and Angela agrees. But Angela added, "And then I said to myself, 'Maybe [my brother] feels the same way, he misses [his wife] in the evening.'" Although two other adults are responsible for the children, the children's father and grandmother, Angela thinks that the key to her nephew's delinquent behavior is the absence of the mother during the evening hours, an absence that leads the husband to go out at night, leaving his children with their elderly grandmother. Angela's judgmental comments about her sister-in-law are probably glossing other unspoken family strains, but Angela's disapproval of her sister-in-law is expressed in a story about the symbols of appropriate motherhood. Earlier in our conversation, Angela had described her sister-in-law as an "ideal mother [whose] house is clean, [and who] cooks so good," and had then launched into the story about how her nephew was sent to Juvenile Hall. Angela concluded:

> [My sister-in-law] likes [to work] in the evening because she can do more work in the daytime at home. Her house *very clean.* . . . And I told [my sister-in-law], I said, "Why you don't work nights?"—"I cannot function right at night," she said. But I don't know what's best. That's why the house don't get clean.

Angela was presenting a morality tale about priorities and motherhood, and she was also presenting her own strategy of being by positing what she presents as the failed strategy represented by her sister-in-law. Despite her disclaimer, Angela clearly feels that she does know what is best, and she invokes the theme of "being there" to present her own strategy of being a mother, a strategy in which she is at home during the day and early evening for her children. . . .

Both "Working Mothers" and "Stay-at-Home Moms"

Mothers who work the night shift use the cloak of night to render their employment less visible. They do not deny the fact that they are employed, but they do try to implement strategies of being that highlight their maternal visibility. The night shift allows "working mothers" to appear to be "stay-at-home moms." At issue is the preservation of a family form in which the mother is available to her children during the day, both as the person who performs symbolically invested activities, such as volunteering at her child's school or taking her children to dance lessons or sports activities, *and* as the person whose very being is symbolically invested—the woman in the house, the mother at home.

Night-shift nurses implement strategies of being employed mothers in three major ways: they limit the visibility of their labor force participation to their children and in the public spheres of their children's lives; they make themselves available to involve their children in symbolically invested activities outside the home, and they position themselves in the culturally appropriate place and time: at home, during the day. All three of these strategies work to highlight their visibility as mothers.

What explains this shared concern with being seen as "at-home moms"? It is not a commonality of cultural, ethnic, or class background. Doris is the daughter of Mexican-immigrant, working-class parents who were both employed while she was growing up. Julia came from an upper-middle-class, Jewish home with a father in the professions and a homemaker mother. Patricia's parents were middle-class African Americans who both held professional positions. Shirley grew up in a working-class, African-American home in which her father was the breadwinner and her mother stayed home and was not employed until Shirley was in elementary school. Janice immigrated to the United States from the Philippines with her college-educated parents, both of whom were employed. What they all face, however, are similar dominant cultural norms about motherhood. From their different backgrounds, they each interact with prevailing definitions of motherhood—they are not creating motherhood from scratch, and they are not immune to the culture around them.

Working the night shift enables these mothers to normalize family life so it looks and feels more like the dominant cultural ideal of a traditional family: a father who goes to work in the morning and a mother who is home during the day, welcomes her children home from school, has dinner on the table for her returning husband, and tucks the children into bed at night. Judith Stacey refers to this family form as the "modern family": "an intact nuclear household unit composed of a male breadwinner, his full-time homemaker wife, and their dependent children" (Stacey 1990:5). In historical terms, Stacey is correct; the prevalence of such families was historically recent and short-lived, as well as being culturally specific. But for the women I interviewed, this family form is conceptualized as traditional. If not a common family form in their modern world, it was still an ideal by which they measured themselves, and the word "traditional" best represents the concept that these "working mothers" were trying to convey.

As a group, they have similar constellations of resources that make night-shift employment a sensible strategy for negotiating norms about motherhood in their constructions of themselves as "working mothers." Except for Shirley, they all have qualifications as registered nurses. Except for Patricia, each relies on her husband for nighttime child care. Unlike the voluntary part-time nurses, their husbands' jobs do not pay

enough or provide the needed benefits that would enable them to work part time. Of course, similar resources are experienced differently by women in differing social locations and familial contexts. What it means, for example, to be the sole support of her family will be different for Julia, whose parents have economic resources she could call on in an emergency, than for Patricia, who is estranged from her parents and has grown children who still turn to her in times of need. They have traveled different paths (Cole 1986), but they talk in remarkably similar ways about how working the night shift enables them to be "working mothers" who are "stay-at-home moms."

REFERENCES

Bose, Christine E. 1987. "Devaluing Women's Work: The Undercount of Women's Employment in 1900 and 1980." Pp. 95–115 in *Hidden Aspects of Women's Work*, edited by Roslyn Feldberg, Christine Bose, and Natalie Sokoloff. New York: Praeger.

Cole, Johnetta B. 1986. "Commonalities and Differences." Pp. 1–30 in *All American Women: Lines That Divide, Ties That Bind*, edited by Johnetta B. Cole. New York: Free Press.

Coltrane, Scott. 1989. "Household Labor and the Routine Production of Gender." *Social Problems* 36:473–90.

Dixon, Ruth B. 1982. "Women in Agriculture: Counting the Labor Force in Developing Countries." *Population and Development Review* 8(3):539–66.

Hertz, Rosanna, and Faith I. T. Ferguson. 1996. "Childcare Choices and Constraints in the United States: Social Class, Race and the Influence of Family Views." *Journal of Comparative Family Studies* 27(2):249–80.

Hochschild, Arlie Russell, and Anne Machung. 1989. *The Second Shift: Working Parents and the Revolution at Home*. New York: Viking.

Ibsen, Henrik. 1958 [1879]. "A Doll's House." Pp. 1–68 in *Four Great Plays by Ibsen*. New York: Bantam.

Kessler-Harris, Alice. 1982. *Out to Work: A History of Wage-Earning Women in the United States*. Oxford: Oxford University Press.

Malone, Beverly L., and Geri Marullo. 1997. "Workforce Trends Among U.S. Registered

Nurses." A report for the International Council of Nurses ICN Workforce Forum. Stockholm, Sweden, September 21–October 1, 1997. ANA Policy Series. Washington, D.C.: American Nurses Association (www.ana.org/readroom/usworker.htm).

Potuchek, Jean L. 1997. *Who Supports the Family? Gender and Breadwinning in Dual-Earner Marriages.* Palo Alto: Stanford University Press.

————. 1988. "Shift Work and Child Care Among Dual-Earner American Parents." *Journal of Marriage and the Family* 50(1):133–48.

————. 1989. "Can We Make Time for Children? The Economy, Work Schedules, and Child Care." *Demography* 26:523–43.

Zavella, Patricia. 1987. *Women's Work and Chicano Families: Cannery Workers of the Santa Clara Valley.* Ithaca: Cornell University Press.

∽ **READING 42** ∾

The Time Divide

American Workers in Cross-National Perspective

Jerry A. Jacobs and Kathleen Gerson with Janet C. Gornick

Although the growth of time pressures between paid work and domestic life has dramatically altered the lives of American workers, many of these trends are not unique to the United States. The rise of employed women, for example, is a worldwide phenomenon that can be found in all economically advanced societies. Yet the United States appears atypical in its response to these basic economic and social transformations, lagging behind most countries in the social support it provides for families, children, and employed parents.

"American Workers and the Cross-National Perspective" is reprinted by permission of the publisher from *The Time Divide: Work, Family, and Gender Inequality* by Jerry A. Jacobs and Kathleen Gerson, pp. 119–120, 126–147, Cambridge, Mass.: Harvard University Press. Copyright © 2004 by the President and Fellows of Harvard College. An earlier version of this essay appeared as "Hours of Paid Work in Dual-Earner Couples" in *Sociological Focus* 35 (2): pp. 169–188.

Comparing the circumstances of U.S. workers to those in other countries who share America's level of economic and social development provides a yardstick by which to measure national changes. By pinpointing the ways in which American workers are similar to, and different from, workers in other countries, a comparative perspective expands the picture provided by historical analysis of work and family change. Cross-national comparisons also provide some clues to the range of policy interventions that might make a difference in the lives of workers. If some aspects of change are shared by all, there is good reason to believe that these trends represent deeply rooted social and economic trends that are not subject to substantial alteration. If, however, the United States looks vastly different from other countries—especially in terms of how it responds to basic economic transformations, there is good reason to conclude that policies can be developed to help Americans better cope with the challenges spawned by change. A comparative perspective allows us to untangle what is endemic to postindustrial development and what is amenable to change. It also provides some hints about how well or poorly policy approaches in other countries can help Americans resolve the dilemmas they confront.

This chapter thus focuses on comparisons between the United States, Canada, and eight European countries using information from the mid-1990s from the Luxembourg Income Study (De Tombeur 1995). We focus on these countries and this time period not only because the information is readily available, but also because these countries share a similar cultural heritage and level of economic development. We compare the average hours of paid work put in jointly by couples as well as the proportion of couples working very long weekly hours. We also assess gender differences in working time within families. . . .

Differences in Yearly Working Time

If accurate measures of working time for American workers are difficult to ascertain, the complexities are magnified for cross-national comparisons. Such comparisons are typically based on annual hours of paid work, an approach that multiplies hours worked per week by weeks worked per year to get a yearly measure for individuals. Although not an ideal measure, annual hours are readily available for a wide range of countries and, consequently, form the starting point for most cross-national comparisons.

We can see from Table 1 that, when working time is measured by annual working hours, American workers stand out. The first column shows that the average American worker puts in 1,976 hours per year, roughly equivalent to a 40-hour week for 50 weeks per year and clearly the greatest number of working hours among all the countries. At the other end of the spectrum, the average German worker puts in 1,556 hours per year, or the equivalent of 35 hours per week for less than 45 weeks, while the average Dutch worker shows only 1,368 annual hours, or the equivalent of 35 hours per week for 39 weeks a year. The most recent OECD data indicate that U.S. workers' hours surpass those of even the notoriously hardworking Japanese.

TABLE 1 Average Annual Hours Worked for Selected Countries, by Gender

Country	A Actual, per Person, 1999	B Full-Time Workers, 1993	C Men, 1994	D Women, 1994
United States	1,976			
Canada	1,777[a]			
Finland	1,765		1,801.5	1,660.6
United Kingdom	1,720	1,952.7	1,973.8	1,469.2
Italy	1,648[b]	1,709.7	1,766.1	1,600.8
Belgium	1,635[b]	1,711.2	1,728.5	1,512.1
Sweden	1,634		1,906.2	1,748.8
France	1,604[b]	1,790.0	1,792.2	1,595.4
Germany	1,556	1,738.7	1,728.5	1,512.1
Netherlands	1,368[b]	1,788.4	1,679.4	1,233.4

Sources: A, OECD 2000 *Employment Outlook;* B, Eurostat 1995, as cited in Lehndorff 2000; C and D, ILO Key Indicators of the Labour Market, 1999.
Note: Countries are listed in order of the figures in Column A.
a. 1997
b. 1998

From the perspective of average annual hours, American workers appear to be harried and overworked compared to the more leisurely work schedules of Europeans. It is not surprising that comparisons of this sort provide fuel for the belief that Americans possess a distinct and unique taste for "workaholism." Commenting on the latest ILO report, which appeared just before Labor Day 2001, the *New York Times* speculated that "the American psyche" and "American culture" explained a national penchant for "overwork" (Greenhouse 2001).

A closer look, however, suggests that the discrepancy between Americans and Europeans, while real, may not be as great as these numbers seem to indicate. The averages in column A of Table 1 include all workers and thus mask some differences among different types of workers, including those on part-time and full-time schedules. In Column B, which includes full-time workers only, the differences between countries become much smaller, with the typical full-time European worker putting in about 1,700– 1,800 hours per year (or about 40 hours per week for 45 weeks). The United Kingdom leads, with 1,953 hours for full-time workers, while Belgium and Italy are nearly tied for the least full-time hours, at just over 1,700. The Netherlands is often noted as the country with the fewest working hours, but this largely stems from the prevalence of part-time employment and does not reflect especially short workweeks among full-time workers. Full-time Dutch workers put in about the same annual hours as those in France, Germany, and a number of other European countries. Although the United States is not included in this ILO series on full-time workers, the fact remains that the average American worker—including both part-timers and full-timers—puts in more hours per year on the job than the typical full-time worker in Europe.

In columns C and D of Table 1, the average annual hours are separated for men and women. From this perspective, the work schedules of European men appear much less leisurely, while European women in different countries appear to have a wide range of average annual hours. German men, for example, put in 1,972 hours per year, or about 42 hours per week for 47 weeks. (In contrast, the *New York Times* reported that the average American worked 499 hours more than their European counterparts.) In all of the European countries except the Netherlands, men work on average between 1,700 and 2,000 hours, while women range from a notable low of 1,233 in the Netherlands to a high of 1,749 in Sweden. Again, it helps to look beyond averages to make sense of differences not only among individual workers but also among countries.

Weekly Working Time

However measured, the annual working time among American workers stands out. One main culprit, of course, is the relative paucity of vacation time. European workers enjoy substantially more time off during the year than Americans do, so their annual working time is proportionately lower even when the length of their workweek is not. But beyond the difference in vacation time over the course of the year, do American workers tend to work longer weekly hours than their European counterparts?

To answer this question, we analyzed data on ten countries from the Luxembourg Income Study (LIS), an international archive of micro-datasets, in order to study patterns of working time. For men, the average workweek in most countries ranges between 40 and 44 hours per week, with only Sweden having a particularly short workweek (results not shown). While average weekly hours in the United States fall at the high end of the range, the average length of the American workweek is not especially distinctive. Where the United States does stand out is in the dispersion among workers in the number of hours worked, especially in the percentage of workers who report working very long workweeks. Over one quarter of American men (26.8 percent) put in more than 50 hours per week on the job, compared with 25.8 percent in Belgium, 17.0 percent in France, 10.6 percent in Finland, and 2.8 percent in Sweden. The United States is at the top of a cluster of several countries having high proportions of men working 50 hours per week or more. Thus, the long workweeks that we have considered throughout this study in the context of the United States [continue] to be a useful focal point for international comparisons. The proportion of U.S. citizens who work long weeks, rather than those having a long average workweek, most clearly sets the United States apart from other countries.

Several countries have experienced increases in the dispersion of working hours since the early 1990s, including Belgium, Germany, the Netherlands, and the United Kingdom. When we conducted this same analysis for an earlier period, around 1990, the United States stood out even more sharply than it did when we focused on more recent years.

The standard workweek has given way to a wider array of formats (OECD 1998; Mutari and Figart 2000). A growth in part-time work, which has swelled the ranks of those working fewer hours, is a large part of this trend. At the other end of the working time continuum, European employers have also pushed for greater flexibility in work arrangements among full-time workers, contributing to a growth in the proportion working many hours. (In the U.S. context, "flexible" work arrangements refer to schemes designed to help workers respond to family concerns; in Europe, however, the term "flexibilization" refers to employers' desire to bend regulations such as maximum-hours rules to enhance productivity and cut labor costs.)

Despite these European trends, the proportion of men and women working long weeks is highest in the United States, where there is far less regulation of wages and hours. The OECD findings (1998) show the United States leading all countries in the proportion of those working long weeks, with the exception of men in the United Kingdom.

More dramatic differences emerge in women's weekly hours. American women report among the longest workweeks in the nine countries—an average of 37.4 hours per week, compared with 34.0 in Germany, 31.6 in Sweden, and 30.4 in the United Kingdom. The Netherlands shows the shortest workweek, with the average Dutch woman working 25.5 hours per week. The United States has the highest percentage of women who work 50 hours per week or more. At 11 percent, those women who work very long weeks are not as numerous as their male counterparts, but they surpass the level in Germany (6.8 percent), the United Kingdom (4.2 percent), the Netherlands (0.2 percent), and Sweden (0.4 percent).

These comparisons suggest that the United States stands out more in terms of the percentage of workers who put in very long weeks than it does in terms of the average workweek. Again, we find that a growing dispersion in working time for women and men emerges as a major feature of the American context.

Part-time jobs have more protections in Europe than they do in the United States, especially since the adoption of the 1997 policy designed to eliminate discrimination against part-time work and to afford job protections to part-time workers (European Union Council Directive 1997; for a detailed discussion of European protections for part-time workers, see Gornick and Meyers 2003). In the United States, part-time jobs tend to be concentrated in occupations that typically offer low wages, few benefits, and little or no job security. The disparity in attractiveness between part-time and full-time jobs is greater in the United States than in many other countries (Gornick and Jacobs 1996; Bardasi and Gornick 2002).

Couples' Joint Working Time

We have seen how the time conflicts facing American workers can be better understood from the perspective of families and households. To place these dynamics in a cross-national perspective, we again need to shift from looking at individuals to looking at the time pressures on entire families. A cross-national focus can tell us how the joint working time of American couples compares with that of couples in other countries.

There are good reasons to believe that dual-earner couples face differing conditions across countries. First, there are considerable differences in the kinds of jobs available, including part-time and flexible work. As important, family-support policies, such as universal day care or paid parental leave, vary widely across countries. Differences in the dynamics of gender equality may also shape the options of couples in different national contexts. Since differences in working time between husbands and wives—especially in families with children—contribute to gender disparities in earnings and career opportunities, it is important to see if some countries have reduced time pressures on couples in a way that promotes, or at least does not undermine, the prospects for gender equality. Understanding how couples apportion paid working time also provides a valuable starting point for identifying social policies that can alleviate domestic time squeezes while supporting egalitarian gender arrangements.

To explore these issues, we focus again on weekly working hours. The week is the best unit of time to use when considering family life, since it corresponds most closely

to families' needs to supervise and care for their children. Annual vacation time, for example, may be helpful in providing a respite from work and caregiving pressures, but annual vacations will not alleviate much of the pressure that families experience on a regular basis.

Weekly hours also provide a more accurate way to make cross-national comparisons, since several factors make it difficult to compare yearly work experiences across countries. Because annual working hours are sensitive to variations in the number of weeks worked, which in turn reflects labor market entrances and exits, countries with relatively low women's labor force participation (or high rates of part-time work) tend to have large numbers of women entering and leaving the labor force and thus produce relatively few annual working hours for women. High or growing levels of unemployment would also tend to reduce annual working hours, as those losing their jobs (or just regaining employment) leave (or enter) the workforce.

In addition to comparing differences in average weekly hours, we also explore cross-national differences in the variability of couples' working time. We have seen how a time divide has emerged among American workers between those putting in very long workweeks and those who work less. Is this division of working time emerging elsewhere, or is it a peculiarly American development? . . .

Couples' Working Time

Because both men and women work slightly more hours in the United States than in other industrialized countries, American couples are likely to put in the most combined time at work as well. Similarly, the proportion of couples who work very long weeks—more than 80, or even 100, hours per week—are likely to be

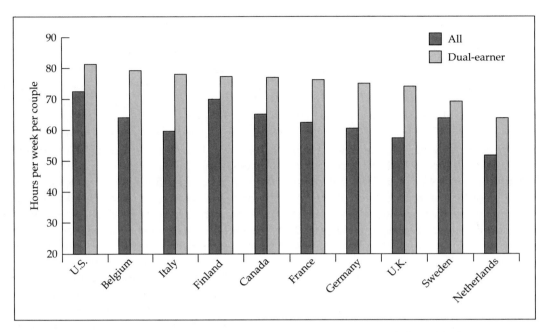

FIGURE 1   Average Joint Hours of Paid Employment for Married Couples, by Country (*Source:* Luxembourg Income Study)

higher in the United States than elsewhere (see Figures 1 and 2).

Figure 1 presents the joint hours of paid work of husbands and wives for all couples in which at least one partner was employed and for dual-earner couples. American couples report the most joint hours of all ten countries included in this analysis. The typical American couple with at least one employed spouse puts in just over 70 (72.3) hours per week.

This high average reflects the fact that, first, the United States has a high percentage of dual-earner couples and, second, the length of the workweek among these couples is relatively long. In terms of the percentage of couples in which both partners work for pay, the United States trails only two Nordic countries—Finland and Sweden—where special efforts have been made to facilitate women's labor force participation. . . .

In half of the countries (Belgium, Canada, France, Germany, and Sweden), the average

married couple spends between 60 and 65 hours a week in paid employment. Even though the majority of couples in these countries have two earners, most work just under 80 hours per week. How couples work this many hours, however, varies from country to country. In Sweden, for example, large numbers of married women work relatively few hours, while in Belgium, fewer employed married women put in longer workweeks. . . .

The Netherlands and the United Kingdom report the shortest average workweeks, with the typical British couple working 57.4 hours per week (or 14.9 fewer hours per week than U.S. couples do). Indeed, the United Kingdom has the third lowest rate of married women's labor force participation (54.6 percent) and the second shortest workweek among dual-earner couples (74.3 hours per week). The truly exceptional case, however, is found in the Netherlands, where only a bare majority of married women work for pay (52.3 percent) and the average workweek among dual-earner couples is 64.0 hours, more than 17 fewer hours per week than in the United States. Despite the similar level of economic development in these countries, the time pressures families face are markedly different in each.

The open bars on Figure 1 present the distribution of working hours among dual-earner couples. U.S. couples put in the longest workweeks, with the average dual-earner couple putting in 81.2 hours per week. In most of the other countries, the figures range from 74 to 79 hours per week, except Sweden and the Netherlands, where dual-earner couples work a combined total of fewer than 70 hours per week.

Figure 2 displays the proportion of couples jointly working many hours for pay. Here again, we see that not only is the average American workweek slightly longer than that of any of the other countries, but the United States also ranks first in the percentage of couples working more than 80 hours per week (68.2 percent) and in the percentage of couples working 100 or more hours per week (12.0 percent). The difference between the United States and the other countries when it comes to the percentage of couples working many hours is even more marked than the comparison of average number of weekly working hours.

Finland, Sweden, and the Netherlands are places where very long workweeks are quite rare. Finland presents an especially interesting comparison, since the average Finnish couple logs nearly as many hours per week as the typical American couple (77.4 for Finland, versus 81.2 for the United States). Yet the Finnish distribution is more tightly clustered, and far fewer Finnish couples put in more than 80 hours per week (25.1 percent), with even fewer working 100 hours per week or more (4.0 percent).

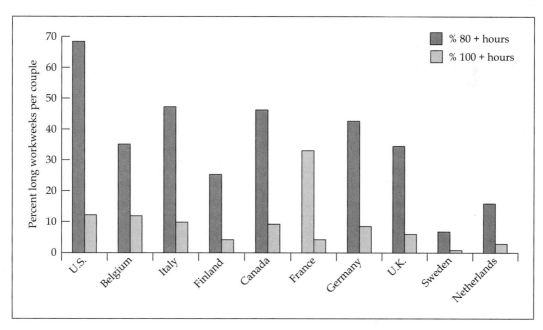

FIGURE 2   Percent of Couples Working Long Weeks, by Country (*Source:* Luxembourg Income Study)

Figures 1 and 2 make it clear that American dual-earner couples, like individual workers, spend more time at the workplace than do their counterparts in other countries. The difference may seem small compared to some countries, such as Finland, but it is substantial compared to others, such as the United Kingdom and the Netherlands. Indeed, dual-earner couples in the United Kingdom put in nearly one fewer person-days per week (6.9 fewer hours) than their American counterparts. Thus, the time demands on dual-earner families vary across countries, and the pressures appear greatest for American couples.

Educational Influences Across Nations

We have seen that American workers with higher educational credentials tend to have longer workweeks than those with less. Can this pattern be found in other national contexts as well? Standard economic theories of labor supply suggest that the higher earning potential of more educated workers would lead them to work more in all societies. Since the United States has comparatively high levels of wage inequality, however, the effect might be larger in this country than elsewhere (Freeman and Bell 1995).

In contrast, sociological and institutional analysis suggests that educational differences in working time will vary in ways that reflect local institutional arrangements, such as legislative measures that affect employment choices (Mutari and Figart 2000). From this perspective, the opportunity as well as the incentive to work many hours may vary in ways that favor the more educated in some places and the less educated in others. It is thus not clear whether the effect of education in America will be the same in other countries.

The structure and organization of educational institutions differ across nations, so it is difficult to compare educational levels across countries. In an attempt to do so, Figure 3 compares the working time of couples in which at least one partner has a college degree or higher with that of couples in which neither partner has a college degree. Countries in

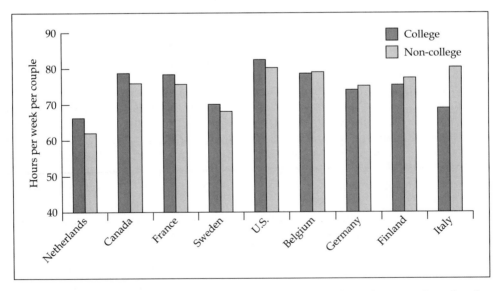

FIGURE 3   Average Joint Hours of Paid Employment of Dual-earner Couples, by Educational Level and Country (*Source:* Luxembourg Income Study)

the figure are ranked in terms of the size of the educational difference in mean hours worked.

Education in the United States is positively associated with the length of the workweek. More highly educated couples in the United States tend to put in more hours working for pay than do their less educated counterparts (82.4 hours versus 80.3 hours). The difference is clearest at the extremes, where the proportion of dual-earner couples working 100 hours per week or more is substantially higher (15.2 percent) than for less educated workers (9.6 percent).

Although college-educated couples are more likely to have the longest workweeks in the United States, the education differential, in percentage terms, is larger in four other countries—the Netherlands, Canada, France, and Sweden. Since these countries have lower wage disparities across the workforce than does the United States, a higher level of income inequality cannot explain the education differential in work hours.

The other countries show a different relationship between education and working time. In Italy and Finland, more educated couples put in substantially *shorter* workweeks than do their less educated peers; and, while not shown here, we find that both husbands and wives in the more educated group report shorter workweeks. In Germany and Belgium, the average workweek does not differ by education level, but the more educated are more likely to put in the largest share of the longest workweeks.

It is tempting to attribute the lengthy working time of highly educated couples to the higher economic rewards they can command, and this is surely part of the story. The United States's surprising rank compared to other countries, however, suggests that other processes are also at work. We must consider noneconomic incentives and local institutional conditions to fully understand why people work the hours they do.

Gender Differences in Working Time

Patterns of working time matter because they have consequences for gender equality as well as for the quality of family life. Very long workdays are certainly not family-friendly, and they are also likely to hinder the opportunities for creating egalitarian time allocations within families. If this is so, the relationship between couples' working time and gender equality is likely to be linked in a curvilinear way. Dual-earner couples with relatively fewer combined working hours will probably depend on small contributions from wives, especially compared to husbands' hours. Couples with many working hours, perhaps over 100 hours per week, are likely to depend substantially on wives' contributions, but these couples are also likely to have husbands putting in the most hours and thus contributing even less to the domestic work of the household. Couples with an intermediate amount of time devoted to paid employment are more likely to have a more equal balance between wives' and husbands' economic contributions.

Do short, intermediate, or long workweeks tend to promote more gender-egalitarian participation in paid work? Again, it is important to note the distribution of working time as well as the average. For married men, the workweek clusters between 41 and 45 hours in all countries except Sweden, which trails at 38.1 hours per week. The United States has the second longest workweek for married men (at 44.8 hours per week, just behind Belgium at 44.9), but it clearly surpasses all of the others in the proportion working 50 hours per week or more. At just under one-third (30.3 percent), the percentage of married men working over 50 hours per week in the United States is nearly triple that in Finland (10.4 percent) and more than ten times as high as in Sweden (2.8 percent).

TABLE 2   Ratio of Wives' to Husbands' Hours of Paid Work Among Dual-Earner Couples, Aged 25–59, by Total Hours of Joint Paid Employment

Country	Total Hours of Joint Paid Employment				
	Total	<60	60–79	80–99	100+
Finland	.93	.54	.96	.91	.83
Sweden	.82	.58	.87	.83	.65
France	.82	.50	.86	.83	.86
Italy	.81	.64	.79	.83	.92
United States	.81	.37	.67	.91	.84
Canada	.79	.43	.78	.87	.85
Belgium	.76	.53	.81	.82	.83
Germany	.71	.41	.67	.87	.77
United Kingdom	.68	.39	.70	.79	.72
Netherlands	.53	.36	.60	.73	.59

Source: Luxembourg Income Study.
Note: Countries are listed in order of the first-column figures.

Married American women (36.4 hours) rank second only to Finnish women (37.2 hours) in the length of their average workweek, while married women in the United Kingdom (30.8 hours per week) and especially the Netherlands (22.4 hours per week) have the shortest average workweeks. And while the United States ties Belgium and Italy for having the highest percentage of married women working over 50 hours per week (10 percent), such long weeks are nearly unknown for married women in Sweden (0.4 percent) and the Netherlands (1.7 percent).

What about cross-national differences in the gender balance of working hours? Table 2 displays this in the ratio of wives' to husbands' average weekly hours. Not surprisingly, gender equality in working hours is high in the United States—absolutely and relatively—among couples without parenting responsibilities (.86), tying with Sweden for second place. Among couples with children under 18, however, American women fare less well. Among parents, the ratio of wives' to husbands' hours falls to .78, and here the United States lags behind Sweden

(.79), Italy (.80), France (.81), and especially Finland (.92) (not shown in table).

What about the link between gender equality and the length of families' working hours? Table 2 shows that in seven of the ten countries, couples with an intermediate number of working hours also have the most equal gender balance in paid working time. In three countries, however, husbands' and wives' contributions are most equal in the families with the most combined hours.

In the United States, the most gender-balanced contributions occur in couples who put in more than 80, but fewer than 100, hours per week. Among couples working fewer than 60 joint hours, wives contribute less than half the time (.37) their husbands do. This ratio rises to .67 among couples working 60–79 hours per week, peaks among couples working 80–99 hours per week (.91) and falls again among those working 100 or more hours per week (.84).

This general pattern also holds for Canada, Germany, the United Kingdom, and the Netherlands. Sweden and Finland show a similar curvilinear pattern, although the gender balance peaks between 60 and 79 hours per week. Indeed, Finnish couples working 60–79 hours have the most gender balance, with wives contributing 96 percent as much time to paid work as their husbands.

In Belgium and France, however, the balance between wives and husbands plateaus after couples reach 60 joint hours of paid work per week, and in Italy, the most equal balance in working time is found among the couples with the most time at the workplace, where the gender ratio increases as total working time rises. Clearly, there is a relationship between gender equality in working time within couples and the length of the joint workweek. And for most counties, the most equal relationships emerge somewhere in the middle, where both husband and wives have found work that takes a moderate amount of time. In most countries, moderation and balance, rather than very long or very short workweeks, appear to promote gender equality as well as to best fit the ideals of most workers, although the balance point at present involves more working time in some countries (the Netherlands, the United Kingdom, the United States, and Germany) than in others (Finland and Sweden).

The Link Between Gender and Parenthood

How does parental status shape couples' working time? Are the effects of parenthood stronger in the United States than elsewhere? And does parenthood have different consequences for women and men? Across countries, parenting is far more likely to influence women's participation than men's (Gornick 1999). Yet it is likely that parenting has an even greater influence among women in the United States, where mothers are less likely to enjoy key institutional supports (such as paid family leave and publicly provided day care) that help parents, especially mothers, integrate work and family than they are in other countries. Scandinavian countries, by contrast, provide paid parental leave for both mothers and fathers, and French families enjoy universally available day care (Henneck 2003).

By comparing the working hours of dual-earner couples with and without children, Figure 4 shows the effect of parental status on working time across countries. When the countries are ranked by the length of the workweek, the United States leads all other countries, whether the measure is the length of the average workweek (for both working parents and childless dual-earner couples) or the percentage working very long workweeks. Among childless couples, weekly hours worked in Belgium and Italy approach those in the United States—exceeding 80 hours in both cases—but American parents report a substantially longer workweek than do their peers in all other countries.

The effect of parenting on couples' total working time varies markedly across the countries. In the United States, working parents put in 2.9 fewer hours per week than do their childless counterparts. In percentage terms, that difference (–3.5 percent) is similar to the Canadian (–3.3 percent) and Swedish (–3.7 percent) patterns. In five countries (Italy, Belgium, Germany, the United Kingdom, and the Netherlands), employed parents put in at least 5 percent fewer hours on the job than do their childless counterparts. In the two other countries, Finland and France, there is hardly any difference between parents and other couples.

We also found that the parenting effect is much larger for mothers than for fathers. (These results can be seen in more detail in Jacobs and Gornick 2002.) Mothers put in less time on the job than other married women in all ten countries. The magnitude

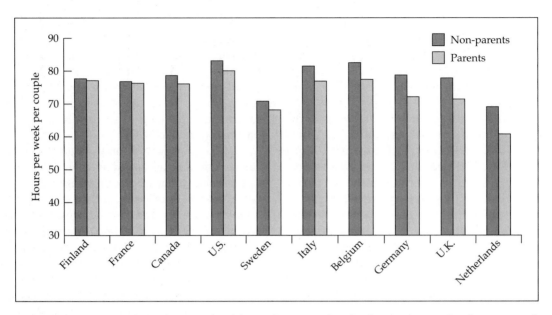

FIGURE 4   Average joint hours of paid employment for dual-earner couples, by parental status and country (*Source:* Luxembourg Income Study)

of the difference ranges from 3.0 percent or less in France and Finland, to 8.6 percent in the United States, to 20 percent or more in Germany, the United Kingdom, and the Netherlands. For husbands, the effects are much smaller and typically in the other direction. Thus, with the exception of Belgium, France, and Italy, fathers put in more hours on the job than other men, but the increase tends to be quite small. (The 1.8 percent increase in Germany is the largest.) Everywhere, the consequences of having children at home are greater for mothers than fathers.

A parenting effect thus exists cross-nationally and applies largely to mothers. Yet there is considerable variation across countries in the degree to which becoming a parent pulls women away from the workplace. The parenting effect among American wives is substantially larger than it is among their peers in Finland and France (where publicly provided day care is widely available), but smaller than in the United Kingdom and three continental European countries (Belgium,

Germany, and the Netherlands). These differences suggest, again, that national contexts—especially the structure of public policies and work institutions—can either facilitate or inhibit women's ability to combine parenting and paid work.

Policies and Institutional Forces Influencing American Working Time

When viewed in cross-national perspective, American dual-earner couples appear to put in the longest workweeks. American husbands have the second highest average number of hours per week (44.8 hours) and, even more distinctively, the greatest percentage working 50 hours or more (30.3 percent). American wives in dual-earner couples also work relatively long weeks (36.4 hours on average) and are most likely to work 50 or more hours per week (10.2 percent). And while American dual-earner couples without children have achieved relative equality in paid working time, the gender balance falls substantially among parents.

What accounts for these differences in working time and, especially, for the distinctive situation of American couples? Our research suggests that cross-national differences in work institutions and public policies may help explain the unusual patterns in the United States. . . .

The Regulation of Working Time

Although the United States is an exception, most industrialized countries regulate the standard as well as the maximum working time for a large proportion of the workforce. In most European countries, collective bargaining agreements establish standard working hours for the majority of workers. Jill Rubery, Mark Smith, and Colette Fagan argue that "national systems of regulation {collective and statutory} can be seen to have a major impact on usual working time" (1998, p. 75). And by setting legal limits on normal weekly hours, weekly overtime hours, and/or total weekly hours, government statutes regulate maximum hours as well. Indeed, of all of the countries we examine in this chapter, only the United States and the United Kingdom have no statutory maximum working time (ILO 1995; OECD 1998). While these direct controls over working time are likely to influence all workers, they are especially important for men, who are more likely to work the maximum possible and less likely to work part-time or pull back from employment to care for children. In most of the countries in our study, collective bargaining agreements covering most of the economy set the standard workweek at between 34 and 40 hours per week. In the United States, however, only 9.0 percent of private-sector workers are unionized (although 37.5 percent of U.S. public sector employees are unionized) (U.S. Bureau of Labor Statistics 2001). In the United States, the regulation of working time falls to the Fair Labor Standards Act, which in 1938 established the 40-hour workweek as the national standard. . . .

As we have seen, the average workweek for men in most European countries in recent years has ranged between 40 and 45 hours per week. European policies thus do more to reduce the prevalence of very long workweeks than they do to reduce the average. The adoption of a 35-hour policy, such as occurred in France, would significantly reduce the average workweek for men in all countries, with the possible exception of the Netherlands. European policies have also succeeded in promoting longer vacations. However, the effort to promote "flexibilization" is eroding the influence of working time regulations in Europe.

Part-Time Work

While government and union regulation of full-time work is likely to place limits on long workweeks, both institutional and labor-supply factors influence the extent of part-time work. A large body of literature shows that rates of part-time work vary markedly across industrialized countries and that part-time work remains predominantly women's work everywhere (OECD 1994, 1999; Rubery, Smith, and Fagan 1998; Gornick 1999).

In theory, the extent to which women prefer part-time work could be ascertained by analyzing rates of "voluntary" part-time work—that is, the percentage of part-time workers who report that they sought part-time hours. In reality, many women who do not "prefer" part-time work in any fundamental way in fact seek part-time work because of substantial constraints on the supply side—for example, a lack of affordable child care of acceptable quality. These part-time workers are counted as "voluntary," strongly suggesting that measured rates of "voluntary part-time work" actually reveal very little about women's preferences (Bardasi and Gornick 2002).

It may be difficult to distinguish the demand-side and supply-side factors that shape levels of part-time work (Hakim 1997; Fagan and O'Reilly 1998; Bardasi and Gornick 2003). We nevertheless agree with Tindara Addabbo's view that "demand-side constraints seem to be the overriding determinants of the level of part-time work" (1997, p. 129). The level of demand for part-time work is in turn shaped by institutional factors, such as the structure of social insurance rules, taxes, and subsidies that reward or penalize the creation of part-time jobs, and the preferences and power of unions.

Many employed wives, especially mothers with young children, seek part-time jobs as a way to balance work and family. In some countries—such as Italy and Finland and, to some extent, the United States—a substantial share of these women may be unable to find suitable part-time work and will work full-time hours instead. Their high rates of full-time employment contribute in turn to the relatively long workweeks of dual-earning couples. In contrast, their counterparts in the United Kingdom, Sweden, and especially the Netherlands face much greater demand for part-time workers and can more easily find part-time jobs; this contributes to shorter average weekly hours for wives and couples alike in those countries.

A prevalence of part-time work, however, constrains the ambitions of women who would prefer to work full-time but cannot find full-time jobs. In countries with a high proportion of part-time women workers, many women are effectively pushed into part-time work. Brendan Burchell, Angela Dale, and Heather Joshi note, for example, that in response to labor shortages in the 1960s, the United Kingdom enacted an official policy of developing part-time work and recruiting married women to fill the jobs. They conclude that the "ramifications of

this are still being experienced today" (1997, p. 211). Since the balance of part-time to full-time jobs is much higher in some countries than in others, wives in countries with limited full-time opportunities are likely to be confined to part-time jobs despite wishes to the contrary. In these cases, the working time of wives is likely to be constrained regardless of the needs or desires of women or their families.

Countries that limit women's chances of finding full-time work thus create an institutional context that dampens women's chances of achieving equality in earnings and career mobility as well as working time. In this instance, at least, American women fare better than many of their European peers.

Child-Care Support

While the preponderance of part-time (over full-time) jobs limits gender egalitarian arrangements, publicly provided child care and educational supports are likely to support mothers' employment and encourage more equality in how couples apportion their working time. Table 3 shows that this is the case. When countries are ranked according to the ratio of married mothers' to married fathers' working time and compared in terms of their child-care provisions for children below primary school age, the United States lags behind most European countries, both in total public slots and in the hours that care is available. Even more striking, all of the countries with more gender egalitarian allocations of working time among parents—Finland, France, Italy, and Sweden—have also made more extensive public investments in child care for young children.

American families face limited access to public care for children below [age] 3, with only 5 percent of infants and toddlers in publicly provided or publicly financed care. Public provisions for preschoolers (children aged 3–5) are more extensive, with

TABLE 3   Availability of Early Childhood Education and Care (ECEC), Mid-1990s

Country (Ratio of Mothers' to Fathers' Hours)		Share of Children Served in Publicly Financed Care		Typical Schedule of Primary form of Care for Children
		Ages 0,1,2	Ages 3, 4, 5	Ages 3, 4, 5
Finland	(.92)	21%	53%	Full day
France	(.81)	23%	99%	Full day
Italy	(.80)	6%	91%	Full day
Sweden	(.79)	33%	72%	Full day
United States	(.78)	5%	54%	Part day
Canada	(.76)	5%	53%	Part day
Belgium	(.73)	30%	95%	Full day
Germany	(.63)	2%	78%	Part day
United Kingdom	(.60)	5%	60%	Mixed
Netherlands	(.46)	8%	71%	Mixed

Source: Meyers and Gornick 2003.
Note: The ordering of the countries corresponds to one indicator of gender equality in working time: the ratio of mothers' to fathers' hours of paid employment.

54 percent of children in some form of public care (including 5-year-olds in kindergarten), but much of this care is available only part of the day. The relatively low levels of publicly provided child care in the United States clearly work against gender egalitarian divisions of working time. Since women continue to perform the lion's share of caregiving, the paucity of child-care supports drives a wedge between husbands' and wives' hours.

Lessons from Abroad

A cross-national perspective enriches our understanding of the situation of American workers and also provides some lessons about the possibilities for achieving greater work-family integration as well as more gender equality. In the search for a model country, however, these twin goals seem elusive; indeed, they also seem to be in conflict.

The Netherlands, for example, has gone furthest in lessening work-family conflict by reducing couples' combined working time,

but only at the price of gender equality in how working time is apportioned. Dutch women typically work part-time and put in shorter weeks than in any other country. In the end, the Dutch supports for family life promote the high degree of economic dependence of Dutch wives. Sweden has created a similar, if less extreme, compromise. Relatively short workweeks for Swedish men and plentiful part-time work for women have helped to reduce work-family conflict, but the gender disparity in working time, especially among working parents, remains substantial. In both cases, family supports have been purchased at the expense of equity, a pattern that in fundamental ways recreates gender inequality even as women enter the world of paid work.

In contrast, Finland has achieved the highest levels of equality in paid working time. Finnish married women work 93 percent as many hours as their husbands, and even working mothers put in 92 percent as many hours on the job as do their husbands. Yet the typical Finnish couple works nearly 80 hours per week. The price of gender equality thus appears to be substantial time pressures in dual-earner families.

Compared to other countries, the United States stands out in terms of both the many hours couples spend at work and the moderate levels of inequality in how they apportion working time. The American labor force has a high proportion of dual-earner couples; relatively long average workweeks, especially among women; and a high proportion of couples who work very long weeks. It ranks above average in paid working time among dual-earner couples with no children, but its relative position drops among working parents.

The prospects for gender equality in the United States appear mixed. Certainly, the very long workweeks that are faced by so many American couples create not only time pressures on families but also inequality in how domestic time is shared. It is not surprising that in the United States, as in most countries, the gender gap in working time peaks among those couples working 100 or more hours per week. More moderate work schedules, in contrast, are more likely to promote greater equality in the working time of husbands and wives while also helping to ease the conflicts between work and private life. And . . . having a moderate number of working hours per week appears to be the shared cultural ideal for most workers.

There is also reason to believe that the institutional conditions of work help account for the distinctive position of American workers and especially for the long workweeks and moderate levels of gender equality found in the United States. The reluctance of American employers and legislators to enact policies that regulate and control working time surely contributes to the many hours Americans put in at the workplace. The relatively high demand for full-time rather than part-time work also contributes to long workweeks, especially among employed women. And, finally, the relative paucity of child-care support for employed parents adds to the pressures and conflicts confronting American families.

Yet these same institutional forces have ambiguous implications for gender arrangements. Long workweeks among men and the lack of child care pose significant obstacles to achieving equality in how couples apportion their time between home and the workplace. Yet the low level of part-time work, especially among American women, enhances egalitarian work commitments—even if it also contributes to time squeezes.

The lessons from abroad appear to be that institutional arrangements and policies matter, but no single policy can suffice. Indeed, institutional constraints and opportunities may work at cross-purposes—especially if the goal is to achieve work-family balance *and* gender equity. Yet this comparative perspective also makes it clear that the squeezes American workers face are not inevitable or inherent in the nature of modern, and particularly professional, work. Like all advanced industrial economies, the United States faces policy choices. Our decisions shape the degree and nature of the dilemmas American workers face.

REFERENCES

Addabbo, Tindara. 1997. "Part-Time Work in Italy," pp. 113–132 in Hans-Peter Blossfeld and Catherine Hakim, eds., *Between Equalization and Marginalization: Women Working Part-Time in Europe and the United States of America.* Oxford: Oxford University Press.

Bardasi, Elena, and Janet C. Gornick. 2002. "Explaining Cross-National Variation in Part-Time/Full-Time Wage Differentials Among Women." Paper presented at conference, Comparative Political Economy of Inequality in OECD Countries, Cornell University, Ithaca, N.Y., April 5–7.

———. 2003. "Women's Part-Time Employment Across Countries: Workers' 'Choices' and Wage Penalties," pp. 209–243 in Brigida Garcia, Richard Anker, and Antonella Pinnelli, eds., *Women in the Labour Market in Changing*

Economies: Demographic Issues. Oxford: Oxford University Press.

Burchell, Brendan, Angela Dale, and Heather Joshi. 1997. "Part-Time Work Among British Women," pp. 210–246 in Hans-Peter Blossfeld and Catherine Hakim, eds., *Between Equalization and Marginalization: Women Working Part-Time in Europe and the United States of America.* Oxford: Oxford University Press.

De Tombeur, Caroline, ed. 1995. *LIS/LES Information Guide*, rev. ed. Luxembourg Income Study, Working Paper Number 7. Luxembourg: Centre d'Etudes de Populations, de Pauvrete et de Politiques Socio-Economiques (CEPS).

European Union Council Directive. 1997. *1997 Directive on Part-Time Work.* Council Directive 97/81/EC. December 15. Brussels.

Fagan, Colette, and Jacqueline O'Reilly. 1998. "Conceptualizing Part-Time Work," pp. 1–31 in Jacqueline O'Reilly and Colette Fagan, eds., *Part-Time Prospects: An International Comparison of Part-Time Work in Europe, North America and the Pacific Rim.* London: Routledge.

Freeman, Richard B., and Linda Bell. 1995. "Why Do American and Germans Work Different Hours?" pp. 101–131 in Friecdrich Buttler, Wolfgang Franz, Ronald Schettkat, and David Soskice, eds., *Institutional Frameworks and Labor Market Performance.* London: Routledge.

Gornick, Janet C. 1999. "Gender Equality in the Labor Market," pp. 210–242 in Diane Sainsbury, ed., *Gender Policy Regimes and Welfare States.* Oxford: Oxford University Press.

Gornick, Janet C., and Jerry A. Jacobs. 1996. "A Cross-National Analysis of the Wages of Part-Time Workers: Evidence from the United States, the United Kingdom, Canada, and Australia." *Work, Employment, and Society* 10 (1): 1–27.

Gornick, Janet C., and Marcia K. Meyers. 2000. "Building the Dual Earner/Dual Career Society: Policy Lessons from Abroad." Paper presented at the Family, Work, and Democracy Conference, Racine, Wisc., December 1.

———. 2003. *Earning and Caring: What Government Can Do to Reconcile Motherhood, Fatherhood, and Employment.* New York: Russell Sage Foundation Press.

Greenhouse, Steven. 2001. "Report Shows Americans Have More 'Labor Days.'" *New York Times,* September 1, p. A-8.

Hakim, Catherine. 1997. "Sociological Perspectives on Part-Time Work," pp. 22–70 in Hans-Peter Blossfeld and Catherine Hakim, eds., *Between Equalization and Marginalization: Women Working Part-Time in Europe and the United States of America.* Oxford: Oxford University Press.

Henneck, Rachel. 2003. "Family Policy in the U.S., Japan, Germany, Italy, and France: Parental Leave, Child Benefits/Family Allowances, Child Care, Marriage/Cohabitation, and Divorce." New York: Council on Contemporary Families Briefing Paper.

ILO (International Labour Office). 1995. *Conditions of Work Digest, Volume 14: Working Time Around the World.* Geneva: ILO.

Jacobs, Jerry A., and Janet C. Gornick. 2002. "Hours of Paid Work in Dual-Earner Couples: The U.S. in Cross-National Perspective." *Sociological Focus* 35 (2): 169–187.

Lehndorff, Steffen. 2000. "Working Time Reduction in the European Union: A Diversity of Trends and Approaches," pp. 38–56 in Lonnie Golden and Deborah M. Figart, eds., *Working Time: International Trends, Theory, and Policy Perspectives.* New York: Routledge.

Meyers, Marcia K., and Janet C. Gornick. 2003. "Public or Private Responsibility? Inequality and Early Childhood Education and Care in the Welfare State." *Journal of Comparative Family Studies* 34 (3): 379–411.

Mutari, Ellen, and Deborah M. Figart. 2000. "The Social Implications of European Work Time Policies: Promoting Gender Equity?" pp. 232–250 in Lonnie Golden and Deborah M. Figart, eds., *Working Time: International Trends, Theory, and Policy Perspectives.* London: Routledge.

OECD (Organization for Economic Cooperation and Development). 1994. *Women and Structural Change: New Perspectives.* Paris: OECD.

———. 1998. "Working Hours: Latest Trends and Policy Initiatives." Chapter 5 in *Employment Outlook.* Paris: OECD.

———. 1999, 2000. *Employment Outlook.* Paris: OECD.

Rubery, Jill, Mark Smith, and Colette Fagan. 1998. "National Working Time Regimes and Equal Opportunities." *Feminist Economics* 4 (1): 71–101.

U.S. Bureau of Labor Statistics. 2000. "Are Managers and Professionals Really Working More?" *Issues in Labor Statistics,* Summary, pp. 1–2 (May 12).

Beach Time, Bridge Time, and Billable Hours

The Temporal Structure of Technical Contracting

James A. Evans, Gideon Kunda, and Stephen R. Barley

Feeling overworked and pressed for time have become familiar complaints among members of the American middle class. Managers and professionals routinely commiserate about working long hours and what those hours cost them and their families. The booming market for advice on managing time effectively and the popularity of academic treatises with titles like *The Overworked American* (Schor, 1991) and *The Time Bind* (Hochschild, 1997) attest to the issue's resonance. In most accounts, temporally greedy organizations are to blame for the "time famine" (Perlow, 1999), and recommended solutions usually involve organizational policies that strike a compromise over how many and which hours employers can lay claim. Some commentators, however, have suggested that employees can gain temporal control by leaving organizational employment for a life in the labor market (Handy, 1989; Kanter, 1989, 1995; Bridges, 1994; Pink, 1998, 2001). The theme of liberation through markets is also found in the recent literature on boundaryless, project-based and portfolio careers, which unfold across rather than within organizations (Faulkner and Anderson, 1987; Mirvis

and Hall, 1994; Arthur and Rousseau, 1996; Jones, 1996; Weick, 1996; Gold and Fraser, 2002). Although scholars have noted a rise in market-oriented careers, they have yet to investigate whether such careers actually grant incumbents more control over their time.

The idea that organizations make unreasonable demands on people's time revolves around two issues: how many and which hours people work. The first issue, how many hours people work, is most fully explored in the literature on "overworked Americans." Interest in the topic burgeoned after Schor (1991) claimed that American men and women were working considerably more hours in the mid-1980s than they had in the 1960s and that growth in the number of weeks that people devote to work explained most of this increase. Although some researchers have disputed Schor's findings on methodological grounds (Robinson and Godbey, 1997), a general consensus has emerged: workers at the lower end of the income distribution often have difficulty finding enough work, while people with higher incomes, especially those in professional and managerial jobs, work more hours than ever before (Coleman and Pencavel, 1993a, 1993b; Bluestone and Rose, 1997, 1998; Jacobs and Gerson, 1998; Reynolds, 2003).

Scholars have offered several explanations for why professionals and managers work so many hours. These explanations range from norms about work (Kunda, 1992; Blair-Loy and Wharton, 2002) and rampant consumerism (Schor, 1991) to the notion that work offers an escape from stressful homes (Hochschild, 1997). Most frequently, however, scholars indict managers and organizations. Schor (1991) and others (Maume and Bellas, 2001) have argued that instead of hiring new employees, organizations prefer to extract longer hours from salaried workers because doing so reduces labor costs. Bluestone and Rose (1997) and Hecksher (1995) claimed that rampant downsizing and increasing job insecurity have led white-collar employees to work longer hours in the hope of avoiding layoffs. Long hours signal the kind of commitment and visibility that employees believe firms demand in return for raises, promotions, and continued employment (Bailyn, 1993; Perlow, 1997).

The second issue, which hours people work, is addressed in the literature on work-family balance under the banner of flexibility. Flexibility can mean many things. Although Kickert (1984) discussed flexibility in the context of strategic planning, he captured flexibility's allure, calling it "the magic word." In the context of dual-career issues, the term usually suggests ceding control to workers over the circumstances of their work by enabling them to vary those circumstances to address personal and family needs and uncertainties (Golden, 2001). The circumstance most often implied in flexibility programs is time. In this paper, flexibility always means temporal flexibility, the ability to determine which and how many hours one works.

Flexibility first became an issue in the mid-1970s when enough middle-class women had entered the managerial and professional workforce to generate concern over dual-career families (e.g., Bailyn, 1970; Rapoport and Rapoport, 1978). In such families, men and women discovered that it was difficult to rear children when both spouses worked more than forty hours a week and when neither could accommodate their work schedules to family needs. As a result, both family and work suffer. When work spills over into the home, workers are more

likely to experience marital conflict, withdraw from their families, and neglect domestic responsibilities (Bolger, Delongis, and Kessler, 1989; Barnett, 1994; Paden and Buehler, 1995; Repetti and Wood, 1997; Bumpus, Crouter, and McHale, 1999). When home spills into the workplace, job satisfaction falls while absenteeism and turnover increase (Goff, Mount, and Jamison, 1990; Higgins, Duxbury, and Irving, 1992; Forthofer et al., 1996). Commentators have argued that in the face of such difficulties, men and women need leeway to adjust their schedules to meet simultaneously the needs of their employers and the needs of their families (Bailyn, 1993; Tausig and Fenwick, 2001).

While American employers have generally resisted calls to limit the number of hours that employees work, since the 1970s they have gradually adopted a variety of programs designed to provide employees with more control over which hours they work. Between two-thirds and four-fifths of all employers report offering flextime programs that allow employees to vary the start and end of their workday and to leave work for family obligations (Osterman, 1995; Daniels, 1997; McShulskis, 1997; Galinsky and Bond, 1998; Greenwald, 1998; Saltzstein, Ting, and Saltzstein, 2001). Yet despite the popularity of flextime, accumulating evidence suggests that no more than a quarter of all eligible employees take advantage of the offering (Galinsky, Bond, and Friedman, 1993; Bond, Galinsky, and Swanberg, 1998; Eaton, 2000; Mead et al., 2000; Golden, 2001; Blair-Loy and Wharton, 2002). Employees are even less likely to use other programs that support greater temporal flexibility, such as the option to work from home or take maternity or paternity leave (Bond, Galinsky, and Swanberg, 1998; O'Mahony and Barley, 1999; Mead et al., 2000).

The discrepancy between employees' professed desire for greater flexibility and their relatively low rates of using flextime has puzzled researchers and policy makers.

Some analysts maintain that the gap simply indicates that people are unable to afford time off from work because of debt, low salaries, and norms of consumption (Schor, 1991). Most researchers, however, explain low utilization in terms of organizational pressures similar to those that account for why employees work long hours. Respondents and informants usually say that managers and peers interpret the use of flexibility programs as evidence of a lack of commitment, motivation, and productivity and that supervisors and mid-level managers routinely deny requests for more flexible work schedules (Bailyn, 1993; Perlow, 1997; Clarkberg and Moen, 2001; Meiksins and Whalley, 2002; Blair-Loy and Wharton, 2002; McBride, 2003). Moreover, in many firms, flexibility programs are stigmatized as women's programs (Schwartz, 1989; Mead et al., 2000; Meiksins and Whalley, 2002), and managers themselves admit that they hesitate to grant employees flexibility because they anticipate shirking (Olson, 1987; Perin, 1991; Kurland and Egan, 1999). In short, commentators argue that firms subject employees to informal pressures and tacit threats of sanction that discourage them from using the flexibility programs formally offered.

Etzioni (1961) and Schein (1972) have argued that organizations bring three types of control to bear on employees to ensure that they fulfill managerial expectations: coercive, remunerative, and normative control. Coercive control rests on the organization's ability to extract compliance by threat, especially the threat of termination or withholding promotions. Remunerative control rests on management's ability to elicit compliance by setting the terms for dispensing salaries, raises, and bonuses. Normative control, the most diffuse of the three, elicits compliance through sustained social and interpersonal pressures to internalize and conform to managerially defined norms and values.

Whereas traditional bureaucracies relied primarily on coercive and remunerative control encoded in rules and procedures (Edwards, 1979), contemporary organizational theorists generally concur that normative control dominates traditional controls in postindustrial organizations, especially high-technology and professional firms (Kunda, 1992; Barker, 1993; Perlow, 1997).

Policies of flexibility explicitly loosen coercive and remunerative control over the employee's time: the firm promises, within reasonable limits, to neither terminate the employee nor withhold recompense and promotions for adopting a more flexible schedule. But these policies do not necessarily remove normative pressures. Managers and coworkers may continue to insist that employees work to expectations that undermine customized schedules. Most explanations for why employees fail to take advantage of flexibility programs, therefore, highlight normative pressures that make it difficult for employees to control their time. Perlow (1999) demonstrated that engineers on development teams feel considerable pressure from management to remain visible by working long and inflexible hours. Similarly, Barker (1993) showed how members of self-managed teams pressure fellow members to disregard family obligations and to work longer hours to finish a job. The unstated proposition in such studies is that more people would avail themselves of flexibility programs, and perhaps even limit the time they spend working, if they could free themselves from the normative control endemic to permanent employment.

Theorists have suggested that one way to escape organizational control is to move into the market. In markets, selling skills to multiple clients, rather than a long-term affiliation with one employer, guarantees a living (Handy, 1989; Kanter, 1989, 1995; Arthur, 1994). Career theorists interested in the notion of boundaryless careers have explored this theme in the academic literature (Arthur, 1994; Mirvis and Hall, 1994; Arthur and Rousseau, 1996). These theorists have accepted the idea that firms can no longer guarantee employment as they once did and that internal labor markets are disintegrating. Drawing inspiration from Hollywood (Jones, 1996), software development (Kanter, 1995), and other project-oriented industries, they have argued that workers in the new economy can attain greater security as well as greater autonomy by configuring their careers around skills that allow them to move freely between organizations.

A popular literature on employability and free agency has advocated an even more extreme movement into the market (Beck, 1992; Bridges, 1994; Caulkin, 1997; Darby, 1997; Pink, 2001). The doctrine of employability exalts consultants, contractors, freelancers, and other free agents who have jettisoned permanent employment in favor of temporary engagements mediated by the market. Like the scholars of boundaryless careers, advocates of free agency claim that markets liberate workers from the shackles of organizational control. Both literatures hold that markets grant considerable flexibility, including the ability for workers to control their time. Writing about boundaryless careers in the software industry where people can easily change employers, Kanter (1995: 56) noted,

> Often no more than buzzwords, flexibility and empowerment take on meaning in software companies where people feel they have real control. . . . Managers can authorize any schedule . . . for people whose knowledge is valuable—for example, having a new mother work two days a week. . . . Employees can design their own three-day, four-day or five-day altered-schedule work weeks.

To support the promise of temporal freedom, advocates of free agency routinely offer readers stories of freelancers who work when they want to work and vacation when they please. "Free agents have less time anxiety than the typical worker," wrote Pink (2001: 109–115). "Independent workers may log about forty hours every week, but how they configure those forty hours is highly fluid. Unlike employees, free agents mostly control the faucet. . . . The free agent way is as much vacation as you can afford and as much work as you need." As these passages illustrate, advocates of boundaryless careers and free agency assert that markets give people control over both how many and which hours they work. They also suggest that temporal flexibility applies to multiple units of time: free agents can choose how to deploy hours within a day, days within a week, or months within a year.

The underlying assumption, in both the academic and popular literatures, is that markets offer individuals greater control over their time because they reduce the relationship between employers and workers to a simple economic exchange between buyers and sellers of skill and time. . . . But market relationships are neither as simple nor as context free as the advocates of boundaryless careers and free agency suggest with their images of frictionless supply and demand for labor (Hirsch and Shanley, 1996).

. . . The rhetoric of markets and free agency inflates the worker's individual freedom and may therefore overestimate the temporal control that workers can achieve by leaving organizations for the market. To explore how workers experience time when they leave permanent employment and how much control they actually achieve over how many and which hours they work, we need to study a population of workers oriented primarily to markets rather than organizations. Technical contractors are one such population.

Technical contractors are the epitome of free agents. They include engineers, software developers, technical writers, and information technology (IT) specialists who sell their services to firms on a project-by-project basis for an hourly wage or a set fee. Their contracts typically last from three to eighteen months. When a contract expires, they move on to another client organization. Although researchers have paid little attention to technical contracting, several recent studies suggest that contractors seek and may even enjoy temporal flexibility. Meiksins and Whalley (2002) reported that technical professionals often turn to contracting because they want more control over their time. Matusik and Fuller (2002) showed that when contractors' skills are in sufficiently high demand, they experience more control over their time. Technical contracting, therefore, appears to offer an ideal context for determining whether and how workers experience flexibility in the absence of organizational control. An even stronger test would be to examine technical contracting during a tight labor market when contractors' bargaining power is enhanced. It was during just such a period that we set out to study the experience of highly skilled technical contractors.

Methods

In the fall of 1997 we embarked on a two-and-a-half year study of how the labor market for technical contractors operates and how participants in that market experience and structure their work and lives. We began with a year of ethnographic observation in three staffing agencies that brokered technical contractors. From this vantage point, we could not only study the agents who brokered the market for contractors, we could also encounter contractors who were seeking jobs and the managers who hired them. Over the course of the year, we developed a substantive understanding of how the market for technical contractors operates, as

well as an initial appreciation for the issues that contractors and their clients face.

Legal institutions and court rulings have shaped the market for technical contractors. In the U.S., employment and tax law are tied to permanent employment. During the 1980s, many firms, including Microsoft, tried to skirt employment taxes and avoid paying benefits by replacing employees with contractors. The Internal Revenue Service (IRS) successfully challenged the practice by taking Microsoft to court. Microsoft subsequently rehired many contractors as permanent employees and let others go. Those who were dismissed sued Microsoft for back benefits and stock options in *Vizcaino v. Microsoft* (97F.3d.1887, 9th Circuit Court, 1996). In 1996, after years of litigation, the court determined that Microsoft had failed to distinguish adequately between contractors and employees and required the firm to pay millions of dollars retroactively for the benefits that contractors would have received had they been employees. The ruling forced other employers to become more cautious about how they played this game. Firms began to differentiate contractors from employees by requiring them to wear special badges, assigning them to less desirable workspaces, and avoiding the appearance of directing contractors' work. To achieve the [last], employers shifted from hiring independent contractors to hiring contractors through staffing agencies. As employers-of-record, staffing agencies shielded companies from legal responsibility for contractors by withholding the contractors' state and federal taxes and thereby appearing, at least on paper, to direct the contractors' work.

Thus, by the time we began collecting data, there were two markets for technical contractors: one for independents who negotiated directly with clients and another for contractors brokered by staffing agencies (commonly called W2s, after the IRS tax form that makes a person an employee in the eyes of the law). Independents and W2s both billed by the hour, but the W2s' bill rate included the agency's markup, which averaged about 30 percent of the total charge.

Although clients rarely hesitated to renew their independent contractors' contracts, they often restricted the duration of a W2's engagement to eighteen months to avoid the appearance of being their employer. Regardless of employment status, however, all contractors' careers were cyclical: all contracts were sooner or later followed by a return to the labor market in search of the next contract. This structure sensitized contractors to both a coarse- and fine-grained flow of time. The coarse grain was defined by the contract cycle and the contractor's choice of how to sequence and space contracts, while the fine grain was measured by the hours of a day and week that contractors worked while on contract.

It was the coarse-grain structure that most clearly set contracting's dynamics apart from permanent employment. Entering the labor market repeatedly to secure new assignments defined the essence of contracting. Both contractors and agents parsed the contractors' time into periods of employment and unemployment, but neither used these terms. Instead, they talked about "being on contract" or "having downtime." "Being on contract" referred to periods when one or more clients compensated a contractor for work. Downtime—also called "beach time," "bench time," or "dead time"—referred to periods between contracts. What distinguished downtime from the notion of unemployment was that downtime was considered normal and inherent to contracting. As the connotative distinction between beach and bench time suggests, downtime could be viewed as a luxury, a time for pleasure and relaxation, for going to the beach. At other times, downtime

was equivalent to sitting on the bench out of play, waiting to return to the game. Coarse-grained flexibility entailed decisions about when and how much downtime to allow and, hence, whether downtime would be spent on the beach or the bench.

Agents and contractors also had a vocabulary for talking about the types of hours that defined the fine-grained flow of a contractor's time. Like lawyers and accountants they spoke of "billable hours," hours of work for which they could charge clients. Hours worked but not billed were known as "unbillable" hours. Unbillable hours were of two types: hours that contractors could have billed but didn't and hours that were necessary for completing the work, but for which they could not ethically or practically bill. Fine-grained flexibility entailed decisions about how many billable and unbillable hours a contractor would accrue in the course of a day or week and when they would work billable hours.

As we learned more about the market for technical contractors, we decided to explore the contractors' experience in depth. Conversations with contractors who were seeking jobs through the agencies we studied suggested that their career histories, their work and business practices, their perceptions of the social world of contracting, and how contracting meshed with their personal and family life were crucial areas for study. To elicit this information, we developed an interview guide . . . consisting of open-ended questions designed to structure our conversations with contractors.

Because there was no representative enumeration of individuals who work as technical contractors, all options for selecting informants posed limitations. We could have convinced a staffing firm to make available the names of the people in its databases, sampled from one of several résumé databanks on the Internet, or sought subscription records from magazines targeted

TABLE 1   Descriptive Statistics for Informants*

Characteristic	Mean	N	S. D.	Min.	Max.
Demographic					
Mean age[†]	43 yrs.		10	25	68
Mean years of post-high-school education[†]	4.2 yrs.		1.4	0	8
Pay rate (in $/hour)[‡]	$68		27	20	125
Male	75%	(49)			
Married[§]	63%	(34)			
With children[¶]	50%	(26)			
Caucasian	75%	(49)			
U.S. citizens	83%	(54)			
California residents	69%	(45)			
Silicon Valley residents	55%	(36)			
Career					
Mean years contracted[†]	6.8 yrs.		4.9	0.5	21
Mean years worked[†]	17.9 Yrs.		8.5	3	44
Mean years contracted / mean years worked[†]	.41 Yrs.		.26	0	1
Independent contractors or corps.	33%	(21)			
On first contract[#]	7%	(5)			
Always contracted[#]	11%	(7)			
Left permanent employment behind[#]	54%	(35)			
Moved back and forth to contracting[#]	25%	(16)			
Technical specialties					
Software developers	29%	(19)			
Hardware designers	8%	(5)			
Database programmers and administrators	18%				
Systems administrators	12%	(8)			
Project managers	5%	(3)			
Technical writers	11%	(7)			
Quality assurance technicians	11%	(7)			
Multimedia (Web)	3%	(2)			
Others	3%	(2)			

*N = 65 individuals. Numbers are drawn from semistructured interview data, and so all of the information is not available on all cases. Numbers in parentheses are the actual number of cases for dummy-variable tabulation.
[†]Only includes data on 64 cases.
[‡]Only includes data on 41 cases.
[§]Only includes data on 54 cases.
[¶]Only includes data on 52 cases.
[#]Only includes data on 63 cases.

at contractors. All of these would have yielded samples biased in different ways. We chose to use a modified snowball sample (Faugier and Sargeant, 1997) . . .

Table 1 reports the distribution of informants across age, marital status, citizen-ship, residency, experience as a contractor, career structure, and occupation. Our informants ranged from 25 to 68 years of age, although most were over forty. Most had a college education, and 25 percent were women.

The majority were U.S. citizens, but only 55 percent resided in the Silicon Valley. Informants represented a variety of occupations and skill levels, from software and hardware engineers to technical writers and quality assurance technicians. The demographic and occupational patterns in table 1 are nearly identical to those reported in Black and Andreini's (1997) survey of IT contractors in the Silicon Valley. . . .

The Contractor's Temporal Experience

Organizational Independence

Before turning to the question of how much control markets give contractors over their time, we must first establish that contractors actually perceive themselves to be free from the normative and coercive shackles of organizational life. Otherwise, we cannot reasonably claim that movement into the market largely restricts clients to using remunerative control. In our interviews, we systematically asked informants why they became contractors. Although their reasons ranged from making more money to escaping boredom, 54 percent told us that they had gradually become frustrated with organizational politics, incompetent management, and inequities in the employment relationship (Kunda, Barley, and Evans, 2002). Our informants eventually turned to contracting to escape organizational control and gain professional autonomy. As one programmer put it:

> [As an employee] I couldn't push back if somebody asked me to do something that was—from an engineering point of view—just clearly stupid. . . . As a contractor I can say, "This is dumb. I'm not going to do it." "This is dumb, I'm not going to do it" is not something you can say as an employee. They basically get to tell you what you do and don't do.

They hold the whip hand over you. Being able to walk away, being independent, having autonomy adds authenticity to your judgment in their eyes.

A majority of informants (70 percent) explicitly told us that they enjoyed considerably more autonomy than they had experienced as permanent employees. In fact, some (35 percent) felt that their freedom from the organization was so great that they sometimes felt like outsiders in the firms where they worked. For many contractors, freedom from organizational control translated directly into the perception of temporal autonomy. They recognized, often in retrospect, just how much of their time employers had extracted for reasons unrelated to the actual requirements of work. A verification engineer recounted:

> When I was a permanent employee I worked a lot of long hours. It was for politics. It wasn't for getting the project done. It was like I was doing this for somebody else's ego, or somebody else's personal or career goals. They could check off, they got this or that done based on my work. . . . There seemed to be this rush to impress people. You were there on the weekends or you came in on a holiday. Like when I worked at Motorola last time, people actually went in on 4th of July—the actual 4th of July!—where they could sign in, and people saw they signed in. I don't see that happening as a contractor.

While gaining control over time was not the primary reason our informants became contractors, over a third (38 percent) told us that being able to control their time was a significant unanticipated benefit. The benefit covered both how many and which hours they worked. Moreover, our informants felt that they had control over both the coarse-and fine-gained flow of their lives. Contractors claimed that the cyclic structure of contracting gave them more options than they had as permanent employees. For instance, a quality control technician explained how contractors could construct a lifestyle unknown to most workers by deciding about how many and which weeks they would work:

> I think contracting gives me the sense of freedom. I feel like if I need to take a lot of time off for something, I can just do it. Finish up what I am doing and just take a lot of time off and not feel obligated to anything. Whereas I think if I worked full time for a company, I would feel like I only have two to three weeks vacation. You know, plan it carefully instead of just like deciding I am going to Mexico and just going and having fun and stuff. I don't like that obligation I guess. I have a lot of obligations being a contractor because I have a lot of responsibility. But at the same time, I know that if I need to leave, I can leave.

Contractors also told us that they were free to set limits on how many and which hours of a day or week they worked. One software engineer testified to his freedom to choose the number of hours he worked:

> As a consultant . . . I'm completely autonomous. I can say, "I really can't do that. I have to leave." As an employee I might find an employer who would be so far thinking as to say, "This employee is going to work 30 hours a week and he's going to get a full salary, maybe even a big salary." Let's say they do that. And then let's say the project is push coming to shove. What are they going to do? "Well, I'm sorry. We really do need you to come in." So they own your ass, and I'm not into that.

A database programmer used the occasion of the interview to make the point that he could decide what he would do with each hour of his day: "I can blow off the afternoon and sit down and talk to you. If I had a real job, I'd have to get an okay from the boss . . . and he's gotta worry about, 'Do we do this against your vacation time' or whatever. Heck, we just do it! The good news is I've got a lot more flexibility in my hours." One of the most accomplished software developers we interviewed made a similar point with respect to her family:

> I can spend time with the kids. I know that we need to get this done, so I'll take the morning and do it. If my husband needs to be someplace, I don't have to be at work at any particular time and I don't have to stay at work for any particular length of time, since the object is getting the job done, not how many hours you're there. So it allows me a lot of flexibility in terms of scheduling. My husband says I'm a much calmer person; because I really don't care that much anymore.

Although, most of our informants perceived themselves to be politically and temporally independent of organizations' control and, hence, able to decide how many and which hours they would devote to work, as researchers have shown (Tausig and Fenwick, 2001; Gareis and Barnett, 2002), there is an important distinction between perceiving that one has temporal flexibility and making use of it. Employees who believe they have temporal flexibility nevertheless work as if they did not. The difference hinges, in part, on organizational pressures but also on how employees make sense of time in the larger context of their lives and careers. To determine whether contractors deploy their flexibility as market advocates predict, we examined how they interpreted the meaning of time as well as the choices they made about its use.

[handwritten margin note: How would/does this differ now?]

The Coarse Grain: Contract Cycles and Vacations

The coarse-grained structure of contractors' time is bound to repeated cycles of contracts and downtime. The essence of coarse-grained choice is how contractors use the time between contracts. The choices that our informants made rested on differences in how they experienced and interpreted that time.

Every informant we interviewed spoke of downtime as an inherent risk of contracting. A few told us that they found the possibility of downtime stressful, if not downright frightening. These tended to be individuals who were new to contracting, who worried about the effect of economic insecurity on their family, or whose spouses were uncomfortable with contracting's risks. One was a young Indian programmer who had recently come to the U.S. to be with her husband. When asked where she "saw herself in a couple of years," she replied, "Two years down the road is too far. I am still thinking, 'Do I have a contract next month?' . . . I stress a lot over whether I will have a job after this. I mean, it is OK to say that the market is good and there is no need to worry. But you do." Another was a technical writer who had experienced several months of downtime that coincided with his wife being laid off from her job. Earlier in his career he had been laid off from a permanent job and was out of work for several months. At the time we interviewed him, he was considering returning to full-time employment because he feared what might happen to his family if he had difficulty maintaining steady work. As he put it, "Say something turns bad and my contract at Cisco is terminated, so what happens? I have my $860 a month mortgage, my $300 a month car payment, my $300 a month food bill, I don't know what else, you know, utilities, electric, gas, water." Ultimately, he did return to full-time employment.

[handwritten margin note: Uncertainty a source of stress for some]

Most contractors, however, took downtime for granted. Although they never scoffed at its possibility, they minimized its threat and spoke as if it were a normal event. These contractors gradually came to accept downtime because experience had taught them that it was rare and that if it occurred, they could generally weather the storm. A programmer who had worked for ten years as a contractor was typical of those whose experience allowed them to come to terms with the possibility of downtime:

[handwritten margin note: most t.c.s not concerned about downtime]

> I used to get really nervous. The six months hiatus [that he once experienced] was really hard on my psyche. I would go into any contract or any job—I had some permanent jobs after that—with fear and trembling. Anytime the boss would say "Hi," I was afraid I was about to get fired. I still have a tiny bit of that. Since then I have never had more than a two-week gap. I have learned that I can make it. If something happens and there is a larger gap, I know that I will make it work out somehow and, second of all, it generally won't be that long.

Perhaps because of the tight labor market, some contractors with substantial experience even treated the possibility of downtime cavalierly, characterizing the process of finding a new job as trivial. "Around here," said one technical writer about life in the Silicon Valley, "If you have seven years experience, you can work literally all the time. You can literally finish a contract at noon and start the next one an hour later. Eat lunch and then go to your next one."

Most of the contractors we interviewed expected that periods of unwanted downtime would last no more than a few weeks, and their experience generally supported that stance. . . .

If one assumes that unwanted downtime was not salient enough for these informants to have mentioned it explicitly, then one is left with the conclusion that at least among the contractors we interviewed, unwanted downtime was rare and of relatively short duration. When facing downtime, contractors took one of three general approaches: they scheduled it, embraced it as an unanticipated gift, or minimized it.

Scheduling downtime. One approach to controlling downtime was to plan it and use it for one's own purposes. A handful of contractors scheduled downtime when they wanted to devote a continuous block of time to learning a new technology or skill. They might use this time for taking formal courses or for studying on their own. Others planned downtime to pursue an avocation. For instance, we interviewed one contractor who sailed with his wife and son on their yacht six months of every year. Another contracted for six to eight months and then turned his attention to photography and scuba diving, which took him to Malaysia and other exotic locations. He had published several books of underwater photography.

Embracing downtime. A second group of informants embraced unanticipated downtime as a spontaneous opportunity for a much-needed break. "It is not uncommon," explained a multimedia designer, "to have a couple of weeks off. But that's OK! Part of the reason I like contract work is that you work on something and when you get done, you get to take a break for a while if you made enough money. It is almost like you can go off on an adventure of some sort." An Oracle database administrator saw downtime in much the same way:

I knew when a contract was coming to an end or, more often, I saw that my contribution was trailing off. So I would tell the client, "I am costing you money and I am really not doing you any good, so why don't we do some documentation and I will hand whatever I am responsible

for over to someone else who will be here for a little longer." And then I look at that as a vacation. And that is another reason, why the money issue isn't just to buy cool toys. It is so I don't have to work 12 months out of the year.

Minimizing downtime. Most informants, however, sought to minimize downtime. They reported that they began searching for a new job as soon as the current contract began to wind down. Usually contractors could anticipate the end of a job by the terms of the contract itself or by the amount of work that was left to do. Experienced contractors pointed to more subtle social cues that allowed them to anticipate even unscheduled terminations. As one systems administrator told us:

And then one day, there's nothing for you to do. You can feel it coming. At one point the manager is around all the time and is really excited. Then the manager just kind of ignores you. Then you know that you have a couple of weeks left. That's when you know they will fire you. Things start slowing down first, although I usually end before they end.

Most informants argued that if they began searching for a new job two to three weeks before the end of their contract, they could almost always secure another in time to avoid downtime. To increase the odds of finding work in such a short period of time, informants employed a number of tactics. One was to work more or less exclusively with a staffing firm that was committed to keeping its contractors employed. A completely different tactic was to play one agency off against another, especially if one's current agency refused to line up a new job until it was clear that the client would not renew. A systems administrator remarked:

What I've encountered is that when I'm nearing the end of a job, the headhunters want me to stay 'til the end of the job. Of course, what that means is that I'll be sitting for a couple of weeks without a paycheck. So I have been forced in most cases to switch to a different headhunter at the end of one particular job so that I can get another lined up before I'm just sitting around for a couple of weeks.

Other contractors employed their personal and professional networks to generate opportunities. Still others made use of the Internet, knowing that staffing firms routinely trolled on-line job listings in search of possible candidates for openings they were trying to fill. As one quality assurance technician told us, this tactic worked particularly well when contractors had skills that were in very high demand, such as the ability to write COBOL during the Y2K scare:

> So anyway, I ended up leaving Toyota. The first thing I did was put my name out on the Internet. Let's see, they sent me home at 12. was on the Internet by 1:30 and I had my first offer by 4 o'clock. It's not hard. Put your name out there. Let 'em know that you can do COBOL and you'll have 500 offers by tomorrow morning.

A final tactic, employed by some contractors, was to work several contracts simultaneously. In fact, one contractor reported having six contracts in play at once. Typically, contractors who held multiple concurrent contracts were software developers and technical writers who worked a significant number of hours from home. These individuals tried to stagger their contracts' end times so that they were never without compensation.

Although none of the informants explicitly gave a name to the period of time at the end of one contract when they began to search for the next, a potentially useful name for this period might be bridge time. With this concept, one can explicitly outline how

contractors who sought to minimize downtime understood the temporal structure of contract work. They saw downtime as a problem instead of an opportunity. Their objective was to incur no downtime involuntarily. They used bridge time to unite two periods of contract time, so that they could, in essence, skip over downtime and ensure continued employment.

The strategies of scheduling, embracing, and minimizing downtime represented different interpretations of the contract cycle. Most informants used one strategy or another. Those who sought to schedule or embrace downtime saw contracting as an opportunity to live a different lifestyle. For schedulers, downtime was a resource to save or spend as they saw fit. For embracers it was a windfall. Those who preferred to minimize downtime, despite how cavalierly they might otherwise talk, implicitly saw the contract cycle as a threat. Their notion of control entailed regaining the security of continual employment by lining up the next contract before the current contract ended so that they could move from one job to the next without incurring time on the bench.

Among our informants, schedulers and embracers were far less common than minimizers. A total of 17 contractors (25 percent) said that they routinely scheduled or embraced downtime for breaks, vacations, or hobbies, even though the vast majority of our informants claimed that the freedom to do so was one of contracting's primary benefits. Yet almost as many informants (13, or 20 percent) said that they had not taken a vacation for a number of years, while another 23 (35 percent) took no more than one or two weeks a year. One technical writer described his summer vacation as a single day between contracts spent going on amusement park rides, interrupted with cell phone calls to his recruiter. A software engineer, when asked what she did outside work, responded, "I've been married for

18 years, and I must say our honeymoon was the last time we took a vacation." A firmware engineer admitted, without regret, "I'm not a real big vacation person. It's not like the family goes for a week someplace twice a year. We don't do that."

In short, even though most contractors felt that contracting offered them more control over their time than did permanent employment, relatively few used this freedom to harness the contract cycle to pursue an alternative lifestyle. Natural breaks between contracts made it possible for contractors to take more time off, but a desire to control the contract cycle led most to avoid doing so. For them, not only were there no paid vacations, but vacations bore a suspicious resemblance to unwanted downtime and what they saw as its consequences: increased expenses, decreased income, and an uncomfortable sense of insecurity and failure.

The Fine Grain

The daily and weekly organization of hours exerted an even more immediate pressure on contractors' temporal choices. Almost every contractor we encountered sold his or her services by the hour. After accounting for the cost of benefits, a contractor's hourly wage was usually 1.5 to 3 times higher than his or her permanent counterparts. Contracts might specify the number of hours per week that contractors would devote to the contract, but they rarely precluded working additional hours or dictated when hours would be spent. Contractors therefore had considerable leeway in choosing how many and which hours to work. A woman who specialized in technical marketing spoke for many of our informants:

> Usually the hours are flexible, so there's a feeling of control. Even though you're working at midnight, you're the one who decided you wanted to work at midnight. I mean I know some companies

are flexible anyway, but when they know you're consulting they're usually more open about you being flexible because they just want the job done. They don't care that you're not there 8:00 to 5:00, they just want results.

Some contractors, like this marketing specialist, used their flexibility to work non-traditional hours. Others exercised flexibility on a weekly basis. These informants valued the freedom to take a day off, and some aspired to work four-day weeks.

Yet, because contractors bore much of the responsibility for deciding when to work and how much to work, they became acutely conscious of how they spent their time. Every hour was a form of capital, which the contractor could invest in a variety of ways. Contractors could invest hours in doing directly compensated work for a client. They could invest hours in unbillable activities that ensured long-term employability: managing their business, developing new skills, or maintaining their networks. Contractors could also invest hours in their families, hobbies, or leisure. The need to make these tradeoffs, often on a daily basis, led contractors to develop an accountant's appreciation for the microeconomics of time. Some contractors set annual targets for the number of billable hours they wanted to work. The baseline was usually a 40-hour week, the standard for a permanent job. A technical writer made the calculations for us:

> Normally, most people work about 2,000 hours a year. Forty-hour weeks, fifty weeks a year. But last year I did about 2,300 hours. We all keep log books of our hours, so it's pretty easy for us to know how many hours we bill. Like lawyers or CPAs, we all know, "Oh, you did 2,400 hours last year," and stuff like that. So then you take 60 times 2,300, you come up with an idea of how much someone makes.

Most informants also worked a sizable number of unbillable hours. Sometimes jobs simply required more time than the terms of the contract allowed. Contractors worked these additional hours because they agreed to provide a deliverable by a certain date, because they could not always estimate the amount of time the work required, or because they felt they needed to adhere to their own standard of excellence. One software developer explained his rationale:

> I end up working more than I charge. Maybe 10 percent more. I usually bill for eight hours a day, but there is so much more you do: you try things, you think. If it doesn't work, you try new things. I guess it averages out to 50 hours a week. Sometimes you need to take an extra week, and often you need to work weekends. . . . You have to meet milestones, show progress. If you haven't, you can't bill.

Contractors also logged unbillable hours because they wanted to make a good impression on the client. By working more hours than they billed or by attending meetings and engaging in other unpaid activities, contractors hoped to signal a level of dedication that would preclude them from being terminated early and ensure a positive recommendation from the client. A project manager explained the tactic:

> I want to make sure that when they are laying off contractors, I am the last one they look at on the list. So I do a lot of things. Like when I came on board for the first two weeks, I probably worked 70 hours a week and billed them for 40. . . . I had been there a week when they noticed that I was there at 6:00 in the morning until 6:00 at night.

In addition to unbillable hours worked for clients, contractors invested considerable time in support activities such as learning new skills, maintaining their professional network, and managing the business aspects of contracting. Contractors realized that they were marketable only to the degree that their skills were in demand. In our informants' occupations, technology changed quickly. New programming languages, new applications, and new hardware were continually making older approaches and technologies obsolete. The majority of informants spoke of the necessity of allocating time to remaining up to date. Contractors employed a wide range of strategies for acquiring new knowledge: they read technically oriented journals and books, they took classes from community colleges and universities, they sought industry certifications, they made use of the Internet, they bought software packages and taught themselves the packages at home, they attended users' groups, and availed themselves of the expertise of other technical specialists in their personal networks. As a mechanical engineer explained, each of these activities absorbed time.

> I need to know what's going around, what's in demand, what's developing, how the software is changing, how the hardware is changing. It takes a lot of research every day, trying to stay ahead. But it's all worth it. I spend at least an hour a day. Maybe 20 minutes at work and about an hour at home—sometimes even two, three, four hours at home—trying to call people, other agencies, job shops, software, hardware companies. I'll ask questions and talk to them: how is the software changing and what's the new version coming out?

In addition to acquiring new skills, all contractors devoted time to business activities. Even contractors who worked primarily through staffing firms actively marketed themselves. Marketing activities ranged from maintaining one's network of contacts to developing brochures, attending meetings of users' groups, going to career fairs, talking to recruiters, and revising résumés and posting them on the Web. In addition, contractors who worked from home typically had a considerable amount of computer equipment to maintain and upgrade. Independent contractors had the additional burden of maintaining tax records and doing other bookkeeping chores. A software developer nicely summarized the amount of time contractors spend in support activities and how these activities inflate the number of hours worked, while decreasing the proportion of hours billed:

I read an article one time, where a good consultant should spend 50 percent of their time learning, and that's what I've been doing lately. I'm spending almost 50 percent of my time trying to keep current—reading the trade magazines, going to the meetings and stuff. You figure I spend 10–15 percent of my time to do marketing, another 10–15 percent of my time to do the housekeeping chores when you've got your own office. Gee, that leaves maybe 15–20 percent of the time that's billable. Think about the rate I'd have to charge if I was working only twenty hours a week. Nobody's going to spend $400 an hour for me. I'm not that good. So, how do you juggle all this?

In short, the fine-grained temporal structure of contracting differed subtantially from most permanent employment. First, contractors had to balance more kinds of time use than their full-time counterparts. Because contractors went to the labor market more frequently, they felt more persistent pressure to invest substantial time in unbillable and support activities than they had as permanent employees. Second, contractors enjoyed more control than most full-time workers over how many and which hours to work. In fact, they confronted an ever-present choice of how to spend every hour. Third, unlike salaried employees, contractors could put a precise value on every hour of the day—their hourly wage. When choosing how to spend their time, contractors could calculate to the penny the opportunity costs of every unbilled or leisure hour.

Finally, unlike employees whose jobs buffer them from the hour-to-hour implications of how they spend their time, contractors were immediately exposed to the consequences of their temporal choices. The number of billable hours that contractors worked translated directly into income. Their investments in unbillable hours affected the probability that clients would extend their contract by making the contractor appear more diligent and by increasing the quality of their work. In this way, unbillable hours increased the odds that a client would provide glowing recommendations. Hours spent in support activities shored up contractors' reputations, skills, and networks, which in turn shaped the outcome of their next encounter with the labor market. These distinctive aspects of the fine-grained structure of contracting combined to focus contractors on the tradeoff between different ways of spending an hour. Generally speaking, contractors approached the tradeoff in two ways. One group evaluated time solely by economic criteria, while another evaluated it more broadly.

Economic evaluators. The temporal logic of contracting conditioned many of our informants to equate time with money. For these contractors, the temptation to maximize income by working as many hours as possible was considerable. As a software developer exclaimed, "When you're a consultant, all you have is your time. You use it or lose it! You can only sell your time, so you need to . . . figure out how to sell the most time! Cause when it's gone, it's gone." Informants reported that they were acutely aware that every hour they failed to work was lost compensation. Another software engineer, who attributed his divorce to contracting, described the experience of wasting time and feeling money pass through his hands: "The funny thing about contracting—I find myself doing this and talking to people [who do it as well]—you develop this mentality. I was one of those guys that said, 'I take a day off—I'm losing 800 dollars. Oh my gosh!'"

A number of informants reported that equating time and money was so ingrained that they could no longer enjoy leisure. One software engineer described taking time off in the middle of the day to chaperone a youth group around San Francisco's Fisherman's Wharf. He described how he lost patience when the children misbehaved. Rather than bemoan his loss of control, he complained about wasted time: "They were really terrible. They spread out in all directions and I ended up with the other chaperone—just the two of us walking around. I was counting those dollars going off. I was really upset about that." He summed up his experience by admitting that as a contractor, "there is a huge temptation to work every hour of the day." Another contractor, a business applications specialist who worked simultaneously for multiple clients, made it abundantly clear that his time was his most valuable resource: "You can do a lot of things to me: you can call me names; you can throw rocks at me; you can shoot at me, and I won't care. Waste my time and I'll drive over you in the parking lot."

In short, many contractors were continuously concerned with the opportunity costs they would incur if they took advantage of the flexibility they perceived themselves to have. As a result, many felt guilty about taking time off. A software developer detailed the experience of doing such a cost/benefit analysis:

[Contracting] is like being a stockbroker. It's not about the fact that you made a million dollars today on your portfolio, it's about the fact that you left 200,000 dollars on the table. If you didn't sell today and waited until tomorrow, or sold earlier, you could have made that 200,000. So this is the lingering thought in your head as a fund manager. . . . The same thing is true in consulting. Time becomes money. When time becomes money, management of that time becomes a critical asset.

A quality assurance technician put the point more succinctly, "I was always hoping that if I could earn more money, I could cut down the number of hours. But because the money is good, I find it very difficult to turn it down."

When contractors used an economic metric as the sole measure of time, they often discounted the worth of other activities whose economic value was difficult to calculate. This was especially true for leisure. When a systems programmer who specialized in mainframes was asked about her life outside work she responded, "What life? I mean I work three weekends out of the month. I work most holidays. I've put in an average of twelve hours a day for the last four years. I work overtime because I want the extra money." When contractors billed 70 or 80 hours a week, they simply had little time left with which to be flexible.

Broad evaluators. Another group of contractors measured time more broadly. They too took economic criteria into account and valued contracting's high wages, but, unlike the economic evaluators, they used contracting's flexibility to set aside time for other purposes. These purposes varied widely. Some sought greater balance between work and family. They spoke about the importance of being available for their children and budgeted their time accordingly. For these informants, flexibility meant not only choosing which hours to work, but also limiting those hours. As one software developer said, "I now am a father. I have two children. And now job one for me is managing my time myself. And that means making the income that I need to make in as little time as possible and not working 40 hours. So I like to work as little as possible. And I don't think employee situations afford that. I work generally 30 hours a week, but I can work 20 hours some weeks. And I like that." For other broad evaluators, work was a necessary evil to be avoided whenever possible. For example, an accomplished programmer remarked candidly when asked why he typically worked only 30 hours a week, "I'm a goof off. . . . I mean I like the rest of my life. It's very important to me. I've adapted to working less than full time." This contractor used the time he bought for himself to write science fiction, pursue his interests in dance, and hang out at the beach. Although he didn't regret his lifestyle, he was fully aware of its cost. "You know," he confided, "Every so often I kick myself 'cause if I'd have put in sixty hours a week for the last five years at these rates I'd have at least a house to my name."

Still other broad evaluators used opportunities for flexibility spontaneously. Like embracers, they valued both work and leisure but did not routinely plan for one or the other. Without reneging on their obligations, they took advantage of possibilities to redefine their schedules as they arose. A business application specialist described this stance:

> I try to maintain some kind of a pattern with clients, because it helps them. But at the same time, I shift my schedule to meet my needs. If we're going to have a couple of days of very good weather, and there are no major conflagrations burning at a client, I'll decide that maybe what I want to do is pack my cameras and get on the road. I'll say

"Hey look, I've got other things going on and instead of me being in on Tuesday and Wednesday, I'm going to be in on Thursday and Friday. I'll see you then unless you have a problem with that." That's what I do usually, 90 percent of the time. Also, if I'm being nonproductive. . . . One day last week was just one of those days where I went to press the "n" on the keyboard and pressed the "q," you know, 37 times in a row—one of those bumble-finger days. My heart wasn't in it that day. I just told the client, "Look, I can stay here and send you a bill, or I can take the afternoon off, go throw rocks at the pigeons in the park or whatever I'm going to go do, and I'll be in better shape tomorrow and you'll get more for your money." And that's the way it is.

Even though broad evaluators had different reasons for doing so, as a group, they did not allow contracting's economic logic to squeeze out the other parts of their lives. They could therefore use the market's flexibility to create temporal rhythms that were consistent with their daily needs and values. On the face of it, broad evaluators had achieved precisely the lifestyle that the free agency literature promises. But broad evaluators were few in number (9, or 14 percent). Most informants worked extremely long hours. In the course of our interviews, three-quarters of our informants estimated the number of hours that they worked each week. Twenty-six percent of the men and 18 percent of the women who estimated their time reported working over 55 hours a week. These figures can be compared with data for full-time technicians, computer scientists, and programmers drawn from the U.S. Department of Labor's Current Population Survey. Hecker (1998) reported that in 1997, only 7 and 3 percent of permanently employed male and female computer scientists, respectively, worked 55 or more hours weekly. Only 4 and 2 percent of male and female technicians worked as long. Even among permanently employed male programmers, a group known for working long hours, only 5 percent worked 55 hours or more each week. . . .

Why Do Contractors Make Such Little Use of Flexibility?

Researchers have repeatedly shown that demographic characteristics play a role in determining the number of hours that people work and whether they make use of flexibility programs (Schor, 1991; Jacobs and Gerson, 1998; Mead et al., 2000; Golden, 2001). One would expect a similar phenomenon among contractors. For example, one might argue that because women assume more family obligations than men, female contractors might structure their time more flexibly than male contractors. One might also expect differences between those who have children and those who do not, although scholars could disagree on the direction of the effect. People with children might exhibit more temporal flexibility because they need to take care of their children; conversely, they might show less temporal flexibility because of the need to maximize family income. The structure of contractors' careers might also matter. For instance, experienced contractors might use their time differently than newcomers because they are less likely to worry about job security and, therefore, have less anxiety about taking vacations and hours off.

Panels A and B of table 2 compare the demographic attributes and careers of informants who had some flexibility, either coarse- or fine-grained, with those who had neither. These data suggest that demographic differences do not provide much leverage in predicting whether our informants made use of their opportunities for temporal control. Only four demographic differences were significant. Contractors who exhibited temporal flexibility were more commonly highly paid Caucasians and independent contractors with more years of contracting experience. These results point to differences in market power (higher wages, Caucasians, and independent contractors) and to the importance of experience in handling the uncertainties of contracting. Notably, sex, marital status, and the presence of children did not seem to distinguish how our informants used their time.

Professional identities and norms of quality offer another plausible explanation for why most contractors did not use the temporal control they perceived themselves to have. Occupational sociologists have shown that professionals are strongly committed to their work (Hughes, 1958; Bucher and Stelling, 1977). Because the professional's identity is tied to his or her work and because professionals typically find their work intrinsically interesting, they tend to work long hours and have a craftsperson's orientation to quality. Moreover, professional norms extend well beyond the confines of organizations: they influence practitioners regardless of work context (Van Mannen and Barley, 1984). Accordingly, one might argue that contractors work long hours and take little time off because they view themselves as committed technical professionals for whom work is a central life interest (Dubin, 1956; Orzack, 1959). But our data do not support this interpretation. We examined all the passages in our transcripts in which contractors explained why they worked long hours for evidence of professional identities and appeals to intrinsic motivation for work. We also searched the transcripts for all mentions of profession and similar words (professionalism, professional, etc.). Only six of our informants voiced such motives as part of

TABLE 2 Attributes of Informants with and Without Flexibility*

Characteristic	Some Flexibility	No Flexibility	t-stat.
A. Demographic			
Mean age (in years)[†]	42.5 yrs.	42.2 yrs.	−.11
Mean education (in post-high-school years)[†]	4.3 yrs.	4.0 yrs.	−.68
Mean pay rate (in \$/hour)[‡]	\$78	\$58	−2.10*
Male	74%	74%	.01
Married[§]	47%	71%	1.65
With Children[¶]	50%	52%	.10
Caucasian	95%	67%	−2.43**
U.S. citizens	89%	80%	.82
California resident	74%	67%	−.54
Bay Area resident	58%	55%	−.22
B. Career structure			
Mean years contracted[†]	8.5 yrs.	6.1 yrs.	−1.78*
Mean years worked[†]	18.1 yrs.	17.2 yrs.	−.37
Years contracted / years worked[†]	.47 yrs.	.40 yrs.	−1.04
Independent contractors or corps.[†]	47%	25%	−1.73
On first contract[#]	11%	7%	−.40
Have always contracted[#]	12%	11%	.18
Left permanent employment behind[#]	58%	51%	−.47
Moved back and forth to contracting[#]	21%	278%	.47
C. Technical specialty (percentage)			
Software developers	42%	21%	−1.68*
Hardware designers	11%	7%	−.44
Database programmers and administrators	26%	17%	−.87
Systems administrators	0%	17%	1.92*
Project managers	0%	7%	1.19
Technical writers	11%	10%	−.12
Quality assurance technicians	11%	12%	.15
Multimedia (Web)	0%	5%	.95
Others	0%	5%	.96

*p < .05; **p < .01; one tailed test.

*N = 60 individuals. Numbers are drawn from semistructured interview data. Thus, some comparisons are based on a subset of the cases. Five informants did not give any information on time use . . .   and were excluded from this table. Contractors with "some flexibility" had fine-, coarse-grained, or both types of flexibility.

[†]Only includes data on 59 cases.

[‡]Only includes data on 36 cases.

[¶]Only includes data on 50 cases.

[§]Only includes data on 48 cases.

[#]Only includes data on 58 cases.

their account for why they worked long hours or eschewed vacations. Professional identities and norms, therefore, did not appear to play a significant role in how the majority of our informants allocated their time. Far more important were the nature of our informants' work and their view of the exchange relationship.

Technical contractors were almost always hired onto a project. Not only did projects have discrete beginnings and endings, but their pace was also patterned. Typically, a project started off slowly and eventually accelerated. By the final third of a project, participants realized that they were running out of time, and the pace became frantic (Gersick, 1988, 1989). This occurred when projects had crises and managers strove to "put out fires" by "throwing bodies at the problem." The bodies usually belonged to contractors. Consequently, contractors typically entered projects precisely when demands on the team's time were greatest. Contractors were expected and paid to do whatever it took to finish the job. Several contractors compared their work with that of a mercenary, entering battle after battle, with heavy expectations balanced by high rewards. Most of our informants agreed with the sentiments expressed by a quality assurance technician, whose avocation was competitive dancing:

There are times when the job is pretty stressful, especially when they come up on their deadlines and they're expecting you to put in 50 plus hours a week and there's problems with the project. They're falling behind. Things aren't going the way they're supposed to. Almost invariably that's what happens. . . . Now [the team's] under the gun. Its like, "We have till January 1, and who knows if we're gonna make it on time." . . . And I think if I weren't doing this, I would go out dancing a lot more often. I would be competing more. . . . But it certainly puts a Kibosh

on that because by the time I get home, and I talk [to my wife] about the bills and whose birthday's coming up next month, very little energy is left for dancing.

The pressure to work long hours created by the fact that contractors usually arrived at "crunch time" was sometimes exacerbated by the nature of the work itself. For example, quality assurance technicians were responsible for running tests on hardware and software. Complex testing could require constantly monitoring the computers on which the tests were running. When running tests, quality assurance technicians would sometimes need to work for stretches of 10 to 15 hours at a time. Systems administrators had responsibility for maintaining networks, the infrastructures whose continual operation was critical to a client's ability to do business. When networks failed or servers crashed, systems administrators had little choice but to work until they fixed the problem. When writing code, software developers, Web designers, and database developers lived in micro-worlds defined entirely by the parameters of the programs they were writing (cf. Kidder, 1981). Writing high-quality, efficient code requires absorption of consciousness that makes designers oblivious to the flow of time. Programmers experience this state as a kind of fixation. A Web designer explained how coding binges sucked up time: "It is very easy for me to become obsessive when it comes to this stuff. I can sit there and do this stuff until 2 A.M. Wake up, go to work, come back and do it until 2 A.M. again. You know, for at least a few days straight. . . . It's something I can't really quit."

Panel C in table 2 suggests how occupations and the tasks they encompass can constrain temporal flexibility. The panel displays the percentage of those with some or no flexibility in eight occupational groups. Compared with contractors with flexibility, contractors without flexibility are more likely to be systems administrators (0 percent vs. 17 percent, $p < .05$), most likely for the reasons discussed above. Despite the fact that software developers could become lost in their work for significant periods of time, they were the most likely occupational group to have some type of temporal flexibility (42 percent vs. 21 percent, $p < .05$). This freedom reflected the fact that coding tasks could be modularized, which freed programmers from a ceaseless temporal regimen and also allowed them to work from home. If the developer was an independent contractor, clients would often require only that he or she deliver completed code by a specified date. How the contractor spent time was irrelevant, so long as he or she delivered the code on time.

Contractors, however, felt that the nature of their work was not nearly as important for how they their allocated time as the exigencies of the exchange relationship. Contractors understood that selling time and skills to a client meant entering a relationship with reciprocal obligations. Clients were obligated to pay contractors but, in return, contractors were obligated to do more than complete a piece of work. They also had to satisfy the client. In the role of customer, clients could make demands that went beyond the letter of the contract, which often translated into demands for additional time. It was precisely because the exchange beneath the contract relationship was remunerative and because current exchanges affected future exchanges that contractors had both immediate and long-term reasons for keeping clients happy, even when this limited contractors' temporal flexibility.

Because contractors sold expertise, the exchange between clients and contractors had overtones of a professional engagement. The ethos of ministering to a client's needs, much as would a doctor or lawyer, was exaggerated by the short-term nature of the contract. Realizing that they hired contractors

as experts allowed clients, as one female software developer put, to adopt an attitude of "OK, you're a consultant. Our employees aren't carrying the load. We're paying you so you do this, this, this, and that." Independent contractors, in particular, found that their obligation to serve clients was broad. Like many independents, an experienced database developer told us he felt he had to be on-call 24 hours a day: "I've had phone calls at 3:00 in the morning. You know, the phone's ringing by the bed at 3:00 in the morning every day because somebody's operation is more important than my life." Contractors who worked several contracts simultaneously found it even more difficult to maintain control over their time while also meeting clients' expectations. A software developer explained:

> On a project it'll be "We need this done. How soon can we get it done?" If I've only got one or two projects, then it's just "Gee, I'm spending all my time working on your project. We'll have it out in a couple weeks." Right now, I've gotten myself into a bind where I've got all these projects. One of them should have been done six months ago. Another's due out March 31. A couple others are expecting stuff in the next two weeks and that's not gonna happen. . . . When I'm concentrating on one project, customers will phone up, "Gee, it broke," and I have to go out and fix it. . . . I don't have 240 percent time.

Even more important than immediate pressures to please the client was the shadow of the future: the fact that contractors relied on clients for referrals and references. Contractors understood that having a reputation as a reliable expert enabled them to negotiate their next contract quickly and successfully. Contractors therefore had incentives to exceed the terms of the contract and to meet clients' demands to protect their reputation and guarantee good references. Informants repeatedly told us that they worked in "small worlds," in which word of performance traveled quickly. A workstation technician, who worked as a W2 and who was moving into quality assurance, explained how concern for her reputation led her to sacrifice her temporal flexibility:

> We're kind of in a heavy point right now. The thing I like about contracting is that it's voluntary. I mean if I don't want to go in, I don't go in. Nobody's telling me to do anything. Nobody's saying, "You have to do this. You have to be here at a certain time." But, say it was a real critical part of the project that needed to be done by Monday, and I decided "Oh, I'm not coming in," and I didn't have a really good reason. I'm still not dinged, but it's filed in the back of somebody's mind and they'll say, "Well, she's not as dependable as we thought she would be" or something like that.

The independent contractor cited above who worked multiple contracts echoed those sentiments: "You must always take responsibility for your projects. If you do a bad job, it will get around and people will stop calling you. When I hear people saying that they want to be a contractor because they want to make lots of money, I think, it's more than that. You have to have a knack for it, and you have to be willing to work weird hours."

Contractors quickly learned that market-based remunerative relationships came with more strings attached than they had originally anticipated. Where they once may have had an employer who could exercise control, they now had clients who had the prerogatives of customers. As in all markets for expertise, reputations built at least partially on client satisfaction lubricated the flow of work. The need to keep clients happy meant that once contractors accepted a contract, they also experienced constraints on contracting's promise of fine-grained flexibility. Although clients had little normative control over how contractors allocated their hours and their days, they owned part of the contractors' reputations. This gave them a kind of coercive control in the present because of the possibility that they could exact retribution in the future when asked by potential employers to provide references. Contractors therefore found exercising fine-grained flexibility more costly than using coarse-grained flexibility. Unlike insisting on temporal autonomy within a contract, taking time off between contracts might lower contractors' annual incomes and deplete their savings, but it did not jeopardize their reputations. For this reason, contractors were more likely to take advantage of the market's coarse-grained flexibility than they were to enjoy its promise of fine-grained freedom.

Discussion

Scholars who study time and flexibility in organizations routinely find that employees feel overworked and desire greater control over their time but take little advantage of the flextime programs available to them. Researchers usually blame this paradox on the normative pressures of organizational life (Kunda, 1992; Barker, 1993; Perlow, 1997). Advocates of employability and free agency contend that people can escape these pressures and regain temporal control by leaving permanent employment for market-based careers that span organizations (Kanter, 1989; Arthur, 1994; Pink, 2001). Our study suggests otherwise. Moving from organizations to markets created new time binds for technical contractors. As the literature would predict, contractors believed they had more control over their time than they had as full-time employees, but this belief rarely led them to limit their hours or schedule their time more flexibly. Few took advantage of contracting's greater opportunity for breaks and vacations, and most worked such long hours each day that there was little time left with which to be flexible, even if they so desired. Thus, despite the absence of normative pressures, our informants exhibited a disjuncture between perceived and realized flexibility similar to that documented by researchers among employees in firms with flexibility programs (Tausig and Fenwick, 2001; Gareis and Barnett, 2002).

The reasons for the disjuncture lay in how the market influenced our informants' interpretations of time and their subsequent choices. First, the contract cycle repeatedly exposed contractors to the possibility of downtime, periods without work and pay. The majority of contractors saw downtime primarily as a period without pay, as opposed to a period without work, and hence sought to avoid or minimize downtime. Second, the market's high wages, which were paid by the hour, led contractors to equate time with money and allowed them to calculate precisely the cost of an hour of leisure or family time. By contrast, the opportunity cost of spending an additional hour at work was more difficult to calculate. Contractors therefore gravitated toward working more rather than fewer hours. Third, the demand for contractors was marked by crisis. The tendency for firms to hire contractors into troubled projects at the last minute exacerbated the contactors' proclivity to work long and inflexible hours. Finally, because reputations were crucial for securing a steady stream of contracts, many contractors put in long, even unbillable hours to ensure solid references and referrals. . . .

Ultimately, our research raises doubts about whether organizational life is really as troublesome for workers' ability to control their time as the literature suggests. Although organizations expose workers to mechanisms of control that contractors appear to escape, organizations also buffer employees from repeated encounters with the labor market. As we have seen, the structure of the labor market constrained most contractors from choosing to work fewer and more flexible hours. Our evidence suggests that contractors may actually work more hours than their full-time counterparts in the same occupations. Our study implies that organizations may conceivably consume less of a worker's time than do markets. Organizational employment may also offer at least as much, if not more, fine-grained control over which hours one works. Were studies to confirm these conjectures, they would not only challenge notions of free agency's promised benefits, they would warrant rethinking a key assumption behind the literature on time binds, namely, that organizations offer only constraints. At the very least, our investigation casts doubt on the claim that market-based careers give workers greater flexibility and control over time. Free agency may lead people to perceive that they have more temporal flexibility, but aside from longer vacations, most will likely never use it. Like bureaucracies, markets are also cages, but cages of a different material. Contractors' choices about beach time, bridge time, and billable hours in the context of work may make it difficult for them to see this.

REFERENCES

Arthur, M. B. 1994. "The boundaryless career: A new perspective for organizational inquiry." Journal of Organizational Behavior, 15: 295–306.

Arthur, M. B., and D. M. Rousseau. 1996. The Boundaryless Career: A New Employment Principle for a New Organizational Era. New York: Oxford University Press.

Bailyn, L. 1970. "Career and family orientations of husbands and wives in relation to marital happiness." Human Relations, 23: 97–113.

1993. Breaking the Mold: Women, Men, and Time in the New Corporate World. New York: Free Press.

Barker, J. R. 1993. "Tightening the iron cage: Concertive control in self-managing teams." Administrative Science Quarterly, 38: 408–437.

Barnett, R. C. 1994. "Home-to-work spillover revisited: A study of full-time employed women in dual-earner couples." Journal of Marriage and the Family, 56: 647–656.

Beck, N. 1992. Shifting Gears: Thriving in the New Economy. Toronto: Harper Collins.

Black, D. S., and R. C. Andreini. 1997. The Information Elite: The Future of the Independent Information Technology Consultant. Redwood Shores, CA: Advanced Technology Staffing.

Blair-Loy, M., and A. Wharton. 2002. "Employees' use of family-responsive policies and the workplace social context." Social Forces, 80: 813–845.

Bluestone, B., and S. Rose. 1997. "Overworked and underemployed: Unraveling an economic enigma." American Prospect, 31: 58–69.

1998. "The macroeconomics of time." Review of Social Economy, 56: 425–441.

Bolger, N., A. Delongis, and R. C. Kessler. 1989. "The contagion of stress across multiple roles." Journal of Marriage and the Family, 51: 175–183.

Bond, J. T., E. Galinsky, and J. E. Swanberg. 1998. The 1997 National Study of the Changing Workforce. New York: Families and Work Institute.

Bridges, W. 1994. Job Shift: How to Prosper in a Workplace Without Jobs. Reading, MA: Addison Wesley.

Bucher, R., and J. G. Stelling. 1977. Becoming Professional. Beverly Hills, CA: Sage.

Bumpus, M. F., A. C. Crouter, and S. M. McHale. 1999. "Work demands of dual-earner couples: Implications for parents' knowledge about children's daily lives in middle childhood." Journal of Marriage and the Family, 61: 465–475.

Caulkin, S. 1997. "Skills, not loyalty, are new key if you want job security." San Francisco Sunday Examiner and Chronicle, September 7 (4): 2.

Clark, J., C. Freeman, and L. Soete. 1981. "Long waves, inventions, and innovations." Futures, August: 308–322.

Clarkberg, M., and P. Moen. 2001. "Understanding the time-squeeze: Married couples' preferred and actual work-hour strategies." American Behavioral Scientist, 44: 1115–1135.

Coleman, M. T., and J. Pencavel. 1993a. "Trends in market work behavior of women since 1940." Industrial and Labor Relations Review, 46: 653–676.

1993b. "Changes in work hours of male employees, 1940–1988." Industrial and Labor Relations Review, 46: 262–283.

Daniels, S. 1997. "Flexible hours, telecommuting increasing." National Underwriting, September 1: 23.

Darby, J. B. 1997. "The ultimate contractor: Lessons from a parallel universe." Contract Professional, 2: 27–32.

Dubin, R. 1956. "Industrial workers' worlds: A study of the 'central life interests' of industrial workers." Social Problems, 3: 131–142.

Eaton, S. C. 2000. "Work and family integration in the biotechnology industry: Implications for employers and firms." Unpublished Ph.D. dissertation, Sloan School of Management, Massachusetts Institute of Technology.

Edwards, R. 1979. Contested Terrain. New York: Basic Books.

Etzioni, A. 1961. A Comparative Analysis of Complex Organizations: On Power, Involvement and Their Correlatives. New York: Free Press.

Faugier, J., and M. Sargeant. 1997. "Sampling hard to reach populations." Journal of Advanced Nursing, 26: 790–797.

Faulkner, R. R. 1987. Music on Demand: Composers and Careers in the Hollywood Film Industry. New Brunswick, NJ: Transaction Books.

Faulkner, R. R., and A. B. Anderson. 1987. "Short-term projects and emergent careers: Evidence from Hollywood." American Journal of Sociology 92: 879–909.

Finlay, W., and J. E. Coverdill. 2002. Headhunters: Matchmaking in the Labor Market. Ithaca, NY: Cornell University Press.

Forthofer, M. S., H. J. Markman, M. Cox, S. Stanley, and R. C. Kessler. 1996. "Associations between marital distress and work loss in a national sample." Journal of Marriage and the Family, 58: 597–605.

Galinsky, E., and J. T. Bond. 1998. The 1998 Business Work-Life Study: A Sourcebook. New York: Families and Work Institute.

Galinsky, E., J. T. Bond, and D. E. Friedman. 1993. National Study of the Changing Workforce. New York: Families and Work Institute.

Gareis, K. C., and R. C. Barnett. 2002. "Under what conditions do long work hours affect psychological distress: A study of full-time and reduced-hours female doctors." Work and Occupations, 29: 483–497.

Gersick, C. J. 1988. "Time and transition in work teams: Toward a new model of group development." Academy of Management Journal, 31: 9–41.

1989. "Marking time: Predictable transitions in task groups." Academy of Management Journal, 32: 274–309.

Goff, S. J., M. K. Mount, and R. L. Jamison. 1990. "Employer supported child care, work/family conflict, and absenteeism: A field study." Personnel Psychology, 43: 793–809.

Gold, M., and J. Fraser. 2002. "Managing self-management: Successful transitions to portfolio careers." Work, Employment and Society, 16: 579–598.

Golden, L. 2001. "Flexible work schedules: Which workers get them?" American Behavioral Scientist, 44: 1157–1178.

Gonos, G. 1997. "The contest over 'employer' status in the postwar United States: The case of temporary help firms." Law and Society Review, 31: 81–110.

Greenwald, J. 1998. "Employers warming up to flexible schedules." Business Insurance, June 15: 3–6.

Handy, C. 1989. The Age of Unreason. Boston: Harvard University Press.

Hecker, D. 1998. "How hours of work affect occupational earnings." Monthly Labor Review, October: 8–18.

Heckscher, C. 1995. White-Collar Blues. New York: Basic Books.

Higgins, C. A., L. E. Duxbury, and R. H. Irving. 1992. "Work-family conflict in the dual-career family." Organizational Behavior and Human Decision Processes, 51: 51–75.

Hirsh, P. M., and M. Shanley. 1996. "The rhetoric of boundaryless—Or how the newly empowered managerial class bought into its own marginalization." In M. B. Arthur and D. M. Rousseau (eds.), The Boundaryless Career: A New Employment Principle for a New Organizational Era: 218–234. New York: Oxford University Press.

Hochschild, A. 1997. The Time Bind: When Work Becomes Home and Home Becomes Work. New York: Metropolitan Books.

Hughes, E. C. 1958. Men and Their Work. Glencoe, IL: Free Press.

Jacobs, J. A., and K. Gerson. 1998. "Who are the overworked Americans?" Review of Social Economy, 56: 422–459.

Jones, C. 1996. "Careers in project networks: The case of the film industry." In M. B. Arthur and D. M. Rousseau (eds.), The Boundaryless Career: A New Employment Principle for a

New Organizational Era: 58–75. New York: Oxford University Press.

Kanter, R. M. 1989. When Giants Learn to Dance: Mastering the Challenge of Strategy, Management, and Careers in the 1990s. New York: Simon and Schuster.

1995. "Nice work if you can get it: The software industry as a model for tomorrow's jobs." American Prospect, 23: 52–58.

Kickert, W. J. M. 1984. "The magic word *flexibility*." International Studies of Management and Organization, 14 (4): 6–31.

Kidder, T. 1981. The Soul of a New Machine. New York: Avon Books.

Kunda, G. 1992. Engineering Culture: Control and Commitment in a High Tech Corporation. Philadelphia: Temple University Press.

Kunda, G., S. R. Barley, and J. A. Evans. 2002. "Why do contractors contract? The experience of highly skilled technical professionals in a contingent labor market." Industrial and Labor Relations Review, 55: 234–261.

Kurland, N. B., and T. D. Egan. 1999. "Telecommuting: Justice and control in the virtual organization." Organization Science, 10: 500–513.

Matusik, S., and S. R. Fuller. 2002. "The nexus of work arrangement preferences and demand for skills: An exploratory examination of alternative work." Paper delivered at the Academy of Management Meeting, Denver, CO.

Maume, D. J., and M. L. Bellas. 2001. "The overworked American or the time bind?: Assessing competing explanations for time spent in paid labor." American Behavioral Scientist, 44: 1137–1156.

McBride, A. 2003. "Reconciling competing pressures for working-time flexibility: An impossible task in the National Health Service." Work, Employment and Society, 17: 159–170.

McShulskis, E. 1997. "Work and family benefits increasingly popular?" HR Magazine, July: 26–29.

Mead, R. J., S. McConville, P. Harmer, M. Lubin, A. Tinsley, J. Chang, and J. McMahon. 2000. The Struggle to Juggle Work and Family. Los Angeles: Center for Labor Research and Education, School of Public Policy and Social Research, UCLA.

Meiksins, P., and P. Whalley. 2002. Putting Work in Its Place: A Quiet Revolution. Ithaca, NY: Cornell University Press.

Mirvis, P. H., and D. T. Hall. 1994. "Psychological success and the boundaryless career." Journal of Organizational Behavior, 15: 365–380.

Olson, M. H. 1987. "Telework: Practical experience and future prospects." In R. E. Kraut (ed.). Technology and the Transformation of White-Collar Work: 135–152. Hillsdale, NJ: Lawrence Erlbaum.

Osterman, P. 1995. "Work/family programs and the employment relationship." Administrative Science Quarterly, 40: 681–700.

O'Mahony, S., and S. R. Barley. 1999. "Do digital telecommunications affect work and organization? The state of our knowledge." In R. I. Sutton and B. M. Staw (eds.), Research in Organizational Behavior, 21: 125–161. Stamford, CT: JAI Press.

Orzack, L. H. 1959. "Work as a 'central life interest' of professionals." Social Problems, 7: 125–132.

Paden, S. L., and C. Buehler. 1995. "Coping with the dual-income lifestyle." Journal of Marriage and the Family, 57: 101–110.

Parker, R. E. 1994. Flesh Peddlers and Warm Bodies: The Temporary Help Industry and Its Workers. New Brunswick, NJ: Rutgers University Press.

Perin, C. 1991. "The moral fabric of the office: Panopticon discourse and schedule flexibilities." In P. S. Tolbert and S. R. Barley (eds.), Research in the Sociology of Organizations, vol. 8: Organizations and Professions: 241–268. Greenwich, CT: JAI Press.

Perlow, L. A. 1997. Finding Time. Ithaca, NY: Cornell University Press.

1999. "The time famine: Toward a sociology of work time." Administrative Science Quarterly, 44: 57–81.

Pink, D. H. 1998. "Free agent nation." Fast Company, December/January: 131–147.

2001. Free Agent Nation: How America's New Independent Workers Are Transforming the Way We Live. New York: Warner Business Books.

Rapoport, R., and R. Rapoport. 1978. Working Couples. New York: Harper.

Repetti, R. L., and J. Wood. 1997. "Effects of daily stress at work on mothers' interactions with preschoolers." Journal of Family Psychology, 11: 90–108.

Reynolds, J. 2003. "You can't always get the hours you want: Mismatches between actual and preferred work hours in the U.S." Social Forces, 81: 1171–1199.

Robinson, J. P., and G. Godbey. 1997. Time for Life: The Surprising Ways Americans Use Their Time. University Park, PA: Pennsylvania State University.

Saltzstein, A. L., Y. Ting, and G. H. Saltzstein. 2001. "Work-family balance and job satisfaction: The impact of family-friendly policies on attitudes of federal government employees." Public Administration Review, 61: 452–467.

Schein, E. H. 1972. Organizational Psychology, 2d ed. Englewood Cliffs, NJ: Prentice-Hall.

Schor, J. B. 1991. The Overworked American: The Unexpected Decline of Leisure. New York: Basic Books.

Schwartz, F. 1989. "Management women and the new facts of life." Harvard Business Review, January/February: 68.

Smelser, N. J., and R. Swedberg. 1994. The Handbook of Economic Sociology. New York: Princeton University Press.

Tausig, M., and R. Fenwick. 2001. "Unbinding time: Alternate work schedules and work-life balance." Journal of Family and Economic Issues, 22: 101–119.

van Duijn, J. J. 1983. The Longwave in Economic Life. London: Allen and Unwin.

Van Maanen, J., and S. R. Barley. 1984. "Occupational communities: Culture and control in organizations." In B. M Staw and L. L. Cummings (eds.), Research in Organizational Behavior, 6: 287–365. Greenwich, CT: JAI Press.

Weick, K. E. 1996. "Enactment and the boundaryless career: Organizing as we work." In M. B. Arthur and D. M. Rousseau (eds.), The Boundaryless Career: A New Employment Principle for a New Organizational Era: 40–57. New York: Oxford University Press.

Discussion Questions for Part V

1. What does Hochschild (Reading 37) mean when she says that love and care have become "the new gold"?

2. In what ways is the United States facing a care deficit? In what ways is the care deficit a global problem?

3. What are some ways to increase the supply of care in our society? What are the advantages and disadvantages of these strategies?

4. Is caring work undervalued? If so, how would you increase the value of this activity?

5. What is Ehrenreich's (Reading 39) critique of the "servant economy"? Do you agree with her disapproval of hiring a paid housecleaner?

6. Are Americans overworked?

7. What are some of the reasons American workers put in longer hours than workers in other industrialized countries?

8. What would a "family-friendly" workplace look like? Is the American workplace becoming more or less family-friendly over time?

9. What kinds of policies should employers offer working parents?

10. What factors make it difficult for men to take advantage of family-friendly policies in the workplace?

11. Should overwork be considered a social problem in the United States? If so, how can this problem be reduced? If not, why not?